Middle School 2-2
학교시험 완벽대비

KB087582

2학기 전과정

적중"100 plus

영어 기출문제집

중2
미래 | 최연희

Best Collection

구성과 특징

교과서의 주요 학습 내용을 중심으로 학습 영역별 특성에 맞춰 단계별로 다양한 학습 기회를 제공하여
단원별 학습능력 평가는 물론 중간 및 기말고사 시험 등에 완벽하게 대비할 수 있도록 내용을 구성

Words & Expressions

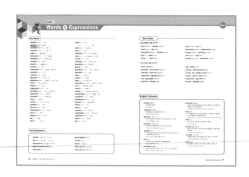

Step1   Key Words 단원별 핵심 단어 설명 및 풀이
         Key Expression 단원별 핵심 숙어 및 관용어 설명
         Word Power 반대 또는 비슷한 뜻 단어 배우기
         English Dictionary 영어로 배우는 영어 단어

Step2   실력평가 단원별 수시평가 대비 주관식, 객관식 문제풀이

Step3   서술형 대비 학업성취도 및 수행능력평가 대비 서술형 문제풀이

Conversation

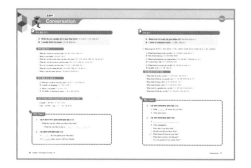

Step1   핵심 의사소통 소통에 필요한 주요 표현 방법 요약
         핵심 Check 기본적인 표현 방법 및 활용능력 확인

Step2   대화문 익히기 교과서 대화문 심층 분석 및 확인

Step3   교과서 확인학습 빈칸 채우기를 통한 문장 완성 능력 확인

Step4   기본평가 시험대비 기초 학습 능력 평가

Step5   실력평가 단원별 수시평가 대비 주관식, 객관식 문제풀이

Step6   서술형 대비 학업성취도 및 수행능력평가 대비 서술형 문제풀이

Grammar

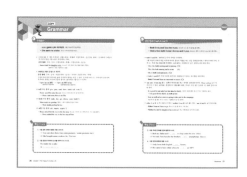

Step1   주요 문법 단원별 주요 문법 사항과 예문을 알기 쉽게 설명

         핵심 Check 기본 문법사항에 대한 이해 여부 확인

Step2   기본평가 시험대비 기초 학습 능력 평가

Step3   실력평가 단원별 수시평가 대비 주관식, 객관식 문제풀이

Step4   서술형 대비 학업성취도 및 수행능력평가 대비 서술형 문제풀이

Reading

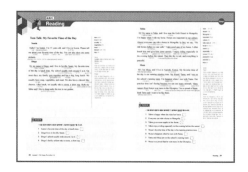

Step1   구문 분석 단원별로 제시된 문장에 대한 구문별 분석과 내용 설명
         확인문제 문장에 대한 기본적인 이해와 인지능력 확인

Step2   확인학습A 빈칸 채우기를 통한 문장 완성 능력 확인

Step3   확인학습B 제시된 우리말을 영어로 완성하여 작문 능력 키우기

Step4   실력평가 단원별 수시평가 대비 주관식, 객관식 문제풀이

Step5   서술형 대비 학업성취도 및 수행능력평가 대비 서술형 문제풀이
         교과서 구석구석 교과서에 나오는 기타 문장까지 완벽 학습

Composition

|영역별 핵심문제|

단어 및 어휘, 대화문, 문법, 독해 등 각 영역별 기출문제의 출제 유형을 분석하여 실전에 대비하고 연습할 수 있도록 문제를 배열

|단원별 예상문제|

기출문제를 분석한 후 새로운 시험 출제 경향을 더하여 새롭게 출제될 수 있는 문제를 포함하여 시험에 완벽하게 대비할 수 있도록 준비

|서술형 실전 및 창의사고력 문제|

학교 시험에서 점차 늘어나는 서술형 시험에 집중 대비하고 고득점을 취득하는데 만전을 기하기 위한 학습 코너

|단원별 모의고사|

영역별, 단계별 학습을 모두 마친 후 실전 연습을 위한 모의고사

교과서 파헤치기

- **단어Test1~3** 영어 단어 우리말 쓰기, 우리말을 영어 단어로 쓰기, 영영풀이에 해당하는 단어와 우리말 쓰기
- **대화문Test1~2** 대화문 빈칸 완성 및 전체 대화문 쓰기
- **본문Test1~5** 빈칸 완성, 우리말 쓰기, 문장 배열연습, 영어 작문하기 복습 등 단계별 반복 학습을 통해 교과서 지문에 대한 완벽한 습득
- **구석구석지문Test1~2** 지문 빈칸 완성 및 전문 영어로 쓰기

Lesson 5

Bravo! Brava!

 의사소통 기능

- 제안하기
  Why don't we see a magic show?

- 약속 정하기
  A: What time shall we meet?
  B: How about 10 o'clock on Saturday?

언어 형식

- 접속사 if
  You will appreciate it better **if** you know the story.

- as + 형용사/부사의 원급 + as
  Turandot is **as cold as** ice.

Words & Expressions

Key Words

- **actually** [ǽktʃuəli] 부 실은, 사실은, 실제로
- **add** [æd] 동 (말을) 덧붙이다, 더하다
- **agree** [əgríː] 동 동의하다
- **already** [ɔːlrédi] 부 이미, 벌써
- **amazing** [əméiziŋ] 형 놀라운
- **anniversary** [æ̀nəvə́ːrsəri] 명 기념일
- **answer** [ǽnsər] 동 대답하다(= reply)
- **appreciate** [əpríːʃièit] 동 감상하다, 감사하다, 진가를 알아보다
- **aria** [άːriə] 명 아리아, 영창
- **beauty** [bjúːti] 명 아름다움, 미
- **brave** [breiv] 형 용감한
- **celebrate** [séləbrèit] 동 기념하다
- **century** [séntʃəri] 명 세기
- **Chinese** [tʃàiníːz] 형 중국의 명 중국인
- **correctly** [kəréktli] 부 정확하게, 바르게
- **dawn** [dɔːn] 명 새벽
- **difficult** [dífikʌlt] 형 어려운
- **discount** [dískaunt] 명 할인
- **fail** [feil] 동 실패하다
- **famous** [féiməs] 형 유명한
- **find** [faind] 동 찾다, 알아내다, 발견하다
- **guess** [ges] 동 추측하다
- **incorrectly** [ìnkəréktli] 부 정확하지 않게, 틀리게
- **Italian** [itǽljən] 명 이탈리아어, 이탈리아인 형 이탈리아의

- **like** [laik] 전 ~처럼
- **marry** [mǽri] 동 ~와 결혼하다
- **mean** [miːn] 동 의미하다
- **moving** [múːviŋ] 형 감동적인
- **ostrich** [ɔ́ːstritʃ] 명 타조
- **part** [paːrt] 명 역할, 배역, 부분
- **perform** [pərfɔ́ːrm] 동 공연하다, 수행하다
- **performance** [pərfɔ́ːrməns] 명 공연
- **place** [pleis] 명 장소
- **play** [plei] 명 연극, 극, 희곡
- **practice** [prǽktis] 동 연습하다
- **princess** [prínsis] 명 공주
- **riddle** [rídl] 명 수수께끼
- **right** [rait] 부 즉시, 곧바로
- **safe** [seif] 형 안전한
- **secret** [síːkrit] 명 비밀
- **stranger** [stréindʒər] 명 낯선 사람, 이방인
- **storyline** [stɔ́ːrilain] 명 줄거리
- **subway** [sʌ́bwèi] 명 지하철
- **suggestion** [səgdʒéstʃən] 명 제안
- **theater** [θíːətər] 명 극장
- **tonight** [tənáit] 부 오늘밤에
- **until** [əntíl] 접 ~할 때까지
- **whole** [houl] 명 전체 형 모든, 전부의

Key Expressions

- **as+형용사+as** ~ …만큼 ~한
- **at first sight** 첫눈에
- **be able to+동사원형** ~할 수 있다
- **be going to+동사원형** ~할 예정이다
- **be late for** ~ ~에 늦다, 지각하다
- **fall in love with** ~ ~와 사랑에 빠지다
- **find out** 알아내다, 발견하다
- **Guess what!** 있잖아.
- **have to+동사원형** ~해야 한다
- **How about+명사** ~? ~은 어때?

- **hurry up** 서두르다
- **in time** 제시간에, 늦지 않게
- **Let's+동사원형** ~. ~하자.
- **nothing more than** ~ ~에 지나지 않는
- **of beauty** 아름다운
- **one day** 어느 날
- **take off** (일을) 쉬다
- **take the subway** 지하철을 타다
- **Why don't you+동사원형** ~? ~하는 게 어때?
- **would like to+동사원형** ~하고 싶다

Word Power

※ 서로 반대되는 뜻을 가진 단어

- □ **brave**(용감한) ↔ **cowardly**(겁이 많은)
- □ **correctly**(정확하게) ↔ **incorrectly**(정확하지 않게)
- □ **difficult**(어려운) ↔ **easy**(쉬운)

- □ **safe**(안전한) ↔ **dangerous**(위험한)
- □ **fail**(실패하다) ↔ **succeed**(성공하다)
- □ **famous**(유명한) ↔ **unknown**(알려지지 않은)

※ 서로 비슷한 뜻을 가진 단어

- □ **answer : reply to** (~에 대답하다)
- □ **moving : touching** (감동적인)
- □ **suggestion : proposal** (제안)

- □ **amazing : surprising** (놀라운)
- □ **famous : well-known** (유명한)
- □ **agree : assent** (동의하다)

English Dictionary

- □ **already** 이미
  → earlier than the time expected
  예상된 시간보다 더 이르게

- □ **amazing** 놀라운
  → very surprising
  매우 놀라운

- □ **anniversary** 기념일
  → a day on which you remember or celebrate something that happened on that day in the past
  과거의 그 날에 일어난 일을 기억하거나 축하하는 날

- □ **appreciate** 진가를 알아보다
  → to understand how good something or someone is
  어떤 것이나 어떤 사람이 얼마나 좋은지 이해하다

- □ **aria** 아리아, 영창
  → a piece of music in an opera sung by one person
  한 사람이 부른 오페라의 음악

- □ **brave** 용감한
  → showing no fear of dangerous or difficult things
  위험하거나 어려운 일에 두려움을 보이지 않는

- □ **celebrate** 축하하다, 기념하다
  → to do something enjoyable on a special occasion
  특별한 경우에 즐거운 어떤 것을 하다

- □ **century** 세기
  → a period of 100 years
  100년

- □ **discount** 할인
  → a reduction in the normal price
  정상 가격에서의 감소

- □ **guess** 추측하다
  → to give an answer to a particular question when you do not have all the facts and so cannot be certain if you are correct
  모든 사실을 가지고 있지 않아서 당신이 옳은지 확신할 수 없을 때 특정한 질문에 답을 하다

- □ **marry** 결혼하다
  → to become the legally accepted husband or wife of someone in an official or religious ceremony
  공식적 또는 종교적 의식에서 합법적으로 인정된 남편이나 아내가 되다

- □ **moving** 감동적인
  → causing strong feelings of sadness or sympathy
  슬픔이나 공감의 강한 감정을 불러일으키는

- □ **perform** 수행하다, 공연하다
  → to do an action or piece of work
  행동이나 작품을 하다

- □ **riddle** 수수께끼
  → a type of question that describes something in a difficult and confusing way and has a clever or funny answer
  어렵고 혼란스러운 방식으로 무언가를 묘사하고 교묘하거나 재미있는 답을 가지는 질문 유형

- □ **secret** 비밀
  → a piece of information that is only known by one person or a few people and should not be told to others
  한 사람이나 몇 사람만 알고 다른 사람에게는 말하지 말아야 하는 정보

- □ **storyline** 줄거리
  → the series of events that happen in a book, film, play, etc.
  책, 영화, 희곡 등에서 일어나는 일련의 사건

서답형

01 다음 짝지어진 두 단어의 관계가 같도록 빈칸에 알맞은 단어를 쓰시오.

> unknown : famous = cowardly : _____

[02~03] 다음 빈칸에 들어갈 말로 가장 적절한 것은?

02

> It's _____. The sun is rising.

① dawn ② crowd ③ drought
④ discount ⑤ aria

중요

03

> Background knowledge will help you to _____ the musical.

① mean ② discount
③ guess ④ appreciate
⑤ celebrate

[04~05] 다음 영영 풀이에 해당하는 단어를 고르시오.

04

> a piece of music in an opera sung by one person

① musical ② century
③ storyline ④ touch
⑤ aria

05

> causing strong feelings of sadness or sympathy

① riddle ② moving
③ brave ④ cowardly
⑤ difficult

중요

06 밑줄 친 부분의 의미가 잘못된 것은?

① Tonight, we are going to perform a musical. (공연하다)
② Why don't we go out to celebrate the New Year? (축하하다)
③ It's our school's 75th anniversary. (기념일)
④ A brave prince falls in love with her at first sight. (사랑에 빠지다)
⑤ He is nothing more than a stranger to her. (결코 ~가 아닌)

서답형

07 다음 밑줄 친 부분과 의미가 비슷한 것을 주어진 철자로 시작하여 쓰시오.

> He becomes the first man to answer all three puzzles.

➡ r_____

서답형

08 다음 두 문장이 같은 뜻이 되도록 빈칸에 알맞은 말을 쓰시오.

> Turandot is a woman of great beauty.
> = Turandot is a very _____ woman.

➡ _____

서답형

09 다음 주어진 우리말에 맞게 빈칸을 채우시오.

(1) 이런, 영화 시간에 늦을 거야.
➡ Oh, we're going to _____ _____ _____ the movie.

(2) 나는 오후에 일을 쉴 수 있을 것 같구나.
➡ I guess I can _____ the afternoon _____.

01 다음 우리말에 맞게 빈칸에 알맞은 단어를 쓰시오.

(1) 학교 끝나고 바로, 네 시에 어때?

➡ How about 4 o'clock, _____
_____ school?

(2) 당신이 맞게 대답한다면 나는 죽는 것에 동의하겠습니다.

➡ If you answer _____, I will
_____ _____ die.

(3) 그녀와 결혼하길 원하는 왕자는 누구든지 반드시 세 가지 수수께끼에 답해야 합니다.

➡ Any prince who wants to _____
her must answer three _____.

02 영어 설명을 읽고, 문장의 빈칸에 들어갈 알맞은 단어를 쓰시오.

> to understand how good something or someone is

(1) Her family doesn't _____ her.

> the series of events that happen in a book, film, play, etc.

(2) Having a clear _____ is very important to movies and novels.

03 다음 〈보기〉에서 빈칸에 공통으로 들어갈 단어를 골라 쓰시오.

┌─ 보기 ─┐
take   be   care   look
└────────┘

• Can I _____ the afternoon off?
• Why don't we _____ the bus?

04 다음 빈칸에 알맞은 단어를 〈보기〉에서 골라 쓰시오. (형태 변화 가능)

┌─ 보기 ─┐
like   famous   celebrate   perform
└────────┘

(1) The prince then sings the _____
_____ aria of the whole opera, "Nessun Dorma."

(2) _____ many other famous operas, *Turandot* is in Italian.

(3) She _____ my birthday last year.

(4) How was our _____?

05 다음 주어진 우리말에 맞게 빈칸을 채우시오. (필요하면 변형하여 쓰시오.)

(1) 수요일에 가면 할인을 받을 수 있어요.

➡ We can get a _____ if we go on a Wednesday.

(2) 그는 그녀에게 단지 낯선 사람일 뿐입니다.

➡ He is _____ _____ _____ a stranger to her.

(3) 만약 실패하면 그는 죽어야 합니다.

➡ If he _____, he must die.

(4) 누군가 그의 이름을 알아낼 때까지 그 누구도 잠들 수 없을 것이다.

➡ No one will go to sleep _____
someone finds out his name.

Conversation

1 제안하기

> **Why don't we see a magic show?** 마술 쇼 보는 게 어때?

- 상대방에게 '함께 ~하자'라고 제안이나 권유할 때에는 'Why don't we ~?'를 사용할 수 있다. 'Why don't you ~?'는 함께 하자는 것이 아니고 상대방에게만 권유하는 것이다.

- **제안하는 다양한 표현**

  Why don't we+동사원형 ~? = Let's+동사원형 ~. = Shall we+동사원형 ~? = How[What] about+동사원형+-ing ~? = What do you say to+동사원형+-ing ~?

제안하기와 답하기

- A: Why don't we go on a bike ride? 함께 자전거 타러 가자.
  B: Yes, let's go. 좋아, 가자.

- A: Why don't you get some sleep? 잠을 좀 자렴.
  B: Yes, I think I should. 네, 그래야겠어요.

- A: What shall we do at the park? 우리 공원에서 뭘 할까?
  B: Why don't we see a magic show? 마술 쇼 보는 게 어때?
  A: That's a good idea. 좋은 생각이야.

핵심 Check

1. 다음 대화의 빈칸에 들어갈 말로 알맞은 것은?

M: _____ The subway will be faster than the bus at this time of day.

W: That's a good idea.

① How do I get to the subway station?
② Let's keep our fingers crossed for him.
③ Shall we take the subway?
④ What happened to the subway?
⑤ What's the matter?

2. 다음 대화의 밑줄 친 부분의 의도로 적절한 것은?

B: Mom, I got only one question wrong on the Korean history exam!

W: Great! I was sure you would do well. <u>Why don't we go out to celebrate tonight?</u>

① 화남 표현하기　② 제안하기　③ 설명하기　④ 의도 표현하기　⑤ 금지하기

2 약속 정하기

> **A** What time shall we meet? 우리 몇 시에 만날까?
> **B** How about 10 o'clock on Saturday? 토요일 10시는 어때?

■ 약속을 정할 때는 What time shall we meet?, 또는 What time should we meet?, Where shall we meet?, Where should we meet? 등의 표현을 써서 몇 시에[어디서] 만날지를 묻고, 시간 및 장소를 제안할 때는 How about ~? What about ~? 등의 표현을 사용한다.

■ 시간과 장소 등의 약속을 정할 때 조동사 'should'를 사용하여 '~할까요?'라는 의미를 전달한다.

• A: What time should we meet? 우리 몇 시에 만날까?
 B: How about 6 o'clock? 6시 어때?
 A: OK. Where should we meet? 좋아. 어디서 만날까?
 B: Let's meet at the subway station. 지하철역에서 만나자.

• A: Let's go on a picnic this weekend. 이번 주말에 소풍가자.
 B: Good idea! What time shall we meet? 좋은 생각이야. 몇 시에 만날래?
 A: How about 10 o'clock on Saturday? 토요일 10시는 어때?
 B: O.K. Let's meet at the subway station. 좋아. 지하철역에서 만나자.

핵심 Check

3. 다음 빈칸에 들어갈 말로 알맞은 것을 <u>모두</u> 고르시오.

M: Karen, let's practice our parts for the school play today.

G: O.K. _____

B: How about 4 o'clock, right after school?

G: Sounds good.

① Where should we meet?
② How about at the park near your place?
③ What time shall we meet?
④ Please tell me where I should go.
⑤ When should we meet?

4. 다음 밑줄 친 문장과 같은 표현을 주어진 철자로 쓰시오.

Sue: What time shall we meet?

Dan: <u>How about 12?</u>

➡ W _____

Listen & Speak 1-A-1

M: Liz, hurry up. ❶It's already 6 o'clock.

W: Oh, ❷we're going to be late for the concert.

M: ❸Why don't we take the subway? The subway will be ❹faster than the bus at this time of day.

W: ❺That's a good idea.

M: Liz, 서둘러. 벌써 여섯 시야.
W: 이런, 우린 콘서트에 늦을 거야.
M: 지하철을 타는 게 어때? 지하철은 지금 이 시간에 버스보다 빠를 거야.
W: 좋은 생각이야.

❶ It은 시간을 나타낼 때 사용하는 비인칭 주어다.
❷ 'be going to+동사원형'은 '~할 것 같다'는 의미고, 'be late for'는 '~에 늦다'는 뜻이다.
❸ 'Why don't we+동사원형?'은 상대방에게 제안을 할 때 사용하는 표현으로 'Shall we+동사원형?'으로 바꾸어 쓸 수 있다.
❹ '비교급+than' 구문으로 '~보다 더 …한'의 의미이다.
❺ 상대가 제안한 말에 대해 동의하는 표현이다.

Check(√) True or False

(1) Liz and her friend are going to take the bus.　　　　　　　　　T ☐ F ☐

(2) Liz is going to go to the concert.　　　　　　　　　　　　　　T ☐ F ☐

Listen & Speak 1-A-2

B: Mom, I got only one question wrong on the Korean history exam!

W: Great! ❶I was sure you would do well. ❷Why don't we go out to celebrate tonight?

B: Yes! Can we ❸have pizza for dinner?

W: Of course, Joe. I'll call your dad.

B: 엄마, 제가 한국사 시험에서 겨우 한 문제만 틀렸어요!
W: 대단해! 네가 잘할 거라고 확신했단다. 오늘밤 축하하러 나가는 건 어때?
B: 좋아요! 저녁으로 피자를 먹어도 되나요?
W: 물론이지, Joe. 아빠에게 전화걸게.

❶ be sure (that) 주어+동사 ~: ~을 확신하다
❷ 'Why don't we+동사원형?'은 상대방에게 제안을 할 때 사용하는 표현으로 'Shall we+동사원형?'으로 바꾸어 쓸 수 있다.
❸ have는 eat의 의미로 사용되었다.

Check(√) True or False

(3) The boy did well on the Korean history exam.　　　　　　　　T ☐ F ☐

(4) The boy's family are going to go out for dinner.　　　　　　　T ☐ F ☐

Listen & Speak 1-B

A: ❶What shall we do at the park?

B: ❷Why don't we see a magic show?

A: That's a good idea.

A: 우리 공원에서 뭘 할까?
B: 마술 쇼를 보는 건 어때?
A: 좋은 생각이야.

❶ What shall we do ~?: 우리 뭘 할까?
❷ 상대방에게 제안을 할 때 사용하는 표현으로 'Shall we+동사원형?', 'Let's+동사원형' 등으로 바꾸어 쓸 수 있다.

Listen & Speak 2-A-1

B: Karen, ❶let's practice our parts for the school play today.

G: O.K. ❷What time shall we meet?

B: ❸How about 4 o'clock, right after school?

G: Sounds good.

❶ Let's+동사원형: '~하자'라는 제안이나 권유의 표현이다.

❷ 시간을 정하는 표현으로 '몇 시에 만날래?'의 뜻이다.

❸ 시간 및 장소를 제안할 때는 'How about ~?', 'What about ~?' 등의 표현을 사용한다.

Listen & Speak 2-A-2

G: Do you want to play badminton together this afternoon, Mark?

B: Sure. ❶Where shall we play?

G: ❷How about at the park near your place?

B: O.K. See you there at 3 o'clock.

❶ 어디서 만날지 장소를 제안하는 표현이다.

❷ 장소를 제안할 때는 'How about ~?', 'What about ~?' 등의 표현을 사용한다.

Listen & Speak 2-B

A: ❶Let's go on a picnic this weekend.

B: Good idea. ❷What time shall we meet?

A: How about 10 o'clock on Saturday?

B: O.K. Let's meet at the subway station. See you there.

❶ Let's+동사원형: '~하자'라는 제안이나 권유의 표현이다.

❷ 몇 시에 만날지 시간을 제안하는 표현이다.

Communicate A

Anna: Dad, ❶guess what! I have no school next Wednesday.

Dad: Really? ❷Why not?

Anna: It's our school's 75th anniversary.

Dad: Oh, I see.

Anna: Can we do something together that day?

Dad: ❸I guess I can take the afternoon off. What do you want to do?

Anna: ❹Why don't we go see a musical at Bravo Theater near your work? We can get a discount if we go on a Wednesday.

Dad: Good idea, Anna! Then, let's just meet at the theater.

Anna: O.K. ❺What time shall we meet?

Dad: How about 12? Then, we can have lunch together, too.

Anna: You're the best, Dad!

❶ 'Guess what!'은 '있잖아'라는 의미로 상대방의 주의를 끌 때 사용하는 표현이다.

❷ 'Why not?'은 Why do you have no school?의 줄임말이다.

❸ 'I guess ~'는 '~할 것 같아'라는 의미다.

❹ 상대방에게 제안을 할 때 사용하는 표현으로 'Shall we+동사원형?', 'Let's+동사원형' 등으로 바꾸어 쓸 수 있다.

❺ 시간을 정하는 표현으로 '몇 시에 만날래?'의 뜻이다.

Communicate B

A: ❶What shall we do this afternoon?

B: ❷Why don't we go see *Wonder Woman*?

A: Good idea! What time shall we meet?

B: How about 4 o'clock?

A: O.K. Let's meet at Moon Theater.

❶ What shall we do ~?: 우리 뭘 할까?

❷ 'Why don't we+동사원형?'은 '~하는 게 어때?'라는 뜻으로 어떤 활동을 함께 하자고 제안할 경우에 사용하는 표현으로 'Let's+동사원형' 등으로 바꾸어 쓸 수 있다.

Progress Check

1. G: Jim, hurry up. It's already 10 o'clock.

   B: Oh, ❶we're going to be late for the movie.

   G: ❷Why don't we take the bus? The bus will be faster than the subway at this time of day.

   B: That's a good idea.

2. B: ❸It's very hot today. ❹Let's go swimming, Julie.

   G: Good idea! Where shall we meet?

   B: ❺How about at the subway station near my place?

   G: O.K. See you there at 11 o'clock.

❶ 'be going to+동사원형'은 '~할 것 같다'는 의미이고, 'be late for'는 '~에 늦다'는 뜻이다.

❷ 'Why don't we+동사원형?'은 '~하는 게 어때?'라는 뜻으로 어떤 활동을 함께 하자고 제안할 경우에 사용한다.

❸ 날씨를 나타내는 비인칭 주어 It이다.

❹ 'Let's+동사원형'은 '~하자'라고 제안을 할 때 사용한다.

❺ 'How about ~?'은 '~는 어때?'라는 표현으로 제안할 때 사용한다.

● 다음 우리말과 일치하도록 빈칸에 알맞은 말을 쓰시오.

Listen & Speak 1-A

1. M: Liz, _____ _____ . It's _____ 6 o'clock.

   W: Oh, we're going to _____ _____ _____ the concert.

   M: _____ _____ _____ _____ the subway? The subway will be _____ _____ the bus at this time of day.

   W: That's a good idea.

2. B: Mom, I got only one question _____ on the Korean history exam!

   W: Great! I was _____ you would do _____ . _____ _____ _____ go out to _____ tonight?

   B: Yes! Can we have pizza _____ dinner?

   W: _____ _____ , Joe. I'll call your dad.

Listen & Speak 1-B

A: What _____ _____ do at the park?

B: _____ _____ _____ see a magic show?

A: That's a _____ _____ .

Listen & Speak 2-A

1. B: Karen, _____ practice our _____ for the school _____ today.

   G: O.K. _____ _____ _____ _____ _____ ?

   B: _____ _____ 4 o'clock, _____ after school?

   G: _____ good.

2. G: Do you want to play badminton together this afternoon, Mark?

   B: Sure. _____ _____ _____ play?

   G: How _____ at the park _____ your place?

   B: O.K. See you there _____ 3 o'clock.

Listen & Speak 2-B

A: _____ go on a picnic this weekend.

B: Good idea. What time _____ we meet?

A: _____ _____ 10 o'clock on Saturday?

B: O.K. _____ _____ at the subway station. See you there.

해석

1. M: Liz, 서둘러. 벌써 여섯 시야.
   W: 이런, 우린 콘서트에 늦을 거야.
   M: 지하철을 타는 게 어때? 지하철은 지금 이 시간에 버스보다 빠를 거야.
   W: 좋은 생각이야.

2. B: 엄마, 제가 한국사 시험에서 겨우 한 문제만 틀렸어요!
   W: 대단해! 네가 잘할 거라고 확신했단다. 오늘 축하하러 나가는 건 어때?
   B: 좋아요! 저녁으로 피자를 먹어도 되나요?
   W: 물론이지, Joe. 아빠에게 전화하마.

A: 우리 공원에서 뭘 할까?
B: 마술 쇼를 보는 건 어때?
A: 좋은 생각이야.

1. B: Karen, 오늘 학교 연극에서 우리 부분을 연습하자.
   G: 좋아. 몇 시에 만날까?
   B: 학교 끝나고 바로, 네 시 어때?
   G: 좋아.

2. G: Mark, 오후에 같이 배드민턴 하지 않을래?
   B: 물론이지. 어디서 할까?
   G: 너희 집 근처 공원은 어때?
   B: 좋아. 세 시에 거기서 보자.

A: 주말에 소풍가자.
B: 좋은 생각이야. 몇 시에 만날래?
A: 토요일 10시는 어때?
B: 좋아. 지하철역에서 만나자. 거기서 봐.

Communicate A

Anna: Dad, _____ what! I have no school next Wednesday.

Dad: Really? _____ _____?

Anna: It's our school's 75th _____.

Dad: Oh, I see.

Anna: Can we do something _____ that day?

Dad: I guess I can _____ the afternoon _____. What do you want to do?

Anna: _____ _____ _____ go see a musical at Bravo Theater near your work? We can _____ a _____ _____ we go on a Wednesday.

Dad: Good idea, Anna! Then, _____ just meet at the theater.

Anna: O.K. What time _____ _____ meet?

Dad: _____ _____ 12? Then, we can have lunch together, too.

Anna: You're the _____, Dad!

Anna: 아빠, 있잖아요! 저는 다음 주 수요일에 수업이 없어요.

아빠: 정말? 왜 없니?

Anna: 75주년 개교 기념일이에요.

아빠: 그렇구나.

Anna: 그날 오후에 같이 뭔가 할 수 있을까요?

아빠: 나는 오후에 휴무를 할 수 있을 것 같구나. 뭘 하고 싶니?

Anna: 아빠 직장 근처 Bravo 극장에서 뮤지컬을 보는 건 어때요? 수요일에 가면 할인을 받을 수 있어요.

아빠: 좋은 생각이구나, Anna! 그럼 바로 극장에서 만나자.

Anna: 좋아요. 몇 시에 만날까요?

아빠: 12시는 어떠니? 그럼 점심도 같이 먹을 수 있단다.

Anna: 최고예요, 아빠!

Communicate B

A: _____ _____ _____ do this afternoon?

B: _____ _____ _____ go see *Wonder Woman*?

A: Good idea! What _____ _____ _____ meet?

B: _____ about 4 o'clock?

A: O.K. _____ meet at Moon Theater.

A: 오늘 오후에 뭘 할까?

B: 원더 우먼을 보러 가는 건 어때?

A: 좋은 생각이야! 몇 시에 만날까?

B: 4시는 어때?

A: 좋아. Moon 극장에서 보자.

Progress Check

1. **G:** Jim, hurry up. It's already 10 o'clock.

   B: Oh, we're going to be late for the movie.

   G: _____ _____ _____ _____ the bus? The bus will be _____ than the subway _____ _____ _____ _____ _____.

   B: That's a good idea.

2. **B:** It's very hot today. _____ _____ _____, Julie.

   G: Good idea! _____ shall we meet?

   B: _____ _____ at the subway station near my place?

   G: O.K. See you there at 11 o'clock.

1. G: Jim, 서둘러. 벌써 10시야.
   B: 이런, 영화 시간에 늦을 거야.
   G: 버스를 타는 게 어때? 지금 이 시간에는 버스가 지하철보다 빠를 거야.
   B: 좋은 생각이야.

2. B: 오늘 굉장히 덥네. 수영하러 가자, Julie.
   G: 좋은 생각이야! 어디서 만날래?
   B: 우리 집 근처 지하철역에서 만나는 게 어때?
   G: 좋아. 11시에 거기서 보자.

[01~03] 다음 대화의 빈칸에 알맞은 말은?

01

B: It's very hot today. Let's go swimming, Julie.

G: Good idea! _____

B: How about at the subway station near my place?

G: O.K. See you there at 11 o'clock.

① Why don't we take the bus?　② What time shall we meet?

③ Let's go there.　④ Where shall we meet?

⑤ Oh, I see.

02

A: Let's go on a picnic this weekend.

B: Good idea. _____

A: How about 10 o'clock on Saturday?

B: O.K. Let's meet at the subway station. See you there.

① Where shall we meet?

② How about at the park near your place?

③ What time shall we meet?

④ What shall we do at the park?

⑤ Why don't we take the subway?

03

M: Liz, hurry up. It's already 6 o'clock.

W: Oh, we're going to be late for the concert.

M: Why don't we take the subway? The subway will be _____ the bus at this time of day.

W: That's a good idea.

① faster than　② more fast than　③ fast than

④ the fastest than　⑤ the faster than

04 자연스러운 대화가 되도록 순서대로 배열하시오.

(A) O.K. See you there at 3 o'clock.

(B) Sure. Where shall we play?

(C) Do you want to play badminton together this afternoon, Mark?

(D) How about at the park near your place?

➡ _____

[01~03] 다음 대화를 읽고 물음에 답하시오.

> A: _____(A)_____ this afternoon?
> B: Why don't we go see *Wonder Woman*?
> A: Good idea! _____(B)_____
> B: How __(C)__ 4 o'clock?
> A: O.K. Let's meet at Moon Theater.

01 빈칸 (A)에 알맞은 말을 고르시오.

① What do you do
② What did you do
③ Where shall we meet
④ What shall we do
⑤ What will you make

02 빈칸 (B)에 알맞은 말을 고르시오.

① Shall we make it at 4?
② What time shall we meet?
③ I'm sorry but I can't.
④ Where shall we meet?
⑤ Why don't we go see a musical?

03 빈칸 (C)에 알맞은 말은?

① about   ② at   ③ for
④ of   ⑤ in

04 밑줄 친 부분과 바꾸어 쓸 수 있는 문장을 모두 고르시오.

> B: It's very hot today. Let's go swimming.
> G: Good idea!

① Why don't we go swimming?
② Are you planning to go swimming?
③ Are you going to go swimming?
④ Shall we go swimming?
⑤ What about going swimming?

05 다음 중 짝지어진 대화가 어색한 것은?

① A: Where shall we play?
　 B: How about at the park near your place?
② A: Let's go on a picnic this weekend.
　 B: Good idea.
③ A: I have no school next Wednesday.
　 B: Really? Why not?
④ A: What time shall we meet?
　 B: How about 1 o'clock?
⑤ A: Jim, hurry up. It's already 10 o'clock.
　 B: What shall we try first?

[06~07] 다음 대화를 읽고 물음에 답하시오.

> B: It's very hot today. ____ⓐ____ go swimming, Julie.
> G: Good idea! ____ⓑ____ shall we meet?
> B: How about at the subway station near my place?
> G: O.K. See you there at 11 o'clock.

06 빈칸 ⓐ, ⓑ에 들어갈 말로 알맞은 것은?

① Let us – What
② Let us – When
③ Let's – What time
④ Let's – Where
⑤ Let's　Whom

서답형

07 다음 영영풀이에 해당하는 단어를 대화에서 찾아 쓰시오.

> a building and the surrounding area where buses or trains stop for people to get on or off

➡ _____

중요

08 다음 대화의 빈칸 (A)에 들어갈 말로 알맞은 것은?

> G: Do you want to play badminton together this afternoon, Mark?
> B: Sure. Where shall we play?
> G: _____(A)_____
> B: O.K. See you there at 3 o'clock.

① How about at the park near your place?
② Let's meet at 3 o'clock.
③ What time shall we meet?
④ I'm playing badminton at the park.
⑤ I'd like to play badminton with you at the park.

[09~12] 다음 대화를 읽고 물음에 답하시오.

> Anna: Dad, guess what! I have no school next Wednesday.
> Dad: Really? Why not?
> Anna: It's our school's 75th anniversary.
> Dad: Oh, I see. (①)
> Anna: Can we do something together that day? (②)
> Dad: ⓐ나는 오후에 휴무를 할 수 있을 것 같구나. What do you want to do?
> Anna: (③) We can get a discount if we go on a Wednesday.
> Dad: Good idea, Anna! Then, let's just meet at the theater. (④)
> Anna: O.K. What time shall we meet?
> Dad: How about 12? Then, we can have lunch together, too. (⑤)
> Anna: You're the best, Dad!

09 위 대화의 ①~⑤ 중 다음 주어진 말이 들어갈 알맞은 곳은?

> Why don't we go see a musical at Bravo Theater near your work?

①   ②   ③   ④   ⑤

서답형

10 다음 영영풀이에 해당하는 단어를 대화에서 찾아 쓰시오.

> a day on which you remember or celebrate something that happened on that day in the past

➡ _____

서답형

11 밑줄 친 ⓐ의 우리말에 맞게 주어진 단어를 알맞게 배열하시오.

> I, guess, take, off, I, can, the afternoon

➡ _____

12 대화의 내용과 일치하지 않는 것은?

① Anna has no school next Wednesday.
② They are talking about getting a discount for a movie.
③ Bravo Theater provides a discount for people on a Wednesday.
④ They will meet at Bravo Theater.
⑤ They will also have lunch together.

서답형

13 대화의 흐름상 빈칸 (A)와 (B)에 들어갈 말로 알맞은 것을 〈보기〉에서 골라 쓰시오.

> ┤ 보기 ├
> right   guess   appreciate   perform
> wrong   suggest   celebrate

> Boy: Mom, I got only one question _____(A)_____ on the Korean history exam!
> Woman: Great! I was sure you would do well. Why don't we go out to _____(B)_____ tonight?
> Boy: Yes! Can we have pizza for dinner?
> Woman: Of course, Joe. I'll call your dad.

➡ (A) _____ (B) _____

[01~02] 다음 대화를 읽고 물음에 답하시오.

> M: Liz, hurry up. It's already 6 o'clock.
> W: Oh, we're going to be late for the concert.
> M: Why don't we take the subway? (A)지하철은 지금 이 시간에 버스보다 빠를 거야.
> W: That's a good idea.

01 What are the speakers going to take?

➡ They _____.

02 밑줄 친 (A)의 우리말에 맞게 주어진 어구를 이용하여 영작하시오.

> this time, day, the subway, the bus, be, will, than, fast, at, of

➡ _____

    _____

03 다음 대화의 밑줄 친 부분을 같은 말로 바꾸어 쓸 때, 주어진 철자로 시작하여 쓰시오.

> A: What shall we do at the park?
> B: Why don't we see a magic show?
> A: That's a good idea.

➡ L_____
➡ S_____
➡ W_____

04 다음 대화에서 괄호 안의 단어를 바르게 배열하시오.

> A: (shall, what, meet, time, we)?
> B: How about 4 o'clock?

➡ _____

[05~07] 다음 대화를 읽고 물음에 답하시오.

> Anna: Dad, guess what! I have no school next Wednesday.
> Dad: Really? Why not?
> Anna: It's our school's 75th anniversary.
> Dad: Oh, I see.
> Anna: Can we do something together that day?
> Dad: I guess I can ___(A)___ the afternoon off. What do you want to do?
> Anna: Why don't we go see a musical at Bravo Theater near your work? We can get a discount if we go on a Wednesday.
> Dad: Good idea, Anna! Then, let's just meet at the theater.
> Anna: O.K. What time shall we meet?
> Dad: How ___(B)___ 12? Then, (C) we can have a lunch together, too.
> Anna: You're the best, Dad!

05 빈칸 (A)와 (B)에 알맞은 단어를 쓰시오.

➡ (A) _____ (B) _____

06 위 대화의 밑줄 친 (C)에서 어법상 틀린 것을 고치시오.

_____ ➡ _____

07 위 대화를 읽고 아래의 표의 빈칸을 완성하시오.

Anna's Next Week Plan		
What: see _____ _____ with _____
When: _____ Wednesday at _____
Where: at _____ _____

Grammar

1 접속사 if

> • You will appreciate it better **if** you know the story.
> 네가 그 이야기를 안다면 더 잘 감상할 것이다.
>
> • **If** he fails, he must die. 만약 실패한다면, 그는 죽어야만 한다.

- 접속사 if는 '만약 ~한다면'이라는 뜻으로, 조건의 부사절을 이끌며, 'if + 주어 + 동사 ~'의 형태로 쓴다. if절이 주절 앞에 오면 if절 뒤에 콤마(,)를 사용하고, 주절 뒤에 오면 콤마(,)를 사용하지 않는다.

  - **If** you miss the bus, you'll be late for school.

    = You'll be late for school **if** you miss the bus. 네가 버스를 놓친다면, 너는 학교에 늦을 것이다.

- 조건 부사절인 if절에서는 현재시제가 미래시제를 대신한다.

  - **If** it **rains** tomorrow, I will stay at home. (○) 내일 비가 온다면, 나는 집에 머물 것이다.

    If it will rain tomorrow, I will stay at home. (✕)

cf. 시간을 나타내는 부사절도 현재시제가 미래시제를 대신한다. 시간을 나타내는 부사절 접속사는 when(~할 때), until(~까지), before, after, as soon as(~하자마자) 등이 있다.

  - No one will go to sleep **until** someone **finds** out his name. (○)

    No one will go to sleep until someone will find out his name. (✕)

cf. if절이 동사의 목적어 자리에 사용되는 명사절일 경우는 미래시제를 사용할 수 있다.

  - I don't know **if** he **will come** tomorrow. 나는 그가 내일 올지 안 올지 모른다.

  - I wonder **if** she **will tell** you the secret. 그녀가 너에게 그 비밀을 말해 줄지 궁금하다.

핵심 Check

1. 괄호 안에서 알맞은 것을 고르시오.

   (1) If it is fine tomorrow, we (will go / go) on a picnic.

   (2) If you (miss / will miss) the bus, you will be late for the movie.

   (3) If you (will be / are) late for the movie, your friend will be very angry!

2. 다음 문장에서 어법상 틀린 곳이 있다면 바르게 고치오.

   (1) If you will exercise every day, you'll stay healthy.

   ➡ _____

   (2) I don't know if he will come to my house tonight.

   ➡ _____

② as + 형용사/부사의 원급 + as

- Turandot is **as** cold **as** ice. Turandot는 얼음처럼 차갑다.
- I can jump **as** high **as** Michael Jordan. 나는 Michael Jordan만큼 높이 점프할 수 있다.

■ 형태: as + 형용사/부사의 원급 + as

■ 의미: ~만큼 …한/하게 (두 대상의 정도가 같음을 나타냄)

  e.g.   She is **as** tall **as** you. 그녀는 너만큼 키가 크다.

      Jane is **as** old **as** Tom. (= Jane and Tom are the same age.)

■ 부정문: not as[so] + 형용사/부사의 원급 + as (~만큼 …하지 않은/않게)

  e.g.   Tom is **not as** tall **as** Amy. Tom은 Amy만큼 키가 크지 않다.

      My bike is **not so** old **as** his bike. 나의 자전거는 그의 자전거만큼 오래되지 않았다.

      Tom is **not as** old **as** Peter. Tom은 Peter만큼 나이가 많지 않다.

      = Tom is **younger than** Peter. Tom은 Peter보다 어리다.

      = Peter is **older than** Tom. Peter는 Tom보다 나이가 많다.

cf. ■ 비교급을 이용한 비교

    두 대상 중 하나가 우위에 있음을 나타낼 때 사용한다.

    형태: 형용사/부사의 비교급 + than ~: ~보다 더 …한/하게

    - Fred is **taller than** I am. Fred는 나보다 더 크다.
    - Cathy is **smarter than** I am. Cathy는 나보다 더 똑똑하다.

  ■ 최상급을 이용한 비교급

    세 개 이상의 대상 중 어느 하나의 정도가 가장 높을 때 사용한다.

    형태: the + 형용사/부사의 최상급: 가장 ~한/ 하게

    - Sujin is **the tallest** of the three. Sujin은 셋 중에서 가장 크다.
    - Here is **the most interesting** place in Busan. 부산에서 가장 흥미로운 장소가 여기에 있다.

핵심 Check

3. 괄호 안에서 알맞은 것을 고르시오.

  (1) A dog is as [cleverer / clever] as a cat.

  (2) Science is as [interestingly / interesting] as history.

4. 다음 빈칸에 공통으로 들어갈 말로 알맞은 것은?

  This car is ＿＿＿＿ cheap ＿＿＿＿ that one.

  ① so   ② as   ③ too   ④ such   ⑤ to

01 다음 문장에서 어법상 <u>어색한</u> 부분을 바르게 고치시오.

(1) This new smartphone is as more expensive as a computer.

_____ ➡ _____

(2) This turtle is as small than a coin.

_____ ➡ _____

(3) If you will answer incorrectly, you will have to marry me.

_____ ➡ _____

(4) If you won't run now, you will miss the bus.

➡ _____

expensive 비싼
turtle 거북
marry 결혼하다
miss 놓치다

02 다음 빈칸에 공통으로 들어갈 말로 알맞은 것은? (대 · 소문자 무시)

• I asked him _____ he could study with me.

• _____ you watch it, you'll enter a fantasy world.

① whether   ② who   ③ which

④ though   ⑤ if

enter 들어가다
fantasy 상상, 공상

03 두 문장을 한 문장으로 만들 때 빈칸에 알맞은 말을 고르시오.

• Sue is 168 cm tall.

• Sam is 168 cm tall, too.

➡ Sue is _____ Sam.

① tall   ② taller than   ③ tall as

④ as tall as   ⑤ as taller as

04 다음 빈칸에 들어갈 말로 알맞은 것은?

• They do not work _____ we do.

① as hard than   ② as hardly as   ③ as hard as

④ hard than   ⑤ as harder as

hard 열심히
hardly 거의 ~ 않다

Grammar 시험대비 실력평가

Step3

01 다음 중 어법상 어색한 문장은?

① His riddle is as difficult as her.
② This shirt isn't so large as that one.
③ Jenny can speak English as fluently as Maria.
④ Sandra is as heavy as Tom.
⑤ This river is as long as the Han River.

서답형

02 다음 대화를 읽고, 빈칸에 알맞은 말을 쓰시오.

> M: Liz, hurry up. It's already 6 o'clock.
> W: Oh, we're going to be late for the concert.
> M: Why don't we take the subway? The subway will be _____ than the bus at this time of day.
> W: That's a good idea.

➡ _____

03 다음 우리말과 일치하도록 알맞게 영작한 것은?

> 네가 약속을 어긴다면, 아무도 너를 믿지 않을 거야.

① Though you break your promises, nobody will trust you.
② Because you will break your promises, nobody will trust you.
③ If you will break your promises, nobody will trust you.
④ If you break your promises, nobody won't trust you.
⑤ If you break your promises, nobody will trust you.

서답형

04 다음 괄호 안에서 알맞은 단어를 고르시오.

(1) Suji is as pretty (so / as) her sister.
(2) Minji is as (taller / tall) as I.
(3) My room is as big as (yours / you).

서답형

05 다음 우리말에 맞게 주어진 어구를 알맞은 순서로 배열하시오. ((1)과 (2)는 if로 문장을 시작하시오.)

(1) 만약 당신이 이어폰을 사용해야 한다면 음악을 크게 틀지 마시오.
(If / play / have to / do / earphones / use / you / your music / not / loud)
➡ _____

(2) 지하철을 놓친다면, 모임에 늦을 거야.
(If / you / you / will be / miss / late / the subway / the meeting / for)
➡ _____

(3) 내 목소리는 너만큼 크다.
(my voice / as / as / yours / loud / is)
➡ _____

(4) Nick은 Peter만큼 빨리 달릴 수 있다.
(Nick / Peter / run / as / as / can / fast)
➡ _____

중요

06 다음 빈칸에 들어갈 알맞은 것은?

> If your friend _____ very angry, you will have to buy her ice cream.

① will be　　② is
③ won't be　　④ will is
⑤ are

07 〈보기〉의 밑줄 친 부분과 쓰임이 같은 것을 모두 고르시오.

> ┤ 보기 ├─
> Tom will be happy <u>if</u> you visit him.

① He asked me <u>if</u> I could play with him.
② I don't know <u>if</u> it will rain tomorrow.
③ I wonder <u>if</u> he will buy a new car.
④ We will play baseball <u>if</u> it doesn't rain tomorrow.
⑤ <u>If</u> he comes back tomorrow, I'll talk to him about the problem.

08 다음 중 어법상 어색한 것은?

① My eyes are as dark as chocolate.
② Fred is as tall as I am.
③ My bike is as old as Tom's bike.
④ Minho speaks English as good as a native speaker.
⑤ Dora is not as fast as I am.

09 다음 우리말을 바르게 영작한 것은?

> 내일 날씨가 맑으면 그들은 바다에 갈 것이다.

① They will go to the sea if it is sunny tomorrow.
② They go to the sea if it will be sunny tomorrow.
③ They go to the sea if it is sunny tomorrow.
④ If it will be sunny tomorrow, they will go to the sea.
⑤ If it was sunny tomorrow, they went to the sea.

서답형

10 어법상 틀린 부분을 찾아 바르게 고치시오.

(1) Juho doesn't study so hard than Dora.
　　_____ ➡ _____

(2) This song sounds as more beautiful as a poem.
　　_____ ➡ _____

(3) I can jump as highly as Michael Jordan.
　　_____ ➡ _____

(4) If she will miss the bus, she won't get here on time.
　　_____ ➡ _____

서답형

11 다음 문장에서 틀린 부분을 찾아 바르게 고치시오.

(1) Your sister is as friend as his.
　　_____ ➡ _____

(2) She can't run as faster as Billy.
　　_____ ➡ _____

12 다음 중 어법상 어색한 것은?

① If he fails, he must die.
② If you answer correctly, I will agree to die.
③ If you answer incorrectly, you will have to marry me.
④ You will appreciate it better if you know the story.
⑤ If you get up early tomorrow morning, you see the sunrise.

13 다음 두 문장을 한 문장으로 바르게 바꾼 것은?

> • Jomin reads many books.
> • Sumin reads many books, too.

① Jomin reads as much books as Sumin.
② Jomin reads as much as Sumin.
③ Jomin reads as many as Sumin's books.
④ Jomin reads as many books as Sumin.
⑤ Jomin reads more books than Sumin does.

서답형
14 다음 괄호 안에서 알맞은 것을 고르시오.

(1) Anne is not (too / as) tall as Judy.
(2) Sumi speaks English as (well / better) as Minsu.
(3) Your house is as small as (I / mine).

서답형
[15~16] 다음 우리말에 맞게 주어진 어구를 이용하여 영작하시오.

15
> 그녀는 깃털만큼 가볍다.
> (light, a feather)

➡ _____

16
> 호랑이는 코끼리만큼 크지 않다.
> (a tiger, so, big, an elephant)

➡ _____

서답형
17 다음 밑줄 친 부분과 바꿔 쓸 수 있는 말을 한 단어로 쓰시오.

> The bus is not <u>as</u> fast as the subway at this time of day.

➡ _____

[18~19] 주어진 어구들을 사용하여 원급 비교 문장으로 바르게 나타낸 것을 모두 고르시오.

18
> This soldier, brave, a lion

① This soldier is so braver as a lion.
② This soldier isn't as brave as a lion.
③ This soldier is as brave as a lion.
④ This soldier is so brave than a lion.
⑤ This soldier is too brave as a lion.

19
> My father, strong, an ox

① My father isn't so strong as an ox.
② My father is stronger than an ox.
③ My father isn't so stronger as an ox.
④ My father is as stronger as an ox.
⑤ My father is as strong as an ox.

서답형
20 우리말에 맞게 괄호 안에서 알맞은 것을 고르시오.

> • 내가 이탈리아에 간다면 나는 피자와 스파게티를 먹을 것이다.
> • 우리가 내일 만나면 무엇을 할 거니?

➡ If I (will go / go) to Italy, I (will eat / eat) pizza and spaghetti.
➡ When we (will meet / meet) tomorrow, what (will / do) you do?

01 다음 두 문장의 의미가 같도록 빈칸을 완성하시오.

> Mina is bigger than Jenny.
> = Jenny _____ Mina.

02 다음 문장에서 어법상 어색한 부분을 고쳐 문장을 다시 쓰시오.

(1) I can finish the work if you will help me.

➡ _____
_____

(2) If school will finish early tomorrow, I will go see a movie.

➡ _____
_____

(3) If my mom will catch a cold, I will do the dishes for her.

➡ _____
_____

03 다음 그림을 보고 주어진 문장을 완성하시오.

(1)
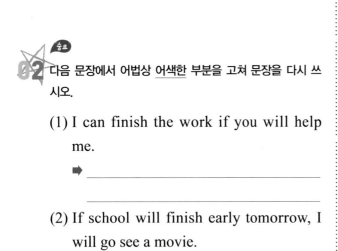

➡ The dog can _____ the ostrich.

(2)

➡ This turtle is _____ small _____ a coin.

04 다음 문장에서 어색한 부분을 찾아 바르게 고치시오.

(1) Your car is as expensive as me.

_____ ➡ _____

(2) Soccer isn't as more popular as baseball in Korea.

_____ ➡ _____

(3) If it won't rain tomorrow, we'll go on a picnic.

_____ ➡ _____

(4) You will fail if you won't study harder from now on.

_____ ➡ _____

05 두 문장을 'as ~ as'를 이용하여 한 문장으로 쓰시오.

(1) • John is 170cm tall.
• Susan is 170cm tall, too.

➡ _____

(2) • This apple is sweet.
• That pineapple is also sweet.

➡ _____

(3) • My bike is old.
• But his bike is older than mine.

➡ _____

(4) • I watch 5 movies every month.
• Kate also watches 5 movies every month.

➡ _____

06 다음 표를 보고 원급 비교를 이용하여 다음 빈칸을 완성하시오.

Name	Tom	Eric	Amy
Age	15	14	15
Height	167cm	167cm	163cm
Weight	58kg	52kg	52kg

(1) Eric is _____ Amy.

(2) Tom is _____ Amy.

(3) Tom is _____ Eric.

07 우리말과 일치하도록 주어진 어구를 알맞은 순서로 배열하시오. (부사절로 문장을 시작하시오.)

(1) 만약 당신이 초콜릿을 너무 많이 먹는다면 당신의 치아가 상할 것이다.

(if / too much / you / eat / your / will / teeth / go / bad / chocolate)

➡ _____

_____

(2) 만약 Fred가 학교에 걸어간다면 40분이 걸릴 것이다.

(Fred / to / if / walks / it / take / school / will / 40 minutes)

➡ _____

(3) 만약 네가 지도를 따라간다면 너는 나의 할머니의 집에 도착할 것이다.

(the / follow / you / get / you'll / if / map / to / my grandma's house)

➡ _____

_____

08 다음 주어진 문장에서 어법상 틀린 부분을 찾아 바르게 고쳐 쓰시오.

> Turandot must find the answer before dawn, but his riddle is as difficult than her. She says to everyone, "No one will go to sleep until someone will find out his name."

➡ _____

➡ _____

09 다음 표를 보고 수지와 민지를 비교하는 글을 완성하시오. (동등비교 구문을 이용할 것.)

이름	나이	키	100m 기록
Suji	14	167 cm	15초
Minji	14	164 cm	12초

(1) Minji is _____ Suji. (나이)

(2) Minji is _____ Suji. (키)

(3) Suji is _____ Minji. (100m 기록)

10 다음 우리말에 맞게 주어진 어구를 이용하여 영작하시오.

(1) 그녀의 여동생은 새끼 고양이만큼 장난꾸러기다. (playful, a kitten)

➡ _____

(2) 우리 집은 묘지만큼이나 조용하다. (home, quiet, a grave)

➡ _____

(3) 나는 내 남동생만큼 키가 크지 않다. (tall, my brother)

➡ _____

Reading

Turandot
The Most Dangerous Love in the World!

Welcome, everyone! Tonight, we are going to perform Giacomo Puccini's opera *Turandot*. Like many other famous operas, *Turandot* is in Italian because opera started in Italy in the 16th century. Before we begin, I'd like to tell you the storyline of the opera *Turandot*. You will appreciate it better if you know the story.

Turandot, a Chinese princess, is a woman of great beauty, but she is as cold as ice. Any prince who wants to marry her must answer three riddles. If he fails, he must die. No one has ever been able to answer them. One day, a brave prince falls in love with her at first sight. He becomes the first man to answer all three riddles.

perform 공연하다, 수행하다
Italian 이탈리아어, 이탈리아인; 이탈리아의
century 100년, 세기
storyline (소설·연극·영화 등의) 줄거리
appreciate 감상하다, 감사하다, 알아주다
riddle 수수께끼
fall in love 사랑에 빠지다, 반하다

확인문제

● 다음 문장이 본문의 내용과 일치하면 T, 일치하지 않으면 F를 쓰시오.

1 Giacomo Puccini composed the opera *Turandot*. ☐

2 *Turandot* is in Italian because Puccini was born in Italy. ☐

3 Many famous operas are in Italian because opera started in Italy. ☐

4 You must appreciate the opera before you know the story. ☐

5 Turandot is a very beautiful Chinese princess. ☐

6 Any prince who wants to marry her must answer four riddles. ☐

7 If the prince fails to answer the riddles, he must die. ☐

8 One day, a brave prince falls in love with her at first sight, but he fails to answer the riddles. ☐

However, Turandot does not want to marry the prince. He is <u>nothing</u>
<u>more than</u> a stranger to her. He then gives her a riddle <u>of his own.</u> He
asks her, "What is my name?" He adds, "If you <u>answer</u> correctly, I will
agree to die. If you answer <u>incorrectly</u>, you will have to marry me."

Turandot must find the answer <u>before</u> dawn, but his riddle is <u>as</u>
<u>difficult as hers.</u> She says to everyone, "<u>No one</u> will go to sleep until
someone <u>finds</u> out his name." The prince then sings <u>the most famous</u>
<u>aria of the whole opera</u>, "Nessun Dorma." It means <u>no one sleeps.</u>

No one sleeps.

No one <u>sleeps</u>, not even you, Princess.

...

My secret is safe.

No one will know my name.

...

At dawn, I will win! I will win!

The prince's name is Calaf. Will the princess learn his name in time?

<u>Let's watch the opera and find out.</u>
= How about watching the opera and finding out?

dawn 새벽, 동틀 녘
aria 아리아, 영창
whole 전체; 모든, 전부의
secret 비밀
safe 안전한
in time 제시간에, 늦지 않게
find out 알아내다, 발견하다

📎 **확인문제**

● 다음 문장이 본문의 내용과 일치하면 T, 일치하지 않으면 <u>F</u>를 쓰시오.

1 Turandot wants to marry the prince. ☐

2 The prince is only a stranger to her. ☐

3 The prince gives Turandot a riddle of his own. ☐

4 If Turandot answers correctly, the prince will marry her. ☐

5 The prince's riddle is as difficult as Turandot's. ☐

6 Turandot will learn the prince's name in time. ☐

● 우리말을 참고하여 빈칸에 알맞은 말을 쓰시오.

1 Turandot _____ _____ _____ Love in the World

2 _____, everyone!

3 Tonight, we are going to _____ Giacomo Puccini's opera *Turandot*.

4 _____ many other famous operas, *Turandot* is _____ _____ because opera started _____ _____ in the 16th century.

5 Before we begin, _____ _____ _____ _____ you the storyline of the opera *Turandot*.

6 You will _____ it better _____ you know the story.

7 Turandot, a Chinese princess, is a woman _____ _____ _____, but she is _____ _____ _____ _____.

8 Any prince _____ wants to _____ _____ must answer three riddles.

9 If he _____, he must die.

10 No one _____ _____ _____ able to answer them.

11 One day, a brave prince _____ _____ _____ _____ her at first sight.

12 He becomes _____ _____ _____ to answer all three riddles.

13 _____, Turandot does not want _____ _____ the prince.

14 He is _____ _____ _____ a stranger to her.

15 He then gives her a riddle _____ _____ _____.

16 He asks her, "_____ is my name?"

17 He _____, "If you answer correctly, I will agree _____

_____. If you answer _____, you will have to marry me."

18 Turandot must find the answer _____ _____, but his riddle is

_____ _____ _____ _____.

19 She says to everyone, "No one will go to sleep _____ someone

_____ _____ his name."

20 The prince then sings _____ _____ _____ _____ of the

whole opera, "Nessun Dorma."

21 It _____ no one sleeps.

22 No one _____.

23 No one sleeps, _____ _____ _____, Princess.

24 My secret is _____.

25 No one _____ _____ my name.

26 _____ _____, I will win! I will win!

27 The _____ name is Calaf.

28 Will the princess learn his name _____ _____?

29 _____ _____ the opera and find out.

16 그는 그녀에게 "제 이름이 무엇입니까?"라고 묻습니다.

17 그는 "당신이 맞게 대답한다면 나는 죽는 것에 동의하겠습니다. 만약 답이 틀리면 당신은 저와 결혼해야 할 것입니다."라고 덧붙입니다.

18 Turandot는 동이 트기 전에 답을 찾아야 하지만 그의 수수께끼는 그녀의 것만큼 어렵습니다.

19 그녀는 모두에게 "누군가 그의 이름을 알아낼 때까지 그 누구도 잠들 수 없다."라고 말합니다.

20 그리고 왕자는 이 오페라 전체에서 가장 유명한 아리아, Nessun Dorma를 부릅니다.

21 그것은 누구도 잠들지 못한다는 뜻입니다.

22 누구도 잠들지 못하네.

23 누구도 잠들지 못하네. 당신조차도, 공주여.

24 나의 비밀은 안전하다네.

25 누구도 나의 이름을 알지 못할 것이네.

26 동틀 녘에, 내가 이길 것이라네! 내가 승리할 것이라네!

27 왕자의 이름은 Calaf입니다.

28 공주는 그의 이름을 제때 알아낼 수 있을까요?

29 오페라를 보고 알아봅시다.

● 우리말을 참고하여 본문을 영작하시오.

1 투란도트, 세상에서 가장 위험한 사랑

➡ _____

2 여러분, 환영합니다!

➡ _____

3 오늘 밤, 우리는 지아코모 푸치니의 오페라 《투란도트》를 공연할 것입니다.

➡ _____

4 다른 많은 유명한 오페라들처럼 《투란도트》는 이탈리아어로 되어 있는데, 오페라가 16세기 이탈리아에서 시작되었기 때문입니다.

➡ _____

5 시작하기 전에 오페라 《투란도트》의 줄거리를 알려 드리려고 합니다.

➡ _____

6 여러분이 줄거리를 알면 이 오페라를 더 잘 감상하게 될 것입니다.

➡ _____

7 중국의 공주 Turandot는 굉장히 아름다운 여인이지만, 그녀는 얼음처럼 차갑습니다.

➡ _____

8 그녀와 결혼하길 원하는 왕자는 누구든지 반드시 세 가지 수수께끼에 답해야 합니다.

➡ _____

9 만약 실패하면 그는 죽어야 합니다.

➡ _____

10 그 누구도 수수께끼에 답할 수 없었습니다.

➡ _____

11 어느 날, 어떤 용감한 왕자가 그녀에게 첫눈에 반합니다.

➡ _____

12 그는 세 수수께끼를 모두 맞힌 첫 번째 사람이 됩니다.

➡ _____

13 그러나 Turandot는 그 왕자와 결혼하길 원하지 않습니다.

➡ _____

14 그는 그녀에게 단지 낯선 사람일 뿐입니다.

➡ _____

15 그러자 그는 그녀에게 자신의 수수께끼를 냅니다.

➡ _____

16 그는 그녀에게 "제 이름이 무엇입니까?"라고 묻습니다.

➡ _____

17 그는 "당신이 맞게 대답한다면 나는 죽는 것에 동의하겠습니다. 만약 답이 틀리면 당신은 저와 결혼해야 할 것입니다."라고 덧붙입니다.

➡ _____

18 Turandot는 동이 트기 전에 답을 찾아야 하지만 그의 수수께끼는 그녀의 것만큼 어렵습니다.

➡ _____

19 그녀는 모두에게 "누군가 그의 이름을 알아낼 때까지 그 누구도 잠들 수 없다."라고 말합니다.

➡ _____

20 그리고 왕자는 이 오페라 전체에서 가장 유명한 아리아, Nessun Dorma를 부릅니다.

➡ _____

21 그것은 누구도 잠들지 못한다는 뜻입니다.

➡ _____

22 누구도 잠들지 못하네.

➡ _____

23 누구도 잠들지 못하네, 당신조차도, 공주여.

➡ _____

24 나의 비밀은 안전하다네.

➡ _____

25 누구도 나의 이름을 알지 못할 것이네.

➡ _____

26 동틀 녘에, 내가 이길 것이라네! 내가 승리할 것이라네!

➡ _____

27 왕자의 이름은 Calaf입니다.

➡ _____

28 공주는 그의 이름을 제때 알아낼 수 있을까요?

➡ _____

29 오페라를 보고 알아봅시다.

➡ _____

[01~03] 다음 글을 읽고 물음에 답하시오.

Welcome, everyone! Tonight, we are going to perform Giacomo Puccini's opera *Turandot*. Like many other famous operas, *Turandot* is in (A)[Italy / Italian] because opera started in Italy in the 16th century. Before we begin, I'd like (B)[to tell / telling] you the storyline of the opera *Turandot*. You will appreciate it better if you (C)[know / will know] the story.

 서답형

01 위 글의 괄호 (A)~(C)에서 문맥이나 어법상 알맞은 낱말을 골라 쓰시오.

➡ (A) _____ (B) _____ (C) _____

02 위 글의 뒤에 올 내용으로 가장 알맞은 것을 고르시오.

① 오페라 《투란도트》의 작곡가 소개
② 오페라에 나오는 이탈리아어 이해하기
③ 이탈리아의 유명한 오페라들 소개
④ 오페라 《투란도트》의 줄거리 소개
⑤ 오페라 《투란도트》의 공연 관람 후기

03 위 글의 내용과 일치하지 <u>않는</u> 것은?

① 오늘 밤, 오페라 《투란도트》를 공연할 것이다.
② 오페라 《투란도트》의 작곡가는 지아코모 푸치니이다.
③ 《투란도트》는 이탈리아어로 되어 있다.
④ 오페라는 16세기 이탈리아에서 시작되었다.
⑤ 이탈리아어를 알면 오페라를 더 잘 감상하게 될 것이다.

[04~06] 다음 글을 읽고 물음에 답하시오.

One day, a brave prince falls in love with her at first sight. He becomes the first man to answer all three riddles.

___Ⓐ___, Turandot does not want to marry the prince. (①) He is nothing more than a stranger to ⓐher. (②) He asks her, "What is ⓑmy name?" (③) He adds, "If ⓒyou answer correctly, I will agree to die. (④) If you answer incorrectly, you will have to marry ⓓme." (⑤)

Turandot must find the answer before dawn, but ⓔhis riddle is as difficult as hers. She says to everyone, "No one will go to sleep until someone finds out his name."

04 위 글의 빈칸 Ⓐ에 들어갈 알맞은 말을 고르시오.

① However ② Therefore
③ In other words ④ For example
⑤ As a result

05 위 글의 흐름으로 보아, 주어진 문장이 들어가기에 가장 적절한 곳은?

> He then gives her a riddle of his own.

① ② ③ ④ ⑤

06 위 글의 밑줄 친 ⓐ~ⓔ 중 가리키는 대상이 같은 것끼리 짝지어진 것은?

① ⓐ – ⓑ ② ⓐ – ⓓ
③ ⓑ – ⓔ ④ ⓒ – ⓓ
⑤ ⓒ – ⓔ

[07~09] 다음 글을 읽고 물음에 답하시오.

Turandot, a Chinese princess, is a woman of great beauty, but she is ⓐas cold as ice. Any prince who wants to marry her must answer three riddles. If he fails, he must die. No one has ever been able to answer them. One day, a brave prince falls in love with her at first sight. He becomes the first man to answer all three riddles.

07 위 글에서 알 수 있는 Turandot의 성격으로 가장 알맞은 것을 고르시오.

① considerate   ② warm-hearted

③ heartless   ④ friendly

⑤ careless

08 위 글의 밑줄 친 ⓐas와 같은 용법으로 쓰인 것은?

① Do as you are told.

② Run as fast as you can.

③ As we go up, the air grows colder.

④ I regarded them as kind helpers.

⑤ As she was tired, she soon fell asleep.

09 위 글을 읽고 대답할 수 없는 질문은?

① Who is Turandot?

② What does Turandot look like?

③ What does the prince who wants to marry Turandot have to do?

④ What are the three riddles that Turandot asks?

⑤ Who becomes the first man to answer all three riddles?

[10~13] 다음 글을 읽고 물음에 답하시오.

Turandot must find the answer ___ⓐ___ dawn, but his riddle is as difficult as hers. She says to everyone, "No one will go to sleep until someone finds out his name."

The prince then sings the most famous aria of the whole opera, "Nessun Dorma." It means no one ___ⓑ___.

No one ___ⓑ___.

No one ___ⓑ___, not even you, Princess.

...

My secret is safe.

No one will know my name.

...

___ⓒ___ dawn, I will win! I will win!

The prince's name is Calaf. Will the princess learn his name in time? Let's watch the opera and ⓓfind out.

10 위 글의 빈칸 ⓐ와 ⓒ에 들어갈 전치사가 바르게 짝지어진 것은?

① at – In   ② before – To

③ before – At   ④ at – To

⑤ on – At

11 위 글의 빈칸 ⓑ에 공통으로 들어갈 알맞은 단어를 고르시오.

① mustn't sleep   ② sleep

③ slept   ④ can't sleep

⑤ sleeps

12 다음 질문에 대한 알맞은 대답을 주어진 단어로 시작하여 쓰시오. (6 단어)

> Q: Why does the prince say "My secret is safe"?
>
> A: Because _____.

➡ _____

서답형

13 위 글의 밑줄 친 ⓓfind out과 바꿔 쓸 수 있는 단어를 본문에서 찾아 쓰시오.

➡ _____

[14~16] 다음 글을 읽고 물음에 답하시오.

I saw *Beauty and the Beast* last Saturday. It is about a beautiful girl and a beast. I enjoyed it a lot. The songs were great, and the love story was as beautiful as a gem. If you like heart-warming stories about love, you will like it, too.

by Lee Minsu on Aug. 12

14 위 글의 종류로 알맞은 것을 고르시오.

① book report   ② essay
③ article   ④ review
⑤ biography

중요

15 위 글의 내용을 다음과 같이 정리하고자 한다. 다음 빈칸에 들어갈 알맞은 말을 고르시오.

Minsu _____ *Beauty and the Beast* to people who like heart-warming stories about love.

① demands   ② recommends
③ expresses   ④ reports
⑤ advises

16 위 글의 영화에 대해 알 수 <u>없는</u> 것은?

① What's the title of it?
② When did Minsu see it?
③ What is the story about?
④ How did Minsu like it?
⑤ With whom did Minsu see it?

[17~19] 다음 글을 읽고 물음에 답하시오.

ⓐ중국의 공주 Turandot는 굉장히 아름다운 여인이지만, 그녀는 얼음처럼 차갑습니다. Any prince who wants to marry her must answer three riddles. If he fails, he must die. No one has ever been able to answer ⓑthem. One day, a brave prince falls in love with her at first sight. He becomes the first man ⓒto answer all three riddles.

서답형

17 위 글의 밑줄 친 ⓐ의 우리말에 맞게 한 단어를 보충하여, 주어진 어휘를 알맞게 배열하시오. (콤마를 사용할 것.)

beauty / Turandot / she / as / is / but / a Chinese princess / ice / as / a woman / cold / is / great

➡ _____
   _____

서답형

18 위 글의 밑줄 친 ⓑthem이 가리키는 것을 본문에서 찾아 쓰시오.

➡ _____

19 위 글의 밑줄 친 ⓒto answer와 to부정사의 용법이 <u>다른</u> 것을 모두 고르시오.

① I want a pen to write it with.
② She was pleased to meet her friend.
③ It was easy for me to do the work.
④ There's not a moment to lose.
⑤ How lucky you are to win the first prize!

[20~23] 다음 글을 읽고 물음에 답하시오.

However, Turandot does not want to marry the prince. He is nothing more than a _____ⓐ_____ to her. He then gives her ⓑa riddle of his own. He asks her, "What is my name?" He adds, "If you answer correctly, I will agree (A)[dying / to die]. If you answer incorrectly, you will have to marry me."

Turandot must find the answer before dawn, but his riddle is as difficult as (B)[her / hers]. She says to everyone, "No one will go to sleep until someone (C)[finds / will find] out his name."

20 위 글의 빈칸 ⓐ에 들어갈 알맞은 말을 고르시오.

① neighbor   ② friend
③ husband   ④ stranger
⑤ co-worker

서답형
21 위 글의 괄호 (A)~(C)에서 어법상 알맞은 낱말을 골라 쓰시오.

➡ (A) _____ (B) _____ (C) _____

서답형
22 위 글의 밑줄 친 ⓑ가 가리키는 것을 본문에서 찾아 쓰시오.

➡ _____

23 위 글의 마지막 부분에서 알 수 있는 'Turandot'의 심경으로 가장 알맞은 것을 고르시오.

① desperate   ② satisfied
③ bored   ④ ashamed
⑤ excited

[24~26] 다음 글을 읽고 물음에 답하시오.

Review of *La La Land*   ★★★★☆
I saw *La La Land* last Friday. It is about the dreams and love of Mia and Sebastian. I enjoyed its beautiful and ⓐmoving songs. ⓑ The story was also as good as the songs. If you are looking for a good musical movie, you should see this movie.

by Kim Jisu on Aug. 11

24 위 글의 밑줄 친 ⓐmoving과 바꿔 쓸 수 있는 말을 고르시오.

① lively   ② cheerful
③ touching   ④ energetic
⑤ depressing

서답형
25 To whom does Jisu recommend *La La Land*? Fill in the blank with the suitable words.

➡ To people who _____
_____.

26 위 글의 밑줄 친 ⓑ와 같은 의미의 문장을 모두 고르시오.

① Not only the story but also the songs were good.
② Not the story but the songs were good.
③ Both the story and the songs were good.
④ Either the story or the songs were good.
⑤ Neither the story nor the songs were good.

[01~03] 다음 글을 읽고 물음에 답하시오.

Welcome, everyone! Tonight, we are going to perform Giacomo Puccini's opera *Turandot*. Like many other famous operas, *Turandot* is in Italian because opera started in Italy in the 16th century. Before we begin, ⓐ I'd like to tell you the storyline of the opera *Turandot*. You will appreciate ⓑit better if you know the story.

01 위 글의 밑줄 친 ⓐ를 우리말로 옮기시오.

➡ _____

02 위 글의 밑줄 친 ⓑ가 가리키는 것을 본문에서 찾아 쓰시오.

➡ _____

03 Why is *Turandot* in Italian? Fill in the blank with the suitable words.

➡ It's because _____
_____.

[04~06] 다음 글을 읽고 물음에 답하시오.

However, Turandot does not want to marry the prince. He is ⓐnothing more than a stranger to her. He then gives her a riddle of his own. He asks her, "What is my name?" He adds, "ⓑIf you answer incorrectly, I will agree to die. If you answer correctly, you will have to marry me."

Turandot must find the answer before dawn, but his riddle is as difficult as hers. She says to everyone, "ⓒNo one will go to sleep until someone finds out his name."

04 위 글의 밑줄 친 ⓐnothing more than과 바꿔 쓸 수 있는 한 단어를 쓰시오.

➡ _____

05 위 글의 밑줄 친 ⓑ에서 흐름상 어색한 부분을 고치시오. (두 군데)

➡ _____, _____

06 위 글의 밑줄 친 ⓒ를 다음과 같이 바꿔 쓸 때 빈칸에 들어갈 알맞은 말을 쓰시오. (5 단어)

➡ People will go to sleep only after _____.

[07~09] 다음 글을 읽고 물음에 답하시오.

ⓐTurandot, a Chinese princess, is a woman of great beauty, but she is as cold as ice. Any prince ___ⓑ___ wants to marry her must answer three riddles. If he fails, he must die. No one has ever been able to answer them. One day, a brave prince falls in love with her at first sight. He becomes the first man to answer all three riddles.

07 위 글의 밑줄 친 ⓐ를 다음과 같이 바꿔 쓸 때 빈칸에 들어갈 알맞은 말을 쓰시오.

➡ Turandot, a Chinese princess, is a _____ woman.

08 위 글의 빈칸 ⓑ에 들어갈 알맞은 말을 쓰시오.

➡ _____

09 다음 문장에서 위 글의 내용과 <u>다른</u> 부분을 찾아서 고치시오.

> • Before a brave prince gives answers to all three riddles, a few princes have been able to give correct answers.

_____ ➡ _____

[10~12] 다음 글을 읽고 물음에 답하시오.

Turandot, a Chinese princess, (A)[is / are] a woman of great beauty, but she is as cold as ice. Any prince who wants to (B)[marry / marry with] her must answer three riddles. If he fails, he must die. No one has ever been able to answer them. One day, a brave prince falls in love with her ⓐ첫눈에. He becomes the first man to (C)[answer / answer to] all three riddles.

10 위 글의 괄호 (A)~(C)에서 어법상 알맞은 낱말을 골라 쓰시오.

➡ (A) _____ (B) _____ (C) _____

11 위 글의 밑줄 친 ⓐ의 우리말을 세 단어로 쓰시오.

➡ _____

12 본문의 내용과 일치하도록 다음 빈칸 (A)와 (B)에 알맞은 단어를 쓰시오.

> Turandot, the Chinese princess, gives (A)_____ _____ to any prince who wants to get married to her. If he doesn't reply to them correctly, he (B)_____ _____.

[13~14] 다음 글을 읽고 물음에 답하시오.

Turandot must find the answer before dawn, but his riddle is as difficult as ____ⓐ____. She says to everyone, "No one will go to sleep until someone finds out his name."

The prince's name is Calaf. Will the princess learn his name ⓑin time? Let's watch the opera and find out.

13 위 글의 빈칸 ⓐ에 she를 알맞은 형태로 쓰시오.

➡ _____

14 위 글의 밑줄 친 ⓑin time과 바꿔 쓸 수 있는 단어를 본문에서 찾아 쓰시오.

➡ _____

[15~16] 다음 글을 읽고 물음에 답하시오.

The prince then gives her a riddle of his own. He asks her, "What is my name?"
He adds, "ⓐ당신이 맞게 대답한다면 나는 죽는 것에 동의하겠습니다. If you answer incorrectly, you will have to marry me."

ⓑTurandot must find the answer before dawn, but his riddle is so difficult as hers. She says to everyone, "No one will go to sleep until someone finds out his name."

15 위 글의 밑줄 친 ⓐ의 우리말에 맞게 한 단어를 보충하여, 주어진 어휘를 알맞게 배열하시오.

> die / answer / if / I / correctly / to / you / agree / ,

➡ _____

16 위 글의 밑줄 친 ⓑ에서 어법상 <u>틀린</u> 부분을 고치시오.

_____ ➡ _____

해석

Link

A: How was our performance?
  ~은 어땠니?

B: It was amazing! Actually, I've seen the musical *Cats* before, and your song
                                        현재완료(경험)

was as <u>great</u> as the musical's.
~만큼 ···한(원급 비교)   = the musical's song

구문해설 • performance 공연 • amazing 놀라운 • actually 사실

A: 우리 공연 어땠어?
B: 굉장했어! 사실, 난 뮤지컬 캣츠를 전에 본 적이 있는데, 너희 노래는 그 뮤지컬의 노래만큼 훌륭했어.

Write

Review of *La La Land*   ★★★★☆

I <u>saw</u> *La La Land* last Friday. It <u>is about</u> the dreams and love of Mia and
과거의 일이라 과거시제 사용함   ~에 관한 것이다

Sebastian. I enjoyed its beautiful and moving songs. The story was also

as good as the songs. If you are looking for a good musical movie, you <u>should</u>
as+원급+as: ~만큼 좋은   조건의 부사절 접속사   ~해야 한다

see this movie.

by Kim Jisu on Aug. 11

구문해설 • enjoy 즐기다 • moving 감동적인 • look for ~을 찾다

라라랜드에 대한 감상

나는 지난 금요일에 라라랜드를 보았어. 그건 Mia와 Sebastian의 꿈과 사랑에 대한 이야기야. 나는 그것의 아름답고 감동적인 노래를 즐겼어. 이야기도 노래만큼이나 좋았지. 좋은 뮤지컬 영화를 찾고 있다면, 이 영화를 봐야 할 거야.

8월 11일, 김지수 씀

Write

Review of *Beauty and the Beast*   ★★★★★

I saw *Beauty and the Beast* last Saturday. It is about a beautiful girl and a beast.
                            on last Saturday(×)   *Beauty and the Beast*

I enjoyed <u>it</u> a lot. The songs were great, and the love story was as beautiful as
        Beauty and the Beast   as+원급+as: 동등비교 표현으로, 두 대상의 동등한 가치를 나타낸다.

a gem. If you <u>like</u> heart-warming stories about love, you will like <u>it</u>, too.
조건의 부사절에서 미래시제 대신 현재시제를 사용   *Beauty and the Beast*

by Lee Minsu on Aug. 12

구문해설 • beauty 아름다움, 미녀 • beast 짐승, 야수 • gem 보석
      • heart-warming 마음이 따뜻해지는

미녀와 야수에 대한 감상

나는 지난 토요일에 미녀와 야수를 봤어. 그건 예쁜 여자 아이와 야수에 대한 이야기야. 나는 그것을 매우 즐겼어. 노래들은 아주 좋았고, 사랑 이야기는 보석만큼 아름다웠어. 마음이 따뜻해지는 사랑 이야기를 좋아한다면, 너도 이걸 좋아할 거야.

8월 12일, 이민수 씀

영역별 핵심문제

01 두 단어의 관계가 나머지 넷과 다른 것은?

① brave – cowardly

② safe – dangerous

③ difficult – easy

④ fail – succeed

⑤ moving – touching

02 밑줄 친 단어와 의미가 같은 것을 고르시오.

> A: How was our performance?
> B: It was very <u>surprising</u>!

① amazing   ② interesting

③ famous   ④ moving

⑤ popular

03 다음 제시된 단어를 사용하여 자연스러운 문장을 만들 수 <u>없는</u> 것은? (형태 변화 가능)

> ┌─ 보기 ─┐
> brave century mean dawn practice

① One day, a _____ prince falls in love with her at first sight.

② Opera started in Italy in the 16th _____.

③ Why don't we _____ the subway?

④ She must find the answer before _____.

⑤ "Nessun Dorma" _____ no one sleeps.

04 사진을 보고 대화의 빈칸에 어울리는 단어를 고르시오.

> B: Mom, I got only one question wrong on the Korean history exam!
> W: Great! I was sure you would do well. Why don't we go out to _____ tonight?
> B: Yes!

① marry   ② appreciate

③ celebrate   ④ leave

⑤ finish

05 우리말에 맞게 빈칸에 알맞은 단어를 쓰시오.

> 학교 끝나고 바로, 네 시 어때?
> How about 4 o'clock, _____ after school?

[06~07] 다음 대화를 읽고 물음에 답하시오.

> G: Do you want to play badminton together this afternoon, Mark?
> B: Sure. __(A)__ shall we play?
> G: __(B)__ about at the park near your place?
> B: O.K. See you there at 3 o'clock.

06 빈칸 (A)와 (B)에 들어갈 말을 쓰시오.

➡ (A) _____ (B) _____

07 위 대화의 목적으로 알맞은 것은?

① to advise   ② to inform

③ to recommend   ④ to make plans

⑤ to appreciate

[08~09] 다음 대화를 읽고 물음에 답하시오.

> A: (A)Why don't we eat pizza after school?
> B: Good idea. (B)몇 시에 만날까?
> A: How about 5 o'clock at the restaurant?
> B: O.K. See you then.

08 밑줄 친 (A)와 바꾸어 쓸 수 없는 표현은?

① Let's eat pizza after school.

② Shall we eat pizza after school?

③ Why are we going to eat pizza after school?

④ How about eating pizza after school?

⑤ What about eating pizza after school?

09 밑줄 친 (B)의 우리말에 맞게 주어진 단어를 이용하여 영어로 쓰시오.

> what, shall, meet

➡ _____

10 주어진 문장 뒤에 이어질 대화의 순서를 바르게 배열하시오.

> What shall we do this afternoon?

> (A) Good idea! What time shall we meet?
> (B) Why don't we go to the art museum?
> (C) How about 2 o'clock?
> (D) O.K. Let's meet in front of the museum.

➡ _____

[11~12] 다음 대화를 읽고 물음에 답하시오.

> Anna: Dad, guess what! I have no school next Wednesday.
> Dad: Really? Why not?
> Anna: It's our school's 75th anniversary.
> Dad: Oh, I see.
> Anna: Can we do something together that day?
> Dad: I guess I can take the afternoon ___(A)___. What do you want to do?
> Anna: Why don't we go see a musical at Bravo Theater near your work? We can get a discount ___(B)___ we go on a Wednesday.
> Dad: Good idea, Anna! Then, let's just meet at the theater.
> Anna: O.K. What time ___(C)___ meet?
> Dad: How about 12? Then, we can have lunch together, too.
> Anna: You're the best, Dad!

11 위 대화의 빈칸 (A)~(C)에 알맞은 말을 쓰시오.

➡ (A) _____ (B) _____ (C) _____

12 위 대화를 읽고 다음 물음에 대해 영어로 답하시오.

> Q: Why does Anna have no school next Wednesday?

➡ Because it's _____.

Grammar

13 우리말에 맞게 주어진 어구를 이용하여 영어로 쓰시오.

> 세상을 위해 뭔가 특별한 일을 한다면, 세상은 변할 것이다. (if / something / the world / do / change / special / for)

➡ _____

_____

14 다음 우리말을 올바르게 영작한 것은?

> 나는 내가 여배우만큼 예쁘다고 생각해.

① I think I am prettier than an actress.
② I think I am so pretty as an actress.
③ I think I am as pretty as an actress.
④ I think I am the prettiest actress.
⑤ I think I am as pretty than an actress.

15 다음 우리말을 주어진 〈조건〉에 맞게 영작하시오.

┌─ 조건 ├─
• 부정어 'not'을 사용할 것.
• 'as+원급+as' 구문을 사용할 것.

> 그는 나만큼 TV를 많이 보지 않는다.

➡ _____ I do.

16 다음 빈칸에 공통으로 들어갈 말은? (대 · 소문자 무시)

(1) You should check _____ it will rain during the trip.
(2) _____ your bag is too heavy, I'll help you to carry it.

① that   ② whether   ③ if
④ when   ⑤ which

17 다음 중 밑줄 친 부분의 쓰임이 다른 것은?

① Do you know if he is a tailor?
② I am not sure if she is Korean or not.
③ They want to know if the answer is right.
④ He wonders if she likes James.
⑤ We will go swimming if the weather is good.

18 다음 중 주어진 문장을 어법상 바르게 고친 것이 아닌 것은?

① My room is as not large as yours.
  → My room is not as large as yours.
② This donkey is as bigger as that horse.
  → This donkey is so big as that horse.
③ I'll join the club if you will teach me how to snowboard.
  → I'll join the club if you teach me how to snowboard.
④ If you will find something valuable, you should keep it in the safe.
  → If you find something valuable, you should keep it in the safe. *safe: 금고
⑤ Her dress looks as love as mine.
  → Her dress looks as lovely as mine.

19 다음 중 어법상 어색한 문장을 고르시오.

① If my mom catches a cold, I will do the dishes for her.
② I can finish the work if you help me.
③ If you want to succeed in life, you will have to study harder.
④ Bills are not so heavy so coins.
⑤ He kicks the ball as hard as he can.

*bill: 지폐

20 다음 중 어법상 바르지 않은 문장은 몇 개인가?

• This tool is not so useful as that one.
• I read as many books as she does.
• The subway is as faster as the train.
• We will go swimming if the weather will be fine tomorrow.
• My mother is as tall as my father.

① 1개   ② 2개   ③ 3개   ④ 4개   ⑤ 5개

21 다음 빈칸에 들어갈 형태로 알맞은 것은?

• If my friends _____ their promises, I will talk to them about it.

① breaks
② will break
③ broken
④ break
⑤ won't break

22 다음 교통수단에 관한 표를 보고 as ~ as를 이용하여 비교하는 문장을 완성하시오.

Transportation	Subway	Bus	Taxi
Speed	60km	80km	80km
Fare	1,200 won	1,200 won	3,000 won

(1) The subway cannot go _____ the bus. (speed)

(2) The bus is _____ the taxi. (speed)

(3) The subway is _____ the bus. (fare)

23 다음 중 의미가 다른 하나는?

① I'm not as old as you.
② You are older than I.
③ I'm younger than you.
④ I am as young as you.
⑤ You are not as young as I.

24 다음 우리말에 맞게 주어진 단어를 이용하여 빈칸을 채우시오.

(1) 그녀의 얼굴은 CD만큼이나 작다. (small)
➡ Her face is _____ a CD.

(2) 나는 그녀만큼 빨리 달릴 수 있다. (fast)
➡ I can _____ she can.

(3) 나는 너만큼 키가 크고 싶어.
➡ I want to be _____ you.

25 다음 문장에서 <u>틀린</u> 것을 바르게 고치시오.

• Justin will not go if Judy won't go.

_____ ➡ _____

26 다음 문장에서 어법상 <u>틀린</u> 부분을 찾아 바르게 고치시오.

(1) I won't wash my car if it will rain.

_____ ➡ _____

(2) I'm not sure if my grandma comes tomorrow.

_____ ➡ _____

Reading

[27~28] 다음 글을 읽고 물음에 답하시오.

Welcome, everyone! Tonight, we are going to _____ⓐ_____ Giacomo Puccini's opera *Turandot*. ⓑLike many other famous operas, *Turandot* is in Italian because opera started in Italy in the 16th century. Before we begin, I'd like to tell you the storyline of the opera *Turandot*. You will appreciate it better if you know the story.

27 위 글의 빈칸 ⓐ에 들어갈 알맞은 말을 고르시오.

① practice
② perform
③ work
④ achieve
⑤ complete

28 위 글의 밑줄 친 ⓑLike와 같은 의미로 쓰인 것을 고르시오.

① Do you like vegetables?
② I like playing tennis.
③ Which pen do you like best?
④ I, like everyone else, make mistakes.
⑤ I like my coffee strong.

[29~31] 다음 글을 읽고 물음에 답하시오.

Turandot, a Chinese princess, is a woman of great beauty, but she is as cold as ice. (①) Any prince who wants to marry her must answer three riddles. (②) If he fails, he must die. (③) No one ⓐhas ever been able to answer them. (④) He becomes the first man to answer all three riddles. (⑤)

29 위 글의 흐름으로 보아, 주어진 문장이 들어가기에 가장 적절한 곳은?

One day, a brave prince falls in love with her at first sight.

①   ②   ③   ④   ⑤

30 위 글의 밑줄 친 ⓐ와 현재완료의 용법이 같은 것을 모두 고르시오.

① I have seen a tiger before.
② He has lost his camera.
③ How many times have you read it?
④ She has just arrived here.
⑤ I have known him for five years.

31 위 글의 내용과 일치하지 않는 것은?

① Turandot는 중국의 공주이다.
② Turandot와 결혼하기를 원하는 왕자는 반드시 세 가지 수수께끼에 답해야 한다.
③ 수수께끼에 답하지 못하는 왕자는 죽어야 한다.
④ 지금까지 수수께끼에 답하지 못해 죽은 왕자는 없다.
⑤ 어느 날, 어떤 용감한 왕자가 Turandot에게 첫눈에 반한다.

[32~33] 다음 글을 읽고 물음에 답하시오.

However, Turandot does not want to marry the prince. He is nothing (A)[more / less] than a stranger to her. ⓐHe then gives her a riddle of his own. He asks her, "What is my name?" He adds, "If you answer correctly, I will (B)[agree / refuse] to die. If you answer incorrectly, you will have to marry me."

Turandot must find the answer before dawn, but his riddle is as (C)[different / difficult] as hers. She says to everyone, "No one will go to sleep until someone finds out his name."

32 위 글의 괄호 (A)~(C)에서 문맥이나 어법상 알맞은 낱말을 골라 쓰시오.

➡ (A) _____ (B) _____ (C) _____

33 다음 중 3형식 문장으로 바꿀 때 필요한 전치사가 밑줄 친 ⓐ와 같은 문장을 모두 고르시오.

① Did he buy you the present?
② She sent Tom an email.
③ Mom made me a birthday cake.
④ He asked me a question.
⑤ Who wrote you the thank-you note?

01 출제율 95% 다음 짝지어진 단어의 관계가 같도록 빈칸에 알맞은 말을 쓰시오.

> proposal : suggestion = reply to : _____

02 출제율 90% 우리말에 맞게 빈칸에 세 단어의 알맞은 말을 쓰시오.

> 금은 단지 돌에 지나지 않는다.
> Gold is _____ a stone.

03 출제율 95% 다음 우리말 해석에 맞게 빈칸을 완성하시오. (철자가 주어진 경우 그 철자로 시작할 것)

(1) 중국의 공주 Turandot는 굉장히 아름다운 여인이지만, 그녀는 얼음처럼 차갑습니다.
  ➡ Turandot, a Chinese princess, is a woman of great _____, but she is as _____ as ice.

(2) 우리는 지아코모 푸치니의 오페라 《투란도트》를 공연할 것입니다.
  ➡ We are going to _____ Giacomo Puccini's opera *Turandot*.

(3) 만약 답이 틀리면 당신은 저와 결혼해야 할 것입니다.
  ➡ If you answer _____, you will have to _____ me.

(4) 어느 날, 어떤 용감한 왕자가 그녀에게 첫눈에 반합니다.
  ➡ One day, a brave prince _____ _____ _____ with her at first _____.

04 출제율 90% 다음 영영풀이에 해당하는 단어는?

> earlier than the time expected

① tomorrow ② already
③ near ④ hardly
⑤ still

[05~07] 다음 대화를 읽고 물음에 답하시오.

A: ⓐLet's go on a picnic this weekend. ①
B: Good idea. ② What time shall we meet? ③
A: ⓑHow about 10 o'clock on Saturday?
B: ④ O.K. ⑤ See you there.

05 출제율 100% 위 대화의 ①~⑤ 중 주어진 문장이 들어갈 알맞은 곳은?

> Let's meet at the subway station.

① ② ③ ④ ⑤

06 출제율 85% 밑줄 친 ⓐ와 같은 의미를 가진 문장을 쓰고자 한다. 괄호 안에 주어진 어구를 알맞게 배열하시오

(1) (go / why / we / on / don't / a picnic / this weekend / ?)
  ➡ _____

(2) (going / what / on / this weekend / a picnic / about / ?)
  ➡ _____

07 출제율 95% 밑줄 친 ⓑ의 목적으로 알맞은 것은?

① 시간 묻기 ② 비교하며 말하기
③ 수정하기 ④ 약속 정하기
⑤ 의도 표현하기

[08~11] 다음 대화를 읽고 물음에 답하시오.

Anna: Dad, _____(A)_____ I have no school next Wednesday.

Dad: Really? Why not?

Anna: It's our school's 75th anniversary.

Dad: Oh, I see.

Anna: Can we do something together that day?

Dad: I guess I can take the afternoon off. What do you want to do?

Anna: Why don't we go see a musical at Bravo Theater near your work? (B)수요일에 가면 할인을 받을 수 있어요.

Dad: Good idea, Anna! Then, let's just meet at the theater.

Anna: O.K. (C)몇 시에 만날까요?

Dad: How about 12? Then, we can have lunch together, too.

Anna: (D)You're the best, Dad!

08 다음 영어 설명을 참고하여, 위 대화의 빈칸 (A)에 들어갈 말을 고르시오.

> used before telling someone something interesting or surprising

① you know why?　② what did it say?
③ of course.　④ well done.
⑤ guess what!

09 밑줄 친 (B)의 우리말과 같도록 다음 문장의 빈칸을 완성하시오.

➡ We can _____ a _____ _____ we go on a Wednesday.

10 밑줄 친 (C)의 우리말을 괄호 안의 단어를 이용하여 영어로 쓰시오.

➡ _____ (shall, meet)

11 밑줄 친 (D)에서 추측할 수 있는 Anna의 기분으로 가장 알맞은 것은?

① sad　② lonely
③ happy　④ relaxed
⑤ ashamed

12 대화의 빈칸에 들어갈 표현으로 적절하지 않은 것은?

> A: Oh, we're going to be late for the concert.
>
> B: _____ The subway will be faster than the bus at this time of the day.

① Let's take the subway.
② How about taking the subway?
③ Are you taking the subway?
④ Why don't we take the subway?
⑤ What about taking the subway?

13 대화의 흐름상 어색한 곳을 고르시오.

> B: Mom, I got only one question ① wrong on the Korean history exam!
>
> W: ②Great! I was sure you would do ③well. Why don't we go out to ④ appreciate tonight?
>
> B: Yes! Can we have pizza for dinner?
>
> W: ⑤Of course, Joe. I'll call your dad.

①　②　③　④　⑤

14 출제율 95%

다음 문장의 빈칸에 공통으로 들어갈 말은?

> • You will be late for the class _____ you miss the subway.
> • _____ the weather is bad, I won't go hiking.

① as[As]
② if[If]
③ because[Because]
④ which[Which]
⑤ though[Though]

15 출제율 85%

다음 표를 보고 틀린 문장을 고르시오.

	Tom	Jane	Mike
나이	15	14	15
키	163	170	170
성적	90	90	70

① Tom is as old as Mike.
② Tom isn't as tall as Jane.
③ Tom is as smart as Jane.
④ Jane is as tall as Mike.
⑤ Jane isn't as smart as Mike.

16 출제율 100%

다음 〈보기〉에서 알맞은 단어를 골라 빈칸에 쓰시오. (필요하면 단어를 변형하시오.)

> ┤ 보기 ├
> study   finish   rain   give
> leave   change   meet   hurry

(1) Can I watch TV if I _____ my homework?
(2) If you _____ this book to him, he will be glad.
(3) If your mom _____ her mind, let me know.

17 출제율 90%

다음 중 어법상 어색한 것은?

① The prince then sings the most famous aria of the whole opera.
② No one will go to sleep until someone will find out his name.
③ My sister is as tall as my father.
④ If you don't give me candy, I will cry!
⑤ If you want to experience something special, come and enjoy the festival.

18 출제율 95%

다음 중 어법상 어색한 것은?

① I can run as fast as Junsu.
② This flower is as pretty as that one.
③ His backpack is as bigger as mine.
④ You are not as smart as I.
⑤ His cell phone is as good as mine.

19 출제율 95%

밑줄 친 부분의 쓰임이 나머지와 다른 것은?

① If he is honest, I'll employ him.
② You can be successful in life if you work hard.
③ I will meet him if he visits you.
④ If you do the work, your parents will be happy.
⑤ Can you tell me if he will come?

20 출제율 90%

다음 〈보기〉의 단어를 이용하여 빈칸에 알맞은 말을 쓰시오.

> ┤ 보기 ├
> well   tall   kind   good   big   heavy

(1) Jinhee is 150cm tall and I am 170cm tall. Jinhee is _____ me.
(2) Katy doesn't sing as _____ as Jessica.
(3) Subin is 65kg and Jongmin is 65kg, too. Subin is _____ Jongmin.

[21~23] 다음 글을 읽고 물음에 답하시오.

Welcome, everyone! Tonight, we are going to perform Giacomo Puccini's opera *Turandot*. Like many other famous operas, *Turandot* is ____ⓐ____ Italian because opera started ____ⓑ____ Italy ____ⓒ____ the 16th century. Before we begin, I'd like to tell you the storyline of the opera *Turandot*. You will ⓓappreciate it better if you know the story.

21 위 글의 빈칸 ⓐ~ⓒ에 공통으로 들어갈 전치사를 고르시오.

① for ② from ③ in
④ at ⑤ on

22 위 글의 밑줄 친 ⓓappreciate와 같은 의미로 쓰인 것을 고르시오.

① This is a great chance to appreciate the architecture of Korea.
② I'd appreciate your help.
③ You won't appreciate how expensive it is.
④ Thanks for coming. I appreciate it.
⑤ I failed to appreciate the distance between the two cities.

23 다음 질문에 대한 알맞은 대답을 주어진 단어로 시작하여 쓰시오. (3 단어)

Q: How will you be able to appreciate the opera *Turandot* better?
A: By _____.

➡ _____

[24~26] 다음 글을 읽고 물음에 답하시오.

ⓐTurandot, a Chinese princess, is a woman of great beauty, but she is as sweet as honey. Any prince who wants to marry her must answer three ____ⓑ____. If he fails, he must die. No one has ever been able to answer them. One day, a brave prince falls in love with her at first sight. He becomes the first man to answer all three ____ⓑ____.

24 위 글의 밑줄 친 ⓐ에서 흐름상 어색한 부분을 고치시오.

_____ ➡ _____

25 주어진 영영풀이를 참고하여 빈칸 ⓑ에 철자 r로 시작하는 단어를 쓰시오.

puzzles or jokes in which you ask a question that seems to be nonsense but which has a clever or amusing answer

➡ _____

26 위 글을 읽고 알 수 없는 것을 고르시오.

① Turandot의 신분
② Turandot의 외모
③ Turandot와 결혼하려는 왕자들이 통과해야만 하는 절차
④ 절차를 통과하지 못한 왕자들이 감수해야 하는 위험
⑤ 절차를 통과하지 못한 왕자들의 숫자

01 주어진 단어를 이용하여 대화의 빈칸을 완성하시오.

> A: Let's go on a picnic this weekend.
> B: Good idea. _____(A)_____ (time, shall, meet)
> A: How about 10 o'clock on Saturday?
> B: O.K. _____(B)_____ (shall, meet)
> A: Let's meet at the subway station. See you there.

➡ (A) _____
　 (B) _____

02 대화의 빈칸에 제안을 하는 표현을 이용하여 6 단어로 문장을 완성하시오.

> M: _____? The subway will be faster than the bus at this time of day.
> W: That's a good idea.

➡ _____

03 (중요) 대화의 빈칸 (A)~(C)에 알맞은 표현을 〈보기〉에서 찾아 쓰시오.

> ┌─── 보기 ───┐
> • Why don't we go see *Wonder Woman*?
> • What shall we do this afternoon?
> • How about 4 o'clock?

> A: (A) _____
> B: (B) _____
> A: Good idea! What time shall we meet?
> B: (C) _____
> A: O.K. Let's meet at Moon Theater.

➡ (A) _____
　 (B) _____
　 (C) _____

04 다음 우리말에 맞게 주어진 단어를 이용하여 빈칸에 알맞은 말을 쓰시오.

(1) 그녀의 반지는 나의 것만큼 비싸다.
　➡ Her ring is _____. (expensive)

(2) Cathy는 Juliet만큼 친절하지 않다.
　➡ Cathy is _____ Juliet. (so, kind)

(3) 그가 내일 여기로 오면, 나에게 데려와.
　➡ If he _____ here tomorrow, _____ him _____ me. (come, take)

05 다음 문장에서 어법상 틀린 부분을 찾아 바르게 고치시오.

(1) If it will rain tomorrow, we won't go on a picnic.
　_____ ➡ _____

(2) I'll call you if I will need your help.
　_____ ➡ _____

06 (중요) 다음 표를 보고 문장의 빈칸을 채우시오.

조건 1: 번호에 해당하는 표현을 찾아 주어, 동사를 포함한 완전한 문장으로 쓰시오.

조건 2: 동등 비교 표현을 이용하여 쓰시오.

	Minho	Mike	Jane
(1) Age	14	13	14
(2) Height	160	160	165
(3) Weight	50	40	50

(1) Minho is _____ Jane.
　 But Mike is _____ Minho.

(2) Minho is _____ Mike.
　 But _____ Jane.

(3) Minho is _____ Jane.
　 But Mike _____ Minho.

07 다음 문장에서 어법상 틀린 부분을 찾아 바르게 고치시오.

> I'll stop talking about it if you won't pay attention to me.

_____ ➡ _____

[08~10] 다음 글을 읽고 물음에 답하시오.

> Turandot, a Chinese princess, is a woman of great beauty, but she is _____ ⓐ _____ . (A) [Some / Any] prince who wants to marry her must answer three riddles. If he fails, he must die. No one has (B)[ever / never] been able to answer them. One day, a brave prince falls in love with her at first (C)[see / sight]. He becomes the first man to answer all three riddles.

08 다음과 같은 뜻이 되도록 위 글의 빈칸 ⓐ에 들어갈 알맞은 말을 as와 ice를 포함하여 쓰시오.

> very cold

➡ _____

09 위 글의 괄호 (A)~(C)에서 문맥이나 어법상 알맞은 낱말을 골라 쓰시오.

➡ (A) _____ (B) _____ (C) _____

10 본문의 내용과 일치하도록 다음 빈칸에 알맞은 단어를 쓰시오. (본문의 단어를 변형하여 쓰시오.)

> All the princes who tried to answer three riddles at the risk of their lives have _____ to answer them except one prince.

[11~13] 다음 글을 읽고 물음에 답하시오.

> However, Turandot does not want to marry the prince. ⓐ그는 그녀에게 던지 낯선 사람일 뿐입니다. He then gives her a riddle of his own. He asks her, "What is my name?" He adds, "If you answer correctly, I will agree to die. If you answer incorrectly, you will have to marry me."
>
> Turandot must find the answer before dawn, but his riddle is as difficult as ⓑhers. She says to everyone, "No one will go to sleep until someone finds out his name."

11 위 글의 밑줄 친 ⓐ의 우리말에 맞게 주어진 어휘를 이용하여 9 단어로 영작하시오.

> nothing

➡ _____

12 위 글의 밑줄 친 ⓑhers가 가리키는 것을 영어로 쓰시오.

➡ _____

13 본문의 내용과 일치하도록 다음 빈칸 (A)와 (B)에 알맞은 단어를 쓰시오.

> If Turandot answers the prince's riddle incorrectly, she will have to (A)_____ _____ . If Turandot answers correctly, he will agree (B)_____ _____ .

01 다음 그림을 보고 놀이동산에서 해야 할 일을 제안하는 대화를 〈보기〉를 참고하여 완성하시오.

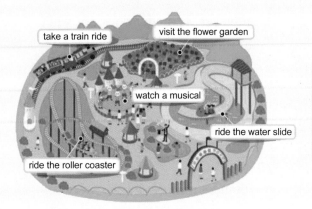

take a train ride
visit the flower garden
watch a musical
ride the water slide
ride the roller coaster

보기
A: What shall we do at the park?
B: Why don't we see a magic show?
A: That's a good idea.

02 다음 그림을 보고 지하철과 버스의 속도와 요금을 비교하는 문장을 'as ~ as'를 이용하여 완성하시오. (fast, expensive를 사용할 것)

Transportation	Subway	Bus
Speed	60km	80km
Fare	1,200 won	1,200 won

(1) _____

(2) _____

03 다음 내용을 바탕으로 영화의 감상문을 쓰시오.

• What is the title? 　*La La Land* • What is it about? 　the dreams and love of Mia and Sebastian	• What did you think about it? 　– beautiful and moving songs 　– a good story

___(A)___ of *La La Land*　　★★★★☆

I saw *La La Land* last Friday. It is about ___(B)___ of Mia and Sebastian. I enjoyed its ___(C)___ songs. The ___(D)___ was also as good as the songs. If you are looking for a good musical movie, you should see this movie.

by Kim Jisu on Aug. 11

단원별 모의고사

01 다음 단어에 대한 영어 설명이 <u>어색한</u> 것은?

① moving: causing strong feelings of sadness or sympathy

② storyline: the series of events that happen in a book, film, play, etc.

③ marry: to become the legally accepted husband or wife of someone in an official or religious ceremony

④ riddle: a type of question that describes something in a difficult and confusing way and has a clever or funny answer

⑤ appreciate: to do something enjoyable on a special occasion

02 다음 우리말 해석에 맞게 알맞은 단어를 쓰시오.

(1) 나는 오후에 휴무를 할 수 있을 것 같구나.

➡ I guess I can _____ the afternoon _____.

(2) Karen, 오늘 학교 연극의 우리 역할을 연습하자.

➡ Karen, let's _____ our parts for the school _____ today.

(3) 오늘 축하하러 나가는 건 어때?

➡ Why _____ we go out to _____ tonight?

[03~04] 다음 글을 읽고 물음에 답하시오.

I saw *La La Land* last Friday. It is about the dreams and love of Mia and Sebastian. (A)나는 그것의 아름답고 감동적인 이야기가 좋았어. The story was also _____ⓐ_____ the songs. If you are looking for a good musical movie, you should see this movie.

03 위 글의 빈칸 ⓐ에 들어갈 말로 알맞은 것은?

① as well as   ② as better as

③ as good as   ④ good as

⑤ the best

04 위 글의 밑줄 친 (A)의 우리말에 맞게 빈칸에 알맞은 단어를 쓰시오. (m으로 시작할 것)

➡ I enjoyed its beautiful and _____ songs.

[05~06] 다음 대화를 읽고 물음에 답하시오.

M: Liz, hurry up. It's already 6 o'clock.

W: Oh, we're going to be late for the concert.

M: Why don't we take the subway? The subway will be faster than the bus at this time of day.

W: That's a good idea.

05 다음 영영풀이에 해당하는 단어를 대화에서 찾아 쓰시오.

> happening or arriving after the planned, expected, usual, or necessary time

➡ _____

06 위 대화를 읽고 답할 수 <u>없는</u> 질문을 고르시오.

① What time is it now?

② Where are they going to go?

③ When does the concert begin?

④ What will they take to go to the concert?

⑤ Which is faster, the subway or the bus?

[07~08] 다음 대화를 읽고 물음에 답하시오.

Joe: Mom, I got only one question ①wrong on the Korean history exam!

Mom: Great! I was sure you would ②do poorly. ③Why don't we go out to ④celebrate tonight?

Joe: Yes! Can we ⑤have pizza for dinner?

Mom: Of course, Joe. I'll call your dad.

07 위 대화의 ①~⑤ 중 어휘의 쓰임이 어색한 것은?

①   ②   ③   ④   ⑤

08 위 대화의 내용과 일치하지 않는 것은?

① Joe took the Korean history exam.
② Joe's mom suggests going out tonight.
③ Joe got only one question wrong on the exam.
④ Joe's mom did well on the exam.
⑤ Joe's family will go out for dinner.

09 다음 중 짝지어진 대화가 어색한 것은?

① A: Why don't we see a magic show?
  B: That's a good idea.
② A: Karen, let's practice our parts for the school play today.
  B: O.K. What time shall we meet?
③ A: Where shall we play?
  B: How about at the park near your place?
④ A: What time shall we meet?
  B: How about at the bus stop?
⑤ A: What shall we do this afternoon?
  B: Why don't we go see *Wonder Woman*?

[10~12] 다음 대화를 읽고 물음에 답하시오.

Anna: Dad, guess what! I have no school next Wednesday.

Dad: Really? _____(A)_____

Anna: It's our school's 75th anniversary.

Dad: Oh, I see.

Anna: Can we do something together that day?

Dad: I guess I can take the afternoon off. (B)뭘 하고 싶니?

Anna: Why don't we go see a musical at Bravo Theater near your work? We can get a discount if we go on a Wednesday.

Dad: Good idea, Anna! Then, let's just meet at the theater.

Anna: O.K. What time shall we meet?

Dad: How about 12? Then, we can have lunch together, too.

Anna: You're the best, Dad!

10 빈칸 (A)에 알맞은 말은?

① You know what?   ② I know.
③ Why not?   ④ Excuse me?
⑤ What are you going to do?

11 밑줄 친 (B)의 우리말에 맞게 주어진 단어를 이용하여 영작하시오.

➡ _____(what / want / do)

12 위 대화의 내용과 일치하지 않는 것은?

① Next Wednesday is Anna's school's 75th anniversary.
② Anna won't go to school next Wednesday.
③ Anna and her dad will go see a movie next Wednesday.
④ Anna and her dad will meet at the theater.
⑤ Anna and her dad will have lunch together.

13 다음 괄호 안의 단어를 알맞은 곳에 넣어 문장을 다시 쓰시오.

(1) Anna is as as Julie. (beautiful)

➡ _____

(2) I will let you go out you do finish your job. (if)

➡ _____

14 다음 주어진 문장은 어법상 <u>틀린</u> 문장이다. 바르게 고친 것이 <u>아닌</u> 것은?

① I am not as braver as Jack.
　→ I am not as brave as Jack.
② He drove so fast as I.
　→ He drove as fast as I
③ Her hair is as long as I.
　→ Her hair is as long as me.
④ This bicycle is as not expensive as that one.
　→ This bicycle is not as expensive as that one.
⑤ If she will go to the island, she will spend all day swimming.
　→ If she goes to the island, she will spend all day swimming.

15 다음 문장에서 어법상 <u>어색한</u> 곳을 찾아 바르게 고치시오.

(1) My room is as not larger as yours.
　_____ ➡ _____
(2) This donkey is as bigger as that horse.
　_____ ➡ _____

16 다음 그림과 같은 의미가 되도록 'as ～ as'를 이용하여 알맞은 단어를 쓰시오.

Tom
Ann

➡ Ann is _____ Tom.

17 다음 두 문장을 한 문장으로 알맞게 바꾼 것은?

- I will go swimming.
- It will not rain tomorrow.

① I will go swimming if it didn't rain tomorrow.
② I will go swimming if it will not rain tomorrow.
③ I go swimming if it will not rain tomorrow.
④ I will go swimming if it does not rain tomorrow.
⑤ I go swimming if it do not rain tomorrow.

18 다음 중 어법상 <u>어색한</u> 것은?

① If it is sunny tomorrow, how about playing soccer?
② If I'm not busy tomorrow, I will go with you.
③ That tower is as high as this tower.
④ This dog is as big as that dog.
⑤ Tennis is as less popular as soccer.

[19~20] 다음 글을 읽고 물음에 답하시오.

Welcome, everyone! Tonight, we are going to perform Giacomo Puccini's opera *Turandot*. Like many other famous operas, *Turandot* is in ___ⓐ___ because opera started in Italy in the 16th century. Before we begin, I'd like to tell you the ⓑstoryline of the opera *Turandot*. You will appreciate it better if you know the story.

19 본문의 한 단어를 변형하여 위 글의 빈칸 ⓐ에 들어갈 알맞은 말을 쓰시오.

➡ _____

20 위 글의 밑줄 친 ⓑstoryline과 바꿔 쓸 수 있는 말을 고르시오.

① theme   ② setting   ③ plot
④ concept   ⑤ subject

[21~22] 다음 글을 읽고 물음에 답하시오.

Turandot, a Chinese princess, is a woman ___ⓐ___ great beauty, but she is as cold as ice. ⓑAny prince who wants to marry her must ask three riddles. If he fails, he must die. No one has ever been able to answer them. One day, a brave prince falls in love ___ⓒ___ her at first sight. He becomes the first man to answer all three riddles.

21 위 글의 빈칸 ⓐ와 ⓒ에 들어갈 전치사가 바르게 짝지어진 것은?

① for – from   ② of – at
③ of – with   ④ for – at
⑤ on – with

22 위 글의 밑줄 친 ⓑ에서 흐름상 어색한 부분을 찾아 고치시오.

_____ ➡ _____

[23~24] 다음 글을 읽고 물음에 답하시오.

However, Turandot does not want to marry the prince. He is nothing more than a stranger to her. He then gives her a riddle of his own. He asks her, "What is my name?" He adds, "If you answer correctly, I will agree ⓐto die. If you answer incorrectly, you will have to marry me."

Turandot must find the answer before dawn, but his riddle is as difficult as hers. She says to everyone, "No one will go to sleep until someone finds out his name."

23 아래 〈보기〉에서 위 글의 밑줄 친 ⓐto die와 문법적 쓰임이 같은 문장의 개수를 고르시오.

┌─ 보기 ┤
① I would be happy to be helpful to you.
② She learned to play the piano.
③ This book is too difficult to read.
④ He has a few friends to play with.
⑤ Her plan is to go to the movies tonight.
└─

① 1개   ② 2개   ③ 3개   ④ 4개   ⑤ 5개

24 위 글의 내용과 일치하지 <u>않는</u> 것은?

① Turandot는 그 왕자와 결혼하기를 원하지 않는다.
② 왕자는 Turandot에게 단지 낯선 사람일 뿐이다.
③ 왕자는 Turandot에게 자신의 수수께끼를 낸다.
④ 만약 Turandot의 답이 틀리면 왕자는 죽는 것에 동의할 것이다.
⑤ Turandot는 동이 트기 전에 수수께끼의 답을 찾아야 한다.

Lesson 6

Food in History

🎙 의사소통 기능

- 선호하는 것 묻고 답하기
  A: Do you prefer summer or winter?
  B: I prefer summer.

- 추천 부탁하기
  Could you recommend a book for me?

🎙 언어 형식

- 수동태
  This dish **was called** tangpyeongchae.

- something/someone+형용사
  King Yeongjo offered them **something special**.

Words & Expressions

교과서

Key Words

- **alone**[əlóun] 부 혼자, 홀로
- **back**[bæk] 명 등
- **beginner**[bigínər] 명 초보자
- **comedy**[kámədi] 명 희극, 코미디
- **cookbook**[kúkbùk] 명 요리책
- **culture**[kʌ́ltʃər] 명 문화
- **dessert**[dizə́ːrt] 명 후식, 디저트
- **different**[dífərənt] 형 다른
- **disappointed**[dìsəpɔ́intid] 형 실망한
- **dish**[diʃ] 명 음식, 요리
- **fried**[fraid] 형 튀긴
- **fried fish** 생선 튀김
- **fried vegetables** 채소 볶음
- **fortune teller** 점쟁이
- **funny**[fʌ́ni] 형 웃긴, 재미있는
- **half**[hæf] 명 반 형 반의, 절반의
- **half-moon**[hǽfmùːn] 명 반달
- **harmony**[háːrməni] 명 화합, 조화
- **hit**[hit] 명 성공, 히트작
- **honesty**[ánisti] 명 정직함
- **however**[hauévər] 부 하지만
- **imaginary**[imǽdʒənèri] 형 상상의, 가상의
- **indoor**[índɔr] 형 실내의
- **ingredient**[ingríːdiənt] 명 재료
- **interesting**[íntərəstiŋ] 형 흥미로운
- **Italian**[itǽljən] 형 이탈리아의
- **kingdom**[kíŋdəm] 명 왕국

- **mainly**[méinli] 부 주로
- **mean**[miːn] 동 의미하다
- **meat**[miːt] 명 육류, 고기
- **offer**[ɔ́ːfər] 동 제안하다, 권하다
- **official**[əfíʃəl] 명 신하, 관리, 공직자
- **order**[ɔ́ːrdər] 동 주문하다
- **outdoor**[áutdɔr] 형 실외의
- **party**[páːrti] 명 정당
- **policy**[páləsi] 명 정책
- **political**[pəlítikəl] 형 정치의, 정당의
- **pot**[pɑt] 명 냄비, 솥
- **prefer**[prifə́ːr] 동 선호하다
- **recently**[ríːsntli] 부 최근에
- **recommend**[rèkəménd] 동 추천하다
- **restaurant**[réstərənt] 명 식당
- **rice flour** 쌀가루
- **scholar**[skálər] 명 학자
- **seafood**[síːfud] 명 해산물
- **servant**[sə́ːrvənt] 명 신하, 하인
- **shape**[ʃeip] 명 모양
- **since**[sins] 전 ~ 이후로
- **special**[spéʃəl] 형 특별한
- **symbolize**[símbəlàiz] 동 상징하다
- **table tennis** 탁구
- **traditional**[trədíʃənl] 형 전통의, 전통적인
- **turtle**[tə́ːrtl] 명 거북
- **vegetable**[védʒətəbl] 명 야채, 채소

Key Expressions

- **be afraid of** ~을 두려워하다
- **become worried about** ~에 대해 걱정하게 되다
- **be named after** ~의 이름을 따서 지어지다
- **by oneself** 혼자서, 홀로(= **alone**)
- **dive into** ~으로 뛰어들다
- **have been to**+장소 ~에 가 본 적이 있다
- **How about**+명사/**-ing**? ~은 어때?

- **I'm thinking of …ing** ~할까 생각 중이야
- **look for** ~을 찾다
- **look like**+명사 ~처럼 보이다
- **on sale** 세일 중
- **on the other hand** 반면에
- **Why don't you**+동사원형 ~? ~하는 게 어때?

Word Power

※ 서로 반대되는 뜻을 가진 어휘

- □ **indoor**(실내의) ↔ **outdoor**(실외의)
- □ **different**(다른) ↔ **same**(같은)

- □ **beginner**(초보자) ↔ **expert**(전문가)
- □ **famous**(유명한) ↔ **unknown**(알려지지 않은)

※ 서로 비슷한 뜻을 가진 단어

- □ **alone** : **by oneself** (혼자)
- □ **offer** : **propose** (제안하다)
- □ **recently** : **lately** (최근에)

- □ **hit** : **success** (성공)
- □ **famous** : **well-known** (유명한)
- □ **imaginary** : **fictional** (가상의, 허구의)

English Dictionary

□ **beginner** 초보자
→ a person who is starting to do something or learn something for the first time
어떤 것을 하기 시작하거나 처음으로 어떤 것을 배우는 사람

□ **culture** 문화
→ the way of life, especially the general customs and beliefs, of a particular group of people at a particular time
특정한 시대에 특정한 집단의 사람들이 갖는 삶의 방식으로 특히 일반적인 관습이나 신념

□ **dessert** 후식
→ sweet food eaten at the end of a meal
식사가 끝났을 때 먹는 단 음식

□ **disappointed** 실망한
→ unhappy because someone or something was not as good as you hoped or expected
누군가나 무언가가 당신이 희망하거나 기대했던 것만큼 좋지 않았기 때문에 행복하지 않은

□ **imaginary** 상상의, 가상의
→ created by and existing only in the mind
생각에 의해 만들어지고 생각 속에서만 존재하는

□ **ingredient** 재료
→ a food that is used with other foods in the preparation of a particular dish
특별한 음식을 준비할 때 다른 음식과 함께 사용되는 음식

□ **kingdom** 왕국
→ a country ruled by a king or queen
왕이나 여왕이 통치하는 나라

□ **official** 관리, 신하
→ a person who has a position of responsibility in an organization
조직에서 책임 있는 지위를 가진 사람

□ **order** 주문하다
→ to ask for something to be made, supplied, or delivered, especially in a restaurant or shop
특히 식당이나 가게에서 만들어지거나, 공급되거나, 배달될 어떤 것을 요청하다

□ **party** 정당
→ an organization of people with particular political beliefs that competes in elections to try to win positions in local or national government
지방이나 국가 정부에서의 지위를 얻기 위해 선거에서 경쟁하는 특정한 정치적 신념을 가진 사람들의 조직

□ **policy** 정책
→ a set of ideas or a plan of what to do in particular situations that has been agreed to officially by a group of people, a government, or a political party
특정한 상황에서 무엇을 해야 하는지에 대한 집단이나 정부, 또는 정당이 공식적으로 동의한 일련의 생각이나 계획

□ **prefer** 선호하다
→ to like, choose, or want one thing rather than another
다른 것보다 하나를 좋아하거나 선택하거나 원하다

□ **recommend** 추천하다
→ to suggest that someone or something would be good or suitable for a particular job or purpose
어떤 사람이나 어떤 것이 특정 직업이나 목적에 좋거나 적합할 것이라고 제안하다

□ **scholar** 학자
→ a person who studies a subject in great detail, especially at a university
특히 대학에서 특정한 과목을 매우 세부적으로 공부하는 사람

□ **servant** 하인, 신하
→ a person who is employed in another person's house, doing jobs such as cooking and cleaning, especially in the past
특히 과거에 다른 사람의 집에 고용되어 요리와 청소와 같은 일을 하는 사람

□ **symbolize** 상징하다
→ to represent something
어떤 것을 나타내다

01 다음 짝지어진 두 단어의 관계가 같도록 빈칸에 알맞은 단어를 쓰시오.

> indoor : outdoor = same : _____

[02~03] 다음 빈칸에 들어갈 말로 가장 적절한 것은?

02

> How did tangpyeongchae and sinseollo get their names? Why does songpyeon look like a half moon? There are many interesting stories about our _____ food.

① new   ② popular
③ traditional   ④ foreign
⑤ imaginary

03 중요

> I have added a special _____ to the food.

① policy   ② party
③ guest   ④ honesty
⑤ ingredient

[04~05] 다음 영영풀이에 해당하는 단어를 고르시오.

04

> an organization of people with particular political beliefs that competes in elections to try to win positions in local or national government

① government   ② party
③ kingdom   ④ state
⑤ official

05

> to like, choose, or want one thing rather than another

① offer   ② order   ③ love
④ prefer   ⑤ differ

06 중요 밑줄 친 부분의 의미가 잘못된 것은?

① The color red <u>symbolizes</u> luck in Chinese culture. (상징하다)
② The government has announced a new <u>policy</u>. (정책)
③ Yulgok was a great <u>scholar</u> of Joseon. (학자)
④ My teacher has <u>recommended</u> the book to me. (명령했다)
⑤ I have been very busy <u>recently</u>. (최근에)

07 다음 〈영어 설명〉을 읽고 빈칸에 알맞은 말을 쓰시오.

> However, the king never listened to him. The scholar was so _____ that he went to live on a mountain.

> <영어 설명> unhappy because someone or something was not as good as you hoped or expected

➡ _____

08 다음 밑줄 친 단어와 같은 뜻을 가진 두 단어를 쓰시오.

> That is because the scholar lived like a sinseon, an imaginary person who lives <u>alone</u> in nature.

➡ _____

01 영영풀이에 해당하는 단어를 〈보기〉에서 찾아 첫 번째 칸에 쓰고, 두 번째 칸에는 우리말 뜻을 쓰시오.

┌─ 보기 ┐
recommend / servant / culture / official / symbolize / order / policy

(1) _____ : a set of ideas or a plan of what to do in particular situations that has been agreed to officially by a group of people, a government, or a political party: _____

(2) _____ : to suggest that someone or something would be good or suitable for a particular job or purpose: _____

(3) _____ : to represent something: _____

02 다음 빈칸에 알맞은 단어를 〈보기〉에서 골라 쓰시오. (형태 변화 가능)

┌─ 보기 ┐
mainly / pot / fortune teller / worry

(1) The king needs a _____ to know the future of his kingdom.

(2) Add some milk and chicken to the _____ .

(3) The king became _____ about his kingdom.

(4) While he lived there by himself, he _____ ate vegetables.

03 영어 설명을 읽고, 문장의 빈칸에 들어갈 알맞은 단어를 쓰시오. (주어진 글자로 시작할 것.)

┌──────────────────────────────┐
not long ago, or at a time that started not long ago
└──────────────────────────────┘

(1) I haven't seen a movie r_____ . Could you recommend a good one?

┌──────────────────────────────┐
a person who studies a subject in great detail, especially at a university
└──────────────────────────────┘

(2) In the time of King Yeonsan, there was a s_____ who was famous for his honesty.

04 우리말과 같은 의미가 되도록 빈칸에 알맞은 단어를 쓰시오.

(1) 정직은 최상의 정책이다.
➡ _____ is the best _____ .

(2) 정당은 그 문제를 해결해야 한다.
➡ The _____ needs to solve the problem.

05 다음 주어진 우리말에 맞게 빈칸을 채우시오. (필요하면 변형하여 쓰시오.)

(1) 백제는 보름달과 같지만 신라는 반달과 같다.
➡ Baekje is like a full moon, but Silla is like a _____ .

(2) 영조는 이 음식처럼 네 당파가 화합을 이루어 일해야 한다는 것을 말하고 싶었다.
➡ Yeongjo wanted to say that the four _____ should work in _____ like this dish.

(3) 그녀는 정부 관리다.
➡ She is an _____ in the government.

교과서

Conversation

① 선호하는 것 묻고 답하기

> **A** Do you prefer summer or winter? 넌 여름이 더 좋으니, 겨울이 더 좋으니?
> **B** I prefer summer. 나는 여름이 더 좋아.

- 둘 중 더 좋아하는 것에 대해 물을 때는 'Do you prefer A or B?' 표현을 쓰고, 답할 때는 'I prefer ~.' 형태로 답한다.
  A와 B 둘 중에 어떤 것을 더 좋아하는지 물을 때 'Which do you prefer, A or B?'라는 표현도 사용한다. prefer는 'like better[more]'로도 바꿀 수 있으므로 'Which do you like better[more], A or B?'라고도 할 수 있다. which가 뒤의 명사를 수식하는 의문형용사로도 쓰일 수 있으므로 'Which sport do you prefer, baseball or tennis?'라고도 할 수 있다.

- **선호하는 것 묻기**

  선호하는 것을 물을 때는 'Would you prefer A or B?'와 같이 말할 수 있다.

  - Would you prefer rice or noodles? 밥을 더 좋아하니, 국수를 더 좋아하니?
  - Which do you prefer, dogs or cats? 개와 고양이 중에서 어떤 것을 더 좋아하니?
    = Which do you like better, dogs or cats?
  - Would you prefer to buy the books or to borrow them from the library?
    너는 책을 사는 것을 더 좋아하니, 도서관에서 책을 빌리는 것을 더 좋아하니?

- **선호 표현하기**

  선호하는 것을 말할 때는 'B보다 A를 더 좋아한다'는 의미의 'prefer A to B'로 표현할 수 있다.

  - I prefer meat to vegetables. 나는 야채보다 고기를 더 좋아해.
    = I would prefer meat to vegetables.
    = I like meat more than vegetables.
  - I prefer to stay in my room rather than (to) go out. 외출하는 것보다 방에 있는 게 더 좋아.

핵심 Check

1. 다음 대화의 빈칸에 공통으로 들어갈 알맞은 것은?

   A: Which do you _____, baseball or soccer?
   B: I _____ soccer to baseball.

   ① choose ② prefer ③ like ④ have ⑤ think

② 추천 부탁하기

> • **Could you recommend a book for me?** 나한테 책 한 권 추천해 줄 수 있나요?

■ '(제게) ~을 추천해 주시겠어요?'라는 뜻으로 상대방에게 추천을 부탁할 때 'Could you recommend ~ (for me)?' 표현을 쓴다.

A: Could you recommend a book for me? 나에게 책 한 권 추천해 줄래?

B: Well, why don't you read *The Flying Pan*? 음. '플라잉 팬' 어때?

A: Great idea! Thanks. 멋진 생각이야! 고마워.

• Could you recommend one for me? 나에게 하나를 추천해 줄래?

• Which book do you recommend? 어떤 책을 추천하니?

■ **추천하기**

추천을 해줄 때는 동사 recommend를 이용하거나 'Why don't you ~?(~은 어때?)'를 이용하여 답을 한다.

• I recommend reading this article. 이 기사를 읽을 것을 추천해.

• I recommend you take a taxi to go there. 네가 그곳에 택시를 타고 갈 것을 추천해.

• I recommend you watch this movie. 네가 이 영화를 볼 것을 추천해.

핵심 Check

2. 다음 빈칸에 들어갈 말로 알맞은 것은?

G: I haven't seen a movie recently. _____ a good one?

B: Why don't you see *Iron Woman* 2? It's a big hit.

① Where could I see   ② How about

③ Could you recommend   ④ Please tell me where I should see

⑤ Could you show me

3. 다음 밑줄 친 문장의 의도로 알맞은 것은?

W: Excuse me. I'm looking for a skirt. <u>Could you recommend one</u>?

M: What color do you like?

W: Blue and pink are my favorite colors.

① 명령하기   ② 추천 부탁하기   ③ 예약하기

④ 능력 묻기   ⑤ 선호 묻기

Listen & Speak 1-A-1

B: Do you have anything for dessert, Aunt May?

W: Yes, Johnny. ❶Do you prefer pie or cake?

B: ❷I prefer cake.

W: O.K. I have some chocolate cake. I'll get you some.

B: May 이모, 디저트로 먹을 만한 게 있나요?
W: 그럼, Johnny. 파이가 더 좋으니, 케이크가 더 좋으니?
B: 전 케이크가 더 좋아요.
W: 알았어. 초콜릿 케이크가 좀 있네. 좀 갖다 줄게.

❶ 둘 중 더 좋아하는 것에 대해 물을 때 사용하는 표현이다.
❷ 선호하는 것을 답할 때 동사 'prefer'를 사용한다.

Check(√) True or False

(1) Johnny likes cake more than pie.   T☐ F☐

(2) Aunt May is going to make chocolate cake for Johnny.   T☐ F☐

Listen & Speak 1-A-2

B: ❶I'm thinking of joining a sports club.

G: ❷Do you prefer indoor or outdoor sports?

B: I prefer indoor sports. I was in the badminton club last year.

G: ❸Why don't you join the table tennis club, then?

B: That's a good idea. Thank you.

B: 나 스포츠 동아리에 가입하려고 생각 중이야.
G: 실내 스포츠가 더 좋아, 야외 스포츠가 더 좋아?
B: 실내 스포츠가 더 좋아. 작년에 배드민턴 동아리에 있었거든.
G: 그럼, 탁구 동아리가 어때?
B: 그게 좋겠다. 고마워.

❶ 'I'm thinking of ...ing'는 '…할 생각 중이야'라는 계획이나 의도를 말할 때 사용하는 표현이다.
❷ A와 B 둘 중에 어떤 것을 더 좋아하는지 물을 때 사용하는 표현으로, 'Which do you prefer, A or B?'라는 표현도 사용한다.
❸ 'Why don't you+동사원형?'은 '…하는 게 어때?'라는 뜻으로 상대방에게 제안할 때 사용한다.

Check(√) True or False

(3) B prefers indoor sports to outdoor sports.   T☐ F☐

(4) G recommends that B should join the table tennis club.   T☐ F☐

Listen & Speak 2-A-1

W: Excuse me. I'm looking for an Italian cookbook. ❶Could you recommend one?

M: Well, have you ever cooked Italian food?

W: No, I haven't, but I want to try. I really like spaghetti.

M: Then, ❷how about this Italian cookbook for beginners? It's ❸on sale now.

W: Good! Thank you. I'll take it.

❶ 추천을 부탁하는 표현이다.
❷ 'how about+명사?'로 '~는 어때?'라는 제안의 표현이다.
❸ '세일 중'이라는 표현이다.

Listen & Speak 2-A-2

G: I haven't seen a movie recently. ❶Could you recommend a good one?

B: ❷Why don't you see *Iron Woman 2*? It's a big hit.

G: Well, I don't like action movies. ❸Can you recommend any good comedies?

B: Then, how about *Funny Families*?

G: That sounds good.

❶ '(제게) ~을 추천해 주시겠어요?'라는 뜻으로 상대방에게 추천을 부탁하는 표현이다.
❷ 'Why don't you+동사원형 ~?'은 '~하는 게 어때?'라는 뜻으로 상대방에게 제안할 때 사용한다.
❸ 상대방에게 추천을 부탁하는 표현이다.

Listen & Speak B

A: ❶Could you recommend a book for me?

B: Well, why don't you read *The Flying Pan*?

A: Great idea. Thanks.

❶ 상대방에게 추천을 부탁하는 표현이다.

Communicate A

Jaden: ❶Have you been to the new Chinese restaurant, Ms. Park?

Ms. Park: Are you talking about the one on Main Street, Jaden?

Jaden: Yes, that's the one. They opened about two weeks ago, right?

Ms. Park: I think so. I went there last Friday with my friends.

Jaden: How was the food?

Ms. Park: It was great. We ordered many different dishes. I really liked the fried vegetables.

Jaden: ❷Could you recommend a dish for me? I'm going there for dinner tonight with my family.

Ms. Park: ❸Do you prefer seafood or meat?

Jaden: I prefer seafood.

Ms. Park: Then, you should try their fried fish. You'll love it!

❶ 'Have you been to ~?'는 '~에 가 본 적이 있니?'라는 뜻이다.
❷ '(제게) ~을 추천해 주시겠어요?'라는 뜻으로 상대방에게 추천을 부탁하는 표현이다.
❸ A와 B 둘 중에 어떤 것을 더 좋아하는지 물을 때 사용하는 표현으로, 'Which do you prefer, A or B?'라는 표현도 사용한다.

Communicate B

M: Could you recommend a Korean restaurant ❶near here?

W: Do you prefer hot or cold food?

M: I prefer cold food.

W: Then, you should ❷try the naengmyeon place at the end of this block.

M: Thank you.

❶ near here: 이 근처에
❷ try: 가 보다

Progress Check

1. G: I'm thinking of getting a pet.
   B: Do you prefer dogs or cats?
   G: I prefer cats. They're so cute.
   B: Great! I can give you ❶one. I have seven cats at home.
   G: Thank you.

2. W: Excuse me. I'm looking for a skirt. Could you recommend one?
   M: What color do you like?
   W: Blue and pink are my favorite colors.
   M: Then, how about this blue ❷one? It's on sale now.
   W: Good! Thank you. I'll ❸take it.

❶ one = a cat
❷ one = skirt
❸ take = buy

다음 우리말과 일치하도록 빈칸에 알맞은 말을 쓰시오.

Listen & Speak 1-A

1. **B:** Do you have _____ for _____, Aunt May?
   W: Yes, Johnny. Do you _____ pie _____ cake?
   B: I _____ cake.
   W: O.K. I have some chocolate cake. I'll _____ you some.

2. **B:** I'm _____ _____ joining a sports club.
   G: Do you _____ _____ _____ _____ sports?
   B: I _____ indoor sports. I was in the badminton club _____ year.
   G: _____ _____ _____ join the table tennis club, then?
   B: That's a good idea. Thank you.

Listen & Speak 2-A

1. **W:** Excuse me. I'm _____ _____ an Italian cookbook. Could you _____ one?
   M: Well, have you ever _____ _____ food?
   W: No, I _____, but I want to try. I really like spaghetti.
   M: Then, _____ _____ this _____ cookbook for _____? It's _____ _____ now.
   W: Good! Thank you. I'll _____ it.

2. **G:** I _____ _____ a movie _____. Could you _____ a good one?
   B: _____ _____ _____ _____ see *Iron Woman 2*? It's a _____ _____.
   G: Well, I don't like _____ movies. Can you _____ any good _____?
   B: Then, _____ about *Funny Families*?
   G: That _____ good.

Listen & Speak B

A: Could you _____ a book for me?
B: Well, _____ _____ _____ read *The Flying Pan*?
A: Great idea. Thanks.

해석

1. **B:** May 이모, 디저트로 먹을 만한 게 있나요?
   W: 그럼, Johnny. 파이가 더 좋으니, 케이크가 더 좋으니?
   B: 전 케이크가 더 좋아요.
   W: 알았어. 초콜릿 케이크가 좀 있네. 좀 갖다 줄게.

2. **B:** 나 스포츠 동아리에 가입하려고 생각 중이야.
   G: 실내 스포츠가 더 좋아, 야외 스포츠가 더 좋아?
   B: 실내 스포츠가 더 좋아. 작년에 배드민턴 동아리에 있었거든.
   G: 그럼, 탁구 동아리가 어때?
   B: 그게 좋겠다. 고마워.

1. **W:** 실례합니다. 이탈리아 요리책을 찾고 있는데요. 추천해 주실 수 있으세요?
   M: 음, 이탈리아 요리를 해 보신 적이 있나요?
   W: 아뇨, 없습니다. 하지만 해 보고 싶어서요. 스파게티를 정말 좋아하거든요.
   M: 그렇다면 초보자들을 위한 이 이탈리아 요리책이 어떨까요? 지금 세일 중이에요.
   W: 좋아요! 감사합니다. 그걸 살게요.

2. **G:** 최근에 영화를 한 편도 못 봤어. 좋은 영화 한 편 추천해 줄래?
   B: 《아이언 우먼 2》 어때? 크게 히트를 치고 있는데.
   G: 글쎄, 액션 영화는 안 좋아해. 괜찮은 코미디 영화 추천해 줄 수 있어?
   B: 그렇다면, 《퍼니 패밀리즈》는 어때?
   G: 그게 좋겠다.

A: 나한테 책 한 권 추천해 줄래?
B: 글쎄, '플라잉 팬' 어때?
A: 아주 좋아. 고마워.

Communicate A

Jaden: _____ you _____ _____ the new Chinese restaurant, Ms. Park?

Ms. Park: Are you _____ _____ the one on Main Street, Jaden?

Jaden: Yes, that's _____ _____. They opened about two weeks _____, right?

Ms. Park: I think _____. I _____ there _____ Friday with my friends.

Jaden: _____ _____ the food?

Ms. Park: It was great. We _____ many _____ _____. I really liked the _____ vegetables.

Jaden: Could you _____ a dish _____ me? I'm going there for dinner _____ with my family.

Ms. Park: Do you _____ seafood _____ meat?

Jaden: I _____ _____.

Ms. Park: Then, you _____ _____ their _____ _____. You'll love it!

Communicate B

M: _____ _____ _____ a Korean restaurant near here?

W: _____ you _____ hot _____ cold food?

M: I _____ cold food.

W: Then, you should _____ the naengmyeon place at the end of this block.

M: Thank you.

Progress Check

1. **G:** _____ _____ _____ getting a pet.

   B: Do you _____ dogs _____ cats?

   G: I _____ cats. They're so cute.

   B: Great! I can give you _____. I have seven cats at home.

   G: Thank you.

2. **W:** Excuse me. I'm _____ _____ a skirt. Could you _____ one?

   M: What _____ do you like?

   W: Blue and pink are my _____ colors.

   M: Then, _____ _____ this blue one? It's _____ _____ now.

   W: Good! Thank you. I'll _____ it.

해석

Jaden: 새로 생긴 중국집에 가 보셨어요, 박 선생님?

박 선생님: 메인 가에 있는 거 말하는 거니, Jaden?

Jaden: 네, 거기요. 한 2주 전쯤에 문을 열었어요, 그렇죠?

박 선생님: 그런 것 같아. 지난 금요일에 친구들과 함께 거기에 갔단다.

Jaden: 음식이 어땠나요?

박 선생님: 훌륭했어. 우린 다양한 음식을 많이 시켰어. 나는 채소볶음이 정말 좋았어.

Jaden: 제게 요리 하나 추천해 주시겠어요? 오늘 저녁에 저녁 식사를 하러 가족들과 함께 그곳에 가거든요.

박 선생님: 너는 해산물을 더 좋아하니, 육류를 더 좋아하니?

Jaden: 전 해산물을 더 좋아해요.

박 선생님: 그럼 그곳의 생선튀김을 먹어 봐. 네가 정말 좋아할 거야!

M: 이 근처에서 한국 음식점 좀 추천해 주실래요?

W: 뜨거운 음식이 더 좋으세요, 차가운 음식이 더 좋으세요?

M: 찬 음식을 더 좋아해요.

W: 그럼, 이 블록 끝에 있는 냉면집에 가 보세요.

M: 감사합니다.

1. **G:** 애완동물을 키울까 해.
   B: 개가 좋아, 아니면 고양이가 좋아?
   G: 나는 고양이가 좋아. 정말 귀엽잖아.
   B: 잘 됐다! 내가 한 마리 줄 수 있어. 집에 일곱 마리나 있거든.
   G: 고마워.

2. **W:** 실례합니다. 치마를 찾고 있는데요. 하나 추천해 주실 수 있나요?
   M: 어떤 색을 좋아하세요?
   W: 파란색과 분홍색을 제일 좋아해요.
   M: 그럼, 이 파란 건 어때요? 지금 세일 중이에요.
   W: 좋아요! 감사합니다. 그걸로 할게요.

01 다음 밑줄 친 우리말에 맞게 빈칸에 알맞은 말을 쓰시오.

> A: <u>나한테 책 한 권 추천해 줄래?</u>
> B: Well, why don't you read *The Flying Pan*?
> A: Great idea. Thanks.

➡ Could you _____ a book _____ me?

[02~03] 대화의 빈칸에 들어갈 말로 알맞은 것은?

02

> B: Do you have anything for dessert, Aunt May?
> W: Yes, Johnny. _____
> B: I prefer cake.
> W: O.K. I have some chocolate cake. I'll get you some.

① Do you want to eat cake?
② Do you have cake?
③ Do you prefer pie or cake?
④ How much do you like chocolate cake?
⑤ Why don't you eat cake?

03

> G: I'm thinking of getting a pet.
> B: Do you prefer dogs or cats?
> G: _____ They're so cute.
> B: Great! I can give you one. I have seven cats at home.
> G: Thank you.

① I prefer cats.　　　② I like dogs most.
③ I don't think so.　　④ How about you?
⑤ I prefer dogs.

04 다음 대화의 밑줄 친 부분의 의도로 알맞은 것은?

> B: We're planning our school's sports day. <u>Do you prefer indoor or outdoor activities?</u>

① 능력 여부 묻기　　② 유감 표현하기　　③ 기대 표현하기
④ 선호 묻기　　　　⑤ 보고하기

[01~02] 다음 대화를 읽고 물음에 답하시오.

> B: _____(A)_____
> G: Do you prefer indoor or outdoor sports?
> B: I prefer indoor sports. I was in the badminton club last year.
> G: _____(B)_____, then?
> B: That's a good idea. Thank you.

01 빈칸 (A)에 알맞은 말을 고르시오.

① I'm planning to play tennis.
② I'm considering joining a soccer club.
③ I'm thinking of buying a tennis racket.
④ I'm thinking of joining a sports club.
⑤ I broke my leg in the soccer game.

02 빈칸 (B)에 들어가기에 어색한 말은?

① How about joining the table tennis club
② Why don't you join the table tennis club
③ What about joining the table tennis club
④ What do you say to joining the table tennis club
⑤ How do you join the table tennis club

03 다음 중 짝지어진 대화가 어색한 것은?

① A: Could you recommend a movie for me?
  B: Well, why don't you watch *Avengers*?
② A: Do you prefer chicken or beef?
  B: I don't like pork.
③ A: I like Chinese food.
  B: Then, I recommend the Chinese restaurant at the Happy Department Store.
④ A: Could you recommend a book for me?
  B: Well, why don't you read *A Good Singer*?
⑤ A: Does Yuna prefer cats or dogs?
  B: She prefers dogs.

서답형

04 대화에서 빈칸에 주어진 〈조건〉대로 문장을 완성하시오.

> B: Do you have anything for dessert, Aunt May?
> W: Yes, Johnny. _____
> B: I prefer cake.

┤ 보기 ├
• 선호를 묻는 표현을 쓸 것
• 'prefer', 'cake', 'pie'를 사용할 것

➡ _____

[05~06] 다음 대화를 읽고 물음에 답하시오.

> W: Excuse me. I'm looking for an Italian cookbook. Could you ___ⓐ___ one?
> M: Well, have you ever cooked Italian food?
> W: No, I haven't, but I want to try. I really like spaghetti.
> M: Then, ___ⓑ___ this Italian cookbook for beginners? It's on sale now.
> W: Good! Thank you. I'll take it.

05 빈칸 ⓐ, ⓑ에 들어갈 말로 알맞은 것은?

① recommend – where can I buy
② recommend – where did you buy
③ recommend – how about
④ advise – what about
⑤ advise – why don't you

06 다음 영영풀이에 해당하는 단어를 대화에서 찾아 쓰시오.

> a person who is starting to do something or learn something for the first time

➡ _____

[07~08] 다음 대화를 읽고 물음에 답하시오.

G: I haven't seen a movie recently. Could you recommend a good one?

B: (A)Why don't you see *Iron Woman 2*? It's a big hit.

G: Well, I don't like action movies. _____(a)_____

B: Then, how about *Funny Families*?

G: That sounds good.

07 위 대화의 빈칸 (a)에 들어갈 말로 알맞은 것은?

① Can you recommend any good comedies?

② Let's see a movie tonight.

③ Where shall we meet?

④ Do you like action movies?

⑤ I'd like to see action movies.

08 밑줄 친 (A)와 바꾸어 쓸 수 있는 것은?

① Why did you see *Iron Woman 2*?

② Are you planning to see *Iron Woman 2*?

③ Are you going to see *Iron Woman 2*?

④ Shall I see *Iron Woman 2*?

⑤ What about seeing *Iron Woman 2*?

[09~11] 다음 대화를 읽고 물음에 답하시오.

Jaden: (A)새로 생긴 중국집에 가 보셨어요, Ms. Park?

Ms. Park: Are you talking about the one on Main Street, Jaden? (①)

Jaden: Yes, that's the one. (②) They opened about two weeks ago, right?

Ms. Park: I think so. I went there last Friday with my friends.

Jaden: How was the food?

Ms. Park: It was great. (③)

Jaden: _____(a)_____ I'm going there for dinner tonight with my family. (④)

Ms. Park: Do you prefer seafood or meat?

Jaden: I prefer seafood. (⑤)

Ms. Park: Then, you should try their fried fish. You'll love it!

09 위 대화의 (①)~(⑤) 중 다음 주어진 말이 들어갈 알맞은 곳은?

> We ordered many different dishes. I really liked the fried vegetables.

①   ②   ③   ④   ⑤

10 위 대화의 빈칸 (a)에 들어갈 말로 알맞은 것은?

① Could you recommend a Japanese restaurant near here?

② Do you prefer sushi or udong?

③ Do you prefer Chinese or Japanese food?

④ Could you recommend a dish for me?

⑤ Why don't you try the new Chinese restaurant?

11 위 대화의 밑줄 친 (A)의 우리말에 맞게 주어진 단어를 배열하시오.

> (been / the / new / restaurant / have / you / to / Chinese)

➡ _____

[01~02] 다음 대화를 읽고 물음에 답하시오.

Man: Could you recommend a Korean restaurant near here?

Woman: (A)뜨거운 음식이 더 좋으세요, 차가운 음식이 더 좋으세요?

Man: I prefer cold food.

Woman: Then, you should try the naengmyeon place at the end of this block.

Man: Thank you.

01 What food is the man going to eat?

➡ _____

02 밑줄 친 (A)의 우리말에 맞게 주어진 단어를 이용하여 영작하시오. (7 words)

> (prefer / hot / cold / food)

➡ _____

03 다음 그림을 보고 주어진 단어를 이용하여 (1)은 선호하는 것을 묻는 말을, (2)는 선호하는 말을 쓰시오.

A: (1)_____
   (rainy days / sunny days)
B: I (2)_____ (sunny days)

04 다음 문장의 우리말에 맞게 단어를 바르게 배열하시오.

> 나한테 책 한 권 추천해 줄 수 있나요?
> (recommend / a / book / could / me / for / you / ?)

➡ _____

[05~06] 다음 대화를 읽고 물음에 답하시오.

Jaden: Have you been to the new Chinese restaurant, Ms. Park?

Ms. Park: Are you talking about the one on Main Street, Jaden?

Jaden: Yes, that's the one. They opened about two weeks ago, right?

Ms. Park: I think so. I went there last Friday with my friends.

Jaden: How was the food?

Ms. Park: It was great. We ordered many different dishes. I really liked the fried vegetables.

Jaden: _____(A)_____ I'm going there for dinner tonight with my family.

Ms. Park: _____(B)_____

Jaden: I prefer seafood.

Ms. Park: Then, you should try their fried fish. You'll love it!

05 위 대화의 빈칸 (A)에 주어진 어구를 이용하여 '제게 요리 하나 추천해 주시겠어요?'라는 표현을 영어로 쓰시오.

> (could / a dish / me)

➡ _____

06 위 대화의 빈칸 (B)에 주어진 조건에 맞게 한 문장을 쓰시오.

> ┤ 조건 ├
> • 선호하는 것을 묻는 표현을 쓸 것.
> • 'seafood'와 'meat'를 사용할 것.

➡ _____
_____

Grammar

1 수동태

- They **called** this dish tangpyeongchae. 〈능동태〉 그들은 이 음식을 탕평채라고 불렀다.
- This dish **was called** tangpyeongchae. 〈수동태〉 이 음식은 탕평채라고 불렸다.

■ 수동태는 주어가 동작의 대상인 문장으로 '주어+be동사+과거분사(+by 행위자)'의 형식을 가지며 '~해지다, …에 의해 ~되다[당하다]'라는 의미이다. 수동태 문장의 주어 자리에는 능동태 문장의 목적어가 오고, by 다음에는 능동태 문장의 주어를 쓴다. 누가 그 동작을 했는지 중요하지 않거나 잘 모를 때, 수동태 문장으로 표현하며 'by+행위자'를 생략한다. 수동태는 현재, 과거, 미래 시제로 쓸 수 있고, 'be동사+과거분사'에서 be동사로 시제를 나타낸다.

■ 4형식 문장의 수동태는 간접목적어와 직접목적어 각각을 주어로 하는 수동태가 가능하다. 직접목적어를 주어로 한 수동태에서는 간접목적어 앞에 특정한 전치사를 써야 한다.
전치사 to를 쓰는 동사는 'bring, give, show, send, tell, teach' 등이고, 전치사 for를 쓰는 동사는 'buy, choose, cook, get, make' 등이며, 전치사 of를 쓰는 동사는 'ask' 등이 있다. 또한 'buy, make, read, write' 등은 직접목적어를 주어로 하는 수동태만 가능하다.

- Her mom **made** her a dress.
  → A dress **was made** for her by her mom. 옷이 그녀의 엄마에 의해 그녀에게 만들어졌다.
  → She was made a dress by her mom. (×)

■ 조동사가 있는 문장의 수동태는 '조동사+be+p.p.' 형식을 갖는다.

- Jake **will send** her an e-mail.
  → An e-mail **will be sent** to her by Jake. 이메일이 Jake에 의해 그녀에게 보내질 것이다.

■ 5형식 문장의 수동태는 목적어와 목적격 보어 자리에 모두 명사가 오더라도 목적어만 수동태의 주어 자리에 올 수 있으며, 목적격 보어 자리에 동사원형이 쓰이면 수동태 문장에서는 to부정사 형태로 바뀌어야 한다.

- The teacher **made** him **do** his homework. 선생님이 그에게 숙제를 하노록 시켰다.
  → He **was made to do** his homework by the teacher.

■ by 이외의 전치사를 사용하는 수동태에 유의한다.

- be interested in: ~에 흥미가 있다
- be covered with: ~로 덮여 있다
- be made of: ~로 만들어지다(물리적 변화)
- be filled with: ~로 가득 차다
- be surprised at: ~에 놀라다
- be made from: ~로 만들어지다(화학적 변화)

핵심 Check

1. 다음 괄호 안에서 알맞은 말을 고르시오.
   (1) The gate (painted / was painted) by John.
   (2) Social studies was taught (for / to) us by Mr. Min.
   (3) They were pleased (for / with) the news.

② something/someone+형용사

> • King Yeongjo offered them something **special**. 영조가 그들에게 특별한 무언가를 권했다.
> • I want to eat something **cold**. 나는 시원한 무언가를 먹고 싶다.

■ 형용사는 보통 명사 앞에 오지만, '-thing, -one, -body'로 끝나는 대명사는 형용사가 뒤에서 수식한다. 이러한 대명사에는 something, someone, somebody, anything, anyone, anybody, nothing, no one, nobody 등이 있다.

- I want something **big** and **baggy**. 크고 헐렁한 것으로 주십시오.
- Did you meet anyone **nice** last weekend? 지난 주말 괜찮은 사람을 만났니?

■ '-thing, -one, -body'로 끝나는 대명사를 to부정사와 형용사가 동시에 수식할 때 어순은 '대명사+형용사+to부정사'이다.

- I have something **important to tell** you. 너에게 할 중요한 이야기가 있다.
- She didn't have anything **nice to say** about him. 그녀는 그에 대해 좋게 말할 게 없었어.

핵심 Check

2. 다음 괄호 안에서 알맞은 말을 고르시오.

(1) Do you have (long anything / anything long)?

(2) (Terrible something / Something terrible) happened last night.

(3) Dr. Ian couldn't find (anyone nice to talk with / anyone to talk with nice).

01 다음 빈칸에 알맞은 것은?

> • J. K. Rowling wrote it.
> → It _____ by J. K. Rowling.

① writes　　　　　② wrote　　　　　③ has written

④ is written　　　⑤ was written

02 괄호 안의 단어를 바르게 배열한 것은?

> We (special, need, something).

① need special something　　② need something special

③ special something need　　④ something special need

⑤ something need special

03 다음 우리말에 맞게 빈칸에 알맞은 말을 쓰시오.

(1) 그 학교는 10년 전에 세워졌다.
　➡ The school _____ _____ ten years ago.

(2) '*Romeo and Juliet*'은 Shakespeare에 의해 쓰여졌다.
　➡ *Romeo and Juliet* _____ _____ by Shakespeare.

(3) 우리는 어떤 재미있는 사람을 찾고 있다. (funny와 someone을 이용할 것.)
　➡ We are looking for _____ _____.

(4) 그는 어떤 중요한 사람임에 틀림없다. (important와 somebody를 이용할 것.)
　➡ He must be _____ _____.

04 다음 문장에서 어법상 어색한 부분을 바르게 고쳐 쓰시오.

(1) His room cleans every day by him.
　_____ ➡ _____

(2) Give me something to read interesting.
　_____ ➡ _____

01 다음 빈칸에 알맞은 것은?

> This toy _____ by my dad.

① makes   ② made
③ to make   ④ was made
⑤ was making

02 다음 중 어법상 어색한 것을 고르시오.

① We need a special plan.
② Is it something good?
③ King Yeongjo offered them something special.
④ Is there anything interesting to buy?
⑤ I don't have reliable anyone.

03 다음 중 수동태로의 전환이 어색한 것은?

① Thomas Edison invented the light bulb.
→ The light bulb was invented by Thomas Edison.
② Her mother often made it for the family.
→ It was often made for the family by her mother.
③ The teacher made us do homework.
→ We were made do homework by the teacher.
④ Her mom chose her a beautiful dress.
→ A beautiful dress was chosen for her by her mom.
⑤ They sold shirts and pants at the shop.
→ Shirts and pants were sold at the shop.

04 다음 중 어법상 옳은 것은?

① My family eats something special on Chuseok.
② How were tangpyeongchae and sinseollo got their names?
③ *The Mona Lisa* painted by Leonardo da Vinci.
④ There was wrong something with my bill.
⑤ The dress will be bought to her by Mary.

05 다음 우리말을 바르게 영작한 것은?

> 오직 33명 만이 그녀에 의해 최종 오디션에 선발되었다.

① Only 33 were chosen with the final audition by her.
② Only 33 were chosen for the final audition by her.
③ Only 33 were chosen of the final audition by her.
④ The final audition was chosen for only 33 by her.
⑤ Only 33 were chosen for her by the final audition.

06 다음 빈칸에 공통으로 들어갈 말로 가장 적절한 것은?

> • The box was filled _____ chocolate bars.
> • I'm not satisfied _____ the customer service.

① at   ② in   ③ of
④ for   ⑤ with

07 다음 대화의 빈칸에 들어갈 말이 바르게 짝지어진 것은?

> M: Did you go to the party last night?
> Who hold the party? And how was it?
> W: It _____ by Dave. It was
> great and I met _____ there.

① was held – someone funny
② held – someone funny
③ was held – funny someone
④ held – funny someone
⑤ holds – anyone funny

서답형

08 다음 괄호 안에서 알맞은 것을 고르시오.

(1) Beautiful flowers were sent (to / for) her by an old man.

(2) A new type of character was made (to / for) the Horde, too.

(3) A lot of questions were asked (to / of) the singer by her fans.

서답형

09 다음 그림을 참고하여 주어진 문장의 빈칸을 알맞게 채우시오.

> A: Did you find _____ at the store?
> B: Yes, I found some funny hats.

➡ _____

중요
10 다음 중 태의 전환이 <u>어색한</u> 것은?

① They advised him to leave the place as soon as possible.
→ He was advised to leave the place as soon as possible by them.

② He made William finish the work by the next day.
→ William was made to finish the work by the next day by him.

③ Gibson gave Jane a present.
→ A present was given for Jane by Gibson.

④ Someone stole my bag.
→ My bag was stolen.

⑤ Mom bought me a smartphone.
→ A smartphone was bought for me by mom.

서답형

11 다음 문장에서 어법상 <u>어색한</u> 부분을 찾아 바르게 고치시오.

(1) In 1964, China's first nuclear test was taken place.
➡ _____

(2) *Two Sisters* painted Auguste Renoir in 1881.
➡ _____

(3) Give me something to drink cold.
➡ _____

(4) They will see her as respectable someone.
➡ _____

12 주어진 문장을 영어로 바르게 옮긴 것은?

> 나는 어젯밤에 아주 놀라운 일이 발생했다고 들었다.

① I heard very surprising anything was happened last night.
② I heard very surprising something happened last night.
③ I heard very surprising something was happened last night.
④ I heard something very surprising happened last night.
⑤ I heard something very surprising was happened last night.

서답형

13 다음 문장을 수동태로 바꿔 쓰시오.

(1) He bought me a nice cap.
⇒ _____
_____

(2) They speak French in France.
⇒ _____
_____

(3) Who draw the picture *The Sunflowers*?
⇒ _____
_____

(4) Marianne made Sam delicious spaghetti last night.
⇒ _____
_____

(5) I heard Emily talking to her friend in class.
⇒ _____
_____

14 다음 문장에서 something이 들어갈 위치로 알맞은 곳은?

> • People avoid others' notice ① when ② they ③ do ④ bad ⑤.

① ② ③ ④ ⑤

15 다음 문장을 수동태로 바르게 바꾼 것은?

> She gave it up in order to support her family.

① It gave up by her in order to support her family.
② It given up by her in order to support her family.
③ It was given up her in order to support her family.
④ It was given by her in order to support her family.
⑤ It was given up by her in order to support her family.

서답형

16 다음 빈칸에 들어갈 말이 바르게 짝지어진 것은?

> • The storyline of the opera *Turandot* will _____ to you by me. (tell)
> • Many fancy cars _____ in Korea. (make) (현재 시제)
> • I _____ the number of side dishes. (surprise) (과거 시제)
> • Susan _____ acting. (interest) (과거 시제)
> • He _____ dust while walking along the road. (cover) (과거 시제)
> • His heart _____ pride at that time. (fill) (과거 시제)

01 다음 문장을 수동태로 바꿔 쓰시오.

(1) Each ingredient symbolized a different political party.

➡ _____

(2) The king never listened to him.

➡ _____

(3) Dan made his son a small sandcastle.

➡ _____

(4) They throw away many computers every year in the United States.

➡ _____

(5) Who wrote the novel, *Christmas Carol*?

➡ _____

02 다음 괄호 안에 주어진 단어를 넣어 문장을 다시 쓰시오.

(1) I want to show something to you. (wonderful)

➡ _____

(2) I want to work with somebody for our business. (honest)

➡ _____

(3) There was nobody at the meeting. (important)

➡ _____

03 다음 문장에서 어법상 어색한 부분을 찾아 바르게 고쳐 다시 쓰시오.

(1) The bench painted the man.

➡ _____

(2) Spicy food is loving by all of my family members.

➡ _____

(3) The bookshelf was made from wood.

➡ _____

(4) Amy was heard sing in front of all the classmates by us.

➡ _____

(5) She was written a long letter by him.

➡ _____

(6) A wedding ring with a small ruby will be bought to her.

➡ _____

04 주어진 말을 이용하여 대화의 빈칸을 채우시오.

> A: Are there any interesting programs on TV tonight?
>
> B: No, there is _____ on TV. (nothing)

➡ _____

05 다음 우리말을 괄호 안에 주어진 어휘를 이용하여 영작하시오.

(1) 그것의 등에 무언가가 쓰여 있었다.
(something, write, back)

➡ _____

_____

(2) 로마는 하루아침에 이루어지지 않았다.
(Rome, build, a day)

➡ _____

(3) 제가 그에게 전화를 해보았지만, 그의 전화기는 꺼져 있었습니다. (call him, his phone, turn off)

➡ _____

(4) 내 숙제는 나에 의해 일요일까지는 끝내져야 한다. (my homework, by Sunday, must, finish)

➡ _____

(5) 나는 Tom에게서 흥미로운 무언가를 들었다.
(interesting, something)

➡ _____

(6) 그 집에는 아무도 행복한 사람이 없을 것이다.
(nobody, that house, there, will)

➡ _____

06 다음 문장에서 어법상 <u>어색한</u> 부분을 찾아 바르게 고치시오.

(1) I'm looking for funny someone.

_____ ➡ _____

(2) Is it always hard to try new something?

_____ ➡ _____

(3) Can I have cold to drink something?

_____ ➡ _____

(4) I could find new nobody there.

_____ ➡ _____

07 다음 문장을 수동태는 능동태로, 능동태는 수동태로 고치시오.

(1) Thomas Edison invented the light bulb.

➡ _____

_____

(2) Mahatma Gandhi is respected by many people.

➡ _____

(3) They canceled all the flights due to the bad weather.

➡ _____

_____

08 주어진 단어를 활용하여 빈칸에 알맞은 말을 쓰시오.

• Artist: Vincent Van Gogh
• Title: *The Starry Night*
• Year: 1889

This picture _____ _____ (paint) by Vincent Van Gogh. It _____ _____ (title) *The Starry Night* and _____ _____ (complete) in 1889.

Reading

A Bite of Korean History

How did tangpyeongchae and sinseollo get their names? Why does

songpyeon <u>look like</u> a half moon? There are many interesting stories
　　　　　　look like+명사: ~처럼 보이다

<u>about</u> our traditional food. Let's dive into the <u>fun</u> history of our food.
~에 관한　　　　　　　　　　　　　　　　　재미있는

bite: 한 입, 소량의 음식

half: 반, 절반; 절반의

dive into: ~으로 뛰어들다

official: 신하, 관리, 공무원

offer: 제의[제안]하다, 권하다

ingredient: (특히 요리 등의) 재료, 성분

symbolize: 상징하다

political: 정치의, 정당의

party: 정당

policy: 정책

Tangpyeongchae

One day, King Yeongjo <u>was having</u> dinner with <u>his</u> officials and
　　　　　　　　　　　　과거진행형 having = eating　　　　영조

offered <u>them</u> <u>something special</u>. It was a dish with four colorful
영조의 신하들　something과 같이 -thing으로 끝나는 대명사를 수식할 때 형용사가 뒤에 온다.

ingredients. <u>Each</u> ingredient symbolized a different <u>political party</u>.
　　　　　　각각의(+단수명사)　　　　　　　　　　　　　　　　　정파

Yeongjo wanted to say <u>that</u> the four parties should work <u>in harmony</u>
　　　　　　　　　　　that 이하는 영조가 말하고 싶었던 것이 무엇인지를 나타내는 목적어　　　　화합을 이루어

<u>like</u> this dish. This dish <u>was called</u> tangpyeongchae. The name came
~와 같이　　　　　　　　be동사+과거분사: ~라고 불렸다(수동의 의미)

from Yeongjo's policy tangpyeongchaek.

확인문제

● 다음 문장이 본문의 내용과 일치하면 T, 일치하지 <u>않으면</u> F를 쓰시오.

1　There are many interesting stories about our traditional food. ☐

2　One day, King Yeongjo was having dinner with his sons. ☐

3　Tangpyeongchae was a dish with four colorful ingredients. ☐

4　Yeongjo said that the four parties should work in harmony by his policy

　　tangpyeongchaek. ☐

Sinseollo

In the time of King Yeonsan, there was a scholar who was famous
~의 시대에   주격 관계대명사
for his honesty. When the king did something wrong, the scholar was
                                          부정대명사+형용사
never afraid of telling him so. However, the king never listened to him.
              동명사   = the king did something wrong
The scholar was so disappointed that he went to live on a mountain.
              so+형용사/부사+that+주어+동사: 너무 ~해서 …하다
While he lived there by himself, he mainly ate vegetables. He made a

special pot to cook many different vegetables together. People called
요리하기 위해서 (목적을 나타내는 to부정사의 부사적 용법)   call A B는 'A를 B라고 부르다'. this pot and
this pot and the food in it sinseollo. That is because the scholar lived
the food in it(목적어). sinseollo(목적격 보어)   바로 앞에 나온 문장 'People called ~ sinseollo.'를 가리킨다.
like a sinseon, an imaginary person who lives alone in nature.
~과 같이   a sinseon과 an imaginary person은 동격

Songpyeon

It was the time of the last king of Baekje. One day, the king and his

servants found a strange turtle. Something was written on its back. It
                                               수동태 구문   = the turtle's
said, "Baekje is like a full moon, but Silla is like a half moon."

The king asked a fortune teller, "What does this mean?"
          → 간접화법: The king asked a fortune teller what that meant.
The fortune teller answered, "A full moon will soon become smaller.

On the other hand, a half moon will grow bigger and become a full
반면에
moon."

The king became worried about his kingdom. However, people of
                                          앞의 내용과 반대되는 상황을 연결하는 접속부사
Silla were very happy to learn this and made rice cakes in the shape of
                         부사적 용법(감정의 원인)
a half moon. Since then, people have enjoyed these half-moon shaped
since: '~ 이래로', 현재완료 시제와 자주 쓰임.   현재완료 시제: 과거부터 현재까지 계속해서 사람들이 송편을 먹고 있다는 의미
rice cakes, songpyeon.

scholar: 학자
honesty: 정직함 cf. honest: 정직한
disappointed: 실망한
by oneself 혼자서, 홀로 (= alone)
mainly: 주로
pot: 냄비, 솥
imaginary: 상상의
servant: 하인, 시종
turtle: 거북
fortune teller: 점술가, 역술인, 점쟁이
kingdom: 왕국

확인문제

● 다음 문장이 본문의 내용과 일치하면 T, 일치하지 않으면 F를 쓰시오.

1 In the time of King Yeonsan, there was a servant who was famous for his honesty. ☐

2 King Yeonsan made a special pot to cook many different vegetables together. ☐

3 The last king of Silla and his servants found a strange turtle. ☐

4 People of Silla made rice cakes in the shape of a half moon. ☐

● 우리말을 참고하여 빈칸에 알맞은 말을 쓰시오.

1 A _____ of Korean History

2 _____ did tangpyeongchae and sinseollo _____ _____ _____ ?

3 _____ does songpyeon _____ _____ a half moon?

4 There are many interesting stories about our _____ _____ .

5 Let's _____ _____ the fun history of our food.

Tangpyeongchae

6 One day, King Yeongjo _____ _____ _____ with his officials and offered them _____ _____ .

7 It was a dish with _____ _____ _____ .

8 Each ingredient symbolized _____ _____ _____ _____ .

9 Yeongjo wanted to say that the four parties should work _____ _____ like this dish.

10 This dish _____ _____ tangpyeongchae.

11 The name _____ _____ Yeongjo's policy tangpyeongchaek.

Sinseollo

12 In the time of King Yeonsan, there was a scholar who _____ _____ _____ his honesty.

13 When the king did _____ _____ , the scholar was never _____ _____ _____ him so.

14 _____ , the king never listened to him.

1	한국 역사 한 입
2	탕평채와 신선로는 어떻게 해서 그런 이름을 얻게 되었을까?
3	송편은 왜 반달 모양일까?
4	우리의 전통 음식에 대한 재미있는 이야기들이 많이 있다.
5	우리 음식의 재미있는 역사 속으로 들어가 보자.

탕평채

6	어느 날, 영조가 그의 신하들과 저녁을 먹다가 그들에게 특별한 무언가를 권했다.
7	그것은 네 가지의 다채로운 재료로 만든 음식이었다.
8	각 재료는 서로 다른 당파를 상징했다.
9	영조는 이 음식처럼 네 당파가 화합을 이루어 일해야 한다는 것을 말하고 싶었다.
10	이 음식은 탕평채라고 불렸다.
11	그 이름은 영조의 정책인 탕평책에서 왔다.

신선로

12	연산군 시대에 정직하기로 유명한 한 학자가 있었다.
13	왕이 무언가를 잘못하면, 그 학자는 왕에게 그렇게 말하는 것을 절대 두려워하지 않았다.
14	그러나 왕은 그의 말에 전혀 귀기울이지 않았다.

15 The scholar was _____ disappointed _____ he went to live on a mountain.

16 While he lived there _____ _____, he mainly ate vegetables.

17 He made _____ _____ _____ to cook many different vegetables together.

18 People _____ this pot and _____ _____ _____ _____ sinseollo.

19 That is _____ the scholar lived _____ a sinseon, an _____ person who lives alone in nature.

Songpyeon

20 It was the time of _____ _____ _____ of Baekje.

21 One day, the king and his servants found _____ _____ _____.

22 Something _____ _____ on its back.

23 It said, "Baekje _____ _____ a full moon, but Silla _____ _____ a half moon."

24 The king asked a fortune teller, "_____ does this _____?"

25 The fortune teller answered, "A full moon will soon become _____.

26 _____ _____ _____ _____, a half moon will _____ _____ and become a full moon."

27 The king became _____ about his kingdom.

28 _____, people of Silla were very happy to learn this and made rice cakes _____ _____ _____ _____ a half moon.

29 _____ _____, people _____ _____ these half-moon shaped rice cakes, songpyeon.

15 학자는 너무 실망하여 산속으로 살러 들어갔다.

16 그곳에서 혼자 사는 동안, 그는 주로 채소를 먹었다.

17 그는 여러 다양한 채소들을 함께 요리하기 위해 특별한 솥을 만들었다.

18 사람들은 이 솥과 그 안의 음식을 신선로라고 불렀다.

19 그것은 그 학자가 마치 자연 속에 홀로 사는 상상의 인물인 신선처럼 살았기 때문이다.

송편

20 백제의 마지막 왕 때였다.

21 어느 날, 왕과 신하들은 이상한 거북을 한 마리 발견했다.

22 그 거북의 등에 무언가가 쓰여 있었다.

23 그것은 "백제는 보름달과 같지만 신라는 반달과 같다."였다.

24 왕은 점술가에게 "이게 무슨 뜻인가?"라고 물었다.

25 점술가는 "보름달은 곧 작아질 것입니다.

26 반면에, 반달은 점점 커져서 보름달이 될 것입니다."라고 답했다.

27 왕은 자신의 왕국이 걱정되었다.

28 그러나 신라 사람들은 이것을 알고 매우 기뻐하며 반달 모양의 떡을 만들었다.

29 그 후로 사람들은 이 반달 모양의 떡인 송편을 즐겨 먹고 있다.

Reading **83**

● 우리말을 참고하여 본문을 영작하시오.

1 한국 역사 한 입

➡ _____

2 탕평채와 신선로는 어떻게 해서 그런 이름을 얻게 되었을까?

➡ _____

3 송편은 왜 반달 모양일까?

➡ _____

4 우리의 전통 음식에 대한 재미있는 이야기들이 많이 있다.

➡ _____

5 우리 음식의 재미있는 역사 속으로 들어가 보자.

➡ _____

Tangpyeongchae 탕평채

6 어느 날, 영조가 그의 신하들과 저녁을 먹다가 그들에게 특별한 무언가를 권했다.

➡ _____

7 그것은 네 가지의 다채로운 재료로 만든 음식이었다.

➡ _____

8 각 재료는 서로 다른 당파를 상징했다.

➡ _____

9 영조는 이 음식처럼 네 당파가 화합을 이루어 일해야 한다는 것을 말하고 싶었다.

➡ _____

10 이 음식은 탕평채라고 불렸다.

➡ _____

11 그 이름은 영조의 정책인 탕평책에서 왔다.

➡ _____

Sinseollo 신선로

12 연산군 시대에 정직하기로 유명한 한 학자가 있었다.

➡ _____

13 왕이 무언가를 잘못하면, 그 학자는 왕에게 그렇게 말하는 것을 절대 두려워하지 않았다.

➡ _____

14 그러나 왕은 그의 말에 전혀 귀 기울이지 않았다.

➡ _____

15 학자는 너무 실망하여 산속으로 살러 들어갔다.

➡ _____

16 그곳에서 혼자 사는 동안, 그는 주로 채소를 먹었다.

➡ _____

17 그는 여러 다양한 채소들을 함께 요리하기 위해 특별한 솥을 만들었다.

➡ _____

18 사람들은 이 솥과 그 안의 음식을 신선로라고 불렀다.

➡ _____

19 그것은 그 학자가 마치 자연 속에 홀로 사는 상상의 인물인 신선처럼 살았기 때문이다.

➡ _____

Songpyeon 송편

20 백제의 마지막 왕 때였다.

➡ _____

21 어느 날, 왕과 신하들은 이상한 거북을 한 마리 발견했다.

➡ _____

22 그 거북의 등에 무언가가 쓰여 있었다.

➡ _____

23 그것은 "백제는 보름달과 같지만 신라는 반달과 같다."였다.

➡ _____

24 왕은 점술가에게 "이게 무슨 뜻인가?"라고 물었다.

➡ _____

25 점술가는 "보름달은 곧 작아질 것입니다.

➡ _____

26 반면에, 반달은 점점 커져서 보름달이 될 것입니다."라고 답했다.

➡ _____

27 왕은 자신의 왕국이 걱정되었다.

➡ _____

28 그러나 신라 사람들은 이것을 알고 매우 기뻐하며 반달 모양의 떡을 만들었다.

➡ _____

29 그 후로 사람들은 이 반달 모양의 떡인 송편을 즐겨 먹고 있다.

➡ _____

[01~04] 다음 글을 읽고 물음에 답하시오.

(A)[How / What] did tangpyeongchae and sinseollo get their names? Why does songpyeon (B)[look / look like] a half moon? There are many (C)[interesting / interested] stories about our traditional ⓐ . ⓑLet's dive into the fun history of our food.

01 위 글의 빈칸 ⓐ에 들어갈 알맞은 말을 고르시오.

① ceremony   ② food
③ culture   ④ holiday
⑤ custom

서답형
02 위 글의 괄호 (A)~(C)에서 문맥이나 어법상 알맞은 낱말을 골라 쓰시오.

➡ (A) _____ (B) _____ (C) _____

03 위 글의 밑줄 친 ⓑ와 의미가 <u>다른</u> 문장을 고르시오.

① How about diving into the fun history of our food?
② Why don't we dive into the fun history of our food?
③ Shall we dive into the fun history of our food?
④ Why do you dive into the fun history of our food?
⑤ What about diving into the fun history of our food?

04 위 글의 뒤에 올 내용으로 가장 알맞은 것을 고르시오.

① 우리 음식을 즐기는 방법
② 전통 문화 계승의 소중함
③ 우리 음식의 재미있는 역사
④ 우리 음식의 조리법
⑤ 미풍양속을 지키는 사례들

[05~07] 다음 글을 읽고 물음에 답하시오.

Tangpyeongchae
One day, King Yeongjo was having dinner with his officials and (a)그들에게 특별한 무언가를 권했다. It was a dish with four colorful ingredients. Each ingredient symbolized a different political ⓐparty. Yeongjo wanted to say that the four parties should work in harmony like this dish. This dish was called tangpyeongchae. The name came from Yeongjo's ___(A)___ tangpyeongchaek.

05 위 글의 빈칸 (A)에 들어갈 알맞은 말을 고르시오.

① recipe   ② justice   ③ custom
④ policy   ⑤ dessert

06 위 글의 밑줄 친 ⓐparty와 같은 의미로 쓰인 것을 고르시오.

① Did you go to the birthday party?
② She belongs to the Democratic Party.
③ She held a dinner party yesterday.
④ He was a third party.
⑤ The school will take a party of 40 children to France.

서답형
07 위 글의 밑줄 친 (a)의 우리말에 맞게 주어진 어휘를 알맞게 배열하시오.

special / them / offered / something

➡ _____

[08~10] 다음 글을 읽고 물음에 답하시오.

Tangpyeongchae

One day, King Yeongjo was having dinner with his officials and offered them something (A)[ordinary / special]. It was a dish with four colorful ingredients. Each (B)[ingredient / ingredients] symbolized (C)[a different / the same] political party. Yeongjo wanted to say that the four parties should work   (A)   harmony like this dish. This dish was called tangpyeongchae. The name came   (B)   Yeongjo's policy tangpyeongchaek.

08 위 글의 빈칸 (A)와 (B)에 들어갈 전치사가 바르게 짝지어진 것은?

① to – from
② on – by
③ in – from
④ to – for
⑤ in – for

09 위 글의 괄호 (A)~(C)에서 문맥이나 어법상 알맞은 낱말을 골라 쓰시오.

➡ (A) _____ (B) _____ (C) _____

10 위 글의 내용과 일치하지 <u>않는</u> 것은?

① 어느 날, 영조가 그의 신하들과 저녁을 먹다가 그들에게 특별한 무언가를 권했다.
② 영조가 권한 것은 네 가지 종류의 음식이었다.
③ 음식의 각 재료는 당파를 상징했다.
④ 영조는 이 음식처럼 네 당파가 화합을 이루어 일해야 한다는 것을 말하고 싶었다.
⑤ 탕평채의 이름은 탕평책을 따서 지어졌다.

[11~13] 다음 글을 읽고 물음에 답하시오.

Sinseollo

In the time of King Yeonsan, there was a scholar who was famous for his honesty. When the king did something wrong, the scholar was never afraid of telling ①him so. However, the king never listened to ②him. The scholar was   ⓐ   disappointed   ⓑ   he went to live on a mountain. While he lived there by ③himself, ④he mainly ate vegetables. ⑤He made a special pot to cook many different vegetables together. People called this pot and the food in it sinseollo. That is because the scholar lived like a sinseon, an imaginary person who lives alone in nature.

11 위 글의 빈칸 ⓐ와 ⓑ에 들어갈 말이 바르게 짝지어진 것은?

① so – as
② such – that
③ too – as
④ so – that
⑤ too – that

12 밑줄 친 ①~⑤ 중에서 가리키는 대상이 나머지 넷과 <u>다른</u> 것은?

①   ②   ③   ④   ⑤

13 위 글의 주제로 알맞은 것을 고르시오.

① a scholar who was famous for his honesty
② King Yeonsan who never listened to the scholar
③ the disappointment of the scholar
④ a sinseon, an imaginary person
⑤ a story behind the food, Sinseollo

[14~16] 다음 글을 읽고 물음에 답하시오.

Songpyeon

It was the time of the last king of Baekje. One day, the king and his servants found a strange turtle. Something was written on its back. It said, "Baekje is like a full moon, but Silla is like a half moon."

The king asked a fortune teller, "What does this mean?"

The fortune teller answered, "A full moon will soon become smaller. On the other hand, a half moon will grow bigger and become a full moon."

The king became worried about his kingdom. However, people of Silla were very happy to learn this and made rice cakes in the shape of a half moon. Since then, people ⓐhave enjoyed these half-moon shaped rice cakes, songpyeon.

14 위 글의 밑줄 친 ⓐhave enjoyed와 현재완료의 용법이 다른 것을 모두 고르시오.

① She has lost her book.
② He has played basketball for two hours.
③ I have learned English since 2013.
④ She hasn't cleaned her room yet.
⑤ I have never seen a whale.

서답형

15 Why did the last king of Baekje become worried about his kingdom? Fill in the blanks with suitable words.

➡ That's because some letters written on a turtle's back said "Baekje is like a ＿＿＿＿ ＿＿＿＿," and a fortune teller said, "A ＿＿＿＿ ＿＿＿＿ will soon become ＿＿＿＿."

16 위 글을 읽고 대답할 수 없는 질문은?

① Who found a strange turtle?
② What did the letters on the turtle's back mean?
③ Was the last king of Baekje satisfied with the letters on the turtle's back?
④ In what shape did people of Silla make rice cakes?
⑤ What fillings for songpyeon did people of Silla use?

[17~19] 다음 글을 읽고 물음에 답하시오.

Sinseollo

In the time of King Yeonsan, there was a scholar who was famous for his honesty. When the king did something wrong, the scholar was never afraid of telling him so. ＿＿ⓐ＿＿, the king never listened to him. (①) The scholar was so disappointed that he went to live on a mountain. (②) While he lived there by himself, he mainly ate vegetables. (③) People called this pot and the food in it sinseollo. (④) That is because the scholar lived like a sinseon, an imaginary person who lives alone in nature. (⑤)

17 위 글의 빈칸 ⓐ에 들어갈 알맞은 말을 고르시오.

① Therefore   ② However
③ For example   ④ In addition
⑤ Moreover

18 위 글의 흐름으로 보아, 주어진 문장이 들어가기에 가장 적절한 곳은?

He made a special pot to cook many different vegetables together.

①   ②   ③   ④   ⑤

19 위 글의 'the scholar'에 대한 설명으로 옳지 <u>않은</u> 것은?

① 연산군 시대에 살았던 정직하기로 유명한 학자였다.

② 왕이 무언가를 잘못하면, 왕에게 그것에 대해 말하는 것을 절대 두려워하지 않았다.

③ 왕이 그의 말에 전혀 귀 기울이지 않자 그는 너무 실망하여 산속으로 들어갔다.

④ 여러 다양한 채소들을 함께 요리하기 위해 특별한 솥을 만들었다.

⑤ 자연 속에 홀로 살면서 신선이 되었다.

[20~22] 다음 글을 읽고 물음에 답하시오.

It was the time of the last king of Baekje. One day, the king and his servants found a strange turtle. Something was written on ⓐits back. It said, "Baekje is like a full moon, but Silla is like a half moon."

The king asked a fortune teller, "What does this mean?"

The fortune teller answered, "A full moon will soon become smaller. On the other hand, a half moon will grow bigger and become a full moon."

The king became ____(A)____ about his kingdom. However, people of Silla were very happy to learn this and made rice cakes in the shape of a half moon. Since then, people have enjoyed these half-moon shaped rice cakes, songpyeon.

20 위 글의 빈칸 (A)에 들어갈 알맞은 말을 고르시오.

① satisfied   ② bored

③ worried   ④ interested

⑤ comfortable

---

21 위 글의 밑줄 친 ⓐits가 가리키는 것을 본문에서 찾아 쓰시오.

➡ _____

22 위 글의 제목으로 알맞은 것을 고르시오.

① Something Was Written on a Turtle's Back!

② Baekje Is Like a Full Moon!

③ Silla Is Like a Half Moon!

④ Don't Worry! A Half Moon Becomes a Full Moon!

⑤ Why Does Songpyeon Look Like a Half moon?

[23~24] 다음 글을 읽고 물음에 답하시오.

Fish Skin Sundae

My family eats something special on Chuseok. (①) It is made of rice, vegetables, and fish skin. (②) It is a kind of sundae. (③) She is from North Korea. (④) When she was young, her mother often made it for the family. (⑤) The food gives us a chance to think about my grandma's home.

23 위 글의 흐름으로 보아, 주어진 문장이 들어가기에 가장 적절한 곳은?

> When I eat this food, I always think of my grandma.

①   ②   ③   ④   ⑤

24 What are the ingredients of fish skin sundae? Answer in English in a full sentence. (7 words)

➡ _____

[01~03] 다음 글을 읽고 물음에 답하시오.

Tangpyeongchae

One day, King Yeongjo was having dinner with his officials and offered ⓐthem something special. It was a dish with four colorful ingredients. Each ingredient symbolized a different political party. Yeongjo wanted to say that the four parties should work ⓑin harmony like this dish. This dish was called tangpyeongchae. The name came from Yeongjo's policy tangpyeongchaek.

01 위 글의 밑줄 친 ⓐthem이 가리키는 것을 본문에서 찾아 쓰시오.

➡ _____

02 위 글의 밑줄 친 ⓑin harmony를 한 단어로 고치시오.

➡ _____

03 본문의 내용과 일치하도록 다음 빈칸 (A)와 (B)에 알맞은 단어를 쓰시오.

> Tangpyeongchae was a dish with (A)_____ colorful ingredients, and each of them symbolized a different (B)_____ _____.

[04~06] 다음 글을 읽고 물음에 답하시오.

Sinseollo

In the time of King Yeonsan, there was a scholar who was famous for his honesty. When the king did something wrong, the scholar was never afraid of telling him ⓐso. However, the king never listened to him.

ⓑ학자는 너무 실망하여 산속으로 살러 들어갔다. While he lived there ⓒby himself, he mainly ate vegetables. He made a special pot to cook many different vegetables together. People called this pot and the food in it sinseollo. That is because the scholar lived like a sinseon, an imaginary person who lives alone in nature.

04 위 글의 밑줄 친 ⓐso가 가리키는 것을 본문에서 찾아 쓰시오.

➡ _____

05 위 글의 밑줄 친 ⓑ의 우리말에 맞게 한 단어를 보충하여, 주어진 어휘를 알맞게 배열하시오.

> on a mountain / he / to live / that / was / went / disappointed / the scholar

➡ _____
_____

06 위 글의 밑줄 친 ⓒby himself와 바꿔 쓸 수 있는 단어를 본문에서 찾아 쓰시오.

➡ _____

[07~09] 다음 글을 읽고 물음에 답하시오.

Songpyeon

It was the time of the last king of Baekje. One day, the king and his servants found a strange turtle. Something was written on its back. It said, "Baekje is ___ⓐ___ a full moon, but Silla is ___ⓑ___ a half moon."

The king asked a fortune teller, "What does this mean?"

The fortune teller answered, "A full moon will soon become smaller. ⓒOn the other hand, a half moon will grow smaller and become a full moon."

The king became worried about his kingdom. However, people of Silla were very happy to learn this and made rice cakes in the shape of a half moon. Since then, people have enjoyed these half-moon shaped rice cakes, songpyeon.

07 위 글의 빈칸 ⓐ와 ⓑ에 공통으로 들어갈 알맞은 말을 쓰시오.

➡ _____

중요
08 위 글의 밑줄 친 ⓒ에서 흐름상 어색한 부분을 찾아 고치시오.

_____ ➡ _____

고난이도
09 위 글의 보름달과 반달이 상징하는 것을 우리말로 쓰시오.

➡ 보름달: _____

반달: _____

[10~11] 다음 글을 읽고 물음에 답하시오.

Tangpyeongchae

One day, King Yeongjo was having dinner with his officials and offered them something special. It was a dish with four colorful ingredients. ⓐ각 재료는 서로 다른 당파를 상징했다. Yeongjo wanted to say that the four parties should work in harmony like this dish. ⓑThis dish was called tangpyeongchae. The name came from Yeongjo's policy tangpyeongchaek.

중요
10 위 글의 밑줄 친 ⓐ의 우리말에 맞게 주어진 어휘를 이용하여 7단어로 영작하시오.

each, symbolized, party

➡ _____

11 위 글의 밑줄 친 ⓑ를 능동태로 고치시오.

➡ _____

[12~13] 다음 글을 읽고 물음에 답하시오.

Songpyeon

It was the time of the last king of Baekje. One day, the king and his servants found a strange turtle. Something was written on its back. It said, "Baekje is like a full moon, but Silla is like a half moon."

The king asked a fortune teller, "What does ⓐthis mean?"

The fortune teller answered, "A full moon will soon become smaller. On the other hand, a half moon will grow bigger and become a full moon."

The king became worried about his kingdom. However, people of Silla were very happy to learn this and made rice cakes in the shape of a half moon. Since then, people have enjoyed these half-moon shaped rice cakes, songpyeon.

12 위 글의 밑줄 친 ⓐthis가 가리키는 것을 영어로 쓰시오.

➡ _____

고난이도
13 Why did people of Silla make rice cakes in the shape of a half moon? Fill in the blanks with suitable words.

➡ That's because some letters written on a turtle's back said "Silla is like a _____ moon," and a fortune teller said, "A _____ moon will grow _____ and become a _____ moon."

Work Together

A: Could you recommend a salad for me?
　　　　추천을 부탁하는 표현

B: We have two salads today. Do you prefer chicken salad or green salad?
　　　　　　　　　　　　둘 중 더 좋아하는 것에 대해 물을 때는 Do you prefer A or B?를 사용한다.

A: I prefer green salad.
　　　선호하는 것을 답할 때

B: O.K. Here you are.
　　　　　　물건을 건네줄 때 쓰는 표현

A: Thank you.

구문해설　• recommend: 추천하다

해석

A: 샐러드 좀 추천해 주시겠습니까?

B: 저희는 오늘 두 가지 샐러드가 있습니다. 닭고기 샐러드가 더 좋으신가요, 야채 샐러드가 더 좋으신가요?

A: 야채 샐러드가 더 좋아요.

B: 네. 여기 나왔습니다.

A: 감사합니다.

Write

Chocolate Songpyeon

My family eats something special on Chuseok. It is made of rice flour,
　　　　　　　　　－thing으로 끝나는 대명사를 수식할 때는 형용사가 뒤에 온다.　　　　　　～으로 만들어진다

chocolate, and nuts. It is a kind of tteok. When I eat this food, I always think
　　　　　　　　　　　　　　　　　　　　　　　　　　　　　빈도부사: 일반동사 앞에 위치

of my little brother. Three years ago, he ate all the fillings for songpyeon,

so we decided to make chocolate songpyeon. This food gives us a chance
　　decide는 to부정사를 목적어로 취한다.

to remember that funny day.
to부정사의 형용사적 용법

구문해설　• rice flour: 쌀가루　• nut: 견과　• filling: (음식의) 소, 속　• remember: 기억하다

초콜릿 송편

나의 가족은 추석에 특별한 것을 먹는다. 그것은 쌀가루, 초콜릿, 그리고 견과로 만들어진다. 그것은 일종의 떡이다. 내가 이 음식을 먹을 때, 나는 항상 나의 남동생을 생각한다. 3년 전, 그가 송편의 모든 소를 먹어서, 우리는 초콜릿 송편을 만들기로 결심했다. 이 음식은 우리에게 그 재미있던 날을 기억할 기회를 준다.

Culture Project

The word *dongporou* comes from the name of the famous Chinese poet Su
└　동격　┘　　　　～에서 생겨나다

Dongpo. During his time in Hangzhou, he invented a way to keep pork fresh
　　　　　during+명사(구), while+절　　　　　　　　　　　　형용사적 용법　keep의 보어로 형용사

for a long time. He made the pork sweet and salty. Afterwards, dongporou or
　　　　　　　　　　　　made의 보어로 형용사　　　　　　　　　　　　　　　즉

dongpo pork became popular across China.
　　　　　　　　　　　～의 전역에서

구문해설　• poet: 시인　• pork: 돼지고기　• salty: 짠, 소금기가 있는　• afterwards: 뒤[나중]에, 그후

동파육이라는 단어는 중국의 유명한 시인인 소동파의 이름에서 나왔다. 그의 시대에 항저우에서, 그는 돼지고기를 오랫동안 신선하게 유지하는 방법을 창안했다. 그는 돼지고기를 달고 짜게 만들었다. 나중에 동파육, 즉 동파 돼지고기는 중국 전역에서 인기 있게 되었다.

영역별 핵심문제

Words & Expressions

01 다음 **두** 단어의 관계가 같도록 빈칸에 알맞은 단어를 쓰시오.

different : same = indoor : _____

02 우리말 해석에 맞게 주어진 글자로 시작하여 문장을 완성하시오.

우리 음식의 재미있는 역사 속으로 들어가 보자.
Let's d_____ _____ the fun history of our food.

03 대화의 빈칸에 어울리는 단어를 고르시오.

One day, King Yeongjo was having dinner with his officials and offered them something special. It was a dish with four colorful ingredients. Each ingredient _____ a different political party.

① offered   ② appreciated
③ symbolized   ④ included
⑤ tasted

04 다음 〈보기〉의 단어를 사용하여 자연스러운 문장을 만들 수 없는 것은?

┌─── 보기 ├──
afraid / policy / prefer / servant / shape
└────────────

① Do you _____ indoor or outdoor sports?
② One day, the king and his _____ found a strange turtle.
③ When the king did something wrong, the scholar was never _____ of telling him so.
④ This dish came from Yeongjo's _____ tangpyeongchaek.
⑤ The story is based on an _____ animal.

05 다음 우리말에 해당하는 단어를 쓰시오. (2 words)

송편은 왜 반달 모양일까?
Why does songpyeon _____ a half moon?

➡ _____

Conversation

[06~07] 다음 대화를 읽고 물음에 답하시오.

W: Excuse me. I'm looking for a skirt.
_____(A)_____
M: What color do you like?
W: Blue and pink are my favorite colors.
M: Then, how about this blue one? (B)그것은 지금 세일 중이에요. (sale / now) (4 words)
W: Good! Thank you. I'll take it.

06 빈칸 (A)에 들어갈 말로 알맞은 것은?

① Do you know where to buy one?
② What's wrong?
③ Can you recommend any good comedies?
④ Could you recommend one?
⑤ Which do you prefer?

07 밑줄 친 (B)의 우리말에 맞게 주어진 단어를 이용하여 쓰시오.

➡ _____

[08~09] 다음 대화를 읽고 물음에 답하시오.

G: _____(A)_____
B: (①) Do you prefer dogs or cats?
G: (②) They're so cute. (③)
B: Great! (④) I can give you one. (⑤) I have seven cats at home.
G: Thank you.

08 빈칸 (A)에 들어갈 말로 알맞은 것은?

① I'm looking for a dog.

② Do you like pets?

③ Why are you getting a pet?

④ Could you recommend a movie for me?

⑤ I'm thinking of getting a pet.

09 위 대화의 (①)~(⑤) 중 주어진 문장이 들어갈 위치로 알맞은 것은?

> I prefer cats.

①   ②   ③   ④   ⑤

10 다음 중 두 사람의 대화가 <u>어색한</u> 것은?

① A: What color do you like?

   B: Blue and pink are my favorite colors.

② A: Do you prefer hot or cold food?

   B: I prefer cold food.

③ A: How was the food?

   B: It was great.

④ A: Excuse me. I'm looking for a skirt. Could you recommend one?

   B: What color do you like?

⑤ A: Could you recommend a restaurant near here?

   B: O.K. I'll try it. Thanks.

[11~12] 다음 대화를 읽고 물음에 답하시오.

> Jaden: Have you been to the new Chinese restaurant, Ms. Park?
>
> Ms. Park: Are you talking about the one on Main Street, Jaden?
>
> Jaden: Yes, that's the one. They opened about two weeks ago, right?
>
> Ms. Park: I think so. I went there last Friday with my friends.

> Jaden: How was the food?
>
> Ms. Park: It was great. We ordered many different dishes. I really liked the fried vegetables.
>
> Jaden: Could you recommend a dish for me? I'm going there for dinner tonight with my family.
>
> Ms. Park: Do you prefer seafood or meat?
>
> Jaden: I prefer seafood.
>
> Ms. Park: Then, you should try their fried fish. You'll love it!

11 위 대화를 읽고 다음 물음에 대해 영어로 답하시오.

> Q: What food does Ms. Park recommend?

➡ _____

12 위 대화의 내용과 일치하지 <u>않는</u> 것은?

① The new Chinese restaurant opened about two weeks ago.

② Ms. Park has been to the new Chinese restaurant.

③ Ms. Park went to the new restaurant with her friends.

④ Ms. Park really liked fried fish.

⑤ Jaden likes seafood more than meat.

Grammar

13 주어진 어휘를 이용하여 다음 우리말에 맞게 빈칸을 채우시오.

> 우리는 특별한 누군가를 찾고 있다.
>
> We are _____. (someone, look, special)

➡ _____

14 다음 주어진 문장과 같은 뜻이 되도록 빈칸을 채우시오.

(1) He chose his son an interesting storybook.

　➡ An interesting storybook _____

　_____ .

(2) A lady asked me the way to the bus stop.

　➡ The way to the bus stop _____

　_____ .

15 다음 중 어법상 올바른 것은?

① The National Museum of Korea built in 1945.

② My wallet had stolen on the crowded subway.

③ She was made leave her family by him.

④ Are you going to do anything special after school?

⑤ Is there available anybody this weekend?

16 다음 빈칸에 들어갈 말을 순서대로 바르게 짝지은 것을 고르시오.

• Did you see _____ ?

• We _____ 45 minutes to solve all the problems by the teacher.

---

① anything red – gave

② red something – were given

③ something red – were given

④ red something – gave

⑤ something red – gave

17 다음 중 어법상 어색한 문장은?

① *The Mona Lisa* was painted by Leonardo da Vinci.

② The soup is smelled good.

③ I am called Big Deer by my classmates because I am good at running.

④ He was seen to dance by his friends.

⑤ Sand castles were built by some children on the beach.

18 다음 빈칸에 공통으로 알맞은 것은?

• I have _____ great for you.

• There's _____ wrong with your computer. It doesn't work well.

---

① anyone　　　　② nobody

③ something　　④ anything

⑤ nothing

19 다음 빈칸에 들어갈 전치사가 나머지와 다른 것은?

① Do you think I'll be satisfied _____ small potatoes?

② These cookies were made _____ my mother.

③ The singer of the year was chosen _____ online voters.

④ This room was cleaned _____ him.

⑤ The mouse was caught _____ the cat.

20 어법상 어색한 것을 찾아 바르게 고쳐 다시 쓰시오.

(1) Ann was seen walk on the street by Jack yesterday.

➡ Ann _____

_____.

21 우리말과 같은 의미가 되도록 빈칸에 알맞은 말을 쓰시오.

> 어젯밤 많은 사람이 하늘에서 이상한 무엇인가를 보았다. (see, strange)
> Last night many people _____ in the sky.

➡ _____

Reading

[22~23] 다음 글을 읽고 물음에 답하시오.

Tangpyeongchae

One day, King Yeongjo was _____ⓐ_____ dinner with his officials and offered them something special. It was a dish with four colorful ingredients. Each ingredient symbolized a different political party. Yeongjo wanted to say that the four parties should work in harmony like this dish. This dish was called tangpyeongchae. The name came from Yeongjo's policy tangpyeongchaek.

22 다음 문장의 빈칸 중에 위 글의 빈칸 ⓐ에 들어갈 단어를 쓸 수 <u>없는</u> 문장을 고르시오.

① We are _____ a good time.

② I'm _____ a book.

③ They are _____ a fight.

④ My mother is _____ trouble with the computer.

⑤ He is _____ a walk.

23 본문의 내용과 일치하도록 다음 빈칸에 알맞은 단어를 쓰시오.

> Yeongjo wanted to say that like the four ingredients of tangpyeongchae, the _____ _____ should work in harmony.

[24~26] 다음 글을 읽고 물음에 답하시오.

Songpyeon

It was the time of the last king of Baekje. One day, the king and his servants found a strange turtle. Something was written on its back. It said, "ⓐ백제는 보름달과 같지만 신라는 반달과 같다."

The king asked a fortune teller, "What does this mean?"

The fortune teller answered, "A full moon will soon become smaller. ____(A)____, a half moon will grow bigger and become a full moon."

The king became worried about his kingdom. However, people of Silla were very happy to learn this and made rice cakes in the shape of a half moon. Since then, people have enjoyed these half-moon shaped rice cakes, songpyeon.

24 위 글의 빈칸 (A)에 들어갈 알맞은 말을 고르시오.

① Likewise   ② Thus

③ In other words   ④ Therefore

⑤ On the other hand

25 위 글의 밑줄 친 ⓐ의 우리말에 맞게 주어진 어휘를 이용하여 13단어로 영작하시오.

> is like, a half moon

➡ _____

26 위 글의 주제로 알맞은 것을 고르시오.

① to tell the fortune with a turtle's back

② the origin of songpyeon shaped the half-moon

③ the important role of a fortune teller

④ the meaning of the shape of the moon

⑤ how to make rice cakes well

[27~29] 다음 글을 읽고 물음에 답하시오.

Sinseollo

In the time of King Yeonsan, there was a scholar who was famous for his honesty. When the king did something wrong, the scholar was never afraid of ⓐtelling him so. However, the king never listened to him. The scholar was so disappointed that he went to live on a mountain. While he lived there by himself, he mainly ate vegetables. He made a special pot to cook many different vegetables together. People called this pot and the food in it sinseollo. ⓑThat is because the scholar lived like a sinseon, an imaginary person who lives alone in nature.

27 위 글의 밑줄 친 ⓐtelling과 문법적 쓰임이 같은 것을 모두 고르시오.

① She smelled something burning.

② I'm proud of being Korean.

③ John is yelling at the dog.

④ I saw him entering the room.

⑤ How about playing outside?

28 위 글의 밑줄 친 ⓑThat이 가리키는 것을 본문에서 찾아 쓰시오.

➡ _____

29 위 글의 내용과 일치하지 <u>않는</u> 것은?

① In the time of King Yeonsan, there was a very honest scholar.

② The king never listened to the advice of the scholar.

③ The scholar went to live on a mountain because he was so disappointed.

④ The scholar made a special pot to cook many different vegetables together with people.

⑤ This pot and the food in it were called sinseollo.

[30~31] 다음 글을 읽고 물음에 답하시오.

Fish Skin Sundae

My family eats something special on Chuseok. It is made __ⓐ__ rice, vegetables, and fish skin. It is a kind of sundae. When I eat this food, I always think of my grandma. She is __ⓑ__ North Korea. When she was young, her mother often made it for the family. The food gives us a chance ⓒto think about my grandma's home.

30 위 글의 빈칸 ⓐ와 ⓑ에 들어갈 전치사가 바르게 짝지어진 것은?

① from – in   ② from – by

③ of – from   ④ into – from

⑤ of – in

31 위 글의 밑줄 친 ⓒto think와 to부정사의 용법이 <u>다른</u> 것을 <u>모두</u> 고르시오.

① We go to school to learn many things.

② I have nothing particular to do today.

③ He was too tired to work any longer.

④ It is good for your health to get up early.

⑤ It is high time to finish your work.

출제율 85%

01 다음 두 단어의 관계가 같도록 빈칸에 알맞은 말을 쓰시오.

> recently : lately = fictional : _____

출제율 95%

02 우리말에 맞게 빈칸에 알맞은 단어를 쓰시오.

> • 점술가는 "보름날은 곧 삭아실 것입니다."라고 답했다.
> The (A)_____ answered, "A full moon will soon become smaller."
> • 어느 날, 영조가 그의 신하들과 저녁을 먹다가 그들에게 특별한 무언가를 권했다.
> One day, King Yeongjo was having dinner with his officials and (B)_____ them something special.

[03~04] 다음 영영풀이에 해당하는 단어를 고르시오.

출제율 95%

03

> unhappy because someone or something was not as good as you hoped or expected

① pleased   ② funny
③ disappointed   ④ alone
⑤ interested

출제율 90%

04

> sweet food eaten at the end of a meal

① dish   ② dessert
③ fried   ④ ingredient
⑤ desert

[05~06] 다음 대화를 읽고 물음에 답하시오.

> Girl: I ①haven't seen a movie recently. Could you recommend a good one?
> Boy: ②Why don't you seeing *Iron Woman 2*? It's ③a big hit.

> Girl: Well, I don't like action movies. Can you recommend ④any good comedies?
> Boy: Then, how about *Funny Families*?
> Girl: That ⑤sounds good.

출제율 100%

05 대화의 ①~⑤ 중 어법상 어색한 것은?

①   ②   ③   ④   ⑤

출제율 95%

06 다음은 위 대화를 요약한 문장이다. 빈칸에 들어갈 알맞은 말을 쓰시오.

> Because the girl hasn't seen a movie recently, she asks the boy to _____ a movie. The girl _____ comedies _____ action movies, so the boy recommends a _____ movie, *Funny Families*.

출제율 95%

07 빈칸에 들어갈 말로 알맞은 것은?

> M: Could you recommend a Korean restaurant near here?
> W: Do you prefer hot or cold food?
> M: _____
> W: Then, you should try the naengmyeon place at the end of this block.
> M: Thank you.

① I like Korean food more than Chinese food.
② I like hot food more than cold food.
③ How about you?
④ I prefer cold food.
⑤ Blue and pink are my favorite colors.

[08~09] 다음 대화를 읽고 물음에 답하시오.

> Jaden: Have you been to the new Chinese restaurant, Ms. Park? (①)
>
> Ms. Park: Are you talking about the one on Main Street, Jaden? (②)
>
> Jaden: Yes, that's the one. (③)
>
> Ms. Park: I think so. I went there last Friday with my friends. (④)
>
> Jaden: How was the food?
>
> Ms. Park: It was great. We ordered many different dishes. I really liked the fried vegetables. (⑤)
>
> Jaden: _____(A)_____ I'm going there for dinner tonight with my family.
>
> Ms. Park: Do you prefer seafood or meat?
>
> Jaden: I prefer seafood.
>
> Ms. Park: Then, you should try their fried fish. You'll love it!

08 위 대화의 (①)~(⑤) 중 주어진 문장이 들어갈 위치로 알맞은 것은?

> They opened about two weeks ago, right?

①   ②   ③   ④   ⑤

09 대화의 빈칸 (A)에 들어갈 표현을 주어진 조건에 맞게 쓰시오.

┌─ 보기 ├─
- '제게 ~을 추천해 주시겠어요?'라는 뜻으로 상대방에게 추천을 부탁하는 표현을 쓸 것.
- 'could', 'a dish', 'me'를 사용할 것.

➡ _____

10 다음 대화의 빈칸에 들어갈 말로 알맞은 것은?

> W: Excuse me. I'm looking for an Italian cookbook. Could you recommend one?
>
> M: Well, have you ever cooked Italian food?
>
> W: No, I haven't, but I want to try. I really like spaghetti.
>
> M: Then, _____ It's on sale now.
>
> W: Good! Thank you. I'll take it.

① how about this cookbook for experts?
② why don't you try the new Indian restaurant in front of the school?
③ I want to know more about Italian food.
④ why don't you go to another bookstore?
⑤ how about this Italian cookbook for beginners?

[11~12] 다음 중 어법상 <u>어색한</u> 것은?

11 ① This teddy bear was made by my father.
② The room was filled with the smell of roses.
③ The baby was named Thomas by the parents.
④ The baby will be looked after my mom while I'm away.
⑤ Ann was made to wash the dishes by her aunt.

12 ① It's something red.
② Is it something small?
③ I hope to meet new somebody.
④ I met someone beautiful today.
⑤ There was not anyone strange there.

13 다음 문장에서 틀린 것을 고쳐 다시 쓰시오.

(1) My father is resembled by me.

➡ _____

(2) I want hot something to eat.

➡ _____

14 우리말 의미에 맞도록 괄호 안의 단어를 이용하여 영작하시오.

(1) 카드에 이상한 무언가가 적혀 있었다. (something, write)

➡ _____

_____

(2) 한국의 역사와 문화는 그것의 전통 음식에서 발견될 수 있다. (find, food)

➡ _____

_____

(3) 그것은 쌀, 야채 그리고 생선 껍질로 만들어진다. (make, fish skin)

➡ _____

_____

[15~16] 다음 글을 읽고 물음에 답하시오.

Tangpyeongchae

One day, King Yeongjo was having dinner with his officials and ⓐoffered them something special. It was a dish with four colorful ingredients. Each ingredient ⓑ symbolized a different political party. Yeongjo wanted to say that the four parties should work in harmony like this dish. This dish was called tangpyeongchae. The name came from Yeongjo's policy tangpyeongchaek.

15 위 글의 밑줄 친 ⓐ를 3형식 문장으로 고치시오.

➡ _____

16 위 글의 밑줄 친 ⓑsymbolized와 바꿔 쓸 수 있는 말을 모두 고르시오.

① represented   ② accepted

③ discussed   ④ mentioned

⑤ stood for

[17~19] 다음 글을 읽고 물음에 답하시오.

Sinseollo

In the time of King Yeonsan, there was a scholar who was famous for his honesty. When the king did something wrong, the scholar was never afraid of telling him so. However, the king never listened to him. The scholar was so disappointed that he went ⓐ to live on a mountain. While he lived there by himself, he mainly ate vegetables. He made a special pot to cook many different vegetables together. People called this pot and the food in it sinseollo. That is because the scholar lived like a sinseon, an imaginary person who lives alone in nature.

17 위 글의 밑줄 친 ⓐto live와 to부정사의 용법이 같은 것을 모두 고르시오.

① I need a house to live in.

② He didn't tell us what to do.

③ She grew up to be a famous musician.

④ It is difficult to understand her feelings.

⑤ I am sorry to give you trouble.

18 위 글의 제목으로 알맞은 것을 고르시오.

① The Cruelty of King Yeonsan

② How Did Sinseollo Get Its Name?

③ The Difficulty of Giving the King Advice

④ The Good Point of Eating Vegetables

⑤ How to Cook Many Different Vegetables Together

19 다음 빈칸 (A)와 (B)에 알맞은 단어를 넣어 신선로에 대한 소개를 완성하시오.

> It was a special pot which was made to cook many (A)_____ _____ together by a scholar who lived (B)_____ on a mountain.

[20~22] 다음 글을 읽고 물음에 답하시오.

Songpyeon

(①) It was the time of the (A)[last / latest] king of Baekje. (②) One day, the king and his servants found a strange turtle. (③) It said, "Baekje is like a full moon, but Silla is like a half moon." (④)

The king asked a fortune teller, "What does this mean?" (⑤)

The fortune teller answered, "A full moon will soon become smaller. On the other hand, a half moon will grow bigger and become a full moon."

The king became (B)[worrying / worried] about his kingdom. ___ⓐ___, people of Silla were very happy to learn this and made rice cakes in the shape of a half moon. Since then, people have enjoyed these half-moon (C)[shaping / shaped] rice cakes, songpyeon.

20 위 글의 빈칸 ⓐ에 들어갈 알맞은 말을 고르시오.

① For example   ② However
③ Besides   ④ That is
⑤ On the one hand

21 위 글의 흐름으로 보아, 주어진 문장이 들어가기에 가장 적절한 곳은?

> Something was written on its back.

①   ②   ③   ④   ⑤

22 위 글의 괄호 (A)~(C)에서 문맥이나 어법상 알맞은 낱말을 골라 쓰시오.

➡ (A) _____ (B) _____ (C) _____

[23~25] 다음 글을 읽고 물음에 답하시오.

Chocolate Songpyeon

ⓐ나의 가족은 추석에 특별한 것을 먹는다. It is made of rice flour, chocolate, and nuts. It is a kind of tteok. When I eat this food, I always think of my little brother. Three years ago, he ate all the fillings for songpyeon, so we decided ___(A)___ chocolate songpyeon. This food gives us a chance to remember that funny day.

23 위 글의 빈칸 (A)에 make를 알맞은 형태로 쓰시오.

➡ _____

24 위 글의 밑줄 친 ⓐ의 우리말에 맞게 주어진 어휘를 이용하여 7단어로 영작하시오.

> eats, something, on

➡ _____

25 위 글을 읽고 알 수 없는 것을 고르시오.

① 필자의 가족이 추석에 먹는 특별한 음식
② 초콜릿 송편의 재료
③ 초콜릿 송편을 먹을 때 생각나는 사람
④ 송편소로 준비했던 견과의 종류
⑤ 초콜릿 송편을 만들게 된 계기

01 다음 대화를 읽고 물음에 답하시오.

> Jaden: Have you been to the new Chinese restaurant, Ms. Park?
>
> Ms. Park: Are you talking about the one on Main Street, Jaden?
>
> Jaden: Yes, that's the one. They opened about two weeks ago, right?
>
> Ms. Park: I think so. I went there last Friday with my friends.
>
> Jaden: How was the food?
>
> Ms. Park: It was great. We ordered many different dishes. I really liked the fried vegetables.
>
> Jaden: Could you recommend a dish for me? I'm going there for dinner tonight with my family.
>
> Ms. Park: Do you prefer seafood or meat?
>
> Jaden: I prefer seafood.
>
> Ms. Park: Then, you should try their fried fish. You'll love it!

(1) Where is the new Chinese restaurant?

➡ _____

(2) Who will Jaden go to the restaurant with?

➡ _____

02 다음 대화의 빈칸에 들어갈 말을 주어진 조건에 맞게 영어로 쓰시오.

> G: I haven't seen a movie recently. Could you recommend a good one?
>
> B: _____ It's a big hit.
>
> G: Well, I don't like action movies. Can you recommend any good comedies?
>
> B: Then, how about *Funny Families*?
>
> G: That sounds good.

┤ 조건 ├
- 'Iron Woman 2'를 제안하는 표현을 사용할 것.
- 숫자와 see를 포함하여 7단어로 쓰시오.

➡ _____

03 다음 대화의 빈칸에 들어갈 말을 주어진 조건에 맞게 영어로 쓰시오.

> B: I'm thinking of joining a sports club.
>
> G: _____
>
> B: I prefer indoor sports. I was in the badminton club last year.
>
> G: Why don't you join the table tennis club, then?
>
> B: That's a good idea. Thank you.

┤ 조건 ├
- 둘 중 더 좋아하는 것에 대해 묻는 표현을 쓸 것.
- 'indoor'와 'outdoor'를 사용하여 7단어로 쓸 것.

➡ _____

04 다음 문장에서 틀린 것을 고쳐 다시 쓰시오.

(1) BTS was appeared on TV last night.

➡ _____

(2) It was made run on city streets and highways.

➡ _____

(3) Sinseollo was called this pot and the food in it by people.

➡ _____

➡ _____

(4) There was new nothing in this magazine.

➡ _____

Sinseollo

In the time of King Yeonsan, there was a scholar who was famous for his honesty. When the king did something wrong, the scholar was never afraid of telling him so. However, the king never listened to him. The scholar was so (A)[disappointing / disappointed] that he went to live on a mountain. While he lived there by himself, he mainly ate vegetables. He made a special pot to cook many different vegetables together. ⓐPeople called this pot and the food in it sinseollo. That is (B)[because / why] thc scholar lived like a sinseon, an (C)[imaginary / imaginative] person who lives alone in nature.

05 위 글의 괄호 (A)~(C)에서 문맥이나 어법상 알맞은 낱말을 골라 쓰시오.

➡ (A) _____ (B) _____ (C) _____

06 Why did the scholar make a special pot? Fill in the blanks with suitable words.

➡ He made a special pot in order that he _____ _____ many different vegetables together.

07 위 글의 밑줄 친 ⓐ를 수동태로 고치시오.

➡ _____
_____

Songpyeon

It was the time of the last king of Baekje. One day, the king and his servants found a strange turtle. Something was written on its back. It said, "Baekje is like a full moon, but Silla is like a half moon."

The king asked a fortune teller, "What does this mean?"

The fortune teller answered, "A full moon will soon become smaller. On the other hand, a half moon will grow bigger and become a full moon."

The king became worried about his kingdom. However, people of Silla were very happy to learn ⓐthis and made rice cakes in the shape of a half moon. Since then, people have enjoyed these half-moon shaped rice cakes, songpyeon.

08 위 글의 밑줄 친 ⓐthis가 가리키는 것을 영어로 쓰시오.

➡ _____
_____

09 Why were people of Silla very happy? Fill in the blanks with the same word.

➡ That's because they believed that the power of Silla would grow _____ like a half moon which will grow _____ and become a full moon.

10 다음 빈칸에 알맞은 단어를 넣어 반달 모양의 송편에 대한 소개를 완성하시오.

People have enjoyed the half-moon shaped rice cakes, songpyeon, since it was made in the shape of a half moon by _____ _____ _____.

01 다음 그림을 보고 음식을 추천하는 말과 선호하는 것을 묻고 답하는 대화를 〈보기〉와 같이 자신의 경우에 맞게 쓰시오.

SALAD	MAIN DISH	DESSERT
chicken salad	seafood spaghetti	chocolate ice cream
green salad	bibimbap	patbingsu

┌ 보기 ┐

A: Could you recommend a salad for me?

D: Do you prefer chicken salad or green salad?

A: I prefer green salad.

02 주어진 동사와 수동태를 사용하여 다양한 문장을 완성하시오.

These pictures/paint	These dresses/make
Hangeul/invent	*Harry Potter*/write

(1) _____

(2) _____

(3) _____

(4) _____

03 다음 내용을 바탕으로 우리 집의 특별한 음식을 소개하는 글을 쓰시오.

1. My family enjoys fish skin sundae on Chuseok.
2. It is made of rice, vegetables, and fish skin.
3. It has a story about my grandma and her home in North Korea.
4. It is special because it gives us a chance to think about my grandma's home.

Fish Skin Sundae

My family eats something special on (A)_____. It is made of rice, vegetables, and (B)_____. It is a kind of sundae. When I eat this food, I always think of my grandma. She is from (C)_____. When she was young, her mother often made it for the family. The food gives us a chance to think about (D)_____.

단원별 모의고사

01 다음 단어에 대한 영어 설명이 <u>어색한</u> 것은?

① culture: the way of life, especially the general customs and beliefs, of a particular group of people at a particular time

② order: to ask for something to be made, supplied, or delivered, especially in a restaurant or shop

③ servant: a person who is employed in another person's house, doing jobs such as cooking and cleaning, especially in the past

④ beginner: a person who is starting to do something or learn something for the first time

⑤ dessert: a food that is used with other foods in the preparation of a particular dish

02 다음 우리말 해석에 맞게 알맞은 단어를 쓰시오.

(1) 학생들은 과학 실험에 몰두했다.
➡ The students _____ into the science experiment.

(2) 우리의 전통 음식에 대한 재미있는 이야기들이 많이 있다.
➡ There are many i_____ stories about our traditional food.

03 다음 영영풀이에 해당하는 단어를 고르시오.

a country ruled by a king or queen

① tradition   ② policy
③ kingdom   ④ scholar
⑤ official

04 다음 글의 빈칸에 들어갈 단어를 영어 설명을 보고 쓰시오.

While the scholar lived there by himself, he mainly ate vegetables. He made a special _____ to cook many different vegetables together.
<영어 설명>
any of various types of container, usually round, especially one used for cooking food

05 대화의 빈칸에 공통으로 들어갈 말은?

B: Do you have anything for dessert, Aunt May?
W: Yes, Johnny. Do you _____ pie or cake?
B: I _____ cake.
W: O.K. I have some chocolate cake. I'll get you some.

① agree   ② think   ③ have
④ recommend   ⑤ prefer

06 주어진 문장에 이어질 글의 순서로 알맞은 것은?

A: Excuse me. I'm looking for a skirt. Could you recommend one?

(A) Then, how about this blue one? It's on sale now.
(B) Blue and pink are my favorite colors.
(C) What color do you like?
(D) Good! Thank you. I'll take it.

① (A) – (B) – (C) – (D)
② (B) – (C) – (A) – (D)
③ (C) – (A) – (D) – (B)
④ (C) – (B) – (A) – (D)
⑤ (D) – (B) – (C) – (A)

07 대화의 밑줄 친 ①~⑤ 중 어휘의 쓰임이 어색한 것은?

> W: Excuse me. I'm ①looking for an Italian cookbook. Could you ②command one?
>
> M: Well, have you ever cooked Italian food?
>
> W: No, I haven't, but I ③want to try. I really ④like spaghetti.
>
> M: Then, how about this Italian cookbook for ⑤beginners? It's on sale now.
>
> W: Good! Thank you. I'll take it.

①   ②   ③   ④   ⑤

08 다음 중 짝지어진 대화가 어색한 것은?

① A: Do you prefer pie or cake?
   B: I prefer cake.

② A: What kind of restaurant do you like to go to?
   B: I like to go to Chinese restaurants.

③ A: Why don't you join the table tennis club, then?
   B: That's a good idea. Thank you.

④ A: I'm thinking of joining a sports club.
   B: I prefer action movies.

⑤ A: Could you recommend a book for me?
   B: Why don't you read *The Flying Pan*?

09 다음 대화의 빈칸에 공통으로 들어갈 말로 알맞은 것은?

> G: I haven't seen a movie recently. Could you _____ a good one?
>
> B: Why don't you see *Iron Woman 2*? It's a big hit.
>
> G: Well, I don't like action movies. Can you _____ any good comedies?
>
> B: Then, how about *Funny Families*?
>
> G: That sounds good.

① have   ② commend   ③ advise
④ bring   ⑤ recommend

[10~12] 다음 대화를 읽고 물음에 답하시오.

> Jaden: Have you been to the new Chinese restaurant, Ms. Park?
>
> Ms. Park: Are you talking about the one on Main Street, Jaden?
>
> Jaden: Yes, that's the one. They opened about two weeks ago, right?
>
> Ms. Park: I think so. I went there last Friday with my friends.
>
> Jaden: How was the food?
>
> Ms. Park: It was great. We ordered many different dishes. I really liked the fried vegetables.
>
> Jaden: Could you recommend a dish for me? I'm going there for dinner tonight with my family.
>
> Ms. Park: Do you prefer seafood or meat?
>
> Jaden: I prefer seafood.
>
> Ms. Park: _____(A)_____ You'll love it!

10 빈칸 (A)에 알맞은 말은?

① Well, why don't you watch *Avengers*?
② I've never been to the Chinese restaurant.
③ Then, you should try their fried fish.
④ Why don't you try the fried vegetables?
⑤ I'd like to order some seafood.

11 다음 질문에 대해 영어로 답하시오.

> Q: What food did Ms. Park like at the restaurant?

➡ She _____.

12 위 대화를 읽고 답할 수 없는 질문은?

① Where is the new Chinese restaurant?

② When did the restaurant open?

③ When did Ms. Park go to the restaurant?

④ How many dishes will Jaden's family order?

⑤ When will Jaden go to the restaurant with his family?

13 다음 주어진 문장을 능동태는 수동태로, 수동태는 능동태로 바꾸시오.

(1) Songpyeon was made in the shape of a half moon by people of Silla.

➡ _____

_____

(2) Did John paint the picture?

➡ _____

(3) Mariel told her daughter a funny story. (2가지로 쓸 것.)

➡ _____

_____

(4) English is spoken in many countries.

➡ _____

14 다음 중 어법상 어색한 것은?

① The tree will be planted by them tomorrow.

② We are waiting for special someone.

③ The scholar was so disappointed that he went to live on a mountain.

④ When the king did something wrong, the scholar was never afraid of telling him so.

⑤ I found this book while I was looking for something interesting at a bookstore.

15 밑줄 친 부분 중 생략할 수 있는 것은?

① This book was read by many children.

② What are you called by your classmates?

③ These flowers were planted by my mom.

④ Is French spoken in Canada by them?

⑤ The book was written by Mina.

16 괄호 안의 어구를 바르게 배열하여 문장을 완성하시오.

(1) I think that (I, something, the class, can, new, learn, at).

➡ _____

(2) (you, today, interesting, heard, have, anything)?

➡ _____

17 다음 중 어법상 적절한 것은?

① The food is made from rice flour, chocolate, and nuts.

② Is there anything new in this magazine?

③ This song wrote a famous musician.

④ I want to drink cold something.

⑤ I want to do special something for my brother's birthday party.

[18~19] 다음 글을 읽고 물음에 답하시오.

Tangpyeongchae

One day, King Yeongjo was having dinner with his officials and offered them something special. It was a dish with four ⓐcolor ingredients. Each ingredient symbolized a different political party. Yeongjo wanted to say that the four parties should work in harmony ⓑlike this dish. This dish was called tangpyeongchae. The name came from Yeongjo's policy tangpyeongchaek.

18 밑줄 친 ⓐ를 알맞은 형태로 고치시오.

➡ _____

19 위 글의 밑줄 친 ⓑlike와 같은 의미로 쓰인 것을 고르시오.

① Look for the things of like shape.
② I like playing the piano.
③ Please make it like this.
④ He studied painting, music, and the like.
⑤ Do as you like.

[20~21] 다음 글을 읽고 물음에 답하시오.

Sinseollo

In the time of King Yeonsan, there was a scholar ___ⓐ___ was famous for his honesty. When the king did something wrong, the scholar was never afraid of telling him so. However, the king never listened to him. The scholar was so disappointed that he went to live on a mountain. While he lived there by himself, he mainly ate vegetables. He made a special pot to cook many different vegetables together. ⓑ사람들은 이 솥과 그 안의 음식을 신선로라고 불렀다. That is because the scholar lived like a sinseon, an imaginary person ___ⓒ___ lives alone in nature.

20 위 글의 빈칸 ⓐ와 ⓒ에 공통으로 들어갈 알맞은 말을 고르시오. (2개)

① who   ② which   ③ whom
④ that   ⑤ what

21 밑줄 친 ⓑ의 우리말에 맞게 주어진 어휘를 이용하여 10단어로 영작하시오.

People, the food, sinseollo

➡ _____

[22~23] 다음 글을 읽고 물음에 답하시오.

Songpyeon

It was the time of the last king of Baekje. One day, the king and his servants found a strange turtle. Something was written on its back. It said, "Baekje is like a full moon, but Silla is like a half moon."

The king asked a fortune teller, "What does this mean?"

The fortune teller answered, "A full moon will soon become smaller. ⓐOn the other hand, a half moon will grow bigger and become a full moon."

The king became worried about his kingdom. However, people of Silla were very happy to learn this and made rice cakes in the shape of a half moon. Since then, people have enjoyed these half-moon shaped rice cakes, songpyeon.

22 위 글의 밑줄 친 ⓐOn the other hand와 바꿔 쓸 수 있는 말을 고르시오.

① Otherwise   ② Whereas
③ Besides   ④ Nevertheless
⑤ In addition

23 위 글의 내용과 일치하지 않는 것은?

① 어느 날, 백제의 마지막 왕과 신하들은 이상한 거북을 한 마리 발견했다.
② 그 거북의 등에 "백제는 보름달과 같지만 신라는 반달과 같다."라는 말이 쓰여 있었다.
③ 왕은 점술가에게 거북의 등에 쓰여 있는 말의 뜻을 물었다.
④ 점술가의 말을 듣고 왕은 자신의 왕국이 걱정되었다.
⑤ 백제 사람들은 반달 모양의 떡을 만들었다.

Think Big, Start Small

의사소통 기능

- 알고 있음 표현하기
  I've heard our music teacher is getting married.
- 상기시켜 주기
  A: I'm going to go hiking.
  B: Don't forget to take a bottle of water.

언어 형식

- 5형식 동사+목적어+형용사
  Add some bleach to **keep the water clear**.
- 사역동사
  Let me just **put** your phone in a glass.

Words & Expressions

Key Words

- **actress** [ǽktris] 명 여배우
- **amazing** [əméiziŋ] 형 놀라운
- **amusement park** 놀이공원
- **bend(–bent–bent)** [bend] 동 구부리다, 휘다
- **blackout** [blǽkaut] 명 대규모 정전 사태
- **bleach** [bli:tʃ] 명 표백제
- **bottle** [bátl] 명 병
- **ceiling** [síːliŋ] 명 천장
- **charity** [tʃǽrəti] 명 자선단체
- **chief** [tʃi:f] 형 주요한 명 우두머리, 부장
- **darkness** [dáːrknis] 명 어둠, 암흑
- **difficult** [dífikʌlt] 형 어려운
- **dim sum** 딤섬(중국식 작은 만두 요리)
- **electricity** [ilektrísəti] 명 전기
- **enough** [inʌ́f] 형 충분한
- **exciting** [iksáitiŋ] 형 흥미로운
- **favorite** [féivərit] 형 가장 좋아하는
- **foundation** [faundéiʃən] 명 재단
- **impossible** [impásəbl] 형 불가능한
- **install** [instɔ́:l] 동 설치하다
- **interesting** [íntərəstiŋ] 형 흥미로운
- **invent** [invént] 동 발명하다
- **last** [læst] 동 지속되다
- **leave(–left–left)** [li:v] 동 떠나다
- **leftover** [léftouvər] 명 남은 음식
- **less** [les] 형 더 적은
- **magic** [mǽdʒik] 형 마법의, 신기한
- **meal** [mi:l] 명 식사
- **packed** [pækt] 형 꽉 들어찬
- **popular** [pápjulər] 형 인기 있는
- **remain** [riméin] 동 남아 있다
- **roof** [ru:f] 명 지붕
- **safe** [seif] 형 안전한
- **save** [seiv] 동 구하다
- **shake(–shook–shaken)** [ʃeik] 동 흔들다, 털다
- **shelter** [ʃéltər] 명 주거지, 쉼터
- **shout** [ʃaut] 동 외치다
- **single** [síŋgl] 형 단 하나의
- **spread(–spread–spread)** [spred] 동 퍼지다
- **surprisingly** [sərpráiziŋli] 부 놀랍게도
- **teach(–taught–taught)** [ti:tʃ] 동 가르치다
- **thing** [θiŋ] 명 (복수형으로) 상황
- **times** [taimz] 명 (반복되는 행위의) ~번
- **village** [vílidʒ] 명 마을
- **whole** [houl] 형 전체의
- **widely** [wáidli] 부 널리, 폭넓게
- **winter break** 겨울 방학
- **work** [wəːrk] 동 작동하다

Key Expressions

- **at least** 최소한, 적어도
- **because of+명사** ~ 때문에
- **be going to부정사** ~할 예정이다
- **not ~ anymore** 더 이상 ~ 않다
- **dry off** ~을 말리다
- **get married** 결혼하다
- **I can't wait to부정사** 빨리 ~하고 싶다
- **just like** ~와 꼭 마찬가지로
- **forget to부정사** ~할 것을 잊다
- **how to부정사** ~하는 방법
- **fill A with B** A를 B로 채우다
- **come up with** ~을 생각해 내다, ~을 만들어 내다
- **have to+동사원형** ~해야 한다
- **light up** ~을 환하게 밝히다
- **pay for** 지불하다
- **thanks to** ~ 덕분에
- **thousands of** 수천의
- **too+형용사+to부정사** 너무 ~해서 …할 수 없다
- **turn off** ~을 끄다
- **turn up** (소리 등을) 높이다

Word Power

※ 서로 반대되는 뜻을 가진 어휘

- difficult (어려운) ↔ easy (쉬운)
- popular (인기 있는) ↔ unpopular (인기 없는)
- possible (가능한) ↔ impossible (불가능한)

- exciting (흥미로운) ↔ boring (지루한)
- safe (안전한) ↔ dangerous (위험한)
- whole (전체의) ↔ partial (일부분의)

※ 서로 비슷한 뜻을 가진 단어

- shout : yell (외치다)
- save : rescue (구하다)
- last : continue (지속하다)

- install : set up (설치하다)
- work : operate (작동하다)
- chief : main (주요한)

English Dictionary

- **blackout** 정전
  → a time when there is no light or power because of an electricity failure
  전기 시스템의 고장으로 빛이나 전력이 없는 때

- **bleach** 표백제
  → a strong chemical used for cleaning things or removing colour from things
  물건을 청소하거나 사물에서 색을 제거하기 위해 사용되는 강한 화학물질

- **charity** 자선, 자선단체
  → a system of giving money, food, or help free to those who are in need because they are ill, poor, or have no home, or any organization that has the purpose of providing money or helping in this way
  병들거나 가난하거나 집이 없기 때문에 어려움에 처한 사람들에게 무료로 돈, 음식 또는 도움을 주는 시스템, 또는 이런 식으로 돈과 도움을 제공할 목적을 가지고 있는 단체

- **ceiling** 천장
  → the inside surface of a room that you can see when you look above you
  위쪽을 바라볼 때 볼 수 있는 방의 안쪽 표면

- **daytime** 낮
  → the period between the time when the sun rises and the time it goes down, or the part of the day that is neither evening nor night
  해가 뜨는 시간과 지는 시간 사이의 기간이나 저녁도 밤도 아닌 하루의 부분

- **electricity** 전기
  → a form of energy that can be produced in several ways and that provides power to devices that create light, heat, etc
  여러 가지 방법으로 생산될 수 있고 빛, 열 등을 만드는 장치에 동력을 제공하는 에너지의 형태

- **install** 설치하다
  → to put furniture, a machine, or a piece of equipment into position and make it ready to use
  가구, 기계 또는 장비를 제 위치에 놓고 사용할 준비가 되게 하다

- **invent** 발명하다
  → to design and/or create something that has never been made before
  이전에 만들어진 적이 없는 어떤 것을 디자인하거나 만들다

- **lamp** 램프, 등
  → a device for giving light, especially one that has a covering
  특히 덮개가 있는 빛을 제공하는 장치

- **last** 지속되다
  → to continue to exist
  계속해서 존재하다

- **roof** 지붕
  → the covering that forms the top of a building, vehicle, etc
  건물이나 차량의 상부를 형성하는 덮개

- **spread** 퍼지다
  → to cover, reach, or have an effect on a wider or increasing area
  더 넓은 또는 증가하는 영역을 덮거나, 도달하거나, 영향을 미치다

 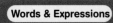

서답형

01 다음 짝지어진 두 단어의 관계가 같도록 빈칸에 알맞은 단어를 쓰시오.

> difficult : easy = partial : _____

[02~03] 다음 빈칸에 들어갈 말로 가장 적절한 것은?

02

> "I can't read a book in my room!" shouted Marco, a boy in a village in the Philippines. His house has no _____ just like all the other houses in the village.

① sunlight   ② roof
③ tradition   ④ electricity
⑤ ceiling

 중요

03

> This amazing plastic bottle is called a Moser lamp because it was _____ by Alfredo Moser.

① invited   ② saved
③ taught   ④ interested
⑤ invented

[04~05] 다음 영영풀이에 해당하는 단어를 고르시오.

04

> a device for giving light, especially one that has a covering

① lamp   ② wheel
③ ceiling   ④ roof
⑤ bottle

05

> a form of energy that can be produced in several ways and that provides power to devices that create light, heat, etc

① device   ② daytime
③ electricity   ④ bleach
⑤ charity

중요

06 밑줄 친 부분의 의미가 잘못된 것은?

① Bend the straw to use it easily. (굽히다)
② Strong lightning can cause a blackout.(정전)
③ Use bleach to make your clothes clean. (표백제)
④ His father is the chief of police. (주요한)
⑤ The daytime gets longer in the summer. (낮)

서답형

[07~08] 우리말 해석에 맞게 주어진 문장의 빈칸에 세 단어의 영어를 쓰시오.

07

> 이 정전들은 그가 집을 밝히는 새로운 방법을 생각해 내도록 만들었다.
> ➡ These blackouts made him _____ a new way to light his house.

08

> 병의 3분의 1은 지붕 위에 남아 있도록 한다.
> ➡ Let _____ the bottle remain above the roof.

01 영영풀이에 해당하는 단어를 〈보기〉에서 찾아 첫 번째 칸에 쓰고, 두 번째 칸에는 우리말 뜻을 쓰시오.

┌─── 보기 ───
│ ceiling / roof / daytime / blackout /
│ bleach
└

(1) _____: the period between the time when the sun rises and the time it goes down, or the part of the day that is neither evening nor night: _____

(2) _____: the inside surface of a room that you can see when you look above you: _____

(3) _____: a time when there is no light or power because of an electricity failure: _____

02 다음 주어진 우리말에 맞게 빈칸을 채우시오. (필요하면 변형하여 쓰시오.)

(1) Moser 램프는 앞으로 오랫동안 많은 사람들의 삶을 밝혀 줄 것이다.
   ➡ Moser lamps will _____ the lives of many people for many years to come. (두 단어로 쓰시오)

(2) 햇빛이 병 속의 물에 의해 굴절되어 방에 퍼진다.
   ➡ Sunlight is _____ by the water in the bottle and _____ around the room.

03 우리말 해석을 읽고, 주어진 철자를 알맞은 순서로 배열하여 빈칸을 채우시오.

(1) 남은 음식을 집에 가져가시겠어요?
   ➡ Do you want to take the _____ home? (e, o, t, e, l, f, r, v)

(2) 필리핀에서 Moser 램프는 My Shelter 재단에 의해 널리 사용된다.
   ➡ In the Philippines, Moser lamps are widely used by the My Shelter _____. (t, d, o, a, f, i, u, n, n, o)

04 다음 빈칸에 알맞은 단어를 〈보기〉에서 골라 쓰시오. (형태 변화 가능)

┌─── 보기 ───
│ wide / chief / bleach / whole
└

(1) She played the _____ scientist in the movie *Jupiter*.

(2) Add some _____ to keep the water clear.

(3) Today, gas is _____ used for cooking.

05 영어 설명을 읽고, 문장의 빈칸에 들어갈 알맞은 단어를 쓰시오.

┌─────────────────────────────────────
│ an empty space in an object, usually with
│ an opening to the object's surface, or an
│ opening that goes completely through an
│ object
└─────────────────────────────────────

(1) Make a _____ in the roof, and push the bottle into the _____.

┌─────────────────────────────────────
│ with special powers or happening in an
│ unusual or unexpected way, or easily or
│ quickly
└─────────────────────────────────────

(2) Surprisingly, it is very easy to make this _____ lamp.

Conversation

1 알고 있음 표현하기

• **I've heard our music teacher is getting married.** 우리 음악 선생님께서 결혼하신다고 들었어.

■ 어떤 사실을 들어서 알고 있음을 말할 때 'I've heard (that) ~.' 표현을 쓴다.

알고 있는지 묻기

• Do you know about ~? / You know ~, don't you?
"~에 관해 알고 있니?" / "너는 ~을 알고 있지, 그렇지 않니?"

• Are you aware of ~? / Have you heard ~? "~을 알고 있니? / ~을 늘었니?"

알고 있음 표현하기

• I've heard that ~. / I heard ~. / I know ~. "나는 ~라고 들었어 / 나는 ~을 알고 있어"

• A: Are you aware of today's lunch menu? 오늘의 점심 메뉴가 뭔지 알고 있니?
  B: I've heard that today's lunch menu is Kimchi fried rice.
  나는 오늘 점심이 김치 볶음밥이라고 들었어.

• I heard you didn't come to school yesterday. 나는 네가 어제 학교에 오지 않았다고 들었어.

핵심 Check

1. 다음 대화의 빈칸에 들어갈 알맞은 것은?

A: Do you know why Ted was absent from school yesterday?

B: _____

① I know he is very healthy.
② I've heard he was sick.
③ He likes to study in his room.
④ I wanted to go to school.
⑤ He feels good today.

② 상기시켜 주기

A I'm going to go hiking. 나는 하이킹을 하러 갈 거야.
B Don't forget to take a bottle of water. 물 한 병 챙기는 것을 잊지 마.

■ '~하는 것을 잊지 마'라는 뜻으로 상대방에게 해야 할 일을 상기시켜 줄 때 'Don't forget to부정사'나 'Remember to부정사'를 사용한다.

- A: Are you ready for your trip to Jejudo? 너는 제주도로 여행 갈 준비되었니?
  B: Not yet. What should I bring? 아직. 내가 무엇을 가져가야만 하니?
  A: Don't forget to bring a camera and a map of Jejudo.
    = Remember to bring a camera and a map of Jejudo.
    카메라와 제주도 지도를 가져가야 할 것을 잊지 마[기억해라].

- A: Don't forget to be quiet in the library. 도서관에서 조용히 하는 것 잊지 마.
  B: I won't forget. 잊지 않을게요.

- A: What will you take with you to a deserted island? 너는 무인도에 무엇을 가져갈 것이니?
  B: I will take a pen and some paper to write a diary. 나는 일기를 쓸 펜과 종이를 가져갈 거야.
  A: Don't forget to take some matches. 성냥을 가져가야 할 것도 잊지 마.

핵심 Check

2. 다음 빈칸에 들어갈 말로 알맞은 것은?

A: I'm going bike riding.
B: Have fun and _____.
A: Okay, I won't.

① it's fine today
② I think we should not make fun of others
③ don't forget to wear a helmet
④ I'm interested in baseball
⑤ I'm going to go on a trip to Jejudo

Listen & Speak 1-A-1

G: ❶Can you turn up the volume on your phone? I like this song.

B: ❷I can't turn it up anymore. It's the highest volume.

G: ❸Let me just put your phone in a glass. ❹I've heard a glass works like a speaker.

B: ❺What an interesting idea! Let's try it now.

G: 네 휴대폰 소리를 키워줄 수 있겠니? 이 노래가 좋아.
B: 소리를 더는 키울 수 없어. 음량이 이미 가장 높은데.
G: 그냥 네 휴대폰을 유리잔 안에 넣게 해 줘. 유리잔이 스피커처럼 쓰인다고 들었어.
B: 재미있는 생각이야! 지금 해 보자.

❶ 상대방에게 요청할 때 사용하는 표현으로 '~해 줄 수 있니?'의 의미다.
❷ 'turn up'은 '볼륨을 높이다'는 의미로 목적어가 대명사(it)일 때 '동사+대명사+부사'의 어순을 취한다. not ~ anymore는 '더 이상 ~ 않다'는 의미다.
❸ 'Let+목적어+동사원형'은 '…가 ~하게 하다'는 의미다.
❹ 어떤 사실을 들어서 알고 있음을 말할 때 'I've heard (that) ~.' 표현을 쓴다. 'work'는 '작동하다'는 의미다.
❺ 감탄문으로 'What+a(n)+형용사+명사+주어+동사 ~!'의 어순을 취한다.

Check(√) True or False

(1) G likes the song from B's phone.　　　　　　　　　T ☐ F ☐

(2) G suggests that B should use a speaker to listen to the song.　　T ☐ F ☐

Listen & Speak 1-A-2

B: ❶I've heard that a movie star is coming to our school.

G: That's right. She's my favorite actress.

B: Oh, who is she?

G: Miranda Kim. She played the chief scientist in the movie *Jupiter*.

B: Wow, ❷I can't wait to see her!

B: 우리 학교에 영화 배우가 온다고 들었어.
G: 맞아. 내가 가장 좋아하는 여배우야.
B: 오, 누군데?
G: Miranda Kim이야. 영화 《주피터》에서 책임 과학자를 연기했어.
B: 우와, 빨리 만나보고 싶은데!

❶ 어떤 사실을 들어서 알고 있음을 말할 때 사용하는 표현으로 '~을 들었다'는 뜻이다. 'is coming'은 현재진행형으로 미래의 일을 나타낸다.
❷ 'I can't wait to부정사'는 '빨리 ~하고 싶어'라는 뜻이다.

Check(√) True or False

(3) B knows a movie star is coming to his school.　　　　　T ☐ F ☐

(4) B saw the movie in which Miranda Kim played the chief scientist the actress coming to his school.

　　　　　　　　　　　　　　　　　　　　　　　　　T ☐ F ☐

Listen & Speak 2-A-1

W: Excuse me, ❶are you finished with your meal?

M: Yes, it was really good.

W: Do you want to take the leftovers home?

M: Yes, please.

W: ❷Don't forget to eat the leftovers by tomorrow.

❶ 'be finished with'는 '~을 마치다, ~을 끝내다'는 의미다.

❷ '~하는 것을 잊지 마'라는 뜻으로 상대방에게 해야 할 일을 상기시켜 줄 때 사용하는 표현이다. 이때 'forget to부정사'는 '~할 것을 잊다'는 미래의 일을 나타낸다.

Listen & Speak 2-A-2

B: ❶What's your plan for this winter break?

G: ❷I'm going to visit Hong Kong with my parents.

B: That sounds exciting. What are you going to do there?

G: I'm going to go to an amusement park. I'm also going to try all kinds of food.

B: Good. ❸Don't forget to try some dim sum.

❶ 미래의 계획을 물어볼 때 사용하는 표현이다.

❷ 'be going to부정사'는 '~할 예정이다'는 뜻으로 미래 계획을 말할 때 사용한다.

❸ '~하는 것을 잊지 마'라는 뜻으로 상대방에게 해야 할 일을 상기시켜 줄 때 사용하는 표현이다.

Communicate A

Yuri: What's wrong, Jaden?

Jaden: My science homework is too difficult.

Yuri: ❶What do you have to do?

Jaden: I need to find a way ❷to save trees.

Yuri: That's easy. ❸I've heard that we can save trees ❹by using less paper.

Jaden: Oh, I think I've heard that, too. Then, I can just ❺stop using paper cups.

Yuri: Yes! You can also use just one paper towel to dry off your hands.

Jaden: That's impossible. I need at least two or three paper towels.

Yuri: Just shake your hands before you use a paper towel. Then, one will be ❻more than enough.

Jaden: Oh, that's a good idea, Yuri! I'll try that next time.

Yuri: Good! Just ❼don't forget to shake your hands at least 10 times.

❶ 'have to부정사'는 '~해야 한다'는 의미다.

❷ 'to save'는 명사 'a way'를 꾸며주는 형용사 용법이다.

❸ 어떤 사실을 들어서 알고 있음을 말할 때 사용하는 표현으로 '~을 들었다'는 뜻이다.

❹ 'by -ing'는 '~함으로써'의 뜻이다.

❺ 'stop -ing'는 '~하는 것을 멈추다'라는 뜻이다.

❻ 'more than enough'는 '충분하고도 남을 거야'라는 뜻이다.

❼ '~하는 것을 잊지 마'라는 뜻으로 상대방에게 해야 할 일을 상기시켜 줄 때 사용하는 표현이다.

Communicate B

A: ❶I've heard that saving electricity is the best way to save the Earth.

B: I've heard that, too. What can we do to save electricity?

A: ❷Why don't we turn off the light when we're not using it?

B: That's a good idea. ❸Don't forget to turn off the light when you leave your room.

❶ 어떤 사실을 들어서 알고 있음을 말할 때 사용하는 표현으로 '~을 들었다'라는 뜻이다.

❷ '~하는 게 어때?'라는 뜻으로 상대방에게 제안할 때 사용한다.

❸ '~하는 것을 잊지 마'라는 뜻으로 상대방에게 해야 할 일을 상기시켜 줄 때 사용하는 표현이다.

Progress Check

1. B: ❶I've heard that a famous baseball player is coming to our school.

   G: That's right. He's my favorite player.

   B: Oh, who is he?

   G: I'm not going to tell you. It's a surprise!

2. B: What's your plan for this winter break?

   G: I'm going to visit Vietnam with my parents.

   B: That sounds exciting. What are you going to do there?

   G: I'm going to spend some time on the beach and eat lots of seafood.

   B: Good. ❷Don't forget to try the fruit there, too.

   G: O.K., I won't forget.

❶ 어떤 사실을 들어서 알고 있음을 말할 때 사용하는 표현이다.

❷ '~하는 것을 잊지 마'라는 뜻으로 상대방에게 해야 할 일을 상기시켜 줄 때 사용하는 표현이다.

● 다음 우리말과 일치하도록 빈칸에 알맞은 말을 쓰시오.

Listen & Speak 1-A

1. G: Can you _____ _____ the volume on your phone? I like this song.

   B: I can't _____ _____ _____ _____. It's the _____ volume.

   G: _____ me just _____ your phone in a glass. _____ _____ a glass _____ _____ a speaker.

   B: _____ _____ _____ _____! _____ try it now.

2. B: _____ _____ that a movie star _____ _____ to our school.

   G: That's right. She's my _____ _____.

   B: Oh, who is she?

   G: Miranda Kim. She _____ the _____ scientist in the movie *Jupiter*.

   B: Wow, I _____ _____ _____ see her!

Listen & Speak 2-A

1. W: Excuse me, are you _____ with your meal?

   M: Yes, it was really _____.

   W: Do you _____ _____ _____ the _____ home?

   M: Yes, please.

   W: _____ _____ _____ _____ the leftovers by tomorrow.

2. B: What's _____ _____ _____ this _____ _____?

   G: _____ _____ _____ visit Hong Kong with my parents.

   B: That sounds _____. What are you _____ _____ there?

   G: I'm _____ _____ _____ to an _____ park. I'm also going to try _____ _____ of food.

   B: Good. _____ _____ _____ _____ some dim sum.

해석

1. G: 네 휴대폰 소리를 키워줄 수 있겠니? 이 노래가 좋아.
   B: 소리를 더는 키울 수 없어. 음량이 이미 가장 높은데.
   G: 그냥 네 휴대폰을 유리잔 안에 넣게 해 줘. 유리잔이 스피커처럼 쓰인다고 들었어
   B: 재미있는 생각이야! 지금 해 보자.

2. B: 우리 학교에 영화 배우가 온다고 들었어.
   G: 맞아. 내가 가장 좋아하는 여배우야.
   B: 오, 누군데?
   G: Miranda Kim이야. 영화 《주피터》에서 책임 과학자를 연기했어.
   B: 우와, 빨리 만나보고 싶은데!

1. W: 실례합니다, 식사를 마치셨나요?
   M: 네, 정말 좋았어요.
   W: 남은 음식을 집에 가져가시겠어요?
   M: 네, 부탁합니다.
   W: 내일까지는 남은 음식을 다 드시는 걸 잊지 마세요.

2. B: 이번 겨울 방학에는 뭘 할 거야?
   G: 부모님과 홍콩에 갈 거야.
   B: 신나겠는걸. 거기서 뭘 할 거니?
   G: 놀이공원에 갈 거야. 그리고 온갖 음식들을 먹어 볼 거야.
   B: 좋은데. 딤섬을 먹어 보는 걸 잊지 마.

Communicate A

Yuri: What's _____, Jaden?

Jaden: My science homework is too _____.

Yuri: What do you _____ _____ do?

Jaden: I need to find a way _____ _____ trees.

Yuri: That's easy. _____ _____ _____ we can save trees _____ _____ _____ paper.

Jaden: Oh, I think _____ _____ _____, _____. Then, I can just _____ _____ paper cups.

Yuri: Yes! You can also use just one paper towel _____ _____ _____ your hands.

Jaden: That's _____. I need _____ _____ two or three paper towels.

Yuri: Just _____ your hands _____ you use a paper towel. Then, one will be _____ _____ _____.

Jaden: Oh, that's a good idea, Yuri! I'll _____ that _____ _____.

Yuri: Good! Just _____ _____ _____ your hands _____ _____ 10 _____.

Communicate B

A: _____ _____ that _____ _____ is the best way _____ _____ the Earth.

B: I've _____ _____, _____. What can we do to _____ electricity?

A: Why don't we _____ _____ the light _____ we're not using it?

B: That's a good idea. _____ _____ to _____ _____ the light _____ you _____ your room.

Progress Check

1. **B:** _____ _____ _____ a famous baseball player _____ _____ to our school.

   G: That's right. He's my _____ player.

   B: Oh, who is he?

   G: I'm not going to tell you. It's a _____!

2. **B:** What's your _____ _____ this winter break?

   G: I'm going _____ _____ Vietnam with my parents.

   B: That _____ _____. What are you going to do there?

   G: I'm going to _____ some time on the _____ and eat lots of _____.

   B: Good. _____ _____ _____ _____ the fruit there, too.

   G: O.K., I _____ _____.

유리: 무슨 일 있니, Jaden?

Jaden: 과학 숙제가 너무 어려워.

유리: 뭘 해야 하는데?

Jaden: 나무들을 살리는 방법을 찾아야 해.

유리: 그건 쉬워. 나는 종이를 덜 사용함으로써 나무들을 살릴 수 있다고 들었어.

Jaden: 아, 나도 들어 본 것 같아. 그럼, 종이컵 쓰는 걸 멈추면 되겠네.

유리: 맞아! 그리고 손을 말리는 데 종이 수건을 한 장만 쓸 수도 있지.

Jaden: 그건 불가능해. 나는 종이 수건이 적어도 두세 장은 필요해.

유리: 종이 수건을 쓰기 전에 손을 털어 봐. 그럼, 한 장으로 충분하고도 남을 거야.

Jaden: 오, 좋은 생각이야, 유리야! 다음에 해 봐야겠어.

유리: 좋아! 손을 적어도 열 번은 털어야 한다는 걸 잊지 마.

A: 전기를 절약하는 게 지구를 살리는 데 가장 좋은 방법이라고 들었어.

B: 나도 들었어. 전기를 절약하기 위해 무엇을 할 수 있을까?

A: 사용하지 않을 때는 전기를 끄는 게 어때?

B: 좋은 생각이야. 방을 나갈 때 불 끄는 것을 잊지 마.

1. B: 유명한 야구 선수가 우리 학교로 온다고 들었어.

   G: 맞아. 그는 내가 가장 좋아하는 선수야.

   B: 오, 누군데?

   G: 말해주지 않을 거야. 놀라게 할 거야!

2. B: 이번 겨울 방학에 무슨 계획이 있니?

   G: 부모님과 함께 베트남에 갈 거야.

   B: 재미있겠다. 거기서 뭘 할 거야?

   G: 바닷가에서 시간을 좀 보내고 해산물을 많이 먹을 거야.

   B: 좋아. 거기 과일을 먹어 보는 것도 잊지 마.

   G: 알겠어, 잊지 않을게.

01 다음 대화의 빈칸에 들어갈 말로 알맞은 것은?

> B: _____
>
> G: That's right. He's my favorite player.
>
> B: Oh, who is he?
>
> G: I'm not going to tell you. It's a surprise!

① I heard you didn't come to school yesterday.

② I've heard the car was invented earlier than the bicycle.

③ I've heard that a famous baseball player is coming to our school.

④ I heard chocolate isn't good for dogs.

⑤ Ted, I've been told Mr. Brown is going back to Canada.

[02~03] 다음 대화를 읽고, 물음에 답하시오.

> W: Excuse me, (A)식사를 마치셨나요?
>
> M: Yes, it was really good.
>
> W: Do you want to take the leftovers home?
>
> M: Yes, please.
>
> W: _____ (B)

02 (A)의 우리말에 맞게 주어진 단어를 알맞은 순서로 배열하시오.

> (finished / you / with / are / your / meal / ?)

➡ _____

03 빈칸 (B)에 들어갈 말로 알맞은 것은?

① Don't remember to eat the leftovers by tomorrow.

② Don't forget eating the leftovers by tomorrow.

③ Remember eating the leftovers by tomorrow.

④ Don't forget to come home until 7.

⑤ Don't forget to eat the leftovers by tomorrow.

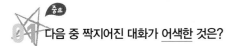

01 다음 중 짝지어진 대화가 어색한 것은?

① A: What's your plan for this winter break?
B: I'm going to visit Hong Kong with my parents.

② A: What's wrong, Jaden?
B: Don't forget to bring my science homework tomorrow.

③ A: You can also use just one paper towel to dry off your hands.
B: That's impossible.

④ A: What can we do to save electricity?
B: Why don't we turn off the light when we're not using it?

⑤ A: Don't forget to try the fruit there, too.
B: O.K., I won't forget.

[02~03] 다음 대화를 읽고 물음에 답하시오.

> G: _____(A)_____ I like this song.
> B: I can't turn it up anymore. It's the highest volume.
> G: Let me just put your phone in a glass. _____(B)
> B: What an interesting idea! Let's try it now.

02 빈칸 (A)에 알맞은 말을 고르시오.

① Can I play soccer with my friends after school?
② Would you turn down the volume on your phone?
③ I think the volume of your phone is high.
④ Can you turn up the volume on your phone?
⑤ What are you interested in?

03 빈칸 (B)에 들어갈 알맞은 말은?

① Be carful to put your phone in a glass
② Do you know about my latest cell phone?
③ I've heard a glass works like a speaker.
④ I've heard you have a nice speaker.
⑤ I use a phone to take pictures.

[04~05] 다음 대화를 읽고 물음에 답하시오.

> B: What's your plan for this winter break?
> G: _____(A)_____ visit Hong Kong with my parents.
> B: That sounds exciting. What are you going to do there?
> G: I'm going to go to an amusement park. I'm also going to try all kinds of food.
> B: Good. _____(B)_____ some dim sum.

04 빈칸 (A), (B)에 들어갈 말로 알맞은 것은?

① I'm going to – Don't remember to try
② I was going to – Don't forget trying
③ I'm going to – Don't forget trying
④ I was going to – Remember trying
⑤ I'm going to – Don't forget to try

서답형
05 다음 영영풀이에 해당하는 단어를 대화에서 찾아 쓰시오.

> a Chinese meal or snack of small dishes including different foods fried or cooked in steam

➡ _____

[06~07] 다음 대화를 읽고 물음에 답하시오.

Yuri: What's wrong, Jaden?

Jaden: My science homework is too difficult.

Yuri: What do you have to do? (①)

Jaden: I need to find a way to save trees.

Yuri: That's easy. I've heard that we can save trees by using less paper. (②)

Jaden: Oh, I think I've heard that, too. Then, I can just stop using paper cups. (③)

Yuri: Yes! You can also use just one paper towel to dry off your hands.

Jaden: That's impossible. (④)

Yuri: Just shake your hands before you use a paper towel. Then, one will be more than enough. (⑤)

Jaden: Oh, that's a good idea, Yuri! I'll try that next time.

Yuri: Good! Just don't forget to shake your hands at least 10 times.

06 위 대화의 (①)~(⑤) 중 다음 주어진 말이 들어갈 알맞은 곳은?

> I need at least two or three paper towels.

①   ②   ③   ④   ⑤

07 위 대화의 내용과 일치하지 <u>않는</u> 것은?

① They are talking about an easy way to save trees.

② Jaden thinks that his science homework is difficult.

③ Jaden has to find a way to save trees.

④ Yuri suggests that Jaden should stop using paper cups and use just one paper towel to dry off his hands.

⑤ Yuri suggests to Jaden that he should shake his hands at least 10 times before he uses a paper towel.

[08~09] 다음 대화를 읽고 물음에 답하시오.

A: I've heard that _____(A)_____ is the best way to save the Earth.

B: I've heard that, too. What can we do to save electricity?

A: _____(B)_____ when we're not using it?

B: That's a good idea. Don't forget to turn off the light when you leave your room.

08 위 대화의 빈칸 (A)에 들어갈 말로 알맞은 것은?

① saving electricity

② saving water

③ using less paper

④ washing hands

⑤ using paper towels

09 빈칸 (B)에 들어갈 말로 알맞은 것은?

① Why did you turn off the light

② Are you planning to turn off the light

③ Why don't we turn off the light

④ Shall I turn off the light

⑤ Don't forget turning off the light

[01~02] 다음 대화를 읽고 물음에 답하시오.

Boy: What's your plan for this winter break?

Girl: I'm going to visit Vietnam with my parents.

Boy: That sounds exciting. What are you going to do there?

Girl: I'm going to spend some time on the beach and eat lots of seafood.

Boy: Good. Don't forget to try the fruit there, too.

Girl: O.K., (A)잊지 않을게(forget).

01 Read the dialogue above and write what the boy suggests the girl do on her trip? (Write 5 words.)

➡ He suggests that _____.

02 밑줄 친 (A)의 우리말에 맞게 주어진 단어를 이용하여 영작하시오. (3단어로 쓸 것)

➡ _____

[03~04] 다음 대화를 읽고 물음에 답하시오.

Yuri: What's wrong, Jaden?

Jaden: My science homework is too difficult.

Yuri: What do you have to do?

Jaden: I need to find a way to save trees.

Yuri: That's easy. (A)나는 종이를 덜 사용함으로써 나무들을 살릴 수 있다고 들었어.

Jaden: Oh, I think I've heard that, too. Then, I can just stop using paper cups.

Yuri: Yes! You can also use just one paper towel to dry off your hands.

Jaden: That's impossible. I need at least two or three paper towels.

Yuri: Just shake your hands before you use a paper towel. Then, one will be more than enough.

Jaden: Oh, that's a good idea, Yuri! I'll try that next time.

Yuri: Good! Just _____ (B)

03 밑줄 친 (A)의 우리말에 맞게 주어진 단어를 이용하여 영어로 쓰시오.

> I've / that / can / by / use / little

➡ _____

04 대화의 빈칸 (B)에 주어진 조건과 우리말 해석에 맞게 한 문장을 쓰시오.

┤ 조건 ├
'forget'을 이용하여 상기시켜 주는 표현을 쓸 것.

┤ 해석 ├
'손을 적어도 열 번은 털어야 한다는 걸 잊지 마'

➡ _____

05 Read the sentence below and fill in the blank to complete the advice that the boy gives to the girl.

> Girl: I'm going to go hiking tomorrow, but I'm worried about bad weather.

➡ Boy: _____ take an umbrella with you.

06 다음 우리말에 맞게 주어진 어휘를 바르게 배열하시오.

> 우리 학교에 영화배우가 온다고 들었어.
> (I've / a movie / heard / star / that / is / to / our school / coming)

➡ _____

Grammar

1 5형식 동사+목적어+형용사

- Add some bleach to **keep** the water **clear**. 물을 깨끗이 유지하기 위해 표백제를 조금 넣어라.
- You'll **find** it **interesting**. 너는 그게 재미있다는 걸 알 거야.

■ '주어+동사+목적어+목적격보어'의 어순으로 이루어진 문장을 5형식 문장이라고 하며, 목적격보어 자리에는 명사, 형용사, to부정사, 현재분사, 과거분사, 동사원형 등 다양한 형태가 올 수 있다. 이때, 목적격보어는 목적어의 특징이나 상태 등을 설명하는 역할을 한다. 형용사를 목적격보어로 취하는 동사에는 find, get, keep, leave, make, paint, think 등이 있다.

- He **made** his daughter a **teacher**. 〈명사〉 그는 그의 딸을 교사로 만들었다.
- She **makes** me **happy**. 〈형용사〉 그녀는 나를 행복하게 해.

■ 목적격 보어를 형용사가 아닌 부사로 쓰지 않도록 주의해야 한다.

- Do you **think** him **honest**? 너는 그가 정직하다고 생각하니?
- This jacket will **keep** you **warm**. 이 재킷이 너를 따뜻하게 해 줄 거야.

■ **5형식 문장과 4형식 문장 비교**

5형식 문장: 주어+동사+목적어+목적격보어

- He **kept** his room **clean**. (his room = clean) 그는 그의 방을 깨끗하게 유지했다.

4형식 문장: 주어+동사+간접목적어+직접목적어

- Her mom **made** her a **dress**. (her ≠ a dress) 그녀의 엄마는 그녀에게 옷을 만들어 주었다.

핵심 Check

1. 다음 우리말에 맞게 빈칸에 알맞은 말을 쓰시오.

(1) 그는 그녀가 유명하게 만들었다.

➡ He made her _____.

(2) 아름다운 꽃들은 그녀를 행복하게 만든다.

➡ Beautiful flowers make her _____.

2 사역동사

> • **Let** me just **put** your phone in a glass. 그냥 네 휴대폰을 유리잔 안에 넣게 해 줘.

- **사역동사**

  - 의미: (목적어)가 ~하게 하다/~하도록 시키다

  - 형태: 사역동사(let/make/have)+목적어+동사원형

- 사역동사는 '사역동사+목적어+목적격보어'의 형태로 '(목적어)가 ~하게 하다/~하도록 시키다'의 뜻을 가지며 사역동사에는 make, have, let이 있다.

  - Mom **made** me **do** the dishes. 엄마는 내게 설거지를 하도록 시켰다.

  - She **let** me **go** home early. 그녀는 내가 집에 일찍 가도록 해 주었다.

- 목적격보어로 동사원형이 오면 능동의 의미로 '~(목적어)가 …(목적격보어)을 하게 하다'의 뜻을 가지며, 과거분사가 오면 수동의 의미로 '~(목적어)가 …(목적격보어)을 당하게[되게] 하다'의 뜻을 갖는다.

  - I **had** him **call** her. 〈능동〉 나는 그가 그녀에게 전화하도록 했다. (그가 전화하는 것으로 능동)

  - He **had** his computer **repaired**. 〈수동〉 그는 그의 컴퓨터가 수리되도록 했다. (컴퓨터가 수리되는 것으로 수동)

- **'help'와 'get'**

  - help는 목적격보어로 동사원형이나 to부정사가 나오며 뜻의 차이는 없다.

  - It **helped** her **forget** life on the streets.
    = It **helped** her **to forget** life on the streets. 그것은 그녀로 하여금 거리에서의 삶을 잊는 데 도움이 되었다.

  - get이 '~하게 하다'라는 사역동사의 뜻으로 쓰일 때 목적격보어로 능동의 의미일 때는 to부정사를, 수동의 의미일 때는 과거분사를 쓴다.

  - He **got** her **to finish** her homework. 〈능동〉 그는 그녀가 숙제를 끝내도록 시켰다.
    = He **had** her **finish** her homework.

  - He **got** his computer **repaired**. 〈수동〉 그는 그의 컴퓨터가 수리되도록 했다.
    = He **had** his computer **repaired**.

핵심 Check

2. 다음 괄호 안에서 알맞은 것을 고르시오.

(1) Dad had me (wash / to wash) his car.

(2) Carol got her house (paint / painted).

(3) Minhee helped me (to do / doing) my homework.

(4) They got him (sign / to sign) the contract.

01 다음 문장에서 어법상 어색한 부분을 바르게 고쳐 쓰시오.

(1) The funny movie made me to laugh.

_____ ➡ _____

(2) I let him finishing cleaning his room.

_____ ➡ _____

(3) The song made me sadly.

_____ ➡ _____

(4) Too much homework makes me tiring.

➡ _____

02 주어진 단어를 어법에 맞게 빈칸에 쓰시오.

(1) She had her son _____ the trash away. (throw)

(2) She had the trash _____ away. (throw)

(3) She got him _____ her at the station. (meet)

(4) He helped his sister _____ her homework. (do)

03 다음 우리말을 영어로 바르게 옮긴 것은?

그 소설은 그녀를 유명하게 만들었다.

① The novel made her famously.

② The novel made her famous.

③ The novel had her famous.

④ She made the novel famous.

⑤ She made the novel famously.

04 주어진 단어를 바르게 배열하여 다음 우리말을 영어로 쓰시오.

• 제게 그녀의 이름을 알게 해 주세요.
  (me / name / know / let / her)

➡ _____

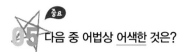
01 다음 빈칸에 알맞은 말이 순서대로 바르게 짝지어진 것은?

> • His parents let him _____ a pet.
> • We had a math test yesterday and found it _____.

① to have – difficultly
② having – difficultly
③ having – difficult
④ have – difficultly
⑤ have – difficult

02 다음 빈칸에 들어갈 말로 적절한 것을 <u>모두</u> 고르시오.

> His neighbor helped him _____ his roof.

① fix   ② fixes   ③ fixed
④ fixing   ⑤ to fix

03 (중요) 다음 빈칸에 알맞은 말을 고르시오.

> Merriam _____ the garden in the backyard very beautiful.

① found   ② called   ③ asked
④ ordered   ⑤ begged

04 (서답형) 주어진 어구를 이용하여 다음 우리말을 영어로 쓰시오. (7단어)

> 그 항아리는 과일을 차갑게 유지할 수 있다. (the pot, keep, the fruit)

➡ _____

05 (중요) 다음 중 어법상 <u>어색한</u> 것은?

① Could you let Cindy know that I'll call her later?
② Finally we got the little child to sit still long enough for photo.
③ Her wish was to have her son's name mention at graduation.
④ It helped him to forget other things.
⑤ I'll make my robot clean my room.

06 (서답형) 괄호 안에서 알맞은 것을 고르시오.

(1) Catherine wanted to have her son (learn / to learn) Chinese.
(2) Let me (see / seeing) if I can get there on time.
(3) Amy got her room (to clean / cleaned).
(4) Did the coach (make / help) the team to win the soccer match?
(5) The teacher gets us (read / to read) many books.
(6) I found the movie (interesting / interestingly).
(7) I tried to do exercise (regular / regularly) and it made me (health / healthy).

07 다음 중 어법상 올바른 문장을 고르시오.

① Add some bleach to keep the water clearly.
② This food will make me healthily.
③ What made you so angry last Saturday?
④ Reading a lot of books will make me well at English.
⑤ This heater will make us stay warmly in winter.

08 다음 중 어법상 바르지 <u>않은</u> 것은?

> I ①had the beef ②cook and ③put ④it ⑤into sandwiches.

①   ②   ③   ④   ⑤

09 다음 문장에서 어법상 틀린 부분을 찾아 바르게 고쳐 쓰시오.

> When I arrived at home, I found my wallet steal.

_____ ➡ _____

[10~11] 다음 우리말을 영어로 바르게 옮긴 것을 고르시오.

10 (2개)

> Ben은 Marie가 의자에 앉도록 도와주었다.

① Ben helped Marie sits on the chair.
② Ben helped Marie sat on the chair.
③ Ben helped Marie sit on the chair.
④ Ben helped Marie to sit on the chair.
⑤ Ben helped Marie sitting on the chair.

11

> 내가 아기를 안전하게 지킬 것이다.

① The baby will keep me safe.
② The baby will keep me safely.
③ The baby will keep I safe.
④ I'll keep the baby safe.
⑤ I'll keep the baby safely.

12 다음 문장의 빈칸에 알맞지 <u>않은</u> 것은?

> Venus _____ her daughter be on a healthy diet.

① made   ② had   ③ let
④ helped   ⑤ got

13 밑줄 친 부분과 용법이 <u>다른</u> 것은?

> Eating vegetables every day will <u>make</u> me healthy.

① She always <u>makes</u> me happy.
② His lie <u>made</u> her angry.
③ She <u>made</u> her son sad.
④ My dad <u>made</u> me a model train.
⑤ The comedy <u>made</u> them laugh.

14 다음 중 어법상 <u>어색한</u> 문장을 <u>모두</u> 고르시오.

① He helped her to carry her cases up the stairs.
② Elizabeth had the meat roast in the garden.
③ Morris got the girl stand up in front of students.
④ Alicia had her daughter take care of her cats.
⑤ Playing soccer always makes Beckham feel excited.

15 다음 중 (A)~(C)에서 어법상 옳은 것끼리 바르게 짝지은 것은?

> • Charlotte made Tom (A)(bake / baking) some cookies for her.
> • Angelina got him (B)(take / to take) some photos of her.
> • Richard had his bike (C)(fix / fixed).

	(A)	(B)	(C)
①	baking	take	fixed
②	baking	to take	fix
③	bake	to take	fix
④	bake	take	fix
⑤	bake	to take	fixed

서답형
16 두 문장의 뜻이 같도록 빈칸에 알맞은 말을 쓰시오.

(1) Kirk found the test difficult.
= Kirk found that _____ _____ _____ difficult.

(2) I think him silly.
= I think that _____ _____ _____.

서답형
17 다음 문장에서 어법상 어색한 부분을 바르게 고치시오.

(1) The police made the thief to wear handcuffs.
_____ ➡ _____

(2) Julie got the man write down 25 things he wanted to do.
_____ ➡ _____

(3) The girl had her purse steal on the train.
_____ ➡ _____

서답형
18 다음 괄호 안에 주어진 어구를 이용하여 우리말을 영어로 옮기시오.

(1) 우리 아버지는 차를 깨끗이 유지하신다. (my father, keep, clean)
➡ _____

(2) 비 오는 날은 나를 슬프게 한다. (rainy days, sad, make)
➡ _____

(3) 그녀의 새 책은 그녀를 유명하게 만들었다. (make, famous)
➡ _____

(4) 나는 내 아이들이 TV를 보게 하지 않을 것이다. (let, watch, TV)
➡ _____

(5) 재미있는 이야기가 나를 웃게 했다. (the funny story, make)
➡ _____

(6) 나는 그 남자에게 내 컴퓨터를 고치도록 했다. (have, the man, fix)
➡ _____

[19~20] 다음 빈칸에 알맞은 말을 고르시오.

19
> My brother _____ my room dirty.

① made ② ordered ③ did
④ asked ⑤ have

20
> My boss _____ a meeting.

① got me arrange
② made me arranged
③ got me arranged
④ made me arrange
⑤ makes I arranged

01 다음 중 어법상 <u>어색한</u> 부분을 찾아 바르게 고쳐 다시 쓰시오.

(1) She made him to finish his work by the next day.

➡ _____

_____

(2) She doesn't let her children playing online games.

➡ _____

_____

(3) I must go to the dry cleaner's to have my suit clean.

➡ _____

_____

(4) Mom got me help my sister with her homework.

➡ _____

_____

(5) I helped him calming down before playing the guitar on the stage.

➡ _____

_____

02 다음 문장의 빈칸에 한 단어씩을 채워 비슷한 뜻을 갖는 문장으로 바꿔 쓰시오.

(1) As I read the book, I felt sad.

= The book made _____ _____.

(2) When he did exercise regularly, he became healthy.

= Regular exercise _____ _____ _____.

03 다음 두 문장을 주어진 〈조건〉에 맞춰 〈보기〉와 같이 한 문장으로 완성하시오.

┤ 보기 ├

• My mom was busy today.

• So, she asked me to prepare dinner tonight.

→ My mom had me prepare dinner tonight.

┤ 조건 ├

1. 동사 have와 repair를 이용할 것.

2. 5 단어로 쓸 것.

• Eric had a broken camera.

• So, he brought it to a repair shop and asked a repairman to repair it.

➡ _____

04 다음 중 어법상 <u>어색한</u> 부분을 찾아 바르게 고쳐 다시 쓰시오.

(1) A strange man broke into my house, but he stole nothing and left it cleanly.

➡ _____

_____

(2) They made Stacy happiness by saying white lies.

➡ _____

(3) He found his new smartphone broke.

➡ _____

(4) At first, Samanda thought William honestly.

➡ _____

(5) This thick blanket will keep you warmly.

➡ _____

05 다음 그림을 참고하여 단어 turn의 알맞은 형태를 빈칸에 채우시오.

➡ I made him _____ up the volume of his smartphone.

07 그림을 보고 괄호 안에 주어진 단어들을 바르게 배열하여 문장을 완성하시오.

(holidays, year, her, lots, next, makes, having, excited, of)

➡ _____

_____

08 다음 문장을 〈보기〉와 같이 사역동사를 이용하여 바꿔 쓰시오.

┌─ 보기 ─┐
Mr. Kim got Jack to open the window.
= Mr. Kim had Jack open the window.
└────────┘

(1) Eve allowed Adam to use her pen.
➡ _____

(2) She forced Dan to follow her advice.
➡ _____

06 〈보기〉에서 의미상 적절한 단어를 골라 빈칸에 알맞은 형태로 쓰시오.

┌─ 보기 ─┐
be   watch   carry   find   clean
└────────┘

(1) The teacher made the students _____ their desks yesterday.

(2) Mom had the heavy box _____ upstairs.

(3) They got him _____ in the prison for a while.

(4) Yesterday I helped Jaden _____ his lost keys.

(5) His parents let him _____ TV after he finishes his homework.

09 다음 괄호 안에 주어진 단어를 이용하여 우리말을 영어로 옮기시오.

(1) 그는 어제 그의 차가 닦여지게 했다. (have, wash)
➡ _____

(2) 우리는 램프를 더 밝게 만들 수 있었다. (can, the lamp, make, bright.)
➡ _____

Reading

교과서

One-Dollar Magic Lamps

"Wow, I can read a book in my room now!" shouted Marco, a boy in a village in the Philippines. His house has no electricity just like all the other houses in the village. People in the village are too poor to pay for electricity. Even during the daytime, they live in darkness because the houses are packed close together. Now things are changing because of a single plastic bottle. One plastic bottle in the ceiling can light up a whole room without using any electricity.

This amazing plastic bottle is called a Moser lamp because it was invented by Alfredo Moser. In 2002, there were many blackouts in his town in Brazil. These blackouts made him come up with a new way to light his house.

A Moser lamp can be made for about one dollar and lasts for about 10 years. It is also very safe. It can never start a house fire. Surprisingly, it is very easy to make this magic lamp.

magic: 마법의, 신기한
lamp: 램프, 등
shout: 외치다
electricity: 전기
village 마을
daytime: 낮, 주간
packed 꽉 들어찬
ceiling: 천장
whole 전체의
blackout 정전 사태
last 지속되다

 확인문제

● 다음 문장이 본문의 내용과 일치하면 T, 일치하지 않으면 F를 쓰시오.

1   Marco's house has no electricity just like all the other houses in the village. ☐

2   During the daytime, they live in the bright room. ☐

3   A Moser lamp can be made for about one dollar and lasts for about 10 years. ☐

4   It is not easy to make this magic lamp. ☐

How to make a Moser lamp from a bottle
how to+동사원형: ~하는 방법

1. Fill a clear plastic bottle with water.
~으로

2. Add some bleach to keep the water clear.
keep+목적어+목적격 보어(5형식): 목적격 보어이 자리에 형용사를 씀. to keep: 부사적 용법

3. Make a hole in the roof, and push the bottle into the hole.

4. Let a third of the bottle remain above the roof.
사역동사 let+목적어+목적격 보어(동사원형): ~이 …하게 하다

5. Sunlight is bent by the water in the bottle and spreads around the
and로 연결된 병렬 구조. spreads 앞에 주어 sunlight가 생략됨.
room.

In the Philippines, Moser lamps are widely used by the My Shelter
수동태
Foundation. The charity also teaches local people how to make and
install the lamps. Thanks to the charity, thousands of homes in the
thousands of+명사: 수천의 ~. cf. hundred. thousand. million 등의 단어가
숫자 뒤에서 단위로 사용될 때: 단수형으로만 사용 e.g. two hundred. three million
Philippines now have Moser lamps. It has also made Moser lamps
= The charity 현재완료 계속 용법   5형식 동사+목적어+목적격보어(형용사)
popular in other countries, such as Argentina, India, and Fiji. Moser
~와 같은
lamps will light up the lives of many people for many years to come.
life의 복수형   앞으로 오랫동안

bleach: 표백제
hole: 구멍
bend: 구부러지다. 휘다 (bend–bent–bent)
spread: 펼치다, (여러 장소로) 퍼뜨리다
thanks to: ~ 덕분에
charity: 자선 단체
install: 설치하다
life: 삶, 생활

확인문제

● 다음 문장이 본문의 내용과 일치하면 T, 일치하지 않으면 F를 쓰시오.

1 To make a Moser lamp from a bottle, you must fill a clear plastic bottle with water. ☐

2 You need to add some bleach to keep the water cool. ☐

3 You must let two thirds of the bottle remain above the roof. ☐

4 Sunlight is bent by the water in the bottle and spreads around the room. ☐

5 The My Shelter Foundation teaches local people how to make and install Moser lamps. ☐

6 Thanks to the My Shelter Foundation, thousands of homes in the Philippines now have Moser lamps. ☐

● 우리말을 참고하여 빈칸에 알맞은 말을 쓰시오.

1 _____ Magic Lamps

2 "Wow, I can read a book in my room now!" shouted Marco, a boy in a village _____ _____ _____.

3 His house _____ _____ _____ just like _____ _____ _____ in the village.

4 People in the village are _____ poor _____ pay for electricity.

5 Even during the daytime, they live in darkness because the houses _____ _____ _____ _____.

6 Now things are changing _____ _____ a single plastic bottle.

7 One plastic bottle in the ceiling can _____ _____ a whole room _____ _____ any electricity.

8 This amazing plastic bottle _____ _____ a Moser lamp _____ it _____ _____ _____ Alfredo Moser.

9 In 2002, there were _____ _____ in his town in Brazil.

10 These blackouts made him _____ _____ _____ a new way to light his house.

11 A Moser lamp can _____ _____ _____ about one dollar and _____ _____ about 10 years.

12 It is also _____ _____.

1	1달러짜리 마법의 전구
2	"우와, 이젠 제 방에서 책을 읽을 수 있어요!" 필리핀의 한 마을에 사는 소년인 Marco가 외쳤다.
3	그의 집은 마을의 다른 모든 집들과 마찬가지로 전기가 없다.
4	마을 사람들은 너무나 가난해서 전기세를 낼 수가 없다.
5	심지어 낮 동안에도, 집들이 빽빽하게 들어차 있어서 그들은 어둠 속에 살아간다.
6	이제 플라스틱병 하나 때문에 상황이 바뀌고 있다.
7	천장에 있는 플라스틱병 하나는 전기를 쓰지 않고 방 전체를 밝힐 수 있다.
8	이 놀라운 플라스틱병은 Moser 램프라고 불리는데, 그것이 Alfredo Moser에 의해 발명되었기 때문이다.
9	2002년, 브라질에 있는 그의 마을에는 정전이 잦았다.
10	이 정전들은 그가 집을 밝히는 새로운 방법을 생각해 내도록 만들었다.
11	Moser 램프는 1달러 정도로 만들 수 있고 10년 정도 지속된다.
12	그것은 또한 매우 안전하다.

13 It can _____ _____ a house fire.

14 Surprisingly, it is very easy _____ _____ this magic lamp.

15 _____ _____ _____ a Moser lamp from a bottle

16 1. _____ a clear plastic bottle _____ water.

17 2. _____ some bleach _____ _____ the water _____ .

18 3. Make a hole in the roof, and _____ the bottle _____ the hole.

19 4. Let _____ _____ of the bottle _____ above the roof.

20 5. Sunlight _____ _____ by the water in the bottle and _____ around the room.

21 In the Philippines, Moser lamps _____ _____ _____ by the My Shelter Foundation.

22 _____ _____ also teaches local people _____ _____ _____ and _____ the lamps.

23 _____ _____ the charity, _____ _____ homes in the Philippines now have Moser lamps.

24 It _____ also _____ Moser lamps popular in other countries, _____ _____ Argentina, India, and Fiji.

25 Moser lamps will light up the lives of many people _____ _____ _____ _____ _____ .

13 그것은 절대 집에 불을 낼 수 없다.

14 놀랍게도, 이 신기한 램프를 만드는 것은 매우 쉽다.

15 병으로 Moser 램프를 만드는 법

16 1. 투명한 플라스틱병에 물을 채운다.

17 2. 물을 깨끗이 유지하기 위해 표백제를 조금 넣는다.

18 3. 지붕에 구멍을 내고, 병을 구멍 안으로 넣는다.

19 4. 병의 3분의 1은 지붕 위에 남아 있도록 한다.

20 5. 햇빛이 병 속의 물에 의해 굴절되어 방에 퍼진다.

21 필리핀에서 Moser 램프는 My Shelter 재단에 의해 널리 사용된다.

22 또한 그 자선단체는 지역 사람들에게 램프를 만들고 설치하는 법을 가르친다.

23 이 자선단체 덕분에, 필리핀의 수천 가구가 이제 Moser 램프를 갖고 있다.

24 그 단체는 아르헨티나, 인도, 피지와 같은 다른 나라들에서도 Moser 램프가 유명해 지도록 만들었다.

25 Moser 램프는 앞으로 오랫동안 많은 사람들의 삶을 밝혀 줄 것이다.

● 우리말을 참고하여 본문을 영작하시오.

1 1달러짜리 마법의 전구

➡ _____

2 "우와, 이젠 제 방에서 책을 읽을 수 있어요!" 필리핀의 한 마을에 사는 소년인 Marco가 외쳤다.

➡ _____

3 그의 집은 마을의 다른 모든 집들과 마찬가지로 전기가 없다.

➡ _____

4 마을 사람들은 너무나 가난해서 전기세를 낼 수가 없다.

➡ _____

5 심지어 낮 동안에도, 집들이 빽빽하게 들어차 있어서 그들은 어둠 속에 살아간다.

➡ _____

6 이제 플라스틱병 하나 때문에 상황이 바뀌고 있다.

➡ _____

7 천장에 있는 플라스틱병 하나는 전기를 쓰지 않고 방 전체를 밝힐 수 있다.

➡ _____

8 이 놀라운 플라스틱병은 Moser 램프라고 불리는데, 그것이 Alfredo Moser에 의해 발명되었기 때문이다.

➡ _____

9 2002년, 브라질에 있는 그의 마을에는 정전이 잦았다.

➡ _____

10 이 정전들은 그가 집을 밝히는 새로운 방법을 생각해 내도록 만들었다.

➡ _____

11 Moser 램프는 1달러 정도로 만들 수 있고 10년 정도 지속된다.

➡ _____

12 그것은 또한 매우 안전하다.

➡ _____

13 그것은 절대 집에 불을 낼 수 없다.

➡ _____

14 놀랍게도, 이 신기한 램프를 만드는 것은 매우 쉽다.

➡ _____

15 병으로 Moser 램프를 만드는 법

➡ _____

16 1. 투명한 플라스틱병에 물을 채운다.

➡ _____

17 2. 물을 깨끗이 유지하기 위해 표백제를 조금 넣는다.

➡ _____

18 3. 지붕에 구멍을 내고, 병을 구멍 안으로 넣는다.

➡ _____

19 4. 병의 3분의 1은 지붕 위에 남아 있도록 한다.

➡ _____

20 5. 햇빛이 병 속의 물에 의해 굴절되어 방에 퍼진다.

➡ _____

21 필리핀에서 Moser 램프는 My Shelter 재단에 의해 널리 사용된다.

➡ _____

22 또한 그 자선단체는 지역 사람들에게 램프를 만들고 설치하는 법을 가르친다.

➡ _____

23 이 자선단체 덕분에, 필리핀의 수천 가구가 이제 Moser 램프를 갖고 있다.

➡ _____

24 그 단체는 아르헨티나, 인도, 피지와 같은 다른 나라들에서도 Moser 램프가 유명해 지도록 만들었다.

➡ _____

25 Moser 램프는 앞으로 오랫동안 많은 사람들의 삶을 밝혀 줄 것이다.

➡ _____

[01~04] 다음 글을 읽고 물음에 답하시오.

"Wow, I can read a book in my room now!" shouted Marco, a boy in a village in the Philippines. (①) His house has no electricity just like all the other houses in the village. (②) People in the village are too poor to pay ___ⓐ___ electricity. (③) Even during the daytime, they live ___ⓑ___ darkness because the houses are packed close together. (④) One plastic bottle in the ceiling can light up a whole room without using any ___ⓒ___ . (⑤)

01 위 글의 빈칸 ⓐ와 ⓑ에 들어갈 전치사가 바르게 짝지어진 것은?

① for – on   ② to – in
③ in – from   ④ for – in
⑤ to – from

02 위 글의 빈칸 ⓒ에 들어갈 말로 가장 옳은 것을 고르시오.

① source   ② electricity
③ chemicals   ④ gas
⑤ rcsource

03 위 글의 흐름으로 보아, 주어진 문장이 들어가기에 가장 적절한 곳은?

> Now things are changing because of a single plastic bottle.

①   ②   ③   ④   ⑤

04 위 글의 내용과 일치하지 않는 것은?

① Marco의 집은 마을의 다른 모든 집들과 마찬가지로 전기가 없다.

② Marco의 마을 사람들은 너무나 가난해서 전기세를 낼 수가 없다.

③ 낮 동안에는 대부분의 마을 사람들의 집안에 햇빛이 들어온다.

④ 이제 플라스틱병 하나 때문에 어둠 속에서 살아가던 상황이 바뀌고 있다.

⑤ 천장에 있는 플라스틱병 하나로 방 전체를 밝힐 수 있다.

[05~07] 다음 글을 읽고 물음에 답하시오.

How to make a Moser lamp from a bottle
1. ___ⓐ___ a clear plastic bottle with water.
2. ___ⓑ___ some bleach to ___ⓒ___ the water clear.
3. ___ⓓ___ a hole in the roof, and ___ⓔ___ the bottle into the hole.
4. (A)Let a third of the bottle remain above the roof.
5. (B)Sunlight is bent by the water in the bottle and spreads around the room.

05 위 글의 빈칸 ⓐ~ⓔ에 들어갈 수 없는 단어를 고르시오. (대·소문자 무시)

① push   ② make   ③ give
④ fill   ⑤ add

서답형
06 위 글의 밑줄 친 (A)를 다음과 같이 바꿔 쓸 때 빈칸에 들어갈 알맞은 말을 쓰시오.

➡ Let _____ of the bottle remain below the roof.

서답형
07 위 글의 밑줄 친 (B)를 능동태로 고치시오.

➡ _____

[08~10] 다음 글을 읽고 물음에 답하시오.

This amazing plastic bottle is called a Moser lamp because it was invented by Alfredo Moser. In 2002, there were many blackouts in his town in Brazil. These blackouts made him come up with a new way ⓐto light his house.

A Moser lamp can be made for about one dollar and _____(A)_____ for about 10 years. It is also very safe. It can never start a house fire. Surprisingly, it is very easy to make this magic lamp.

서답형

08 주어진 영영풀이를 참고하여 빈칸 (A)에 철자 l로 시작하는 단어를 알맞은 형태로 쓰시오.

to continue to be able to be used for a particular length of time

➡ _____

09 위 글의 밑줄 친 ⓐto light와 to부정사의 용법이 다른 것을 모두 고르시오.

① To take a walk is good for the health.
② John needed someone to help him.
③ He stopped his car to check the engine.
④ She was sad to hear the news.
⑤ I have much homework to finish by tomorrow.

중요

10 위 글의 제목으로 알맞은 것을 고르시오.

① Various Uses of a Plastic Bottle
② Alfredo Moser, the Inventor of the Moser Lamp
③ The Cheap and Safe Magic Lamp
④ Blackouts Caused the Invention of a Lamp
⑤ The Amazing Effect of a Creative Idea

[11~14] 다음 글을 읽고 물음에 답하시오.

In the Philippines, Moser lamps are widely used by the My Shelter Foundation. The charity also teaches local people how to make and install the lamps. ___ⓐ___ the charity, ⓑ필리핀의 수천 가구 now have Moser lamps. It has also made Moser lamps popular in other countries, ⓒsuch as Argentina, India, and Fiji. Moser lamps will light ___ⓓ___ the lives of many people for many years to come.

중요

11 위 글의 빈칸 ⓐ에 들어갈 알맞은 말을 고르시오.

① Instead of   ② Without
③ In place of   ④ Thanks to
⑤ Unlike

서답형

12 위 글의 밑줄 친 ⓑ의 우리말을 다음 주어진 단어를 이용하여 여섯 단어로 쓰시오.

of, home

➡ _____

서답형

13 위 글의 밑줄 친 ⓒsuch as와 바꿔 쓸 수 있는 단어를 쓰시오.

➡ _____

14 위 글의 빈칸 ⓓ에 들어갈 알맞은 말을 고르시오.

① up   ② to
③ for   ④ from
⑤ with

[15~18] 다음 글을 읽고 물음에 답하시오.

How to make a Moser lamp from a bottle

1. Fill a clear plastic bottle   ⓐ   water.
2. Add some bleach ⓑ<u>to keep</u> the water clear.
3. Make a hole in the roof, and push the bottle   ⓒ   the hole.
4. ⓓ<u>Let a third of the bottle to remain above the roof.</u>
5. Sunlight is bent by the water in the bottle and spreads around the room.

⭐ **중요**

15 위 글의 빈칸 ⓐ와 ⓒ에 들어갈 전치사가 바르게 짝지어진 것은?

① in – from
② with – from
③ in – into
④ to – by
⑤ with – into

16 아래 보기에서 위 글의 밑줄 친 ⓑto keep과 to부정사의 용법이 <u>다른</u> 것의 개수를 고르시오.

┤ 보기 ├
① Give me something to write on.
② I went to London to meet my uncle.
③ She worked hard to be a professor.
④ She is planning to visit her uncle.
⑤ You had better come early to get seats.

① 1개　② 2개　③ 3개　④ 4개　⑤ 5개

서답형

17 위 글의 밑줄 친 ⓓ에서 어법상 틀린 부분을 찾아 고치시오.

_____ ➡ _____

⭐ **중요**

18 다음 중 '플라스틱병으로 Moser 램프를 만드는 법'을 올바르게 이해하지 <u>못한</u> 사람을 고르시오.

① 성민: 불투명한 플라스틱병에 물을 채워 넣어야 한다.

② 재희: 표백제를 조금 넣는 이유는 물을 깨끗이 유지하기 위해서이다.
③ 보람: 지붕에 구멍을 내고, 병을 구멍 안으로 넣어야 한다.
④ 형규: 병의 3분의 1은 지붕 위에 남아 있도록 해야 한다.
⑤ 민수: 햇빛이 병 속의 물에 의해 굴절되어 방에 퍼지게 된다.

[19~21] 다음 글을 읽고 물음에 답하시오.

In the Philippines, Moser lamps are widely used by the My Shelter Foundation. The charity also teaches local people how to make and ⓐ<u>install</u> the lamps. Thanks to the charity, thousands of homes in the Philippines now have Moser lamps. It has also made Moser lamps popular in other countries, such as Argentina, India, and Fiji. Moser lamps will light up the lives of many people for many years ⓑ<u>to come</u>.

서답형

19 위 글의 밑줄 친 ⓐinstall 앞에 생략된 말을 쓰시오.

➡ _____

20 아래 〈보기〉에서 위 글의 밑줄 친 ⓑto come과 문법적 쓰임이 <u>다른</u> 것의 개수를 고르시오.

┤ 보기 ├
① I think it necessary to do the work now.
② Sujin is happy to meet her old friends.
③ We are ready to leave for London.
④ He promised me to send a postcard to me from Paris.
⑤ This apron has no pocket to put things in.

① 1개　② 2개　③ 3개　④ 4개　⑤ 5개

위 글의 주제로 알맞은 것을 고르시오.

① the strong points of the Moser lamps
② people who work for the My Shelter Foundation
③ the remarkable activities of the My Shelter Foundation
④ the popularity of the Moser lamps
⑤ the long-lasting power of the Moser lamps

[22~24] 다음 글을 읽고 물음에 답하시오.

This amazing plastic bottle is called a Moser lamp because it was invented by Alfredo Moser. In 2002, there were many blackouts in his town in Brazil. These blackouts made him come up with a new way to light his house.

A Moser lamp can be made for ⓐabout one dollar and lasts for about 10 years. It is also very safe. ⓑIt can never start a house fire. Surprisingly, it is very easy to make this magic lamp.

22 위 글의 밑줄 친 ⓐabout과 같은 의미로 쓰인 것을 고르시오.

① Tell me all about it.
② It costs about $10.
③ The film is about poor boys.
④ There is nobody about.
⑤ What is he about?

서답형

23 위 글의 밑줄 친 ⓑIt이 가리키는 것을 본문에서 찾아 쓰시오.

➡ _____

24 위 글을 읽고 대답할 수 없는 질문은?

① What's the name of the amazing plastic bottle?
② Why did Alfredo Moser come up with a new way to light his house?
③ Is it expensive to make a Moser lamp?
④ How long does a Moser lamp last?
⑤ How long docs it takc to make a Moser lamp?

[25~27] 다음 글을 읽고 물음에 답하시오.

You can make ⓐa lot of things with a CD case. You can even make a grass container. First, fill half of the CD case with soil and water, and put grass seeds into the soil. Second, close the case and tape all of the sides. Finally, leave it in the sun (A)[during / for] about ten days. Now, your grass container is ready. It will make you (B)[happy / happily] when the grass (C)[grows / will grow].

서답형

25 위 글의 괄호 (A)~(C)에서 어법상 알맞은 낱말을 골라 쓰시오.

➡ (A) _____ (B) _____ (C) _____

26 위 글의 밑줄 친 ⓐa lot of와 바꿔 쓸 수 없는 말을 고르시오.

① lots of   ② many
③ plenty of   ④ a number of
⑤ much

서답형

27 CD 케이스로 잔디를 기르는 용기를 만드는 법을 우리말로 설명하시오.

➡ (1) _____
(2) _____
(3) _____

[01~03] 다음 글을 읽고 물음에 답하시오.

"Wow, I can read a book in my room now!" shouted Marco, a boy in a village in the Philippines. His house has no electricity just like all the other houses in the village. ⓐ People in the village are too poor to pay for electricity. Even during the daytime, they live in darkness ⓑ집들이 빽빽하게 들어차 있어서. Now things are changing because of a single plastic bottle. One plastic bottle in the ceiling can light up a whole room without using any electricity.

01 위 글의 밑줄 친 ⓐ를 다음과 같이 바꿔 쓸 때 빈칸에 들어갈 알맞은 말을 쓰시오.

➡ People in the village are _____ poor _____ they _____ pay for electricity.

02 위 글의 밑줄 친 ⓑ의 우리말에 맞게 한 단어를 보충하여, 주어진 어휘를 알맞게 배열하시오.

| together / packed / the houses / close / because |

➡ _____

03 다음 문장에서 위 글의 내용과 다른 부분을 찾아서 고치시오.

| Now people in Marco's village can light up a whole room with using some electricity by installing one plastic bottle in the ceiling. |

_____ ➡ _____

[04~06] 다음 글을 읽고 물음에 답하시오.

This amazing plastic bottle is called a Moser lamp because it was invented by Alfredo Moser. In ⓐ2002, there were many blackouts in his town in Brazil. These blackouts made him come up with ⓑa new way to light his house.

A Moser lamp can be made for about one dollar and lasts for about 10 years. It is also very safe. It can never start a house fire. Surprisingly, ⓒit is very easy to make this magic lamp.

04 위 글의 밑줄 친 ⓐ2002를 영어로 읽는 법을 쓰시오.

➡ _____

05 위 글의 밑줄 친 ⓑa new way to light his house가 가리키는 것을 본문에서 찾아 쓰시오.

➡ _____

06 위 글의 밑줄 친 ⓒ를 다음과 같이 바꿔 쓸 때 빈칸에 들어갈 알맞은 말을 쓰시오.

➡ (1) _____ _____ this magic lamp is very easy

(2) _____ this magic lamp is very easy

(3) _____ is very easy to make

[07~08] 다음 글을 읽고 물음에 답하시오.

In the Philippines, ⓐMoser lamps are widely used by the My Shelter Foundation. The charity also teaches local people how to make and install the lamps. Thanks to the charity, thousands of homes in the Philippines now have Moser lamps. ⓑIt has also made Moser lamps popularly in other countries, such as Argentina, India, and Fiji. Moser lamps will light up the lives of many people for many years to come.

07 위 글의 밑줄 친 ⓐ를 능동태로 고치시오.

➡ _____

또는 _____

08 위 글의 밑줄 친 ⓑ에서 어법상 틀린 부분을 찾아 고치시오.

_____ ➡ _____

[09~11] 다음 글을 읽고 물음에 답하시오.

This amazing plastic bottle is called a Moser lamp because it was invented by Alfredo Moser. In 2002, there were many blackouts in his town in Brazil. ⓐThese blackouts made him come up with a new way to light his house.
ⓑMoser 램프는 1달러 정도로 만들 수 있고 10년 정도 지속된다. It is also very safe. It can never start a house fire. Surprisingly, it is very easy to make this magic lamp.

09 위 글의 밑줄 친 ⓐ를 다음과 같이 바꿔 쓸 때 빈칸에 들어 갈 알맞은 말을 쓰시오.

➡ _____ these blackouts, he came up with a new way to light his house.

10 위 글의 밑줄 친 ⓑ의 우리말에 맞게 한 단어를 보충하여, 주어진 어휘를 알맞게 배열하시오.

lasts / a Moser lamp / for about 10 years / about one dollar / can be made / and

➡ _____

_____

11 위 글에 나타난 Moser lamp의 장점 네 가지를 우리말로 쓰 시오.

➡ (1) _____ (2) _____
(3) _____ (4) _____

[12~13] 다음 글을 읽고 물음에 답하시오.

In the Philippines, Moser lamps are (A)[wide / widely] used by the My Shelter Foundation. The charity also teaches local people (B)[how / what] to make and install the lamps. ⓐThanks to the charity, thousands of homes in the Philippines now have Moser lamps. It has also made Moser lamps popular in other countries, such as Argentina, India, and Fiji. Moser lamps will (C)[light up / lighten up] the lives of many people for many years to come.

12 위 글의 괄호 (A)~(C)에서 문맥이나 어법상 알맞은 낱말을 골라 쓰시오.

➡ (A) _____ (B) _____ (C) _____

13 위 글의 밑줄 친 ⓐ를 다음과 같이 바꿔 쓸 때 빈칸에 들어 갈 알맞은 말을 쓰시오.

➡ The charity makes it possible for thousands of homes in the Philippines _____ now.

교과서

구석구석

Link - Share

We thought we could make the lamp brighter with a glass bottle. We made one
　　　　　we 앞에 접속사 that 생략　　　　　　　　　　　　　[도구·수단] ~으로, ~을 사용하여

lamp out of a plastic bottle and another lamp out of a glass bottle. All the other
　　　　~으로 (= from)　　　　　　　　　another+단수 명사　　　　　　　　　다른 모든 단계들(복수에 주의)

steps were the same. We learned that the glass bottle lamp was brighter than
　　　　　　　　　　　　　　　　　알았다　　　　　　　　　　　　　　　　비교급

the plastic bottle lamp.

구문해설　• make A out of B: B로 A를 만들다

해석

> 우리는 우리가 램프를 유리병으로 더 밝게 만들 수 있다고 생각했다. 우리는 플라스틱병으로 램프를 하나 만들고 유리병으로 또 다른 하나를 만들었다. 다른 모든 단계는 똑같았다. 우리는 유리병 램프가 플라스틱병 램프보다 더 밝다는 것을 알았다.

Write

You can make a lot of things with a CD case. You can even make a grass
　　　　　　　= many

container. First, fill half of the CD case with soil and water, and put grass
　　　　　　　　└ fill A with B: A를 B로 채우다 ┘

seeds into the soil. Second, close the case and tape all of the sides. Finally,
　　　　　　　　　　　　　　(동사) 닫다　　　　　　　　　　　　　　　= Lastly

leave it in the sun for about ten days. Now, your grass container is ready.
　　= the case　　　　　약

It will make you happy when the grass grows.
5형식 구문으로, 목적격보어의 자리에 형용사 happy를 쓰는 것이 적절하다.

구문해설　• container: 그릇, 용기　• seed: 씨, 씨앗　• tape: (테이프로) 붙이다; 테이프

> 당신은 CD 케이스로 많은 것들을 만들 수 있다. 당신은 심지어 잔디를 기르는 용기를 만들 수도 있다. 먼저 CD 케이스의 절반을 흙과 물로 채우고, 잔디 씨앗을 흙 안에 넣어라. 두 번째, 케이스를 닫고 모든 옆면에 테이프를 붙여라. 마지막으로, 햇빛이 비치는 곳에 약 10일 동안 놓아 두어라. 이제, 당신의 잔디를 기르는 용기가 준비되었다. 잔디가 자랄 때 그것은 당신을 행복히 만들이 줄 것이다.

Culture Project - Share

We'd like to talk about a pot-in-pot cooler. It keeps food fresh without
~하고 싶다(= want to)　　　　　　　　　　　　　　　keep+목적어+목적격보어(형용사)

electricity. It's very easy to make one. First, put a pot inside a larger pot. Then,
　　　　　　　　　가주어　　　　진주어

pour sand and water between these pots. Just let the water dry off, and it'll
　　　　　　　　　　　　　　　　　　　　let(사역동사)+목적어+동사원형

cool the food.

구문해설　• cooler 냉장고　• fresh 신선한　• electricity 전기　• pot 항아리　• inside ~ 안에
　　　　　　• pour 붓다　• dry off 마르다

> 우리는 pot-in-pot cooler (항아리 냉장고)에 대해 이야기하고 싶다. 그것은 전기 없이 식품을 신선하게 유지할 수 있다. 그것을 만드는 것은 매우 쉽다. 우선, 항아리 하나를 더 큰 항아리에 넣는다. 그리고 항아리들 사이에 모래와 물을 넣는다. 물이 그저 마르게 두면, 그것이 음식을 시원하게 할 것이다.

Words & Expressions

01 다음 주어진 두 단어의 관계가 같도록 빈칸에 주어진 철자로 단어를 쓰시오.

> shout : yell = set up : i_____

02 우리말에 맞게 밑줄 친 'hang'을 이용하여 빈칸을 완성하시오.

> 옷걸이에 옷을 거는 것을 잊지 마.
> Don't forget to hang your clothes on the
> _____.

03 다음 〈보기〉의 단어를 사용하여 자연스러운 문장을 만들 수 없는 것은?

> ┌ 보기 ┐
> volume / install / leftovers / lamp / forward

① Can you turn down the _____, please?
② Don't _____ rumors about other people.
③ It is good to take the _____ home to avoid waste.
④ Turn on the _____ when it gets dark.
⑤ Let's step _____ to take a closer look.

04 다음 빈칸에 어울리는 단어를 고르시오.

> His house has no electricity just like all the other houses in the village. People in the village are too poor to _____ electricity.

① save
② invent
③ turn off
④ dry off
⑤ pay for

05 다음 우리말에 해당하는 단어를 주어진 철자로 시작하여 쓰시오.

> 이제 플라스틱병 하나 때문에 상황이 바뀌고 있다.
> Now t_____ are changing because of a single plastic bottle.

Conversation

[06~07] 다음 대화를 읽고 물음에 답하시오.

> W: Excuse me, ⓐare you finished with your meal?
> M: Yes, it was ⓑreally good.
> W: Do you want to ⓒtake the leftovers home?
> M: Yes, please.
> W: ⓓDon't forget eating the leftovers ⓔby tomorrow.

06 위 대화의 ⓐ~ⓔ 중 어법상 어색한 것은?

① ⓐ ② ⓑ ③ ⓒ ④ ⓓ ⑤ ⓔ

07 다음에 주어진 영어 설명에 해당하는 단어를 위 대화에서 찾아 그 단어와 뜻을 쓰시오.

> <영어 설명> food remaining after a meal

➡ _____

[08~09] 다음 대화를 읽고 물음에 답하시오.

> B: What's your plan for this winter break? (①)
> G: I'm going to visit Hong Kong with my parents. (②)
> B: That sounds exciting. (③)
> G: I'm going to go to an amusement park. (④) I'm also going to try all kinds of food. (⑤)
> B: Good. _____(A)

08 위 대화의 (①)~(⑤) 중 주어진 문장이 들어갈 위치로 알맞은 것은?

> What are you going to do there?

①   ②   ③   ④   ⑤

09 빈칸 (A)에 들어갈 말로 알맞은 것은?

① Don't forget to bring your lunch.
② Don't forget to return those books.
③ Don't forget to try some dim sum.
④ Don't forget to visit my grandma.
⑤ Don't forget to go hiking.

10 다음 중 두 사람의 대화가 어색한 것은?

① A: Excuse me, are you finished with your meal?
   B: Yes, it was really good.
② A: I've heard that a movie star is coming to our school.
   B: That's right. She's my favorite actress.
③ A: Don't forget to recycle the cans and bottles.
   B: Sure, I will.
④ A: I've heard you didn't come to school yesterday.
   B: I got a bad cold.
⑤ A: I've heard the car was invented earlier than the bicycle.
   B: Really? That's interesting.

[11~12] 다음 대화를 읽고 물음에 답하시오.

> Yuri: What's wrong, Jaden?
> Jaden: My science homework is too difficult.
> Yuri: What do you have to do?
> Jaden: I need to find a way to save trees.
> Yuri: That's easy. I've heard that we can save trees by using less paper.
> Jaden: Oh, I think I've heard that, too. Then, I can just stop using paper cups.
> Yuri: Yes! You can also use just one paper towel to dry off your hands.
> Jaden: That's impossible. I need at least two or three paper towels.
> Yuri: Just shake your hands before you use a paper towel. Then, one will be more than enough.
> Jaden: Oh, that's a good idea, Yuri! I'll try that next time.
> Yuri: Good! Just don't forget to shake your hands at least 10 times.

11 다음 물음에 대한 답을 대화에서 찾아 9단어의 영어로 답하시오.

> Q: What does Yuri suggest to Jaden?

➡ _____

12 위 대화를 읽고 답할 수 없는 질문은?

① What are the speakers talking about?
② What does Jaden have to do for his science homework?
③ How can we use only one paper towel to dry off our hands?
④ According to Yuri, how can we save trees?
⑤ How many paper towels does Yuri use a day?

Grammar

13 다음 중 어법상 바르지 <u>않은</u> 것은?

① Please let me go.

② I had my hair cut at a famous salon last week.

③ I saw him getting on a bus.

④ Mom made me wash the dishes after dinner.

⑤ He got his car wash yesterday.

14 다음 그림을 보고 괄호 안에 주어진 어휘를 이용하여 빈칸에 알맞은 말을 쓰시오.

My father made me _____ the tree.
(plant)

15 주어진 어휘를 알맞게 배열하여 다음 우리말을 영어로 옮기시오.

그녀는 텔레비전이 시간 낭비라고 생각해서 그녀의 아이들이 TV를 보게 하지 않는다.
(she, she, her children, a waste, television, TV, time, is, watch, doesn't, thinks, let, so, of)

➡ _____

_____

16 다음 문장을 주어진 어휘로 시작하는 문장으로 바꿔 쓰시오.

(1) When my daughter was born, I was happy.

➡ My daughter's birth made
_____. (2단어)

(2) When she heard about the accident, she got nervous.

➡ Hearing about the accident made
_____. (2단어)

17 다음 빈칸에 공통으로 들어갈 말로 가장 알맞은 것은?

- She couldn't _____ them silent.
- Mike, _____ your room clean.

① ask   ② find   ③ keep
④ take   ⑤ tell

18 다음 중 어법상 바른 문장의 개수는?

ⓐ My brother got his robot to do his homework.

ⓑ I heard my name called.

ⓒ My parents won't let me to go out late at night.

ⓓ It will help me improving my English.

ⓔ I'll make my robot tell funny stories.

ⓕ Being sick makes me sad.

ⓖ Eating an apple a day can make us healthily.

ⓗ My father always keeps his car clean and shiny.

ⓘ I like the music because it always makes me relaxed.

① 2개   ② 3개   ③ 4개   ④ 5개   ⑤ 6개

19 다음 빈칸에 공통으로 들어갈 말은?

> • Sunny days _____ me happy.
> • I'll _____ my robot cook for me.

① have   ② find   ③ let
④ make   ⑤ take

[20~21] 다음 빈칸에 알맞은 것은?

20

> Eddie's room is not tidy. I'll make him keep it _____.

① clean   ② cleans   ③ cleaned
④ cleaning   ⑤ to clean

21

> Emily had her boy friend _____ some games with her sisters.

① play   ② plays   ③ played
④ playing   ⑤ to play

22 다음 밑줄 친 단어의 쓰임이 주어진 문장과 같은 것은?

> He made me wash his car yesterday.

① Harry wanted to make me a bowl of spaghetti.
② The heavy snowstorm made us stay at home.
③ They wonder if taking a foot bath can make us relaxed.
④ We made him captain.
⑤ Do you know what made her upset?

Reading

[23~24] 다음 글을 읽고 물음에 답하시오.

> "Wow, I can read a book in my room now!" shouted Marco, a boy in a village in the

Philippines. His house has no electricity just ⓐlike all the other houses in the village. People in the village are too poor to pay for electricity. Even during the daytime, they live in darkness because the houses are packed close together. Now things are changing because of a single plastic bottle. One plastic bottle in the ceiling can light up a whole room without ___(A)___ any electricity.

23 위 글의 빈칸 (A)에 use를 알맞은 형태로 쓰시오.

➡ _____

24 위 글의 밑줄 친 ⓐlike와 같은 의미로 쓰인 것을 모두 고르시오.

① He ran like the wind.
② They responded in like manner.
③ I like to paint in my spare time.
④ What do you like about him?
⑤ She acts like a fool.

[25~27] 다음 글을 읽고 물음에 답하시오.

> This amazing plastic bottle is called a Moser lamp because it was invented by Alfredo Moser. In 2002, there were many blackouts in his town in Brazil. These blackouts made him come up with a new way to light his house.
>
> A Moser lamp can be made for about one dollar and lasts for about 10 years. It is also very safe. It can never start a house fire. Surprisingly, it is very easy ⓐto make this magic lamp.

25 What made Alfredo Moser come up with a new way to light his house? Fill in the blanks with suitable words.

➡ _____ in his town in Brazil in 2002 made him do so.

26 위 글의 밑줄 친 ⓐto make와 to부정사의 용법이 다른 것을 모두 고르시오.

① He decided to sell his car.
② He is looking for friends to go camping with.
③ My dream is to become a famous actor.
④ That club is not easy to join.
⑤ I found it useless to teach him math.

27 위 글의 내용과 일치하지 않는 것은?

① 이 놀라운 플라스틱병은 발명가의 이름을 따서 Moser 램프라고 불린다.
② 2002년, 브라질에 있는 Alfredo Moser의 마을에는 정전이 잦았다.
③ Moser 램프는 1달러 정도로 만들 수 있고 10년 정도 지속된다.
④ Moser 램프는 매우 안전해서 절대 집에 불을 낼 수 없다.
⑤ 이 신기한 램프를 만드는 것은 다소 어렵다.

[28~30] 다음 글을 읽고 물음에 답하시오.

1. Fill a clear plastic bottle with water.
2. Add some ___ⓐ___ to keep the water (A) [clear / clearly].
3. Make a hole in the roof, and push the bottle into the hole.
4. Let (B)[a third / a thirds] of the bottle remain above the roof.
5. Sunlight (C)[bends / is bent] by the water in the bottle and spreads around the room.

28 주어진 영영풀이를 참고하여 빈칸 ⓐ에 철자 b로 시작하는 단어를 쓰시오.

a chemical that is used to make cloth white

➡ _____

29 위 글의 괄호 (A)~(C)에서 어법상 알맞은 낱말을 골라 쓰시오.

➡ (A) _____ (B) _____ (C) _____

30 위 글의 제목으로 가장 알맞은 것을 고르시오.

① How to Use a Clear Plastic Bottle
② Are There Any Ways to Use Natural Resources?
③ Is It Easy to Make a Hole in the Roof?
④ How to Make a Moser Lamp from a Bottle
⑤ We Must Use Sunlight Effectively!

[31~32] 다음 글을 읽고 물음에 답하시오.

You can make a lot of things with a wire hanger. You can even make a book holder. First, bend a wire hanger in the middle. Second, bend both ends up and forward. ___ⓐ___, bend down the top part of the hanger. Now, your book holder is ready. ⓑIt will keep your hands free.

31 위 글의 빈칸 ⓐ에 들어갈 알맞은 말을 모두 고르시오.

① Lastly   ② At last
③ In the end   ④ Finally
⑤ As a result

32 위 글의 밑줄 친 ⓑIt이 가리키는 것을 본문에서 찾아 쓰시오.

➡ _____

단원별 예상문제

출제율 85%

01 다음 두 단어의 관계가 같도록 빈칸에 알맞은 말을 쓰시오.

> popular : unpopular = dangerous : _____

출제율 95%

02 우리말에 맞게 빈칸 (A), (B)에 알맞은 단어를 쓰시오.

> • 심지어 낮 동안에도, 집들이 빽빽하게 들어차 있어서 그들은 어둠 속에 살아간다.
> Even during the daytime, they live in darkness because the houses are (A)_____ close together.
> • 이 자선단체 덕분에, 필리핀의 수천 가구가 이제 Moser 램프를 갖고 있다.
> (B)_____ the charity, thousands of homes in the Philippines now have Moser lamps.

[03~04] 다음 영영풀이에 해당하는 단어를 찾으시오.

출제율 90%

03

> a strong chemical used for cleaning things or removing colour from things

① lamp   ② thing
③ bleach   ④ magic
⑤ paint

출제율 90%

04

> to cover, reach, or have an effect on a wider or increasing area

① cross   ② last
③ shout   ④ spend
⑤ spread

[05~06] 다음 대화를 읽고 물음에 답하시오.

> G: Can you ①turn up the volume on your phone? I like this song.
> B: I can't ②turn up it anymore. It's ③the highest volume.
> G: Let me just put your phone in a glass. ④I've heard a glass works like a speaker.
> B: ⑤What an interesting idea! Let's (A)try it now.

출제율 100%

05 위 대화의 ①~⑤ 중 어법상 어색한 것은?

①   ②   ③   ④   ⑤

출제율 90%

06 위 대화의 밑줄 친 (A)try it이 의미하는 것을 본문에서 찾아 6단어로 쓰시오.

➡ _____

출제율 95%

07 다음 대화의 빈칸에 들어갈 말로 알맞은 것은?

> B: I've heard that a movie star is coming to our school.
> G: That's right. She's my favorite actress.
> B: Oh, who is she?
> G: Miranda Kim. She played the chief scientist in the movie *Jupiter*.
> B: Wow, _____

① I can't wait to see her!
② don't forget to take something to eat.
③ don't forget to take lots of rest.
④ I know that.
⑤ how wonderful you are!

출제율 95%

08 다음 대화의 밑줄 친 우리말에 맞게 주어진 단어를 알맞은 순서로 배열하시오.

> **A:** I've heard that saving electricity is the best way to save the Earth.
> **B:** I've heard that, too. What can we do to save electricity?
> **A:** Why don't we turn off the light when we're not using it?
> **B:** That's a good idea. 방을 나갈 때 불 끄는 것을 잊지 마. (turn off / when / don't / to / you / leave / forget / the light / your room)

➡ _____

_____

[09~10] 다음 대화를 읽고 물음에 답하시오.

> **Yuri:** What's wrong, Jaden?
> **Jaden:** My science homework is too difficult.
> **Yuri:** What do you have to do?
> **Jaden:** I need to find a way to ⓐsave trees.
> **Yuri:** That's easy. I've heard that we can save trees by using ⓑless paper.
> **Jaden:** Oh, I think I've heard that, too. Then, I can just ⓒstop using paper cups.
> **Yuri:** Yes! You can also use just one paper towel to dry off your hands.
> **Jaden:** That's ⓓpossible. I need at least two or three paper towels.
> **Yuri:** Just shake your hands before you use a paper towel. Then, _____(A)_____.
> **Jaden:** Oh, that's a good idea, Yuri! I'll try that next time.
> **Yuri:** Good! Just ⓔdon't forget to shake your hands at least 10 times.

출제율 90%

09 위 대화의 빈칸 (A)에 들어갈 말로 알맞은 것은?

① you will have to save trees
② you will need more paper towels
③ you will stop using paper cups
④ your hands will be dried up faster
⑤ one will be more than enough

출제율 95%

10 위 대화의 밑줄 친 ⓐ~ⓔ 중, 어휘의 쓰임이 어색한 것은?

① ⓐ　　② ⓑ　　③ ⓒ　　④ ⓓ　　⑤ ⓔ

[11~12] 어법상 바른 문장을 모두 고르시오.

출제율 95%

11 ① You'd better have the tooth pulled out.
② Let him joining your club.
③ He made me to introduce myself.
④ She had Mike called me.
⑤ She got me to walk her dog.

출제율 100%

12 ① We found the window break.
② I saw him sang in front of students.
③ She left him alone.
④ The novel made her famous.
⑤ Let's keep the room clean.

출제율 90%

13 다음 우리말을 주어진 어휘를 이용하여 영작하시오.

(1) 이 영화는 그 배우들을 유명하게 만들었다. (make, famous)

➡ _____

(2) 내 부모님은 내가 열심히 공부하도록 시키신다. (make, hard)

➡ _____

14 다음 문장에서 어법상 틀린 부분을 찾아 바르게 고치시오.

> He got me wash the dishes.

➡ _____ ➡ _____

[15~16] 다음 글을 읽고 물음에 답하시오.

"Wow, I can read a book in my room now!" shouted Marco, a boy in a village in the Philippines. His house has no electricity just like all the other houses in the village. ⓐ마을 사람들은 너무나 가난해서 전기세를 낼 수가 없다. Even (A)[during / while] the daytime, they live in darkness because the houses are (B)[packing / packed] close together. Now things are changing because of a single plastic bottle. One plastic bottle in the ceiling can light up a whole room without using (C)[any / no] electricity.

15 위 글의 밑줄 친 ⓐ의 우리말에 맞게 주어진 어휘를 이용하여 11단어로 영작하시오.

> people, too, pay for

➡ _____

16 위 글의 괄호 (A)~(C)에서 어법상 알맞은 낱말을 골라 쓰시오.

➡ (A) _____ (B) _____ (C) _____

[17~19] 다음 글을 읽고 물음에 답하시오.

(A)This amazing plastic bottle is called a Moser lamp because it was invented ① by Alfredo Moser. ②In 2002, there were many blackouts in his town in Brazil. These blackouts made him come up ③with a new way to light his house.

A Moser lamp can be made ④by about one dollar and lasts ⑤for about 10 years. It is also very safe. It can never start a house fire. Surprisingly, ⓐit is very easy to make this magic lamp.

17 위 글의 밑줄 친 ①~⑤ 중 전치사의 쓰임이 어색한 것을 찾아 고치시오.

_____ 번 ➡ _____

18 위 글의 밑줄 친 ⓐit과 문법적 쓰임이 다른 것을 모두 고르시오.

① I gave it to her.
② It is impossible to master English in a month or two.
③ They considered it impossible for us to climb the mountain.
④ How far is it from here to the station?
⑤ It is strange that he says so.

19 위 글을 읽고 밑줄 친 (A)This amazing plastic bottle에 대해 알 수 없는 것을 고르시오.

① 이름 ② 발명가 ③ 발명 동기
④ 제작비 ⑤ 제작 방법

[20~21] 다음 글을 읽고 물음에 답하시오.

How to make a Moser lamp from a bottle
1. Fill a clear plastic bottle with water.
2. Add some bleach ⓐ물을 깨끗이 유지하기 위해.
3. Make a hole in the roof, and push the bottle into the hole.
4. Let a third of the bottle remain above the roof.
5. Sunlight is bent by the water in the bottle and spreads around the room.

출제율 90%

20 위 글의 밑줄 친 ⓐ의 우리말을 다섯 단어로 쓰시오.

➡ _____

출제율 100%

21 위 글을 읽고 대답할 수 <u>없는</u> 질문은?

① What do you need to make a Moser lamp?
② Why do you need to add some bleach?
③ Where do you install a Moser lamp?
④ How long does it take to install a Moser lamp?
⑤ How does a Moser lamp operate?

[22~24] 다음 글을 읽고 물음에 답하시오.

In the Philippines, Moser lamps are widely used by the My Shelter ⓐFoundation. ⓑ또한 그 자선단체는 지역 사람들에게 램프를 만들고 설치하는 법을 가르친다. Thanks to the charity, thousands of homes in the Philippines now have Moser lamps. It has also made Moser lamps popular in other countries, such as Argentina, India, and Fiji. Moser lamps will light up the lives of many people for many years to come.

출제율 85%

22 위 글의 밑줄 친 ⓐFoundation과 같은 의미로 쓰인 것을 고르시오.

① These stories have no foundation.
② They are getting enough financial support from a religious foundation.
③ The organization has grown enormously since its foundation in 1955.
④ The rumour is totally without foundation.
⑤ The holiday is also called the National Foundation Day of Korea.

출제율 95%

23 위 글의 밑줄 친 ⓑ의 우리말에 맞게 한 단어를 보충하여, 주어진 어휘를 알맞게 배열하시오.

to make / also / the lamps / local people / teaches / and / the charity / install

➡ _____

_____

출제율 100%

24 다음 중 'My Shelter Foundation'의 활동에 대한 설명으로 옳지 <u>않은</u> 것을 고르시오.

① 필리핀에서 My Shelter Foundation에 의해 Moser 램프가 널리 사용된다.
② 지역 사람들에게 램프를 만드는 법을 가르친다.
③ 지역 사람들에게 램프를 설치하는 법을 가르친다.
④ 필리핀의 수만 가구가 이제 Moser 램프를 갖게 해주었다.
⑤ 아르헨티나, 인도, 피지와 같은 다른 나라들에서도 Moser 램프가 유명해지도록 만들었다.

[01~02] 다음 대화를 읽고 물음에 답하시오.

Yuri: What's wrong, Jaden?

Jaden: My science homework is too difficult.

Yuri: What do you have to do?

Jaden: I need to find a way to save trees.

Yuri: That's easy. _____ (A)

Jaden: Oh, I think I've heard that, too. Then, I can just stop using paper cups.

Yuri: Yes! You can also use just one paper towel to dry off your hands.

Jaden: That's impossible. I need at least two or three paper towels.

Yuri: (B)종이 수건을 쓰기 전에 손을 털어 봐. Then, one will be more than enough.

Jaden: Oh, that's a good idea, Yuri! I'll try that next time.

Yuri: Good! Just don't forget to shake your hands at least 10 times.

01 위 대화의 빈칸 (A)에 들어갈 표현을 주어진 〈조건〉에 맞게 영어로 쓰시오.

┤ 조건 ├

• 어떤 사실을 들어서 알고 있음을 말할 때 사용하는 표현을 쓸 것

• 'hear'를 이용하여 현재완료로 표현할 것

• 'that'절에 'save trees', 'by', 'less'를 이용하여 '우리가 종이를 덜 사용함으로써 나무들을 살릴 수 있다'는 우리말에 맞게 쓸 것

➡ _____

02 위 대화의 밑줄 친 우리말에 맞게 주어진 단어를 알맞은 순서로 배열하시오.

hands / before / shake / just / your / you / a / use / paper / towel

➡ _____

03 다음 문장의 빈칸에 들어갈 말을 주어진 〈조건〉에 맞게 영어로 쓰시오.

B: What's your plan for this winter break?

G: I'm going to visit Vietnam with my parents.

B: That sounds exciting. What are you going to do there?

G: I'm going to spend some time on the beach and eat lots of seafood.

B: Good. _____, too.

G: O.K., I won't forget.

┤ 조건 ├

• 상대방에게 상기시키는 표현을 쓸 것

• '~할 것을 잊지 마'라는 뜻으로 쓸 것

• 'try the fruit there'라는 표현을 사용할 것

➡ _____

04 다음 우리말을 주어진 어휘를 이용하여 영작하시오.

(1) 나는 사촌의 생일잔치에 가고 싶지 않았으나 엄마가 나를 가도록 하셨다. (my cousin, my mom, make)

➡ _____

_____

(2) 그들은 그들의 집이 칠해지도록 시켰다. (have, their house, paint)

➡ _____

_____

(3) 그 선물은 그 아이들을 종일 행복하게 해 주었다. (present, make, all day long)

➡ _____

_____

05 다음 문장에서 어법상 <u>어색한</u> 것을 고쳐 다시 쓰시오.

(1) The noise kept me wake.

➤ _____

(2) He found the exam difficultly.

➤ _____

(3) These blackouts made him to come up with a new way to light his house.

➤ _____

_____

(4) He had his computer repair yesterday.

➤ _____

(5) Help me taking some pictures of them.

➤ _____

[06~08] 다음 글을 읽고 물음에 답하시오.

ⒶThis amazing plastic bottle is called a Moser lamp because it was invented by Alfredo Moser. In 2002, there were many blackouts in his town in Brazil. These blackouts made him come up with a new way to light his house.

A Moser lamp can be made for about one dollar and lasts for about 10 years. It is also very safe. It can never start a house fire. Surprisingly, it is very easy to make this magic lamp.

06 위 글의 밑줄 친 @를 능동태로 고치시오.

➤ _____

_____

07 주어진 영영풀이에 해당하는 단어를 위 글에서 찾아 쓰시오.

> periods of time during which the electricity supply to a place is temporarily cut off

➤ _____

08 본문의 내용과 일치하도록 다음 빈칸에 알맞은 단어를 쓰시오.

> We can say that a Moser lamp is _____ _____ because it can never start a house fire.

[09~10] 다음 글을 읽고 물음에 답하시오.

In the Philippines, Moser lamps are widely used by the My Shelter Foundation. @The charity also teaches local people how to make and install the lamps. ⒷThanks to the charity, thousand of homes in the Philippines now have Moser lamps. It has also made Moser lamps popular in other countries, such as Argentina, India, and Fiji. Moser lamps will light up the lives of many people for many years to come.

09 위 글의 밑줄 친 @The charity가 가리키는 것을 본문에서 찾아 쓰시오.

➤ _____

10 위 글의 밑줄 친 Ⓑ에서 어법상 틀린 부분을 찾아 고치시오.

_____ ➤ _____

01 상자 안의 Plan과 Advice를 읽고 어울리는 것끼리 연결하여, 계획과 조언을 말하는 대화를 〈보기〉와 같이 작성하시오.

Plan	Advice
go to Gyeongju go on a field trip	visit the National Museum take something to eat

---

보기

- Plan: go hiking   • Advice: take a bottle of water
A: I'm going to go hiking.
B: Don't forget to take a bottle of water.
A: O.K., I won't forget.

---

02 다음 문장을 make를 이용하여 비슷한 의미의 문장으로 바꿔 쓰시오.

(1) Mom told me to do the dishes this morning.
(2) The doctor ordered him to stop smoking.
(3) Miranda asked her husband to buy some fruit.

(1) _____
(2) _____
(3) _____

03 다음 내용을 바탕으로 자신이 만들고 싶은 물건에 관한 글을 쓰시오.

a book holder
1. Bend a wire hanger in the middle.
2. Bend both ends up and forward.
3. Bend down the top part of the hanger.
4. Put your book on the book holder.

You can make a lot of things with a (A)_____. You can even make a book holder. First, (B)_____ a wire hanger in the middle. Second, bend (C)_____ up and forward. Finally, bend down the (D)_____ of the hanger. Now, your book holder is ready. It will keep your hands (E)_____.

단원별 모의고사

01 다음 단어에 대한 영어 설명이 <u>어색한</u> 것은?

① roof: the covering that forms the top of a building, vehicle, etc

② last: to continue to exist

③ invent: to design and/or create something that has never been made before

④ install: to put furniture, a machine, or a piece of equipment into position and make it ready to use

⑤ surprisingly: including a lot of different places, people, subjects, etc

02 다음 우리말에 맞게 빈칸에 알맞은 단어를 쓰시오.

(1) 나는 나무를 심기 위해 구멍을 파고 있다.

➡ I am digging a _____ to plant a tree.

(2) 전선을 구부릴 때 적절한 도구를 사용해라.

➡ Use the right tools when you bend a _____.

03 다음 영영풀이에 해당하는 단어를 고르시오.

a system of giving money, food, or help free to those who are in need because they are ill, poor, or have no home, or any organization that has the purpose of providing money or helping in this way

① company   ② charity

③ kingdom   ④ government

⑤ foundation

04 빈칸에 들어갈 단어를 영어 설명을 보고 주어진 철자로 시작하여 쓰시오.

This a_____ plastic bottle is called a Moser lamp because it was invented by Alfredo Moser.

<영어 설명>

extremely surprising

05 대화의 빈칸에 들어갈 말은?

B: I've heard that a famous baseball player is coming to our school.

G: That's right. He's my favorite player.

B: Oh, who is he?

G: I'm not going to tell you. _____

① I won't forget.

② I've heard that, too.

③ Sorry to hear that.

④ It's a surprise!

⑤ I had a great time there.

06 주어진 문장에 이어질 글의 순서로 알맞은 것은?

W: Excuse me, are you finished with your meal?

(A) Yes, please.

(B) Do you want to take the leftovers home?

(C) Yes, it was really good.

(D) Don't forget to eat the leftovers by tomorrow.

① (A) – (B) – (C) – (D)

② (B) – (C) – (A) – (D)

③ (C) – (A) – (D) – (B)

④ (C) – (B) – (A) – (D)

⑤ (D) – (B) – (C) – (A)

07 대화의 밑줄 친 ①~⑤ 중 어휘의 쓰임이 어색한 것은?

A: I've heard that ①saving electricity is the best way to ②save the Earth.

B: I've heard that, too. What can we do to save electricity?

A: Why don't we ③turn off the light when we're not using it?

B: That's a good idea. Don't ④forget to turn off the light when you ⑤enter your room.

①   ②   ③   ④   ⑤

08 다음 중 짝지어진 대화가 어색한 것은?

① A: I'm going to the supermarket.

    B: Don't forget to buy some toilet paper. We're running out of it.

② A: Tom, are you finished with your art homework?

    B: Yes, I'm almost done.

③ A: I've heard the school soccer team won the soccer match.

    B: Really? That's nice.

④ A: I've heard the school gym is going to open next month.

    B: I will, thanks.

⑤ A: You know what? I've heard the car was invented earlier than the bicycle.

    B: Really? That's interesting.

[09~10] 다음 대화를 읽고 요약문의 빈칸을 완성하시오.

09

B: What's your plan for this winter break?

G: I'm going to visit Hong Kong with my parents.

B: That sounds exciting. What are you going to do there?

G: I'm going to go to an amusement park. I'm also going to try all kinds of food.

B: Good. Don't forget to try some dim sum.

⬇

The girl is going to visit Hong Kong with _____ during this _____. She is going to go to an _____, and she will also try all kinds of _____. And the boy suggests that she try some _____.

10

B: I've heard that a movie star is coming to our school.

G: That's right. She's my favorite actress.

B: Oh, who is she?

G: Miranda Kim. She played the chief scientist in the movie *Jupiter*.

B: Wow, I can't wait to see her!

⬇

The boy has _____ that a _____ is coming to their school. Actually, the movie star is the girl's _____ _____. Her name is Miranda Kim, and she _____ the _____ scientist in the movie *Jupiter*.

[11~12] 다음 대화를 읽고 물음에 답하시오.

Yuri: What's wrong, Jaden?

Jaden: My science homework is too difficult.

Yuri: What do you have to do?

Jaden: I need to find a way to save trees.

Yuri: That's easy. _____(A)_____

Jaden: Oh, I think I've heard that, too. Then, I can just stop using paper cups.

Yuri: Yes! You can also use just one paper towel to dry off your hands.

Jaden: That's impossible. I need at least two or three paper towels.

Yuri: Just shake your hands before you use a paper towel. Then, one will be more than enough.

Jaden: Oh, that's a good idea, Yuri! I'll try that next time.

Yuri: Good! Just don't forget to shake your hands at least 10 times.

11 빈칸 (A)에 알맞은 말은?

① I've heard that drinking coffee very often isn't good for our health.

② I've never been to the Chinese restaurant.

③ I've heard that we can save trees by using less paper.

④ I've heard that we have to plant as many trees as possible.

⑤ I've heard that using paper cups is a way to save the earth.

12 위 대화를 읽고 다음 질문에 대해 영어로 답하시오.

Q: How can we use only one paper towel to dry off our hands?

➡ We can _____
_____ .

13 다음 그림을 보고 괄호 안에 주어진 어휘를 이용하여 주어진 대화의 빈칸을 한 단어씩 알맞게 채우시오.

A: Did you like the sandwich?
B: Yes, I did. Having delicious sandwiches always makes _____ _____. (happy)

14 다음 중 어법상 바르지 <u>않은</u> 것은?

① I don't want to have my picture take by a stranger.

② Don't make me say that again.

③ I won't let the cake be touched.

④ Let's keep the classroom clean.

⑤ The song has made him popular.

15 다음 중 어법상 <u>어색한</u> 부분을 바르게 고치시오.

(1) They took care of the apartment and kept it tidily.

_____ ➡ _____

(2) Dad had the tree plant.

_____ ➡ _____

16 주어진 문장의 밑줄 친 부분과 용법이 <u>다른</u> 하나는?

My brother always <u>makes</u> me clean the room.

① The dance <u>makes</u> me pleased.

② Playing the game <u>made</u> me excited.

③ Her mom <u>made</u> her a dress.

④ I will <u>make</u> her call you tomorrow.

⑤ He <u>made</u> me buy the book.

17 다음 글에서 어법상 틀린 부분을 찾아 바르게 고쳐 쓰시오.

Sam really wanted a dog, but his parents didn't let him to have a pet.

_____ ➡ _____

[18~20] 다음 글을 읽고 물음에 답하시오.

"Wow, I can read a book in my room now!" shouted Marco, a boy in a village in (A) [Philippines / the Philippines]. His house has no electricity just like all the other houses in the village. People in the village are _____ⓐ_____ poor _____ⓑ_____ pay for electricity. Even during the daytime, they live in darkness (B) [because / because of] the houses are packed close together. Now things are changing (C) [because / because of] a single plastic bottle. One plastic bottle in the ceiling can light up a whole room without using any electricity.

18 위 글의 빈칸 ⓐ와 ⓑ에 들어갈 알맞은 말을 고르시오.

① so – that
② too – to
③ such – that
④ so – as to
⑤ enough – to

19 위 글의 괄호 (A)~(C)에서 어법상 알맞은 낱말을 골라 쓰시오.

➡ (A) _____ (B) _____

(C) _____

20 Does a plastic bottle in the ceiling need any electricity to light up a whole room? Answer in English in a full sentence. (3 words)

➡ _____

[21~22] 다음 글을 읽고 물음에 답하시오.

This amazing plastic bottle is called a Moser lamp ⓐbecause it was invented by Alfredo Moser. In 2002, there were many blackouts in his town in Brazil. ⓑThese blackouts made him to come up with a new way to light his house.

A Moser lamp can be made for about one dollar and lasts for about 10 years. It is also very safe. It can never start a house fire. Surprisingly, it is very easy to make this magic lamp.

21 위 글의 밑줄 친 ⓐ를 능동태로 고치시오.

➡ _____

22 위 글의 밑줄 친 ⓑ에서 어법상 틀린 부분을 찾아 고치시오.

_____ ➡ _____

[23~24] 다음 글을 읽고 물음에 답하시오.

In the Philippines, Moser lamps are widely used by the My Shelter Foundation. The charity also teaches local people how to make and install the lamps. Thanks to the charity, thousands of homes in the Philippines now have Moser lamps. It has also made Moser lamps popular in other countries, such as Argentina, India, and Fiji. Moser lamps will light up the lives of many people for many years to come.

23 What enables thousands of homes in the Philippines to have Moser lamps now? Answer in English. (5 words)

➡ _____

24 위 글의 내용과 일치하지 <u>않는</u> 것은?

① In the Philippines, the My Shelter Foundation widely uses Moser lamps.
② The My Shelter Foundation teaches local people how to make the lamps.
③ The My Shelter Foundation teaches local people how to install the lamps.
④ Thousands of homes in the Philippines now have Moser lamps by the help of the My Shelter Foundation.
⑤ Many people of the Philippines have made Moser lamps popular in other countries.

Lesson

8

Have Fun This Winter!

의사소통 기능

- 관심 있는 것 말하기
  I'm interested in reading history books.

- 빈도 묻고 답하기
  A: How often do you clean your room?
  B: I clean my room once a week.

언어 형식

- 지각동사
  Gunnar **saw the river ice cracking**.

- tell/want/ask+목적어+to부정사
  Gunnar **told Balto to continue** on.

Words & Expressions

Key Words

- **around**[əráund] 부 대략
- **arrive**[əráiv] 동 도착하다
- **awesome**[ɔ́:səm] 형 굉장한, 엄청난
- **bark**[bɑːrk] 동 (개가) 짖다
- **broadcast**[brɔ́:dkæst] 명 방송
- **cage**[keidʒ] 명 우리
- **celebrate**[séləbrèit] 동 기념하다, 축하하다
- **climb**[klaim] 동 오르다, 올라가다
- **cover**[kʌ́vər] 동 가다, 이동하다
- **crack**[kræk] 동 갈라지다, 금이 가다
- **disease**[dizíːz] 명 질병, 병, 질환
- **favorite**[féivərit] 형 가장 좋아하는
- **frozen**[fróuzn] 형 얼어붙은
- **gorilla**[gərílə] 명 고릴라
- **granddaughter**[grǽndɔ̀:tər] 명 손녀, 외손녀
- **grandparent**[grǽndpɛ̀ərənt] 명 조부모
- **grandparents' place** 소무보님 댁
- **happen**[hǽpən] 동 발생하다, 일어나다
- **heart-warming** 가슴 따뜻한
- **heavy snow** 폭설
- **highlight**[háilait] 명 하이라이트, 가장 흥미로운 부분
- **hockey**[háki] 명 하키
- **interesting**[íntərəstiŋ] 형 흥미로운
- **language**[lǽŋgwidʒ] 명 언어

- **lead dog** 선두 개, 우두머리 개
- **live**[laiv] 형 생방송의, 생중계의
- **medicine**[médsn] 명 약
- **neck**[nek] 명 목
- **outdoor**[áutdər] 형 실외의
- **popular**[pápjulər] 형 인기 있는
- **race**[reis] 동 경주하다, 달리다 명 경주, 질주
- **reach**[riːtʃ] 동 도달하다, 닿다
- **rescue**[réskjuː] 동 구하다, 구조하다
- **relay**[ríːlei] 명 릴레이 경주, 계주
- **save**[seiv] 동 구하다
- **shout**[ʃaut] 동 외치다
- **sled**[sled] 명 썰매
- **slip**[slip] 동 미끄러지다
- **snowstorm**[snóustɔ̀:rm] 명 눈보라
- **special**[spéʃəl] 형 특별한
- **spread**[spred] 동 (사람들 사이로) 퍼지다
- **table tennis** 탁구
- **terrible**[térəbl] 형 끔찍한
- **trail**[treil] 명 코스, 흔적
- **the Winter Olympics** 동계올림픽
- **weekend**[wíːkend] 명 주말
- **winter break** 겨울 방학

Key Expressions

- **at least** 적어도
- **be good at** ~을 잘하다
- **be interested in** ~에 관심이 있다
- **be sure to**부정사 반드시 ~하다
- **continue on** 계속하다
- **get[become]+형용사** ~하게 되다
- **Good for you!** 잘됐다!
- **go on a trip** 여행을 가다
- **go skating** 스케이트 타러 가다
- **go sledding** 썰매 타러 가다

- **go swimming** 수영하러 가다
- **I can't wait to**부정사 빨리 ~하고 싶다
- **in memory of** ~을 기념[추모]하여
- **just in time** 제때
- **keep -ing** 계속 ~하다
- **once a month** 한 달에 한 번
- **on the trail** 루트[코스]를 따라가는
- **right away** 곧바로, 즉시
- **take part in** ~에 참여[참가]하다
- **take place** 개최되다, 일어나다

Word Power

※ 서로 반대되는 뜻을 가진 어휘

- [ ] **climb** (올라가다) ↔ **descend** (내려오다)
- [ ] **popular** (인기 있는) ↔ **unpopular** (인기 없는)
- [ ] **special** (특별한) ↔ **general** (일반적인)

- [ ] **reach** (도달하다) ↔ **leave** (떠나다)
- [ ] **terrible** (끔찍한) ↔ **awesome** (굉장한)
- [ ] **continue** (계속하다) ↔ **stop** (멈추다)

※ 서로 비슷한 뜻을 가진 단어

- [ ] **shout** : **yell** (외치다)
- [ ] **save** : **rescue** (구하다)
- [ ] **arrive in[at]** : **reach** (도착하다)

- [ ] **crack** : **break**, **split** (갈라지다)
- [ ] **slip** : **slide** (미끄러지다)
- [ ] **happen** : **take place** (일어나다, 발생하다)

English Dictionary

- [ ] **continue** 계속하다
  → to keep happening, existing, or doing something, or to cause something or someone to do this
  계속 일어나거나, 존재하거나, 무언가를 하거나, 혹은 무언가나 누군가가 이런 일을 하게 하다

- [ ] **crack** 금이 가다, 갈라지다
  → to break or to make something break, either so that it gets lines on its surface, or so that it breaks into pieces
  표면에 금이 가게 하거나 조각으로 부수기 위해 무언가를 깨다

- [ ] **disease** 질병
  → illness of people, animals, plants, etc., caused by infection or a failure of health rather than by an accident
  사고에 의해서라기보다는 감염이나 건강 쇠약으로 야기되는 사람, 동물, 식물 등이 아픈 것

- [ ] **medicine** 약
  → a substance, especially in the form of a liquid or a pill, that is a treatment for illness or injury
  특히 액체 또는 알약의 형태로, 질병 또는 부상의 치료제인 물질

- [ ] **race** 경주
  → a competition in which all the competitors try to be the fastest and to finish first
  모든 경쟁자들이 가장 빠르게 먼저 끝내려고 하는 시합

- [ ] **reach** 도달하다
  → to arrive at a place, especially after spending a long time or a lot of effort travelling
  특히 이동하면서 많은 시간이나 많은 노력을 소모한 후에 어떤 장소에 도착하다

- [ ] **relay** 릴레이 경주, 계주
  → a running or swimming race between two or more teams in which each person in the team runs or swims part of the race
  팀 내의 각 사람이 경주의 일부를 달리거나 수영하는 두 개 이상의 팀 간의 달리기 또는 수영 경주

- [ ] **rescue** 구하다
  → to help someone or something out of a dangerous, harmful, or unpleasant situation
  위험하거나, 해롭거나, 불쾌한 상황에서 나오도록 누군가나 어떤 것을 돕다

- [ ] **sled** 썰매
  → an object used for travelling over snow and ice with long, narrow strips of wood or metal
  길고 좁은 나무 조각이나 금속 조각으로 눈과 얼음 위를 여행하는 데 사용되는 물체

- [ ] **snowstorm** 눈보라
  → a heavy fall of snow that is blown by strong winds
  강한 바람에 의해 날리는 폭설

- [ ] **spread** 퍼지다
  → to cover, reach, or have an effect on a wider or increasing area
  더 넓은 또는 증가하는 영역을 덮거나, 도달하거나, 영향을 미치다

- [ ] **take place** 개최되다, 일어나다
  → to happen, especially after being planned or arranged
  특히 계획되거나 준비된 후에 발생하다

- [ ] **terrible** 끔찍한
  → extremely severe in a way that causes harm or damage
  해나 손상을 야기하는 식으로 극도로 심각한

- [ ] **trail** 흔적, 코스
  → a long line or a series of marks that have been left by someone or something
  긴 줄 또는 누군가 혹은 무언가에 의해 남겨진 일련의 표시

01 다음 짝지어진 두 단어의 관계가 같도록 빈칸에 알맞은 단어를 쓰시오.

> crack : split = save : _____

[02~03] 다음 빈칸에 들어갈 말로 가장 적절한 것은?

02
> In early March every year, the world's biggest sled dog race _____ in Alaska.

① slips ② spreads
③ takes part ④ rescues
⑤ takes place

03
> One cold winter day in 1925, a terrible thing happened in Nome. Some children got very sick, and the _____ kept spreading.

① cage ② disease
③ sled ④ medicine
⑤ race

[04~05] 다음 영영 풀이에 해당하는 단어를 고르시오.

04
> to help someone or something out of a dangerous, harmful, or unpleasant situation

① crack ② reach
③ continue ④ rescue
⑤ shout

05
> a competition in which all the competitors try to be the fastest and to finish first

① device ② history
③ race ④ team
⑤ snowstorm

06 밑줄 친 부분의 의미가 잘못된 것은?

① Be sure to watch MBS Sports to enjoy our live broadcasts. (생중계)
② A terrible snowstorm hit us, but we continued on our way. (계속했다)
③ The old wall has started to crack. (갈라지다)
④ Go straight until you reach the main street. (도달하다)
⑤ This trail will lead us to the top of this mountain. (계단)

07 밑줄 친 단어와 가장 가까운 의미를 가진 것은?

> Each team has to cover about 1,800 km from Anchorage to Nome.

① hide ② reveal
③ travel ④ envelop
⑤ wrap

08 우리말 해석에 맞게 빈칸에 알맞은 말을 세 단어로 쓰시오.

> 21개의 개 팀이 릴레이에 참여했다.
> ➡ Twenty-one dog teams were _____.

01 영영풀이에 해당하는 단어를 〈보기〉에서 찾아 첫 번째 칸에 쓰고, 두 번째 칸에는 우리말 뜻을 쓰시오.

┌─ 보기 ──────────────────┐
│ climb / continue / language / sled /   │
│ disease   │
└─────────────────────────┘

(1) _____ : to keep happening, existing, or doing something, or to cause something or someone to do this : _____

(2) _____ : illness of people, animals, plants, etc., caused by infection or a failure of health rather than by an accident: _____

(3) _____ : an object used for travelling over snow and ice with long, narrow strips of wood or metal: _____

02 〈중요〉 다음 우리말 해석에 맞게 주어진 단어를 활용하여 빈칸을 채우시오. (두 단어로 쓰시오)

(1) 몇몇 아이들이 매우 아팠고 병이 계속 퍼졌다.
➡ Some children got very sick, and the disease _____ . (spread)

(2) 놈의 사람들은 당장 약이 필요했지만 마을에는 약이 하나도 없었다.
➡ The people of Nome needed medicine _____ , but the town did not have any. (away)

03 우리말 해석에 맞게 주어진 철자를 알맞은 순서로 배열하여 빈칸을 채우시오.

(1) 수영을 얼마나 자주 하러 가는데?
➡ How _____ do you go swimming? (t, n, o, f, e)

(2) 아이디타로드 경주는 Nome을 구한 개들을 기념하여 1973년에 시작되었다.
➡ The Iditarod Race began in 1973 in _____ of the dogs that saved Nome. (m, m, o, y, e, r)

04 〈중요〉 다음 빈칸에 알맞은 단어를 〈보기〉에서 골라 쓰시오.

┌─ 보기 ──────────────────┐
│ illness / medicine / outdoor / sled / reach │
└─────────────────────────┘

(1) My little brother likes to ride his _____ .

(2) Go straight until you _____ the main street.

(3) Take this _____ , and you will get better soon.

05 〈고난이도〉 영어 설명을 읽고 빈칸에 들어갈 알맞은 단어를 쓰시오.

┌─────────────────────────┐
│ (1) a program on the radio or on television │
│ (2) the best or most exciting, entertaining, │
│   or interesting part of something   │
└─────────────────────────┘

Be sure to watch MBS Sports to enjoy our live (1)_____ from 6 p.m. to 11 p.m. At 11 p.m. every night, you can also enjoy our (2)_____ of the most interesting games of the day.

Conversation

교과서

1 관심있는 것 말하기

> • **I'm interested in reading history books.** 나는 역사책들을 읽는 것에 관심이 있다.

■ 자신이 관심 있는 것에 대해 말할 때는 'I'm interested in ~.' 표현을 쓴다. in 뒤에는 명사구를 사용한다.

관심을 표현할 때

- I'm into sports. 나는 정말 스포츠에 흥미가 있어.
- I'm interested in languages. 나는 언어에 관심이 있어.
- My main interest is cars. 나의 주요 관심사는 자동차야.
- I enjoy cooking. 나는 요리하는 것을 즐겨.
- I like[love] taking pictures. 나는 사진 찍는 것을 좋아해.
- I am interested in K-pop. = I have an interest in K-pop. = I am fascinated by K-pop.
  저는 K-pop에 관심이 있습니다.

관심에 대해 물을 때

- Are you interested in science? 너는 과학에 관심이 있니?
- Are you interested in taking pictures? 너는 사진을 찍는 데 관심이 있니?
- What are you interested in? = What are you into? = What are your main interests?
  너는 무엇에 관심이 있니?

핵심 Check

1. 다음 대화의 빈칸에 들어갈 말로 알맞지 <u>않은</u> 것은?

   A: What are you interested in?

   B: _____

   ① I have an interest in cooking.
   ② I enjoy listening to music.
   ③ I want to be a singer.
   ④ I'm interested in baseball.
   ⑤ I'm into cooking.

166 Lesson 8. Have Fun This Winter!

② 빈도 묻고 답하기

> **A** How often do you clean your room? 너는 얼마나 자주 네 방을 청소하니?
>
> **B** I clean my room once a week. 일주일에 한 번 청소해.

■ '얼마나 자주 ~을 하니?'를 물을 때는 'How often do you ~?' 표현을 쓰고, 답할 때는 always, usually, sometimes, often, never 등의 빈도부사를 이용하거나, every day[weekend], once[twice / three times] a week[month] 등의 표현으로 빈도를 나타낸다.

- A: How often do you exercise? 너는 얼마나 자주 운동하니?

  B: I exercise almost every day. How about you? 나는 거의 매일 운동해. 너는?

  A: I never exercise. 나는 절대로 운동하지 않아.

- A: How often do you eat fast food? 너는 얼마나 자주 패스트푸드를 먹니?

  B: Every Saturday. 매주 토요일마다.

- A: How often do you brush your teeth? 너는 얼마나 자주 양치질을 하니?

  B: Three times a day. 하루에 3번.

핵심 Check

2. 다음 빈칸에 들어갈 말로 알맞은 것은?

A: How often do you exercise?

B: _____

① It takes two hours to run around the village.
② I think exercise is good for your health.
③ Four times a week.
④ It's too far away from here.
⑤ I'm going to go to the gym.

3. 다음 주어진 우리말 해석에 맞게 빈칸에 알맞은 말을 쓰시오.

A: How often do you get a haircut?

B: 한 달에 한 번.

➡ _____

Listen & Speak 1-A-1

B: What are you doing?

G: ❶I'm listening to old pop songs.

B: Oh, do you like old pop songs?

G: No, ❷I'm not interested in them. I just want to sing my grandma's favorite songs at her birthday party next week.

B: Wow, ❸what a nice granddaughter!

B: 뭐 하고 있어?
G: 오래된 팝송들을 듣고 있어.
B: 오, 오래된 팝송들을 좋아하니?
G: 아니, 거기에 관심이 있지는 않아. 그냥 다음 주 할머니 생신에 할머니께서 가장 좋아하시는 노래들을 불러 드리고 싶어.
B: 우와, 정말 착한 손녀구나!

❶ 현재진행형으로 '~하고 있는 중이다'라는 뜻이다.
❷ be not interested in ~'은 관심이 없음을 나타내는 표현이다. 전치사 in 다음에는 대명사나 명사가 온다.
❸ 'What a+형용사+명사!' 형태로 감탄문을 나타낸다.

Check(√) True or False

(1) G doesn't like old pop songs.　　　　　　　　　　　　　　　T ☐ F ☐

(2) G wants to sing her grandma the songs which her grandma likes most.　T ☐ F ☐

Listen & Speak 1-A-2

M: ❶Are you interested in watching the Winter Olympics? Then, ❷ be sure to watch MBS Sports to enjoy our live broadcasts from 6 p.m. to 11 p.m. At 11 p.m. every night, you can also enjoy our highlights of ❸the most interesting games of the day.

M: 동계 올림픽을 보는 것에 관심이 있나요? 그럼, 오후 6시에서 11시까지 하는 MBS Sports의 경기 생중계를 꼭 보세요. 또한 매일 밤 11시에, 여러분은 그날 가장 흥미진진했던 경기의 하이라이트를 즐길 수 있습니다.

❶ 관심에 대해 물어보는 표현으로 'Are you interested in ~?'을 사용한다. 전치사 in 다음에는 동사 'watch'를 동명사 'watching'으로 바꾸어 준다.
❷ 'be sure to부정사'는 '반드시 ~하다'라는 뜻이다.
❸ 형용사 'interesting'의 최상급은 the most interesting이다.

Check(√) True or False

(3) The speaker may be an announcer working for MBS.　　　　　　T ☐ F ☐

(4) You can enjoy the highlights of the most interesting games all day long.　T ☐ F ☐

Listen & Speak 2-A-1

G: ❶What's your favorite sport, James?

B: I don't like sports much, but I sometimes go swimming.

G: ❷How often do you go swimming?

B: ❸Not very often. I only go swimming once a month.

❶ 상대방의 관심사를 묻는 표현이다.

❷ '얼마나 자주 ~을 하니?'의 뜻으로 빈도를 묻는 표현이다.

❸ 빈도를 묻는 말에 대한 답으로 '그렇게 자주는 아니야.'의 뜻으로, 빈도부사를 이용하여 답할 수 있다.

Listen & Speak 2-A-2

B: ❶Do you have any special plans for this weekend, Hana?

G: Well, I'm going to play table tennis with my dad and brother.

B: ❸How often do you play?

G: Every weekend. I love playing table tennis. How about you?

B: I like playing soccer. I enjoy outdoor sports.

❶ 미래의 계획을 물어볼 때 사용하는 표현이다.

❷ 'be going to부정사'는 '~할 예정이다'는 뜻으로 미래 계획을 말할 때 사용한다.

❸ '얼마나 자주 ~을 하니?'를 묻는 말로 빈도를 나타낸다.

Communicate A

Anna: Do you have any special plans for the winter break?

Suho: I'm going to go to my grandparents' place in Pyeongchang. ❶I'll go skating and sledding there. I love winter sports.

Anna: Good for you! I love winter sports, too. My favorite is ice hockey.

Suho: Oh, ❷I've never played ice hockey, but ❸I'm interested in learning how to play it.

Anna: Really? I can teach you ❹how to play.

Suho: That's awesome. Is ice hockey the most popular sport in Canada?

Anna: Yes, it is. ❺Everyone I know loves watching it and playing it.

Suho: ❻How often did you play ice hockey when you were in Canada?

Anna: I played at least two or three times a week in the winter.

Suho: Wow, I'm sure you're really good at ice hockey. ❼I can't wait to learn from you.

❶ 'go -ing' 형태로 '~하러 가다'라는 뜻이다.

❷ 현재완료 형태로 '~해 본 적이 없어'라는 과거 경험을 말하는 표현이다.

❸ 자신이 관심 있는 것에 대해 말할 때 사용하는 표현으로 'be interested in+명사/동명사'를 사용한다.

❹ 'how(의문사)+to부정사'는 '~하는 방법'이란 뜻이다.

❺ everyone은 단수 취급하므로 단수 동사 loves를 사용한다. I know는 목적격 관계대명사절로 주어 Everyone을 수식한다.

❻ 빈도를 묻는 표현으로 '얼마나 자주 ~을 하니?'의 뜻이다.

❼ 'I can't wait to부정사'는 '빨리 ~하고 싶어'의 뜻이다.

Communicate B

A: ❶What winter sport are you interested in?

B: ❷I'm interested in ice skating.

A: How often do you go ice skating?

B: I go ❸once or twice a month.

❶ 상대방에게 무엇에 관심이 있는지 묻는 표현이다.

❷ 자신이 관심 있는 것에 대해 말할 때 사용하는 표현이다.

❸ 빈도를 묻는 말에 대한 답으로 '한 달에 한두 번'의 뜻이다.

Progress Check

1. B: What are you doing?

   G: I'm practicing badminton.

   B: ❶Do you like playing badminton?

   G: No, ❷I'm not interested in it. I just want to pass the badminton test next week.

   B: O.K. Good luck!

2. G: ❶What's your favorite TV show, Jason?

   B: I don't watch TV, but I listen to the radio.

   G: How often do you listen to the radio?

   B: Almost every day.

3. M: ❸It's important to show your love for the people around you. How often do you tell everyone in your family ❹that you love them?

❶ 상대방의 관심사를 묻는 표현이다.

❷ '~에 관심이 없다'는 뜻이다.

❸ 가주어(It) ~ 진주어(to부정사) 구문이다.

❹ tell의 직접목적어로 사용된 that절이다.

● 다음 우리말과 일치하도록 빈칸에 알맞은 말을 쓰시오.

Listen & Speak 1-A

1. **B:** _____ are you _____?

   G: I'm _____ _____ old pop songs.

   B: Oh, _____ old pop songs?

   G: No, _____ _____ _____ _____ them. I just want _____ _____ my grandma's _____ songs at her birthday party next week.

   B: Wow, _____ _____ _____ granddaughter!

2. **M:** _____ _____ _____ _____ _____ the Winter Olympics? Then, _____ _____ _____ _____ MBS Sports to enjoy our live broadcasts from 6 p.m. to 11 p.m. At 11 p.m. _____ _____, you can also _____ our _____ of _____ _____ _____ games of the day.

Listen & Speak 2-A

1. **W:** What's your _____ sport, James?

   B: I don't like sports much, but I sometimes _____ _____.

   G: _____ _____ do you _____ _____?

   B: _____ _____ _____. I only _____ _____ _____ _____ _____.

2. **B:** Do you have _____ for this weekend, Hana?

   G: Well, I'm going _____ _____ table tennis with my dad and brother.

   B: _____ _____ do you play?

   G: _____ _____. I love playing table tennis. _____ _____ you?

   B: I _____ _____ soccer. I enjoy _____ sports.

해석

1. B: 뭐 하고 있어?
   G: 오래된 팝송들을 듣고 있어.
   B: 오, 오래된 팝송들을 좋아하니?
   G: 아니, 거기에 관심이 있지는 않아. 그냥 다음 주 할머니 생신에 할머니께서 가장 좋아하시는 노래들을 불러 드리고 싶어.
   B: 우와, 정말 착한 손녀구나!

2. M: 동계 올림픽을 보는 것에 관심이 있나요? 그럼, 오후 6시에서 11시까지 하는 MBS Sports의 경기 생중계를 꼭 보세요. 또한 매일 밤 11시에, 여러분은 그날 가장 흥미진진했던 경기의 하이라이트를 즐길 수 있습니다.

1. G: James, 가장 좋아하는 스포츠가 뭐야?
   B: 스포츠를 많이 좋아하지는 않지만, 가끔 수영하러 가.
   G: 수영을 얼마나 자주 하러 가는데?
   B: 그렇게 자주 아니야. 한 달에 한 번만 가.

2. B: 하나야, 이번 주말에 특별한 계획 있어?
   G: 음, 우리 아빠와 남동생하고 탁구를 할 거야.
   B: 얼마나 자주 하는데?
   G: 매주 주말. 탁구 하는 걸 정말 좋아하거든. 너는 어때?
   B: 나는 축구 하는 걸 좋아해. 야외 스포츠가 좋아.

Communicate A

Anna: Do you have any _____ _____ for the _____ _____?

Suho: I'm going _____ _____ to my grandparents' _____ in Pyeongchang. I'll _____ _____ and _____ there. I love winter sports.

Anna: _____ for you! I love winter sports, too. My _____ is ice hockey.

Suho: Oh, I've _____ _____ ice hockey, but _____ _____ _____ _____ how _____ _____ it.

Anna: Really? I can teach you _____ _____ _____.

Suho: That's _____. Is ice hockey _____ _____ _____ sport in Canada?

Anna: Yes, it is. _____ I know _____ watching it and _____ it.

Suho: _____ _____ did you play ice hockey _____ you were in Canada?

Anna: I played _____ _____ two or _____ _____ a week in the winter.

Suho: Wow, _____ _____ you're really _____ _____ ice hockey. I _____ _____ _____ learn from you.

Communicate B

A: _____ _____ _____ are you _____ _____?

B: I'm _____ _____ ice skating.

A: _____ _____ _____ you go ice skating?

B: I go _____ or twice _____ _____.

Progress Check

1. **B:** What are you doing?
   G: I'm practicing badminton.
   B: Do you like _____ badminton?
   G: No, I'm _____ _____ _____ it. I just want _____ _____ the badminton test next week.
   B: O.K. _____ _____!

2. **G:** What's your _____ TV show, Jason?
   B: I don't watch TV, but I _____ _____ the radio.
   G: _____ _____ do you listen to the radio?
   B: _____ every day.

3. **M:** _____ important _____ _____ _____ your love for the people around you. _____ _____ do you _____ everyone in your family _____ you love them?

해석

Anna: 너는 겨울 방학 때 특별한 계획이 있니?

수호: 나는 평창에 계신 할머니 할아버지 댁에 갈 거야. 거기서 스케이트와 썰매를 타러 갈 거야. 난 겨울 스포츠를 정말 좋아하거든.

Anna: 잘됐다! 나도 겨울 스포츠를 정말 좋아해. 내가 제일 좋아하는 것은 아이스하키야.

수호: 오, 나는 아이스하키를 해 본 적은 없지만, 하는 법을 배우는 데에는 관심이 있어.

Anna: 정말? 내가 어떻게 하는지 가르쳐 줄 수 있어.

수호: 정말 잘 됐다. 캐나다에서는 아이스하키가 가장 인기 있는 스포츠니?

Anna: 응, 맞아. 내가 아는 모든 사람들은 아이스하키를 보는 것과 직접 하는 것을 정말 좋아해.

수호: 너는 캐나다에 있을 때 아이스하키를 얼마나 자주 했니?

Anna: 겨울에는 일주일에 적어도 두세 번은 했어.

수호: 우와, 네가 아이스하키를 정말 잘 할 거라고 확신해. 너한테 빨리 배우고 싶다.

A: 어떤 겨울 스포츠에 관심이 있니?
B: 스케이트 타기에 관심이 있어.
A: 얼마나 자주 스케이트 타러 가?
B: 한 달에 한두 번 가.

1. B: 뭐 하고 있어?
   G: 배드민턴을 연습하고 있어.
   B: 배드민턴 하는 걸 좋아해?
   G: 아니, 관심이 있지는 않아. 그냥 다음주에 있는 배드민턴 시험에 통과하고 싶어.
   B: 그렇구나. 행운을 빌어!

2. G: Jason, 네가 가장 좋아하는 TV 쇼는 뭐니?
   B: TV를 보지는 않지만, 라디오는 들어.
   G: 얼마나 자주 라디오를 들어?
   B: 거의 매일.

3. M: 당신의 사랑을 주변 사람들에게 보여주는 것은 중요합니다. 당신은 얼마나 자주 가족 모두에게 사랑한다고 말해 주나요?

01 다음 대화의 빈칸에 들어갈 말로 알맞은 것은?

> G: What's your favorite sport, James?
> B: I don't like sports much, but I sometimes go swimming.
> G: _____
> B: Not very often. I only go swimming once a month.

① How long do you swim?

② When do you go swimming?

③ How far is the swimming pool from here?

④ IIow often do you go swimming?

⑤ How do you go to swimming pool?

[02~03] 다음 대화를 읽고 물음에 답하시오.

> B: What are you doing?
> G: I'm listening to old pop songs.
> B: Oh, do you like old pop songs?
> G: No, _____(A)_____ I just want to sing my grandma's favorite songs at her birthday party next week.
> B: Wow, (B)넌 정말 착한 손녀구나!

02 빈칸 (A)에 들어갈 말로 알맞은 것은?

① I'm into old pop songs. ② I'm not interested in them.

③ I'm interested in them. ④ I'm not interested in musicals.

⑤ I'm not interested in it.

03 밑줄 친 (B)의 우리말에 맞게 주어진 단어를 이용하여 영어로 쓰시오. (4 words)

> (nice / what)

➡ _____

04 다음 대화의 밑줄 친 부분의 의도로 알맞은 것은?

> B: How often do you play?
> G: Every weekend. I love playing table tennis. How about you?

① 능력 여부 묻기 ② 유감 표현하기 ③ 기대 표현하기

④ 빈도 묻기 ⑤ 보고하기

Conversation 시험대비 실력평가

Step5

01 다음 중 짝지어진 대화가 <u>어색한</u> 것은?

① A: How often do you clean your room?
B: I clean my room once a week.

② A: What are you interested in?
B: I'm interested in Korean dramas.

③ A: What's your favorite sport, James?
B: I don't like sports much,

④ A: How often do you listen to the radio?
B: For two hours.

⑤ A: What winter sport are you interested in?
B: I'm interested in ice skating.

[02~03] 다음 대화를 읽고 물음에 답하시오.

B: _____(A)_____, Hana?
G: Well, I'm going to play table tennis with my dad and brother.
B: How often do you play?
G: Every weekend. I love playing table tennis. How about you?
B: I like playing soccer. _____(B)_____

서답형

02 위 대화의 빈칸 (A)에 주어진 〈조건〉대로 문장을 완성하시오.

┌─ 조건 ─┐
• 이번 주말 계획을 묻는 말을 쓸 것.
• 'any special plans'를 사용할 것.

➡ _____

03 위 대화의 빈칸 (B)에 들어갈 말로 알맞은 것은?

① I'm not interested in outdoor sports.
② I enjoy outdoor sports.
③ I don't like playing baseball.
④ I'm interested in indoor sports.
⑤ I prefer indoor sports to outdoor ones.

04 다음 대화의 빈칸에 들어갈 말로 알맞은 것은?

G: _____, James?
B: I don't like sports much, but I sometimes go swimming.
G: How often do you go swimming?
B: Not very often. I only go swimming once a month.

① What are you interested in
② What makes you think so
③ What's your favorite sport
④ Are you interested in music
⑤ Do you like to go swimming

[05~06] 다음 대화를 읽고 물음에 답하시오.

B: What are you ①doing?
G: ②I'm listening to old pop songs.
B: Oh, do you like old pop songs?
G: No, I'm not ③interested in them. I just want ④to sing my grandma's favorite songs at her birthday party next week.
B: Wow, ⑤how a nice granddaughter!

05 밑줄 친 ①~⑤ 중 어법상 <u>어색한</u> 것은?

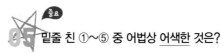

① ② ③ ④ ⑤

Conversation **173**

서답형

06 다음 영영풀이에 해당하는 단어를 대화에서 찾아 쓰시오.

> best liked or most enjoyed

➡ _____

[07~08] 다음 대화를 읽고 물음에 답하시오.

Anna: Do you have any special plans for the winter break?

Suho: I'm going to go to my grandparents' place in Pyeongchang. I'll go skating and sledding there. I love winter sports.

Anna: Good for you! I love winter sports, too. My favorite is ice hockey.

Suho: Oh, I've never played ice hockey, but _____ (A) _____

Anna: Really? I can teach you how to play.

Suho: That's awesome. Is ice hockey the most popular sport in Canada?

Anna: Yes, it is. Everyone I know loves watching it and playing it.

Suho: How often did you play ice hockey when you were in Canada?

Anna: I played at least two or three times a week in the winter.

Suho: Wow, I'm sure you're really good at ice hockey. I can't wait to learn from you.

---

07 위 대화의 빈칸 (A)에 들어갈 말로 알맞은 것은?

① my favorite winter sport is skiing.

② I'm interested in watching the Winter Olympics.

③ I'm interested in drawing cartoons.

④ I'm interested in learning how to play it.

⑤ I only go swimming once a month.

중요

08 위 대화를 읽고 답할 수 <u>없는</u> 질문은?

① Where is Suho going to go during winter break?

② What is Suho going to do in Pyeongchang?

③ How often did Anna play ice hockey when she was in Canada?

④ What winter sport is Suho interested in learning?

⑤ What winter sport is popular in Korea?

[09~10] 다음 대화를 읽고 물음에 답하시오.

M: _____ (A) _____ Then, be sure to watch MBS Sports to enjoy our ____(a)____ broadcasts from 6 p.m. to 11 p.m. At 11 p.m. every night, you can also enjoy our ____(b)____ of the most interesting games of the day.

서답형

09 위 대화의 빈칸 (A)에 주어진 〈조건〉에 맞게 영어로 쓰시오.

> ┤ 조건 ├
> • 동계 올림픽을 보는 데 관심 있는지 묻는 표현을 쓸 것
> • 'interested'를 사용하고, 'watch the Winter Olympics'를 활용할 것

➡ _____

중요

10 빈칸 (a)와 (b)에 들어갈 말로 알맞은 것은?

① living – highlights

② living – spotlights

③ live – highlights

④ live – spotlights

⑤ alive – highlights

[01~02] 다음 대화를 읽고 물음에 답하시오.

> James: Do you have any special plans for this weekend, Hana?
>
> Hana: Well, I'm going to play table tennis with my dad and brother.
>
> James: (A)얼마나 자주 하는데? (play)
>
> Hana: Every weekend. I love playing table tennis. How about you?
>
> James: I like playing soccer. I enjoy outdoor sports.

01 What sport does Hana play and how often does she play it? (6단어의 한 문장으로 쓰시오.)

➡ _____

02 밑줄 친 (A)의 우리말에 맞게 주어진 단어를 이용하여 영작하시오. (5단어로 쓸 것)

➡ _____

[03~04] 다음 대화를 읽고 물음에 답하시오.

> Anna: Do you have any special plans for the winter break?
>
> Suho: I'm going to go to my grandparents' place in Pyeongchang. I'll go skating and sledding there. I love winter sports.
>
> Anna: Good for you! I love winter sports, too. My favorite is ice hockey.
>
> Suho: Oh, I've never played ice hockey, but _____ (A) _____.
>
> Anna: Really? I can teach you how to play.
>
> Suho: That's awesome. Is ice hockey the most popular sport in Canada?

> Anna: Yes, it is. (B) 내가 아는 모든 사람들은 아이스하키를 보는 것과 직접 하는 것을 정말 좋아해.
>
> Suho: How often did you play ice hockey when you were in Canada?
>
> Anna: I played at least two or three times a week in the winter.
>
> Suho: Wow, I'm sure you're really good at ice hockey. I can't wait to learn from you.

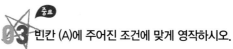

03 빈칸 (A)에 주어진 조건에 맞게 영작하시오.

> ┤ 조건 ├
> • 관심을 표현하기
> • how + to부정사를 사용할 것
> • 'learn', 'play it'을 이용할 것

➡ _____

04 밑줄 친 (B)의 우리말 해석에 맞게 주어진 단어를 알맞은 순서로 배열하시오.

> (everyone / watching / I / playing / know / loves / it / and / it)

➡ _____

05 다음 글을 읽고 마지막 문장의 질문에 답을 하시오. (주어진 단어를 이용할 것)

> M: It's important to show your love for the people around you. How often do you tell everyone in your family that you love them?

➡ I tell them that _____.
(every day)

교과서
Grammar

① 지각동사

> • Gunnar **saw** the river ice **cracking**. Gunnar는 강의 얼음이 갈라지는 것을 보았다.

■ 지각동사는 지각을 묘사할 때 사용하는 동사로 '보다, 듣다, 느끼다'의 의미를 갖는 see, look at, watch, hear, listen to, feel 등의 동사를 말하며, 일반적으로 '지각동사+목적어'의 형태나, '지각동사+목적어+목적격보어'의 형태로 많이 쓰인다. 지각동사의 목적격보어로는 보통 동사원형이나 현재분사(동사+-ing)가 온다. 두 목적격보어의 차이는 현재분사에 진행의 의미가 들어간다는 점이다.

  • I **saw** Tom **get** into his car. 나는 Tom이 차 안으로 들어가는 것을 보았다. **〈동사원형: 동작 전체〉**

  • I **saw** Tom **getting** into his car. 나는 Tom이 차 안으로 들어가고 있는 것을 보았다. **〈현재분사: 진행의 의미를 강조〉**

■ '지각동사+목적어+원형부정사[현재분사]'로 쓰이는 경우에는 목적어와 목적격보어는 능동 관계가 되며, '지각동사+목적어+과거분사'로 쓰이는 경우에는 목적어와 목적격보어의 관계는 수동이다.

  • I **heard** him **call[calling]** my name. 나는 그가 내 이름을 부르는 것을 들었다. **〈원형부정사[현재분사]: 목적어와 목적격보어가 능동 관계〉**

  • I **heard** my name **called**. 나는 내 이름이 불리는 것을 들었다. **〈과거분사: 목적어와 목적격보어가 수동 관계〉**

■ 사역동사 make, have, let과 혼동하지 않도록 한다. 사역동사도 목적어와 목적격보어를 취하지만, 사역동사의 목적격보어로는 현재분사가 나오지 않는다.

  • He **made** me **do** the dishes. 그는 나에게 설거지를 하라고 시켰다.

  • He **had** his bike **repaired**. 그는 그의 자전거가 수리되도록 했다.

핵심 Check

1. 다음 괄호 안에서 알맞은 말을 고르시오.

 (1) I saw my sister (draw / to draw) a butterfly.

 (2) I heard my sister (opening / to open) the window.

 (3) I noticed him (injuring / injured).

2 tell/want/ask+목적어+to부정사

> • Gunnar **told** Balto **to continue** on. Gunnar는 Balto에게 계속 가라고 말했다.

■ 동사 다음에 목적어와 to부정사가 쓰여 '(목적어)에게 …하기를 말하다/원하다/요청하다'라는 의미를 나타낸다. 목적어 다음의 to부정사가 목적격보어이다.

■ to부정사를 목적격보어로 취하는 동사

tell, ask, expect, hope, want, advise, allow, enable, get, permit 등

  • He **told** me **to throw** away the trash. 그는 내게 쓰레기를 버리라고 말했다.

  • Mary **asked** me **to play** the piano. Mary는 내게 피아노를 쳐달라고 부탁했다.

■ 목적격보이로 쓰인 to부정사의 부정형은 'not to 동사원형'으로 쓴다.

  • I **wanted** him **not to do** it again. 나는 그가 그것을 다시 하지 않기를 바랐다.

■ 동사에 따른 목적격보어

지각동사 (see, hear 등)	동사원형, 현재분사, 과거분사
사역동사 (make, have, let)	동사원형, 과거분사
tell, want, ask 등	to부정사
make, keep, find 등	형용사

핵심 Check

2. 다음 괄호 안에서 알맞은 것을 고르시오.

  (1) I asked my sister (draw / to draw) a tree.

  (2) I told my sister (opening / to open) the window.

  (3) I wanted him (listening / to listen) to me.

01 다음 문장에서 어법상 어색한 부분을 바르게 고쳐 쓰시오.

(1) I saw a man took a picture.

_____ ➡ _____

(2) He heard some birds to sing.

_____ ➡ _____

(3) She asked me mailing the letter.

_____ ➡ _____

(4) Hana told me to not lose heart.

_____ ➡ _____

02 주어진 단어를 어법에 맞게 빈칸에 쓰시오.

(1) They heard the dog _____. (bark)

(2) He looked at the house _____ blue. (paint)

(3) We went there to watch it _____. (burn)

(4) Ben felt the snow _____ with his hands. (melt)

03 다음 우리말을 영어로 바르게 옮긴 것은?

> 경찰관은 그들에게 멈추라고 말했다.

① The police officer told them stop.
② The police officer told them stopped.
③ The police officer told them stopping.
④ The police officer told them to stop.
⑤ The police officer told them to stopping.

04 주어진 단어에 한 단어를 추가하고 바르게 배열하여 다음 우리말을 영어로 쓰시오.

> • 그는 빵이 타는 냄새를 맡고 그녀에게 토스터를 끄라고 말했다.
> (he, her, the bread, the toaster, burning, turn, smelled, told, and, off)

➡ _____

01 다음 빈칸에 알맞은 말이 순서대로 바르게 짝지어진 것은?

> • I saw two girls _____ coffee.
> • My friend wants mc _____ a walk with him.

① drink – take
② drank – taking
③ drank – to take
④ drinking – taking
⑤ drinking – to take

02 다음 빈칸에 들어갈 말로 적절한 것을 <u>모두</u> 고르시오.

> He thought he heard someone _____ for help.

① cries   ② cry   ③ cried
④ crying   ⑤ to cry

03 다음 빈칸에 들어갈 말로 적절한 것을 고르시오.

> I asked him _____ the door.

① to close   ② closing   ③ closed
④ closes   ⑤ close

서답형

04 주어진 단어를 이용하여 다음 우리말을 영어로 쓰시오. (10단어)

> 우리는 Kate가 사랑스러운 노래를 부르는 것을 들었다.
> (hear / lovely)

➡ _____

05 다음 중 어법상 바르지 <u>않은</u> 것은?

① Our teacher tells us to read lots of books.
② She asked me to join the club with her.
③ The doctor advised him not smoke and drink.
④ My friend wants me to write a letter to her.
⑤ My mom allowed me to watch TV after dinner.

서답형

06 괄호 안에서 알맞은 것을 고르시오.

(1) I heard someone (sing / sang) a song.
(2) I was surprised to see him (to meet / meeting) a client in person there.
(3) Elisa listened to the wood (popping / popped) as it burned.
(4) Melanie smelled something (burn / burning) in the kitchen.
(5) Did you make him (fix / fixed) your computer?
(6) He told Balto (to continue / continue) on.
(7) Mike asked Yuri (closing / to close) the window.
(8) Her mother warned her (to not / not to) talk to strangers.

07 다음 중 어법상 바르지 않은 것은?

> I ①heard ②someone ③to play the piano ④late ⑤at night.

①   ②   ③   ④   ⑤

서답형

08 다음 문장에서 어법상 틀린 부분을 찾아 바르게 고쳐 쓰시오.

> Sue's mom wants Sue reads more history books.

_____ ➡ _____

[09~10] 다음 우리말을 영어로 바르게 옮긴 것을 고르시오.

09 (2 개)

> 나는 내 남동생이 내 이메일을 읽고 있는 것을 보았다.

① I saw my brother reads my e-mail.
② I saw my brother to read my e-mail.
③ I saw my brother read my e-mail.
④ I saw my brother reading my e-mail.
⑤ I saw my brother to reading my e-mail.

10

> 내가 너를 박물관까지 데려다 주길 원하니?

① Do you want me take you to the museum?
② Do you want me to take you to the museum?
③ Do you want me taking you to the museum?
④ Do you want me to taking you to the museum?
⑤ Do you want me you took to the museum?

11 다음 중 어법상 바르지 않은 것은?

① Alex gets angry when he sees his brother using his phone.
② She could feel somebody touching her shoulder.
③ The students listened to Ruth introduce herself.
④ I watched him to sleep soundly on the sofa.
⑤ I heard a girl singing on my way to school.

12 다음 (A)~(C)에서 어법상 옳은 것끼리 바르게 짝지은 것은?

> • I saw a woman (A)(riding / to ride) a scooter.
> • Did you listen to him (B)(tell / to tell) interesting stories?
> • He found the bird under the tree (C)(injure / injured).

	(A)	(B)	(C)
①	to ride	tell	injure
②	to ride	to tell	injurcd
③	riding	tell	injured
④	riding	tell	injure
⑤	riding	to tell	injure

서답형

13 다음 대화의 빈칸에 알맞은 말을 3단어로 쓰시오.

> A: I can't find Edan anywhere. Do you know if he went out?
> B: I think so. I heard _____ .

➡ _____

14 다음 빈칸에 들어갈 괄호 안에 주어진 동사의 형태가 <u>다른</u> 하나는?

① We told the children _____ basketball in the park. (play)

② Sheryll got her boy friend _____ for her outside. (wait)

③ I didn't allow them _____ everything on television. (watch)

④ Tell me what made you _____ today. (smile)

⑤ Tim asked me _____ him with his homework. (help)

서답형
15 다음 문장에서 어법상 <u>어색한</u> 부분을 바르게 고치시오.

(1) A gorilla saw him to fall inside and caught him.

_____ ➡ _____

(2) They watched me uploaded the report on the Internet.

_____ ➡ _____

(3) I will have him to check your computer.

_____ ➡ _____

(4) My mom wants me clean my desk every day.

_____ ➡ _____

(5) We asked Minho helped us with our art project.

_____ ➡ _____

(6) I told him bringing his passport next time.

_____ ➡ _____

서답형
16 다음 그림을 보고 괄호 안의 동사를 이용하여 주어진 문장의 빈칸을 알맞게 채우시오.

I asked him _____ for some information on the Internet. (search)

중요
17 다음 주어진 문장의 밑줄 친 부분과 쓰임이 같은 것은?

I told him <u>to come</u> early.

① She was happy <u>to meet</u> him.

② My plan is <u>to visit</u> London this year.

③ We asked her <u>to help</u> us.

④ It is important <u>to exercise</u> regularly.

⑤ I need a pen <u>to write</u> with.

서답형
18 다음 괄호 안에 주어진 단어를 이용하여 우리말을 영어로 옮기시오.

(1) Alex는 종종 학교로 가는 길에 새들이 노래하는 것을 듣는다. (often, on his way)

➡ _____

_____

(2) 무언가 타고 있는 냄새가 난다. (smell, something, I, burn)

➡ _____

_____

(3) 그는 내게 그와 결혼해 달라고 요청했다. (ask, marry)

➡ _____

Grammar **181**

01 다음 문장에서 어법상 어색한 부분을 바르게 고쳐 다시 쓰시오.

(1) Alex usually gives a hand when he sees someone carrys something heavy.

➡ _____

_____

(2) A neighbor finally heard the dog to bark and called 911.

➡ _____

_____

(3) Tim just felt the ground shook.

➡ _____

_____

(4) He heard his name calling.

➡ _____

_____

(5) The Greek general ordered a soldier telling the people of Athens about their victory.

➡ _____

_____

(6) Years of training enabled him won the match.

➡ _____

_____

(7) I expect you keep good company when you go abroad.

➡ _____

_____

02 다음 두 문장이 비슷한 의미를 갖도록 빈칸을 알맞은 말로 채우시오.

They said to him, "Please be careful."
→ They asked him _____ .

➡ _____

03 다음 두 문장을 〈보기〉와 같이 지각동사를 이용하여 한 문장으로 완성하시오.

┌─ 보기 ┐
• He saw his son.
• His son was sleeping on the sofa.
→ He saw his son sleeping on the sofa.
└────────┘

• We watched a man.
• He was running outside.

➡ _____

04 다음 두 문장이 비슷한 의미가 되도록 빈칸에 알맞은 말을 쓰시오.

(1) I think that you had better come to my birthday party.
➡ I want you _____ to my birthday party.

(2) Sam told her that she must not forget to turn off the light.
➡ Sam warned her _____ to turn off the light.

(3) The teacher said to her students that they should clean the classroom every day.
➡ The teacher ordered her students _____ the classroom every day.

(4) She said to Jaden that he should eat more vegetables.
➡ She advised Jaden _____ more vegetables.

(5) I said to her, "We believe you are a good painter. You can do it."
➡ I encouraged her _____ a good painter.

05 다음 그림을 참고하여 단어 listen을 알맞은 형태로 빈칸에 쓰시오.

➡ I saw a girl _____ to the music.

⭐중요
06 〈보기〉에서 의미상 적절한 단어를 골라 빈칸에 알맞은 형태로 쓰시오.

┌─── 보기 ───┐
paint   carry   touch   be

(1) He told the children _____ quiet.
(2) He saw the house _____ on his way to the shopping mall.
(3) She felt someone _____ her.
(4) Mom had him _____ the chairs.

07 다음 우리말을 괄호 안에 주어진 어휘를 이용하여 주어진 단어 수대로 영작하시오.

(1) 나는 누군가 나의 이름을 부르고 있는 것을 들었다. (someone, call, 6단어)
➡ _____

(2) Kate는 무언가가 타고 있는 냄새를 맡았다. (something, burn, 4단어)
➡ _____

(3) Jake는 그의 동생이 자기의 전화기를 사용하고 있는 것을 발견했다. (find, brother, use, his phone, 7단어)
➡ _____

(4) 그가 돌아와서 그것이 도난당했다는 것을 알았을 때 그는 매우 화가 났다. (come back, steal, see, get, angry, very, 12단어)
➡ _____
_____

(5) 우리 담임 선생님은 우리에게 늘 학교에 제시간에 오라고 말씀하신다. (our teacher, always, on time, 11단어)
➡ _____
_____

(6) 그는 내가 그 일에 참여하는 것을 용납하지 않을 것이다. (will, permit, take part, 10단어)
➡ _____

(7) 나는 그에게 문을 닫지 말아달라고 부탁했다. (ask, close, the door, 8단어)
➡ _____

(8) 그녀는 내가 컴퓨터 게임을 하도록 했다. (let, computer games, 6단어)
➡ _____

08 그림을 보고 괄호 안에 주어진 단어들을 바르게 배열하여 문장을 완성하시오.

Jaden's mom _____ after finishing homework. (him, allow, watch TV)

The Most Heart-Warming Winter Sport

In early March every year, the world's biggest sled dog race <u>takes</u>
개최된다
<u>place</u> in Alaska. <u>It</u> is <u>called</u> the Iditarod Trail Sled Dog Race. <u>Around</u>
= the world's biggest sled dog race   수동태(be+p.p)   약
80 teams of 12 to 16 dogs <u>take part in</u> this race. Each team has to cover
~에 참여한다   each: 각각의, each+단수명사, 동사도 단수 형태로 쓰임.
about 1,800 km from Anchorage to Nome. The race can take <u>more than</u>
~ 이상
two weeks, and the teams often race through snowstorms. The Iditarod
Race began in 1973 <u>in memory of the dogs that</u> saved Nome.
~을 기념하여   주격 관계대명사
   One cold winter day in 1925, a terrible thing happened in Nome.
Some children <u>got</u> very sick, and the disease <u>kept spreading.</u> The
= became   keep+동사-ing: 계속 ~하다
people of Nome needed medicine <u>right away</u>, but <u>the town</u> did not have
즉시, 당장   = Nome
<u>any.</u> Someone had to get <u>it</u> from a hospital in Anchorage. <u>Because of</u>
= any medicine   medicine   ~ 때문에
the heavy snow, a dog sled relay was the only way <u>to get</u> the medicine
to부정사의 형용사적 용법
from Anchorage to Nome. Soon, the race to Nome began.
   Twenty-one dog teams were in the relay. <u>On</u> January 27, the first
날짜 앞에 on을 쓴다.
team left, and <u>the others</u> waited at different points. Gunnar was the
나머지 전체를 가리킴.
driver of the 20th team. The strongest dog on his team was Balto, <u>so</u> he
그래서(접속사)
<u>made Balto his lead dog.</u>
make+목적어+목적격보어(명사): 목적어를 ~으로 만들다

race: 경주
trail: 자국, 흔적, 오솔길, (특정 목적을 위
     해 따라 가는) 루트[코스]
snowstorm: 눈보라
terrible: 끔찍한
medicine: 약
relay: 릴레이 경주, 계주

📎 **확인문제**

● 다음 문장이 본문의 내용과 일치하면 T, 일치하지 <u>않으면</u> F를 쓰시오.

1 The world's biggest sled dog race takes place in Alaska in early March every
   year. ▢

2 Around 12 to 16 teams of 80 dogs take part in the Iditarod Trail Sled Dog Race. ▢

3 A dog sled relay was the only way to get the medicine from Anchorage to
   Nome. ▢

4 The other teams waited at the same points. ▢

When Gunnar and Balto finally got the medicine, the snow was
~할 때, 시간의 부사절을 이끄는 접속사

so heavy that Gunnar could not see his own hands. However, Balto
so+형용사+that절: 너무 ~해서 …하다   (접속부사) 그러나

was able to stay on the trail. When they were crossing a frozen river,
        (특징 목적을 위한) 루트[코스]를 따라가는   과거신행형

Balto suddenly stopped. Then, Gunnar saw the river ice cracking.
                                    지각동사 see는 목적격보어로 동사원형이나 현재분사가 올 수 있다.

The whole team was saved because Balto stopped just in time. When
                                                          제때에

Balto and Gunnar reached the final team, they were sleeping. Gunnar

told Balto to continue on.
tell+목적어+to부정사: ~에게 …하라고 말하다

   "Here's the medicine, Doctor!" shouted Gunnar. On February 2,

Gunnar and his team finally arrived in Nome. The town was saved.

This heart-warming story is now celebrated every year by the Iditarod
본문 전체에 걸쳐 나온, 개썰매를 통해 놈을 구한 이야기를 말한다.

Race, the biggest sled dog race in the world.
the Iditarod Race와 the biggest sled dog race in the world는 동격

crack: 갈라지다, 금이 가다

reach: ~에 이르다[닿다/도달하다]

continue: 계속되다, 계속하다

📎 **확인문제**

● 다음 문장이 본문의 내용과 일치하면 T, 일치하지 <u>않으면</u> F를 쓰시오.

1 When Gunnar and Balto finally got the medicine, Gunnar could not see his own

   hands because of the heavy snow. ⬚

2 Balto wasn't able to stay on the trail. ⬚

3 The whole team was saved because Balto saw the river ice cracking and stopped

   just in time. ⬚

4 When Balto and Gunnar reached the final team, they were ready to start. ⬚

5 This heart-warming story is now celebrated every month by the Iditarod Race, the

   biggest sled dog race in the world. ⬚

● 우리말을 참고하여 빈칸에 알맞은 말을 쓰시오.

1 The _____ Heart-Warming Winter Sport

2 In early March every year, the world's biggest sled dog race _____ _____ in Alaska.

3 _____ _____ _____ the Iditarod Trail Sled Dog Race.

4 Around 80 teams of 12 to 16 dogs _____ _____ _____ this race.

5 Each team _____ _____ _____ about 1,800 km from Anchorage to Nome.

6 The race can _____ more than two weeks, and the teams often _____ _____ _____.

7 The Iditarod Race began in 1973 _____ _____ _____ the dogs that saved Nome.

8 One cold winter day in 1925, _____ _____ _____ _____ in Nome.

9 Some children got very sick, and the disease _____ _____.

10 The people of Nome needed medicine _____ _____, but the town _____ _____ _____ _____.

11 Someone _____ _____ _____ _____ from a hospital in Anchorage.

12 Because of the heavy snow, a dog sled relay was the only way _____ _____ _____ _____ from Anchorage to Nome.

13 Soon, _____ _____ _____ _____ began.

14 Twenty-one dog teams were _____ _____ _____.

1 가장 가슴 따뜻한 겨울 스포츠

2 매년 3월 초에 알래스카 (Alaska)에서는 세계 최대의 개 썰매 경주가 열린다.

3 그것은 아이디타로드 개썰매 경주(Iditarod Trail Sled Dog Race)라고 불린다.

4 12~16마리 개로 구성된 80여 팀이 이 경주에 참여한다.

5 각 팀은 앵커리지(Anchorage) 에서 놈(Nome)까지 약 1,800 km를 달려야 한다.

6 이 경주는 2주 이상 걸릴 수 있 으며, 팀들은 종종 눈보라를 뚫 고 경주한다.

7 아이디타로드 경주는 놈을 구한 개들을 기념하여 1973년에 시작 되었다.

8 1925년의 어느 추운 겨울날, 놈 마을에서는 끔찍한 일이 일어났 다.

9 몇몇 아이들이 매우 아팠고 병 이 계속 퍼졌다.

10 놈의 사람들은 당장 약이 필요 했지만 마을에는 약이 하나도 없었다.

11 누군가는 앵커리지에 있는 병원 에서 약을 가져와야 했다.

12 폭설 때문에 개썰매 릴레이가 앵커리지에서 놈으로 약을 가져 오는 유일한 방법이었다.

13 곧, 놈으로 향하는 질주가 시작 되었다.

14 21개의 개 팀이 릴레이에 참여 했다.

15 On January 27, the first team left, and _____ _____ waited _____ _____ _____.

16 Gunnar was the driver _____ _____ _____ _____.

17 The strongest dog on his team was Balto, so he _____ Balto _____ _____ _____.

18 When Gunnar and Balto finally got the medicine, the snow was _____ heavy _____ Gunnar _____ _____ see his own hands.

19 _____, Balto was able to _____ _____ _____ _____.

20 When they were crossing a _____ river, Balto suddenly stopped.

21 Then, Gunnar saw the river ice _____.

22 The whole team _____ _____ because Balto stopped _____ _____ _____.

23 When Balto and Gunnar _____ the final team, they were sleeping.

24 Gunnar told Balto _____ _____ _____.

25 "_____ the medicine, Doctor!" _____ Gunnar.

26 _____ February 2, Gunnar and his team finally _____ _____ Nome.

27 The town _____ _____.

28 This heart-warming story _____ _____ _____ every year by the Iditarod Race, _____ _____ _____ _____ _____ in the world.

---

15 1월 27일에 첫 번째 팀이 출발했고, 나머지 팀들은 서로 다른 지점에서 기다렸다.

16 Gunnar는 20번째 팀의 몰이꾼이었다.

17 그의 팀에서 가장 강한 개는 Balto였기 때문에, 그는 Balto를 그의 선두 개로 삼았다.

18 Gunnar와 Balto가 마침내 약을 받았을 때, 눈발이 너무 거세서 Gunnar는 자신의 손조차도 볼 수 없었다.

19 그러나, Balto는 코스를 제대로 따라갈 수 있었다.

20 그들이 얼어붙은 강을 건너고 있을 때 Balto는 갑자기 멈췄다.

21 그때, Gunnar는 강의 얼음이 갈라지는 것을 보았다.

22 Balto가 바로 제때 멈췄기 때문에 팀 전체가 목숨을 구할 수 있었다.

23 Balto와 Gunnar가 마지막 팀에 다다랐을 때, 그들은 자고 있었다.

24 Gunnar는 Balto에게 계속 가라고 말했다.

25 "여기 약이 있습니다. 의사 선생님!"이라고 Gunnar가 소리쳤다.

26 2월 2일에 Gunnar와 그의 팀은 마침내 놈에 도착했다.

27 놈 마을 사람들은 목숨을 구할 수 있었다.

28 이 가슴 따뜻한 이야기는 세계에서 가장 큰 개썰매 경주인 아이디타로드 경주를 통해 오늘날 매년 기념되고 있다.

● 우리말을 참고하여 본문을 영작하시오.

1 가장 가슴 따뜻한 겨울 스포츠

➡ _____

2 매년 3월 초에 알래스카(Alaska)에서는 세계 최대의 개썰매 경주가 열린다.

➡ _____

3 그것은 아이디타로드 개썰매 경주(Iditarod Trail Sled Dog Race)라고 불린다.

➡ _____

4 12~16마리 개로 구성된 80여 팀이 이 경주에 참여한다.

➡ _____

5 각 팀은 앵커리지(Anchorage)에서 놈(Nome)까지 약 1,800 km를 달려야 한다.

➡ _____

6 이 경주는 2주 이상 걸릴 수 있으며, 팀들은 종종 눈보라를 뚫고 경주한다.

➡ _____

7 아이디타로드 경주는 놈을 구한 개들을 기념하여 1973년에 시작되었다.

➡ _____

8 1925년의 어느 추운 겨울날, 놈 마을에서는 끔찍한 일이 일어났다.

➡ _____

9 몇몇 아이들이 매우 아팠고 병이 계속 퍼졌다.

➡ _____

10 놈의 사람들은 당장 약이 필요했지만 마을에는 약이 하나도 없었다.

➡ _____

11 누군가는 앵커리지에 있는 병원에서 약을 가져와야 했다.

➡ _____

12 폭설 때문에 개썰매 릴레이가 앵커리지에서 놈으로 약을 가져오는 유일한 방법이었다.

➡ _____

13 곧, 놈으로 향하는 질주가 시작되었다.

➡ _____

14 21개의 개 팀이 릴레이에 참여했다.

➡ _____

15 1월 27일에 첫 번째 팀이 출발했고, 나머지 팀들은 서로 다른 지점에서 기다렸다.

➡ _____

16 Gunnar는 20번째 팀의 몰이꾼이었다.

➡ _____

17 그의 팀에서 가장 강한 개는 Balto였기 때문에, 그는 Balto를 그의 선두 개로 삼았다.

➡ _____

18 Gunnar와 Balto가 마침내 약을 받았을 때, 눈발이 너무 거세서 Gunnar는 자신의 손조차도 볼 수 없었다.

➡ _____

_____

19 그러나, Balto는 코스를 제대로 따라갈 수 있었다.

➡ _____

20 그들이 얼어붙은 강을 건너고 있을 때 Balto는 갑자기 멈췄다.

➡ _____

21 그때, Gunnar는 강의 얼음이 갈라지는 것을 보았다.

➡ _____

22 Balto가 바로 제때 멈췄기 때문에 팀 전체가 목숨을 구할 수 있었다.

➡ _____

23 Balto와 Gunnar가 마지막 팀에 다다랐을 때, 그들은 자고 있었다.

➡ _____

24 Gunnar는 Balto에게 계속 가라고 말했다.

➡ _____

25 "여기 약이 있습니다, 의사 선생님!"이라고 Gunnar가 소리쳤다.

➡ _____

26 2월 2일에 Gunnar와 그의 팀은 마침내 놈에 도착했다.

➡ _____

27 놈 마을 사람들은 목숨을 구할 수 있었다.

➡ _____

28 이 가슴 따뜻한 이야기는 세계에서 가장 큰 개썰매 경주인 아이디타로드 경주를 통해 오늘날 매년 기념되고 있다.

➡ _____

_____

[01~04] 다음 글을 읽고 물음에 답하시오.

ⓐIn early March every year, the world's biggest sled dog race is taken place in Alaska. It is called the Iditarod Trail Sled Dog Race. ⓑAround 80 teams of 12 to 16 dogs take part in ⓒthis race. Each team has to cover about 1,800 km from Anchorage to Nome. The race can take more than two weeks, and the teams often race through snowstorms. The Iditarod Race began in 1973 in memory of the dogs that saved Nome.

서답형

01 위 글의 밑줄 친 ⓐ에서 어법상 틀린 부분을 찾아 고치시오.

_____ ➡ _____

02 위 글의 밑줄 친 ⓑAround와 같은 의미로 쓰인 것을 고르시오.

① I could hear laughter all around.
② They walked around the lake.
③ There were papers lying around all over the floor.
④ He arrived around five o'clock.
⑤ The house is built around a central courtyard.

서답형

03 위 글의 밑줄 친 ⓒthis race가 가리키는 것을 본문에서 찾아 쓰시오.

➡ _____

중요

04 위 글의 내용과 일치하지 않는 것은?

① 매년 3월 초에 알래스카에서는 세계 최대의 개썰매 경주가 열린다.
② 12~16마리 개로 구성된 80여 팀이 경주에 참여한다.

③ 개썰매 경주에 참여한 각 팀은 앵커리지에서 놈까지 약 1,800 km를 달려야 한다.
④ 이 개썰매 경주는 2주 이상 걸릴 수 있으며, 팀들은 종종 눈보라를 뚫고 경주한다.
⑤ 아이디타로드 경주는 앵커리지를 구한 개들을 기념하여 1973년에 시작되었다.

[05~08] 다음 글을 읽고 물음에 답하시오.

When Gunnar and Balto finally got the medicine, the snow was so heavy that Gunnar could not see his own hands. ___(A)___, Balto was able to stay on the trail. When they were crossing a frozen river, Balto suddenly stopped. Then, ⓐGunnar는 강의 얼음이 갈라지는 것을 보았다. The whole team was saved because Balto stopped just in time. When Balto and Gunnar reached the final team, they were sleeping. Gunnar told Balto ___(B)___ on.

"Here's the medicine, Doctor!" shouted Gunnar. On February 2, Gunnar and his team finally arrived in Nome. ⓑThe town saved. This heart-warming story is now celebrated every year by the Iditarod Race, the biggest sled dog race in the world.

05 위 글의 빈칸 (A)에 들어갈 알맞은 말을 고르시오.

① In addition   ② However
③ As a result   ④ For example
⑤ Thus

서답형

06 위 글의 빈칸 (B)에 continue를 알맞은 형태로 쓰시오.

➡ _____

서답형

07 위 글의 밑줄 친 ⓐ의 우리말에 맞게 주어진 어휘를 이용하여 6단어로 영작하시오.

> crack

➡ _____

서답형

08 위 글의 밑줄 친 ⓑ에서 어법상 틀린 부분을 찾아 고치시오.

_____ ➡ _____

[09~11] 다음 글을 읽고 물음에 답하시오.

One cold winter day in 1925, a terrible thing happened in Nome. (①) Some children got very sick, and the disease kept ⓐ____. (②) Someone had to get it from a hospital in Anchorage. (③) Because of the heavy snow, a dog sled relay was the only way to get the medicine from Anchorage to Nome. (④) Soon, the race to Nome began. (⑤)

Twenty-one dog teams were in the relay. On January 27, the first team left, and the others waited at different points. Gunnar was the driver of the 20th team. The strongest dog on his team was Balto, so he made Balto his lead dog.

서답형

09 위 글의 빈칸 ⓐ에 spread를 알맞은 형태로 쓰시오.

➡ _____

10 위 글의 흐름으로 보아, 주어진 문장이 들어가기에 가장 적절한 곳은?

> The people of Nome needed medicine right away, but the town did not have any.

① ② ③ ④ ⑤

중요

11 위 글의 주제로 알맞은 것을 고르시오.

① a terrible thing which happened in Nome
② people who needed medicine right away
③ a dog sled relay, the only way to get the medicine from Anchorage to Nome
④ twenty-one dog teams which were in the relay
⑤ the other teams waiting at different points

[12~14] 다음 글을 읽고 물음에 답하시오.

One cold winter day, a man left home ⓐto get wood for a fire.

He slipped and broke his neck. He could not move, but no one was near him.

His dog came ⓑto his rescue. She barked and barked for 19 hours.

A neighbor finally heard the dog barking and called 911.

12 위 글의 밑줄 친 ⓐto get과 to부정사의 용법이 다른 것을 고르시오. (2개)

① I have no book to read.
② He awoke to find himself famous.
③ He went abroad to study economics.
④ It is difficult to know oneself.
⑤ I am glad to meet you.

서답형

13 Why couldn't the man move? Answer in English. (7 words)

➡ _____

서답형

14 위 글의 밑줄 친 ⓑ와 같은 뜻이 되도록 to부정사를 써서 바꿔 쓰시오.

➡ _____

[15~17] 다음 글을 읽고 물음에 답하시오.

One cold winter day in 1925, a terrible thing happened in Nome. Some children got very sick, and the disease kept spreading. The people of Nome needed medicine ⓐ right away, but the town did not have any. Someone had to get it from a hospital in Anchorage. ⓑBecause of the heavy snow, a dog sled relay was the only way to get the medicine from Anchorage to Nome. Soon, the race to Nome began.

Twenty-one dog teams were in the relay. On January 27, the first team left, and the others waited at different points. Gunnar was the driver of the 20th team. ⓒ그의 팀에서 가장 강한 개는 Balto였기 때문에, 그는 Balto를 그의 선두 개로 삼았다.

15 위 글의 밑줄 친 ⓐright away와 바꿔 쓸 수 <u>없는</u> 말을 고르시오.

① immediately   ② at once
③ closely   ④ right now
⑤ without delay

서답형

16 위 글의 밑줄 친 ⓑ를 Because를 사용하여 바꿔 쓰시오.

➡ _____

서답형

17 위 글의 밑줄 친 ⓒ의 우리말에 맞게, 주어진 어휘를 알맞게 배열하시오.

> made / on his team / Balto / the strongest dog / Balto / his lead dog / so / was / he

➡ _____
_____

[18~20] 다음 글을 읽고 물음에 답하시오.

(A)[In / On] early March every year, the world's biggest sled dog race takes place in Alaska. ⓐIt is called the Iditarod Trail Sled Dog Race. Around 80 teams of 12 to 16 dogs take part in this race. Each team has to ⓑ cover about 1,800 (B)[km / kilometer] from Anchorage to Nome. The race can (C)[spend / take] more than two weeks, and the teams often race through snowstorms. The Iditarod Race began in 1973 in memory of the dogs that saved Nome.

서답형

18 위 글의 괄호 (A)~(C)에서 어법상 알맞은 낱말을 골라 쓰시오.

➡ (A) _____ (B) _____ (C) _____

서답형

19 위 글의 밑줄 친 ⓐ를 능동태로 고치시오.

➡ _____

20 위 글의 밑줄 친 ⓑcover와 같은 의미로 쓰인 것을 고르시오.

① Did she <u>cover</u> her face with her hands?
② The surveys <u>cover</u> all sides of the business.
③ The cars <u>cover</u> 200 miles a day.
④ The BBC will <u>cover</u> all the major games of the tournament.
⑤ He will <u>cover</u> the loss with insurance.

[21~24] 다음 글을 읽고 물음에 답하시오.

When Gunnar and Balto finally got the medicine, the snow was so heavy that Gunnar could not see his own hands. However, Balto was able to stay ____ⓐ____ the trail. When they were crossing a frozen river, Balto suddenly stopped. Then, Gunnar saw the river ice cracking. The whole team was saved because Balto stopped just in time. When Balto and Gunnar reached the final team, they were sleeping. Gunnar told Balto to continue ____ⓑ____.

"Here's the medicine, Doctor!" shouted Gunnar. ____ⓒ____ February 2, Gunnar and his team finally arrived in Nome. The town was saved. This heart-warming story is now celebrated every year by the Iditarod Race, the biggest sled dog race in the world.

21 위 글의 빈칸 ⓐ~ⓒ에 공통으로 들어갈 전치사를 고르시오. (대·소문자 무시)

① from
② by
③ in
④ for
⑤ on

22 What's the Iditarod Race? Answer in English in a full sentence. (9~10 words)

➡ _____

23 위 글의 제목으로 알맞은 것을 고르시오.

① Gunnar Couldn't See His Own Hands
② Balto Was Able to Stay on the Trail
③ The Team Was Saved Thanks to Balto
④ Gunnar Finally Arrived in Nome
⑤ The Origin of the Iditarod Race

24 위 글을 읽고 대답할 수 <u>없는</u> 질문은?

① When did Gunnar and Balto get the medicine?
② Why couldn't Gunnar see his own hands?
③ When Balto and Gunnar reached the final team, why did Gunnar tell Balto to continue going?
④ When did Gunnar and his team finally arrive in Nome?
⑤ Was the town saved?

[25~27] 다음 글을 읽고 물음에 답하시오.

One summer day, there were lots of people around a gorilla cage at a zoo.
A boy was ____ⓐ____ excited ____ⓑ____ he climbed over the wall.
One of the gorillas saw him falling inside and caught him.
ⓒShe ⓓtook care of the boy until help arrived.

25 위 글의 빈칸 ⓐ와 ⓑ에 들어갈 알맞은 말을 쓰시오.

➡ ⓐ _____ ⓑ _____

26 위 글의 밑줄 친 ⓒShe가 가리키는 것을 본문에서 찾아 쓰시오.

➡ _____

27 위 글의 밑줄 친 ⓓtook care of와 바꿔 쓸 수 있는 말을 쓰시오.

➡ _____

[01~02] 다음 글을 읽고 물음에 답하시오.

In early March every year, the world's biggest sled dog race ⓐtakes placc in Alaska. It is called the Iditarod Trail Sled Dog Race. Around 80 teams of 12 to 16 dogs take part in this race. Each tcam has to covcr about ⓑ1,800 km from Anchorage to Nome. The race can take more than two weeks, and the teams often race through snowstorms. The Iditarod Race began in 1973 ⓒ~을 기념하여 the dogs that saved Nome.

중요

01 위 글의 밑줄 친 ⓐtakes place와 바꿔 쓸 수 있도록 hold를 변형하여 쓰시오.

➡ _____

02 위 글의 밑줄 친 ⓑ를 읽는 법을 영어로 쓰시오.

➡ _____

[03~05] 다음 글을 읽고 물음에 답하시오.

When Gunnar and Balto finally got the medicine, ⓐthe snow was so heavy that Gunnar could not see his own hands. However, Balto was able to stay on the trail. When they were crossing a frozen river, Balto suddenly stopped. Then, Gunnar saw the river ice cracking. The whole team was saved because Balto stopped just in time. When Balto and Gunnar reached the final team, they were sleeping. Gunnar told Balto to continue on.

"Here's the medicine, Doctor!" shouted Gunnar. On February 2, Gunnar and his team finally ⓑarrived in Nome. ⓒThe town was saved.

중요

03 위 글의 밑줄 친 ⓐ를 다음과 같이 바꿔 쓸 때 빈칸에 들어갈 알맞은 말을 쓰시오.

➡ the snow was _____ heavy for Gunnar _____ see his own hands

04 위 글의 밑줄 친 ⓑarrived in과 바꿔 쓸 수 있는 단어를 본문에서 찾아 쓰시오.

➡ _____

05 위 글의 밑줄 친 ⓒThe town이 가리키는 것을 본문에서 찾아 쓰시오.

➡ _____

[06~08] 다음 글을 읽고 불음에 답하시오.

One cold winter day in ⓐ1925, a terrible thing happened in Nome. Some children got very sick, and the disease kept spreading. The people of Nome needed medicine right away, but the town did not have any. ⓑSomeone must get it from a hospital in Anchorage. Because of the heavy snow, a dog sled relay was the only way to get the medicine from Anchorage to Nome. Soon, the race to Nome began.

Twenty-one dog teams were in the relay. ___(A)___ January 27, the first team left, and the others waited at different points. Gunnar was the driver of the 20th team. The strongest dog on his team was Balto, so he made Balto his lead dog.

06 위 글의 빈칸 (A)에 들어갈 알맞은 전치사를 쓰시오.

➡ _____

07 위 글의 밑줄 친 ⓐ1925를 읽는 법을 영어로 쓰시오.

➡ _____

08 위 글의 밑줄 친 ⓑ에서 어법상 틀린 부분을 찾아 고치시오.

_____ ➡ _____

[09~11] 다음 글을 읽고 물음에 답하시오.

One cold winter day in 1925, a terrible thing happened in Nome. Some children got very sick, and the disease kept spreading. The people of Nome needed medicine right away, but the town did not have ⓐany. Someone had to get it from a hospital in Anchorage. (A)[Because / Because of] the heavy snow, a dog sled relay was the only way to get the medicine from Anchorage to Nome. Soon, the race to Nome began.

Twenty-one dog teams were in the relay. On January 27, the first team left, and (B)[others / the others] waited at different points. Gunnar was the driver of the 20th team. The strongest dog on his team was Balto, (C)[as / so] he made Balto his lead dog.

09 위 글의 괄호 (A)~(C)에서 문맥이나 어법상 알맞은 낱말을 골라 쓰시오.

➡ (A) _____ (B) _____ (C) _____

10 위 글의 밑줄 친 ⓐany 뒤에 생략된 말을 쓰시오.

➡ _____

11 본문의 내용과 일치하도록 다음 빈칸 (A)와 (B)에 알맞은 단어를 쓰시오.

> When the people of Nome needed medicine right away, a (A)_____ _____ _____ was the only way to get the medicine from Anchorage to Nome. Soon, the race to Nome began and (B)_____ _____ _____ took part in the relay.

[12~13] 다음 글을 읽고 물음에 답하시오.

When Gunnar and Balto finally got the medicine, the snow was so heavy that Gunnar could not see his own hands. However, Balto was able to stay on the trail. When they were crossing a frozen river, Balto suddenly stopped. ⓐThen, Gunnar saw the river ice to crack. The whole team was saved because Balto stopped just in time. When Balto and Gunnar reached the final team, they were sleeping. Gunnar told Balto to continue on.

"Here's the medicine, Doctor!" shouted Gunnar. On February 2, Gunnar and his team finally arrived in Nome. The town was saved. ⓑThis heart-warming story is now celebrated every year by the Iditarod Race, the biggest sled dog race in the world.

12 위 글의 밑줄 친 ⓐ에서 어법상 틀린 부분을 찾아 고치시오.

_____ ➡ _____

13 위 글의 밑줄 친 ⓑ를 능동태로 고치시오.

➡ _____
_____

Link - Share

Are you interested in <u>learning</u> the history of the marathon? The first marathon
전치사의 목적어(동명사)

<u>was run by</u> Pheidippides in 490 B.C. The Greek army in Marathon <u>ordered</u>
수동태 to부정사를 목적격보어로 받는 동사

him <u>to tell</u> the people of Athens about their victory. He ran 40 km <u>from</u>
목적격보어 ~에서

Marathon <u>to</u> Athens.
…까지

구문해설 · army: 군대, 육로 · victory: 승리

> 마라톤의 역사를 배우는 것에 관심이 있나요? 최초의 마라톤은 **Pheidippides**에 의해 기원전 490년에 달려졌습니다. 마라톤에 있던 그리스 군대는 그들의 승리에 관해 아테네의 사람들에게 말하라고 그에게 명령했습니다. 그는 마라톤에서 아테네까지 40km를 달렸습니다.

Write

One cold winter day, a man left home <u>to get</u> wood for a fire. He <u>slipped</u> and
to부정사의 부사적 용법(목적) slip의 과거

broke his neck. He could not move, but <u>no one was</u> near him. His dog came
아무도 없었다

<u>to his rescue</u>. <u>She</u> barked and barked for 19 hours. A neighbor <u>finally</u> heard the
= to rescue him = His dog = at last

dog <u>barking</u> and called 911.
지각동사 hear의 목적격보어로 쓰인 현재분사

구문해설 · slip: 미끄러지다 · neck: 목 · rescue: 구하다, 구조하다 · bark: (개가) 짖다

> 어느 추운 겨울날, 한 남자가 불을 피울 나무를 구하기 위해 집을 떠났다. 그는 미끄러져서 목을 부러뜨렸다. 그는 움직일 수 없었지만, 그 주변에 아무도 없었다. 그의 개가 그를 구하기 위해 왔다. 그녀는 19시간 동안 짖고 또 짖었다. 한 이웃이 마침내 개가 짖는 소리를 듣고 911에 전화했나.

Culture Project - Share

Every winter, you can see many people <u>jumping</u> into the sea at Haeundae
every+단수 명사 지각동사+목적어+현재분사: '…가 ~하는 것을 보다'

Beach. <u>It's</u> a way of wishing for good health in the New Year.
= Jumping into the sea

구문해설 · jump into: ~로 뛰어들다 · beach: 해변 · way: 방법 · wish: 바라다
· New Year: 새해

> 매년 겨울, 많은 사람들이 해운대 해변에서 바다로 뛰어드는 모습을 볼 수 있다. 이것은 새해에 건강하기를 비는 방법이다.

01 다음 두 단어의 관계가 같도록 빈칸에 주어진 철자로 단어를 쓰시오.

> shout : yell = arrive in[at] : _____

02 우리말에 맞게 빈칸을 완성하시오.

> 그 경주는 2주 이상 걸릴 수 있으며, 팀들은 종종 눈보라를 뚫고 경주한다.
> ➡ The race can _____ more than two weeks, and the teams often race through _____s.

03 〈보기〉의 단어를 사용하여 자연스러운 문장을 만들 수 없는 것은? (대·소문자 무시)

> ─┤ 보기 ├─
> medicine / polar / heart-warming / terrible / victory

① The car racer started to drive faster to catch up with the _____ car.
② _____ bears are large and white.
③ She cried when she heard the _____ story.
④ I had a _____ dream last night.
⑤ Our _____ will be remembered forever.

04 다음 우리말에 해당하는 단어를 세 단어로 쓰시오.

> 아이디타로드 경주는 Nome을 구한 개들을 기념하여 1973년에 시작되었다.
> The Iditarod Race began in 1973 _____ the dogs that saved Nome.

05 다음 빈칸에 어울리는 말을 고르시오.

> _____ the heavy snow, a dog sled relay was the only way to get the medicine from Anchorage to Nome.

① Because   ② Despite
③ Though   ④ Because of
⑤ In spite of

06 다음 글의 ⓐ～ⓔ 중 어법상 어색한 것은?

> M: ⓐIt's important ⓑshow your love for the people around you. ⓒHow often do you tell everyone in your family ⓓthat you love ⓔthem?

① ⓐ   ② ⓑ   ③ ⓒ   ④ ⓓ   ⑤ ⓔ

[07~08] 다음 대화를 읽고 물음에 답하시오.

> A: What winter sport are you interested in?
> B: _____(A)
> A: How often do you go ice skating?
> B: (B)한 달에 한두 번 가.

07 위 대화의 빈칸 (A)에 들어갈 표현을 〈조건〉에 맞게 쓰시오.

> ─┤ 보기 ├─
> • 'ice skating'에 관심을 나타내는 표현을 쓸 것
> • 명사 'an interest'를 사용할 것

➡ _____

08 위 대화의 밑줄 친 (B)의 우리말에 맞게 주어진 단어를 이용하여 쓰시오.

> go / twice

➡ _____

09 두 사람의 대화가 <u>어색한</u> 것은?

① A: Are you interested in reading novels?
   B: Yes, reading novels is my favorite.
② A: What are you doing?
   B: I'm listening to old pop songs.
③ A: What TV programs are you interested in?
   B: I'm fascinated by Korean history and culture.
④ A: How often do you watch comedy programs?
   B: I watch them every day.
⑤ A: Sumi, are you interested in watching movies?
   B: Yes, I am.

[10~11] 다음 대화를 읽고 물음에 답하시오.

G: _____(A)_____, James?
B: I don't like sports much, but I sometimes go swimming.
G: How often do you go swimming?
B: Not very often. _____(B)_____

10 빈칸 (A)에 들어갈 말로 알맞은 것은?

① What are you going to do
② Are you interested in watching movies
③ What are you doing
④ What's your favorite sport
⑤ Do you have any special plans for this weekend

11 빈칸 (B)에 들어갈 말로 알맞은 것은?

① I only go swimming once a month.
② I always go swimming.
③ I'm not interested in going swimming.
④ I'll go skating and sledding.
⑤ I go swimming almost every day.

[12~13] 다음 대화를 읽고 물음에 답하시오.

Anna: Do you have any special plans for the winter break?
Suho: I'm going to go to my grandparents' place in Pyeongchang. I'll go skating and sledding there. I love winter sports.
Anna: Good for you! I love winter sports, too. My favorite is ice hockey.
Suho: Oh, I've never played ice hockey, but I'm interested in learning how to play it.
Anna: Really? I can teach you how to play.
Suho: That's awesome. Is ice hockey the most popular sport in Canada?
Anna: Yes, it is. Everyone I know loves watching it and playing it.
Suho: _____(A)_____ when you were in Canada?
Anna: I played at least two or three times a week in the winter.
Suho: Wow, I'm sure you're really good at ice hockey. I can't wait to learn from you.

12 위 대화의 빈칸 (A)에 들어갈 말로 알맞은 것은?

① What did you usually do
② What city did you live in
③ What were you interested in
④ Were you into ice hockey
⑤ How often did you play ice hockey

13 위 대화의 내용과 일치하지 <u>않는</u> 것은?

① Suho is going to his grandparents' place during the winter vacation.
② Both Suho and Anna love winter sports.
③ Suho goes skating two or three times a week in the winter.
④ Ice hockey is the most popular sport in Canada.
⑤ Suho thinks Anna is really good at ice hockey.

Grammar

14 다음 빈칸에 알맞은 말이 순서대로 짝지어진 것은?

> • Gunnar saw the river ice _____ .
> • Mr. Kim told me _____ on time.

① crack – come
② cracks – comes
③ cracked – came
④ to crack – coming
⑤ cracking – to come

15 다음 그림을 보고 괄호 안에 주어진 어휘를 이용하여 빈칸에 알맞은 말을 쓰시오.

> I saw David _____ fishing with his father. (go)

16 다음 중 어법상 바르지 <u>않은</u> 것은?

① She made me bake the bread yesterday.
② I watched her talked on the phone.
③ Did you see the man walking his dog?
④ They asked Molly to help them.
⑤ Anne told me to stay longer.

17 다음 주어진 문장의 밑줄 친 부분과 쓰임이 같은 것은?

> I caught him <u>reading</u> my diary.

① We spent a few days at the shelter, <u>waiting</u> for the heavy snow to stop.
② When they were <u>crossing</u> a frozen river, Balto suddenly stopped.
③ I saw him <u>walking</u> across the street.
④ My dream was <u>becoming</u> a B-boy dancer.
⑤ Some children got very sick, and the disease kept <u>spreading</u>.

18 다음 두 문장을 〈보기〉와 같이 한 문장으로 고쳐 쓰시오.

> ┤ 보기 ├
> • I saw her.
> • She was crossing the road.
> = I saw her crossing the road.

(1) • He looked at the baby.
　• The baby was sleeping on the bed.
　➡ _____

(2) • I heard Amy.
　• She was locking her room.
　➡ _____

19 다음 문장에서 어법상 어색한 부분을 찾아 바르게 고쳐 다시 쓰시오.

(1) Do you want me believing that false story?

➡ _____

(2) Can you ask him return the book to the library tomorrow?

➡ _____
_____

(3) I heard somebody cried while I took a walk to the park.

➡ _____

(4) I saw Ann to wait for a bus at the bus stop.

➡ _____
_____

Reading

[20~22] 다음 글을 읽고 물음에 답하시오.

In early March every year, the world's biggest sled dog race takes place in Alaska. It is called the Iditarod Trail Sled Dog Race. Around 80 teams of 12 to 16 dogs take part in this race. Each team has to cover ⓐabout 1,800 km ___(A)___ Anchorage to Nome. The race can take more than two weeks, and the teams often race ___(B)___ snowstorms. The Iditarod Race began in 1973 in memory of the dogs that saved Nome.

20 위 글의 빈칸 (A)와 (B)에 들어갈 전치사가 바르게 짝지어진 것은?

① for – through   ② from – by
③ at – in   ④ at – in
⑤ from – through

21 위 글의 밑줄 친 ⓐabout과 바꿔 쓸 수 있는 단어를 본문에서 찾아 쓰시오.

➡ _____

22 위 글을 읽고 대답할 수 없는 질문은?

① When does the world's biggest dog race take place?
② What is the world's biggest sled dog race called?
③ How many teams take part in this race?
④ How long does it take for the winning team of the race to finish it?
⑤ When did the Iditarod Race begin?

[23~25] 다음 글을 읽고 물음에 답하시오.

One cold winter day in 1925, a terrible thing happened in Nome. Some children got very sick, and the disease kept spreading. The people of Nome needed medicine right away, but the town did not have any. Someone had to get it from a hospital in Anchorage. Because of the heavy snow, a dog sled relay was the only way ⓐto get the medicine from Anchorage to Nome. Soon, the race to Nome began.

Twenty-one dog teams were in the relay. On January 27, the first team left, and ___(A)___ waited at different points. Gunnar was the driver of the 20th team. The strongest dog on his team was Balto, so he made Balto his lead dog.

23 위 글의 빈칸 (A)에 들어갈 알맞은 말을 고르시오.

① one   ② the other
③ another   ④ the others
⑤ others

24 아래 〈보기〉에서 위 글의 밑줄 친 ⓐto get과 문법적 쓰임이 같은 것의 개수를 고르시오.

┌─ 보기 ┐
① I was surprised to see my cousin there.
② I want something cold to drink.
③ It is difficult to answer the question.
④ He use the computer to do his homework.
⑤ Is there a knife to cut this bread with?
└──────┘

① 1개 ② 2개 ③ 3개 ④ 4개 ⑤ 5개

25 위 글의 내용과 일치하지 않는 것은?

① 1925년의 어느 추운 겨울날, 놈 마을의 몇몇 아이들이 매우 아팠고 병이 계속 퍼졌다.
② 놈의 사람들은 당장 약이 필요했지만 마을에는 약이 하나도 없었다.
③ 폭설 때문에 개썰매 릴레이가 앵커리지에서 놈으로 약을 가져오는 유일한 방법이었다.
④ 21개의 개 팀이 릴레이에 참여했다.
⑤ 1월 27일에 첫 번째 팀이 출발했고, 나머지 팀들은 모두 같은 지점에서 기다렸다.

[26~27] 다음 글을 읽고 물음에 답하시오.

When Gunnar and Balto finally got the medicine, the snow was so heavy that Gunnar could not see his own hands. However, ⓐ Balto는 코스를 제대로 따라갈 수 있었다. When they were crossing a frozen river, Balto suddenly stopped. Then, Gunnar saw the river ice cracking. The whole team was saved because Balto stopped just in time. When Balto and Gunnar reached the final team, they were sleeping. Gunnar told Balto to continue on.

"Here's the medicine, Doctor!" shouted Gunnar. On February 2, Gunnar and his team ⓑfinally arrived in Nome. The town was saved. This heart-warming story is now celebrated every year by the Iditarod Race, the biggest sled dog race in the world.

26 위 글의 밑줄 친 ⓐ의 우리말에 맞게 주어진 어휘를 이용하여 8단어로 영작하시오.

┌──────────────────────┐
│   able, stay, trail   │
└──────────────────────┘

➡ _____

27 위 글의 밑줄 친 ⓑfinally와 바꿔 쓸 수 없는 말을 모두 고르시오.

① at last   ② in the end
③ at least   ④ in the long run
⑤ actually

[28~29] 다음 글을 읽고 물음에 답하시오.

One summer day, there were lots of people around a gorilla cage at a zoo.
A boy was so (A)[exciting / excited] that he climbed over the wall.
One of the (B)[gorilla / gorillas] saw him (C)[to fall / falling] inside and ___ⓐ___ him.
She took care of the boy until help arrived.

28 위 글의 괄호 (A)~(C)에서 문맥이나 어법상 알맞은 낱말을 골라 쓰시오.

➡ (A) _____ (B) _____ (C) _____

29 위 글의 빈칸 ⓐ에 catch를 알맞은 형태로 쓰시오.

➡ _____

01 출제율 85%
다음 두 단어의 관계가 같도록 빈칸에 알맞은 말을 쓰시오.
(a로 시작하여 쓸 것.)

> popular : unpopular = terrible : _____

02 출제율 95%
우리말에 맞게 빈칸에 알맞은 단어를 쓰시오.

> • 그의 팀에서 가장 강한 개는 Balto였기 때문에, 그는 Balto를 그의 선두 개로 삼았다.
> ➡ The strongest dog on his team was Balto, so he made Balto his (A)_____ dog.
> • 그들이 얼어붙은 강을 건너고 있을 때 Balto는 갑자기 멈췄다.
> ➡ When they were crossing a (B)_____ river, Balto suddenly stopped.

[03~04] 다음 영영풀이에 해당하는 단어를 찾으시오.

03 출제율 90%

> to break or to make something break, either so that it gets lines on its surface, or so that it breaks into pieces

① cost ② slip
③ crack ④ reach
⑤ cut

04 출제율 90%

> to cover, reach, or have an effect on a wider or increasing area

① cross ② spread
③ shout ④ spend
⑤ save

05 출제율 100%
자연스러운 대화가 되도록 알맞은 순서로 배열한 것은?

> (A) I'm interested in ice skating.
> (B) How often do you go ice skating?
> (C) What sport are you interested in?
> (D) I go once or twice a month.

① (A) – (B) – (D) – (C)
② (B) – (A) – (C) – (D)
③ (C) – (A) – (B) – (D)
④ (C) – (D) – (A) – (D)
⑤ (D) – (A) – (B) – (D)

06 출제율 90%
다음 글의 밑줄 친 우리말에 맞게 주어진 〈조건〉을 보고 영작하시오.

> M: 크리스마스에 이런 가난한 사람들을 돕는 것은 중요합니다.

┤ 조건 ├
• 가주어, 진주어 to부정사를 이용할 것.
• 'these', 'help', 'at'을 사용할 것.

➡ _____

07 출제율 95%
빈칸에 들어갈 말로 알맞은 것은?

> G: What's your favorite TV show, Jason?
> B: I don't watch TV, but I listen to the radio.
> G: _____
> B: Almost every day.

① How often do you watch it?
② How often do you clean your room?
③ How many times a week do you play soccer?
④ How often do you listen to the radio?
⑤ How long have you been interested in listening to the radio?

08 다음 대화를 읽고 아래의 요약문을 완성하시오.

> B: What are you doing?
> G: I'm listening to old pop songs.
> B: Oh, do you like old pop songs?
> G: No, I'm not interested in them. I just want to sing my grandma's favorite songs at her birthday party next week.
> B: Wow, what a nice granddaughter!

⬇

> The girl is listening to _____ to sing her _____ songs at her _____ next week.

[09~10] 다음 대화를 읽고 물음에 답하시오.

> Anna: Do you have any special plans for the winter break?
> Suho: I'm going to go to my grandparents' place in Pyeongchang. (A)거기서 스케이트와 썰매를 타러 갈 거야. I love winter sports.
> Anna: Good for you! I love winter sports, too. My favorite is ice hockey.
> Suho: Oh, I've never played ice hockey, but I'm interested ⓐin learning how to play it.
> Anna: Really? I can teach you ⓑhow to play.
> Suho: That's awesome. Is ice hockey ⓒthe most popular sport in Canada?
> Anna: Yes, it is. Everyone I know ⓓlove watching it and playing it.
> Suho: How often did you play ice hockey when you were in Canada?
> Anna: I played at least ⓔtwo or three times a week in the winter.
> Suho: Wow, I'm sure you're really good at ice hockey. I can't wait to learn from you.

09 위 대화의 밑줄 친 ⓐ~ⓔ 중, 어법상 어색한 것은?

① ⓐ ② ⓑ ③ ⓒ ④ ⓓ ⑤ ⓔ

10 위 대화의 밑줄 친 (A)의 우리말에 맞게 주어진 단어를 활용하여 영작하시오.

> go / skate / sled

➡ _____

11 다음 빈칸에 들어갈 말이 바르게 짝지어진 것은?

> • I saw the moon _____ from my bedroom window.
> • This problem is easy _____ for everybody to solve.

① rising – too
② rising – enough
③ rose – too
④ rose – enough
⑤ rise – to

[12~13] 다음 중 어법상 어색한 문장을 고르시오.

12 ① I felt somebody look at me.
② In Canada, you can see many people to sail on the ice in small boats.
③ I smell something burning.
④ He was listening to her play the piano.
⑤ I heard them yelling each other.

13 ① My parents want me to do better next time.
② Ms. Lee told her dog to bring her the stick.
③ Simon encouraged his son studying science harder.
④ She asked me to speak slowly.
⑤ My mom made me clean my room.

14 빈칸에 들어갈 말이 바르게 짝지어진 것은? (출제율 90%)

> • Mr. Kim tells his students _____ lunch tomorrow.
> • Every winter, you can see many people _____ into the sea at Haeundae Beach.

① bring – jumping
② bring – to jump
③ to bring – jumping
④ to bring – to jump
⑤ to bringing – jumped

15 다음 중 어법상 틀린 문장의 개수는? (출제율 100%)

> ⓐ The doctor told him not to eat salty food.
> ⓑ We never allow our children playing with toy guns.
> ⓒ I didn't expect her to dance with me last night.
> ⓓ I want you coming to my birthday party.
> ⓔ We heard a baby crying loudly.
> ⓕ We watched an old man to run outside.
> ⓖ We were so surprised to see the snow to fall from the sky.

① 1개   ② 2개   ③ 3개   ④ 4개   ⑤ 5개

16 주어진 단어를 이용하여 다음 우리말을 영어로 쓰시오. (출제율 90%)

> 나는 Jake가 농구하는 것을 보았다.
> (see, play)

➡ _____

17 다음 우리말을 영어로 바르게 옮긴 것은? (출제율 95%)

> 그에게 그것을 고쳐 달라고 부탁해 보는 게 어때?

① Why don't you ask him fixes it?
② Why don't you ask him fix it?
③ Why don't you ask him fixing it?
④ Why don't you ask him to fix it?
⑤ Why don't you ask him to fixing it?

[18~20] 다음 글을 읽고 물음에 답하시오.

> In early March every year, the world's biggest sled dog race takes place in Alaska. It is called the Iditarod Trail Sled Dog Race. ⓐ12~16마리 개로 구성된 80여 팀이 이 경주에 참여한다. Each team has to cover about 1,800 km from Anchorage to Nome. The race can take ⓑmore than two weeks, and the teams often race through snowstorms. The Iditarod Race began in 1973 in memory of the dogs ⓒthat saved Nome.

18 위 글의 밑줄 친 ⓐ의 우리말에 맞게 한 단어를 보충하여, 주어진 어휘를 알맞게 배열하시오. (출제율 95%)

> this race / of / dogs / 80 teams / 12 / 16 / take part in / around

➡ _____

_____

19 위 글의 밑줄 친 ⓑmore than과 바꿔 쓸 수 있는 한 단어를 쓰시오. (출제율 90%)

➡ _____

20 위 글의 밑줄 친 ⓒthat과 문법적 쓰임이 같은 것을 모두 고르시오.

① He is the greatest novelist that has ever lived.
② The fact is that he said so.
③ I'm glad that I found you.
④ He was the first man that came here.
⑤ It is natural that they should respect each other.

[21~23] 다음 글을 읽고 물음에 답하시오.

ⓐOne cold winter day in 1925, a terrible thing was happened in Nome. Some children got very sick, and the disease kept spreading. The people of Nome needed medicine right away, but the town did not have any. Someone had to get it from a hospital in Anchorage. Because of the heavy snow, a dog sled relay was the only way to get the medicine from Anchorage to Nome. Soon, the race to Nome began.

Twenty-one dog teams were in the relay. On January 27, the first team left, and the others waited at different points. Gunnar was the driver of the 20th team. The strongest dog on his team was Balto, so ⓑhe made Balto his lead dog.

21 위 글의 밑줄 친 ⓐ에서 어법상 틀린 부분을 찾아 고치시오.

_____ ➡ _____

22 위 글의 밑줄 친 ⓑhe가 가리키는 것을 본문에서 찾아 쓰시오.

➡ _____

23 위 글을 읽고 대답할 수 없는 질문은?

① When did a terrible thing happen in Nome?
② Did the town have any medicine?
③ How many dog teams were in the dog sled relay?
④ Why was Gunnar the driver of the 20th team?
⑤ What was the name of the strongest dog on Gunnar's team?

[24~25] 다음 글을 읽고 물음에 답하시오.

One cold winter day, a man left home to get wood for a fire.
He slipped and broke his neck. He could not move, but no one was near him.
His dog came to his rescue. ⓐShe barked and barked for 19 hours.
A neighbor finally heard the dog barking and called 911.

24 위 글의 밑줄 친 ⓐShe가 가리키는 것을 본문에서 찾아 쓰시오.

➡ _____

25 위 글의 내용과 일치하지 않는 것은?

① 어느 추운 겨울날, 한 남자가 불을 피울 나무를 구하기 위해 집을 떠났다.
② 그는 미끄러져서 목이 부러졌다.
③ 그는 움직일 수 없었지만, 그 주변에 아무도 없었다.
④ 그는 19시간 동안 계속 고함을 질렀다.
⑤ 한 이웃이 911에 전화했다.

[01~02] 다음 대화를 읽고 물음에 답하시오.

Anna: Do you have any special plans for the winter break?

Suho: I'm going to go to my grandparents' place in Pyeongchang. I'll go skating and sledding there. I love winter sports.

Anna: Good for you! I love winter sports, too. My favorite is ice hockey.

Suho: Oh, I've never played ice hockey, but I'm interested in learning how to play it.

Anna: Really? I can teach you how to play.

Suho: That's awesome. Is ice hockey the most popular sport in Canada?

Anna: Yes, it is. Everyone I know loves watching it and playing it.

Suho: _____ (A) _____

Anna: I played ice hockey at least two or three times a week in the winter.

Suho: Wow, I'm sure you're really good at ice hockey. I can't wait to learn from you.

01 위 대화의 빈칸 (A)에 들어갈 표현을 주어진 〈조건〉과 밑줄 친 Anna의 대답을 참고하여 영어로 쓰시오.

┤ 조건 ├
• '얼마나 자주 ~을 했니?'라고 빈도를 묻는 표현을 쓸 것.
• 'when'을 이용하여 '캐나다에 있었을 때'를 사용할 것.

➡ _____
_____

02 위 대화의 요약문의 빈칸을 완성하시오.

The girl and the boy both like _____.
The boy is going to go to Pyeongchang

and _____ and _____ there _____ the winter break. The girl likes _____. The boy is interested in _____ ice hockey, so the girl is going to teach him _____ it.

03 다음 대화의 빈칸 (A)와 (B)에 들어갈 말을 주어진 조건에 맞게 영어로 쓰시오.

A: _____ (A) _____
B: I'm interested in comedy programs.
A: _____ (B) _____
B: I watch them every day.

┤ 조건 ├
• (A)는 'interested'를 사용하여 '어떤 TV 프로그램에 관심이 있는지' 묻는 표현을 쓸 것.
• (B)는 대명사 'them'을 사용하여 '얼마나 자주 코미디 프로그램을 보는지' 묻는 표현을 쓸 것.

➡ (A) _____
(B) _____

04 다음 대화를 요약하여 한 문장으로 쓸 때 빈칸을 알맞게 채우시오.

(1) Dad: Minji, are you hungry?
Minji: Yes, Dad. I want to have pizza. Will you order one for me?
➡ Minji asked _____.

(2) Stuart: We will go to the beach tomorrow. Don't forget to wear suncream.
Susie: Okay, I will.
➡ Stuart told Susie _____.

05 다음 두 문장을 하나의 문장으로 쓰시오.

(1) • Julia closed the door.
   • Did you hear it?
   ➡ _____

(2) • Ms. Park saw her son.
   • He was reading a book.
   ➡ _____

[06~07] 다음 글을 읽고 물음에 답하시오.

One cold winter day in 1925, a terrible thing happened in Nome. ⓐ몇몇 아이들이 매우 아팠고 병이 계속 퍼졌다. The people of Nome needed medicine right away, but the town did not have any. Someone had to get it from a hospital in Anchorage. Because of the heavy snow, a dog sled relay was the only way to get the medicine from Anchorage to Nome. Soon, the race to Nome began.

Twenty-one dog teams were in the relay. On January 27, the first team left, and the others waited at different points. Gunnar was the driver of the 20th team. ⓑThe strongest dog on his team was Balto, so he made Balto his lead dog.

06 위 글의 밑줄 친 ⓐ의 우리말에 맞게 주어진 어휘를 이용하여 10단어로 영작하시오.

> got, sick, disease, kept

➡ _____

_____

07 위 글의 밑줄 친 ⓑ를 다음과 같이 바꿔 쓸 때 빈칸에 들어갈 알맞은 말을 쓰시오.

➡ _____ the strongest dog on his team was Balto, he made Balto his lead dog.

[08~10] 다음 글을 읽고 물음에 답하시오.

When Gunnar and Balto finally got the medicine, the snow was so heavy that Gunnar could not see his own hands. However, Balto was able to stay on the trail. When they were (A)[crossing / crossed] a frozen river, Balto suddenly stopped. Then, Gunnar saw the river ice cracking. The whole team was saved because Balto stopped ⓐ바로 제때. When Balto and Gunnar (B)[reached / reached to] the final team, they were sleeping. Gunnar told Balto to continue on.

"Here's the medicine, Doctor!" shouted Gunnar. On February 2, Gunnar and his team finally arrived in Nome. The town was saved. This (C)[heart-warming / heart-warmed] story is now celebrated every year by the Iditarod Race, the biggest sled dog race in the world.

08 위 글의 괄호 (A)~(C)에서 문맥이나 어법상 알맞은 낱말을 골라 쓰시오.

➡ (A) _____ (B) _____ (C) _____

09 위 글의 밑줄 친 ⓐ의 우리말을 세 단어로 쓰시오.

➡ _____

10 본문의 내용과 일치하도록 다음 빈칸 (A)와 (B)에 알맞은 단어를 쓰시오.

In spite of all the difficulties, Gunnar and his team finally arrived in Nome and (A)_____ the town. This heart-warming story is now (B)_____ every year by the Iditarod Race, the biggest sled dog race in the world.

창의사고력 서술형 문제

01 다음에 주어진 일을 얼마나 자주 하는지 묻고 대답하는 말을 〈보기〉와 같이 세 문장을 완성하시오.

> **[What]**
> • clean your room   • wash your hands   • play the piano   • go on a trip
> **[How often]**
> • once a week   • very often   • three times a day   • twice a month

> ┌─ 보기 ─┐
>
> • What: go to the movies   • How often: twice a month
> A: How often do you go to the movies?
> B: I go to the movies twice a month.

02 〈보기〉에 주어진 어휘와 지각동사를 이용하여 공원에서 볼 수 있는 다양한 사람들을 묘사하는 문장을 세 문장 이상 쓰시오.

> ┌─ 보기 ─┐
>
> ride a bike   eat a piece of pizza
> take a picture   wait for someone

(1) _____
(2) _____
(3) _____
(4) _____

03 다음 내용을 바탕으로 감동적인 이야기를 담은 네 컷 만화의 대본을 쓰시오.

> **Characters:** a boy, his parents, a gorilla
> **Setting:** on a summer day at a zoo
> **Beginning:** A boy climbed over the wall to see the gorillas.
> **Middle:** A gorillas saw him falling inside and caught him.
> **End:** The gorilla took care of him until help arrived.

> One summer day, there were lots of people around a gorilla cage (A)_____.
> A boy was so excited that he climbed (B)_____.
> One of the gorillas saw him (C)_____ inside and caught him.
> She (D)_____ the boy until help arrived.

단원별 모의고사

01 다음 단어에 대한 영어 설명이 어색한 것은?

① reach: to arrive at a place, especially after spending a long time or a lot of effort travelling

② terrible: extremely severe in a way that causes harm or damage

③ medicine: a substance, especially in the form of a liquid or a pill, that is a treatment for illness or injury

④ race: a running or swimming race between two or more teams in which each person in the team runs or swims part of the race

⑤ snowstorm: a heavy fall of snow that is blown by strong winds

02 다음 우리말에 맞게 빈칸에 알맞은 단어를 쓰시오.

(1) 너는 겨울 방학 때 특별한 계획이 있니?
➡ Do you have any _____ plans for the winter break?

(2) 그는 미끄러져 목이 부러졌다.
➡ He _____ and broke his neck

03 다음 영영풀이에 해당하는 단어를 고르시오.

a long line or a series of marks that have been left by someone or something

① rescue ② trail
③ crack   ④ memory
⑤ relay

04 주어진 우리말에 맞게 빈칸에 알맞은 단어를 쓰시오. (단, 분사 형태로 쓸 것)

그들이 얼어붙은 강을 건너고 있을 때 Balto는 갑자기 멈췄다. 그때, Gunnar는 강의 얼음이 갈라지는 것을 보았다.

➡ When they were crossing a ⓐ_____ river, Balto suddenly stopped. Then, Gunnar saw the river ice ⓑ_____.

05 다음 대화의 빈칸에 들어갈 알맞은 말은?

B: Do you have any special plans for this weekend, Hana?

G: Well, I'm going to play table tennis with my dad and brother.

B: How often do you play?

G: _____ I love playing table tennis. How about you?

B: I like playing soccer. I enjoy outdoor sports.

① I don't like sports much.
② I'm interested in playing table tennis.
③ Every weekend.
④ I play table tennis.
⑤ I had a great time.

06 다음 대화의 빈칸에 들어갈 말로 어색한 것은?

B: What are you doing?

G: I'm listening to old pop songs.

B: Oh, do you like old pop songs?

G: Yes, _____

① I'm into old pop songs.
② I enjoy old pop songs.
③ I like old pop songs.
④ I don't listen to pop songs very often.
⑤ I have an interest in old pop songs.

07 다음 대화의 빈칸에 들어갈 말로 적절한 것은?

> B: What are you doing?
> G: I'm practicing badminton.
> B: Do you like playing badminton?
> G: _____ I just want to pass the badminton test next week.
> B: O.K. Good luck!

① Yes, I love playing badminton.
② No, I don't. I'm into playing badminton.
③ I play badminton twice a week.
④ What makes you think so?
⑤ No, I'm not interested in it.

08 다음 중 짝지어진 대화가 어색한 것은?

① A: Are you interested in dolphins?
   B: Yes, I'm interested in smart animals.
② A: How often do you eat fast food?
   B: Eating fast food is not good for your health.
③ A: Jimin, are you interested in sports?
   B: No, I'm not.
④ A: What are you interested in?
   B: I'm interested in art.
⑤ A: How often do you exercise?
   B: I never exercise.

[09~10] 다음 대화를 읽고 아래 요약문의 빈칸을 완성하시오.

09

> G: What's your favorite sport, James?
> B: I don't like sports much, but I sometimes go swimming.
> G: How often do you go swimming?
> B: Not very often. I only go swimming once a month.

⬇

James _____ sports much, but he goes _____ _____ a _____.

10

> B: Do you have any special plans for this weekend, Hana?
> G: Well, I'm going to play table tennis with my dad and brother.
> B: How often do you play?
> G: Every weekend. I love playing table tennis. How about you?
> B: I like playing soccer. I enjoy outdoor sports.

⬇

Hana is going to play _____ with her dad and brother _____. She plays table tennis _____.

[11~12] 다음 대화를 읽고 물음에 답하시오.

> Anna: Do you have any special plans for the winter break?
> Suho: I'm going to go to my grandparents' place in Pyeongchang. I'll go skating and sledding there. I love winter sports.
> Anna: Good for you! I love winter sports, too. My favorite is ice hockey.
> Suho: Oh, I've never played ice hockey, but I'm interested in learning how to play it.
> Anna: Really? I can teach you how to play.
> Suho: That's awesome. Is ice hockey the most popular sport in Canada?
> Anna: Yes, it is. Everyone I know loves watching it and playing it.
> Suho: How often did you play ice hockey when you were in Canada?
> Anna: I played at least two or three times a week in the winter.
> Suho: Wow, I'm sure you're really good at ice hockey. (A)너한테 빨리 배우고 싶다.

11 위 대화를 읽고 다음 질문에 영어로 답하시오.

> Q: What winter sport is Suho interested in learning?

➡ _____

12 위 대화의 밑줄 친 (A)의 우리말에 맞게 주어진 조건에 따라 영어로 쓰시오.

┌─── 조건 ───┐
• 'can't wait'을 사용할 것.
└─────────────┘

➡ _____

13 다음 중 밑줄 친 부분의 쓰임이 바르지 <u>못한</u> 것은?

① Jaden asks Minji <u>to review</u> his Korean essay after school.
② She advised me <u>staying</u> in bed for a few days.
③ They won't let you <u>use</u> a plastic bag.
④ I saw her <u>crying</u> in the room.
⑤ He told me <u>to send</u> the card.

14 다음 중 어법상 바르지 <u>않은</u> 것은?

① I heard her opened the window.
② She saw James talk on the phone.
③ They watched Pheidippides running from Marathon to Athens.
④ I felt the ground shake.
⑤ He listened to her sing a song.

15 주어진 단어를 이용하여 다음 우리말을 영어로 쓰시오.

(1) 그는 누군가가 자기를 보고 있는 것을 느꼈다.
(feel, someone, look)

➡ _____

(2) 나는 그에게 여권을 가져오라고 말했다.
(tell, bring, his passport)

➡ _____

16 다음 문장에서 어법상 어색한 부분을 바르게 고치시오.

(1) I saw an old woman to walk her dog.
_____ ➡ _____
(2) I heard my sister cried.
_____ ➡ _____
(3) Have you ever heard Russian speaking?
_____ ➡ _____
(4) I want my parents listening to me more.
_____ ➡ _____
(5) Ms. Kim told us being not late for class.
_____ ➡ _____

17 다음 빈칸에 fix를 어법에 맞게 쓰시오.

> • I watched him _____ my computer.
> • I saw my computer _____.

[18~20] 다음 글을 읽고 물음에 답하시오.

> In early March every year, the world's biggest sled dog race takes place in Alaska. ⓐ<u>It</u> is called the Iditarod Trail Sled Dog Race. Around 80 teams of 12 to 16 dogs ⓑ<u>take part in</u> this race. Each team has to cover about 1,800 km from Anchorage to Nome. The race can take more than two weeks, and the teams often race through snowstorms. The Iditarod Race began in 1973 in memory of the dogs that saved Nome.

18 위 글의 밑줄 친 ⓐlt이 가리키는 것을 본문에서 찾아 쓰시오.

➡ _____

19 위 글의 밑줄 친 ⓑtake part in과 바꿔 쓸 수 있는 말을 모두 고르시오.

① take place   ② participate in
③ perform   ④ carry out
⑤ join

20 위 글을 읽고 the Iditarod Trail Sled Dog Race에 대해 알 수 없는 것을 고르시오.

① 개최 시기   ② 개최 장소
③ 참가팀의 규모   ④ 개의 품종
⑤ 시작 연도

[21~22] 다음 글을 읽고 물음에 답하시오.

One cold winter day ①in 1925, a (A) [terrible / terrific] thing happened in Nome. Some children got very sick, and the disease kept spreading. The people of Nome needed medicine right away, but the town did not have (B)[any / none]. Someone had to get it ②from a hospital in Anchorage. Because of the heavy snow, a dog sled relay was the only way to get the medicine from Anchorage to Nome. Soon, the race ③to Nome began.

Twenty-one dog teams were in the relay. On January 27, the first team left, and the others waited ④at different points. Gunnar was the driver of the (C)[20 / 20th] team. The strongest dog ⑤from his team was Balto, so he made Balto his lead dog.

21 위 글의 밑줄 친 ①~⑤에서 전치사의 쓰임이 적절하지 않은 것을 찾아 알맞게 고치시오.

_____ 번 ➡ _____

22 위 글의 괄호 (A)~(C)에서 문맥이나 어법상 알맞은 낱말을 골라 쓰시오.

➡ (A) _____ (B) _____ (C) _____

[23~25] 다음 글을 읽고 물음에 답하시오.

When Gunnar and Balto finally got the medicine, ⓐ눈발이 너무 거세서 Gunnar는 자신의 손조차도 볼 수 없었다. However, Balto was able to stay on the trail. When they were crossing a frozen river, Balto suddenly stopped. Then, Gunnar saw the river ice cracking. The whole team was saved because Balto stopped just in time. When Balto and Gunnar reached the final team, they were sleeping. Gunnar told Balto to continue on.

"Here's the medicine, Doctor!" shouted Gunnar. On February 2, Gunnar and his team finally arrived in Nome. The town _____(A)_____. This heart-warming story is now celebrated every year by the Iditarod Race, the biggest sled dog race in the world.

23 위 글의 빈칸 (A)에 save를 알맞은 형태로 쓰시오.

➡ _____

24 위 글의 밑줄 친 ⓐ의 우리말에 맞게 한 단어를 보충하여, 주어진 어휘를 알맞게 배열하시오.

Gunnar / heavy / the snow / that / his own hands / could not see / was

➡ _____
_____

25 위 글의 내용과 일치하지 않는 것은?

① Gunnar와 Balto가 마침내 약을 받았을 때, 눈발이 너무 거셌다.
② Balto는 코스를 제대로 따라갈 수 없었다.
③ Balto와 Gunnar가 마지막 팀에 다다랐을 때, 그들은 자고 있었다.
④ Gunnar는 Balto에게 계속 가라고 말했다.
⑤ 2월 2일에 Gunnar와 그의 팀은 마침내 놈에 도착했다.

중간 + 기말
적중100 plus

영어 기출문제집

영어 중 2

미래 | 최연희

Best Collection

내용문의 중등영어발전소 적중100 편집부 TEL 070-7707-0457

INSIGHT
on the textbook

교과서 파헤치기

영어 기출 문제집

적중 100 plus
2학기 전과정

영어 중 2

미래 | 최연희

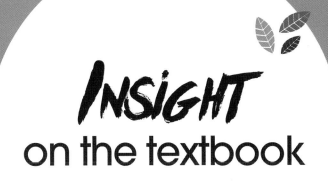

INSIGHT
on the textbook
교과서 파헤치기

※ 다음 영어를 우리말로 쓰시오.

01 practice _____

02 subway _____

03 appreciate _____

04 brave _____

05 century _____

06 actually _____

07 marry _____

08 dawn _____

09 perform _____

10 fail _____

11 storyline _____

12 riddle _____

13 princess _____

14 celebrate _____

15 already _____

16 performance _____

17 secret _____

18 correctly _____

19 suggestion _____

20 famous _____

21 guess _____

22 incorrectly _____

23 stranger _____

24 discount _____

25 difficult _____

26 mean _____

27 amazing _____

28 ostrich _____

29 add _____

30 anniversary _____

31 right _____

32 safe _____

33 theater _____

34 whole _____

35 hurry up _____

36 be late for ~ _____

37 Why don't you+동사원형 ~? _____

38 would like to+동사원형 _____

39 as+형용사+as ~ _____

40 fall in love with ~ _____

41 nothing more than ~ _____

42 in time _____

43 find out _____

Step2

※ 다음 우리말을 영어로 쓰시오.

01	비밀	
02	추측하다	
03	세기	
04	정확하지 않게	
05	실은, 사실은	
06	공주	
07	용감한	
08	타조	
09	할인	
10	감상하다, 감사하다	
11	낯선 사람, 이방인	
12	정확하게, 바르게	
13	동의하다	
14	연극, 극, 희곡	
15	줄거리	
16	이미, 벌써	
17	기념일	
18	~와 결혼하다	
19	공연하다, 수행하다	
20	실패하다	
21	전체, 모든, 전부의	

22	지하철	
23	(말을) 덧붙이다, 더하다	
24	기념하다	
25	유명한	
26	안전한	
27	공연	
28	제안	
29	연습하다	
30	감동적인	
31	어려운	
32	놀라운	
33	수수께끼	
34	아름다움, 미	
35	~에 늦다, 지각하다	
36	제시간에, 늦지 않게	
37	알아내다, 발견하다	
38	서두르다	
39	~와 사랑에 빠지다	
40	(일을) 쉬다	
41	어느 날	
42	첫눈에	
43	~하고 싶다	

※ 다음 영영풀이에 알맞은 단어를 <보기>에서 골라 쓴 후, 우리말 뜻을 쓰시오.

1 _____ : a period of 100 years: _____

2 _____ : earlier than the time expected: _____

3 _____ : to do an action or piece of work: _____

4 _____ : very surprising: _____

5 _____ : the series of events that happen in a book, film, play, etc.: _____

6 _____ : a piece of music in an opera sung by one person: _____

7 _____ : showing no fear of dangerous or difficult things: _____

8 _____ : a reduction in the normal price: _____

9 _____ : to understand how good something or someone is: _____

10 _____ : to do something enjoyable on a special occasion: _____

11 _____ : causing strong feelings of sadness or sympathy: _____

12 _____ : to give an answer to a particular question when you do not have all the facts and so cannot be certain if you are correct: _____

13 _____ : a piece of information that is only known by one person or a few people and should not be told to others: _____

14 _____ : to become the legally accepted husband or wife of someone in an official or religious ceremony: _____

15 _____ : a day on which you remember or celebrate something that happened on that day in the past: _____

16 _____ : a type of question that describes something in a difficult and confusing way and has a clever or funny answer: _____

보기			
marry	celebrate	secret	moving
amazing	discount	century	aria
guess	anniversary	appreciate	perform
riddle	storyline	already	brave

※ 다음 우리말과 일치하도록 빈칸에 알맞은 말을 쓰시오.

Listen & Speak 1-A

1. **M:** Liz, _____ _____. It's _____ 6 o'clock.

   W: Oh, we're _____ _____ _____ _____ _____ _____ the concert.

   M: _____ _____ _____ _____ the subway? The subway will be _____ _____ the bus at this time of day.

   W: That's a _____ _____.

2. **B:** Mom, I _____ _____ one question _____ on the Korean history exam!

   W: Great! I was _____ you would do _____. _____ _____ _____ _____ _____ _____ _____ tonight?

   B: Yes! Can we _____ _____ _____ dinner?

   W: _____ _____, Joe. I'll call your dad.

Listen & Speak 1-B

A: _____ _____ _____ _____ at the park?

B: _____ _____ _____ _____ a magic show?

A: That's _____ _____ _____.

Listen & Speak 2-A

1. **B:** Karen, _____ _____ our _____ for the _____ _____ today.

   G: O.K. _____ _____ _____ _____ _____ _____?

   B: _____ _____ 4 o'clock, _____ _____ _____ _____?

   G: _____ good.

2. **G:** Do you want to _____ _____ together this afternoon, Mark?

   B: Sure. _____ _____ _____ _____ play?

   G: _____ _____ at the park _____ your place?

   B: O.K. _____ _____ _____ _____ 3 o'clock.

Listen & Speak 2-B

A: _____ _____ _____ _____ _____ _____ _____ this weekend.

B: Good idea. _____ _____ _____ _____ _____ _____?

A: _____ _____ 10 o'clock _____ Saturday?

B: O.K. _____ _____ at the subway station. See you there.

해석

1. M: Liz, 서둘러. 벌써 여섯 시야.
   W: 이런, 우린 콘서트에 늦을 거야.
   M: 지하철을 타는 게 어때? 지하철은 지금 이 시간에 버스보다 빠를 거야.
   W: 좋은 생각이야.

2. B: 엄마, 제가 한국사 시험에서 겨우 한 문제만 틀렸어요!
   W: 대단해! 네가 잘할 거라고 확신했단다. 오늘 축하하러 나가는 건 어때?
   B: 좋아요! 저녁으로 피자를 먹어도 되나요?
   W: 물론이지, Joe. 아빠에게 전화하마.

A: 우리 공원에서 뭘 할까?
B: 마술 쇼를 보는 건 어때?
A: 좋은 생각이야.

1. B: Karen, 오늘 학교 연극에서 우리 부분을 연습하자.
   G: 좋아. 몇 시에 만날까?
   B: 학교 끝나고 바로, 네 시 어때?
   G: 좋아.

2. G: Mark, 오후에 같이 배드민턴 하지 않을래?
   B: 물론이지. 어디서 할까?
   G: 너희 집 근처 공원은 어때?
   B: 좋아. 세 시에 거기서 보자.

A: 주말에 소풍가자.
B: 좋은 생각이야. 몇 시에 만날래?
A: 토요일 10시는 어때?
B: 좋아. 지하철역에서 만나자. 거기서 봐.

Communicate A

Anna: Dad, _____ _____! I _____ _____ _____ next Wednesday.

Dad: Really? _____ _____?

Anna: It's our school's 75th _____.

Dad: Oh, I see.

Anna: Can we do something _____ that day?

Dad: I guess I can _____ the afternoon _____. _____ do you _____ _____ do?

Anna: _____ _____ _____ _____ _____ a musical at Bravo Theater _____ _____ _____? We can _____ a _____ _____ we _____ _____ _____ _____ _____.

Dad: Good idea, Anna! Then, _____ _____ _____ at the theater.

Anna: O.K. What time _____ _____ meet?

Dad: _____ _____ 12? Then, we can _____ _____ together, too.

Anna: You're the _____, Dad!

Communicate B

A: _____ _____ _____ do this afternoon?

B: _____ _____ _____ go see *Wonder Woman*?

A: Good idea! What _____ _____ _____ _____ _____?

B: _____ _____ 4 o'clock?

A: O.K. _____ _____ at Moon Theater.

Progress Check

1. **G:** Jim, _____ _____. It's _____ 10 o'clock.

   B: Oh, we're going to _____ _____ _____ the movie.

   G: _____ _____ _____ _____ the bus? The bus will be _____ _____ the subway _____ _____ _____ _____ _____.

   B: That's a _____ _____.

2. **B:** It's very _____ _____. _____ _____ _____, Julie.

   G: Good idea! _____ _____ we _____?

   B: _____ _____ at the subway station near my place?

   G: O.K. _____ you _____ at 11 o'clock.

Anna: 아빠, 있잖아요! 저는 다음 주 수요일에 수업이 없어요.
아빠: 정말? 왜 없니?
Anna: 75주년 개교 기념일이에요.
아빠: 그렇구나.
Anna: 그날 오후에 같이 뭔가 할 수 있을까요?
아빠: 나는 오후에 휴무를 할 수 있을 것 같구나. 뭘 하고 싶니?
Anna: 아빠 직장 근처 Bravo 극장에서 뮤지컬을 보는 건 어때요? 수요일에 가면 할인을 받을 수 있어요.
아빠: 좋은 생각이구나, Anna! 그럼 바로 극장에서 만나자.
Anna: 좋아요. 몇 시에 만날까요?
아빠: 12시는 어떠니? 그럼 점심도 같이 먹을 수 있단다.
Anna: 최고예요, 아빠!

A: 오늘 오후에 뭘 할까?
B: 원더 우먼을 보러 가는 건 어때?
A: 좋은 생각이야! 몇 시에 만날까?
B: 4시는 어때?
A: 좋아. Moon 극장에서 보자.

1. G: Jim, 서둘러. 벌써 10시야.
   B: 이런, 영화 시간에 늦을 거야.
   G: 버스를 타는 게 어때? 지금 이 시간에는 버스가 지하철보다 빠를 거야.
   B: 좋은 생각이야.

2. B: 오늘 굉장히 덥네. 수영하러 가자, Julie.
   G: 좋은 생각이야! 어디서 만날래?
   B: 우리 집 근처 지하철역에서 만나는 게 어때?
   G: 좋아. 11시에 거기서 보자.

※ 다음 우리말에 맞도록 대화를 영어로 쓰시오.

Listen & Speak 1-A

1. M: _____
   W: _____
   M: _____
   _____
   W: _____

2. B: _____
   W: _____
   _____
   B: _____
   W: _____

Listen & Speak 1-B

A: _____
B: _____
A: _____

Listen & Speak 2-A

1. B: _____
   G: _____
   B: _____
   G: _____

2. G: _____
   B: _____
   G: _____
   B: _____

Listen & Speak 2-B

A: _____
B: _____
A: _____
B: _____

해석

1. M: Liz, 서둘러. 벌써 여섯 시야.
   W: 이런, 우린 콘서트에 늦을 거야.
   M: 지하철을 타는 게 어때? 지하철은 지금 이 시간에 버스보다 빠를 거야.
   W: 좋은 생각이야.

2. B: 엄마, 제가 한국사 시험에서 겨우 한 문제만 틀렸어요!
   W: 대단해! 네가 잘할 거라고 확신했단다. 오늘 축하하러 나가는 건 어때?
   B: 좋아요! 저녁으로 피자를 먹어도 되나요?
   W: 물론이지, Joe. 아빠에게 전화하마.

A: 우리 공원에서 뭘 할까?
B: 마술 쇼를 보는 건 어때?
A: 좋은 생각이야.

1. B: Karen, 오늘 학교 연극에서 우리 부분을 연습하자.
   G: 좋아. 몇 시에 만날까?
   B: 학교 끝나고 바로, 네 시 어때?
   G: 좋아.

2. G: Mark, 오후에 같이 배드민턴 하지 않을래?
   B: 물론이지. 어디서 할까?
   G: 너희 집 근처 공원은 어때?
   B: 좋아. 세 시에 거기서 보자.

A: 주말에 소풍가자.
B: 좋은 생각이야. 몇 시에 만날래?
A: 토요일 10시는 어때?
B: 좋아. 지하철역에서 만나자. 거기서 봐.

Step2

Communicate A

Anna: _____

Dad: _____

Anna: _____

Dad: _____

Anna: _____

Dad: _____

Anna: _____
_____

Dad: _____

Anna: _____

Dad: _____

Anna: _____

Anna: 아빠, 있잖아요! 저는 다음 주 수요일에 수업이 없어요.
아빠: 정말? 왜 없니?
Anna: 75주년 개교 기념일이에요.
아빠: 그렇구나.
Anna: 그날 오후에 같이 뭔가 할 수 있을까요?
아빠: 나는 오후에 휴무를 할 수 있을 것 같구나. 뭘 하고 싶니?
Anna: 아빠 직장 근처 Bravo 극장에서 뮤지컬을 보는 건 어때요? 수요일에 가면 할인을 받을 수 있어요.
아빠: 좋은 생각이구나, Anna! 그럼 바로 극장에서 만나자.
Anna: 좋아요. 몇 시에 만날까요?
아빠: 12시는 어떠니? 그럼 점심도 같이 먹을 수 있단다.
Anna: 최고예요, 아빠!

Communicate B

A: _____

B: _____

A: _____

B: _____

A: _____

A: 오늘 오후에 뭘 할까?
B: 원더 우먼을 보러 가는 건 어때?
A: 좋은 생각이야! 몇 시에 만날까?
B: 4시는 어때?
A: 좋아. Moon 극장에서 보자.

Progress Check

1. G: _____
B: _____
G: _____
_____
B: _____

2. B: _____
G: _____
B: _____
G: _____

1. G: Jim, 서둘러. 벌써 10시야.
B: 이런, 영화 시간에 늦을 거야.
G: 버스를 타는 게 어때? 지금 이 시간에는 버스가 지하철보다 빠를 거야.
B: 좋은 생각이야.

2. B: 오늘 굉장히 덥네. 수영하러 가자, Julie.
G: 좋은 생각이야! 어디서 만날래?
B: 우리 집 근처 지하철역에서 만나는 게 어때?
G: 좋아. 11시에 거기서 보자.

※ 다음 우리말과 일치하도록 빈칸에 알맞은 것을 골라 쓰시오.

1 Turandot The _____ _____ Love in the _____
　A. Dangerous　　B. Most　　C. World

2 _____, _____!
　A. everyone　　B. welcome

3 Tonight, we are _____ to _____ Giacomo Puccini's _____ *Turandot*.
　A. perform　　B. going　　C. opera

4 _____ many _____ famous operas, *Turandot* is in _____ _____ opera started in Italy in the 16th century.
　A. because　　B. like　　C. Italian　　D. other

5 _____ we begin, I'd _____ to tell you the _____ of the opera *Turandot*.
　A. like　　B. before　　C. storyline

6 You will _____ it _____ _____ you know the story.
　A. better　　B. if　　C. appreciate

7 Turandot, a Chinese princess, is a woman _____ great _____, but she is as _____ _____ ice.
　A. of　　B. cold　　C. beauty　　D. as

8 Any prince _____ wants to _____ her _____ answer three riddles.
　A. marry　　B. who　　C. must

9 If he _____, he must _____.
　A. die　　B. fails

10 No one _____ ever _____ _____ to answer them.
　A. able　　B. been　　C. has

11 _____ day, a brave prince _____ in love with her _____ first _____.
　A. falls　　B. sight　　C. one　　D. at

12 He _____ the first man to _____ all three _____.
　A. answer　　B. becomes　　C. riddles

13 _____, Turandot does not want to _____ the _____.
　A. marry　　B. however　　C. prince

14 He is _____ _____ _____ a stranger to her.
　A. than　　B. nothing　　C. more

15 He _____ gives her a riddle _____ his _____.
　A. of　　B. then　　C. own

1 투란도트, 세상에서 가장 위험한 사랑

2 여러분, 환영합니다!

3 오늘 밤, 우리는 지아코모 푸치니의 오페라 《투란도트》를 공연할 것입니다.

4 다른 많은 유명한 오페라들처럼 《투란도트》는 이탈리아어로 되어 있는데, 오페라가 16세기 이탈리아에서 시작되었기 때문입니다.

5 시작하기 전에 오페라 《투란도트》의 줄거리를 알려 드리려고 합니다.

6 여러분이 줄거리를 알면 이 오페라를 더 잘 감상하게 될 것입니다.

7 중국의 공주 Turandot는 굉장히 아름다운 여인이지만, 그녀는 얼음처럼 차갑습니다.

8 그녀와 결혼하길 원하는 왕자는 누구든지 반드시 세 가지 수수께끼에 답해야 합니다.

9 만약 실패하면 그는 죽어야 합니다.

10 그 누구도 수수께끼에 답할 수 없었습니다.

11 어느 날, 어떤 용감한 왕자가 그녀에게 첫눈에 반합니다.

12 그는 세 수수께끼를 모두 맞힌 첫 번째 사람이 됩니다.

13 그러나 Turandot는 그 왕자와 결혼하길 원하지 않습니다.

14 그는 그녀에게 단지 낯선 사람일 뿐입니다.

15 그러자 그는 그녀에게 자신의 수수께끼를 냅니다.

16 He _____ her, "_____ is my name?"
    A. what   B. asks

17 He _____, "If you answer _____, I will agree to _____. If you answer _____, you will have to marry me."
    A. correctly   B. die   C. adds   B. incorrectly

18 Turandot must find the answer _____ _____, but his riddle is _____ difficult as _____.
    A. dawn   B. hers   C. as   D. before

19 She says to everyone, "No one will go _____ sleep _____ someone _____ _____ his name."
    A. out   B. finds   C. until   D. to

20 The prince then sings the _____ _____ _____ of the _____ opera, "Nessun Dorma."
    A. most   B. whole   C. famous   D. aria

21 It _____ no one _____.
    A. sleeps   B. means

22 _____ one _____.
    A. sleeps   B. no

23 No _____ sleeps, _____ _____ you, Princess.
    A. even   B. one   C. not

24 My _____ is _____.
    A. safe   B. secret

25 _____ one _____ _____ my name.
    A. know   B. will   C. no

26 _____ _____, I _____ win! I will win!
    A. will   B. at   C. dawn

27 The _____ name _____ Calaf.
    A. is   B. prince's

28 Will the princess _____ his name _____ _____?
    A. time   B. learn   C. in

29 Let's _____ the opera and _____ _____.
    A. out   B. watch   C. find

---

16 그는 그녀에게 "제 이름이 무엇입니까?"라고 묻습니다.

17 그는 "당신이 맞게 대답한다면 나는 죽는 것에 동의하겠습니다. 만약 답이 틀리면 당신은 저와 결혼해야 할 것입니다."라고 덧붙입니다.

18 Turandot는 동이 트기 전에 답을 찾아야 하지만 그의 수수께끼는 그녀의 것만큼 어렵습니다.

19 그녀는 모두에게 "누군가 그의 이름을 알아낼 때까지 그 누구도 잠들 수 없다."라고 말합니다.

20 그리고 왕자는 이 오페라 전체에서 가장 유명한 아리아, Nessun Dorma를 부릅니다.

21 그것은 누구도 잠들지 못한다는 뜻입니다.

22 누구도 잠들지 못하네.

23 누구도 잠들지 못하네, 당신조차도, 공주여.

24 나의 비밀은 안전하다네.

25 누구도 나의 이름을 알지 못할 것이네.

26 동틀 녘에, 내가 이길 것이라네! 내가 승리할 것이라네!

27 왕자의 이름은 Calaf입니다.

28 공주는 그의 이름을 제때 알아낼 수 있을까요?

29 오페라를 보고 알아봅시다.

※ 다음 우리말과 일치하도록 빈칸에 알맞은 말을 쓰시오.

1 Turandot _____ _____ _____ Love in the _____

2 _____, _____!

3 Tonight, we _____ _____ _____ _____ Giacomo Puccini's opera *Turandot*.

4 _____ many _____ _____ _____, *Turandot* is _____ _____ _____ opera started _____ _____ in the _____ _____.

5 Before we begin, _____ _____ _____ _____ you the _____ _____ _____ _____ *Turandot*.

6 You will _____ it _____ _____ you know the story.

7 Turandot, a Chinese princess, is a woman _____ _____ _____, but she is _____ _____ _____ _____.

8 Any prince _____ wants to _____ _____ must answer _____ _____.

9 If he _____, he _____ _____.

10 No one _____ _____ _____ _____ _____ _____ answer them.

11 One day, a brave prince _____ _____ _____ _____ her _____ _____ _____.

12 He becomes _____ _____ _____ _____ _____ all three riddles.

13 _____, Turandot does not want _____ _____ the prince.

14 He is _____ _____ _____ a stranger to her.

15 He then gives _____ _____ _____ _____ _____.

---

1 투란도트, 세상에서 가장 위험한 사랑

2 여러분, 환영합니다!

3 오늘 밤, 우리는 지아코모 푸치니의 오페라 《투란도트》를 공연할 것입니다.

4 다른 많은 유명한 오페라들처럼 《투란도트》는 이탈리아어로 되어 있는데, 오페라가 16세기 이탈리아에서 시작되었기 때문입니다.

5 시작하기 전에 오페라 《투란도트》의 줄거리를 알려 드리려고 합니다.

6 여러분이 줄거리를 알면 이 오페라를 더 잘 감상하게 될 것입니다.

7 중국의 공주 Turandot는 굉장히 아름다운 여인이지만, 그녀는 얼음처럼 차갑습니다.

8 그녀와 결혼하길 원하는 왕자는 누구든지 반드시 세 가지 수수께끼에 답해야 합니다.

9 만약 실패하면 그는 죽어야 합니다.

10 그 누구도 수수께끼에 답할 수 없었습니다.

11 어느 날, 어떤 용감한 왕자가 그녀에게 첫눈에 반합니다.

12 그는 세 수수께끼를 모두 맞힌 첫 번째 사람이 됩니다.

13 그러나 Turandot는 그 왕자와 결혼하길 원하지 않습니다.

14 그는 그녀에게 단지 낯선 사람일 뿐입니다.

15 그러자 그는 그녀에게 자신의 수수께끼를 냅니다.

16 He _____ _____, "_____ is my name?"

17 He _____, "If you answer _____, I will _____ _____

_____. If you answer _____, you will _____ _____

_____ me."

18 Turandot must find the answer _____ _____, but his riddle is

_____ _____ _____ _____ _____.

19 She says to everyone, "No one will _____ _____ _____

_____ someone _____ _____ his name."

20 The prince then sings _____ _____ _____ _____ of the

_____ _____, "Nessun Dorma."

21 It _____ no one _____.

22 _____ one _____.

23 No one sleeps, _____ _____ _____, Princess.

24 _____ _____ is _____.

24 _____ _____ _____ _____ my name.

26 _____ _____, I _____ _____! I will win!

27 The _____ _____ is Calaf.

28 _____ the princess _____ his name _____ _____?

29 _____ _____ the opera and _____ _____.

16 그는 그녀에게 "제 이름이 무엇입니까?"라고 묻습니다.

17 그는 "당신이 맞게 대답한다면 나는 죽는 것에 동의하겠습니다. 만약 답이 틀리면 당신은 저와 결혼해야 할 것입니다."라고 덧붙입니다.

18 Turandot는 동이 트기 전에 답을 찾아야 하지만 그의 수수께끼는 그녀의 것만큼 어렵습니다.

19 그녀는 모두에게 "누군가 그의 이름을 알아낼 때까지 그 누구도 잠들 수 없다."라고 말합니다.

20 그리고 왕자는 이 오페라 전체에서 가장 유명한 아리아, Nessun Dorma를 부릅니다.

21 그것은 누구도 잠들지 못한다는 뜻입니다.

22 누구도 잠들지 못하네.

23 누구도 잠들지 못하네, 당신조차도, 공주여.

24 나의 비밀은 안전하다네.

25 누구도 나의 이름을 알지 못할 것이네.

26 동틀 녘에, 내가 이길 것이라네! 내가 승리할 것이라네!

27 왕자의 이름은 Calaf입니다.

28 공주는 그의 이름을 제때 알아낼 수 있을까요?

29 오페라를 보고 알아봅시다.

※ 다음 문장을 우리말로 쓰시오.

1 Turandot The Most Dangerous Love in the World

➡ _____

2 Welcome, everyone!

➡ _____

3 Tonight, we are going to perform Giacomo Puccini's opera *Turandot*.

➡ _____

4 Like many other famous operas, *Turandot* is in Italian because opera started in Italy in the 16th century.

➡ _____

5 Before we begin, I'd like to tell you the storyline of the opera *Turandot*.

➡ _____

6 You will appreciate it better if you know the story.

➡ _____

7 Turandot, a Chinese princess, is a woman of great beauty, but she is as cold as ice.

➡ _____

8 Any prince who wants to marry her must answer three riddles.

➡ _____

9 If he fails, he must die.

➡ _____

10 No one has ever been able to answer them.

➡ _____

11 One day, a brave prince falls in love with her at first sight.

➡ _____

12 He becomes the first man to answer all three riddles.

➡ _____

13 However, Turandot does not want to marry the prince.

➡ _____

14 He is nothing more than a stranger to her.

➡ _____

15 He then gives her a riddle of his own.

➡ _____

16 He asks her, "What is my name?"

➡ _____

17 He adds, "If you answer correctly, I will agree to die. If you answer incorrectly, you will have to marry me."

➡ _____

18 Turandot must find the answer before dawn, but his riddle is as difficult as hers.

➡ _____

19 She says to everyone, "No one will go to sleep until someone finds out his name."

➡ _____

20 The prince then sings the most famous aria of the whole opera, "Nessun Dorma."

➡ _____

21 It means no one sleeps.

➡ _____

22 No one sleeps.

➡ _____

23 No one sleeps, not even you, Princess.

➡ _____

24 My secret is safe.

➡ _____

25 No one will know my name.

➡ _____

26 At dawn, I will win! I will win!

➡ _____

27 The prince's name is Calaf.

➡ _____

28 Will the princess learn his name in time?

➡ _____

29 Let's watch the opera and find out.

➡ _____

Step4

※ 다음 괄호 안의 단어들을 우리말에 맞도록 바르게 배열하시오.

1 (Turandot / Most / The / Love / Dangerous / the / in / World)
➡ _____

2 (everyone! / welcome,)
➡ _____

3 (we / tonight, / going / are / perform / to / Puccini's / Giacomo / *Turandot.* / opera)
➡ _____

4 (many / like / famous / other / operas, / is / *Turandot* / Italian / in / opera / because / in / started / Italy / the / century. / 16th / in)
➡ _____

5 (we / before / begin, / like / I'd / tell / to / the / you / of / storyline / *Turandot.* / opera / the)
➡ _____

6 (will / you / it / appreciate / better / you / if / know / story. / the)
➡ _____

7 (a / Turandot, / princess, / Chinese / a / is / woman / great / of / beauty, / but / is / she / cold / as / ice. / as)
➡ _____

8 (prince / any / wants / who / marry / to / her / answer / must / riddles. / three)
➡ _____

9 (he / if / fails, / he / die. / must)
➡ _____

10 (one / no / ever / has / been / to / able / them. / answer)
➡ _____

11 (day, / one / brave / a / prince / falls / love / in / her / with / sight. / first / at)
➡ _____

12 (becomes / he / first / the / to / man / answer / all / riddles. / three)
➡ _____

13 (Turandot / however / not / does / to / want / prince. / the / marry)
➡ _____

14 (is / he / more / nothing / a / than / stranger / her. / to)
➡ _____

15 (then / he / gives / a / her / riddel / own. / his / of)
➡ _____

1 투란도트, 세상에서 가장 위험한 사랑

2 여러분, 환영합니다!

3 오늘 밤, 우리는 지아코모 푸치니의 오페라 《투란도트》를 공연할 것입니다.

4 다른 많은 유명한 오페라들처럼 《투란도트》는 이탈리아어로 되어 있는데, 오페라가 16세기 이탈리아에서 시작되었기 때문입니다.

5 시작하기 전에 오페라 《투란도트》의 줄거리를 알려 드리려고 합니다.

6 여러분이 줄거리를 알면 이 오페라를 더 잘 감상하게 될 것입니다.

7 중국의 공주 Turandot는 굉장히 아름다운 여인이지만, 그녀는 얼음처럼 차갑습니다.

8 그녀와 결혼하길 원하는 왕자는 누구든지 반드시 세 가지 수수께끼에 답해야 합니다.

9 만약 실패하면 그는 죽어야 합니다.

10 그 누구도 수수께끼에 답할 수 없었습니다.

11 어느 날, 어떤 용감한 왕자가 그녀에게 첫눈에 반합니다.

12 그는 세 수수께끼를 모두 맞힌 첫 번째 사람이 됩니다.

13 그러나 Turandot는 그 왕자와 결혼하길 원하지 않습니다.

14 그는 그녀에게 단지 낯선 사람일 뿐입니다.

15 그러자 그는 그녀에게 자신의 수수께끼를 냅니다.

16 (asks / he / her, / is / "what / name?" / my)

➡ _____

17 (adds, / he / you / "if / answer / correctly, / will / I / die. / to / agree / you / if / incorrectly, / answer / will / you / to / have / me." / marry)

➡ _____

_____

18 (must / Turandot / find / answer / the / dawn, / before / his / but / as / is / riddle / difficult / hers. / as)

➡ _____

_____

19 (says / she / everyone, / to / one / "no / go / will / sleep / to / someone / until / out / finds / name." / his)

➡ _____

_____

20 (prince / the / sings / then / most / the / aria / famous / of / opera, / whole / the / Dorma." / "Nessun)

➡ _____

_____

21 (means / it / one / sleeps. / no)

➡ _____

22 (sleeps. / one / no)

➡ _____

23 (one / no / sleeps, even / not / Princess. / you,)

➡ _____

24 (secret / safe. / is / my)

➡ _____

25 (one / no / know / will / name. / my)

➡ _____

26 (dawn, / at / will / I / win! / will / I / win!)

➡ _____

27 (prince's / the / is / Calaf. / name)

➡ _____

28 (the / will / learn / princess / name / his / time? / in)

➡ _____

29 (watch / let's / opera / the / out. / find / and)

➡ _____

16 그는 그녀에게 "제 이름이 무엇입니까?"라고 묻습니다.

17 그는 "당신이 맞게 대답한다면 나는 죽는 것에 동의하겠습니다. 만약 답이 틀리면 당신은 저와 결혼해야 할 것입니다."라고 덧붙입니다.

18 Turandot는 동이 트기 전에 답을 찾아야 하지만 그의 수수께끼는 그녀의 것만큼 어렵습니다.

19 그녀는 모두에게 "누군가 그의 이름을 알아낼 때까지 그 누구도 잠들 수 없다."라고 말합니다.

20 그리고 왕자는 이 오페라 전체에서 가장 유명한 아리아, Nessun Dorma를 부릅니다.

21 그것은 누구도 잠들지 못한다는 뜻입니다.

22 누구도 잠들지 못하네.

23 누구도 잠들지 못하네. 당신조차도, 공주여.

24 나의 비밀은 안전하다네.

25 누구도 나의 이름을 알지 못할 것이네.

26 동틀 녘에, 내가 이길 것이라네! 내가 승리할 것이라네!

27 왕자의 이름은 Calaf입니다.

28 공주는 그의 이름을 제때 알아낼 수 있을까요?

29 오페라를 보고 알아봅시다.

※ 다음 우리말을 영어로 쓰시오.

1 투란도트, 세상에서 가장 위험한 사랑

➡ _____

2 여러분, 환영합니다!

➡ _____

3 오늘 밤, 우리는 지아코모 푸치니의 오페라 《투란도트》를 공연할 것입니다.

➡ _____

4 다른 많은 유명한 오페라들처럼 《투란도트》는 이탈리아어로 되어 있는데, 오페라가 16세기 이탈리아에서 시작되었기 때문입니다.

➡ _____

5 시작하기 전에 오페라 《투란도트》의 줄거리를 알려 드리려고 합니다.

➡ _____

6 여러분이 줄거리를 알면 이 오페라를 더 잘 감상하게 될 것입니다.

➡ _____

7 중국의 공주 Turandot는 굉장히 아름다운 여인이지만, 그녀는 얼음처럼 차갑습니다.

➡ _____

8 그녀와 결혼하길 원하는 왕자는 누구든지 반드시 세 가지 수수께끼에 답해야 합니다.

➡ _____

9 만약 실패하면 그는 죽어야 합니다.

➡ _____

10 그 누구도 수수께끼에 답할 수 없었습니다.

➡ _____

11 어느 날, 어떤 용감한 왕자가 그녀에게 첫눈에 반합니다.

➡ _____

12 그는 세 수수께끼를 모두 맞힌 첫 번째 사람이 됩니다.

➡ _____

13 그러나 Turandot는 그 왕자와 결혼하길 원하지 않습니다.

➡ _____

14 그는 그녀에게 단지 낯선 사람일 뿐입니다.

➡ _____

15 그러자 그는 그녀에게 자신의 수수께끼를 냅니다.

➡ _____

16 그는 그녀에게 "제 이름이 무엇입니까?"라고 묻습니다.

   ➡ _____

17 그는 "당신이 맞게 대답한다면 나는 죽는 것에 동의하겠습니다. 만약 답이 틀리면 당신은 저와 결혼해야 할 것입니다."라고 덧붙입니다.

   ➡ _____

_____

18 Turandot는 동이 트기 전에 답을 찾아야 하지만 그의 수수께끼는 그녀의 것만큼 어렵습니다.

   ➡ _____

19 그녀는 모두에게 "누군가 그의 이름을 알아낼 때까지 그 누구도 잠들 수 없다."라고 말합니다.

   ➡ _____

20 그리고 왕자는 이 오페라 전체에서 가장 유명한 아리아, Nessun Dorma를 부릅니다.

   ➡ _____

21 그것은 누구도 잠들지 못한다는 뜻입니다.

   ➡ _____

22 누구도 잠들지 못하네.

   ➡ _____

23 누구도 잠들지 못하네, 당신조차도, 공주여.

   ➡ _____

24 나의 비밀은 안전하다네.

   ➡ _____

25 누구도 나의 이름을 알지 못할 것이네.

   ➡ _____

26 동틀 녘에, 내가 이길 것이라네! 내가 승리할 것이라네!

   ➡ _____

27 왕자의 이름은 Calaf입니다.

   ➡ _____

28 공주는 그의 이름을 제때 알아낼 수 있을까요?

   ➡ _____

29 오페라를 보고 알아봅시다.

   ➡ _____

※ 다음 우리말과 일치하도록 빈칸에 알맞은 말을 쓰시오.

Link

1. A: _____ was _____ _____?

2. B: It was _____! Actually, I've _____ the musical *Cats* before, and your song was _____ _____ _____ the _____.

1. A: 우리 공연 어땠어?
2. B: 굉장했어. 사실, 뮤지컬 캣츠를 전에 본 적이 있는데, 너희 노래는 뮤지컬의 노래만큼 대단했어.

Write

1. _____ _____ *La La Land*

2. I _____ *La La Land* _____ _____.

3. It _____ _____ the _____ and _____ of Mia and Sebastian.

4. I enjoyed _____ _____ and _____ _____.

5. The story _____ _____ _____ _____ _____ the songs.

6. If you _____ _____ _____ a good musical movie, you _____ _____ this movie.

7. _____ Kim Jisu _____ Aug. 11

1. 라라랜드에 대한 감상
2. 나는 지난 금요일에 라라랜드를 보았다.
3. 그건 Mia와 Sebastian의 꿈과 사랑에 대한 이야기야.
4. 나는 그것의 아름답고 감동적인 노래를 즐겼어.
5. 이야기도 노래만큼이나 좋았지.
6. 좋은 뮤지컬 영화를 찾고 있다면, 이 영화를 봐야 할 거야.
7. 8월 11일, 김지수 씀

Write

1. _____ _____ *Beauty and the Beast*

2. I _____ *Beauty and the Beast* _____ _____.

3. It is about a _____ _____ and a _____.

4. I enjoyed _____ _____ _____.

5. The songs were great, and the love story was _____ _____ _____ _____ _____.

6. If you _____ _____ _____ about love, you _____ _____ it, _____.

7. _____ Lee Minsu _____ _____. 12

1. 미녀와 야수에 대한 감상
2. 나는 지난 토요일에 미녀와 야수를 봤어.
3. 그건 예쁜 여자아이와 야수에 대한 이야기야.
4. 나는 그것을 매우 즐겼어.
5. 노래들은 아주 좋았고, 사랑 이야기는 보석만큼 아름다웠어.
6. 마음이 따뜻해지는 사랑 이야기를 좋아한다면, 너도 이걸 좋아할 거야.
7. 8월 12일, 이민수 씀

※ 다음 우리말을 영어로 쓰시오.

Link

1. A: 우리 공연 어땠어?

   ➡ _____

2. B: 굉장했어. 사실, 뮤지컬 캣츠를 전에 본적이 있는데, 너희 노래는 뮤지컬의 노래만큼 대단했어.

   ➡ _____

Write

1. 라라랜드에 대한 감상

   ➡ _____

2. 나는 지난 금요일에 라라랜드를 보았다.

   ➡ _____

3. 그건 Mla와 Sebastian의 꿈과 사랑에 대한 이야기야.

   ➡ _____

4. 나는 그것의 아름답고 감동적인 노래를 즐겼어.

   ➡ _____

5. 이야기도 노래만큼이나 좋았지.

   ➡ _____

6. 좋은 뮤지컬 영화를 찾고 있다면, 이 영화를 봐야 할 거야.

   ➡ _____

7. 8월 11일, 김지수 씀

   ➡ _____

Write

1. 미녀와 야수에 대한 감상

   ➡ _____

2. 나는 지난 토요일에 미녀와 야수를 봤어.

   ➡ _____

3. 그건 예쁜 여자아이와 야수에 대한 이야기야.

   ➡ _____

4. 나는 그것을 매우 즐겼어.

   ➡ _____

5. 노래들은 아주 좋았고, 사랑 이야기는 보석만큼 아름다웠어.

   ➡ _____

6. 마음이 따뜻해지는 사랑 이야기를 좋아한다면, 너도 이걸 좋아할 거야.

   ➡ _____

7. 8월 12일, 이민수 씀

   ➡ _____

※ 다음 영어를 우리말로 쓰시오.

01 beginner

02 seafood

03 disappointed

04 fortune teller

05 alone

06 back

07 prefer

08 half-moon

09 policy

10 culture

11 funny

12 meat

13 scholar

14 honesty

15 traditional

16 imaginary

17 offer

18 indoor

19 recently

20 ingredient

21 recommend

22 symbolize

23 servant

24 dish

25 harmony

26 special

27 kingdom

28 order

29 shape

30 mainly

31 official

32 different

33 outdoor

34 political

35 on sale

36 on the other hand

37 be afraid of

38 look like+명사

39 by oneself

40 dive into

41 become worried about

42 have been to+장소

43 be named after

※ 다음 우리말을 영어로 쓰시오.

01 전통의, 전통적인

02 문화

03 해산물

04 주로

05 제안하다, 권하다

06 신하, 관리, 공직자

07 다른

08 신하, 하인

09 실내의

10 특별한

11 재료

12 혼자, 홀로

13 등

14 선호하다

15 초보자

16 웃긴, 재미있는

17 정치의, 정당의

18 점쟁이

19 반의, 절반(의)

20 실망한

21 추천하다

22 상징하다

23 화합, 조화

24 정책

25 주문하다

26 성공, 히트작

27 정직함

28 반달

29 상상의, 가상의

30 학자

31 왕국

32 실외의

33 정당

34 최근에

35 세일 중

36 ~처럼 보이다

37 ~을 두려워하다

38 ~으로 뛰어들다

39 반면에

40 혼자서, 홀로

41 ~의 이름을 따서 지어지다

42 ~할까 생각 중이다

43 ~에 대해 걱정하다

※ 다음 영영풀이에 알맞은 단어를 <보기>에서 골라 쓴 후, 우리말 뜻을 쓰시오.

1 _____ : sweet food eaten at the end of a meal: _____
2 _____ : a country ruled by a king or queen: _____
3 _____ : to represent something: _____
4 _____ : created by and existing only in the mind: _____
5 _____ : a person who is starting to do something or learn something for the first time: _____
6 _____ : to like, choose, or want one thing rather than another: _____
7 _____ : a food that is used with other foods in the preparation of a particular dish: _____
8 _____ : a person who has a position of responsibility in an organization: _____
9 _____ : a person who studies a subject in great detail, especially at a university: _____
10 _____ : to suggest that someone or something would be good or suitable for a particular job or purpose: _____
11 _____ : a person who is employed in another person's house, doing jobs such as cooking and cleaning, especially in the past: _____
12 _____ : the way of life, especially the general customs and beliefs, of a particular group of people at a particular time: _____
13 _____ : unhappy because someone or something was not as good as you hoped or expected: _____
14 _____ : an organization of people with particular political beliefs that competes in elections to try to win positions in local or national government: _____
15 _____ : to ask for something to be made, supplied, or delivered, especially in a restaurant or shop: _____
16 _____ : a set of ideas or a plan of what to do in particular situations that has been agreed to officially by a group of people, a government, or a political party: _____

보기	servant	kingdom	prefer	recommend
	policy	order	culture	ingredient
	dessert	scholar	beginner	party
	symbolize	disappointed	official	imaginary

※ 다음 우리말과 일치하도록 빈칸에 알맞은 말을 쓰시오.

Listen & Speak 1-A

1. **B:** Do you have _____ for _____, Aunt May?
   W: Yes, Johnny. Do you _____ pie _____ cake?
   B: I _____ cake.
   W: O.K. I have some chocolate cake. I'll _____ you _____ .

2. **B:** I'm _____ _____ _____ a sports club.
   G: Do you _____ _____ _____ _____ sports?
   B: I _____ indoor sports. I was in the badminton club _____ year.
   G: _____ _____ _____ the table tennis club, then?
   B: That's a _____ _____ . Thank you.

Listen & Speak 2-A

1. **W:** _____ me. I'm _____ _____ an Italian cookbook. Could you _____ one?
   M: Well, _____ you ever _____ _____ food?
   W: No, I _____ , but I want _____ _____ . I really like spaghetti.
   M: Then, _____ this _____ cookbook for _____ ? It's _____ _____ now.
   W: Good! Thank you. I'll _____ it.

2. **G:** I _____ _____ a movie _____ . Could you _____ a good one?
   B: _____ _____ _____ see *Iron Woman 2*? It's a _____ _____ .
   G: Well, I don't like _____ movies. Can you _____ any good _____ ?
   B: Then, _____ _____ *Funny Families*?
   G: That _____ good.

Listen & Speak B

A: Could you _____ a book _____ _____ ?
B: Well, _____ _____ _____ _____ *The Flying Pan*?
A: Great idea. Thanks.

1. **B:** May 이모, 디저트로 먹을 만한 게 있나요?
   W: 그럼, Johnny. 파이가 더 좋으니, 케이크가 더 좋으니?
   B: 전 케이크가 더 좋아요.
   W: 알았어. 초콜릿 케이크가 좀 있네. 좀 갖다 줄게.

2. **B:** 나 스포츠 동아리에 가입하려고 생각 중이야.
   G: 실내 스포츠가 더 좋아, 야외 스포츠가 더 좋아?
   B: 실내 스포츠가 더 좋아. 작년에 배드민턴 동아리에 있었거든.
   G: 그럼, 탁구 동아리가 어때?
   B: 그게 좋겠다. 고마워.

1. **W:** 실례합니다. 이탈리아 요리책을 찾고 있는데요. 추천해 주실 수 있으세요?
   M: 음, 이탈리아 요리를 해 보신 적이 있나요?
   W: 아뇨, 없습니다. 하지만 해 보고 싶어서요. 스파게티를 정말 좋아하거든요.
   M: 그렇다면 초보자들을 위한 이 이탈리아 요리책이 어떨까요? 지금 세일 중이에요.
   W: 좋아요! 감사합니다. 그걸 살게요.

2. **G:** 최근에 영화를 한 편도 못 봤어. 좋은 영화 한 편 추천해 줄래?
   B: 《아이언 우먼 2》 어때? 크게 히트를 치고 있는데.
   G: 글쎄, 액션 영화는 안 좋아해. 괜찮은 코미디 영화 추천해 줄 수 있어?
   B: 그렇다면, 《퍼니 패밀리즈》는 어때?
   G: 그게 좋겠다.

A: 나한테 책 한 권 추천해 줄래?
B: 글쎄, '플라잉 팬' 어때?
A: 아주 좋아. 고마워.

Communicate A

Jaden: _____ you _____ _____ the new Chinese restaurant, Ms. Park?

Ms. Park: Are you _____ _____ the one on Main Street, Jaden?

Jaden: Yes, that's _____ _____. They opened _____ two weeks _____, _____?

Ms. Park: I think _____. I _____ there _____ Friday with my friends.

Jaden: _____ _____ the food?

Ms. Park: It was great. We _____ many _____ _____. I really liked the _____ vegetables.

Jaden: Could you _____ a dish _____ me? I'm going there for dinner _____ _____ my family.

Ms. Park: Do you _____ seafood _____ meat?

Jaden: I _____ _____.

Ms. Park: Then, you _____ _____ their _____ _____. You'll love it!

Communicate B

M: _____ _____ _____ _____ a Korean restaurant _____ here?

W: _____ you _____ hot _____ cold food?

M: I _____ cold food.

W: Then, you should _____ the naengmyeon place _____ _____ _____ _____ this block.

M: Thank you.

Progress Check

1. **G:** _____ _____ _____ _____ _____ a pet.

   B: Do you _____ dogs _____ cats?

   G: I _____ cats. They're so _____.

   B: Great! I can _____ _____ _____. I have seven cats at home.

   G: Thank you.

2. **W:** Excuse me. I'm _____ _____ a skirt. Could you _____ one?

   M: _____ _____ do you _____?

   W: Blue and pink are my _____ _____.

   M: Then, _____ _____ this blue one? It's _____ _____ now.

   W: Good! Thank you. I'll _____ it.

Jaden: 새로 생긴 중국집에 가 보셨어요, 박 선생님?

박 선생님: 메인 가에 있는 거 말하는 거니, Jaden?

Jaden: 네, 거기요. 한 2주 전쯤에 문을 열었어요, 그렇죠?

박 선생님: 그런 것 같아. 지난 금요일에 친구들과 함께 거기에 갔었단다.

Jaden: 음식이 어땠나요?

박 선생님: 훌륭했어. 우린 다양한 음식을 많이 시켰어. 나는 채소볶음이 정말 좋았어.

Jaden: 제게 요리 하나 추천해 주시겠어요? 오늘 저녁에 저녁 식사를 하러 가족들과 함께 그곳에 가거든요.

박 선생님: 너는 해산물을 더 좋아하니, 육류를 더 좋아하니?

Jaden: 전 해산물을 더 좋아해요.

박 선생님: 그럼 그곳의 생선튀김을 먹어 봐. 네가 정말 좋아할 거야!

M: 이 근처에서 한국 음식점 좀 추천해 주실래요?

W: 뜨거운 음식이 더 좋으세요, 차가운 음식이 더 좋으세요?

M: 찬 음식을 더 좋아해요.

W: 그럼, 이 블록 끝에 있는 냉면집에 가 보세요.

M: 감사합니다.

1. G: 애완동물을 키울까 해.

   B: 개가 좋아, 아니면 고양이가 좋아?

   G: 나는 고양이가 좋아. 정말 귀엽잖아.

   B: 잘 됐다! 내가 한 마리 줄 수 있어. 집에 일곱 마리나 있거든.

   G: 고마워.

2. W: 실례합니다. 치마를 찾고 있는데요. 하나 추천해 주실 수 있나요?

   M: 어떤 색을 좋아하세요?

   W: 파란색과 분홍색을 제일 좋아해요.

   M: 그럼, 이 파란 건 어때요? 지금 세일 중이에요.

   W: 좋아요! 감사합니다. 그걸로 할게요.

대화문 Test

※ 다음 우리말에 맞도록 대화를 영어로 쓰시오.

Listen & Speak 1-A

1. B: _____
   W: _____
   B: _____
   W: _____

2. B: _____
   G: _____
   B: _____
   G: _____
   B: _____

Listen & Speak 2-A

1. W: _____
   M: _____
   W: _____
   M: _____
   W: _____

2. G: _____
   B: _____
   G: _____
   B: _____
   G: _____

Listen & Speak B

A: _____
B: _____
A: _____

1. B: May 이모, 디저트로 먹을 만한 게 있나요?
   W: 그럼, Johnny. 파이가 더 좋으니, 케이크가 더 좋으니?
   B: 전 케이크가 더 좋아요.
   W: 알았어. 초콜릿 케이크가 좀 있네. 좀 갖다 줄게.

2. B: 나 스포츠 동아리에 가입하려고 생각 중이야.
   G: 실내 스포츠가 더 좋아, 야외 스포츠가 더 좋아?
   B: 실내 스포츠가 더 좋아. 작년에 배드민턴 동아리에 있었거든.
   G: 그럼, 탁구 동아리가 어때?
   B: 그게 좋겠다. 고마워.

1. W: 실례합니다. 이탈리아 요리책을 찾고 있는데요. 추천해 주실 수 있으세요?
   M: 음, 이탈리아 요리를 해 보신 적이 있나요?
   W: 아뇨, 없습니다, 하지만 해 보고 싶어서요. 스파게티를 정말 좋아하거든요.
   M: 그렇다면 초보자들을 위한 이 이탈리아 요리책이 어떨까요? 지금 세일 중이에요.
   W: 좋아요! 감사합니다. 그걸 살게요

2. G: 최근에 영화를 한 편도 못 봤어. 좋은 영화 한 편 추천해 줄래?
   B: 《아이언 우먼 2》 어때? 크게 히트를 치고 있는데.
   G: 글쎄, 액션 영화는 안 좋아해. 괜찮은 코미디 영화 추천해 줄 수 있어?
   B: 그렇다면, 《퍼니 패밀리즈》는 어때?
   G: 그게 좋겠다.

A: 나한테 책 한 권 추천해 줄래?
B: 글쎄, '플라잉 팬' 어때?
A: 아주 좋아. 고마워.

Communicate A

Jaden: _____

Ms. Park: _____

Jaden: _____

Ms. Park: _____

Jaden: _____

Ms. Park: _____

_____

Jaden: _____

_____

Ms. Park: _____

Jaden: _____

Ms. Park: _____

Jaden: 새로 생긴 중국집에 가 보셨어
요, 박 선생님?

박 선생님: 메인 가에 있는 거 말하는 거
니, Jaden?

Jaden: 네, 거기요. 한 2주 전쯤에 문을
열었어요, 그렇죠?

박 선생님: 그런 것 같아. 지난 금요일에
친구들과 함께 거기에 갔었단다.

Jaden: 음식이 어땠나요?

박 선생님: 훌륭했어. 우린 다양한 음식
을 많이 시켰어. 나는 채소볶음이
정말 좋았어.

Jaden: 제게 요리 하나 추천해 주시겠
어요? 오늘 저녁에 저녁 식사를 하
러 가족들과 함께 그곳에 가거든요.

박 선생님: 너는 해산물을 더 좋아하니,
육류를 더 좋아하니?

Jaden: 전 해산물을 더 좋아해요.

박 선생님: 그럼 그곳의 생선튀김을 먹
어 봐. 네가 정말 좋아할 거야!

Communicate B

M: _____

W: _____

M: _____

W: _____

M: _____

M: 이 근처에서 한국 음식점 좀 추천해
주실래요?

W: 뜨거운 음식이 더 좋으세요, 차가운
음식이 더 좋으세요?

M: 찬 음식을 더 좋아해요.

W: 그럼, 이 블록 끝에 있는 냉면집에
가 보세요.

M: 감사합니다.

Progress Check

1. G: _____

B: _____

G: _____

B: _____

G: _____

2. W: _____

M: _____

W: _____

M: _____

W: _____

1. G: 애완동물을 키울까 해.
   B: 개가 좋아, 아니면 고양이가 좋
   아?
   G: 나는 고양이가 좋아. 정말 귀엽잖
   아.
   B: 잘 됐다! 내가 한 마리 줄 수 있
   어. 집에 일곱 마리나 있거든.
   G: 고마워.

2. W: 실례합니다. 치마를 찾고 있는
   데요. 하나 추천해 주실 수 있나
   요?
   M: 어떤 색을 좋아하세요?
   W: 파란색과 분홍색을 제일 좋아해
   요.
   M: 그럼, 이 파란 건 어때요? 지금
   세일 중이에요.
   W: 좋아요! 감사합니다. 그걸로 할게
   요.

※ 다음 우리말과 일치하도록 빈칸에 알맞은 것을 골라 쓰시오.

1 A _____ of _____ _____

A. History   B. Bite   C. Korean

2 _____ did tangpyeongchae and sinseollo _____ their _____?

A. get   B. how   C. names

3 Why does songpyeon _____ _____ a _____ moon?

A. like   B. half   C. look

4 _____ _____ many interesting stories about our _____ _____.

A. are   B. food   C. traditional   D. there

5 _____ _____ _____ the fun history of our food.

A. into   B. dive   C. let's

Tangpyeongchae

6 One day, King Yeongjo was _____ dinner with his _____ and offered them _____ _____.

A. something   B. having   C. special   D. officials

7 It was a _____ with four _____ _____.

A. colorful   B. dish   C. ingredients

8 _____ ingredient _____ a different _____ party.

A. symbolized   B. political   C. each

9 Yeongjo wanted to say _____ the four parties should work _____ _____ _____ this dish.

A. harmony   B. that   C. like   D. in

10 This dish _____ _____ tangpyeongchae.

A. called   B. was

11 The name _____ _____ Yeongjo's _____ tangpyeongchaek.

A. policy   B. from   C. came

Sinseollo

12 In the _____ of King Yeonsan, there _____ a scholar who was _____ _____ his honesty.

A. famous   B. for   C. time   D. was

13 When the king did _____ _____, the scholar was never _____ of _____ him so.

A. afraid   B. something   C. telling   D. wrong

14 _____, the king never _____ _____ him.

A. listened   B. however   C. to

1	한국 역사 한 입
2	탕평채와 신선로는 어떻게 해서 그런 이름을 얻게 되었을까?
3	송편은 왜 반달 모양일까?
4	우리의 전통 음식에 대한 재미 있는 이야기들이 많이 있다.
5	우리 음식의 재미있는 역사 속으로 들어가 보자.

탕평채

6	어느 날, 영조가 그의 신하들과 저녁을 먹다가 그들에게 특별한 무언가를 권했다.
7	그것은 네 가지의 다채로운 재료로 만든 음식이었다.
8	각 재료는 서로 다른 당파를 상징했다.
9	영조는 이 음식처럼 네 당파가 화합을 이루어 일해야 한다는 것을 말하고 싶었다.
10	이 음식은 탕평채라고 불렸다.
11	그 이름은 영조의 정책인 탕평책에서 왔다.

신선로

12	연산군 시대에 정직하기로 유명한 한 학자가 있었다.
13	왕이 무언가를 잘못하면, 그 학자는 왕에게 그렇게 말하는 것을 절대 두려워하지 않았다.
14	그러나 왕은 그의 말에 전혀 귀기울이지 않았다.

15 The scholar was _____ disappointed _____ he went to live _____ a mountain.

    A. that   B. on   C. so

16 _____ he lived there _____ _____, he _____ ate vegetables.

    A. himself   B. mainly   C. while   D. by

17 He made a _____ _____ to cook many _____ vegetables together.

    A. pot   B. different   C. special

18 People _____ this _____ and the food _____ it sinseollo.

    A. in   B. pot   C. called

19 That is _____ the scholar lived _____ a sinseon, an _____ person who lives _____ in nature.

    A. like   B. alone   C. because   D. imaginary

Songpyeon

20 It was the _____ of the _____ _____ of Baekje.

    A. last   B. time   C. king

21 _____ day, the king and his _____ found a _____ turtle.

    A. strange   B. one   C. servants

22 _____ was _____ on its _____.

    A. back   B. something   C. written

23 It said, "Baekje is _____ a _____ moon, but Silla is like a _____ moon."

    A. like   B. half   C. full

24 The king asked a _____ _____, "_____ does this _____?"

    A. fortune   B. mean   C. teller   D. what

25 The _____ teller answered, "A _____ moon will soon _____ _____.

    A. become   B. full   C. fortune   D. smaller

26 _____ the _____ hand, a half moon will _____ _____ and become a full moon."

    A. grow   B. other   C. on   D. bigger

27 The king _____ _____ _____ his kingdom.

    A. worried   B. became   C. about

28 _____, people of Silla were very happy _____ learn this and made rice cakes _____ the _____ of a half moon.

    A. shape   B. to   C. in   D. however

29 _____ _____, people _____ enjoyed these half-moon _____ rice cakes, songpyeon.

    A. shaped   B. since   C. have   D. then

---

15 학자는 너무 실망하여 산속으로 살러 들어갔다.

16 그곳에서 혼자 사는 동안, 그는 주로 채소를 먹었다.

17 그는 여러 다양한 채소들을 함께 요리하기 위해 특별한 솥을 만들었다.

18 사람들은 이 솥과 그 안의 음식을 신선로라고 불렀다.

19 그것은 그 학자가 마치 자연 속에 홀로 사는 상상의 인물인 신선처럼 살았기 때문이다.

송편

20 백제의 마지막 왕 때였다.

21 어느 날, 왕과 신하들은 이상한 거북을 한 마리 발견했다.

22 그 거북의 등에 무언가가 쓰여 있었다.

23 그것은 "백제는 보름달과 같지만 신라는 반달과 같다."였다.

24 왕은 점술가에게 "이게 무슨 뜻인가?"라고 물었다.

25 점술가는 "보름달은 곧 작아질 것입니다.

26 반면에, 반달은 점점 커져서 보름달이 될 것입니다."라고 답했다.

27 왕은 자신의 왕국이 걱정되었다.

28 그러나 신라 사람들은 이것을 알고 매우 기뻐하며 반달 모양의 떡을 만들었다.

29 그 후로 사람들은 이 반달 모양의 떡인 송편을 즐겨 먹고 있다.

※ 다음 우리말과 일치하도록 빈칸에 알맞은 말을 쓰시오.

1 A _____ of _____ _____

2 _____ did tangpyeongchae and sinseollo _____ _____
_____?

3 _____ does songpyeon _____ _____ a _____ _____?

4 _____ _____ many interesting stories about our _____
_____.

5 Let's _____ _____ the fun history of our food.

Tangpyeongchae

6 One day, King Yeongjo _____ _____ _____ with his
_____ and _____ them _____ _____.

7 It was a dish _____ _____ _____ _____ _____.

8 Each ingredient symbolized _____ _____ _____ _____.

9 Yeongjo wanted to say that the four parties should work _____
_____ _____ this dish.

10 This dish _____ _____ tangpyeongchae.

11 The name _____ _____ Yeongjo's policy tangpyeongchaek.

Sinseollo

12 In the time of King Yeonsan, there _____ _____ _____ _____
who _____ _____ _____ his honesty.

13 When the king did _____ _____, the scholar _____
_____ _____ _____ _____ him so.

14 _____, the king never _____ _____ him.

1 한국 역사 한 입

2 탕평채와 신선로는 어떻게 해서 그런 이름을 얻게 되었을까?

3 송편은 왜 반달 모양일까?

4 우리의 전통 음식에 대한 재미있는 이야기들이 많이 있다.

5 우리 음식의 재미있는 역사 속으로 들어가 보자.

탕평채

6 어느 날, 영조가 그의 신하들과 저녁을 먹다가 그들에게 특별한 무언가를 권했다.

7 그것은 네 가지의 다채로운 재료로 만든 음식이었다.

8 각 재료는 서로 다른 당파를 상징했다.

9 영조는 이 음식처럼 네 당파가 화합을 이루어 일해야 한다는 것을 말하고 싶었다.

10 이 음식은 탕평채라고 불렸다.

11 그 이름은 영조의 정책인 탕평책에서 왔다.

신선로

12 연산군 시대에 정직하기로 유명한 한 학자가 있었다.

13 왕이 무언가를 잘못하면, 그 학자는 왕에게 그렇게 말하는 것을 절대 두려워하지 않았다.

14 그러나 왕은 그의 말에 전혀 귀 기울이지 않았다.

15 The scholar was _____ disappointed _____ he went to live on a mountain.

16 _____ he lived there _____ _____, he mainly ate vegetables.

17 He made _____ _____ _____ to cook many different vegetables _____.

18 People _____ this pot and _____ _____ _____ _____ sinseollo.

19 That is _____ the scholar lived _____ a sinseon, an _____ person who _____ _____ in nature.

Songpyeon

20 It was the time of _____ _____ _____ of Baekje.

21 One day, the king and his _____ found _____ _____ _____.

22 Something _____ _____ _____ _____ _____ _____.

23 It said, "Baekje _____ _____ a _____ _____, but Silla _____ _____ a _____ _____."

24 The king asked a fortune teller, "_____ does this _____?"

25 The _____ _____ answered, "A full moon will soon _____ _____.

26 _____ _____ _____ _____, a half moon will _____ _____ and _____ a _____ _____."

27 The king _____ _____ _____ his kingdom.

28 _____, people of Silla were very happy to learn this and made rice cakes _____ _____ _____ _____ a half moon.

29 _____ _____, people _____ _____ these half-moon _____ _____, songpyeon.

15 학자는 너무 실망하여 산속으로 살러 들어갔다.

16 그곳에서 혼자 사는 동안, 그는 주로 채소를 먹었다.

17 그는 여러 다양한 채소들을 함께 요리하기 위해 특별한 솥을 만들었다.

18 사람들은 이 솥과 그 안의 음식을 신선로라고 불렀다.

19 그것은 그 학자가 마치 자연 속에 홀로 사는 상상의 인물인 신선처럼 살았기 때문이다.

송편

20 백제의 마지막 왕 때였다.

21 어느 날, 왕과 신하들은 이상한 거북을 한 마리 발견했다.

22 그 거북의 등에 무언가가 쓰여 있었다.

23 그것은 "백제는 보름달과 같지만 신라는 반달과 같다."였다.

24 왕은 점술가에게 "이게 무슨 뜻인가?"라고 물었다.

25 점술가는 "보름달은 곧 작아질 것입니다.

26 반면에, 반달은 점점 커져서 보름달이 될 것입니다."라고 답했다.

27 왕은 자신의 왕국이 걱정되었다.

28 그러나 신라 사람들은 이것을 알고 매우 기뻐하며 반달 모양의 떡을 만들었다.

29 그 후로 사람들은 이 반달 모양의 떡인 송편을 즐겨 먹고 있다.

※ 다음 문장을 우리말로 쓰시오.

1 ▶ A Bite of Korean History

➡ _____

2 ▶ How did tangpyeongchae and sinseollo get their names?

➡ _____

3 ▶ Why does songpyeon look like a half moon?

➡ _____

4 ▶ There are many interesting stories about our traditional food.

➡ _____

5 ▶ Let's dive into the fun history of our food.

➡ _____

Tangpyeongchae

6 ▶ One day, King Yeongjo was having dinner with his officials and offered them something special.

➡ _____

7 ▶ It was a dish with four colorful ingredients.

➡ _____

8 ▶ Each ingredient symbolized a different political party.

➡ _____

9 ▶ Yeongjo wanted to say that the four parties should work in harmony like this dish.

➡ _____

10 ▶ This dish was called tangpyeongchae.

➡ _____

11 ▶ The name came from Yeongjo's policy tangpyeongchaek.

➡ _____

Sinseollo

12 ▶ In the time of King Yeonsan, there was a scholar who was famous for his honesty.

➡ _____

13 ▶ When the king did something wrong, the scholar was never afraid of telling him so.

➡ _____

14 ▶ However, the king never listened to him.

➡ _____

15 The scholar was so disappointed that he went to live on a mountain.

➡ _____

16 While he lived there by himself, he mainly ate vegetables.

➡ _____

17 He made a special pot to cook many different vegetables together.

➡ _____

18 People called this pot and the food in it sinseollo.

➡ _____

19 That is because the scholar lived like a sinseon, an imaginary person who lives alone in nature.

➡ _____

Songpyeon

20 It was the time of the last king of Baekje.

➡ _____

21 One day, the king and his servants found a strange turtle.

➡ _____

22 Something was written on its back.

➡ _____

23 It said, "Baekje is like a full moon, but Silla is like a half moon."

➡ _____

24 The king asked a fortune teller, "What does this mean?"

➡ _____

25 The fortune teller answered, "A full moon will soon become smaller.

➡ _____

26 On the other hand, a half moon will grow bigger and become a full moon."

➡ _____

27 The king became worried about his kingdom.

➡ _____

28 However, people of Silla were very happy to learn this and made rice cakes in the shape of a half moon.

➡ _____

29 Since then, people have enjoyed these half-moon shaped rice cakes, songpyeon.

➡ _____

※ 다음 괄호 안의 단어들을 우리말에 맞도록 바르게 배열하시오.

1 (Bite / A / History / of / Korean)
➡ _____

2 (did / how / sinseollo / and / tangpyeongchae / their / get / names?)
➡ _____

3 (does / why / look / songpyeon / like / half / moon? / a)
➡ _____

4 (are / there / interesting / many / about / stories / traditional / our / food.)
➡ _____

5 (dive / let's / into / fun / the / of / history / food. / our)
➡ _____

Tangpyeongchae

6 (day, / one / Yeongjo / King / having / was / with / dinner / officials / his / and / them / offered / something / special.)
➡ _____
_____

7 (was / it / dish / a / four / with / ingredients. / colorful)
➡ _____

8 (ingredient / each / a / symbolized / political / different / party.)
➡ _____

9 (Yeongjo / to / wanted / say / that / four / the / parties / work / should / harmony / in / this / like / dish.)
➡ _____

10 (dish / this / called / was / tangpyeongchae.)
➡ _____

11 (name / the / from / came / policy / Yeongjo's / tangpyeongchaek.)
➡ _____

Sinseollo

12 (the / in / of / time / Yeonsan, / King / was / there / who / a / scholar / was / for / famous / his / for / honesty.)
➡ _____
_____

13 (the / when / king / something / did / wrong, / scholar / the / never / was / of / afraid / telling / so. / him)
➡ _____
_____

14 (the / however, / king / listened / never / him. / to)
➡ _____

1 한국 역사 한 입

2 탕평채와 신선로는 어떻게 해서 그런 이름을 얻게 되었을까?

3 송편은 왜 반달 모양일까?

4 우리의 전통 음식에 대한 재미 있는 이야기들이 많이 있다.

5 우리 음식의 재미있는 역사 속 으로 들어가 보자.

탕평채

6 어느 날, 영조가 그의 신하들과 저녁을 먹다가 그들에게 특별한 무언가를 권했다.

7 그것은 네 가지의 다채로운 재 료로 만든 음식이었다.

8 각 재료는 서로 다른 당파를 상 징했다.

9 영조는 이 음식처럼 네 당파가 화합을 이루어 일해야 한다는 것을 말하고 싶었다.

10 이 음식은 탕평채라고 불렸다.

11 그 이름은 영조의 정책인 탕평 책에서 왔다.

신선로

12 연산군 시대에 정직하기로 유명 한 한 학자가 있었다.

13 왕이 무언가를 잘못하면, 그 학 자는 왕에게 그렇게 말하는 것 을 절대 두려워하지 않았다.

14 그러나 왕은 그의 말에 전혀 귀 기울이지 않았다.

15 (scholar / the / so / was / disappointed / he / that / to / went / live / on / mountain. / a)

➡ _____

16 (he / while / there / lived / himself, / by / mainly / he / vegetables. / ate)

➡ _____

17 (made / he / special / a / to / pot / many / cook / vegetables / different / together.)

➡ _____

18 (called / people / pot / this / and / food / the / it / in / sinseollo.)

➡ _____

19 (is / that / because / scholar / the / like / lived / sinseon, / a / imaginary / an / person / who / alone / lives / nature. / in)

➡ _____

Songpyeon

20 (was / it / time / the / of / last / the / Baekje. / king / of)

➡ _____

21 (day, / one / king / the / and / servants / his / a / found / turtle. / strange)

➡ _____

22 (was / something / on / written / back. / its)

➡ _____

23 (said, / it / "Baekje / like / is / full / a / moon, / but / is / Silla / half / a / moon." / like)

➡ _____

24 (king / the / a / asked / teller, / fortune / "what / this / does / mean?")

➡ _____

25 (fortune / the / teller / answered, / "full / a / moon / soon / will / smaller. / become)

➡ _____

26 (the / on / hand, / other / half / a / moon / grow / will / and / bigger / become / moon." / full / a)

➡ _____

27 (king / the / worried / became / about / kingdom. / his)

➡ _____

28 (people / however, / Silla / of / very / were / to / happy / this / learn / and / rice / made / cakes / the / in / shape / a / of / moon. / half)

➡ _____

_____

29 (then, / since / have / people / these / enjoyed / shaped / half-moon / rice / songpyeon. / cakes,)

➡ _____

_____

15 학자는 너무 실망하여 산속으로 살러 들어갔다

16 그곳에서 혼자 사는 동안, 그는 주로 채소를 먹었다.

17 그는 여러 다양한 채소들을 함께 요리하기 위해 특별한 솥을 만들었다.

18 사람들은 이 솥과 그 안의 음식을 신선로라고 불렀다.

19 그것은 그 학자가 마치 자연 속에 홀로 사는 상상의 인물인 신선처럼 살았기 때문이다.

송편

20 백제의 마지막 왕 때였다.

21 어느 날, 왕과 신하들은 이상한 거북을 한 마리 발견했다.

22 그 거북의 등에 무언가가 쓰여 있었다.

23 그것은 "백제는 보름달과 같지만 신라는 반달과 같다."였다.

24 왕은 점술가에게 "이게 무슨 뜻인가?"라고 물었다.

25 점술가는 "보름달은 곧 작아질 것입니다.

26 반면에, 반달은 점점 커져서 보름달이 될 것입니다."라고 답했다.

27 왕은 자신의 왕국이 걱정되었다.

28 그러나 신라 사람들은 이것을 알고 매우 기뻐하며 반달 모양의 떡을 만들었다.

29 그 후로 사람들은 이 반달 모양의 떡인 송편을 즐겨 먹고 있다.

※ 다음 우리말을 영어로 쓰시오.

1 한국 역사 한 입

➡ _____

2 탕평채와 신선로는 어떻게 해서 그런 이름을 얻게 되었을까?

➡ _____

3 송편은 왜 반달 모양일까?

➡ _____

4 우리의 전통 음식에 대한 재미있는 이야기들이 많이 있다.

➡ _____

5 우리 음식의 재미있는 역사 속으로 들어가 보자.

➡ _____

Tangpyeongchae 탕평채

6 어느 날, 영조가 그의 신하들과 저녁을 먹다가 그들에게 특별한 무언가를 권했다.

➡ _____

7 그것은 네 가지의 다채로운 재료로 만든 음식이었다.

➡ _____

8 각 재료는 서로 다른 당파를 상징했다.

➡ _____

9 영조는 이 음식처럼 네 당파가 화합을 이루어 일해야 한다는 것을 말하고 싶었다.

➡ _____

10 이 음식은 탕평채라고 불렸다.

➡ _____

11 그 이름은 영조의 정책인 탕평책에서 왔다.

➡ _____

Sinseollo 신선로

12 연산군 시대에 정직하기로 유명한 한 학자가 있었다.

➡ _____

13 왕이 무언가를 잘못하면, 그 학자는 왕에게 그렇게 말하는 것을 절대 두려워하지 않았다.

➡ _____

14 그러나 왕은 그의 말에 전혀 귀 기울이지 않았다.

➡ _____

15 학자는 너무 실망하여 산속으로 살러 들어갔다.

➡ _____

16 그곳에서 혼자 사는 동안, 그는 주로 채소를 먹었다.

➡ _____

17 그는 여러 다양한 채소들을 함께 요리하기 위해 특별한 솥을 만들었다.

➡ _____

18 사람들은 이 솥과 그 안의 음식을 신선로라고 불렀다.

➡ _____

19 그것은 그 학자가 마치 자연 속에 홀로 사는 상상의 인물인 신선처럼 살았기 때문이다.

➡ _____

Songpyeon 송편

20 백제의 마지막 왕 때였다.

➡ _____

21 어느 날, 왕과 신하들은 이상한 거북을 한 마리 발견했다.

➡ _____

22 그 거북의 등에 무언가가 쓰여 있었다.

➡ _____

23 그것은 "백제는 보름달과 같지만 신라는 반달과 같다."였다.

➡ _____

24 왕은 점술가에게 "이게 무슨 뜻인가?"라고 물었다.

➡ _____

25 점술가는 "보름달은 곧 작아질 것입니다.

➡ _____

26 반면에, 반달은 점점 커져서 보름달이 될 것입니다."라고 답했다.

➡ _____

27 왕은 자신의 왕국이 걱정되었다.

➡ _____

28 그러나 신라 사람들은 이것을 알고 매우 기뻐하며 반달 모양의 떡을 만들었다.

➡ _____

29 그 후로 사람들은 이 반달 모양의 떡인 송편을 즐겨 먹고 있다.

➡ _____

※ 다음 우리말과 일치하도록 빈칸에 알맞은 말을 쓰시오.

Work Together

1. A: _____ _____ _____ a salad for me?

2. B: We have two salads today. _____ _____ _____ chicken salad _____ green salad?

3. A: I _____ green salad.

4. B: O.K. _____ _____ _____.

5. A: _____ you.

Write

1. _____ Songpyeon

2. My family eats _____ _____ on Chuseok.

3. It _____ _____ _____ rice _____, chocolate, and _____.

4. It is _____ _____ _____ tteok.

5. _____ I eat this food, I _____ _____ _____ my little brother.

6. Three years _____, he ate all the _____ for songpyeon, so we _____ _____ _____ chocolate songpyeon.

7. This food gives us a _____ _____ _____ that funny day.

Culture Project

1. The word *dongporou* _____ _____ the name of the _____ _____ _____ Su Dongpo.

2. _____ his time in Hangzhou, he invented a way _____ _____ pork fresh _____ _____ _____ _____.

3. He made the pork _____ _____ _____.

4. _____, dongporou _____ dongpo pork _____ _____ _____ China.

※ 다음 우리말을 영어로 쓰시오.

Work Together

1. A: 샐러드 좀 추전해 주시겠습니까?
   ➡ _____

2. B: 저희는 오늘 두 가지 샐러드가 있습니다. 닭고기 샐러드가 더 좋으신가요, 야채 샐러드가 더 좋으신가요?
   ➡ _____

3. A: 야채 샐러드가 더 좋아요.
   ➡ _____

4. B: 네. 여기 나왔습니다.
   ➡ _____

5. A: 감사합니다.
   ➡ _____

Write

1. 초콜릿 송편
   ➡ _____

2. 나의 가족은 추석에 특별한 것을 먹는다.
   ➡ _____

3. 그것은 쌀가루, 초콜릿, 그리고 견과로 만들어진다.
   ➡ _____

4. 그것은 일종의 떡이다.
   ➡ _____

5. 내가 이 음식을 먹을 때, 나는 항상 나의 남동생을 생각한다.
   ➡ _____

6. 3년 전, 그가 송편의 모든 소를 먹어서, 우리는 초콜릿 송편을 만들기로 결심했다.
   ➡ _____

7. 이 음식은 우리에게 그 재미있던 날을 기억할 기회를 준다.
   ➡ _____

Culture Project

1. 동파육이라는 단어는 중국의 유명한 시인인 소동파의 이름에서 나왔다.
   ➡ _____

2. 그의 시대에 항저우에서, 그는 돼지고기를 오랫동안 신선하게 유지하는 방법을 창안했다.
   ➡ _____

3. 그는 돼지고기를 달고 짜게 만들었다.
   ➡ _____

4. 나중에 동파육, 곧 동파 돼지고기는 중국 전역에서 인기 있게 되었다.
   ➡ _____

※ 다음 영어를 우리말로 쓰시오.

01 single _____

02 chief _____

03 darkness _____

04 spread _____

05 electricity _____

06 foundation _____

07 amusement park _____

08 blackout _____

09 shelter _____

10 impossible _____

11 ceiling _____

12 widely _____

13 bend _____

14 charity _____

15 install _____

16 shout _____

17 invent _____

18 shake _____

19 magic _____

20 leftover _____

21 whole _____

22 bleach _____

23 enough _____

24 packed _____

25 popular _____

26 surprisingly _____

27 remain _____

28 roof _____

29 safe _____

30 village _____

31 work _____

32 save _____

33 less _____

34 amazing _____

35 pay for _____

36 at least _____

37 light up _____

38 not ~ anymore _____

39 forget to부정사 _____

40 turn up _____

41 thanks to _____

42 come up with _____

43 just like _____

※ 다음 우리말을 영어로 쓰시오.

01	구부리다, 휘다	
02	천장	
03	흔들다, 털다	
04	자선단체	
05	어둠, 암흑	
06	어려운	
07	전체의	
08	대규모 정전 사태	
09	널리, 폭넓게	
10	남은 음식	
11	주요한; 우두머리, 부장	
12	더 적은	
13	불가능한	
14	외치다	
15	전기	
16	단 하나의	
17	작동하다	
18	구하다	
19	놀이공원	
20	재단	
21	지붕	

22	마법의, 신기한	
23	주거지, 쉼터	
24	마을	
25	인기 있는	
26	설치하다	
27	남아 있다	
28	안전한	
29	지속되다	
30	놀랍게도	
31	표백제	
32	꽉 들어찬	
33	충분한	
34	발명하다	
35	~을 환하게 밝히다	
36	~ 덕분에	
37	더 이상 ~ 않다	
38	~을 말리다	
39	지불하다	
40	~할 것을 잊다	
41	~을 생각해 내다, ~을 만들어 내다	
42	(소리 등을) 높이다	
43	A를 B로 채우다	

※ 다음 영영풀이에 알맞은 단어를 <보기>에서 골라 쓴 후, 우리말 뜻을 쓰시오.

1 _____ : to continue to exist: _____

2 _____ : a very small town located in a country area: _____

3 _____ : the covering that forms the top of a building, vehicle, etc.: _____

4 _____ : food that has not been finished at a meal: _____

5 _____ : a time when there is no light or power because of an electricity failure: _____

6 _____ : to keep someone or something safe from death, harm, loss, etc.: _____

7 _____ : the inside surface of a room that you can see when you look above you: _____

8 _____ : liked or enjoyed by a large number of people: _____

9 _____ : a device for giving light, especially one that has a covering: _____

10 _____ : to cover, reach, or have an effect on a wider or increasing area: _____

11 _____ : to design and/or create something that has never been made before: _____

12 _____ : a strong chemical used for cleaning things or removing colour from things: _____

13 _____ : to put furniture, a machine, or a piece of equipment into position and make it ready to use: _____

14 _____ : the period between the time when the sun rises and the time it goes down, or the part of the day that is neither evening nor night: _____

15 _____ : a form of energy that can be produced in several ways and that provides power to devices that create light, heat, etc.: _____

16 _____ : a system of giving money, food, or help free to those who are in need because they are ill, poor, or have no home, or any organization that has the purpose of providing money or helping in this way _____

보기

charity	blackout	roof	village
bleach	install	spread	leftover
ceiling	electricity	daytime	save
last	lamp	invent	popular

※ 다음 우리말과 일치하도록 빈칸에 알맞은 말을 쓰시오.

Listen & Speak 1-A

1. **G:** Can you _____ _____ the volume on your phone? I like this song.

   B: I can't _____ _____ _____ _____ . It's the _____ volume.

   G: _____ me just _____ your phone in a glass. _____ _____ a glass _____ _____ a speaker.

   B: _____ _____ _____ _____ ! _____ try it now.

2. **B:** _____ _____ that a movie star _____ _____ to our school.

   G: That's _____ . She's my _____ _____ .

   B: Oh, who is she?

   G: Miranda Kim. She _____ the _____ _____ in the movie *Jupiter*.

   B: Wow, I _____ _____ _____ _____ her!

Listen & Speak 2-A

1. **W:** Excuse me, are you _____ with your _____ ?

   M: Yes, it was really _____ .

   W: Do you _____ _____ _____ the _____ home?

   M: Yes, _____ .

   W: _____ _____ _____ _____ the leftovers by tomorrow.

2. **B:** What's _____ _____ this _____ _____ ?

   G: _____ _____ visit Hong Kong _____ _____ _____ .

   B: That _____ _____ . What are you _____ _____ there?

   G: I'm _____ _____ _____ to an _____ park. I'm also going _____ _____ _____ _____ of food.

   B: Good. _____ _____ _____ _____ some dim sum.

1. G: 네 휴대폰 소리를 키워줄 수 있겠니? 이 노래가 좋아.
   B: 소리를 더는 키울 수 없어. 음량이 이미 가장 높은데.
   G: 그냥 네 휴대폰을 유리잔 안에 넣게 해 줘. 유리잔이 스피커처럼 쓰인다고 들었어.
   B: 재미있는 생각이야! 지금 해 보자.

2. B: 우리 학교에 영화 배우가 온다고 들었어.
   G: 맞아. 내가 가장 좋아하는 여배우야.
   B: 오, 누군데?
   G: Miranda Kim이야. 영화 《주피터》에서 책임 과학자를 연기했어.
   B: 우와, 빨리 만나보고 싶은데!

1. W: 실례합니다, 식사를 마치셨나요?
   M: 네, 정말 좋았어요.
   W: 남은 음식을 집에 가져가시겠어요?
   M: 네, 부탁합니다.
   W: 내일까지는 남은 음식을 다 드시는 걸 잊지 마세요.

2. B: 이번 겨울 방학에는 뭘 할 거야?
   G: 부모님과 홍콩에 갈 거야.
   B: 신나겠는걸. 거기서 뭘 할 거니?
   G: 놀이공원에 갈 거야. 그리고 온갖 음식들을 먹어 볼 거야.
   B: 좋은데. 딤섬을 먹어 보는 걸 잊지 마.

Communicate A

Yuri: _____ _____, Jaden?

Jaden: My science homework is too _____.

Yuri: What do you _____ _____ do?

Jaden: I need to find _____ _____ _____ _____ trees.

Yuri: That's easy. _____ _____ _____ we _____ _____ trees _____ _____ _____ paper.

Jaden: Oh, I think _____ _____ _____ _____, _____. Then, I can just _____ _____ _____ _____ _____.

Yuri: Yes! You _____ _____ _____ just one paper towel _____ _____ _____ your hands.

Jaden: That's _____. I need _____ _____ two or three paper towels.

Yuri: Just _____ your hands _____ you use a paper towel. Then, one will be _____ _____ _____.

Jaden: Oh, that's a good idea, Yuri! I'll _____ that _____ _____.

Yuri: Good! Just _____ _____ _____ _____ your hands _____ _____ 10 _____.

Communicate B

A: _____ _____ _____ that _____ _____ is the _____ _____ _____ _____ the Earth.

B: I've _____ _____, _____. What can we do to _____ _____?

A: _____ _____ we _____ _____ the light _____ we're not using it?

B: That's a good idea. _____ _____ to _____ _____ the light _____ you _____ your room.

Progress Check

1. **B:** _____ _____ _____ a famous baseball player _____ _____ to our school.

   G: That's right. He's _____ _____ _____.

   B: Oh, who is he?

   G: I'm _____ _____ _____ tell you. It's a _____!

2. **B:** What's your _____ this _____ _____?

   G: I'm going _____ _____ Vietnam _____ my parents.

   B: That _____ _____. What are you _____ to do there?

   G: I'm going to _____ some time on the _____ and eat lots of _____.

   B: Good. _____ _____ _____ _____ the fruit there, too.

   G: O.K., I _____ _____.

유리: 무슨 일 있니, Jaden?
Jaden: 과학 숙제가 너무 어려워.
유리: 뭘 해야 하는데?
Jaden: 나무들을 살리는 방법을 찾아야 해.
유리: 그건 쉬워. 나는 종이를 덜 사용함으로써 나무들을 살릴 수 있다고 들었어.
Jaden: 아, 나도 들어 본 것 같아. 그럼, 종이컵 쓰는 걸 멈추면 되겠네.
유리: 맞아! 그리고 손을 말리는 데 종이 수건을 한 장만 쓸 수도 있지.
Jaden: 그건 불가능해. 나는 종이 수건이 적어도 두세 장은 필요해.
유리: 종이 수건을 쓰기 전에 손을 털어 봐. 그럼, 한 장으로 충분하고도 남을 거야.
Jaden: 오, 좋은 생각이야, 유리야! 다음에 해 봐야겠어.
유리: 좋아! 손을 적어도 열 번은 털어야 한다는 걸 잊지 마.

A: 전기를 절약하는 게 지구를 살리는 데 가장 좋은 방법이라고 들었어.
B: 나도 들었어. 전기를 절약하기 위해 무엇을 할 수 있을까?
A: 사용하지 않을 때는 전기를 끄는 게 어때?
B: 좋은 생각이야. 방을 나갈 때 불 끄는 것을 잊지 마.

1. B: 유명한 야구 선수가 우리 학교로 온다고 들었어.
   G: 맞아. 그는 내가 가장 좋아하는 선수야.
   B: 오, 누군데?
   G: 말해주지 않을 거야. 놀라게 할 거야!

2. B: 이번 겨울 방학에 무슨 계획이 있니?
   G: 부모님과 함께 베트남에 갈 거야.
   B: 재미있겠다. 거기서 뭘 할 거야?
   G: 바닷가에서 시간을 좀 보내고 해산물을 많이 먹을 거야.
   B: 좋아. 거기 과일을 먹어 보는 것도 잊지 마.
   G: 알겠어, 잊지 않을게.

Step2

※ 다음 우리말에 맞도록 대화를 영어로 쓰시오.

Listen & Speak 1-A

1. G: _____
   B: _____
   G: _____
   B: _____

2. B: _____
   G: _____
   B: _____
   G: _____
   B: _____

해석

1. G: 네 휴대폰 소리를 키워줄 수 있겠니? 이 노래가 좋아.
   B: 소리를 더는 키울 수 없어. 음량이 이미 가장 높은데.
   G: 그냥 네 휴대폰을 유리잔 안에 넣게 해 줘. 유리잔이 스피커처럼 쓰인다고 들었어.
   B: 재미있는 생각이야! 지금 해 보자.

2. B: 우리 학교에 영화 배우가 온다고 들었어.
   G: 맞아. 내가 가장 좋아하는 여배우야.
   B: 오, 누군데?
   G: Miranda Kim이야. 영화 《주피터》에서 책임 과학자를 연기했어.
   B: 우와, 빨리 만나보고 싶은데!

Listen & Speak 2-A

1. W: _____
   M: _____
   W: _____
   M: _____
   W: _____

2. B: _____
   G: _____
   B: _____
   G: _____
   B: _____

1. W: 실례합니다, 식사를 마치셨나요?
   M: 네, 정말 좋았어요.
   W: 남은 음식을 집에 가져가시겠어요?
   M: 네, 부탁합니다.
   W: 내일까지는 남은 음식을 다 드시는 걸 잊지 마세요.

2. B: 이번 겨울 방학에는 뭘 할 거야?
   G: 부모님과 홍콩에 갈 거야.
   B: 신나겠는걸. 거기서 뭘 할 거니?
   G: 놀이공원에 갈 거야. 그리고 온갖 음식들을 먹어 볼 거야.
   B: 좋은데. 딤섬을 먹어 보는 걸 잊지 마.

Communicate A

Yuri: _____

Jaden: _____

Yuri: _____

Jaden: _____

Yuri: _____

Jaden: _____

Yuri: _____

Jaden: _____

Yuri: _____

_____

Jaden: _____

Yuri: _____

유리: 무슨 일 있니, Jaden?
Jaden: 과학 숙제가 너무 어려워.
유리: 뭘 해야 하는데?
Jaden: 나무들을 살리는 방법을 찾아야 해.
유리: 그건 쉬워. 나는 종이를 덜 사용함으로써 나무들을 살릴 수 있다고 들었어.
Jaden: 아, 나도 들어 본 것 같아. 그럼, 종이컵 쓰는 걸 멈추면 되겠네.
유리: 맞아! 그리고 손을 말리는 데 종이 수건을 한 장만 쓸 수도 있지.
Jaden: 그건 불가능해. 나는 종이 수건이 적어도 두세 장은 필요해.
유리: 종이 수건을 쓰기 전에 손을 털어 봐. 그럼, 한 장으로 충분하고도 남을 거야.
Jaden: 오, 좋은 생각이야, 유리야! 다음에 해 봐야겠어.
유리: 좋아! 손을 적어도 열 번은 털어야 한다는 걸 잊지 마.

Communicate B

A: _____

B: _____

A: _____

B: _____

A: 전기를 절약하는 게 지구를 살리는 데 가장 좋은 방법이라고 들었어.
B: 나도 들었어. 전기를 절약하기 위해 무엇을 할 수 있을까?
A: 사용하지 않을 때는 전기를 끄는 게 어때?
B: 좋은 생각이야. 방을 나갈 때 불 끄는 것을 잊지 마.

Progress Check

1. B: _____

G: _____

B: _____

G: _____

2. B: _____

G: _____

B: _____

G: _____

B: _____

G: _____

1. B: 유명한 야구 선수가 우리 학교로 온다고 들었어.
   G: 맞아. 그는 내가 가장 좋아하는 선수야.
   B: 오, 누군데?
   G: 말해주지 않을 거야. 놀라게 할 거야!

2. B: 이번 겨울 방학에 무슨 계획이 있니?
   G: 부모님과 함께 베트남에 갈 거야.
   B: 재미있겠다. 거기서 뭘 할 거야?
   G: 바닷가에서 시간을 좀 보내고 해산물을 많이 먹을 거야.
   B: 좋아. 거기 과일을 먹어 보는 것도 잊지 마.
   G: 알겠어, 잊지 않을게.

※ 다음 우리말과 일치하도록 빈칸에 알맞은 것을 골라 쓰시오.

1 _____ Magic _____

A. Lamps   B. One-Dollar

2 "Wow, I can _____ a book in my room now!" _____ Marco, a boy in a _____ in the Philippines.

A. shouted   B. village   C. read

3 His house has no _____ just _____ all the _____ houses in the _____.

A. other   B. village   C. like   D. electricity

4 People in the village are _____ poor _____ _____ for electricity.

A. pay   B. to   C. too

5 Even _____ the _____, they live in darkness _____ the houses are _____ close together.

A. because   B. daytime   C. packed   D. during

6 Now _____ are changing _____ _____ a _____ plastic bottle.

A. of   B. because   C. single   D. things

7 One plastic bottle in the ceiling can _____ _____ a whole room _____ _____ any electricity.

A. without   B. light   C. using   D. up

8 This amazing plastic bottle is _____ a Moser lamp _____ it was _____ _____ Alfredo Moser.

A. invented   B. called   C. by   D. because

9 In 2002, _____ _____ many _____ in his town in Brazil.

A. blackouts   B. were   C. there

10 These blackouts made him _____ up _____ a new _____ to _____ his house.

A. come   B. light   C. with   D. way

11 A Moser lamp can be _____ _____ about one dollar and _____ for _____ 10 years.

A. for   B. made   C. about   D. lasts

12 It is _____ very _____.

A. safe   B. also

---

1 1달러짜리 마법의 전구

2 "우와, 이젠 제 방에서 책을 읽을 수 있어요!" 필리핀의 한 마을에 사는 소년인 Marco가 외쳤다.

3 그의 집은 마을의 다른 모든 집들과 마찬가지로 전기가 없다.

4 마을 사람들은 너무나 가난해서 전기세를 낼 수가 없다.

5 심지어 낮 동안에도, 집들이 빽빽하게 들어차 있어서 그들은 어둠 속에 살아간다.

6 이제 플라스틱병 하나 때문에 상황이 바뀌고 있다.

7 천장에 있는 플라스틱병 하나는 전기를 쓰지 않고 방 전체를 밝힐 수 있다.

8 이 놀라운 플라스틱병은 Moser 램프라고 불리는데, 그것이 Alfredo Moser에 의해 발명되었기 때문이다.

9 2002년, 브라질에 있는 그의 마을에는 정전이 잦았다.

10 이 정전들은 그가 집을 밝히는 새로운 방법을 생각해 내도록 만들었다.

11 Moser 램프는 1달러 정도로 만들 수 있고 10년 정도 지속된다.

12 그것은 또한 매우 안전하다.

13 It can _____ _____ a house _____ .

    A. fire   B. start   C. never

14 _____ , it is very _____ to _____ this magic lamp.

    A. easy   B. surprisingly   C. make

15 _____ to _____ a Moser lamp _____ a bottle

    A. from   B. how   C. make

16 1. _____ a _____ plastic bottle _____ water.

    A. with   B. fill   C. clear

17 2. _____ some bleach _____ _____ the water _____ .

    A. clear   B. keep   C. add   D. to

18 3. Make a hole in the _____ , and _____ the bottle _____ the _____ .

    A. hole   B. into   C. push   D. roof

19 4. _____ a _____ of the bottle _____ _____ the roof.

    A. remain   B. third   C. let   D. above

20 5. Sunlight _____ _____ by the water in the bottle and _____ _____ the room.

    A. spreads   B. bent   C. around   D. is

21 _____ the Philippines, Moser lamps are _____ _____ _____ the My Shelter Foundation.

    A. used   B. by   C. in   D. widely

22 The _____ also teaches _____ people _____ to make and _____ the lamps.

    A. install   B. charity   C. how   D. local

23 _____ _____ the charity, _____ _____ homes in the Philippines now have Moser lamps.

    A. of   B. thanks   C. thousands   D. to

24 It _____ also _____ Moser lamps popular in _____ countries, _____ as Argentina, India, and Fiji.

    A. has   B. other   C. made   D. such

25 Moser lamps will _____ _____ the lives of many people _____ many _____ to come.

    A. for   B. light   C. years   D. up

---

13 그것은 절대 집에 불을 낼 수 없다.

14 놀랍게도, 이 신기한 램프를 만드는 것은 매우 쉽다.

15 병으로 Moser 램프를 만드는 법

16 1. 투명한 플라스틱병에 물을 채운다.

17 2. 물을 깨끗이 유지하기 위해 표백제를 조금 넣는다.

18 3. 지붕에 구멍을 내고, 병을 구멍 안으로 넣는다.

19 4. 병의 3분의 1은 지붕 위에 남아 있도록 한다.

20 5. 햇빛이 병 속의 물에 의해 굴절되어 방에 퍼진다.

21 필리핀에서 Moser 램프는 My Shelter 재단에 의해 널리 사용된다.

22 또한 그 자선단체는 지역 사람들에게 램프를 만들고 설치하는 법을 가르친다.

23 이 자선단체 덕분에, 필리핀의 수천 가구가 이제 Moser 램프를 갖고 있다.

24 그 단체는 아르헨티나, 인도, 피지와 같은 다른 나라들에서도 Moser 램프가 유명해 지도록 만들었다.

25 Moser 램프는 앞으로 오랫동안 많은 사람들의 삶을 밝혀 줄 것이다.

※ 다음 우리말과 일치하도록 빈칸에 알맞은 말을 쓰시오.

1 _____ _____ Lamps

2 "Wow, I can read a book in my room now!" _____ Marco, a boy in a village _____ _____ _____ .

3 His house _____ _____ _____ just like _____ _____ _____ _____ in the village.

4 People in the village are _____ poor _____ _____ _____ _____ .

5 Even _____ the daytime, they live in darkness _____ the houses _____ _____ _____ _____ .

6 Now things _____ _____ _____ _____ a single plastic bottle.

7 One plastic bottle _____ _____ _____ can _____ _____ a whole room _____ _____ any electricity.

8 This amazing plastic bottle _____ _____ a Moser lamp _____ it _____ _____ _____ Alfredo Moser.

9 In 2002, there _____ _____ _____ in his town in Brazil.

10 These blackouts made him _____ _____ _____ a new _____ _____ _____ his house.

11 A Moser lamp can _____ _____ _____ about one dollar and _____ _____ _____ 10 years.

12 It is also _____ _____ .

1 1달러짜리 마법의 전구

2 "우와, 이젠 제 방에서 책을 읽을 수 있어요!" 필리핀의 한 마을에 사는 소년인 Marco가 외쳤다.

3 그의 집은 마을의 다른 모든 집들과 마찬가지로 전기가 없다.

4 마을 사람들은 너무나 가난해서 전기세를 낼 수가 없다.

5 심지어 낮 동안에도, 집들이 빽빽하게 들어차 있어서 그들은 어둠 속에 살아간다.

6 이제 플라스틱병 하나 때문에 상황이 바뀌고 있다.

7 천장에 있는 플라스틱병 하나는 전기를 쓰지 않고 방 전체를 밝힐 수 있다.

8 이 놀라운 플라스틱병은 Moser 램프라고 불리는데, 그것이 Alfredo Moser에 의해 발명되었기 때문이다.

9 2002년, 브라질에 있는 그의 마을에는 정전이 잦았다.

10 이 정전들은 그가 집을 밝히는 새로운 방법을 생각해 내도록 만들었다.

11 Moser 램프는 1달러 정도로 만들 수 있고 10년 정도 지속된다.

12 그것은 또한 매우 안전하다.

13 It can _____ _____ a house fire.

14 Surprisingly, it is very easy _____ _____ this magic lamp.

15 _____ _____ _____ a Moser lamp from a bottle

16 1. _____ a clear plastic bottle _____ water.

17 2. _____ some _____ _____ _____ the water _____ .

18 3. Make a hole in the roof, and _____ the bottle _____ the hole.

19 4. Let _____ _____ of the bottle _____ _____ the roof.

20 5. Sunlight _____ _____ _____ the water in the bottle and _____ _____ the room.

21 In the Philippines, Moser lamps _____ _____ _____ by the My Shelter Foundation.

22 _____ _____ also teaches local people _____ _____ _____ and _____ the lamps.

23 _____ _____ the charity, _____ _____ homes in the Philippines now have Moser lamps.

24 It _____ also _____ Moser lamps popular in _____ _____ , _____ _____ Argentina, India, and Fiji.

25 Moser lamps will _____ _____ the lives of many people _____ _____ _____ _____ _____ .

13 그것은 절대 집에 불을 낼 수 없다.

14 놀랍게도, 이 신기한 램프를 만드는 것은 매우 쉽다.

15 병으로 Moser 램프를 만드는 법

16 1. 투명한 플라스틱병에 물을 채운다.

17 2. 물을 깨끗이 유지하기 위해 표백제를 조금 넣는다.

18 3. 지붕에 구멍을 내고, 병을 구멍 안으로 넣는다.

19 4. 병의 3분의 1은 지붕 위에 남아 있도록 한다.

20 5. 햇빛이 병 속의 물에 의해 굴절되어 방에 퍼진다.

21 필리핀에서 Moser 램프는 My Shelter 재단에 의해 널리 사용된다.

22 또한 그 자선단체는 지역 사람들에게 램프를 만들고 설치하는 법을 가르친다.

23 이 자선단체 덕분에, 필리핀의 수천 가구가 이제 Moser 램프를 갖고 있다.

24 그 단체는 아르헨티나, 인도, 피지와 같은 다른 나라들에서도 Moser 램프가 유명해 지도록 만들었다.

25 Moser 램프는 앞으로 오랫동안 많은 사람들의 삶을 밝혀 줄 것이다.

※ 다음 문장을 우리말로 쓰시오.

1 One-Dollar Magic Lamps

➡ _____

2 "Wow, I can read a book in my room now!" shouted Marco, a boy in a village in the Philippines.

➡ _____

3 His house has no electricity just like all the other houses in the village.

➡ _____

4 People in the village are too poor to pay for electricity.

➡ _____

5 Even during the daytime, they live in darkness because the houses are packed close together.

➡ _____

6 Now things are changing because of a single plastic bottle.

➡ _____

7 One plastic bottle in the ceiling can light up a whole room without using any electricity.

➡ _____

8 This amazing plastic bottle is called a Moser lamp because it was invented by Alfredo Moser.

➡ _____

9 In 2002, there were many blackouts in his town in Brazil.

➡ _____

10 These blackouts made him come up with a new way to light his house.

➡ _____

11 A Moser lamp can be made for about one dollar and lasts for about 10 years.

➡ _____

12 It is also very safe.

➡ _____

13 It can never start a house fire.

➡ _____

14 Surprisingly, it is very easy to make this magic lamp.

➡ _____

15 How to make a Moser lamp from a bottle

➡ _____

16 1. Fill a clear plastic bottle with water.

➡ _____

17 2. Add some bleach to keep the water clear.

➡ _____

18 3. Make a hole in the roof, and push the bottle into the hole.

➡ _____

19 4. Let a third of the bottle remain above the roof.

➡ _____

20 5. Sunlight is bent by the water in the bottle and spreads around the room.

➡ _____

21 In the Philippines, Moser lamps are widely used by the My Shelter Foundation.

➡ _____

22 The charity also teaches local people how to make and install the lamps.

➡ _____

23 Thanks to the charity, thousands of homes in the Philippines now have Moser lamps.

➡ _____

24 It has also made Moser lamps popular in other countries, such as Argentina, India, and Fiji.

➡ _____

25 Moser lamps will light up the lives of many people for many years to come.

➡ _____

Step4

※ 다음 괄호 안의 단어들을 우리말에 맞도록 바르게 배열하시오.

1 (Magic / One-Dollar / Lamps)
➡ _____

2 ("wow, / can / I / a / read / book / my / in / room / now!" / Marco, / shouted / boy / a / in / village / a / in / Philippines. / the)
➡ _____
_____

3 (house / his / no / has / just / electricity / like / the / all / other / in / houses / village. / the)
➡ _____

4 (in / people / the / village / too / are / poor / pay / to / electricity. / for)
➡ _____

5 (during / even / daytime, / the / live / they / darkness / in / because / houses / the / packed / are / together. / close)
➡ _____
_____

6 (things / now / changing / are / of / because / a / plastic / single / bottle.)
➡ _____

7 (plastic / one / in / bottle / the / ceiling / light / can / up / a / room / whole / using / without / electricity. / any)
➡ _____
_____

8 (amazing / this / bottle / plastic / called / is / Moser / a / lamp / it / because / invented / was / by / Moser. / Alfredo)
➡ _____
_____

9 (2002, / in / were / there / blcakouts / many / his / in / town / Brazil. / in)
➡ _____

10 (blackouts / these / him / made / come / with / up / a / way / new / light / to / house. / his)
➡ _____

11 (Moser / a / lamp / be / can / for / made / about / dollar / one / and / for / lasts / about / years. / 10)
➡ _____
_____

12 (is / it / also / safe. / very)
➡ _____

1 1달러짜리 마법의 전구

2 "우와, 이젠 제 방에서 책을 읽을 수 있어요!" 필리핀의 한 마을에 사는 소년인 Marco가 외쳤다.

3 그의 집은 마을의 다른 모든 집들과 마찬가지로 전기가 없다.

4 마을 사람들은 너무나 가난해서 전기세를 낼 수가 없다.

5 심지어 낮 동안에도, 집들이 빽빽하게 들어차 있어서 그들은 어둠 속에 살아간다.

6 이제 플라스틱병 하나 때문에 상황이 바뀌고 있다.

7 천장에 있는 플라스틱병 하나는 전기를 쓰지 않고 방 전체를 밝힐 수 있다.

8 이 놀라운 플라스틱병은 Moser 램프라고 불리는데, 그것이 Alfredo Moser에 의해 발명되었기 때문이다.

9 2002년, 브라질에 있는 그의 마을에는 정전이 잦았다.

10 이 정전들은 그가 집을 밝히는 새로운 방법을 생각해 내도록 만들었다.

11 Moser 램프는 1달러 정도로 만들 수 있고 10년 정도 지속된다.

12 그것은 또한 매우 안전하다.

13 (it / never / can / a / start / fire. / house)

➡ _____

14 (surprisingly, / is / it / easy / very / make / to / magic / this / lamp.)

➡ _____

15 (to / how / a / make / lamp / Moser / a / from / bottle)

➡ _____

16 (1. / a / fill / plastic / clear / with / bottle / water.)

➡ _____

17 (2. / some / add / to / bleach / the / keep / clear. / water)

➡ _____

18 (3. / a / make / hole / the / in / roof, / and / the / push / into / bottle / hole. / the)

➡ _____

19 (4. / a / let / of / third / the / remain / bottle / above / roof. / the)

➡ _____

20 (5. / is / sunlight / bent / by / water / the / in / bottle / and / spreads / the / around / room.)

➡ _____

21 (the / in / Philippines, / lamps / Moser / widely / are / by / used / the / Shelter / My / Foundation.)

➡ _____

22 (charity / the / teaches / also / people / local / to / how / make / and / the / install / lamps.)

➡ _____

23 (to / thanks / charity, / the / of / thousands / homes / the / in / now / Philippines / have / lamps. / Moser)

➡ _____

➡ _____

24 (has / it / made / also / lamps / Moser / in / popular / countries, / other / as / such / India, / Argentina, / Fiji. / and)

➡ _____

➡ _____

25 (lamps / Moser / light / will / up / lives / the / many / of / for / people / years / many / come. / to)

➡ _____

➡ _____

13 그것은 절대 집에 불을 낼 수 없다.

14 놀랍게도, 이 신기한 램프를 만드는 것은 매우 쉽다.

15 병으로 Moser 램프를 만드는 법

16 1. 투명한 플라스틱병에 물을 채운다.

17 2. 물을 깨끗이 유지하기 위해 표백제를 조금 넣는다.

18 3. 지붕에 구멍을 내고, 병을 구멍 안으로 넣는다.

19 4. 병의 3분의 1은 지붕 위에 남아 있도록 한다.

20 5. 햇빛이 병 속의 물에 의해 굴절되어 방에 퍼진다.

21 필리핀에서 Moser 램프는 My Shelter 재단에 의해 널리 사용된다.

22 또한 그 자선단체는 지역 사람들에게 램프를 만들고 설치하는 법을 가르친다.

23 이 자선단체 덕분에, 필리핀의 수천 가구가 이제 Moser 램프를 갖고 있다.

24 그 단체는 아르헨티나, 인도, 피지와 같은 다른 나라들에서도 Moser 램프가 유명해 지도록 만들었다.

25 Moser 램프는 앞으로 오랫동안 많은 사람들의 삶을 밝혀 줄 것이다.

※ 다음 우리말을 영어로 쓰시오.

1 1달러짜리 마법의 전구

➡ _____

2 "우와, 이젠 제 방에서 책을 읽을 수 있어요!" 필리핀의 한 마을에 사는 소년인 Marco가 외쳤다.

➡ _____

3 그의 집은 마을의 다른 모든 집들과 마찬가지로 전기가 없다.

➡ _____

4 마을 사람들은 너무나 가난해서 전기세를 낼 수가 없다.

➡ _____

5 심지어 낮 동안에도, 집들이 빽빽하게 들어차 있어서 그들은 어둠 속에 살아간다.

➡ _____

6 이제 플라스틱병 하나 때문에 상황이 바뀌고 있다.

➡ _____

7 천장에 있는 플라스틱병 하나는 전기를 쓰지 않고 방 전체를 밝힐 수 있다.

➡ _____

8 이 놀라운 플라스틱병은 Moser 램프라고 불리는데, 그것이 Alfredo Moser에 의해 발명되었기 때문이다.

➡ _____

9 2002년, 브라질에 있는 그의 마을에는 정전이 잦았다.

➡ _____

10 이 정전들은 그가 집을 밝히는 새로운 방법을 생각해 내도록 만들었다.

➡ _____

11 Moser 램프는 1달러 정도로 만들 수 있고 10년 정도 지속된다.

➡ _____

12 그것은 또한 매우 안전하다.

➡ _____

13 그것은 절대 집에 불을 낼 수 없다.

➡ _____

14 놀랍게도, 이 신기한 램프를 만드는 것은 매우 쉽다.

➡ _____

15 병으로 Moser 램프를 만드는 법

➡ _____

16 1. 투명한 플라스틱병에 물을 채운다.

➡ _____

17 2. 물을 깨끗이 유지하기 위해 표백제를 조금 넣는다.

➡ _____

18 3. 지붕에 구멍을 내고, 병을 구멍 안으로 넣는다.

➡ _____

19 4. 병의 3분의 1은 지붕 위에 남아 있도록 한다.

➡ _____

20 5. 햇빛이 병 속의 물에 의해 굴절되어 방에 퍼진다.

➡ _____

21 필리핀에서 Moser 램프는 My Shelter 재단에 의해 널리 사용된다.

➡ _____

22 또한 그 자선단체는 지역 사람들에게 램프를 만들고 설치하는 법을 가르친다.

➡ _____

23 이 자선단체 덕분에, 필리핀의 수천 가구가 이제 Moser 램프를 갖고 있다.

➡ _____

24 그 단체는 아르헨티나, 인도, 피지와 같은 다른 나라들에서도 Moser 램프가 유명해 지도록 만들었다.

➡ _____

25 Moser 램프는 앞으로 오랫동안 많은 사람들의 삶을 밝혀 줄 것이다.

➡ _____

※ 다음 우리말과 일치하도록 빈칸에 알맞은 말을 쓰시오.

Link-Share

1. We thought we could _____ _____ _____ _____ with a glass bottle.

2. We made one lamp _____ _____ a plastic bottle and _____ _____ out of a glass bottle.

3. _____ _____ _____ _____ were the same.

4. We _____ _____ the glass bottle lamp was _____ _____ the plastic bottle lamp.

1. 우리는 우리가 램프를 유리병으로 더 밝게 만들 수 있다고 생각했다.
2. 우리는 플라스틱병으로 램프를 하나 만들고 유리병으로 또 다른 하나를 만들었다.
3. 다른 모든 단계는 똑같았다.
4. 우리는 유리병 램프가 플라스틱병 램프보다 더 밝다는 것을 알았다.

Write

1. You can make _____ _____ _____ things _____ a CD case.

2. You _____ _____ _____ a grass container.

3. First, _____ _____ _____ the CD case with soil and water, and _____ grass seeds _____ the soil.

4. Second, _____ the case and tape _____ _____ _____ _____.

5. _____, leave _____ in the sun _____ _____ ten days.

6. Now, your grass container _____ _____.

7. It will _____ _____ _____ when the grass grows.

1. 당신은 CD 케이스로 많은 것들을 만들 수 있다.
2. 당신은 심지어 잔디를 기르는 용기를 만들 수도 있다.
3. 먼저 CD 케이스의 절반을 흙과 물로 채우고, 잔디 씨앗을 흙 안에 넣어라.
4. 두 번째, 케이스를 닫고 모든 옆면에 테이프를 붙여라.
5. 마지막으로, 햇빛이 비치는 곳에 약 10일 동안 놓아 두어라.
6. 이제, 당신의 잔디를 기르는 용기가 준비되었다.
7. 잔디가 자랄 때 그것은 당신을 행복하게 만들어 줄 것이다.

Culture Project-Share

1. We'd _____ _____ _____ about a pot-in-pot cooler.

2. It _____ _____ _____ without electricity.

3. _____'s very easy _____ _____ one.

4. First, _____ a pot _____ a larger pot.

5. Then, _____ sand and water _____ these pots.

6. Just _____ the water _____ _____, and it'll _____ the food.

1. 우리는 pot-in-pot cooler(항아리 냉장고)에 대해 이야기하고 싶다.
2. 그것은 전기 없이 식품을 신선하게 유지할 수 있다.
3. 그것을 만드는 것은 매우 쉽다.
4. 우선, 항아리 하나를 더 큰 항아리에 넣는다.
5. 그리고 항아리들 사이에 모래와 물을 넣는다.
6. 물이 그저 마르게 두면, 그것이 음식을 시원하게 할 것이다.

※ 다음 우리말을 영어로 쓰시오.

Link -Share

1. 우리는 우리가 램프를 유리병으로 더 밝게 만들 수 있다고 생각했다.
➡ _____

2. 우리는 플라스틱병으로 램프를 하나 만들고 유리병으로 또 다른 하나를 만들었다.
➡ _____

3. 다른 모든 단계는 똑같았다.
➡ _____

4. 우리는 유리병 램프가 플라스틱병 램프보다 더 밝다는 것을 알았다.
➡ _____

Write

1. 당신은 CD 케이스로 많은 것들을 만들 수 있다.
➡ _____

2. 당신은 심지어 잔디를 기르는 용기를 만들 수도 있다.
➡ _____

3. 먼저 CD 케이스의 절반을 흙과 물로 채우고, 잔디 씨앗을 흙 안에 넣어라.
➡ _____

4. 두 번째, 케이스를 닫고 모든 옆면에 테이프를 붙여라.
➡ _____

5. 마지막으로, 햇빛이 비치는 곳에 약 10일 동안 놓아 두어라.
➡ _____

6. 이제, 당신의 잔디를 기르는 용기가 준비되었다.
➡ _____

7. 잔디가 자랄 때 그것은 당신을 행복하게 만들어 줄 것이다.
➡ _____

Culture Project-Share

1. 우리는 pot-in-pot cooler(항아리 냉장고)에 대해 이야기하고 싶다.
➡ _____

2. 그것은 전기 없이 식품을 신선하게 유지할 수 있다.
➡ _____

3. 그것을 만드는 것은 매우 쉽다.
➡ _____

4. 우선, 항아리 하나를 더 큰 항아리에 넣는다.
➡ _____

5. 그리고 항아리들 사이에 모래와 물을 넣는다.
➡ _____

6. 물이 그저 마르게 두면, 그것이 음식을 시원하게 할 것이다.
➡ _____

※ 다음 영어를 우리말로 쓰시오.

01 bark _____

02 crack _____

03 shout _____

04 awesome _____

05 reach _____

06 sled _____

07 relay _____

08 special _____

09 celebrate _____

10 grandparents' place _____

11 save _____

12 heart-warming _____

13 snowstorm _____

14 outdoor _____

15 rescue _____

16 spread _____

17 around _____

18 frozen _____

19 popular _____

20 race _____

21 lead dog _____

22 cover _____

23 granddaughter _____

24 slip _____

25 trail _____

26 broadcast _____

27 highlight _____

28 language _____

29 cage _____

30 happen _____

31 medicine _____

32 disease _____

33 heavy snow _____

34 terrible _____

35 once a month _____

36 take place _____

37 right away _____

38 continue on _____

39 take part in _____

40 in memory of _____

41 keep -ing _____

42 be sure to부정사 _____

43 get[become]+형용사 _____

※ 다음 우리말을 영어로 쓰시오.

01 굉장한, 엄청난

02 (개가) 짖다

03 폭설

04 갈라지다, 금이 가다

05 질병, 병, 질환

06 언어

07 미끄러지다

08 눈보라

09 끔찍한

10 목

11 얼어붙은

12 발생하다, 일어나다

13 대략

14 가슴 따뜻한

15 코스, 흔적

16 경주하다, 달리다

17 기념하다, 축하하다

18 도달하다, 닿다

19 (사람들 사이로) 퍼지다

20 구하다, 구조하다

21 방송

22 우리

23 썰매

24 약

25 실외의

26 인기 있는

27 구하다

28 외치다

29 특별한

30 오르다, 올라가다

31 생방송의, 생중계의

32 썰매 타러 가다

33 선두 개

34 손녀, 외손녀

35 ~에 참여[참가]하다

36 ~을 기념[추모]하여

37 곧바로, 즉시

38 계속 ~하다

39 개최되다, 일어나다

40 적어도

41 ~에 관심이 있다

42 한 달에 한 번

43 여행을 가다

※ 다음 영영풀이에 알맞은 단어를 <보기>에서 골라 쓴 후, 우리말 뜻을 쓰시오.

1 _____ : a heavy fall of snow that is blown by strong winds: _____

2 _____ : extremely severe in a way that causes harm or damage: _____

3 _____ : to cover, reach, or have an effect on a wider or increasing area: _____

4 _____ : to happen, especially after being planned or arranged: _____

5 _____ : a competition in which all the competitors try to be the fastest and to finish first: _____

6 _____ : a long line or a series of marks that have been left by someone or something: _____

7 _____ : to keep happening, existing, or doing something, or to cause something or someone to do this: _____

8 _____ : a structure made of metal bars or wire in which animals or birds are kept: _____

9 _____ : to help someone or something out of a dangerous, harmful, or unpleasant situation: _____

10 _____ : a substance, especially in the form of a liquid or a pill, that is a treatment for illness or injury: _____

11 _____ : to slide a short distance by accident so that you fall or nearly fall: _____

12 _____ : to arrive at a place, especially after spending a long time or a lot of effort travelling: _____

13 _____ : an object used for travelling over snow and ice with long, narrow strips of wood or metal: _____

14 _____ : illness of people, animals, plants, etc., caused by infection or a failure of health rather than by an accident: _____

15 _____ : to break or to make something break, either so that it gets lines on its surface, or so that it breaks into pieces: _____

16 _____ : a running or swimming race between two or more teams in which each person in the team runs or swims part of the race: _____

보기			
race	reach	crack	rescue
disease	relay	continue	medicine
terrible	snowstorm	take place	cage
sled	spread	trail	slip

※ 다음 우리말과 일치하도록 빈칸에 알맞은 말을 쓰시오.

Listen & Speak 1-A

1. B: _____ are you _____?

   G: I'm _____ _____ old pop songs.

   B: Oh, _____ _____ _____ old pop songs?

   G: No, _____ _____ _____ _____ them. I just want _____ _____ m y _____ _____ _____ at her birthday party next week.

   B: Wow, _____ _____ _____ granddaughter!

2. M: _____ _____ _____ _____ _____ _____ the Winter Olympics? Then, _____ _____ _____ _____ MBS Sports to enjoy our _____ _____ from 6 p.m. to 11 p.m. At 11 p.m. _____ _____, you can also _____ our _____ of _____ _____ _____ games of the day.

1. B: 뭐 하고 있어?
   G: 오래된 팝송들을 듣고 있어.
   B: 오, 오래된 팝송들을 좋아하니?
   G: 아니, 거기에 관심이 있지는 않아. 그냥 다음 주 할머니 생신에 할머니께서 가장 좋아하시는 노래들을 불러 드리고 싶어.
   B: 우와, 정말 착한 손녀구나!

2. M: 동계 올림픽을 보는 것에 관심이 있나요? 그럼, 오후 6시에서 11시까지 하는 MBS Sports의 경기 생중계를 꼭 보세요. 또한 매일 밤 11시에, 여러분은 그날 가장 흥미진진했던 경기의 하이라이트를 즐길 수 있습니다.

Listen & Speak 2-A

1. W: What's your _____ sport, James?

   B: I don't like sports much, but I _____ _____ _____.

   G: _____ _____ do you _____ _____?

   B: _____ _____ _____. I only _____ _____ _____ _____ _____.

2. B: Do you have _____ _____ _____ for this weekend, Hana?

   G: Well, I'm _____ _____ _____ _____ _____ with my dad and brother.

   B: _____ _____ do you _____?

   G: _____ _____. I love _____ table tennis. _____ _____ you?

   B: I _____ soccer. I _____ _____ sports.

1. G: James, 가장 좋아하는 스포츠가 뭐야?
   B: 스포츠를 많이 좋아하지는 않지만, 가끔 수영하러 가.
   G: 수영을 얼마나 자주 하러 가는데?
   B: 그렇게 자주는 아니야. 한 달에 한 번만 가.

2. B: 하나야, 이번 주말에 특별한 계획 있어?
   G: 음, 우리 아빠와 남동생하고 탁구를 할 거야.
   B: 얼마나 자주 하는데?
   G: 매주 주말. 탁구 하는 걸 정말 좋아하거든. 너는 어때?
   B: 나는 축구 하는 걸 좋아해. 야외 스포츠가 좋아.

Communicate A

Anna: Do you have any _____ _____ for the _____ _____?

Suho: I'm going _____ _____ to my _____ _____ in Pyeongchang. I'll _____ _____ and _____ there. I love _____ _____.

Anna: _____ _____ you! I love winter sports, too. My _____ is ice hockey.

Suho: Oh, I've _____ _____ ice hockey, but _____ _____ _____ how _____ _____ it.

Anna: Really? I can teach you _____ _____ _____.

Suho: That's _____. Is ice hockey _____ _____ _____ sport in Canada?

Anna: Yes, it is. _____ I know _____ watching it and _____ it.

Suho: _____ _____ did you play ice hockey _____ you were in Canada?

Anna: I played _____ _____ two or _____ _____ a week in the winter.

Suho: Wow, _____ _____ you're really _____ _____ ice hockey. I _____ _____ _____ _____ from you.

Communicate B

A: _____ _____ _____ are you _____ _____?

B: I'm _____ _____ _____ _____.

A: _____ _____ _____ _____ you go ice skating?

B: I go _____ or _____ _____ _____.

Progress Check

1. **B:** What _____ you _____?
   G: I'm _____ _____.
   B: Do you like _____ badminton?
   G: No, I'm _____ _____ _____ it. I just want _____ _____ the badminton test _____ _____.
   B: O.K. _____ _____!

2. **G:** What's your _____ TV show, Jason?
   B: I don't watch TV, but I _____ _____ the radio.
   G: _____ _____ do you _____ _____ the radio?
   B: _____ _____ _____.

3. **M:** _____ important _____ _____ your love for the people around you. _____ _____ do you _____ everyone in your family _____ you love them?

Anna: 너는 겨울 방학 때 특별한 계획이 있니?

수호: 나는 평창에 계신 할머니 할아버지 댁에 갈 거야. 거기서 스케이트와 썰매를 타러 갈 거야. 난 겨울 스포츠를 정말 좋아하거든.

Anna: 잘됐다! 나도 겨울 스포츠를 정말 좋아해. 내가 제일 좋아하는 것은 아이스하키야.

수호: 오, 나는 아이스하키를 해 본 적은 없지만, 하는 법을 배우는 데에는 관심이 있어.

Anna: 정말? 내가 어떻게 하는지 가르쳐 줄 수 있어.

수호: 정말 잘 됐다. 캐나다에서는 아이스하키가 가장 인기 있는 스포츠니?

Anna: 응, 맞아. 내가 아는 모든 사람들은 아이스하키를 보는 것과 직접 하는 것을 정말 좋아해.

수호: 너는 캐나다에 있을 때 아이스하키를 얼마나 자주 했니?

Anna: 겨울에는 일주일에 적어도 두세 번은 했어.

수호: 우와, 네가 아이스하키를 정말 잘 할 거라고 확신해. 너한테 빨리 배우고 싶다.

A: 어떤 겨울 스포츠에 관심이 있니?
B: 스케이트 타기에 관심이 있어.
A: 얼마나 자주 스케이트 타러 가?
B: 한 달에 한두 번 가.

1. **B:** 뭐 하고 있어?
   G: 배드민턴을 연습하고 있어.
   B: 배드민턴 하는 걸 좋아해?
   G: 아니, 관심이 있지는 않아. 그냥 다음주에 있는 배드민턴 시험에 통과하고 싶어.
   B: 그렇구나. 행운을 빌어!

2. **G:** Jason, 네가 가장 좋아하는 TV 쇼는 뭐니?
   B: TV를 보지는 않지만, 라디오는 들어.
   G: 얼마나 자주 라디오를 들어?
   B: 거의 매일.

3. **M:** 당신의 사랑을 주변 사람들에게 보여주는 것은 중요합니다. 당신은 얼마나 자주 가족 모두에게 사랑한다고 말해 주나요?

대화문 Test

※ 다음 우리말에 맞도록 대화를 영어로 쓰시오.

Listen & Speak 1-A

1. B: _____

   G: _____

   B: _____

   G: _____
   _____

   B: _____

2. M: _____
   _____
   _____
   _____

Listen & Speak 2-A

1. G: _____

   B: _____

   G: _____

   B: _____

2. B: _____

   G: _____

   B: _____

   G: _____

   B: _____

---

1. B: 뭐 하고 있어?
   G: 오래된 팝송들을 듣고 있어.
   B: 오, 오래된 팝송들을 좋아하니?
   G: 아니, 거기에 관심이 있지는 않아. 그냥 다음 주 할머니 생신에 할머니께서 가장 좋아하시는 노래들을 불러 드리고 싶어.
   B: 우와, 정말 착한 손녀구나!

2. M: 동계 올림픽을 보는 것에 관심이 있나요? 그럼, 오후 6시에서 11시까지 하는 MBS Sports의 경기 생중계를 꼭 보세요. 또한 매일 밤 11시에, 여러분은 그날 가장 흥미진진했던 경기의 하이라이트를 즐길 수 있습니다.

1. G: James, 가장 좋아하는 스포츠가 뭐야?
   B: 스포츠를 많이 좋아하지는 않지만, 가끔 수영하러 가.
   G: 수영을 얼마나 자주 하러 가는데?
   B: 그렇게 자주는 아니야. 한 달에 한 번만 가.

2. B: 하나야, 이번 주말에 특별한 계획 있어?
   G: 음, 우리 아빠와 남동생하고 탁구를 할 거야.
   B: 얼마나 자주 하는데?
   G: 매주 주말. 탁구 하는 걸 정말 좋아하거든. 너는 어때?
   B: 나는 축구 하는 걸 좋아해. 야외 스포츠가 좋아.

Communicate A

Anna: _____

Suho: _____

_____

Anna: _____

Suho: _____

_____

Anna: _____

Suho: _____

Anna: _____

Suho: _____

Anna: _____

Suho: _____

Communicate B

A: _____

B: _____

A: _____

B: _____

Progress Check

1. B: _____

   G: _____

   B: _____

   G: _____

   B: _____

2. G: _____

   B: _____

   G: _____

   B: _____

3. M: _____

   _____

Anna: 너는 겨울 방학 때 특별한 계획이 있니?

수호: 나는 평창에 계신 할머니 할아버지 댁에 갈 거야. 거기서 스케이트와 썰매를 타러 갈 거야. 난 겨울 스포츠를 정말 좋아하거든.

Anna: 잘됐다! 나도 겨울 스포츠를 정말 좋아해. 내가 제일 좋아하는 것은 아이스하키야.

수호: 오, 나는 아이스하키를 해 본 적은 없지만, 하는 법을 배우는 데에는 관심이 있어.

Anna: 정말? 내가 어떻게 하는지 가르쳐 줄 수 있어.

수호: 정말 잘 됐다. 캐나다에서는 아이스하키가 가장 인기 있는 스포츠니?

Anna: 응, 맞아. 내가 아는 모든 사람들은 아이스하키를 보는 것과 직접 하는 것을 정말 좋아해.

수호: 너는 캐나다에 있을 때 이이스하키를 얼마나 자주 했니?

Anna: 겨울에는 일주일에 적어도 두세 번은 했어.

수호: 우와, 네가 아이스하키를 정말 잘 할 거라고 확신해. 너한테 빨리 배우고 싶다.

A: 어떤 겨울 스포츠에 관심이 있니?
B: 스케이트 타기에 관심이 있어.
A: 얼마나 자주 스케이트 타러 가?
B: 한 달에 한두 번 가.

1. B: 뭐 하고 있어?
   G: 배드민턴을 연습하고 있어.
   B: 배드민턴 하는 걸 좋아해?
   G: 아니, 관심이 있지는 않아. 그냥 다음주에 있는 배드민턴 시험에 통과하고 싶어.
   B: 그렇구나. 행운을 빌어!

2. G: Jason, 네가 가장 좋아하는 TV 쇼는 뭐니?
   B: TV를 보지는 않지만, 라디오는 들어.
   G: 얼마나 자주 라디오를 들어?
   B: 거의 매일.

3. M: 당신의 사랑을 주변 사람들에게 보여주는 것은 중요합니다. 당신은 얼마나 자주 가족 모두에게 사랑한다고 말해 주나요?

※ 다음 우리말과 일치하도록 빈칸에 알맞은 것을 골라 쓰시오.

1 _____ _____ _____ Winter Sport

A. Heart-Warming   B. Most   C. The

2 In _____ March every year, the world's _____ sled dog race _____ _____ in Alaska.

A. take   B. early   C. place   D. biggest

3 _____ _____ _____ the Iditarod Trail Sled Dog Race.

A. is   B. it   C. called

4 _____ 80 teams of 12 _____ 16 dogs take _____ in this race.

A. to   B. part   C. around

5 Each team _____ to _____ about 1,800 km _____ Anchorage to Nome.

A. cover   B. from   C. has

6 The race can _____ more _____ two weeks, and the teams often race _____ _____.

A. through   B. take   C. snowstorms   D. than

7 The Iditarod Race began in 1973 _____ _____ of the dogs that _____ Nome.

A. memory   B. saved   C. in

8 One _____ winter day in 1925, a _____ thing _____ in Nome.

A. happened   B. cold   C. terrible

9 Some children _____ very sick, and the disease _____ _____.

A. kept   B. got   C. spreading

10 The people of Nome _____ medicine _____ _____, but the town did not have _____.

A. away   B. any   C. right   D. needed

11 Someone _____ _____ get it _____ a hospital in Anchorage.

A. to   B. from   C. had

12 _____ of the _____ snow, a dog sled relay was the only _____ to get the _____ from Anchorage to Nome.

A. heavy   B. medicine   C. because   D. way

13 Soon, the _____ to Nome _____.

A. race   B. began

14 _____ dog teams were _____ the _____.

A. relay   B. twenty-dog   C. in

1 가장 가슴 따뜻한 겨울 스포츠

2 매년 3월 초에 알래스카 (Alaska)에서는 세계 최대의 개 썰매 경주가 열린다.

3 그것은 아이디타로드 개썰매 경주(Iditarod Trail Sled Dog Race)라고 불린다.

4 12~16마리 개로 구성된 80여 팀이 이 경주에 참여한다.

5 각 팀은 앵커리지(Anchorage) 에서 놈(Nome)까지 약 1,800 km를 달려야 한다.

6 이 경주는 2주 이상 걸릴 수 있 으며, 팀들은 종종 눈보라를 뚫 고 경주한다.

7 아이디타로드 경주는 놈을 구한 개들을 기념하여 1973년에 시작 되었다.

8 1925년의 어느 추운 겨울날, 놈 마을에서는 끔찍한 일이 일어났 다.

9 몇몇 아이들이 매우 아팠고 병 이 계속 퍼졌다.

10 놈의 사람들은 당장 약이 필요 했지만 마을에는 약이 하나도 없었다.

11 누군가는 앵커리지에 있는 병원 에서 약을 가져와야 했다.

12 폭설 때문에 개썰매 릴레이가 앵커리지에서 놈으로 약을 가져 오는 유일한 방법이었다.

13 곧, 놈으로 향하는 질주가 시작 되었다.

14 21개의 개 팀이 릴레이에 참여 했다.

15 _____ January 27, the first team left, and the _____ waited _____ different _____.

    A. others   B. on   C. points   D. at

16 Gunnar was the driver _____ the _____ _____.

    A. of   B. team   C. 20th

17 The _____ dog on his team was Balto, so he _____ Balto his _____ dog.

    A. made   B. strongest   C. lead

18 When Gunnar and Balto _____ got the medicine, the snow was _____ heavy _____ Gunnar could not see his _____ hands.

    A. that   B. own   C. finally   D. so

19 _____, Balto was able to _____ on the _____.

    A. stay   B. however   C. trail

20 When they were _____ a _____ river, Balto suddenly _____.

    A. frozen   B. stopped   C. crossing

21 Then, Gunnar _____ the river ice _____.

    A. cracking   B. saw

22 The _____ team was saved _____ Balto stopped _____ in time.

    A. because   B. whole   C. just

23 When Balto and Gunnar _____ the _____ team, they were _____.

    A. sleeping   B. final   C. reached

24 Gunnar _____ Balto to _____ _____.

    A. continue   B. told   C. on

25 "_____ the _____, Doctor!" _____ Gunnar.

    A. shouted   B. here's   C. medicine

26 _____ February 2, Gunnar and his team finally _____ _____ Nome.

    A. in   B. on   C. arrived

27 The town _____ _____.

    A. saved   B. was

28 This heart-warming story _____ now _____ every year by the Iditarod Race, the _____ _____ dog race in the world.

    A. biggest   B. celebrated   C. is   D. sled

---

15 1월 27일에 첫 번째 팀이 출발했고, 나머지 팀들은 서로 다른 지점에서 기다렸다.

16 Gunnar는 20번째 팀의 몰이꾼이었다.

17 그의 팀에서 가장 강한 개는 Balto였기 때문에, 그는 Balto를 그의 선두 개로 삼았다.

18 Gunnar와 Balto가 마침내 약을 받았을 때, 눈발이 너무 거세서 Gunnar는 자신의 손조차도 볼 수 없었다.

19 그러나, Balto는 코스를 제대로 따라갈 수 있었다.

20 그들이 얼어붙은 강을 건너고 있을 때 Balto는 갑자기 멈췄다.

21 그때, Gunnar는 강의 얼음이 갈라지는 것을 보았다.

22 Balto가 바로 제때 멈췄기 때문에 팀 전체가 목숨을 구할 수 있었다.

23 Balto와 Gunnar가 마지막 팀에 다다랐을 때, 그들은 자고 있었다.

24 Gunnar는 Balto에게 계속 가라고 말했다.

25 "여기 약이 있습니다. 의사 선생님!"이라고 Gunnar가 소리쳤다.

26 2월 2일에 Gunnar와 그의 팀은 마침내 놈에 도착했다.

27 놈 마을 사람들은 목숨을 구할 수 있었다.

28 이 가슴 따뜻한 이야기는 세계에서 가장 큰 개썰매 경주인 아이디타로드 경주를 통해 오늘날 매년 기념되고 있다.

※ 다음 우리말과 일치하도록 빈칸에 알맞은 말을 쓰시오.

1 The ＿＿＿＿ ＿＿＿＿＿ Winter Sport

2 In early March ＿＿＿ ＿＿＿, the world's ＿＿＿ ＿＿＿ ＿＿＿ race ＿＿＿ ＿＿＿ in Alaska.

3 ＿＿＿ ＿＿＿ ＿＿＿ the Iditarod Trail Sled Dog Race.

4 ＿＿＿ 80 teams of 12 to 16 dogs ＿＿＿ ＿＿＿ ＿＿＿ this race.

5 Each team ＿＿＿ ＿＿＿ ＿＿＿ about 1,800 km ＿＿＿ Anchorage ＿＿＿ Nome.

6 The race can ＿＿＿ ＿＿＿ ＿＿＿ two weeks, and the teams often ＿＿＿ ＿＿＿ ＿＿＿.

7 The Iditarod Race began in 1973 ＿＿＿ ＿＿＿ ＿＿＿ the dogs that saved Nome.

8 One cold winter day in 1925, ＿＿＿ ＿＿＿ ＿＿＿ ＿＿＿ in Nome.

9 Some children ＿＿＿ very ＿＿＿, and the disease ＿＿＿ ＿＿＿.

10 The people of Nome needed medicine ＿＿＿ ＿＿＿, but the town ＿＿＿ ＿＿＿ ＿＿＿ ＿＿＿.

11 Someone ＿＿＿ ＿＿＿ ＿＿＿ ＿＿＿ ＿＿＿ from a hospital in Anchorage.

12 ＿＿＿ ＿＿＿ the heavy snow, a dog sled relay was the only way ＿＿＿ ＿＿＿ ＿＿＿ ＿＿＿ from Anchorage to Nome.

13 Soon, ＿＿＿ ＿＿＿ ＿＿＿ ＿＿＿ began.

14 Twenty-one dog teams were ＿＿＿ ＿＿＿ ＿＿＿.

1 가장 가슴 따뜻한 겨울 스포츠

2 매년 3월 초에 알래스카 (Alaska)에서는 세계 최대의 개 썰매 경주가 열린다.

3 그것은 아이디타로드 개썰매 경주(Iditarod Trail Sled Dog Race)라고 불린다.

4 12~16마리 개로 구성된 80여 팀이 이 경주에 참여한다.

5 각 팀은 앵커리지(Anchorage)에서 놈(Nome)까지 약 1,800 km를 달려야 한다.

6 이 경주는 2주 이상 걸릴 수 있으며, 팀들은 종종 눈보라를 뚫고 경주한다.

7 아이디타로드 경주는 놈을 구한 개들을 기념하여 1973년에 시작되었다.

8 1925년의 어느 추운 겨울날, 놈 마을에서는 끔찍한 일이 일어났다.

9 몇몇 아이들이 매우 아팠고 병이 계속 퍼졌다

10 놈의 사람들은 당장 약이 필요했지만 마을에는 약이 하나도 없었다.

11 누군가는 앵커리지에 있는 병원에서 약을 가져와야 했다.

12 폭설 때문에 개썰매 릴레이가 앵커리지에서 놈으로 약을 가져오는 유일한 방법이었다.

13 곧, 놈으로 향하는 질주가 시작되었다.

14 21개의 개 팀이 릴레이에 참여했다.

15 On January 27, the first team left, and _____ _____ waited _____ _____ _____ .

16 Gunnar was the driver _____ _____ _____ _____ .

17 The _____ _____ on his team was Balto, so he _____ Balto _____ _____ _____ .

18 When Gunnar and Balto finally got the medicine, the snow was _____ heavy _____ Gunnar _____ _____ see his own hands.

19 _____ , Balto was _____ _____ _____ _____ _____ .

20 When they were crossing a _____ river, Balto _____ _____ .

21 Then, Gunnar saw the river ice _____ .

22 The whole team _____ _____ because Balto stopped _____ _____ _____ .

23 When Balto and Gunnar _____ the final team, they were sleeping.

24 Gunnar told Balto _____ _____ _____ .

25 " _____ the _____ , Doctor!" _____ Gunnar.

26 _____ February 2, Gunnar and his team finally _____ _____ Nome.

27 The town _____ _____ .

28 This heart-warming story _____ _____ _____ every year by the Iditarod Race, _____ _____ _____ in the world.

15 1월 27일에 첫 번째 팀이 출발했고, 나머지 팀들은 서로 다른 지점에서 기다렸다.

16 Gunnar는 20번째 팀의 몰이꾼이었다.

17 그의 팀에서 가장 강한 개는 Balto였기 때문에, 그는 Balto를 그의 선두 개로 삼았다.

18 Gunnar와 Balto가 마침내 약을 받았을 때, 눈발이 너무 거세서 Gunnar는 자신의 손조차도 볼 수 없었다.

19 그러나, Balto는 코스를 제대로 따라갈 수 있었다.

20 그들이 얼어붙은 강을 건너고 있을 때 Balto는 갑자기 멈췄다.

21 그때, Gunnar는 강의 얼음이 갈라지는 것을 보았다.

22 Balto가 바로 제때 멈췄기 때문에 팀 전체가 목숨을 구할 수 있었다.

23 Balto와 Gunnar가 마지막 팀에 다다랐을 때, 그들은 자고 있었다.

24 Gunnar는 Balto에게 계속 가라고 말했다.

25 "여기 약이 있습니다, 의사 선생님!"이라고 Gunnar가 소리쳤다.

26 2월 2일에 Gunnar와 그의 팀은 마침내 놈에 도착했다.

27 놈 마을 사람들은 목숨을 구할 수 있었다.

28 이 가슴 따뜻한 이야기는 세계에서 가장 큰 개썰매 경주인 아이디타로드 경주를 통해 오늘날 매년 기념되고 있다.

※ 다음 문장을 우리말로 쓰시오.

1 The Most Heart-Warming Winter Sport

➡ _____

2 In early March every year, the world's biggest sled dog race takes place in Alaska.

➡ _____

3 It is called the Iditarod Trail Sled Dog Race.

➡ _____

4 Around 80 teams of 12 to 16 dogs take part in this race.

➡ _____

5 Each team has to cover about 1,800 km from Anchorage to Nome.

➡ _____

6 The race can take more than two weeks, and the teams often race through snowstorms.

➡ _____

7 The Iditarod Race began in 1973 in memory of the dogs that saved Nome.

➡ _____

8 One cold winter day in 1925, a terrible thing happened in Nome.

➡ _____

9 Some children got very sick, and the disease kept spreading.

➡ _____

10 The people of Nome needed medicine right away, but the town did not have any.

➡ _____

11 Someone had to get it from a hospital in Anchorage.

➡ _____

12 Because of the heavy snow, a dog sled relay was the only way to get the medicine from Anchorage to Nome.

➡ _____

13 Soon, the race to Nome began.

➡ _____

14 Twenty-one dog teams were in the relay.

➡ _____

15 On January 27, the first team left, and the others waited at different points.

➡ _____

16 Gunnar was the driver of the 20th team.

➡ _____

17 The strongest dog on his team was Balto, so he made Balto his lead dog.

➡ _____

18 When Gunnar and Balto finally got the medicine, the snow was so heavy that Gunnar could not see his own hands.

➡ _____

19 However, Balto was able to stay on the trail.

➡ _____

20 When they were crossing a frozen river, Balto suddenly stopped.

➡ _____

21 Then, Gunnar saw the river ice cracking.

➡ _____

22 The whole team was saved because Balto stopped just in time.

➡ _____

23 When Balto and Gunnar reached the final team, they were sleeping.

➡ _____

24 Gunnar told Balto to continue on.

➡ _____

25 "Here's the medicine, Doctor!" shouted Gunnar.

➡ _____

26 On February 2, Gunnar and his team finally arrived in Nome.

➡ _____

27 The town was saved.

➡ _____

28 This heart-warming story is now celebrated every year by the Iditarod Race, the biggest sled dog race in the world.

➡ _____

※ 다음 괄호 안의 단어들을 우리말에 맞도록 바르게 배열하시오.

1 (Most / The / Winter / Heart-Warming / Sport)
➡ _____

2 (early / in / every / March / year, / world's / the / sled / biggest / dog / takes / race / place / Alaska. / in)
➡ _____
_____

3 (is / it / the / called / Trail / Iditarod / Dog / Sled / Race.)
➡ _____

4 (80 / around / of / teams / 12 / to / dogs / 16 / part / take / race. / in / this)
➡ _____

5 (team / each / to / has / cover / 1,800km / about / to / Anchorage / from / Nome.)
➡ _____

6 (race / the / take / can / than / more / weeks, / two / and / teams / the / race / often / snowstorms. / through)
➡ _____
_____

7 (Iditarod / the / Race / in / began / 1973 / memory / in / the / of / dogs / saved / that / Nome.)
➡ _____

8 (cold / one / day / winter / 1925, / in / terrible / a / thing / in / happened / Nome.)
➡ _____

9 (children / some / very / got / sick, / and / disease / the / spreading. / kept)
➡ _____

10 (people / the / of / needed / Nome / right / away, / medicine / the / but / town / not / did / any. / have)
➡ _____
_____

11 (had / someone / get / to / it / from / in / hospital / a / Anchorage.)
➡ _____

12 (of / because / the / snow, / heavy / dog / a / sled / was / relay / only / the / to / way / get / medicine / the / to / Anchorage / from / Nome.)
➡ _____
_____

13 (soon, / race / the / Nome / to / began.)
➡ _____

14 (dog / twenty-one / were / teams / in / relay. / the)
➡ _____

1 가장 가슴 따뜻한 겨울 스포츠

2 매년 3월 초에 알래스카 (Alaska)에서는 세계 최대의 개 썰매 경주가 열린다.

3 그것은 아이디타로드 개썰매 경주(Iditarod Trail Sled Dog Race)라고 불린다.

4 12~16마리 개로 구성된 80여 팀이 이 경주에 참여한다.

5 각 팀은 앵커리지(Anchorage) 에서 놈(Nome)까지 약 1,800 km를 달려야 한다.

6 이 경주는 2주 이상 걸릴 수 있 으며, 팀들은 종종 눈보라를 뚫 고 경주한다.

7 아이디타로드 경주는 놈을 구한 개들을 기념하여 1973년에 시작 되었다.

8 1925년의 어느 추운 겨울날, 놈 마을에서는 끔찍한 일이 일어났 다.

9 몇몇 아이들이 매우 아팠고 병 이 계속 퍼졌다.

10 놈의 사람들은 당장 약이 필요 했지만 마을에는 약이 하나도 없었다.

11 누군가는 앵커리지에 있는 병원 에서 약을 가져와야 했다.

12 폭설 때문에 개썰매 릴레이가 앵커리지에서 놈으로 약을 가져 오는 유일한 방법이었다.

13 곧, 놈으로 향하는 질주가 시작 되었다.

14 21개의 개 팀이 릴레이에 참여 했다.

15 (January / on / 27, / team / the / first / left, / and / others / the / waited / different / points. / at)

➡ _____

16 (was / Gunnar / the / of / driver / the / team. / 20th)

➡ _____

17 (the / dog / strongest / on / team / his / was / so / Balto, / made / he / his / Balto / dog. / lead)

➡ _____

18 (Gunnar / when / and / finally / Balto / the / got / medicine, / snow / the / was / heavy / so / that / could / Gunnar / see / not / own / hands. / his)

➡ _____

19 (Balto / however, / able / was / to / on / stay / trail. / the)

➡ _____

20 (they / when / crossing / were / a / river, / frozen / suddenly / Balto / stopped.)

➡ _____

21 (Gunnar / then, / the / saw / ice / river / cracking.)

➡ _____

22 (whole / the / team / saved / was / because / stopped / Balto / in / time. / just)

➡ _____

23 (Balto / when / and / reached / Gunnar / the / team, / final / were / they / sleeping.)

➡ _____

24 (told / Gunnar / Balto / continue / to / on.)

➡ _____

25 (the / "here's / Doctor!" / medicine, / Gunnar. / shouted)

➡ _____

26 (February / on / 2, / Gunnar / and / team / his / arrived / finally / Nome. / in)

➡ _____

27 (town / the / saved. / was)

➡ _____

28 (heart-warming / this / story / now / is / every / celebrated / year / by / Iditarod / the / Race, / biggest / the / dog / sled / race / the / world. / in)

➡ _____

_____

15 1월 27일에 첫 번째 팀이 출발했고, 나머지 팀들은 서로 다른 지점에서 기다렸다.

16 Gunnar는 20번째 팀의 몰이꾼이었다.

17 그의 팀에서 가장 강한 개는 Balto였기 때문에, 그는 Balto를 그의 선두 개로 삼았다.

18 Gunnar와 Balto가 마침내 약을 받았을 때, 눈발이 너무 거세서 Gunnar는 자신의 손조차도 볼 수 없었다.

19 그러나, Balto는 코스를 제대로 따라갈 수 있었다.

20 그들이 얼어붙은 강을 건너고 있을 때 Balto는 갑자기 멈췄다.

21 그때, Gunnar는 강의 얼음이 갈라지는 것을 보았다.

22 Balto가 바로 제때 멈췄기 때문에 팀 전체가 목숨을 구할 수 있었다.

23 Balto와 Gunnar가 마지막 팀에 다다랐을 때, 그들은 자고 있었다.

24 Gunnar는 Balto에게 계속 가라고 말했다.

25 "여기 약이 있습니다, 의사 선생님!"이라고 Gunnar가 소리쳤다.

26 2월 2일에 Gunnar와 그의 팀은 마침내 놈에 도착했다.

27 놈 마을 사람들은 목숨을 구할 수 있었다.

28 이 가슴 따뜻한 이야기는 세계에서 가장 큰 개썰매 경주인 아이디타로드 경주를 통해 오늘날 매년 기념되고 있다.

※ 다음 우리말을 영어로 쓰시오.

1 가장 가슴 따뜻한 겨울 스포츠

➡ _____

2 매년 3월 초에 알래스카(Alaska)에서는 세계 최대의 개썰매 경주가 열린다.

➡ _____

3 그것은 아이디타로드 개썰매 경주(Iditarod Trail Sled Dog Race)라고 불린다.

➡ _____

4 12~16마리 개로 구성된 80여 팀이 이 경주에 참여한다.

➡ _____

5 각 팀은 앵커리지(Anchorage)에서 놈(Nome)까지 약 1,800 km를 달려야 한다.

➡ _____

6 이 경주는 2주 이상 걸릴 수 있으며, 팀들은 종종 눈보라를 뚫고 경주한다.

➡ _____

7 아이디타로드 경주는 놈을 구한 개들을 기념하여 1973년에 시작되었다.

➡ _____

8 1925년의 어느 추운 겨울날, 놈 마을에서는 끔찍한 일이 일어났다.

➡ _____

9 몇몇 아이들이 매우 아팠고 병이 계속 퍼졌다.

➡ _____

10 놈의 사람들은 당장 약이 필요했지만 마을에는 약이 하나도 없었다.

➡ _____

11 누군가는 앵커리지에 있는 병원에서 약을 가져와야 했다.

➡ _____

12 폭설 때문에 개썰매 릴레이가 앵커리지에서 놈으로 약을 가져오는 유일한 방법이었다.

➡ _____

13 곧, 놈으로 향하는 질주가 시작되었다.

➡ _____

14 21개의 개 팀이 릴레이에 참여했다.

➡ _____

15 1월 27일에 첫 번째 팀이 출발했고, 나머지 팀들은 서로 다른 지점에서 기다렸다.

➡ _____

16 Gunnar는 20번째 팀의 몰이꾼이었다.

➡ _____

17 그의 팀에서 가장 강한 개는 Balto였기 때문에, 그는 Balto를 그의 선두 개로 삼았다.

➡ _____

18 Gunnar와 Balto가 마침내 약을 받았을 때, 눈발이 너무 거세서 Gunnar는 자신의 손조차도 볼 수 없었다.

➡ _____

_____

19 그러나, Balto는 코스를 제대로 따라갈 수 있었다.

➡ _____

20 그들이 얼어붙은 강을 건너고 있을 때 Balto는 갑자기 멈췄다.

➡ _____

21 그때, Gunnar는 강의 얼음이 갈라지는 것을 보았다.

➡ _____

22 Balto가 바로 제때 멈췄기 때문에 팀 전체가 목숨을 구할 수 있었다.

➡ _____

23 Balto와 Gunnar가 마지막 팀에 다다랐을 때, 그들은 자고 있었다.

➡ _____

24 Gunnar는 Balto에게 계속 가라고 말했다.

➡ _____

25 "여기 약이 있습니다, 의사 선생님!"이라고 Gunnar가 소리쳤다.

➡ _____

26 2월 2일에 Gunnar와 그의 팀은 마침내 놈에 도착했다.

➡ _____

27 놈 마을 사람들은 목숨을 구할 수 있었다.

➡ _____

28 이 가슴 따뜻한 이야기는 세계에서 가장 큰 개썰매 경주인 아이디타로드 경주를 통해 오늘날 매년 기념되고 있다.

➡ _____

_____

※ 다음 우리말과 일치하도록 빈칸에 알맞은 말을 쓰시오.

Link-Share

1. _____ you _____ _____ _____ the history of the marathon?

2. The first marathon _____ _____ _____ Pheidippides in 490 _____.

3. The Greek army in Marathon _____ _____ _____ _____ the people of Athens about their victory.

4. He _____ 40 km _____ Marathon _____ Athens.

1. 마라톤의 역사를 배우는 것에 관심이 있나요?
2. 최초의 마라톤은 Pheidippides에 의해 기원전 490년에 달려졌습니다.
3. 마라톤에 있던 그리스 군대는 그들의 승리에 관해 아테네의 사람들에게 말하라고 그에게 명령했습니다.
4. 그는 마라톤에서 아테네까지 40km를 달렸습니다.

Write

1. One cold winter day, a man _____ home _____ _____ _____ for a fire.

2. He _____ and _____ _____ _____.

3. He could _____ _____, but _____ _____ was _____ him.

4. His dog _____ _____ _____ _____.

5. She _____ _____ _____ _____ 19 hours.

6. A neighbor finally _____ _____ _____ _____ and _____ 911.

1. 어느 추운 겨울날, 한 남자가 불을 피울 나무를 구하기 위해 집을 떠났다.
2. 그는 미끄러져서 목을 부러뜨렸다.
3. 그는 움직일 수 없었지만, 그 주변에 아무도 없었다.
4. 그의 개가 그를 구하기 위해 왔다.
5. 그녀는 19시간 동안 짖고 또 짖었다.
6. 한 이웃이 마침내 개가 짖는 소리를 듣고 911에 전화했다.

Culture Project-Share

1. _____ _____, you can _____ _____ _____ _____ into the sea at Haeundae Beach.

2. It's _____ _____ _____ _____ for good health in the New Year.

1. 매년 겨울, 많은 사람들이 해운대 해변에서 바다로 뛰어 드는 모습을 볼 수 있다.
2. 이것은 새해에 건강하기를 비는 방법이다.

Step2

※ 다음 우리말을 영어로 쓰시오.

Link-Share

1. 바라톤의 역사를 배우는 것에 관심이 있나요?

   ➡ _____

2. 최초의 마라톤은 Pheidippides에 의해 기원전 490년에 달려졌습니다.

   ➡ _____

3. 마라톤에 있던 그리스 군대는 그들의 승리에 관해 아테네의 사람들에게 말하라고 그에게 명령했습니다.

   ➡ _____

4. 그는 마라톤에서 아테네까지 40km를 달렸습니다.

   ➡ _____

Write

1. 어느 추운 겨울날, 한 남자가 불을 피울 나무를 구하기 위해 집을 떠났다.

   ➡ _____

2. 그는 미끄러져서 목을 부러뜨렸다.

   ➡ _____

3. 그는 움직일 수 없었지만, 그 주변에 아무도 없었다.

   ➡ _____

4. 그의 개가 그를 구하기 위해 왔다.

   ➡ _____

5. 그녀는 19시간 동안 짖고 또 짖었다.

   ➡ _____

6. 한 이웃이 마침내 개가 짖는 소리를 듣고 911에 전화했다.

   ➡ _____

Culture Project-Share

1. 매년 겨울, 많은 사람들이 해운대 해변에서 바다로 뛰어 드는 모습을 볼 수 있다.

   ➡ _____

2. 이것은 새해에 건강하기를 비는 방법이다.

   ➡ _____

MEMO

MEMO

MEMO

적중100 plus

2학기 전과정

영어 기출 문제집

Lesson 5

Bravo! Brava!

시험대비 실력평가   p.08

01 brave   02 ①   03 ④   04 ⑤

05 ②   06 ⑤   07 (r)iddles

08 beautiful   09 (1) be late for   (2) take, off

01 둘은 반의어 관계이다. 알려지지 않은 : 유명한 = 겁 많은 : 용감한

02 새벽이다. 해가 떠오르고 있어.

03 배경 지식은 당신이 뮤지컬을 감상하는 데 도움이 될 것이다.

04 한 사람에 의해 불러지는 오페라의 음악

05 슬픔이나 공감의 강한 감정을 불러일으키는

06 nothing more than은 '~에 지나지 않'의 뜻이다.

07 puzzle = riddle: 수수께끼

08 'of+추상명사'는 형용사와 뜻이 같다.

09 (1) be late for: ~에 늦다 (2) take off: (일을) 쉬다

서술형 시험대비   p.09

01 (1) right after   (2) correctly, agree to   (3) marry, riddles   02 (1) appreciate   (2) storyline

03 take   04 (1) most famous   (2) Like

(3) celebrated   (4) performance

05 (1) discount   (2) nothing more than   (3) fails

(4) until[till]

01 (1) right는 부사로 '바로'의 뜻이다. (2) correctly는 부사로 '맞게, 올바르게'의 뜻이고, '~에 동의하다'는 'agree to+동사원형'을 사용한다. (3) '~와 결혼하다'는 marry가 적절하다. 수수께끼는 three가 있으므로 복수형이 적절하다.

02 (1) 어떤 것이나 어떤 사람이 얼마나 좋은지 이해하다 (2) 책, 영화, 희곡 등에서 일어나는 일련의 사건

03 take off: 일을 쉬다, take+교통수단: ~을 타다

04 (1) of the whole opera(전체 오페라 중에서)와 호응이 되려면 'the+최상급' 형태가 적절하다. (2) like는 전치사로 '~와 같이'의 의미로 사용이 되었다. (3) celebrate: (특별한 날·경사 등을) 축하하다, 기념하다 / '그녀는 작년에 내 생일을 축하해 줬다.'는 의미로 과거시제가 적절하다. (4) 소유격 our 뒤에 명사형이 적절하므로 동사 perform의 명사형인 performance가 맞다.

05 (1) discount: 할인 (2) nothing more than: ~에 지나지 않은 (3) fail: 실패하다 (4) until[till]: ~할 때까지

교과서 Conversation

핵심 Check   p.10~11

1 ③   2 ②   3 ③, ⑤

4 (W)hat about

교과서 대화문 익히기

Check(√) True or False   p.12

1 F   2 T   3 T   4 T

교과서 확인학습   p.14~15

Listen & Speak 1-A

1 hurry up, already / be late for / Why don't we take / faster than

2 wrong / sure, well, Why don't we, celebrate / for / Of course

Listen & Speak 1-B

shall we / Why don't we / good idea

Listen & Speak 2-A

1 let's, parts, play / What time shall we meet / How about, right / Sounds

2 Where shall we / about, near / at

Listen & Speak 2-B

Let's / shall / How about / Let's meet

Communicate A

guess / Why not / anniversary / together / take, off / Why don't we, get, discount if / let's / shall we / How about / best

Communicate B

What shall we / Why don't we / time shall we / How / Let's

Progress Check

1 Why don't we take, faster, at this time of day

2 Let's go swimming / Where / How about

시험대비 기본평가   p.16

01 ④   02 ③   03 ①

04 (C) → (B) → (D) → (A)

01 B의 대답이 '지하철역에서 만나는 게 어때?'라고 했으므로 G는 어디서 만날지 묻는 말이 적절하다.

02 A의 답으로 보아 B는 몇 시에 만날지 묻고 있다는 것을 알 수 있다.

03 비교급 구문으로 faster than이 적절하다.

04 (C) '배드민턴 하지 않을래?'라는 제안 → (B) 승낙의 표현과 이디서 할 것인지 묻고 → (D) 장소 제안 → (A) 동의

시험대비 실력평가 p.17~18

01 ④　　　02 ②　　　03 ①
04 ①, ④, ⑤　05 ⑤　　06 ④　　07 station
08 ①　　　09 ③　　　10 anniversary
11 I guess I can take the afternoon off.　12 ②
13 (A) wrong　(B) celebrate

01 B가 '원더 우먼을 보러 가는 게 어때?'라고 답하는 걸로 보아 A는 오후에 무엇을 할 것인지 묻는 것을 알 수 있다.

02 B의 대답으로 보아 시간 약속을 정하는 표현이 적절하다.

03 '~이 어때?'라는 의미로 How about ~?을 사용한다.

04 '~하는 게 어때?', '~하자'는 표현으로 Let's+동사원형 ~, Shall we+동사원형 ~?, Why don't we+동사원형 ~?, What about+동사원형+-ing ~? 등을 사용할 수 있다.

05 ⑤ 'A: 서둘러. 벌써 10시야.' 'B: 먼저 무엇을 시도해 볼까?'라는 대답은 자연스럽지 못하다.

06 ⓐ '~하자'는 의미로 Let's가 적절하다. ⓑ 만날 장소를 묻는 말이 적절하다.

07 사람들이 타거나 내리기 위해 버스나 기차가 멈추는 건물이나 주변 지역

08 B의 물음은 어디서 배드민턴을 할지 장소를 묻고 있으므로 빈칸에는 장소를 제안하는 말이 적절하다.

09 아빠의 'What do you want to do?'라는 말 다음에 '뮤지컬을 보러 가는 게 어때요?'라는 말이 적절하다.

10 과거의 그 날에 일어난 일을 기억하거나 축하하는 날

11 '~일 것 같다'는 I guess로 문장을 시작한다. '휴무를 하다'는 표현으로 take the afternoon off를 사용한다.

12 Anna와 그녀의 아빠는 다음 주 수요일에 대한 계획에 대해 말하고 있다.

13 대화의 내용은 아들이 한국사 시험에서 한 문제만 틀려서 축하하기 위해 저녁에 외식을 간다는 내용이다.

서술형 시험대비 p.19

01 are going to take the subway
02 The subway will be faster than the bus at this time of day.

03 (L)et's see a magic show.
(S)hall we see a magic show?
(W)hat about seeing a magic show?
04 What time shall we meet
05 (A) take　(B) about
06 have a lunch → have lunch
07 a musical, Dad / next, 12 / Bravo Theater

01 지하철이 버스보다 빠르기 때문에 지하철을 탈 것이다.

02 '~보다 빠르다'는 의미로 비교급 than을 이용한다.

03 '~하는 게 어때?', '~하자'는 표현으로 Let's+동사원형 ~, Shall we+동사원형 ~?, Why don't we+동사원형 ~?, What about+동사원형+-ing ~? 등을 사용할 수 있다.

04 약속을 정하는 표현으로 '몇 시에 만날래?'의 의미다.

05 (A)는 '(일을) 쉬다'는 의미로 take off를 사용한다. (B)는 시간을 정하는 표현으로 How about을 사용하여 '12시 어때?'라는 의미이다.

06 식사 이름 앞에는 부정관사 a를 붙이지 않는다.

07 다음 주 수요일 12시에 Bravo 극장에서 아빠와 뮤지컬을 본다.

교과서
Grammar

핵심 Check p.20~21

1 (1) will go　(2) miss　(3) are
2 (1) will exercise → exercise　(2) 틀린 곳 없음
3 (1) clever　(2) interesting　　　4 ②

시험대비 기본평가 p.22

01 (1) more expensive → expensive　(2) than →
as　(3) will answer → answer　(4) won't → don't
02 ⑤　　　03 ④　　　04 ③

01 (1) 'as+원급+as' 구문으로 원급인 expensive를 써야 한다.
(2) 원급 비교는 'as+원급+as'를 사용하므로 than을 as로 고친다. (3), (4) 조건의 부사절을 이끄는 접속사 if절에는 미래시제 대신 현재시제를 사용해야 한다.

02 asked의 직접목적어 자리에 사용된 명사절 접속사 if와 조건을 나타내는 부사절 접속사 if가 적절하다.

03 두 대상의 정도가 같음을 나타낼 때 'as+원급(형용사/부사)+as'를 사용한다.

04 'as+원급(형용사/부사)+as'를 사용하고, 비교급(harder)은 than과 함께 사용된다. hardly는 부사로 '거의 ~ 않다'는 의미이다.

01 ①   02 faster   03 ⑤

04 (1) as   (2) tall   (3) yours

05 (1) If you have to use earphones, do not play your
     music loud.

    (2) If you miss the subway, you will be late for the
      meeting.

    (3) My voice is as loud as yours.

    (4) Nick can run as fast as Peter.

06 ②   07 ④, ⑤   08 ④   09 ①

10 (1) than → as   (2) more beautiful → beautiful

    (3) highly → high   (4) will miss → misses

11 (1) friend → friendly   (2) faster → fast

12 ⑤   13 ④   14 (1) as   (2) well

    (3) mine   15 She is as light as a feather.

16 A tiger is not so big as an elephant.

17 so   18 ②, ③   19 ①, ⑤

20 go, will eat / meet, will

01 ① 두 대상을 비교할 때는 비교의 대상이 동일해야 한다. His
riddle과 her riddle을 비교해야 하므로 her를 hers(= her
riddle)로 고쳐야 한다.

02 대화의 흐름상 지하철이 버스보다 더 빠르다(faster)는 의미가
적절하다.

03 '~한다면'의 의미로 조건의 부사절 접속사 if가 적절하고, 조건
의 부사절에는 미래시제 대신 현재시제를 사용해야 한다.

04 (1), (2) 'as+원급(형용사/부사)+as' 형태를 사용한다. (3) 두
대상을 비교할 때는 비교의 대상이 동일해야 한다. my room과
your room을 비교해야 하므로 소유대명사 yours가 적절하다.

05 (1), (2) if가 있는 부사절은 '접속사(If)+주어+동사 ~, 주
어+동사 …'의 어순으로 쓴다. (3), (4) 'as+원급(형용사/부
사)+as' 형태를 사용한다.

06 조건의 부사절에서는 미래시제 대신 현재시제를 사용해야 한다.

07 보기의 if는 조건의 부사절이다. ①, ②, ③은 동사의 목적어 자
리에 사용된 명사절 접속사로 '~인지 아닌지'의 뜻이다.

08 두 대상의 동등함을 나타낼 때 'as+원급(형용사/부사)+as' 형태
를 사용한다. ④번은 '민호는 원어민만큼 영어를 잘한다.'는 의
미로 동사 speaks를 수식하는 부사 well이 적절하다.

09 조건의 부사절에서는 미래시제 대신 현재시제를 사용하지만, 주
절에는 미래의 의미일 때 미래시제 will을 사용해야 한다.

10 (1) 두 대상의 동등함을 나타낼 때 'as+원급(형용사/부사)+as'
형태를 사용해야 한다. (2) 'as+원급(형용사/부사)+as' 형태가
적절하므로 비교급을 원급으로 바꾸어야 한다. (3) 'as+원급(형
용사/부사)+as' 형태로 부사 highly는 '매우, 대단히'의 의미이
므로, '높이, 높게'의 의미를 가진 high로 바꾸어야 한다. (4) 조
건의 부사절에서는 미래시제 대신 현재시제를 사용한다. 주어가
she(3인칭 단수)이므로 misses가 적절하다.

11 (1) 'as+원급(형용사/부사)+as' 형태를 사용해야 하므로, 명사
friend를 형용사 friendly로 바꾸어야 한다. (2) 'as+원급(형
용사/부사)+as' 형태로 비교급 faster를 fast로 바꾼다.

12 ⑤ 조건의 부사절에서는 미래시제 대신 현재시제를 사용하지
만, 주절에는 미래의 의미일 때 미래시제 will을 사용해야 한다.
you see the sunrise는 you will see ~.가 되어야 한다.

13 두 대상 간의 동등함을 나타낼 때 'as+원급(형용사/부사)+as'
형태를 사용한다. book은 셀 수 있는 명사이므로 much가 아니
라 many로 수식한다.

14 (1), (2): 두 대상 간의 동등함을 나타내는 동등비교는 'as+원
급(형용사/부사)+as' 형태를 사용해야 한다. (3) 두 대상을 비
교할 때는 비교하는 대상이 동일해야 한다. Your house와 my
house가 비교되어야 하므로 소유대명사 mine이 적절하다.

15 두 대상 간의 동등함을 나타내는 동등비교는 'as+원급(형용사/
부사)+as' 형태를 사용해야 한다.

16 동등비교는 'as+원급+as' 형태를 취하지만 부정문에서는 'not
so+원급+as'를 사용할 수 있다.

17 동등 비교인 'as+원급(형용사/부사)+as'는 부정문에서는 'not
as[so]+원급+as'로 사용할 수 있다.

18 동등비교는 'as+원급(형용사/부사)+as'형태를 취한다.

19 동등비교인 'as+원급(형용사/부사)+as' 형태를 취하고, 부정문
에서는 'not as[so]+원급+as'를 취한다.

20 조건이나 시간의 부사절에서는 미래시제 대신 현재시제를 사용
하지만, 주절에는 미래의 의미일 때 미래시제 will을 사용해야
한다.

01 isn't as[so] big as

02 (1) I can finish the work if you help me.

    (2) If school finishes early tomorrow, I will go see a
      movie.

    (3) If my mom catches a cold, I will do the dishes
      for her.

03 (1) run as fast as   (2) as, as

04 (1) me → mine[my car]   (2) more popular →
popular   (3) won't → doesn't   (4) won't → don't

05 (1) John is as tall as Susan.

    (2) This apple is as sweet as that pineapple.

    (3) My bike is not so[as] old as his[his bike].

    (4) I watch as many movies as Kate.

06 (1) as heavy as   (2) as old as   (3) as tall as

07 (1) If you eat too much chocolate, your teeth will
     go bad.

    (2) If Fred walks to school, it will take 40 minutes.

(3) If you follow the map, you'll get to my
    grandma's house.

08 than her → as hers / will find → finds

09 (1) as old as (2) not so[as] tall as
   (3) not so[as] fast as

10 (1) Her sister is as playful as a kitten.
   (2) My home is as quiet as a grave.
   (3) I'm not so[as] tall as my brother.

01 Mina가 Jenny보다 몸집이 더 크기 때문에 Jenny는 Mina만
   큼 크지 않다는 'not as[so]+원급+as'가 적절하다.

02 조건의 부사절에서는 미래시제 대신 현재시제를 사용하지만, 주
   절에는 미래의 의미일 때 미래시제 will을 사용해야 한다.

03 위의 그림은 두 대상 간의 동등한 성질을 나타내고 있으므로 'as+
   원급(형용사/부사)+as' 형태를 사용한다.

04 (1) 두 대상을 비교할 때는 비교하는 대상이 동일해야 한다.
   Your car와 my car가 비교되어야 하므로 소유대명사 mine
   이나 my car가 적절하다. (2) 'as+원급(형용사/부사)+as'를
   사용하므로 원급 popular가 적절하다. (3) 조건 부사절에서는
   미래시제 대신 현재시제를 사용하므로 won't를 3인칭 단수형
   doesn't로 고친다. (4) 조건 부사절에서는 미래시제 대신 현재
   시제를 사용하므로 won't를 don't로 고친다.

05 두 대상 간의 동등한 성질을 나타내고 있으므로 'as+원급(형용
   사/부사)+as' 형태를 사용한다. 그리고 부정문은 'not as[so]+
   원급+as' 형태를 사용한다.

06 (1) Eric과 Amy가 동일한 것은 몸무게이므로 형용사 heavy
   를 이용한다. (2) Tom과 Amy가 동일한 것은 나이이므로 형용
   사 old를 이용한다. (3) Tom과 Eric이 동일한 것은 키이므로
   형용사 tall을 이용하여 'as+원급+as' 형태를 사용한다.

07 부사절로 시작하는 문장의 형태는 '접속사(If)+주어+동사 ~, 주
   어+동사 …'이다. 조건의 부사절에는 미래시제 대신 현재시제를
   사용한다.

08 첫 번째 틀린 부분은 as difficult 뒤에는 as가 적절하고, 두
   대상을 비교할 때는 비교 대상이 같아야 하므로 his riddle과
   her riddle을 비교해야 한다. 그러므로 소유대명사 hers가 적
   절하다. 두 번째 틀린 부분은 시간을 나타내는 부사절에는 미래
   시제 대신 현재시제를 사용해야 하므로 will find를 finds로
   고친다.

09 (1) 수지와 민지는 나이가 같으므로 'as old as'를 사용한다.
   (2) 민지가 수지보다 키가 크지 않기 때문에 부정문 'not so[as]
   tall as'를 사용한다. (3) 수지가 민지보다 빠르지 않기 때문에
   'not so[as] fast as'를 사용한다.

10 두 대상 간의 동등한 성질을 나타내고 있으므로 'as+원급(형용
   사/부사)+as' 형태를 사용한다. 그리고 부정문은 'not as[so]+
   원급+as' 형태를 사용한다.

[교과서]
Reading

확인문제   p.28

1 T 2 F 3 T 4 F 5 T 6 F 7 T 8 F

확인문제   p.29

1 F 2 T 3 T 4 F 5 T 6 F

교과서 확인학습 A   p.30~31

01 The Most Dangerous   02 Welcome
03 perform   04 Like, in Italian, in Italy
05 I'd like to tell   06 appreciate, if
07 of great beauty, as cold as ice
08 who, marry her   09 fails
10 has ever been   11 falls in love with
12 the first man   13 However, to marry
14 nothing more than   15 of his own
16 What   17 adds, to die, incorrectly
18 before dawn, as difficult as hers
19 until, finds out   20 the most famous aria
21 means   22 sleeps
23 not even you   24 safe
25 will know   26 At dawn
27 prince's   28 in time
29 Let's watch

교과서 확인학습 B   p.32~33

1 Turandot The Most Dangerous Love in the World
2 Welcome, everyone!
3 Tonight, we are going to perform Giacomo
  Puccini's opera Turandot.
4 Like many other famous operas, Turandot is in
  Italian because opera started in Italy in the 16th
  century.
5 Before we begin, I'd like to tell you the storyline of
  the opera Turandot.
6 You will appreciate it better if you know the story.
7 Turandot, a Chinese princess, is a woman of great
  beauty, but she is as cold as ice.
8 Any prince who wants to marry her must answer
  three riddles.
9 If he fails, he must die.
10 No one has ever been able to answer them.

11 One day, a brave prince falls in love with her at first sight.

12 He becomes the first man to answer all three riddles.

13 However, Turandot does not want to marry the prince.

14 He is nothing more than a stranger to her.

15 He then gives her a riddle of his own.

16 He asks her, "What is my name?"

17 He adds, "If you answer correctly, I will agree to die. If you answer incorrectly, you will have to marry me."

18 Turandot must find the answer before dawn, but his riddle is as difficult as hers.

19 She says to everyone, "No one will go to sleep until someone finds out his name."

20 The prince then sings the most famous aria of the whole opera, "Nessun Dorma."

21 It means no one sleeps.

22 No one sleeps.

23 No one sleeps, not even you, Princess.

24 My secret is safe.

25 No one will know my name.

26 At dawn, I will win! I will win!

27 The prince's name is Calaf.

28 Will the princess learn his name in time?

29 Let's watch the opera and find out.

시험대비 실력평가
p.34~37

01 (A) Italian (B) to tell (C) know 02 ④
03 ⑤ 04 ① 05 ② 06 ③
07 ③ 08 ② 09 ④ 10 ③
11 ⑤ 12 no one will know his name
13 learn 14 ④ 15 ② 16 ⑤
17 Turandot, a Chinese princess, is a woman of great beauty, but she is as cold as ice.
18 three riddles 19 ②, ③, ⑤
20 ④ 21 (A) to die (B) hers (C) finds
22 What is my name? 23 ① 24 ③
25 are looking for a good musical movie 26 ①, ③

01 (A) '이탈리아어로'라고 해야 하므로 Italian이 적절하다. in Italy: 이탈리아에서, in Italian: 이탈리아어로, (B) would like 다음에는 동명사가 아니라 to부정사를 써야 하므로 to tell이 적절하다. (C) 조건 부사절에서는 현재시제가 미래시제를 대용하므로 know가 적절하다.

02 시작하기 전에 '오페라 《투란도트》의 줄거리를 알려 드리려고

한다'고 했으므로, ④번이 적절하다.

03 '줄거리'를 알면 이 오페라를 더 잘 감상하게 될 것이라고 했다.

04 앞에 나오는 내용과 상반되는 내용이 뒤에 이어지므로 However가 가장 적절하다. ② 그러므로, ③ 즉, 다시 말해, ④ 예를 들어, ⑤ 그 결과

05 주어진 문장의 a riddle of his own에 주목한다. ②번 다음 문장의 질문을 가리키므로 ②번이 적절하다.

06 ⓐ, ⓒ: Turandot, ⓑ, ⓓ, ⓔ: the prince

07 Turandot는 얼음처럼 차갑고 세 가지 수수께끼에 답하지 못한 왕자들은 죽어야 한다고 했기 때문에 성격이 '무정하고 비정하다'고 하는 것이 적절하다. heartless: 무정한, 비정한, ① 사려 깊은, ② 마음이 따뜻한, ⑤ 부주의한

08 ⓐ와 ②번: [보통 as ... as ~로 형용사·부사 앞에서] …와 같은 정도로, 마찬가지로 (앞의 as는 지시부사, 뒤의 as는 접속사), ① …한 대로(접속사), ③ [비례] …함에 따라, …할수록(접속사), ④ …이라고, …으로(전치사), ⑤ …이므로, …이기 때문에(접속사)

09 ④ Turandot가 물어보는 세 가지 수수께끼가 무엇인지는 대답할 수 없다. ① She is a Chinese princess. ② She is a woman of great beauty. ③ He must answer three riddles. ⑤ A brave prince who falls in love with her at first sight.

10 ⓐ Turandot는 동이 트기 '전에' 답을 찾아야 한다. ⓒ '동틀 녘에', 내가 이길 것이라고 하는 것이 적절하다.

11 글의 흐름상 현재시제로 써야 하고, no one의 경우 3인칭 단수 취급을 하므로 동사 sleep에 -s를 붙인 형태를 쓰는 것이 적절하다.

12 '누구도 그의 이름을 알지 못할 것이기' 때문이다.

13 공주는 그의 이름을 제때 '알아낼' 수 있을까요? 오페라를 보고 '알아봅시다.'라고 했으므로, learn으로 바꿀 수 있다. find out 알아내다, 발견하다

14 위 글은 '감상문'이다. review (책·연극·영화 등에 대한) 논평[비평], 감상문, ① 독후감, ② 수필, ③ (신문·잡지의) 글, 기사, ⑤ 전기

15 recommend: 추천[천거]하다, 권고[권장]하다, 민수는 미녀와 야수를 마음이 따뜻해지는 사랑 이야기를 좋아하는 사람들에게 '추천한다.' ① 요구하다, ③ 표현하다, ④ 보고하다, ⑤ 충고하다

16 ⑤ 민수가 누구와 그것을 보았는지는 알 수 없다. ① Beauty and the Beast. ② Last Saturday. ③ It is about a beautiful girl and a beast. ④ He enjoyed it a lot.

17 'of'를 보충하고, Turandot와 a Chinese princess는 동격이므로 a Chinese princess 앞뒤로 콤마를 찍는 것이 적절하다. of+추상명사 = 형용사

18 '세 가지 수수께끼'를 가리킨다.

19 ⓒ와 ①, ④는 형용사적 용법, ②, ⑤ 부사적 용법, ③ 명사적 용법

20 ④ Turandot는 그 왕자의 이름도 모르기 때문에, 그는 그녀에게 단지 '낯선 사람'일 뿐이라고 하는 것이 적절하다. ① 이웃, ⑤ 동료

21 (A) agree는 to부정사를 목적어로 취하므로 to die가 적절하다. (B) 그의 수수께끼는 '그녀의 것'만큼 어렵다고 해야 하므로 hers가 적절하다. (C) 시간을 나타내는 부사절에서는 현재시제가 미래시제를 대신하므로 finds가 적절하다.

22 왕자가 낸 수수께끼는 "제 이름이 무엇입니까?"이다.

23 Turandot는 동이 트기 전에 답을 찾아야 하지만 그의 수수께끼는 그녀의 것만큼 어렵다고 했기 때문에, Turandot의 심경은 절박하다고 하는 것이 직질하다. desperate: 필사적인, 절박한, ② 만족스러운, ③ 지루한, ④ 부끄러운, ⑤ 흥분한

24 ⓐ와 ③: 감동적인, ① 활기[생기] 넘치는, ② 발랄한, 쾌활한, ④ 정력[활동]적인, ⑤ 우울하게 만드는, 우울한

25 '좋은 뮤지컬 영화를 찾고 있는 사람들'에게 추천하고 있다.

26 ① not only A but also B: A뿐만 아니라 B도, ② not A but B: A가 아니라 B, ③ both A and B: A와 B 둘 다, ④ either A or B: A와 B 둘 중 하나, ⑤ neither A nor B: A와 B 둘 다 아닌

서술형 시험대비 p.38~39

01 나는 여러분에게 오페라 〈투란도트〉의 줄거리를 알려 드리려고 합니다.   02 the opera *Turandot*

03 opera started in Italy in the 16th century

04 only

05 incorrectly → correctly, correctly → incorrectly

06 someone finds out his name

07 very beautiful   08 who 또는 that

09 a few → no   10 (A) is   (B) marry   (C) answer

11 at first sight   12 (A) three riddles   (B) must die

13 hers   14 before dawn

15 If you answer correctly, I will agree to die.

16 so → as

---

01 would like to+동사원형: ~하고 싶다

02 '오페라 《투란도트》'를 가리킨다.

03 《투란도트》가 이탈리아어로 되어 있는 이유는 '오페라가 16세기 이탈리아에서 시작되었기' 때문이다.

04 nothing more than: ~에 지나지 않는, ~에 불과한

05 "당신이 '맞게' 대답한다면 나는 죽는 것에 동의하겠습니다. 만약 답이 '틀리면' 당신은 저와 결혼해야 합니다."라고 고치는 것이 적절하다.

06 '누군가 그의 이름을 알아낼 때까지 그 누구도 잠들 수 없다'는 것은 '누군가 그의 이름을 알아낸' 후에야 사람들이 잠들 수 있다는 뜻이다.

07 of+추상명사 = 형용사, of great beauty = very beautiful

---

08 주격 관계대명사 who 또는 that이 적절하다.

09 그 누구도 수수께끼에 답할 수 없었고 어떤 용감한 왕자가 세 수수께끼를 모두 맞힌 첫 번째 사람이 된다고 했기 때문에, 'a few'를 'no'로 고치는 것이 적절하다.

10 (A) Turandot와 a Chinese princess는 동격으로 단수로 취급해야 하므로 is가 적절하다. (B) marry는 타동사이므로 전치사 없이 바로 목적어를 써야 하므로 marry가 적절하다. (C) answer는 타동사이므로 전치사 없이 바로 목적어를 써야 하므로 answer가 적절하다.

11 at first sight: 첫눈에, 언뜻 보기에

12 중국의 공주 Turandot는 자기와 결혼하기를 원하는 어떤 왕사에게도 '세 가지 수수께끼'를 낸다. 만약 그가 그것들에 올바르게 대답하지 못하면, 그는 '죽어야 한다.'

13 그의 수수께끼는 '그녀의 것'만큼 어렵다고 해야 하므로 'hers'가 적절하다.

14 '제때에'는 '동이 트기 전에'를 가리킨다.

15 'will'을 보충하면 된다.

16 'as+원급+as'를 사용하여 '그의 수수께끼가 그녀의 수수께끼만큼 어렵다'라고 하는 것이 적절하다. 부정문에서는 'not so+원급+as'도 가능하다.

영역별 핵심문제 p.41~45

01 ⑤   02 ①   03 ③   04 ③

05 right   06 (A) Where   (B) How[What]

07 ④   08 ③   09 What time shall we meet?   10 (B) → (A) → (C) → (D)

11 (A) off   (B) if   (C) shall we

12 her school's 75th anniversary

13 If you do something special for the world, the world will change.

14 ③   15 He doesn't watch TV as[so] much as

16 ③   17 ⑤   18 ②

19 ④   20 ②   21 ④

22 (1) as[so] fast as   (2) as fast as   (3) as cheap as

23 ④   24 (1) as small as   (2) run as fast as   (3) as tall as   25 won't → doesn't

26 (1) will rain → rains   (2) comes → will come

27 ②   28 ④   29 ④   30 ①, ③

31 ④   32 (A) more   (B) agree   (C) difficult

33 ②, ⑤

---

01 ① 용감한 – 겁 많은, ② 안전한 – 위험한, ③ 어려운 – 쉬운, ④ 실패하다 – 성공하다 / 모두 반의어 관계이고 ⑤는 두 단어 모두 '감동적인'이라는 뜻의 유의어 관계이다.

02 surprising '놀라운' = amazing

03 ① brave: 용감한 / 어느 날, 어떤 용감한 왕자가 그녀에게 첫눈에 반합니다. ② century: 세기 / 오페라는 16세기에 이탈리아

7

에서 시작되었다. ③ '지하철을 타는 게 어때?'라는 의미로 동사 take가 자연스럽다. ④ dawn: 새벽 / 그녀는 동이 트기 전에 답을 찾아야 한다. ⑤ mean: 의미하다 / Nessun Dorma는 누구도 잠들지 못한다는 뜻이다.

04 celebrate: 축하하다

05 right는 부사로 '바로'의 의미로 사용된다.

06 (A) G의 말로 보아 B는 배드민턴을 칠 장소를 묻고 있다. (B) 상대방에게 제안할 때 사용하는 표현으로 How[What] about ~?을 사용한다.

07 위 대화는 오후에 친구와 무엇을 할 것인지에 대한 계획을 세우는 내용이다.

08 제안할 때 사용하는 표현으로 Why don't we+동사원형?, Let's+동사원형., Shall we+동사원형?, How[What] about+동사-ing?가 있다.

10 오늘 오후에 무엇을 할 건지 묻는 말에, (B) 미술관에 가는 게 어떠냐고 제안을 한다. (A) '좋아'라는 동의의 말을 하고 만날 시간을 물어본다. (C) 2시가 어떤지 시간을 제안하고 (D) 마지막으로 승낙의 표현과 함께 미술관 앞에서 만나자고 제안한다.

11 (A)는 take와 호응하여 '(일을) 쉬다'는 의미로 off를 사용하고, (B)는 의미상 '~한다면'의 의미를 가지는 조건의 부사절 접속사 if가 적절하다. (C)는 시간을 제안할 때 사용하는 표현으로 What time shall we ~?가 적절하다.

13 조건의 부사절에서는 미래시제 대신 현재시제를 사용하고, 주절에는 미래시제를 그대로 사용한다.

14 '~만큼 …한'의 의미로 'as+원급+as'를 사용한다. 부정문에서는 'not as[so]+원급+as'를 사용하지만, 긍정문에서는 as 대신 so를 사용하지 않는다.

15 TV를 보지 않는다는 일반동사 watch의 부정문을 사용해서 He doesn't watch TV를 쓰고, 그 다음 '~만큼 …하게'의 의미로 'as[so]+원급+as' 구문을 이용한다. 이때 watch를 수식하는 부사 much가 적절하다.

16 (1)은 check의 목적어 자리에 사용되는 접속사 if(~인지 아닌지), (2)는 조건의 부사절 접속사 if(만일 ~라면)가 적절하다.

17 ①~④는 동사의 목적어를 이끄는 명사절 접속사 if로 '~인지 아닌지'의 의미이고, ⑤는 조건의 부사절 접속사 if로 '만일 ~라면'의 의미다.

18 ②는 'as+원급+as' 구문으로 so를 as로 바꾸어야 한다.

19 ④ '~만큼 …하지 않다'는 의미로 'not as[so]+원급+as' 구문이 적절하다. 'so heavy so'를 'so[as] heavy as'로 바꾸어야 한다.

20 The subway is as faster as the train.은 as fast as가 되어야 하고, We will go swimming if the weather will be fine tomorrow.는 조건의 부사절에서 미래시제 대신 현재시제를 사용하므로 will be를 is로 고쳐야 한다.

21 조건의 부사절에서는 미래시제 대신 현재시제를 사용하므로 break가 적절하다. 복수 주어 my friends이므로 breaks는 적절하지 않다.

22 (1)은 지하철이 버스보다 빠르지 않기 때문에 'not as[so]+원급+as' 구문을 이용하고, (2)는 버스가 택시와 속도가 같으므로 'as+원급+as' 구문을 이용한다. (3)은 지하철이 버스와 요금이 같기 때문에 'as cheap as'가 자연스럽다.

23 ④는 '나는 너만큼 어리다.'라는 의미이고, 나머지는 모두 '네가 나보다 나이가 많다.'라는 의미이다.

24 '~만큼 …한[하게]'의 의미는 'as+원급+as' 구문을 이용한다.

25 조건을 나타내는 부사절에서는 미래시제 대신 현재시제를 사용해야 하므로, 미래시제 won't를 3인칭 단수 현재형인 doesn't로 바꾸어야 한다.

26 (1) 소선의 부사절에서는 미래시세 내신 현새시세를 사용하고, (2) be sure의 목적어 자리에 사용된 명사절 접속사 if는 미래시제를 사용할 수 있다.

27 시작하기 전에 오페라를 더 잘 '감상하도록' 《투란도트》의 줄거리를 알려 드리려고 한다고 말했기 때문에, 오페라 《투란도트》를 '공연할' 것이라고 하는 것이 적절하다. perform: 공연하다, ① 연습하다, ③ 잘되어 가다, 작동하다, ④ 이루다, 성취하다, ⑤ 완료하다, 끝마치다

28 ⓑ와 ④번은 '~과 같이'라는 의미의 전치사로 사용되었다. 나머지는 다 '~을 좋아하다'라는 의미의 동사이다.

29 ④번 다음 문장의 He에 주목한다. 주어진 문장의 a brave prince를 받고 있으므로 ④번이 적절하다.

30 ⓐ와 ①, ③번은 경험 용법, ② 결과 용법, ④ 완료 용법, ⑤ 계속 용법

31 ④ 수수께끼에 답하지 못하면 죽어야 하는데, 그 누구도 수수께끼에 답할 수 없었다고 했기 때문에, 지금까지 수수께끼에 도전했던 왕자들은 다 죽었다.

32 (A) 그는 그녀에게 '단지 낯선 사람일 뿐'이라고 해야 하므로 more가 적절하다. nothing more than: ~에 지나지 않는, nothing less than: 다름 아닌 바로, (B) 당신이 맞게 대답한다면 나는 죽는 것에 '동의하겠다'고 해야 하므로 agree가 적절하다. refuse: 거절하다, (C) 그의 수수께끼는 그녀의 것만큼 '어렵다'고 해야 하므로 difficult가 적절하다. different: 다른

33 give, send, write는 3형식으로 고칠 때 'to'를 사용한다. ①, ③ buy, make는 for를 사용한다. ④ ask는 of를 사용한다. ⑤ thank-you note: 감사장

단원별 예상문제 p.46~49

01 answer **02** nothing more than
03 (1) beauty, cold (2) perform (3) incorrectly, marry
  (4) falls in love, sight
04 ② **05** ⑤
06 (1) Why don't we go on a picnic this weekend?
  (2) What about going on a picnic this weekend?
07 ④ **08** ⑤ **09** get, discount if

10 What time shall we meet?   11 ③

12 ③   13 ④   14 ②   15 ⑤

16 (1) finish   (2) give   (3) changes   17 ②

18 ③   19 ⑤   20 (1) not as[so] tall as

(2) well   (3) as heavy as   21 ③   22 ①

23 knowing the story   24 as sweet as honey →

as cold as ice   25 riddles   26 ⑤

---

01 둘은 유의어 관계이다. 제안 : 대답하다

02 nothing more than ~: ~에 지나지 않는

03 (1) of+추상명사 = 형용사. of beauty = beautiful(아름다운) (2) perform: 공연하다 (3) incorrectly: 올바르지 않게, 틀리게, marry: 결혼하다 (4) fall in love: 사랑에 빠지다. at first sight: 첫눈에

04 예상된 시간보다 더 이르게

05 ⑤번 뒤의 문장에 나오는 See you there.에서 there가 the subway station을 가리키므로 ⑤가 적절하다.

06 상대에게 제안을 할 때 사용하는 표현으로 Let's+동사원형, Why don't we+동사원형?, What about+동명사/명사? 등이 있다.

07 시간이나 장소를 정할 때 How about이나 What about을 이용한다.

08 흥미롭거나 놀라운 일을 말하기 전에 사용되는 표현

09 get a discount: 할인받다, if: ~한다면

10 제안할 때 사용하는 표현으로 shall we ~를 이용하고 시간을 묻는 표현인 What time으로 문장을 시작한다.

12 '~하자'는 제안이나 권유의 의미로 사용할 수 없는 표현은 ③번이다.

13 대화의 흐름상 한국사 시험에서 한 문제 틀린 것에 대해 오늘 밤 축하하러 나가자는 의미로 celebrate가 적절하다. appreciate는 '감상하다'라는 뜻이다.

14 '만일 ~한다면'의 의미로 조건을 나타내는 접속사 if가 적절하다.

15 ⑤ Jane은 Mike보다 성적이 높기 때문에 Mike isn't as smart as Jane.으로 쓰는 것이 적절하다.

16 조건의 부사절에서는 의미가 미래라 할지라도 현재시제를 사용한다.

17 ② 시간을 나타내는 부사절에서는 미래시제 대신 현재시제를 사용한다. will find를 finds로 고쳐야 한다.

18 ③ as ~ as 사이에는 형용사나 부사의 원급을 사용해야 한다. bigger를 big으로 고쳐야 한다.

19 ⑤번은 tell의 직접목적어 자리에 사용된 명사절 접속사 if다. '~인지 아닌지'로 해석한다.

20 두 대상 간의 동등함을 나타낼 때 'as+원급+as'를 사용한다. 부정문은 '~만큼 …하지 않은'의 의미로 'not as[so]+원급+as'를 사용한다.

21 in Italian: 이탈리아어로, in Italy: 이탈리아에서, in the 16th century: 16세기에

22 ④와 ①번은 감상하다, architecture: 건축학[술], 건축 양식, ②와 ④ 고마워하다, ③과 ⑤ (제대로) 인식하다

23 여러분이 '줄거리를 알면' 이 오페라를 더 잘 감상하게 될 것이다. 전치사 By 다음에 동명사로 쓰는 것이 적절하다.

24 수수께끼에 답하는 데 실패하면 죽어야 한다고 했기 때문에, 그녀는 '얼음처럼 차갑다' 하는 것이 적절하다.

25 riddle: 수수께끼, 터무니없는 것 같지만 영리하거나 재미있는 대답을 지닌 질문을 하는 수수께끼나 농담

26 ⑤ 절차를 통과하지 못한 왕자들이 몇 명인지는 대답할 수 없다. ① 중국의 공주, ② 굉장히 아름답다. ③ 반드시 세 가지 수수께끼에 답해야 한다. ④ 만약 세 가지 수수께끼에 답하지 못하면 죽어야 한다.

서술형 실전문제   p.50~51

01 (A) What time shall we meet?

(B) Where shall we meet?

02 Why don't we take the subway

03 (A) What shall we do this afternoon?

(B) Why don't we go see *Wonder Woman*?

(C) How about 4 o'clock?

04 (1) as expensive as mine[my ring]

(2) not so kind as   (3) comes, take, to

05 (1) will rain → rains   (2) will need → need

06 (1) as old as, not as[so] old as

(2) as tall as, Mike[Minho] is not as[so] tall as

(3) as heavy as, is not as[so] heavy as

07 won't pay → don't pay   08 as cold as ice

09 (A) Any   (B) ever   (C) sight   10 failed

11 He is nothing more than a stranger to her.

12 her riddles   13 (A) marry him   (B) to die

---

01 약속을 정할 때 사용하는 표현으로, (A)는 만날 시간을 (B)는 만날 장소를 물어보는 표현이 적절하다.

02 제안을 할 때 'Why don't we+동사원형?'을 이용한다.

03 (A)에는 무엇을 할 것인지 묻는 말로 대화를 시작하는 것이 적절하다. (B)는 구체적으로 무엇을 할 것인지 제안하는 표현이 적절하다. (C)는 '몇 시에 만날래?'라는 물음에 시간을 정하는 표현이 적절하다.

04 (1) 두 대상 간의 동일한 것을 나타낼 때 'as+원급+as'를 사용하고, 비교하는 대상은 같아야 하므로 her ring과 my ring을 비교해야 한다. (2) '~만큼 …하지 않다'는 의미로 'not so[as]+원급+as' 구문을 사용한다. (3) 조건의 부사절에서는 미래시제 대신 현재시제를 사용한다. take A to B는 A를 B로 데려오다라는 의미다.

05 조건 부사절에서는 미래시제 대신 현재시제를 사용한다.

06 두 대상 간의 동일한 것을 나타낼 때 'as+원급+as'를 사용한다. '~만큼 …하지 않다'는 의미로 'not so[as]+원급+as' 구문을

사용한다.

07 조건 부사절에서는 미래시제 대신 현재시제를 사용한다.

08 as cold as ice = very cold

09 (A) 그녀와 결혼하길 원하는 왕자는 '누구든지'라고 해야 하므로 Any가 적절하다. 긍정문의 any: '어떤 ~이라도', some+셀 수 있는 명사 복수: '약간의', some+셀 수 있는 명사 단수: '어떤(a certain)', (B) 부정의 의미인 No one이 주어이므로 ever가 적절하다. (C) 그녀에게 '첫눈에' 반한다고 해야 하므로 sight가 적절하다. at first sight: 첫눈에

10 목숨을 걸고 세 가지 수수께끼에 답하려고 시도했던 모든 왕자들이 한 왕자를 제외하고는 다 '실패했다.' at the risk of one's life: 목숨을 걸고, except: ~을 제외하고는

11 nothing more than: ~에 지나지 않는, ~에 불과한

12 '그녀의 수수께끼들'을 가리킨다.

13 만약 Turandot가 왕자의 수수께끼에 틀리게 대답한다면 그녀는 '그와 결혼해야 한다.' 만약 Turandot가 맞게 대답한다면 그는 '죽는 것에' 동의할 것이다.

창의사고력 서술형 문제   p.52

|모범답안|

01 (1) A: What shall we do at the park?
     B: Why don't we ride the roller coaster?
     A: That's a good idea.
   (2) A: What shall we do at the park?
     B: Why don't we visit the flower garden?
     A: That's a good idea.
02 (1) The subway fare is as expensive as the bus fare.
   (2) The subway is not so[as] fast as the bus.
03 (A) Review   (B) the dreams and love
   (C) beautiful and moving   (D) story

단원별 모의고사   p.53~56

01 ⑤   02 (1) take, off   (2) practice, play
(3) don't, celebrate   03 ③   04 moving
05 late   06 ③   07 ②   08 ④
09 ④   10 ③
11 What do you want to do?   12 ③
13 (1) Anna is as beautiful as Julie.
   (2) I will let you go out if you do finish your job.
14 ③   15 (1) as not larger → not as large as
(2) as bigger as → as big as   16 not as[so] tall as
17 ④   18 ⑤   19 Italian   20 ③
21 ③   22 ask → answer   23 ②
24 ④

---

01 ⑤의 appreciate는 'to understand how good something or someone is' (어떤 것이나 어떤 사람이 얼마나 좋은지 이해하다)라는 설명이 적절하다. to do something enjoyable on a special occasion은 celebrate에 대한 설명이다.

02 (1) take off: (일을) 쉬다 (2) practice: 연습하다, play: 연극 (3) Why don't we ~?: ~하는 게 어때?, celebrate: 축하하다

03 빈칸에는 be동사 뒤에 형용사가 보어로 와야 하므로 ①은 적절하지 못하다. as와 as 사이에는 형용사 원급 형태 good이 적절하다. ⑤의 the best는 셋 이상에서 '가장 ~한'의 의미인 최상급이다.

04 moving: 감동적인

05 '계획되고, 예상되고, 일상적인 또는 필요한 시간 후에 발생하거나 도착하는', 즉 '늦은'의 의미이다.

06 콘서트가 언제 시작되는지는 대화에 언급되어 있지 않다.

07 한국사 시험에서 한 문제만 틀렸다고 했으므로, 시험을 못 본 것이 아니라 잘 봤다는 것을 알 수 있다. poorly를 well로 바꾸어야 한다.

08 ④ 시험을 잘 본 사람은 Joe다.

09 '몇 시에 만날래?'라는 물음에 장소를 말하는 것은 어색하다.

10 다음 주 수요일에 학교를 가지 않는다는 말에 이유를 물어보는 것이 자연스럽다.

11 의문사 what으로 문장을 시작하고, '~하고 싶다'는 'want to+동사원형'을 이용한다.

12 ③ Ann과 아빠는 뮤지컬을 보러 갈 것이다.

13 (1) 'as+원급+as' 구문으로 형용사 beautiful은 as와 as 사이에 넣는다. (2) 접속사 if 뒤에는 '주어+동사'가 나와야 한다.

14 ③ 두 대상인 Her hair와 my hair를 비교하는 문장이므로 I를 mine이나 my hair로 바꾸어야 한다.

15 'as+원급+as' 구문으로, 원급은 형용사와 부사를 사용해야 한다.

16 Ann이 Tom보다 키가 작으므로 'not so[as]+원급+as' 구문을 사용한다.

17 조건의 부사절에서는 미래시제 대신 현재시제를 사용하지만 주절에는 미래시제를 그대로 사용한다.

18 ⑤번은 '테니스는 축구만큼 인기가 없다'는 의미로 is not as[so] popular as가 되어야 한다.

19 'Italy'의 언어를 나타내는 'Italian'을 쓰는 것이 적절하다. in Italian: 이탈리아어로

20 storyline: (소설·연극·영화 등의) 줄거리, ③ plot: (소설, 극, 영화 등의) 구성[플롯/줄거리], ① 주제, 테마, ② 배경, ④ 개념, ⑤ (논의 등의) 주제[대상/화제]

21 ⓐ of+추상명사 = 형용사, of great beauty = very beautiful, ⓒ fall in love with: ~와 사랑에 빠지다

22 그녀와 결혼하길 원하는 왕자는 누구든지 반드시 세 가지 수수께끼에 '답해야' 한다고 해야 하므로 ask를 answer로 고치는 것이 적절하다.

23 ⓐ와 ②, ⑤는 명사적 용법, ①, ③은 부사적 용법, ④는 형용사적 용법

24 ④ 만약 Turandot의 답이 틀리면 '그녀는 왕자와 결혼해야 한다.'

Food in History

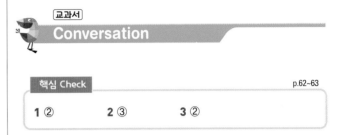

시험대비 실력평가 p.60

01 different   02 ③   03 ⑤   04 ②
05 ④   06 ④   07 disappointed
08 by himself

01 둘은 반의어 관계이다. 실내의 : 실외의 = 같은 : 다른
02 탕평채와 신선로, 송편에 대해 말하고 있으므로 전통 음식이 적절하다.
03 나는 음식에 특별한 재료를 더했다.
04 지방이나 국가 정부에서의 지위를 얻기 위해 선거에서 경쟁하는 특정한 정치적 신념을 가진 사람들의 조직은 '정당'이다.
05 다른 것보다 어떤 하나를 좋아하거나 선택하거나 원하다
06 'recommend'는 '추천하다'는 뜻이다.
07 누군가나 무언가가 당신이 희망하거나 기대했던 것만큼 좋지 않았기 때문에 행복하지 않은
08 'alone'은 '혼자'의 뜻으로 'by oneself'와 같다. 신선은 일반적으로 남자를 가리키므로 himself를 쓰는 것이 적절하다.

서술형 시험대비 p.61

01 (1) policy, 정책   (2) recommend, 추천하다
   (3) symbolize, 상징하다
02 (1) fortune teller   (2) pot   (3) worried   (4) mainly
03 (1) (r)ecently   (2) (s)cholar
04 (1) Honesty, policy   (2) party
05 (1) half moon   (2) parties, harmony   (3) official

01 (1) 특정한 상황에서 무엇을 해야 하는지에 대한 집단이나 정부, 또는 정당이 공식적으로 동의한 일련의 생각이나 계획 (2) 어떤 사람이나 어떤 것이 특정 직업이나 목적에 좋거나 적합할 것이라고 제안하다 (3) 어떤 것을 나타내다
02 (1) 왕은 왕국의 미래를 알기 위해 점쟁이가 필요하다. (2) 우유 약간과 닭고기를 냄비에 넣어라. (3) 왕은 그의 왕국이 걱정이 되었다. '~에 관해 걱정하다'는 'be worried about'이다. 동사 worry를 become 동사 뒤에 사용하기 위해 형용사 worried 로 바꾸어 준다. (4) 그가 혼자 그곳에 사는 동안, 그는 주로 채소를 먹었다.
03 (1) 얼마 전, 혹은 얼마 전에 시작된 때에: 최근에 (2) 특히 대학에서 특정한 과목을 매우 세부적으로 공부하는 사람: 학자
04 (1) 정직, 정직함: honesty, 정책: policy (2) 정당: party

05 (1) half moon: 반달 (2) party: 정당, four와 함께 쓰여서 복수 명사로 parties가 적절하다. in harmony: 조화롭게(3) official: 관리

교과서 Conversation

핵심 Check p.62~63

1 ②   2 ③   3 ②

교과서 대화문 익히기

Check(√) True or False p.64

1 T   2 F   3 T   4 T

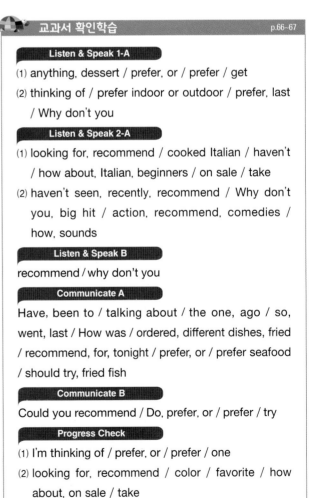

교과서 확인학습 p.66~67

Listen & Speak 1-A
(1) anything, dessert / prefer, or / prefer / get
(2) thinking of / prefer indoor or outdoor / prefer, last / Why don't you

Listen & Speak 2-A
(1) looking for, recommend / cooked Italian / haven't / how about, Italian, beginners / on sale / take
(2) haven't seen, recently, recommend / Why don't you, big hit / action, recommend, comedies / how, sounds

Listen & Speak B
recommend / why don't you

Communicate A
Have, been to / talking about / the one, ago / so, went, last / How was / ordered, different dishes, fried / recommend, for, tonight / prefer, or / prefer seafood / should try, fried fish

Communicate B
Could you recommend / Do, prefer, or / prefer / try

Progress Check
(1) I'm thinking of / prefer, or / prefer / one
(2) looking for, recommend / color / favorite / how about, on sale / take

11

01 recommend, for   02 ③   03 ①

04 ④

01 '(제게) ~을 추천해 주시겠어요?'라는 뜻으로 상대방에게 추천을 부탁할 때 'Could you recommend ~ (for me)?' 표현을 쓴다.

02 B의 답으로 보아 빈칸에는 어느 것을 더 좋아하는지 묻는 말이 적절하다.

03 B의 마지막 말에서 일곱 마리의 고양이 중 한 마리를 주겠다는 말로 보아 G는 고양이를 좋아한다는 것을 알 수 있다.

04 Do you prefer A or B?는 상대방의 선호를 묻는 표현이다.

01 ④   02 ⑤   03 ②

04 Do you prefer pie or cake?   05 ③

06 beginner   07 ①   08 ⑤

09 ③   10 ④

11 Have you been to the new Chinese restaurant

01 빈칸 다음의 G의 말과 실내 스포츠를 좋아한다는 B의 대답으로 보아 '스포츠 동아리에 가입할 생각 중이다.'라는 말이 가장 적절하다.

02 ⑤는 '탁구 동아리에 어떻게 가입하니?'라는 뜻이고, 나머지는 모두 '~하는 게 어때?'라고 제안하는 표현이다.

03 ② 'A: 치킨을 좋아하니 소고기를 좋아하니?'라는 물음에 'B: 나는 돼지고기를 좋아하지 않아.'라는 대답은 자연스럽지 못하다.

04 둘 중 더 좋아하는 것에 대해 물을 때는 'Do you prefer A or B?' 표현을 쓴다.

05 ⓐ '추천해 주실 수 있으세요?'라는 뜻으로 recommend가 적절하다. ⓑ 제안하는 말로 '~은 어때?'라는 how about이 적절하다.

06 '어떤 것을 하기 시작하거나 처음으로 어떤 것을 배우는 사람'은 '초보자'를 의미한다.

07 G가 액션 영화는 좋아하지 않는다는 말에 B가 'Funny Families는 어때?'라고 말하는 것으로 보아 빈칸에는 추천을 부탁하는 말이 적절하다.

08 '~하는 게 어때?'라는 표현으로 'Why don't you+동사원형 ~?', 'What about+동사원형+-ing' 등을 사용할 수 있다.

09 '음식은 어땠나요?'라고 묻는 Jaden의 말 다음에 오는 Ms. Park의 답변에 들어가는 것이 적절하다.

10 빈칸 (a) 다음에 Ms. Park이 '해산물을 더 좋아하니, 육류를 더 좋아하니?'라고 묻고 있기 때문에 빈칸에는 음식을 추천해 달라는 말이 적절하다.

11 현재완료 의문문(Have+주어+과거분사 ~?)을 이용하여 문장을 쓴다.

01 He is going to eat naengmyeon.

02 Do you prefer hot or cold food?

03 (1) Do you prefer rainy days or sunny days?

    (2) prefer sunny days

04 Could you recommend a book for me?

05 Could you recommend a dish for me?

06 Do you prefer[Which do you prefer,] seafood or meat?

01 남자는 어떤 음식을 먹을 예정인가?

02 둘 중 더 좋아하는 것에 대해 물을 때는 Do you prefer A or B? 표현을 쓴다.

03 둘 중 더 좋아하는 것에 대해 물을 때는 Do you prefer A or B? 표현을 쓴다. 선호하는 것을 답할 때는 'I prefer ~'을 사용한다.

04 '제게 ~을 추천해 주시겠어요?'라는 뜻으로 상대방에게 추천을 부탁할 때 'Could you recommend ~ for me?' 표현을 쓴다.

교과서

Grammar

1 (1) was painted   (2) to   (3) with

2 (1) anything long   (2) Something terrible

   (3) anyone nice to talk with

01 ⑤   02 ②

03 (1) was built   (2) was written   (3) someone funny

    (4) somebody important

04 (1) cleans → is cleaned

    (2) to read interesting → interesting to read

01 동사를 시제에 맞게 'be+pp'로 바꾸고 수동태 문장의 주어 자리에는 능동태 문장의 목적어가 오고, by 다음에는 능동태 문장의 주어를 목적격으로 쓴다.

02 '-thing'으로 끝나는 대명사는 형용사가 뒤에서 수식한다. 동사 다음에 '-thing+형용사'를 쓴다.

03 (1) 수동태는 'be+pp'의 형태이다. (2) 책 이름은 단수로 취급하며 과거에 씌여진 것이므로 과거로 쓴다. (3), (4) '-one, -body'로 끝나는 대명사는 형용사가 뒤에서 수식한다.

04 (1) 방이 청소되는 것이므로 수동태가 적절하다. (2) '-thing'으로 끝나는 대명사를 형용사와 to부정사가 동시에 수식하는 경우 '대명사+형용사+to부정사'의 어순임에 유의한다.

시험대비 실력평가   p.75~77

01 ④	02 ⑤	03 ③	04 ①
05 ②	06 ⑤	07 ①	

08 (1) to (2) for (3) of   09 anything funny

10 ③

11 (1) In 1964, China's first nuclear test took place.

(2) *Two Sisters* was painted by Auguste Renoir in 1881.

(3) Give me something cold to drink.

(4) They will see her as someone respectable.

12 ④

13 (1) A nice cap was bought for me by him.

(2) French is spoken in France (by them).

(3) By whom was the picture *The Sunflowers* drawn?

(4) Delicious spaghetti was made for Sam by Marianne last night.

(5) Emily was heard talking to her friend in class by me.

14 ④   15 ⑤

16 be told / are made / was surprised at / was interested in / was covered with / was filled with

01 This toy가 만들어지는 것이므로 수동태가 적절하다.

02 '-one, -body'로 끝나는 대명사는 형용사가 뒤에서 수식한다. I don't have anyone reliable.

03 ③ 목적격보어가 원형부정사인 경우 수동태 문장에서는 to부정사로 바뀐다.

04 ② How did tangpyeongchae and sinseollo get their names? ③ The Mona Lisa was painted by Leonardo da Vinci. ④ There was something wrong with my bill. ⑤ The dress will be bought for her by Mary.

05 목적어 only 33를 수동태의 주어로 한 구문이다.

06 be satisfied with: ~에 만족하다 be filled with: ~로 가득 차다

07 Dave에 의해 개최되는 것이므로 수동태가 적절하고 '-one'으로 끝나는 대명사는 형용사가 뒤에서 수식한다.

08 직접목적어를 주어로 한 수동태에서 간접목적어 앞에 (1) send는 전치사 to를, (2) make는 전치사 for를, (3) ask는 전치사 of를 쓴다.

09 의문문이므로 anything을 쓰고 '-thing'으로 끝나는 대명사이므로 funny가 뒤에서 수식하도록 한다.

10 ③ give는 간접목적어 앞에 전치사 to를 붙인다.

11 (1) take place는 자동사이므로 수동태로 쓰이지 않는다. (2) *Two Sisters*(두 자매)가 그려지는 것이므로 수동태가 적절하다. (3) '-thing'으로 끝나는 대명사를 형용사와 to부정사가 동시에 수식하는 경우 '대명사+형용사+to부정사'의 어순이다. (4) '-one'으로 끝나는 대명사는 형용사가 뒤에서 수식한다.

12 '-thing'으로 끝나는 대명사는 형용사가 뒤에서 수식하며 happen은 자동사이므로 수동태로 쓰이지 않는다.

13 (1), (2) 동사를 'be+pp'로 바꾸고 수동태 문장의 주어 자리에는 능동태 문장의 목적어가 오고, by 다음에는 능동태 문장의 주어를 목적격으로 쓴다. 일반 주어인 by them은 생략할 수 있다. (3) 수동태를 의문문 형태로 만들 때는 주어와 be동사의 위치를 바꾼다. by whom은 의문사로 취급하여 문장의 맨 앞에 써야 한다. (4) 직접목적어를 주어로 한 수동태에서 made는 간접목적어 앞에 전치사 for를 쓴다. 또한 간접목적어를 주어로 수동태를 만들지 않는다. (5) 시제가 heard로 과거형이므로 was heard으로 쓰고, 목적격보어 talking은 그대로 써준다.

14 '-thing'으로 끝나는 대명사를 수식하는 형용사는 대명사 뒤에 위치한다.

15 give up은 구동사로 하나의 단어처럼 취급하여 be given up으로 나타낸다. up이나 by를 빠뜨리지 않도록 주의한다.

16 줄거리가 말해지고, 자동차가 만들어지는 것이므로 수동태가 적절하다. be surprised at: ~에 놀라다 be interested in: ~에 흥미가 있다, be covered with: ~로 덮여 있다 be filled with: ~로 가득 차다

서술형 시험대비   p.78~79

01 (1) A different political party was symbolized by each ingredient.

(2) He was never listened to by the king.

(3) A small sandcastle was made for his son by Dan.

(4) Many computers are thrown away every year in the United States.

(5) By whom was the novel, *Christmas Carol*, written?

02 (1) I want to show something wonderful to you.

(2) I want to work with somebody honest for our business.

(3) There was nobody important at the meeting.

03 (1) The bench was painted by the man. 또는 The man painted the bench.

(2) Spicy food is loved by all of my family members.

(3) The bookshelf was made of wood.

(4) Amy was heard to sing in front of all the classmates by us.

(5) A long letter was written (to) her by him. 또는 He wrote her a long letter.

(6) A wedding ring with a small ruby will be bought for her.

04 nothing interesting

05 (1) Something was written on its back.

(2) Rome was not built in a day.

(3) I called him, but his phone was turned off.

(4) My homework must be finished by me by Sunday.

(5) I heard something interesting from Tom.

(6) There will be nobody happy in that house.

06 (1) funny someone → someone funny

(2) new something → something new

(3) cold to drink something → something cold to drink

(4) new nobody → nobody new

07 (1) The light bulb was invented by Thomas Edison.

(2) Many people respect Mahatma Gandhi.

(3) All the flights were canceled due to the bad weather (by them).

08 was painted, was titled, was completed

---

01 (1) 수동태는 'be+pp'의 형태이다. (2) 전치사 to의 목적어를 주어로 수동태로 바꾼다. (3) make는 직접목적어를 주어로 하는 수동태만 가능하며 간접목적어 앞에 for를 써야 한다. (4) throw away는 구동사로 하나의 단어처럼 취급하여 be thrown away로 나타낸다. away나 by를 빠뜨리지 않도록 주의한다. (5) 의문사 who가 by whom으로 바뀌어 문두에 쓰이는 것에 주의한다.

02 '-thing, -one, -body'로 끝나는 부정대명사는 형용사가 뒤에서 수식한다.

03 (1) The bench를 주어로 하면 수동태가, the man을 주어로 하면 능동태가 적절하다. (2) Spicy food가 무엇을 사랑하는 것이 아니므로 진행형이 아닌 수동태가 적절하다. (3) be made of: ~로 만들어지다(물리적 변화), be made from: ~로 만들어지다(화학적 변화) (4) 목적격보어가 원형부정사인 경우, 수동태 문장에서는 to부정사로 바뀐다. (5) write는 직접목적어를 주어로 하는 수동태만 가능하다. (6) buy는 직접목적어를 주어로 한 수동태에서는 간접목적어 앞에 for를 쓰고 미래 시제의 수동태는 'will be+과거분사'이다.

04 '-thing'으로 끝나는 부정대명사는 형용사가 뒤에서 수식한다.

05 (1) 수동태는 '주어+be동사+동사의 과거분사+by+행위자'의 형식이다. 누가 그 동작을 했는지 중요하지 않거나 잘 모를 때 'by+행위자'를 생략한다. (2) 수동태의 부정은 'be+not+과거분사'이다. (3) turn off를 하나의 단위처럼 생각해서 'be turned off'로 써야 한다. (4) 조동사가 있는 문장의 수동태는 '조동사+be+p.p.' 형식을 갖는다. (5), (6) '-thing, -body'로 끝나는 대명사는 형용사가 뒤에서 수식한다.

06 '-thing, -one, -body'로 끝나는 대명사는 형용사가 뒤에서 수식한다. 형용사와 to부정사가 동시에 수식하는 경우 '대명사+형용사+to부정사'의 어순에 유의한다.

07 능동태를 수동태로 바꿀 때 동사를 'be+p.p.'로 바꾸고 수동태 문장의 주어 자리에는 능동태 문장의 목적어가 오고, by 다음에는 능동태 문장의 주어를 목적격으로 쓴다. 일반 주어인 by them은 생략할 수 있다.

08 이 그림은 Vincent Van Gogh에 의해 그려졌다. 이것은 '별이 빛나는 밤(*The Starry Night*)'이라는 제목이 붙여졌고 1889년에 완성되었다.

Reading

확인문제   p.80

1 T 2 F 3 T 4 F

확인문제   p.81

1 F 2 F 3 F 4 T

교과서 확인학습 A   p.82~83

01 Bite   02 How, get their names
03 Why, look like   04 traditional food
05 dive into
06 was having dinner, something special
07 four colorful ingredients
08 a different political party 09 in harmony
10 was called   11 came from
12 was famous for
13 something wrong, afraid of telling
14 However   15 so, that
16 by himself   17 a special pot
18 called, the food in it
19 because, like, imaginary 20 the last king
21 a strange turtle   22 was written
23 is like, is like   24 What, mean
25 smaller

26 On the other hand, grow bigger

27 worried

28 However, in the shape of

29 Since then, have enjoyed

---

26 On the other hand, a half moon will grow bigger and become a full moon."

27 The king became worried about his kingdom.

28 However, people of Silla were very happy to learn this and made rice cakes in the shape of a half moon.

29 Since then, people have enjoyed these half-moon shaped rice cakes, songpyeon.

교과서 확인학습 B
p.84~85

1 A Bite of Korean History

2 How did tangpyeongchae and sinseollo get their names?

3 Why does songpyeon look like a half moon?

4 There are many interesting stories about our traditional food.

5 Let's dive into the fun history of our food.

6 One day, King Yeongjo was having dinner with his officials and offered them something special.

7 It was a dish with four colorful ingredients.

8 Each ingredient symbolized a different political party.

9 Yeongjo wanted to say that the four parties should work in harmony like this dish.

10 This dish was called tangpyeongchae.

11 The name came from Yeongjo's policy tangpyeongchaek.

12 In the time of King Yeonsan, there was a scholar who was famous for his honesty.

13 When the king did something wrong, the scholar was never afraid of telling him so.

14 However, the king never listened to him.

15 The scholar was so disappointed that he went to live on a mountain.

16 While he lived there by himself, he mainly ate vegetables.

17 He made a special pot to cook many different vegetables together.

18 People called this pot and the food in it sinseollo.

19 That is because the scholar lived like a sinseon, an imaginary person who lives alone in nature.

20 It was the time of the last king of Baekje.

21 One day, the king and his servants found a strange turtle.

22 Something was written on its back.

23 It said, "Baekje is like a full moon, but Silla is like a half moon."

24 The king asked a fortune teller, "What does this mean?"

25 The fortune teller answered, "A full moon will soon become smaller.

시험대비 실력평가
p.86~89

01 ②

02 (A) How   (B) look like   (C) interesting   03 ④

04 ③   05 ④   06 ②

07 offered them something special   08 ③

09 (A) special   (B) ingredient   (C) a different

10 ②   11 ④   12 ①   13 ⑤

14 ①, ④, ⑤   15 full moon, full moon, smaller

16 ⑤   17 ②   18 ③   19 ⑤

20 ③   21 a strange turtle

22 ⑤   23 ③

24 They are rice, vegetables, and fish skin.

---

01 ② 탕평채, 신선로, 송편은 우리의 전통 '음식'이다. ① 의식, ③ 문화, ④ 명절, ⑤ 풍습

02 (A) '어떻게 해서'라고 해야 하므로 How가 적절하다. (B) 뒤에 명사가 있으므로 look like가 적절하다. look+형용사, look like+명사: ~처럼 보이다, (C) '재미있는' 역사라고 해야 하므로 interesting이 적절하다.

03 Let's 동사원형 ~. = How about ~ing ~? = What about ~ing ~? = Why don't we 동사원형 ~? = Shall we 동사원형 ~?: ~하는 게 어때?

04 본문 끝에서 '우리 음식의 재미있는 역사 속으로 들어가 보자.'라고 하고 있다.

05 ④ '탕평책'은 영조의 정책이다. policy: 정책, ① 조리[요리]법, ② 정의, ③ 풍습, ⑤ 후식

06 ⓐ와 ②번: 정당, ①, ③ 파티, ④ 관계자, 당사자, a third party: (이해관계가 없는) 제삼자, ⑤ (여행방문 등을 함께 하는) 단체

07 something과 같이 -thing으로 끝나는 대명사를 수식할 때는 형용사가 뒤에 온다.

08 (A) in harmony: (~와) 조화되어, 협조하여 (B) come from: ~에서 생겨나다

09 (A) '특별한' 무언가를 권했다고 해야 하므로 special이 적절하다. ordinary: 보통의, 일상적인, (B) each 뒤에 단수 명사를 써야 하므로 ingredient가 적절하다. (C) '서로 다른' 당파를 상

15

징했다고 해야 하므로 **different**가 적절하다.

10 영조가 권한 것은 '네 가지 종류의 음식'이 아니라 '네 가지의 다채로운 재료로 만든 음식'이었다.

11 so+형용사/부사+that+주어+동사: 너무 ~해서 …하다

12 ①의 him은 King Yeonsan을, 나머지는 다 the scholar를 가리킨다.

13 이 글은 신선로라는 이름이 생기게 된 유래에 관한 글이므로, 주제로는 '신선로라는 음식의 뒷이야기'가 적절하다.

14 ⓐ와 ②, ③번: 계속 용법, ① 결과 용법, ④ 완료 용법, ⑤ 경험 용법

15 거북의 등에 "백제는 '보름달'과 같다."라는 글자가 써져 있었는데, 점술가가 "'보름달'은 곧 '작아질' 것입니다."라고 말했기 때문이다.

16 ⑤ 신라 사람들이 송편의 소로 무엇을 사용했는지는 대답할 수 없다. filling: (음식의) 소, 속, ① The last king of Baekje and his servants did. ② They meant that a full moon will soon become smaller, on the other hand, a half moon will grow bigger and become a full moon. ③ No. ④ In the shape of a half moon.

17 앞에 나오는 내용과 상반되는 내용이 뒤에 이어지므로 However가 가장 적절하다. ① 그러므로, ④, ⑤: 게다가, 더욱이

18 ③번 다음 문장의 this pot에 주목한다. 주어진 문장의 a special pot을 받고 있으므로 ③번이 적절하다..

19 학자가 신선이 된 것이 아니라, 사람들이 솥과 그 안의 음식을 신선로라고 불렀던 이유가 그 학자가 마치 자연 속에 홀로 사는 상상의 인물인 신선처럼 살았기 때문이라고 했다.

20 점술가가 "보름달은 곧 작아질 것입니다."라고 답했기 때문에, 왕은 자신의 왕국이 '걱정되었다'고 하는 것이 적절하다.

21 '이상한 거북'을 가리킨다.

22 이 글은 송편을 반달 모양으로 만들게 된 기원에 관한 글이므로, 제목으로는 '송편은 왜 반달 모양일까?'가 적절하다.

23 ③번 다음 문장의 She가 주어진 문장의 my grandma를 가리키므로 ③번이 적절하다.

24 재료는 쌀, 채소, 그리고 생선 껍질이다.

서술형 시험대비   p.90~91

01 his officials   02 harmoniously

03 (A) four   (B) political party

04 the king did something wrong

05 The scholar was so disappointed that he went to live on a mountain.

06 alone   07 like   08 smaller → bigger

09 백제는 세력이 약해질 것이다. / 신라는 세력이 커질 것이다.

---

10 Each ingredient symbolized a different political party.

11 People[They] called this dish tangpyeongchae.

12 Baekje is like a full moon, but Silla is like a half moon.

13 half, half, bigger, full

01 '그의 신하들'을 가리킨다.

02 in+추상명사 = 부사, in harmony = harmoniously: 조화되어

03 당평채는 '네 가지의' 다채로운 재료로 만든 음식이었고, 각 재료는 서로 다른 '당파'를 상징했다.

04 '왕이 무언가를 잘못한 것'을 가리킨다.

05 'so'를 보충하면 된다.

06 by himself = alone: 혼자서, 홀로

07 be like: ~와 같다

08 반달은 점점 '커져서' 보름달이 될 것이라고 하는 것이 적절하다.

09 보름달은 약해지는 백제의 세력을, 반달은 강해지는 신라의 세력을 상징한다.

10 each 뒤에 단수 명사를 쓰는 것이 적절하다.

11 People[They]을 주어로 하여 고치는 것이 적절하다.

12 "백제는 보름달과 같지만 신라는 반달과 같다."는 거북의 등에 쓰여 있는 말을 가리킨다.

13 거북의 등에 "신라는 '반달'과 같다."라는 글자가 써져 있었는데, 점술가가 "'반달'은 점점 '커져서' 보름달이 될 것입니다."라고 말했기 때문이다.

영역별 핵심문제   p.93~97

01 outdoor   02 (d)ive into   03 ③   04 ⑤

05 look like   06 ④   07 It's on sale now.

08 ⑤   09 ②   10 ⑤

11 She recommends the fried fish.

12 ④   13 looking for someone special

14 (1) was chosen for his son by him

   (2) was asked of me by a lady

15 ④   16 ③   17 ②

18 ③   19 ①

20 was seen to walk on the street by Jack yesterday

21 saw something strange   22 ②

23 four parties   24 ⑤

25 Baekje is like a full moon, but Silla is like a half moon.

26 ②   27 ②, ⑤

28 People called this pot and the food in it sinseollo.

29 ④   30 ③   31 ①, ③, ④

01 반의어 관계다. 실내의 : 실외의

02 dive into: …로 뛰어들다, …에 몰두하다

03 '각 재료는 서로 다른 당파를 상징했다.'는 뜻으로 'symbolized'가 알맞다.

04 ① prefer: 선호하다 / 실내 스포츠가 더 좋아, 야외 스포츠가 더 좋아? ② servant: 신하 / 어느 날, 왕과 신하는 이상한 거북을 한 마리 발견했다. ③ afraid: 두려워하는 / 왕이 무언가를 잘못하면, 그 학자는 왕에게 그렇게 말하는 것을 절대 두려워하지 않았다 ④ policy: 정책 / 그 이름은 영조의 정책인 탕평책에서 왔다. ⑤ imaginary: 상상의 / 이 이야기는 상상의 동물에 근거한다.

05 look like+명사: ~처럼 보이다

06 치마를 찾고 있다고 했기 때문에 추천해 달라는 말이 적절하다.

07 '세일 중'은 'on sale'을 쓴다.

08 대화의 내용상 '애완동물을 기를까 생각 중이야.'가 적절하다.

09 they가 cats를 가리키므로 (②)에 들어가는 것이 적절하다.

10 근처의 식당을 추천해 달라는 말에 '좋아. 시도해 볼게. 고마워.'라고 말하는 것은 자연스럽지 않다.

12 Ms. Park은 야채볶음을 좋아했다.

13 '-one'으로 끝나는 대명사는 형용사가 뒤에서 수식한다.

14 능동태의 목적어가 주어 자리에 있으므로 수동태로 쓴다. (1) choose는 직접목적어를 주어로 수동태로 만들 때 간접목적어 앞에 전치사 for를, (2) ask는 of를 쓴다.

15 ① The National Museum of Korea was built in 1945. ② My wallet was stolen (by someone) on the crowded subway. ③ She was made to leave her family by him. ⑤ Is there anybody available this weekend?

16 첫 문장은 '-thing'으로 끝나는 대명사는 형용사가 뒤에서 수식하므로 something red, 두 번째 문장은 by로 보아 수동태로 쓰인 were given이 적절하다.

17 상태나 소유를 나타내는 동사(have, smell, become, resemble 등)는 수동태로 쓸 수 없다. The soup smells good.으로 써야 한다.

18 '-thing, -body, -one'으로 끝나는 대명사는 형용사가 뒤에서 수식하는데 빈칸에 알맞은 것이 사람은 아니므로 ①과 ②는 답이 아니고, 두 번째 문장에서 의미상 '무언가가 잘못되었다'는 말이 자연스러우므로 something이 적절하다.

19 be satisfied with: ~에 만족하다. 나머지는 전치사 by를 쓴다.

20 목적격보어가 원형부정사인 경우, 수동태 문장에서는 to부정사로 바뀐다.

21 '-thing'으로 끝나는 대명사는 형용사가 뒤에서 수식한다.

22 ⓐ having, ② have는 '가지다'는 뜻일 때는 진행형으로 쓸 수 없다. ① (시간 등을) 보내다, 지내다, ③, ④, ⑤ [보통 동작·행위를 나타내는 부정관사가 달린 명사를 목적어로 하여] (~을) 하다, ④ 경험하다

23 영조는 '네 당파'가 탕평채의 네 가지 재료처럼 화합을 이루어 일

24 보름달은 곧 작아질 것이지만, 반면에 반달은 점점 커져서 보름달이 될 것이라고 해야 하므로 'On the other hand'가 적절하다. on the other hand: 다른 한편으로는, 반면에 ① 똑같이, ② 이와 같이, ③ 즉, 다시 말해, ④ 그러므로

25 is like: ~와 같다

26 이 글은 송편을 반달 모양으로 만들게 된 기원에 관한 글이다.

27 ⓐ와 ②, ⑤번: 동명사, ①, ③, ④: 현재분사

28 앞 문장의 내용을 가리킨다.

29 학자는 산속에서 '혼자' 살았고, 여러 다양한 채소들을 함께 요리하기 위해 특별한 솥을 만들었다.

30 ⓐ be made of: ~으로 만들어지다(물리적 변화), be made from: 화학적 변화 ⓑ be from: ~ 출신이다

31 ⓒ와 ②, ⑤: 형용사적 용법, ①, ③: 부사적 용법, ④ 명사적 용법

해야 한다는 것을 말하고 싶었다.

단원별 예상문제   p.98~101

01 imaginary   02 (A) fortune teller   (B) offered

03 ③   04 ②   05 ②

06 recommend, prefers, to, comedy

07 ④   08 ③

09 Could you recommend a dish for me?

10 ⑤   11 ④   12 ③

13 (1) I resemble my father.

   (2) I want something hot to eat.

14 (1) Something strange was written on the card.

   (2) Korean history and culture can be found in its traditional food.

   (3) It is made of rice, vegetables, and fish skin.

15 offered something special to them

16 ①, ⑤   17 ③, ⑤   18 ②

19 (A) different vegetables   (B) alone   20 ②

21 ③   22 (A) last   (B) worried   (C) shaped

23 to make

24 My family eats something special on Chuseok.

25 ④

---

01 둘은 유의어 관계이다. 최근에, 허구의

02 (A) fortune teller: 점술가 (B) offer: 제안하다

03 누군가나 또는 무언가가 당신이 희망하거나 기대했던 것만큼 좋지 않았기 때문에 행복하지 않은: 실망한

04 식사가 끝났을 때 먹는 단 음식: 디저트

05 ②번의 'Why don't you'는 뒤에 동사원형이 나온다.

06 소녀는 최근에 영화를 보지 않았기 때문에 소년에게 영화를 추천해 달라고 요청한다. 소녀는 액션 영화보다 코미디를 더 좋아한다. 그래서 소년은 코미디 영화인 *Funny Families*를 추천한다.

07 냉면을 먹어 보라고 말하므로 차가운 음식을 좋아한다.

08 주어진 문장 '약 2주 전에 문을 열었어요, 그렇죠?'라는 말에 'I thinks so.'라는 동의의 말이 오는 (③)이 적절하다.

09 추천을 부탁할 때 'Could you recommend ~ (for me)?' 표현을 쓴다.

10 요리를 해 본 적이 없다고 한 말에 대해 초보자를 위한 요리책을 제안하는 표현이 적절하다.

11 The baby will be looked after by my mom while I'm away. look after가 하나의 단위처럼 쓰여서 'will be looked after by'의 형태로 써야 한다.

12 '-thing, -one, -body'로 끝나는 대명사는 형용사가 뒤에서 수식한다.

13 (1) 상태나 소유를 나타내는 동사(have, become, resemble 등)는 수동태로 쓸 수 없다. (2) '-thing'으로 끝나는 대명사를 형용사와 to부정사가 동시에 수식하는 경우 '대명사+형용사+to 부정사'의 어순이다.

14 (1) '-thing'으로 끝나는 대명사는 형용사가 뒤에서 수식하며 '적혀 있는' 것이므로 수동태가 적절하다. (2) 조동사가 있는 문장의 수동태는 '조동사+be+p.p.' 형식을 갖는다. (3) be made of: ~로 만들어지다(물리적 변화), be made from: ~로 만들어지다(화학적 변화)

15 offer는 'to'를 사용하여 3형식으로 고친다.

16 symbolize = represent = stand for: 상징하다, ② (기꺼이) 받아들이다, ③ 상의[의논/논의]하다, ④ 언급하다

17 ⓐ와 ③, ⑤: 부사적 용법, ① 형용사적 용법, ②, ④ 명사적 용법

18 이 글은 신선로라는 이름이 생기게 된 유래에 관한 글이므로, 제목으로는 '신선로는 어떻게 해서 그런 이름을 얻게 되었을까?'가 적절하다. ① cruelty: 잔인함

19 그것은 산속에서 '혼자' 살던 학자에 의해 여러 '다양한 채소들을' 함께 요리하기 위해 만들어진 특별한 솥이다.

20 앞에 나오는 내용과 상반되는 내용이 뒤에 이어지므로 However가 적절하다. ③ 게다가, ④ 즉, ⑤ 한편으로는

21 주어진 문장의 Something에 주목한다. ③번 다음 문장의 내용이므로 ③번이 적절하다.

22 (A) 백제의 '마지막' 왕 때였다고 해야 하므로 last가 적절하다. last: 마지막의, latest: 최근의, (B) 감정을 나타내는 동사는 수식받는 명사가 감정을 느끼게 되는 경우에 과거분사를 써야 하므로 worried가 적절하다. (C) 반달 '모양으로 만들어진' 떡이라는 뜻이므로 과거분사 shaped가 적절하다.

23 decide는 to부정사를 목적어로 취한다.

24 something과 같이 -thing으로 끝나는 대명사를 수식할 때는 형용사가 뒤에 온다.

25 '송편소로 준비했던 견과의 종류'는 알 수 없다. ① 초콜릿 송편, ② 쌀가루, 초콜릿, 그리고 견과, ③ 남동생, ⑤ 3년 전, 남동생이 송편의 모든 소를 먹었기 때문이다.

---

01 (1) It is on Main Street.

 (2) He will go there with his family.

02 Why don't you see *Iron Woman 2*?

03 Do you prefer indoor or outdoor sports?

04 (1) BTS appeared on TV last night.

 (2) It was made to run on city streets and highways.

 (3) This pot and the food in it were called sinseollo by people.

 (4) There was nothing new in this magazine.

05 (A) disappointed (B) because (C) imaginary

06 could[might] cook

07 This pot and the food in it were called sinseollo (by people).

08 a half moon will grow bigger and become a full moon

09 bigger, bigger 10 people of Silla

---

01 (1) 새로 생긴 중국 식당은 어디에 있는가? (2) Jaden은 누구와 식당에 갈 것인가?

02 제안을 할 때 'Why don't you+동사원형 ~?'을 이용한다.

03 선호하는 것을 물을 때 'Do you prefer A or B?' 구문을 이용한다.

04 (1) appear는 자동사이므로 수동태로 쓰이지 않는다. (2) 목적격보어가 원형부정사인 경우, 수동태 문장에서는 to부정사로 바뀐다. (3) 목적어와 목적격 보어 자리에 모두 명사가 오더라도 목적어만 수동태의 주어 자리에 올 수 있다. (4) '-thing'으로 끝나는 대명사는 형용사가 뒤에서 수식한다.

05 (A) 감정을 나타내는 동사는 수식받는 명사가 감정을 느끼게 되는 경우에 과거분사를 써야 하므로 disappointed가 적절하다. (B) 그 학자가 신선처럼 살았기 '때문'이라고 해야 하므로 because가 적절하다. because+이유, why+결과, (C) '상상의' 인물인 신선이라고 해야 하므로 imaginary가 적절하다. imaginary: 상상의, imaginative: 상상력이 풍부한

06 그는 여러 다양한 채소들을 함께 '요리하기 위해' 특별한 솥을 만들었다. in order that 주어 can[may] 동사원형 ~: ~하기 위하여

07 this pot and the food in it을 주어로 하여 고치는 것이 적절하다.

08 '반달은 점점 커져서 보름달이 될 것'이라는 내용을 가리킨다.

09 그들은 점점 '커져서' 보름달이 되는 반달처럼 신라의 힘이 '커질' 것이라고 믿었기 때문이다.

10 반달 모양의 떡이 '신라 사람들'에 의해 만들어진 이래로 사람은 반달 모양의 떡인 송편을 즐겨 먹고 있다.

|모범답안|

01 (1) A: Could you recommend a main dish for me?
　　　　 B: Do you prefer seafood spaghetti or
　　　　　 bibimbap?
　　　　 A: I prefer bibimbap.
　　 (2) A: Could you recommend a dessert for me?
　　　　 B: Do you prefer chocolate ice cream or
　　　　　 patbingsu?
　　　　 A: I prefer patbingsu.

02 (1) These pictures were painted by my sister.
　　 (2) These dresses were made by a famous
　　　　 designer.
　　 (3) Hangeul was invented by King Sejong.
　　 (4) *Harry Potter* was written by J. K. Rowling.

03 (A) Chuseok　(B) fish skin　(C) North Korea
　　 (D) my grandma's home

단원별 모의고사　　　　p.105~108

01 ⑤　　　　02 (1) dived[dove] (2) (i)nteresting
03 ③　　　04 pot　　05 ⑤　　　06 ④
07 ②　　　08 ④　　　09 ⑤　　　10 ③
11 liked the fried vegetables　　　　12 ④
13 (1) People of Silla made songpyeon in the shape
　　　 of a half moon.
　　 (2) Was the picture painted by John?
　　 (3) Her daughter was told a funny story by Mariel.
　　　 A funny story told to her daughter by Mariel.
　　 (4) People[They] speak English in many countries.
14 ②　　　　15 ④
16 (1) I can learn something new at the class
　　 (2) Have you heard anything interesting today
17 ②　　　　18 colorful　19 ③　　　20 ①, ④
21 People called this pot and the food in it sinseollo.
22 ②　　　　23 ⑤

01 ⑤번은 'ingredient'에 관한 설명이다.

02 (1) dive into: ~에 몰두하다, ~에 빠져들다 (2) interesting:
흥미로운

03 왕이나 여왕이 통치하는 나라

04 일반적으로 둥글고, 특히 음식을 요리하기 위해 사용되는 다 양
한 형태의 용기

05 파이와 케이크 중에서 선호하는 것을 물을 때 사용하는 것은
'prefer'이다.

06 A가 옷을 추천해 달라고 하자 (C) 좋아하는 색을 묻고 (B) 이에
답하고 (A) 세일 중인 선호하는 색 제품을 권하자 (D) 이에 응하

는 순서가 자연스럽다

07 command는 '명령하다'는 뜻이고, 문맥상 '추천하다'는
'recommend'가 적절하다.

08 스포츠 클럽에 가입할 생각 중이라는 말에 액션영화를 더 좋아
한다는 대답은 자연스럽지 않다.

09 '추천하다'는 recommend가 적절하다.

10 Jaden이 해산물을 더 좋아한다고 했기 때문에 Ms. Park은 해
산물을 추천해 줄 것이다.

11 Ms. Park은 식당에서 어떤 음식을 좋아했나?

12 Jaden의 가족이 식당에서 얼마나 많은 요리를 주문할지는 언급
되어 있지 않다.

13 (1) 동사를 'be+pp'로 바꾸고 수동태 문장의 주어 자리에는 능동
태 문장의 목적어가 오고, by 다음에는 능동태 문장의 주어를 목
적격으로 쓴다. (2) 의문문의 수동태는 능동태의 의문문을 평서
문으로 바꾼 후 이것을 수동태로 고치고, 다시 의문문으로 바꾸면
쉽다. (3) 4형식 문장의 수동태는 간접목적어와 직접목적어 각각
을 주어로 하는 수동태가 가능하며 직접목적어를 주어로 한 수동
태에서 tell 동사는 간접목적이 앞에 전치사 to를 쓴다. (4) 일반
인이 주어인 능동태 문장의 수동태에서는 흔히 'by+목적격'이 생
략된다. 특히 누가 그 동작을 했는지 중요하지 않거나 잘 모를 때,
수동태 문장으로 표현한다.

14 '-one'으로 끝나는 대명사는 형용사가 뒤에서 수식한다. We
are waiting for someone special.

15 일반 사람이 주어인 능동태를 수동태로 바꿀 때 'by+일반 사람'
은 생략 가능하다.

16 '-thing'으로 끝나는 대명사는 형용사가 뒤에서 수식한다.

17 ① The food is made of rice flour, chocolate, and
nuts. ③ This song was written by a famous musician.
④ I want to drink something cold. ⑤ I want to do
something special for my brother's birthday party.

18 color의 형용사형은 colorful이다.

19 ⓐ와 ③번: ~와 (똑)같이[마찬가지로], ~처럼(전치사), ① [외
관·형태·성질 등이] 같은(형용사), ②, ⑤: 좋아하다(동사), ④
비슷한 것(명사), and the like: 기타 같은 종류의 것(etc.보다
형식적인 표현)

20 주격 관계대명사 who나 that이 적절하다.

21 5형식 문장으로 쓰는 것이 적절하다.

22 ② 반면에, 다른 한 편으로 (두 가지 사실을 비교·대조할 때 씀),
① (만약) 그렇지 않으면, ③ 게다가, ④ 그렇기는 하지만, 그럼
에도 불구하고, ⑤ 게다가

23 '신라 사람들'이 반달 모양의 떡을 만들었다.

Think Big, Start Small

교과서 Conversation

시험대비 실력평가   p.112

01 whole   02 ④   03 ⑤   04 ①
05 ③   06 ④   07 come up with
08 a[one] third of

01 둘은 반의어 관계이다. 어려운 : 쉬운 = 일부분의 : 전체의
02 방에서 책을 읽을 수 없다고 소리치고 있으므로 그의 집에 전기
   가 없다는 것이 적절하다.
03 Alfredo Moser에 의해 발명되었다가 적절하다.
04 '특히 덮개가 있는 빛을 제공하는 장치'의 의미로 'lamp(등, 램
   프)'가 적절하다.
05 '여러 가지 방법으로 생산될 수 있고 빛, 열 등을 만드는 장치에
   동력을 제공하는 에너지의 형태'라는 의미로 '전기'가 적절하다.
06 ④의 'chief'는 명사로 사용되었다. '장, 우두머리'의 의미이다.
07 'come up with'는 '~을 생각해 내다'라는 뜻이다.
08 '~의 1/3'은 'a[one] third of'를 사용한다.

서술형 시험대비   p.113

01 (1) daytime, 낮   (2) ceiling, 천장   (3) blackout, 정전
02 (1) light up   (2) bent, spreads
03 (1) leftover   (2) Foundation
04 (1) chief   (2) bleach   (3) widely
05 (1) hole, hole   (2) magic

01 (1) 해가 뜨는 시간과 지는 시간 사이의 기간이나 저녁도 밤도
   아닌 하루의 부분 (2) 위쪽을 바라볼 때 볼 수 있는 방의 안쪽 표
   면 (3) 전기 시스템의 고장으로 빛이나 전력이 없는 때
02 (1) light up: ~을 밝히다 (2) bend가 수동태로 과거분사 bent
   가 적절하고, '퍼지다'는 'spread'를 사용하고 주어가 3인칭 단
   수 'sunlight'이므로 'spreads'로 쓴다.
03 (1) 남은 음식: leftover (2) 재단: foundation
04 (1) 그녀는 영화 '주피터'에서 책임 과학자를 연기했어. (2) 물
   을 깨끗이 유지하기 위해 표백제를 조금 넣어라. (3) 오늘날 가
   스는 요리할 때 널리 쓰인다. / 형용사 'wide'는 동사 'is used'
   를 수식할 때 부사 'widely'가 되어야 한다.
05 (1) 물체의 표면에 개구부가 있거나 물체를 완전히 관통하는 개
   구부가 있는 물체의 빈 공간 (2) 특별한 힘을 가진 또는 비정상
   적이거나 예상치 못한 방식으로 또는 쉽게 또는 빠르게 발생하
   는

핵심 Check   p.114~115

1 ②   2 ③

교과서 대화문 익히기

Check(√) True or False   p.116

1 T   2 F   3 T   4 F

교과서 확인학습   p.118~119

Listen & Speak 1-A
(1) turn up, turn it up anymore, highest / Let, put, I've
heard, works like / What an interesting idea, Let's
(2) I've heard, is coming / favorite actress / played,
chief / can't wait to

Listen & Speak 2-A
(1) finished, good, want to take, leftovers / Don't
forget to eat
(2) your plan for, winter break / I'm going to /
exciting, going to do / going to go, amusement,
all kinds / Don't forget to try

Communicate A
wrong / difficult / have to / to save / I've heard that, by
using less / I've heard that, too, stop using / to dry off /
impossible, at least / shake, before, more than enough
/ try, next time / don't forget to shake, at least, times

Communicate B
I've heard, saving electricity, to save / heard that, too,
save / turn off, when / Don't forget, turn off, when,
leave

Progress Check
(1) I've heard that, is coming / favorite / surprise
(2) plan for / to visit / sounds exciting / spend,
beach, seafood / Don't forget to try / won't forget

시험대비 기본평가   p.120

01 ③   02 are you finished with your meal?   03 ⑤

01 빈칸에는 어떤 사실을 들어서 알고 있음을 말하는 표현이 온다.
   B의 마지막 말에 'who is he?'라고 그가 누군지 모르고 있기
   때문에 ⑤는 자연스럽지 않다.
02 be동사 의문문으로 'be finished with'는 '~을 마치다'는 의미다.
03 (B)에는 'Don't forget to부정사'를 이용하여 '~할 것을 잊지
   마라'는 당부의 말이 적절하다. remember / forget + 동명사
   는 '~한 것을 기억하다[잊다]'의 뜻으로 과거의 일을 나타낸다.

01 ②   02 ④   03 ③   04 ⑤
05 dim sum   06 ④   07 ④   08 ①
09 ③

01 'A: 무슨 일 있어?'라는 물음에 'B: '내일 내 과학 숙제 가져올 것을 잊지 마.'라는 대답은 자연스럽지 못하다.

02 B의 첫 번째 말에서 더 이상 볼륨을 올릴 수 없다고 했으므로 빈칸 (A)는 볼륨을 올려달라는 부탁의 말이 적절하다.

03 B의 마지막 말에 '정말 재미있는 생각이야!'라고 말하는 것으로 보아 빈칸에는 '유리잔이 스피커처럼 작동한다.'는 말이 적절하다.

04 (A) 미래의 계획을 말할 때 'I'm going to부정사'를 사용하고, (B) '~할 것을 잊지 마'라는 상기시켜 주는 표현으로 'Don't forget to부정사'나 'Remember to부정사'를 사용한다.

05 튀기거나 증기로 익힌 여러 음식을 포함하는 중국식 식사 또는 간단한 간식 요리

06 Yuri의 '손을 말리는 데 종이 수건을 한 장만 쓸 수도 있지.'라는 말에 대한 Jaden의 반응으로 (④)가 적절하다.

07 종이컵을 사용하는 것을 멈추는 것은 Jaden이 한 말이다.

08 대화의 내용상 '전기를 절약하는 것'이 적절하다.

09 '~하는 게 어때?', '~하자'는 표현으로 'Why don't we+동사원형 ~?'을 사용할 수 있다.

01 she try the fruit there   02 I won't forget.
03 I've heard that we can save trees by using less paper.
04 don't forget to shake your hands at least 10 times.
05 Don't forget to
06 I've heard that a movie star is coming to our school.

01 소년은 여행에서 과일을 먹어 보라고 제안하고 있다.

02 '~하지 않을 거야'는 will not의 축약형 won't를 사용하여 3단어로 만든다.

03 'I've heard (that) ~.' 표현을 이용하고, '~함으로써'는 'by -ing'를 사용한다. '덜' 사용한다는 것은 little을 비교급 less로 바꾸어 준다.

05 소녀는 날씨가 나쁠까봐 걱정을 하고 있으므로 '우산을 가져갈 것을 잊지 마.'라는 충고가 적절하다. '~하는 것을 잊지 마'라는 뜻으로 상대방에게 해야 할 일을 상기시켜 줄 때 'Don't forget to부정사'를 사용한다.

06 어떤 사실을 들어서 알고 있음을 말할 때 'I've heard (that) ~.' 표현을 쓴다. 현재진행형 'is coming'이 미래의 일을 나타낼 때 사용될 수 있다.

Grammar

1 (1) famous   (2) happy
2 (1) wash   (2) painted   (3) to do   (4) to sign

01 (1) to laugh → laugh   (2) finishing → finish
     (3) sadly → sad   (4) tiring → tired
02 (1) throw   (2) thrown   (3) to meet
     (4) do(또는 to do)
03 ②   04 Let me know her name.

01 (1), (2) 사역동사의 목적어와 목적격보어의 관계가 능동일 경우 목적격보어로 원형부정사를 쓰는 것이 적절하다. (3) 동사 make의 보어로 부사가 아닌 형용사가 적절하다. (4) 내가 지치게 되는 것이므로 tired가 적절하다.

02 (1) 사역동사의 목적격보어는 목적어와의 관계가 능동일 경우 원형부정사가 쓰인다. (2) 사역동사의 목적격보어는 목적어와의 관계가 수동일 경우 과거분사가 쓰인다. (3) get이 '~하게 하다'라는 사역동사의 뜻으로 쓰일 때에는 목적격보어로 to부정사를 쓴다. (4) help는 목적격보어로 동사원형이나 to부정사가 나오며 뜻의 차이는 없다.

03 동사 make의 보어로 부사가 아닌 형용사가 적절하며 소설이 그녀를 유명하게 만든 것이므로 The novel이 주어가 되어야 한다.

04 사역동사 let의 목적격보어로 목적어와의 관계가 능동일 경우 원형부정사를 쓴다.

01 ⑤   02 ①, ⑤   03 ①
04 The pot can keep the fruit cold.   05 ③
06 (1) learn   (2) see   (3) cleaned   (4) help
     (5) to read   (6) interesting   (7) regularly, healthy
07 ③   08 ②   09 steal → stolen
10 ③, ④   11 ④   12 ⑤   13 ④
14 ②, ③   15 ⑤
16 (1) the test was   (2) he is silly
17 (1) to wear → wear   (2) write → to write
     (3) steal → stolen
18 (1) My father keeps his car clean.
     (2) Rainy days make me sad.
     (3) Her new book made her famous.

(4) I will not let my children watch TV.

(5) The funny story made me laugh.

(6) I had the man fix my computer.

19 ①　　　**20** ④

01 목적어와의 관계가 능동이므로 사역동사 let의 목적격보어로 원형부정사가 적절하고, 동사 found의 보어로 부사가 아닌 형용사가 적절하다.

02 help는 준사역동사로 목적어와 목적격보어의 관계가 능동일 경우 목적격보어로 원형부정사 또는 to부정사를 취한다.

03 5형식을 만들 수 있는 동사로 형용사를 목적격보어로 받을 수 있는 동사가 나와야 한다. call은 call A B(명사) 형태로 쓰이며, ask, order, beg 등은 목적격보어로 to부정사가 나온다.

04 '주어+동사+목적어+목적격보어'의 어순으로 쓰는데 동사 keep의 목적격보어로 형용사를 써야 하는 것에 주의한다.

05 이름이 불리는 것으로 목적어와의 관계가 수동이므로 사역동사 have의 목적격보어로 과거분사가 적절하다. Her wish was to have her son's name mentioned at graduation.

06 (1), (2) 사역동사 have와 let의 목적격보어로 동사원형이 적절하다. (3) 방이 청소되는 것이므로 목적격보어로 수동의 의미를 갖는 과거분사가 적절하다. (4) help는 준사역동사로 목적격보어로 원형부정사 또는 to부정사를 받는다. (5) get이 '~하게 하다'라는 사역동사의 뜻으로 쓰일 때에는 목적격보어로 to부정사를 쓴다. (6) 동사 find의 목적격보어로 형용사가 적절하다. (7) 첫 번째 괄호에는 동사를 수식하는 부사가 알맞으므로 regularly, 두 번째 괄호에는 keep의 목적격보어로 형용사를 쓴다.

07 목적격보어로 부사가 아닌 형용사가 사용된다는 것에 주의한다. ④ well은 부사이므로 형용사 good이 적절하다. Reading a lot of books will make me good at English.

08 소고기가 무엇을 요리하는 것이 아니라 요리되도록 하는 것이므로 사역동사 have의 목적격보어로 과거분사 cooked를 쓰는 것이 적절하다.

09 지갑이 무엇을 훔치는 것이 아니라 훔쳐진[도난당한] 것이므로 수동의 의미를 갖는 과거분사가 적절하다.

10 Marie가 의자에 앉는 것으로 목적어와의 관계가 능동이므로 사역동사 help의 목적격보어로 원형부정사 혹은 to부정사가 적절하다.

11 '주어(I)+동사(keep)+목적어(the baby)+목적격보어(safe)'의 어순으로 쓰는데 동사 keep의 목적격보어로 형용사를 써야 하는 것에 주의한다.

12 get은 사역동사의 뜻으로 쓰일 때 목적어와 목적격보어의 관계가 능동일 경우 목적격보어로 to부정사를 쓴다.

13 ④번은 4형식으로 쓰였고 나머지는 5형식이다.

14 ② Elizabeth had the meat roasted in the garden. ③ Morris got the girl to stand up in front of students.

15 (A) 사역동사 make의 목적어와 목적격보어의 관계가 능동이

므로 원형부정사가 적절하다. (B) 동사 get의 목적어와 목적격보어의 관계가 능동이므로 to부정사가 적절하다. (C) 사역동사의 목적어와 목적격보어의 관계가 수동이므로 과거분사가 적절하다.

16 목적어와 목적격보어를 that절의 주어와 동사로 써서 문장을 바꿔 쓴다.

17 (1) 목적어와 목적격보어의 관계가 능동이므로 목적격보어로 원형부정사가 적절하다. (2) 목적어와 목적격보어의 관계가 능동이므로 get의 목적격보어로 to부정사가 적절하다. (3) 목적어와 목적격보어의 관계가 수동이므로 목적격보어로 과거분사가 적절하다. handcuffs: 수갑

18 (1)~(3) '주어+동사+목적어+목적격보어'의 어순으로 쓰는데 동사의 목적격보어로 형용사를 써야 하는 것에 주의한다. (4), (5), (6) 목적어와 목적격보어의 관계가 능동이므로 사역동사의 목적격보어로 원형부정사를 이용한다.

19 형용사를 목적격보어로 받을 수 있는 동사가 나와야 한다.

20 get은 사역동사의 뜻으로 쓰일 때 목적어와 목적격보어의 관계가 능동일 경우 목적격보어로 to부정사를 쓴다.

서술형 시험대비
p.130~131

01 (1) She made him finish his work by the next day.

(2) She doesn't let her children play online games.

(3) I must go to the dry cleaner's to have my suit cleaned.

(4) Mom got me to help my sister with her homework.

(5) I helped him calm[to calm] down before playing the guitar on the stage.

02 (1) me sad　(2) made him healthy

03 Eric had his camera repaired by a repairman.

04 (1) A strange man broke into my house, but he stole nothing and left it clean.

(2) They made Stacy happy by saying white lies.

(3) He found his new smartphone broken.

(4) At first, Samanda thought William honest.

(5) This thick blanket will keep you warm.

05 turn

06 (1) clean　(2) carried　(3) to be　(4) find[to find]

(5) watch

07 Having lots of holidays next year makes her excited.

08 (1) Eve let Adam use her pen.

(2) She made Dan follow her advice.

09 (1) He had his car washed yesterday.

(2) We could make the lamp brighter.

01 (1), (2) 목적어와 목적격보어의 관계가 능동이므로 목적격보어로 원형부정사가 적절하다. (3) 목적어와 목적격보어의 관계가 수동이므로 목적격보어로 과거분사가 적절하다. (4) get이 사역동사의 뜻으로 쓰일 때 목적격보어로 to부정사를 쓴다. (5) help는 목적격보어로 동사원형이나 to부정사가 나온다.

02 (1) 책을 읽으며 슬펐다는 내용을 목적어와 형용사를 목적격보어로 하는 5형식으로 나타낸다. (2) 운동해서 건강하게 되었다는 내용을 목적어와 형용사를 목적격보어로 하는 5형식으로 나타낸다.

03 사역동사의 목적어와 목적격보어의 관계가 수동일 경우 목적격보어로 과거분사를 쓴다.

04 (1) 동사 leave의 목적격보어로 부사가 아닌 형용사가 적절하다. (2) 동사 make의 목적격보어로 명사가 아닌 형용사가 적절하다. (3) 목적어와 목적격보어의 관계가 수동이므로 목적격보어로 과거분사가 적절하다. (4), (5) 동사 think, keep의 목적격보어로 부사가 아닌 형용사가 적절하다. break into: 침입하다 blanket: 담요

05 사역동사 make의 목적어와 목적격보어의 관계가 능동이므로 목적격보어로 원형부정사가 적절하다.

06 (1) 사역동사의 목적어와 목적격보어의 관계가 능동이므로 목적격보어로 원형부정사가 적절하다. (2) 목적어와 목적격보어의 관계가 수동이므로 목적격보어로 과거분사가 적절하다. (3) get은 사역동사의 의미로 쓰일 수 있지만 목적격보어로 to부정사가 나온다. (4) help는 준사역동사로 목적격보어로 원형부정사 또는 to부정사가 나온다. (5) 사역동사의 목적어와 목적격보어의 관계가 능동이므로 목적격보어로 원형부정사가 적절하다.

07 '주어+동사+목적어+목적격보어'의 어순으로 쓰며 동사의 목적격보어로 형용사를 써야 하는 것에 주의한다.

08 get은 have, allow는 let, force는 make와 같은 의미로 쓰인다.

09 (1) 목적어와 목적격보어의 관계가 수동이므로 목적격보어로 과거분사로 쓴다. (2) '주어+동사+목적어+목적격보어'의 어순으로 쓰며 동사의 목적격보어로 형용사를 쓴다. 또한 '더 밝게'이므로 비교급으로 써야 한다.

Reading

확인문제   p.132

1 T   2 F   3 T   4 F

확인문제   p.133

1 T   2 F   3 F   4 T   5 T   6 T

교과서 확인학습 A
p.134~135

01 One-Dollar   02 in the Philippines
03 has no electricity, all the other houses
04 too, to   05 are packed close together
06 because of   07 light up, without using
08 is called, because, was invented by
09 many blackouts   10 come up with
11 be made for, lasts for
12 very safe   13 never start
14 to make   15 How to make
16 Fill, with   17 Add, to keep, clear
18 push, into   19 a third, remain
20 is bent, spreads   21 are widely used
22 The charity, how to make, install
23 Thanks to, thousands of
24 has, made, such as   25 for many years to come

교과서 확인학습 B
p.136~137

1 One-Dollar Magic Lamps
2 "Wow, I can read a book in my room now!" shouted Marco, a boy in a village in the Philippines.
3 His house has no electricity just like all the other houses in the village.
4 People in the village are too poor to pay for electricity.
5 Even during the daytime, they live in darkness because the houses are packed close together.
6 Now things are changing because of a single plastic bottle.
7 One plastic bottle in the ceiling can light up a whole room without using any electricity.
8 This amazing plastic bottle is called a Moser lamp because it was invented by Alfredo Moser.
9 In 2002, there were many blackouts in his town in Brazil.
10 These blackouts made him come up with a new way to light his house.
11 A Moser lamp can be made for about one dollar and lasts for about 10 years.
12 It is also very safe.
13 It can never start a house fire.
14 Surprisingly, it is very easy to make this magic lamp.
15 How to make a Moser lamp from a bottle

16 1. Fill a clear plastic bottle with water.

17 2. Add some bleach to keep the water clear.

18 3. Make a hole in the roof, and push the bottle into the hole.

19 4. Let a third of the bottle remain above the roof.

20 5. Sunlight is bent by the water in the bottle and spreads around the room.

21 In the Philippines, Moser lamps are widely used by the My Shelter Foundation.

22 The charity also teaches local people how to make and install the lamps.

23 Thanks to the charity, thousands of homes in the Philippines now have Moser lamps.

24 It has also made Moser lamps popular in other countries, such as Argentina, India, and Fiji.

25 Moser lamps will light up the lives of many people for many years to come.

시험대비 실력평가
p.138~141

01 ④　　02 ②　　03 ④　　04 ③
05 ③　　06 two-thirds
07 The water in the bottle bends sunlight
08 lasts　　09 ①, ③, ④　　10 ③　　11 ④
12 thousands of homes in the Philippines
13 like　　14 ①　　15 ⑤　　16 ②
17 to remain → remain　　18 ①　　19 how to
20 ④　　21 ③　　22 ②
23 A Moser lamp　　24 ⑤
25 (A) for　(B) happy　(C) grows　　26 ⑤
27 (1) CD 케이스의 절반을 흙과 물로 채우고, 잔디 씨앗을 흙 안에 넣는다.
　 (2) 케이스를 닫고 모든 옆면에 테이프를 붙인다.
　 (3) 햇빛이 비치는 곳에 약 10일 동안 놓아둔다.

01 ⓐ pay for: ~의 대금을 지불하다, ⓑ in darkness: 어둠 속에

02 '전기'를 쓰지 않고 방 전체를 밝힐 수 있다고 하는 것이 적절하다. ① (사물의) 원천, 근원, ③ 화학 약품, ⑤ 자원

03 ④번 다음 문장의 One plastic bottle에 주목한다. 주어진 문장의 a single plastic bottle을 가리키므로 ④번이 적절하다.

04 낮 동안에도, 집들이 빽빽하게 들어차 있어서 그들은 어둠 속에 살아간다.

05 ⓒ에는 keep을 쓰는 것이 적절하다. ⓐ Fill, ⓑ Add, ⓓ Make, ⓔ push

06 two-thirds: 3분의 2, 병의 3분의 1은 지붕 위에 남아 있도록 한다. = 병의 '3분의 2'는 지붕 아래에 남아 있도록 한다.

07 'The water in the bottle'을 주어로 해서 고치는 것이 적절하다.

08 last: (기능이) 지속되다, 특정한 시간 동안 계속해서 사용될 수 있다.

09 ⓐ와 ②, ⑤: 형용사적 용법, ① 명사적 용법, ③, ④ 부사적 용법

10 ③ 이 글은 값싸고 매우 안전한 Moser 램프에 관한 글이므로, 제목으로는 '값싸고 안전한 신기한 램프'가 적절하다.

11 이 자선단체 '덕분에', ①, ③: ⋯ 대신에, ② ⋯ 없이, ⋯이 없다면, ⑤ ⋯와는 달리

12 thousands of+명사: 수천의 ~

13 such as = like: 예를 들어, ⋯와 같은

14 light up: ~을 환하게 밝히다

15 ⓐ fill A with B: A를 B로 채우다, ⓒ push A into B: A를 B에 넣다

16 ⓑ와 ②, ③, ⑤는 부사적 용법, ① 형용사적 용법, ④ 명사적 용법

17 사역동사 let+목적어+목적격보어(동사원형): ~이 ⋯하게 하다

18 투명한 플라스틱병에 물을 채워 넣어야 하므로, 올바르게 이해하지 못한 사람은 성민이다.

19 install은 teaches와 병렬 구문이 아니라, how to make and how to install에서 중복되는 'how to'를 생략한 것이다.

20 ⓑ와 ⑤: 형용사적 용법, ①, ④: 명사적 용법, ②, ③: 부사적 용법

21 이 글은 My Shelter 재단의 여러 활약에 관한 글이므로, 주제로는 'My Shelter 재단의 놀랄 만한 활약들'이 가장 적절하다. remarkable: 놀랄 만한, 놀라운, 주목할 만한, long-lasting: 오래 지속되는

22 ⓐ와 ②번: 약, ~쯤(부사), ①, ③ ⋯에 대한(전치사), ④ 주위에, 근처에, 가까이에(부사 = around), ⑤ ⋯에 종사하여, ⋯에 착수하여(전치사)

23 'Moser 램프'를 가리킨다.

24 Moser lamp를 만드는 데 얼마나 오래 걸리는지는 대답할 수 없다. ① A Moser lamp. ② Because in 2002, there were many blackouts in his town in Brazil. ③ No. ④ For about 10 years.

25 (A) 약 '10일' 동안이라고 해야 하므로 for가 적절하다. during+기간을 나타내는 명사, for+숫자, (B) 'make+목적어+목적격보어'의 형태로 쓰인 5형식 구문으로, 목적격보어의 자리에 형용사 happy를 쓰는 것이 적절하다. (C) 때를 나타내는 부사절에서는 현재시제가 미래시제를 대신하므로, grows가 적절하다.

26 뒤에 복수 명사가 나오므로 much로는 바꿔 쓸 수 없다.

27 First, Second, Finally 다음의 내용을 쓰는 것이 적절하다.

01 so, that, can't

02 because the houses are packed close together.

03 with using some electricity → without using any electricity

04 two thousand (and) two   05 A Moser lamp

06 (1) to make   (2) making   (3) this magic lamp

07 the My Shelter Foundation widely uses Moser lamps / the My Shelter Foundation uses Moser lamps widely

08 popularly → popular   09 Because of

10 A Moser lamp can be made for about one dollar and lasts for about 10 years.

11 (1) 1달러 정도로 만들 수 있다.   (2) 10년 정도 지속된다.
        (3) 매우 안전하다.   (4) 만드는 것이 매우 쉽다.

12 (A) widely   (B) how   (C) light up

13 to have Moser lamps

---

01 too+형용사+to부정사 = so+형용사+that+주어+cannot ...: 너무 ~하여 …할 수 없다

02 'are'를 보충하면 된다. be packed: 들어차다

03 천장에 플라스틱병 하나를 설치함으로써 '전기를 쓰지 않고' 방 전체를 밝힐 수 있다고 하는 것이 적절하다.

04 연도는 보통 두 자리씩 끊어서 읽지만, 2000년부터는 보통 'two thousand ~(미국식)', 'two thousand and ~(영국식)'로 읽는다.

05 'Moser 램프'를 가리킨다.

06 to부정사나 동명사를 주어로 해서 고치거나, make의 목적어인 this magic lamp를 주어로 해서 고치는 것이 적절하다.

07 부사 widely는 타동사 앞이나 목적어 뒤에 쓰는 것이 적절하다.

08 make+목적어+목적격보어'의 형태로 쓰인 5형식 구문으로, 목적격보어의 자리에 형용사를 쓰는 것이 적절하다.

09 이 정전들은 그가 집을 밝히는 새로운 방법을 생각해 내도록 만들었다. = 이 정전들 '때문에', 그는 집을 밝히는 새로운 방법을 생각해 냈다. Because of, Due to 등 이유를 나타내는 말을 쓰는 것이 적절하다.

10 'for'를 보충하면 된다.

11 두 번째 단락의 내용을 쓰는 것이 적절하다.

12 (A) 동사를 꾸며주므로 부사 widely가 적절하다. (B) '어떻게' 램프를 만드는지를 가르치는 것이므로 how가 적절하다. (C) 많은 사람들의 삶을 '밝혀 줄' 것이라고 해야 하므로 light up이 적절하다. light up: ~ 를 환하게 밝히다, lighten up: 기운 내다, lighten: (일·부채·걱정 등을) 가볍게 해주다, 밝아[환해]지다

13 가목적어, 진목적어 구문으로 고치는 것이 적절하다.

---

01 (i)nstall   02 hanger   03 ②   04 ⑤

05 (t)hings   06 ④   07 leftovers : 남은 음식

08 ③   09 ③   10 ③

11 Shake your hands before you use a paper towel.

12 ⑤   13 ⑤   14 plant

15 She thinks television is a waste of time, so she doesn't let her children watch TV.

16 (1) me happy   (2) her nervous   17 ③

18 ⑤   19 ④   20 ①   21 ①

22 ②   23 using   24 ①, ⑤

25 Many blackouts   26 ②, ④   27 ⑤

28 bleach   29 (A) clear   (B) a third   (C) is bent

30 ④   31 ①, ④   32 your book holder

---

01 유의어 관계다. 외치다 : 설치하다

02 'hang'은 동사로 '걸다'는 뜻이고, 'hanger'는 명사로 '옷걸이'이다..

03 ① volume: 음량 / 음량을 줄여 주시겠요? ② spread: 퍼뜨리다 / 다른 사람들에 대한 소문을 퍼뜨리지 마라. ③ leftovers: 남은 음식 / 낭비를 막기 위해 남은 음식을 집으로 가져가는 것이 좋다. ④ lamp: 램프, 등 / 어두울 때 등을 켜라. ⑤ forward: 앞으로 / 더 자세히 보기 위해 앞으로 가자.

04 마을 사람들은 너무나 가난해서 전기세를 낼 수가 없다. pay for: ~을 지불하다

05 'thing'은 '상황'이란 의미가 있다. 복수 동사 'are'가 사용이 되었으므로 복수형 'things'를 쓴다.

06 '~할 것을 잊지 마'라는 의미로 'forget to부정사'를 사용한다. 'forget -ing'는 '~한 것을 잊다'는 의미가 된다. ⓔ는 '내일까지'라는 시간의 부사구다.

07 영어 설명: 식사 후에 남은 음식

08 무엇을 할 것인지에 관한 물음에 '놀이동산에 갈 거야'라고 말하고 있으므로 (③)이 적절하다.

09 G의 '온갖 음식을 먹어 볼 거야.'라는 말에 '딤섬을 먹어 보는 걸 잊지 마.'라고 상기시켜 주는 말이 적절하다.

10 A가 '캔과 병을 재활용할 것을 잊지 마.'라고 말할 때 B가 '물론이야. 잊을게'라고 말하는 것은 어색하다. 'I won't.'가 적절하다.

11 질문: 유리는 Jaden에게 무엇을 제안했나요? 종이 수건을 사용하기 전에 손을 털라고 제안하고 있다.

12 유리가 하루에 얼마나 많은 종이 수건을 사용하는지는 대화에 언급되어 있지 않다.

13 목적어와 목적격보어의 관계가 수동이므로 과거분사를 써야 한다. He got his car washed yesterday.

14 사역동사의 목적격보어로 '나무를 심는' 능동의 의미가 필요하므로 원형부사가 적절하다.

15 사역동사 let의 목적격보어로 목적어와의 관계가 능동일 경우 원형부정사를 쓴다.

16 (1), (2) 딸이 태어나서 행복했고, 사고에 대해 듣고 초조하게 되었으므로 동사 make를 이용하여 행복하게 만들고 초조하게 만들었다고 '주어+동사+목적어+목적격보어'의 형식으로 쓴다. 목적격보어로 형용사를 쓰는 것에 유의한다.

17 문맥에 맞게 형용사를 목적격보어로 받는 동사는 keep이다.

18 ⓒ My parents won't let me go out late at night. ⓓ It will help me (to) improve my English. ⓖ Eating an apple a day can make us healthy.

19 make는 5형식 문장에서 목적격보어로 명사, 형용사, 동사원형을 쓸 수 있다.

20 keep의 목적격보어로 형용사가 적절하다. clean은 동사로도 쓰이지만 형용사로도 쓰인다.

21 사역동사 have의 목적격보어로 목적어와의 관계가 능동이므로 원형부정사가 적절하다.

22 주어진 문장과 ②번의 make는 사역동사로 그 쓰임이 같다.

23 전치사 뒤에 동명사를 쓰는 것이 적절하다.

24 ⓐ와 ①, ⑤번: …와 (똑)같이[마찬가지로], …처럼(전치사), ② 비슷한(형용사), ③, ④: 좋아하다(동사)

25 2002년, 브라질에 있는 그의 마을의 '많은 정전들'이 그가 집을 밝히는 새로운 방법을 생각해 내도록 만들었다.

26 ⓑ와 ①, ③, ⑤: 명사적 용법, ② 형용사적 용법, ④ 부사적 용법

27 이 신기한 램프를 만드는 것은 매우 쉽다.

28 bleach: 표백제, 천을 하얗게 만들기 위해 사용되는 화학 물질

29 (A) keep+목적어+목적격보어(5형식): 목적격보어의 자리에 형용사를 써야 하므로 clear가 적절하다. (B) 분자가 2이상일 때부터 분모에 s를 붙이므로 a third가 적절하다. (C) 뒤에 by가 있고, 햇빛이 병 속의 물에 의해 '굴절된다'고 해야 하므로 수동태 is bent가 적절하다. bend: 구부러지다, 구부리다

30 위 글은 '병으로 Moser 램프를 만드는 법'에 관한 글이다.

31 ① 마지막으로, 끝으로(무엇을 열거하면서 마지막 요소 앞에 붙이는 말), ④ Finally: 마지막으로, 마침내 ②, ③: 마침내, ⑤: 결과적으로

32 '당신의 독서대'를 가리킨다.

단원별 예상문제
p.150~153

01 safe 　　02 (A) packed　(B) Thanks to
03 ③ 　　04 ⑤ 　　05 ②
06 put my phone in a glass 　　07 ①
08 Don't forget to turn off the light when you leave your room.
09 ⑤ 　　10 ④ 　　11 ①, ⑤ 　　12 ③, ④, ⑤

13 (1) This movie made the actors famous.
　 (2) My parents made me study hard.
14 wash → to wash
15 People in the village are too poor to pay for electricity.
16 (A) during　(B) packed　(C) any
17 ④, for 　　18 ①, ③, ④ 　　19 ⑤
20 to keep the water clear[clean]
21 ④ 　　22 ②
23 The charity also teaches local people how to make and install the lamps.
24 ④

01 둘은 반의어 관계이다. 인기 있는 : 인기 없는 = 위험한 : 안전한

02 (A) packed: 꽉 들어찬 (B) thanks to: ~ 덕분에

03 물건을 청소하거나 사물에서 색을 제거하는 데 사용되는 강한 화학물질

04 '더 넓은 또는 증가하는 영역을 덮거나, 도달하거나, 영향을 미치다'라는 의미로 'spread(퍼지다)'가 적절하다.

05 ②번의 'turn up'은 '동사+부사'로 이루어진 이어동사로 인칭대명사가 목적어일 때는 '동사+대명사+부사'의 어순으로 써야 한다. 'turn up it'을 'turn it up'으로 고쳐야 한다.

06 '지금 해 보자'라는 말은 '휴대폰을 유리 속에 넣어 보자'는 것을 의미한다.

07 유명 여배우가 학교로 온다는 소식에 빨리 만나보고 싶다는 말이 자연스럽다.

08 '~하는 것을 잊지 마'는 'Don't forget to부정사'를 사용한다.

09 위의 대화에서 Yuri는 종이 수건을 한 장만 사용하는 방법에 대해 이야기하고 있다. 종이 수건을 사용하기 전에 손을 털면 '종이 수건 한 장이면 충분할 거야'라는 말이 자연스럽다.

10 손을 말리기 위해 종이 수건 한 장만 사용할 수 있다는 말에 적어도 두세 장의 종이 수건이 필요하다고 했기 때문에 ⓓ는 'impossible'이 적절하다.

11 ② Let him join your club. ③ He made me introduce myself. ④ She had Mike call me.

12 ① We found the window broken. ② I saw him sing[singing] in front of students.

13 (1) '주어+동사+목적어+목적격보어(형용사)'의 어순으로 쓴다.
　 (2) 사역동사의 목적격보어로 동사원형을 쓴다.

14 get은 목적격보어로 to부정사가 적절하다.

15 too+형용사+to부정사: 너무 ~하여 …할 수 없다

16 (A) during+기간을 나타내는 명사, while+주어+동사, (B) pack은 '(사람, 물건으로) 빽빽히 채우다'는 뜻이므로, 수동태로 써서 '빽빽하게 들어차 있다'고 하는 것이 적절하다. be packed: 들어차다, (C) '전기를 쓰지 않고'라는 부정의 뜻이 되어야 하는데, 빈칸 앞에 without이 있으므로 부정을 나타내는

'no'를 또 쓰는 것은 적절하지 않다.

17 about one dollar는 행위자가 아니라 '1달러 정도'라는 뜻이므로, for로 고치는 것이 적절하다.

18 ⓐ와 ②, ⑤번: 가주어, ① 목적어, ③ 가목적어, ④ 비인칭 주어

19 '제작 방법'은 알 수 없다. ① Moser lamp, ② Alfredo Moser, ③ 2002년, 브라질에 있는 Alfredo Moser의 마을에는 정전이 잦았기 때문에, 그가 집을 밝히는 새로운 방법을 생각해 내게 되었다. ④ 1달러 정도

20 keep+목적어+목적격보어(5형식): 목적격보어의 자리에 형용사를 쓰는 것이 적절하다.

21 Moser lamp를 설치하는 데 얼마나 오래 걸리는지는 대답할 수 없다. ① We need a clear plastic bottle, water, and some bleach. ② To keep the water clear. ③ In the roof. ⑤ Sunlight is bent by the water in the bottle and spreads around the room. operate: 작동되다

22 'ⓐ와 ②번: 재단, ①, ④: (일의 바탕이 되는) 토대[기반/근거], ③, ⑤: 설립, 창립, National Foundation Day: 건국기념일

23 'how'를 보충하면 된다. also는 일반동사 앞에 쓰는 것이 적절하다.

24 필리핀의 '수천' 가구가 이제 Moser 램프를 갖게 해주었다.

🦉 서술형 실전문제　　　　　p.154~155

01 I've heard that we can save trees by using less paper.

02 Just shake your hands before you use a paper towel.

03 Don't forget to try the fruit there

04 (1) I didn't want to go to my cousin's birthday party, but my mom made me go.
(2) They had their house painted.
(3) The present made the children happy all day long.

05 (1) The noise kept me awake.
(2) He found the exam difficult.
(3) These blackouts made him come up with a new way to light his house.
(4) He had his computer repaired yesterday.
(5) Help me (to) take some pictures of them.

06 People call this amazing plastic bottle a Moser lamp

07 blackouts　　　　　**08** very safe

09 the My Shelter Foundation

10 thousand → thousands

---

02 just로 동사 shake를 수식하여 just shake로 문장을 시작한다 (명령문). '~ 전에'라는 접속사 before 뒤에 '주어+동사' 어순으로 'you use a paper towel'을 쓴다.

03 '~할 것을 잊지 마'라는 뜻으로 상대방에게 해야 할 일을 상기시켜 줄 때 'Don't forget to부정사'를 사용한다.

04 (1) make의 목적격보어로 목적어와의 관계가 능동이므로 원형부정사를 쓴다. (2) had의 목적격보어는 목적어와의 관계가 수동이므로 과거분사를 쓴다. (3) '주어+동사+목적어+목적격보어(형용사)'의 어순으로 쓴다.

05 (1) 동사 keep의 목적격보어로 동사원형이 아닌 형용사가 적절하다. (2) 동사 find의 목적격보어로 부사가 아닌 형용사가 적절하다. (3) 사역동사 make의 목적격보어로 목적어와의 관계가 능동이므로 원형부정사를 써야 한다. (4) 사역동사 have의 목적격보어로 목적어와의 관계가 수동이므로 과거분사를 써야 한다. (5) help는 목적격보어로 동사원형이나 to부정사가 나오며 뜻의 차이는 없다.

06 People을 주어로 해서 고치는 것이 적절하다.

07 blackout: 정전, 어떤 지역에 대한 전기 공급이 일시적으로 끊기는 기간

08 Moser 램프는 절대 집에 불을 낼 수 없기 때문에, '매우 안전하다'고 말할 수 있다.

09 'My Shelter 재단'을 가리킨다.

10 thousands of+명사: 수천의 ~, cf. hundred, thousand, million 등의 단어가 숫자 뒤에서 단위로 사용될 때는 단수형으로만 사용한다. e.g. two hundred, three million

---

🐇 창의사고력 서술형 문제　　　　　p.156

|모범답안|

01 (1) A: I'm going to go to Gyeongju.
　　　 B: Don't forget to visit the National Museum.
　　　 A: O.K., I won't forget.
(2) A: I'm going to go on a field trip.
　　　 B: Don't forget to take something to eat.
　　　 A: O.K., I won't forget.

02 (1) Mom made me do the dishes this morning.
(2) The doctor made him stop smoking.
(3) Miranda made her husband buy some fruit.

03 (A) wire hanger　　(B) bend
(C) both ends　　(D) top part　　(E) free

🐞 단원별 모의고사　　　　　p.157~160

01 ⑤	02 (1) hole　(2) wire	03 ②
04 (a)mazing	05 ④	06 ④
07 ⑤	08 ④	

09 her parents, winter break, amusement park, food, dim sum

10 heard, movie star, favorite actress, played, chief

11 ③

12 shake our hands before we use a paper towel

13 me happy   14 ①

15 (1) tidily → tidy   (2) plant → planted

16 ③   17 to have → have   18 ②

19 (A) the Philippines   (B) because   (C) because of

20 No, it doesn't.

21 because Alfredo Moser invented it

22 to come → come

23 The My Shelter Foundation does.   24 ⑤

01 ⑤번은 'widely'에 관한 설명이다. 'surprisingly'에 대한 영어 설명은 'unexpectedly or in a way that is unusual(예상치 못하거나 특이한 방식으로)'이다.

02 (1) hole: 구멍 (2) wire: 전선

03 병들거나 가난하거나 집이 없기 때문에 어려움에 처한 사람들에게 무료로 돈, 음식 또는 도움을 주는 시스템, 또는 이런 식으로 돈과 도움을 제공할 목적을 가지고 있는 단체

04 '매우 놀라운'의 의미를 가진 'amazing'이 적절하다.

05 그가 누군지 묻는 B의 말에 '말해주지 않을 거야.'라고 말하고 있으므로 빈칸에는 '놀라게 할 거야!'라는 'It's a surprise!'가 적절하다.

06 식사를 마쳤는지 묻는 말에 (C) 정말 맛있었다고 답하고, (B) 남은 음식을 집으로 가져가고 싶은지 묻고 (A) 부탁한다고 말하고 나서 마지막으로 (D) 내일까지 남은 음식 먹으라고 상기시켜주는 말을 하는 것이 자연스럽다.

07 전기를 절약하는 방법에 관한 대화로, 방을 떠날 때 불을 끄는 것을 잊지 마라는 의미가 적절하다. 'enter'를 'leave'로 바꾸어야 한다.

08 다음 달에 체육관이 개장한다는 말에 '그렇게 할게. 고마워.'라고 답하는 것은 어색하다.

11 Jaden이 종이 컵 사용을 줄일 수 있다고 말하고 있으므로 종이를 덜 사용하는 것에 대한 내용이 오는 것이 적절하다.

12 손을 말리기 위해서 어떻게 종이 수건 한 장만 사용할 수 있는가? → 종이 수건을 사용하기 전에 손을 털라고 말하고 있다.

13 make 동사로 '주어+동사+목적어+목적격보어(형용사)'의 형식을 이용한다.

14 사역동사의 목적어와 목적격보어가 수동의 관계에 있을 경우 목적격보어로 과거분사를 쓴다..

15 (1) 동사 keep의 목적격보어로 부사가 아닌 형용사가 적절하다. (2) 사역동사의 목적어와 목적격보어가 수동의 관계에 있을 경우 목적격보어로 과거분사를 쓴다.

16 ③은 4형식으로 쓰였고 주어진 문장과 나머지는 모두 목적어와

목적격보어가 있는 5형식이다.

17 사역동사의 목적격보어로 동사원형이 적절하다.

18 too+형용사+to부정사: 너무 ~하여 …할 수 없다

19 (A) 나라 이름이 복수형일 때는 the를 붙여야 하므로 the Philippines가 적절하다. (B)와 (C) 'because+주어+동사', 'because of+명사'이므로 (B)는 because가, (C)는 because of가 적절하다.

20 천장에 있는 플라스틱병 하나는 '전기를 쓰지 않고' 방 전체를 밝힐 수 있다.

21 Alfredo Moser를 주어로 해서 고치는 것이 적절하다.

22 사역동사 make+목적어+목적격보어(동사원형)

23 'My Shelter 재단' 덕분에, 필리핀의 수천 가구가 이제 Moser 램프를 갖고 있다. enable+목적어+to부정사: (사람에게) ~할 수 있게 하다

24 '그 단체(My Shelter 재단)'가 아르헨티나, 인도, 피지와 같은 다른 나라들에서도 Moser 램프가 인기가 있도록 만들었다.

Have Fun This Winter!

나 가장 흥미진진하거나, 재미있거나 흥미로운 부분
[해석] 오후 6시에서 11시까지 하는 MBS Sports의 경기 생중계를 꼭 보세요. 또한 매일 밤 11시에, 여러분은 그날 가장 흥미진진했던 경기의 하이라이트를 즐길 수 있습니다.

시험대비 실력평가   p.164

01 rescue   02 ⑤   03 ②   04 ④
05 ③   06 ⑤   07 ③
08 in the relay

01 둘은 유의어 관계이다. 갈라지다, 구하다
02 매년 3월 초에 알래스카(Alaska)에서는 세계 최대의 개썰매 경주가 열린다(take place).
03 1925년의 어느 추운 겨울날, 놈 마을에서는 끔찍한 일이 일어났다. 몇몇 아이들이 매우 아팠고 병(disease)이 계속 퍼졌다.
04 '위험하거나, 해롭거나, 불쾌한 상황에서 나오도록 누군가 어떤 것을 돕다'라는 의미로 'rescue(구조하다)'가 적절하다.
05 모든 경쟁자들이 가장 빠르고 먼저 끝내려고 하는 시합
06 'trail'은 '코스, 흔적, 오솔길'의 의미이다.
07 '각 팀은 앵커리지(Anchorage)에서 놈(Nome)까지 약 1,800 km를 달려야 한다.'는 뜻으로 '이동하다'는 'travel'이 적절하다.
08 'be in the relay'는 '릴레이에 참가하다'는 의미다.

서술형 시험대비   p.165

01 (1) continue, 계속하다   (2) disease, 질병
    (3) sled, 썰매
02 (1) kept spreading   (2) right away
03 (1) often   (2) memory
04 (1) sled   (2) reach   (3) medicine
05 (1) broadcasts   (2) highlights

01 (1) 계속 일어나거나, 존재하거나, 무언가를 하거나, 혹은 무언가나 누군가가 이런 일을 하게 하다 (2) 사고에 의해서라기보다는 감염이나 건강 쇠약으로 야기되는 사람, 동물, 식물 등이 아픈 것 (3) 길고 좁은 나무 조각이나 금속 조각으로 눈과 얼음 위를 여행하는 데 사용되는 물체
02 (1) keep -ing: 계속해서 ~하다, spread를 동명사로 바꾸어 준다. (2) 'right away'가 '당장'의 뜻이다. 같은 표현으로 'right now', 'at once' 등이 있다.
03 (1) 자주: often (2) 기념, 기억: memory
04 (1) 내 남동생은 썰매 타는 것을 좋아한다. (2) 메인 가에 도착할 때까지 곧장 가세요. (3) 이 약을 먹으면 곧 좋아질 거야.
05 (1) 라디오나 TV에 나오는 프로그램 (2) 어떤 것의 가장 좋거

교과서 Conversation

핵심 Check   p.166~167

1 ③   2 ③   3 Once a month.

교과서 대화문 익히기

Check(√) True or False   p.168

1 T   2 T   3 T   4 F

교과서 확인학습   p.170~171

Listen & Speak 1-A
(1) What, doing / listening to / do you like / I'm not interested in, to sing, favorite / what a nice
(2) Are you interested in watching, be sure to watch, every night, enjoy, highlights, the most interesting

Listen & Speak 2-A
(1) favorite / go swimming / How often, go swimming / Not very often, go swimming once a month
(2) any special plans / to play / How often / Every weekend, How about / like playing, outdoor

Communicate A
special plans, winter break / to go, place, go skating, sledding / Good, favorite / never played, I'm interested in learning, to play / how to play / awesome, the most popular / Everyone, loves, playing / How often, when / at least, three times / I'm sure, good at, can't wait to

Communicate B
What winter sport, interested in / interested in / How often do / once, a month

Progress Check
(1) playing / not interested in, to pass / Good luck
(2) favorite / listen to / How often / Almost
(3) It's, to show, How often, tell, that

p.172

01 ④　　　　02 ②
03 what a nice granddaughter!　　　　04 ④

01 B의 마지막 말이 빈도를 나타내는 'Not very often.'이므로 빈칸의 질문은 빈도를 묻는 말이 적절하다.

02 '오래된 팝송들을 좋아하니?'라는 물음에 'No'로 대답하고 있기 때문에 부정문이 적절하고, old pop songs는 복수 명사로 대명사 'them'으로 나타내는 것이 적절하다.

03 형용사와 명사가 있을 때 What으로 시작하는 감탄문을 사용한다. 'What+a(n)+형용사+명사+주어+동사' 어순으로 영작한다.

04 'How often do you ~?'는 '얼마나 자주 ~을 하니?'라는 빈도를 물을 때 사용한다.

p.173~174

01 ④
02 Do you have any special plans for this weekend
03 ②　　　　04 ③　　　　05 ⑤
06 favorite　　07 ④　　　　08 ⑤
09 Are you interested in watching the Winter Olympics?　　　　10 ③

01 'A: 얼마나 자주 라디오를 듣니?'라는 물음에 'B: '2시간 동안.'이라는 대답은 자연스럽지 못하다. 'For two hours.'는 'How long do you listen to the radio?'에 대한 답으로 적절하다.

02 미래 계획을 묻는 표현으로 'Do you have any plans ~?'를 이용한다.

03 G가 '딱구 하는 걸 정말 좋아하거든. 너는 어때?'라는 말에 '축구하는 걸 좋아해.'라고 말하고 있으므로 빈칸에는 '야외 스포츠를 즐겨.'가 적절하다.

04 B의 대답이 '스포츠를 많이 좋아하지는 않지만, 가끔 수영하러 가.'라는 말에서 G의 빈칸은 가장 좋아하는 스포츠를 묻는 말이 가장 적절하다.

05 감탄문에서 how를 이용할 경우는 'How+형용사(+주어+동사)~!' 어순을 취하고, what은 'What+a(n)+형용사+명사(+주어+동사)~!' 어순을 취한다. how를 what으로 고쳐야 한다.

06 '가장 좋아하거나 가장 즐기는'의 뜻을 가지는 'favorite'가 적절하다.

07 빈칸 다음에 Anna가 '어떻게 하는지 가르쳐 줄 수 있어.'라고 말하고 있으므로 Suho가 아이스하키를 하는 법을 배우는 데에는 관심이 있다는 ④번이 가장 적절하다.

08 대화의 내용에는 한국에서 인기 있는 겨울 스포츠에 대한 것은 없다.

09 '~에 관심이 있다'는 'be interested in' 표현을 쓴다. 전치사 in 뒤에는 동사 watch를 동명사 watching으로 써야 한다.

10 (a)는 형용사 '생방송인, 실황의' 뜻을 가진 'live'가 적절하고, (b)는 그날의 가장 흥미로운 경기의 '하이라이트'가 적절하다. 'spotlight'는 '환한 조명'이란 뜻이다.

p.175

01 She plays table tennis every weekend.
02 How often do you play?
03 I'm interested in learning how to play it
04 Everyone I know loves watching it and playing it.
05 I love them every day

01 질문: 하나는 어떤 스포츠를 하며 얼마나 자주 하는가?

02 'How often do you ~?'는 '얼마나 자주 ~을 하니?'라는 빈도를 물을 때 사용한다.

03 'I'm interested in'을 쓰고, in 뒤에 동명사 learning을 사용한다. learning의 목적어로 how to play it을 쓴다.

04 Everyone이 주어, 'I know'가 'everyone'을 수식하는 관계대명사절 역할을 한다. everyone이 주어라 단수 동사 loves가 오고 love의 목적어로 동명사 watching과 playing을 쓴다.

05 질문: 당신은 얼마나 자주 가족 모두에게 사랑한다고 말해 주나요?

교과서

Grammar

p.176~177

1 (1) draw　(2) opening　(3) injured
2 (1) to draw　(2) to open　(3) to listen

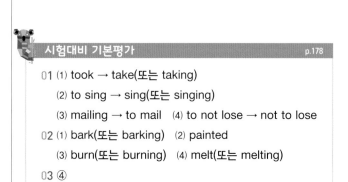

p.178

01 (1) took → take(또는 taking)
　 (2) to sing → sing(또는 singing)
　 (3) mailing → to mail　(4) to not lose → not to lose
02 (1) bark(또는 barking)　(2) painted
　 (3) burn(또는 burning)　(4) melt(또는 melting)
03 ④
04 He smelled the bread burning and told her to turn off the toaster.

01 (1), (2) 지각동사의 목적어가 목적격보어의 행위의 주체가 될 경우 목적격보어로 원형부정사나 현재분사를 쓰는 것이 적절하다. (3) ask의 목적격보어로 to부정사가 적절하다. (4) to부정사의 부정형은 'not to 동사원형'으로 쓴다.

02 (1) 지각동사의 목적격보어는 목적어와의 관계가 능동일 경우 원형부정사나 현재분사가 쓰인다. (2) 지각동사의 목적격보어는 목적어와의 관계가 수동일 경우 과거분사가 쓰인다. (3) 그것이 타는 것이므로 burnt가 아닌 burn 또는 burning이 적절하다. (4) 눈이 녹는 것이므로 능동의 의미를 나타내는 melt 또는 melting이 적절하다. melt: 녹다, 용해하다

03 tell의 목적격보어로 to부정사가 적절하다.

04 to를 추가하여 목적격보어로 현재분사를 쓰고 tell의 목적격보어로 to부정사를 쓴다.

시험대비 실력평가 p.179~181

01 ⑤   02 ②, ④   03 ①

04 We heard Kate sing[singing] a lovely song.

05 ③

06 (1) sing   (2) meeting   (3) popping   (4) burning
   (5) fix   (6) to continue   (7) to close   (8) not to

07 ③   08 reads → to read   09 ③, ④

10 ②   11 ④   12 ③

13 him go[going] out   14 ④

15 (1) to fall → fall(또는 falling)
   (2) uploaded → upload(또는 uploading)
   (3) to check → check   (4) clean → to clean
   (5) helped → to help   (6) bringing → to bring

16 to search   17 ③

18 (1) Alex often hears birds sing[singing] on his way
      to school.
   (2) I smell something burning.
   (3) He asked me to marry him.

01 목적어와의 관계가 능동이므로 지각동사의 목적격보어로 원형부정사 혹은 현재분사가 적절하고 want의 목적격보어로 to부정사가 적절하다.

02 hear는 지각동사이므로 목적격보어로 원형부정사 혹은 현재분사, 과거분사를 받는다. someone이 우는 주체가 되므로 cry 또는 crying이 적절하다.

03 ask의 목적격보어로 to부정사가 적절하다.

04 지각동사 hear의 목적어와 목적격보어의 관계가 능동이므로 목적격보어로 원형부정사 혹은 현재분사를 쓰는 것이 적절하다.

05 advise의 목적격보어로 to부정사가 적절하다. The doctor advised him not to smoke and drink.

06 (1)~(3) 지각동사 hear, see, listen to의 목적격보어로 현재분사나 원형부정사가 적절하다. (4) smell은 목적격보어로 현재분사가 적절하다. (5) make는 사역동사이므로 목적격보어로 원형부정사가 적절하다. (6), (7) tell, ask의 목적격보어로 to부정사가 적절하다. (8) 목적격보어로 쓰인 to부정사의 부정형은 'not to 동사원형'으로 쓴다.

07 지각동사 hear의 목적격보어이므로 현재분사나 원형부정사가 적절하다.

08 want의 목적격보어로 to부정사가 적절하다.

09 목적어와의 관계가 능동이므로 지각동사의 목적격보어로 원형부정사 혹은 현재분사가 적절하다.

10 want의 목적격보어로 to부정사가 적절하다.

11 지각동사 watch의 목적격보어로 원형부정사 혹은 현재분사가 적절하다. I watched him sleep[sleeping] soundly on the sofa. soundly: (수면 상태가) 푹, 깊이

12 (A) 지각동사의 목적어와 목적격보어의 관계가 능동이므로 현재분사가 적절하다. (B) 지각동사의 목적어와 목적격보어의 관계가 능동이므로 원형부정사가 적절하다. (C) 동사 find의 목적어와 목적격보어의 관계가 수동이므로 과거분사가 적절하다.

13 Edan이 나가는 소리를 들었냐는 의미이다. 목적어와 목적격보어의 관계가 능동이므로 원형부정사 또는 현재분사로 써야 한다.

14 make는 사역동사이므로 목적격보어로 동사원형이 나와야 하며 나머지는 모두 목적격보어로 to부정사가 나와야 한다.

15 (1), (2) 지각동사의 목적격보어로 원형부정사나 현재분사가 적절하다. (3) 사역동사 have의 목적격보어로 원형부정사가 적절하다. (4) want의 목적격보어로 to부정사가 적절하다. (5) ask의 목적격보어로 to부정사가 적절하다. (6) tell의 목적격보어로 to부정사가 적절하다.

16 ask의 목적격보어로 to부정사가 적절하다.

17 주어진 문장과 ③번은 명사적 용법으로 목적격보어로 쓰였다. ① 부사적 용법(원인) ② 명사적 용법(보어) ④ 명사적 용법(진주어) ⑤ 형용사적 용법

18 (1) 지각동사의 목적격보어로 원형부정사나 현재분사를 이용한다. (2) smell은 목적격보어로 현재분사를 쓴다. (3) ask의 목적격보어로 to부정사를 쓴다.

서술형 시험대비 p.182~183

01 (1) Alex usually gives a hand when he sees someone carry[carrying] something heavy.
   (2) A neighbor finally heard the dog bark(barking) and called 911.
   (3) Tim just felt the ground shake[shaking].
   (4) He heard his name called.
   (5) The Greek general ordered a soldier to tell the people of Athens about their victory.
   (6) Years of training enabled him to win the match.

(7) I expect you to keep good company when you go abroad.

02 to be careful

03 We watched a man running outside.

04 (1) to come   (2) not to forget   (3) to clean
   (4) to eat   (5) to be

05 listen(또는 listening)

06 (1) to be   (2) painted   (3) touch[touching]
   (4) carry

07 (1) I heard someone call[calling] my name.
   (2) Kate smelled something burning.
   (3) Jake found his brother using his phone.
   (4) He got very angry when he came back and saw it stolen.
   (5) Our teacher always tells us to come to school on time.
   (6) He will not permit me to take part in it.
   (7) I asked him not to close the door.
   (8) She let me play computer games.

08 allowed him to watch TV

01 (1)~(3) 지각동사의 목적어와 목적격보어의 관계가 능동이므로 목적격보어로 원형부정사 혹은 현재분사가 적절하다 (4) 지각동사의 목적어와 목적격보어의 관계가 수동이므로 과거분사가 적절하다. (5)~(7) order, enable, expect의 목적격보어로 to부정사가 적절하다.

02 ask는 목적격보어로 to부정사를 쓴다.

03 지각동사 watch의 목적어가 목적격보어의 행위의 주체이므로 목적격보어로 원형부정사나 현재분사를 쓸 수 있지만 진행형의 문장이므로 목적격보어로 현재분사가 더 적절하다.

04 want, warn, order, advise, encourage의 목적격보어로 to부정사가 나오며 to부정사의 부정은 'not to 동사원형'이다.

05 지각동사 see의 목적어 a girl과 목적격보어의 관계가 능동이므로 목적격보어로 원형부정사나 현재분사가 적절하다.

06 (1) tell은 to부정사를 목적격보어로 받는다. (2) 지각동사의 목적어와 목적격보어의 관계가 수동일 때 목적격보어로 과거분사가 적절하다. (3) 지각동사의 목적어와 목적격보어의 관계가 능동일 때 목적격보어로 원형부정사나 현재분사가 적절하다. (4) 사역동사 have는 원형부정사를 목적격보어로 받는다.

07 (1) 지각동사의 목적어와 목적격보어의 관계가 능동이므로 원형부정사가 적절하다. (2) smell은 목적격보어로 현재분사가 적절하다. (3) '그의 동생이 전화기를 사용하고 있는 것'이므로 목적격보어로 현재분사가 적절하다. (4) 지각동사의 목적어와 목적격보어의 관계가 수동이므로 과거분사가 적절하다. (5), (6) tell, permit, ask는 목적격보어로 to부정사를 쓴다. (7) to부정사의 부정형은 'not to 동사원형'으로 쓴다. (8) let은 사역동사이므로 목적격보어로 동사원형을 쓴다.

08 allow는 목적격보어로 to부정사를 쓴다.

교과서
Reading

확인문제   p.184

1 T   2 F   3 T   4 F

확인문제   p.185

1 T   2 F   3 T   4 F   5 F

교과서 확인학습 A   p.186~187

01 Most   02 takes place
03 It is called   04 take part in
05 has to cover
06 take, race through snowstorms
07 in memory of   08 a terrible thing happened
09 kept spreading
10 right away, did not have any
11 had to get it   12 to get the medicine
13 the race to Nome   14 in the relay
15 the others, at different points
16 of the 20th team   17 made, his lead dog
18 so, that, could not   19 However, stay on the trail
20 frozen   21 cracking
22 was saved, just in time
23 reached   24 to continue on
25 Here's, shouted   26 On, arrived in
27 was saved
28 is now celebrated, the biggest sled dog race

교과서 확인학습 B   p.188~189

1 The Most Heart-Warming Winter Sport
2 In early March every year, the world's biggest sled dog race takes place in Alaska.
3 It is called the Iditarod Trail Sled Dog Race.
4 Around 80 teams of 12 to 16 dogs take part in this race.
5 Each team has to cover about 1,800 km from Anchorage to Nome.
6 The race can take more than two weeks, and the teams often race through snowstorms.
7 The Iditarod Race began in 1973 in memory of the dogs that saved Nome.
8 One cold winter day in 1925, a terrible thing happened in Nome.

9 Some children got very sick, and the disease kept spreading.

10 The people of Nome needed medicine right away, but the town did not have any.

11 Someone had to get it from a hospital in Anchorage.

12 Because of the heavy snow, a dog sled relay was the only way to get the medicine from Anchorage to Nome.

13 Soon, the race to Nome began.

14 Twenty-one dog teams were in the relay.

15 On January 27, the first team left, and the others waited at different points.

16 Gunnar was the driver of the 20th team.

17 The strongest dog on his team was Balto, so he made Balto his lead dog.

18 When Gunnar and Balto finally got the medicine, the snow was so heavy that Gunnar could not see his own hands.

19 However, Balto was able to stay on the trail.

20 When they were crossing a frozen river, Balto suddenly stopped.

21 Then, Gunnar saw the river ice cracking.

22 The whole team was saved because Balto stopped just in time.

23 When Balto and Gunnar reached the final team, they were sleeping.

24 Gunnar told Balto to continue on.

25 "Here's the medicine, Doctor!" shouted Gunnar.

26 On February 2, Gunnar and his team finally arrived in Nome.

27 The town was saved.

28 This heart-warming story is now celebrated every year by the Iditarod Race, the biggest sled dog race in the world.

시험대비 실력평가
p.190~193

01 is taken → takes   02 ④
03 the Iditarod Trail Sled Dog Race   04 ⑤
05 ②   06 to continue
07 Gunnar saw the river ice cracking.
08 saved → was saved   09 spreading
10 ②   11 ③   12 ①, ④
13 Because he slipped and broke his neck.
14 to rescue him   15 ③
16 Because it snowed heavily

17 The strongest dog on his team was Balto, so he made Balto his lead dog.

18 (A) In (B) km (C) take

19 People[They] call it the Iditarod Trail Sled Dog Race.

20 ③   21 ⑤

22 It's the biggest sled dog race in the world.

23 ⑤   24 ①   25 ⓐ so ⓑ that

26 One of the gorillas

27 looked after 또는 cared for

01 take place는 자동사로 쓰이므로 수동태는 적절하지 않다. take place: 개최되다[일어나다]

02 ⓑ와 ④번: 약 …, …쯤(부사), ① 사방에(서), 빙 둘러(부사), ②둥글게, 빙돌아(전치사), ③ 이리저리, 여기저기(부사), ⑤ 둘레에, 주위에(전치사)

03 '아이디타로드 개썰매 경주'를 가리킨다.

04 아이디타로드 경주는 '놈'을 구한 개들을 기념하여 1973년에 시작되었다.

05 Gunnar는 자신의 손조차도 볼 수 없었다. '그러나', Balto는 코스를 제대로 따라갈 수 있었다라고 하는 것이 적절하다. ① 게다가, ③ 결과적으로, ④ 예를 들면, ⑤ 이렇게 하여, 그러므로

06 tell+목적어+to부정사

07 지각동사 see는 목적격보어로 동사원형이나 현재분사가 올 수 있으나, 여기서는 진행 중이므로 현재분사가 적절하다.

08 놈 마을 사람들의 목숨이 구해진 것이므로 수동태로 쓰는 것이 적절하다.

09 keep ~ing: 계속해서 ~하다

10 ②번 다음 문장의 it에 주목한다. 주어진 문장의 medicine을 가리키므로 ②번이 적절하다.

11 이 글은 폭설로 인해 '앵커리지에서 놈으로 약을 가져오는 유일한 방법이었던 개썰매 릴레이'에 관한 글이다.

12 ⓐ와 ②, ③, ⑤는 부사적 용법, ① 형용사적 용법, ④ 명사적 용법

13 미끄러져서 목이 부러졌기 때문이다.

14 to his rescue: 그를 구하기 위해

15 ③ 밀접하게, 친밀하게, 나머지는 모두 '즉시, 당장'

16 because of+명사(구), because+절

17 'so'는 접속사로 쓰여 '그래서'의 의미로 결과의 절을 이끈다. make+목적어+목적격보어(명사): 목적어를 ~으로 만들다

18 (A) 월 앞에는 In을 쓰는 것이 적절하다. (B) 약자로 쓸 때는 앞에 복수 숫자가 나오더라도 km으로 쓰고, 풀어 쓰면 kilometers를 쓰는 것이 적절하다. (C) 2주 이상 '걸릴 수' 있다고 해야 하므로 take가 적절하다. spend: (시간을 어떻게·어디서) 보내다, 지내다(주어는 보통 사람), take: (얼마의 시간이) 걸리다

19 People이나 They를 주어로 해서 고치는 것이 적절하다.

20 ⓑ와 ③번: <어떤 일정한 거리를> 가다, ① (감추거나 보호하기 위해) 씌우다[가리다], ② 다루다, 포함시키다, ④ (텔레비전, 신문 등을 위해) 취재[방송/보도]하다, ⑤ (비용 등을) 충당하다, (보험을 걸어서) 보호하다

21 ⓐ on the trail: (특정 목적을 위한) 루트[코스]를 따라가는, ⓑ continue on: 계속하다 ⓒ 날짜가 있으면 on을 쓰는 것이 적절하다.

22 '세계에서 가장 큰 개썰매 경주'이다.

23 이 글은 'Gunnar와 그의 팀의 가슴 따뜻한 이야기가 아이디타로드 경주를 통해 오늘날 매년 기념되고 있다.'는 내용의 글이므로, 제목으로는 'Iditarod Race의 기원'이 적절하다.

24 ① 언제 Gunnar와 Balto가 약을 받았는지는 대답할 수 없다. ② Because the snow was so heavy. ③ Because they were sleeping. ④ On February 2. ⑤ Yes.

25 so+형용사+that절: 너무 ~해서 …하다

26 '고릴라들 중의 한 마리'를 가리킨다.

27 take care of = look after = care for: ~을 돌보다

서술형 시험대비
p.194~195

01 is held
02 one thousand (and) eight hundred kilometers
03 too, to　04 reached　05 Nome　06 On
07 nineteen twenty-five　08 must → had to
09 (A) Because of　(B) the others　(C) so
10 medicine
11 (A) dog sled relay　(B) twenty-one dog teams
12 to crack → cracking
13 The Iditarod Race, the biggest sled dog race in the world, now celebrates this heart-warming story every year.

---

01 take place = be held: 열리다

02 km를 풀어 쓰면 kilometers라고 쓰는 것이 적절하다.

03 so ~that 주어 can't ... = too ~ to ...: 너무나 ~해서 …할 수 없다

04 arrive in = reach: ~에 도착하다

05 'Nome'을 가리킨다.

06 날짜가 있으면 on을 쓰는 것이 적절하다.

07 연도는 보통 두 자리씩 끊어 읽는다. 십 단위와 단 단위 사이에는 보통 하이픈을 쓴다.

08 과거 시제로 써야 하므로 'must'의 과거 'had to'로 고치는 것이 적절하다.

09 (A) 'because of+명사(구)', 'because+절'이므로 Because of가 적절하다. (B) 나머지 전체를 나타낼 때는 'the'를 써야 하므

로 the others가 적절하다. (C) 'as+주어+동사: ~이기 때문에', 'so+주어+동사: 그래서'의 의미로 결과의 절을 이끌므로, so가 적절하다.

10 당장 약이 필요했지만, 마을에는 '약'이 하나도 없었다.

11 놈의 사람들이 당장 약이 필요했을 때, '개썰매 릴레이'가 앵커리지에서 놈으로 약을 가져오는 유일한 방법이었다. 곧, 놈으로 향하는 질주가 시작되었고 '21개의 개 팀'이 릴레이에 참여했다.

12 지각동사 see는 목적격보어로 동사원형이나 현재분사가 올 수 있으나 진행중인 한 시점을 가리킬 때는 현재분사를 써야 한다.

13 The Iditarod Race, the biggest sled dog race in the world를 주어로 해서 고치는 것이 적절하다.

영역별 핵심문제
p.197~201

01 reach　　02 take, snowstorm　　03 ①
04 in memory of　　05 ④　　06 ②
07 I have an interest in ice skating.
08 I go once or twice a month.
09 ③　　10 ④　　11 ①　　12 ⑤
13 ③　　14 ⑤　　15 go(또는 going)
16 ②　　17 ③
18 (1) He looked at the baby sleeping on the bed.
　(2) I heard Amy locking her room.
19 (1) Do you want me to believe that false story?
　(2) Can you ask him to return the book to the library tomorrow?
　(3) I heard somebody cry[crying] while I took a walk to the park.
　(4) I saw Ann wait[waiting] for a bus at the bus stop.
20 ⑤　　21 around　　22 ④
23 ④　　24 ②　　25 ⑤
26 Balto was able to stay on the trail.　27 ③, ⑤
28 (A) excited　(B) gorillas　(C) falling　29 caught

---

01 유의어 관계이다. 외치다 : 도착[도달]하다

02 take+시간: 시간이 걸리다, snowstorm: 눈보라

03 ① lead: 선두 / 카 레이서는 선두 차량을 따라잡기 위해 더 빨리 운전하기 시작했다. ② polar: 북극의 / 북극곰은 크고 희다. ③ heart-warming: 가슴 따뜻한 / 그녀는 가슴 따뜻한 이야기를 듣고 울었다. ④ terrible: 끔찍한 / 어젯밤에 끔찍한 꿈을 꾸었다. ⑤ victory: 승리 / 우리의 승리는 영원히 기억될 것이다.

04 in memory of: ~을 기념하여

05 폭설 때문에 개썰매 릴레이가 앵커리지에서 Nome으로 약을 가져오는 유일한 방법이었다. / 명사 'the heavy snow'가 있기 때문에 접속사 because는 적절하지 않다.

06 '가주어(It) ~ 진주어(to부정사) …' 구문으로 ⓑ의 동사

'show'를 'to show'로 바꾸어야 한다. ⓓ는 목적격 관계대명사
고, ⓔ는 'everyone in your family'를 가리키는 대명사다.

07 '~에 관심이 있다'는 'have an interest in ~' = 'be interested in ~' 등으로 나타낼 수 있다.

09 A가 '어떤 TV프로그램에 관심이 있니?'라고 묻는 말에 B가 '한국의 역사와 문화에 매료되었어.'라고 말하는 것은 어색하다.

10 James가 '스포츠는 좋아하지 않지만 때때로 수영하러 가.'라고 말하는 것을 보아 (A)에는 무엇에 관심이 있는지를 묻 는 말이 적절하다.

11 얼마나 자주 수영을 가는지 묻는 말에 'Not very often(그렇게 자주는 아니야.)'라고 말하고 있으므로 ①번이 적절하다.

12 Anna의 답에서 일주일에 두세 번 경기를 한다고 했으므로 빈칸은 얼마나 자주 무엇을 하는지 묻는 말이 적절하다.

13 수호가 일주일에 두세 번 스케이트를 타러 가는지는 대화에 언급되어 있지 않다.

14 첫 문장에는 목적격보어로 현재분사가 나와야 한다. 두 번째 문장에서 want의 목적격보어로 to부정사가 적절하다.

15 지각동사의 목적어가 목적격보어의 행위의 주체가 될 경우 목적격보어로 원형부정사나 현재분사를 쓴다.

16 I watched her talk[talking] on the phone.

17 주어진 문장과 ③번은 목적격보어로 쓰인 현재분사이다. 각각 ① 분사구문, ② 진행형을 만드는 현재분사, ④와 ⑤는 동명사이다.

18 지각동사의 목적어와 목적격보어의 관계가 능동이며, 진행형으로 쓰이고 있으므로 목적격보어로 현재분사를 이용한다.

19 (1), (2) want와 ask는 목적격보어로 to부정사가 나와야 한다. (3), (4) hear, see의 목적어와 목적격보어의 관계가 능동이므로 현재분사나 원형부정사가 적절하다.

20 (A) from A to B: A부터 B까지, (B) through snowstorms: 눈보라를 뚫고

21 about = around: 약 …, …쯤(부사)

22 ④ 경주의 우승팀이 경주를 끝내는 데 얼마나 오래 걸리는지는 대답할 수 없다. ① In early March every year. ② It is called the Iditarod Trail Sled Dog Race. ③ Around 80 teams of 12 to 16 dogs do. ⑤ In 1973.

23 나머지 전체를 나타낼 때는 'the'를 써야 하므로 the others가 적절하다.

24 ⓐ와 ②, ⑤: 형용사적 용법, ①, ④: 부사적 용법, ③: 명사적 용법

25 1월 27일에 첫 번째 팀이 출발했고, 나머지 팀들은 '서로 다른' 지점에서 기다렸다.

26 on the trail: (특정 목적을 위한) 루트[코스]를 따라가는

27 finally = at last = in the end = in the long run: 마침내[드디어] ③ 적어도, ⑤ 실제로, 정말로

28 (A) 감정을 나타내는 동사는 수식받는 명사가 감정을 느끼게 되

는 경우에 과거분사를 써야 하므로 excited가 적절하다. (B) '~ 중의 하나'는 'one of the 복수명사'로 써야 하므로 gorillas가 적절하다. (C) 지각동사 see는 목적격 보어로 동사원형이나 현재분사가 올 수 있으므로 falling이 적절하다.

29 과거시제로 쓰는 것이 적절하다.

단원별 예상문제　　　　　　　　　　p.202~205

01 awesome　　　　　　02 (A) lead　(B) frozen
03 ③　　　　04 ②　　　　05 ③
06 It's important to help these poor people at Christmas.　　　　　　　　07 ④
08 old pop songs, grandma's favorite, birthday party
09 ④　　　　10 I'll go skating and sledding there.
11 ②　　　　12 ②　　　13 ③　　　14 ③
15 ④　　　　16 I saw Jake play[playing] basketball.
17 ④
18 Around 80 teams of 12 to 16 dogs take part in this race.
19 over　　　　20 ①, ④
21 was happened → happened　　　22 Gunnar
23 ④　　　　24 His dog　　　　25 ④

01 반의어 관계이다. 인기 있는 : 인기 없는 = 끔찍한 : 멋진, 굉장한

02 (A) lead: 선두 (B) frozen: 얼어붙은

03 '표면에 금이 가게 하거나 조각으로 부수기 위해 무언가를 깨다'의 의미로 'crack(갈라지다)'이 적절하다.

04 '더 넓은 또는 증가하는 영역을 덮거나, 도달하거나, 영향을 미치다'라는 의미로 'spread(퍼지다)'가 적절하다.

05 (C) 어떤 운동에 관심이 있는지 묻는 말에 대한 응답으로 (A) 아이스 스케이팅에 관심이 있다고 답하고, (B) 그것을 얼마나 자주하는지 묻고 그에 대한 응답 (D)가 마지막에 오는 것이 적절하다.

06 '가주어 ~ 진주어' 구문을 이용하여 'It is important to help ~'로 문장을 시작한다.

07 B의 답으로 보아 라디오를 듣는 빈도를 묻는 말이 적절하다.

08 소녀는 다음 주 할머니의 생일 파티에서 할머니가 가장 좋아하는 노래를 불러주기 위해 오래된 팝송을 듣고 있다.

09 everyone은 단수 취급하므로 동사 'love'를 단수 동사인 'loves'로 바꾸어야 한다.

10 '~하러 가다'는 의미로 'go –ing'를 이용한다.

11 첫 번째 문장에서는 지각동사의 목적격보어로 원형부정사나 현재분사가 적절하다. 두 번째 문장에서는 '형용사[부사]+enough+to 동사원형(= so+형용사[부사]+that+주어+can ...)' 구문이 적절하다.

12 지각동사의 목적어와 목적격보어의 관계가 능동일 경우 목적격보어로 원형부정사나 현재분사를 쓴다.

13 encourage의 목적격보어로 to부정사가 적절하다.

14 첫 번째 빈칸은 tell의 목적격보어로 to부정사를 쓴다. 두 번째 빈칸에는 지각동사의 목적격보어로 원형부정사나 현재분사를 쓴다.

15 ⓑ We never allow our children to play with toy guns. ⓓ I want you to come to my birthday party. ⓕ We watched an old man run[running] outside. ⓖ We were so surprised to see the snow falling[fall] from the sky.

17 ask의 목적격보어로 to부정사가 적절하다.

18 'to'를 보충하면 된다. 12 to 16: 12 내지 16, 12~16

19 more than = over: ~ 이상

20 ⓒ와 ①, ④번: 관계대명사, ②, ③, ⑤: 접속사

21 happen은 수동태로 쓸 수 없는 자동사이다.

22 'Gunnar'를 가리킨다.

23 Gunnar가 왜 20번째 팀의 몰이꾼이었는지는 대답할 수 없다. ① One cold winter day in 1925. ② No. ③ Twenty-one dog teams were in it. ⑤ Balto.

24 '그의 개'를 가리킨다.

25 그의 개가 19시간 동안 짖고 또 짖었다.

01 How often did you play ice hockey when you were in Canada?

02 go skating, sledding, during, ice hockey, learning how to play, how to play

03 (A) What TV programs are you interested in?
　　(B) How often do you watch them?

04 (1) her dad to order pizza　(2) to wear suncream

05 (1) Did you hear Julia close[closing] the door?
　　(2) Ms. Park saw her son read[reading] a book.

06 Some children got very sick, and the disease kept spreading.

07 As[Because]

08 (A) crossing　(B) reached　(C) heart-warming

09 just in time　　　　　10 (A) saved　(B) celebrated

01 '얼마나 자주 ~을 하니?'는 'How often do you ~?' 형태이고, Anna의 대답에서 played라고 과거시제를 사용하고 있으므로 'How often did you play ~?'를 사용한다. when은 접속사로 '주어+동사' 어순으로 쓴다.

03 (A) 의문형용사 'what'이 명사 TV programs를 수식하는 역할을 한다. (B)는 '얼마나 자주 ~을 하니?'는 'How often do you ~?' 형태를 사용한다.

04 ask, tell은 목적격보어로 to부정사를 쓴다.

05 지각동사의 목적어와 목적격보어의 관계가 능동이므로 목적격보어로 원형부정사나 현재분사가 적절하다.

06 keep ~ing: 계속해서 ~하다

07 이유를 나타내는 접속사 as, because, since 등을 쓰는 것이 적절하다.

08 (A) '건너고 있을 때'라고 해야 하므로 crossing이 적절하다. (B) reach는 타동사이므로 전치사 없이 reached로 쓰는 것이 적절하다. (C) '가슴을 따뜻하게 하는' 이야기라는 뜻이므로 heart-warming이 적절하다.

09 just in time: 바로 제때

10 모든 어려움에도 불구하고 Gunnar와 그의 팀은 마침내 놈에 도착해서 놈 마을 사람들의 목숨을 '구할 수' 있었다. 이 가슴 따뜻한 이야기는 세계에서 가장 큰 개썰매 경주인 아이디타로드 경주를 통해 오늘날 매년 '기념되고' 있다.

[모범답안]

01 (1) A: How often do you clean your room?
　　　　B: I clean my room once a week.
　　(2) A: How often do you wash your hands?
　　　　B: I wash my hands very often.
　　(3) A: How often do you play the piano?
　　　　B: I play the piano three times a day.

02 (1) I saw a lady ride[riding] a bike.
　　(2) I watched a girl eat[eating] a piece of pizza.
　　(3) I saw a boy take[taking] a picture.
　　(4) I looked at a man wait[waiting] for someone.

03 (A) at a zoo　(B) over the wall　(C) falling
　　(D) took care of

01 ④　　　　02 (1) special　(2) slipped　　　03 ②

04 ⓐ frozen　ⓑ cracking　　05 ③　　　　06 ④

07 ⑤　　　　08 ②

09 doesn't like, swimming once, month

10 table tennis, this weekend, every weekend

11 He is interested in learning how to play ice hocky.

12 I can't wait to learn from you.

13 ②　　　　　14 ①

15 (1) He felt someone look[looking] at him.
　　(2) I told him to bring his passport.

16 (1) to walk → walking[walk]
　　(2) cried → cry[crying]　(3) speaking → spoken
　　(4) listening → to listen　(5) being not → not to be

17 fix[fixing] / fixed
18 the world's biggest sled dog race 19 ②, ⑤
20 ④   21 ⑤, on
22 (A) terrible (B) any (C) 20th
23 was saved
24 the snow was so heavy that Gunnar could not
  see his own hands
25 ②

01 ④번은 'relay'에 관한 설명이다. 'race'에 대한 영어 설명은 'a competition in which all the competitors try to be the fastest and to finish first(모든 경쟁자들이 가장 빠르고 먼저 끝내려고 하는 시합)'이다.

02 (1) special: 특별한 (2) slip: 미끄러지다, 과거형이기 때문에 '단모음+단자음'으로 끝나는 단어는 자음을 한 번 더 쓰고 –ed를 붙인다.

03 '긴 줄 또는 누군가 혹은 무언가에 의해 남겨진 일련의 표시'란 의미로 '흔적, 코스'를 의미하는 'trail'이 적절하다.

04 ⓐ는 '얼어붙은'의 의미를 가진 'frozen'을 쓰고, ⓑ는 '지각동사(saw)+목적어+현재분사(cracking)'를 사용한다.

05 '얼마나 자주 탁구를 치니?'라는 말에 빈도를 나타내는 답이 적절하다.

06 오래된 팝송을 좋아한다는 긍정의 답 다음에 오래된 팝송에 관심이 있다는 말이 오는 것이 적절하다.

07 빈칸 다음에 '단지 다음 주에 있는 배드민턴 시험에 통과하고 싶어.'라고 말하고 있으므로 배드민턴에 관심이 없다는 부정의 말이 적절하다.

08 얼마나 자주 패스트푸드를 먹는지 묻는 말에 패스트푸드를 먹는 것은 건강에 좋지 않다고 말하는 것은 자연스럽지 못하다.

11 수호는 아이스하키를 하는 방법을 배우는 데 관심이 있다.

12 '빨리 ~하고 싶다'는 표현은 'I can't wait to부정사'를 사용한다.

13 advise의 목적격보어로 to부정사가 적절하다.

14 지각동사의 목적어와 목적격보어가 능동의 관계에 있을 경우 목적격보어로 원형부정사나 현재분사를 쓴다.

15 (1) 지각동사의 목적어와 목적격보어가 능동의 관계에 있을 경우 목적격보어로 원형부정사나 현재분사를 쓴다. (2) tell의 목적격보어로 to부정사를 쓴다.

16 (1), (2) 지각동사의 목적어와 목적격보어가 능동의 관계에 있을 경우 목적격보어로 원형부정사나 현재분사를 쓴다. (3) 지각동사의 목적어와 목적격보어가 수동의 관계에 있을 경우 목적격보어로 과거분사를 쓴다. (4), (5) want, tell의 목적격보어로 to부정사가 적절하다. to부정사의 부정형은 'not to 동사원형'으로 쓴다.

17 그가 내 컴퓨터를 고치는 주체이므로 현재분사나 원형부정사를 쓰고, 내 컴퓨터가 '고쳐진 것'이므로 과거분사 fixed를 쓰는 것

이 적절하다.

18 '세계 최대의 개썰매 경주'를 가리킨다.

19 take part in = participate in = join: ~에 참여[참가]하다, ① (특히 미리 준비되거나 계획된 일이) 개최되다[일어나다], ③, ④: (일·과제·의무 등을) 행하다[수행하다/실시하다]

20 개의 품종은 알 수 없다. ① 매년 3월 초, ② 알래스카, ③ 12·16미리 개로 구성된 80여 팀, ⑤ 1973년

21 '소속'을 나타내는 'on'으로 고치는 것이 적절하다.

22 (A) '끔찍한' 일이 일어났다고 해야 하므로 terrible이 적절하다. terrific: 아주 좋은, 멋진, (B) 부정문이므로 any가 적절하다. (C) '20번째' 팀이라고 해야 하므로 20th가 적절하다.

23 목숨이 구해진 것이므로 수동태로 쓰는 것이 적절하다.

24 'so'를 보충하면 된다.

25 Balto는 코스를 제대로 따라갈 수 있었다.

교과서 파헤치기

단어 TEST Step 1   p.02

01 연습하다   02 지하철
03 진가를 알아보다, 감상하다, 감사하다   04 용감한
05 세기   06 실은, 사실은, 실제로
07 ~와 결혼하다   08 새벽   09 공연하다, 수행하다
10 실패하다   11 줄거리   12 수수께끼
13 공주   14 기념하다   15 이미, 벌써
16 공연   17 비밀   18 정확하게, 바르게
19 제안   20 유명한   21 추측하다
22 정확하지 않게, 틀리게   23 낯선 사람, 이방인
24 할인   25 어려운   26 의미하다
27 놀라운   28 타조
29 (말을) 덧붙이다, 더하다   30 기념일
31 즉시, 곧바로   32 안전한   33 극장
34 전체, 모든, 전부의   35 서두르다   36 ~에 늦다, 지각하다
37 ~하는 게 어때?   38 ~하고 싶다   39 …만큼 ~한
40 ~와 사랑에 빠지다   41 ~에 지나지 않는
42 제시간에, 늦지 않게   43 알아내다, 발견하다

단어 TEST Step 2   p.03

01 secret   02 guess   03 century
04 incorrectly   05 actually   06 princess
07 brave   08 ostrich   09 discount
10 appreciate   11 stranger   12 correctly
13 agree   14 play   15 storyline
16 already   17 anniversary   18 marry
19 perform   20 fail   21 whole
22 subway   23 add   24 celebrate
25 famous   26 safe   27 performance
28 suggestion   29 practice   30 moving
31 difficult   32 amazing   33 riddle
34 beauty   35 be late for ~   36 in time
37 find out   38 hurry up   39 fall in love with ~
40 take off   41 one day   42 at first sight
43 would like to+동사원형

단어 TEST Step 3   p.04

1 century, 세기   2 already, 이미
3 perform, 수행하다, 공연하다   4 amazing, 놀라운
5 storyline, 줄거리   6 aria, 아리아, 영창   7 brave, 용감한
8 discount, 할인   9 appreciate, 진가를 알아보다

---

10 celebrate, 축하하다, 기념하다   11 moving, 감동적인
12 guess, 추측하다   13 secret, 비밀   14 marry, 결혼하다
15 anniversary, 기념일   16 riddle, 수수께끼

대화문 TEST Step 1   p.05~06

Listen & Speak 1-A

1 hurry up, already / going to be late for / Why don't we take, faster than / good idea
2 got only, wrong / sure, well, Why don't we go out to celebrate / have pizza for / Of course

Listen & Speak 1-B

What shall we do / Why don't we see / a good idea

Listen & Speak 2-A

1 let's practice, parts, school play / What time shall we meet / How about, right after school / Sounds
2 play badminton / Where shall we / How about, near / See you there at

Listen & Speak 2-B

Let's go on a picnic / What time shall we meet / How about, on / Let's meet

Communicate A

guess what, have no school / Why not / anniversary / together / take, off, What, want to / Why don't we go see, near your work, get, discount if, go on a Wednesday / let's just meet / shall we / How about, have lunch / best

Communicate B

What shall we / Why don't we / time shall we meet / How about / Let's meet

Progress Check

1 hurry up, already / be late for / Why don't we take, faster than, at this time of day / good idea
2 hot today, Let's go swimming / Where shall, meet / How about / See, tere

대화문 TEST Step 2   p.07~08

Listen & Speak 1-A

1 M: Liz, hurry up. It's already 6 o'clock.
   W: Oh, we're going to be late for the concert.
   M: Why don't we take the subway? The subway will be faster than the bus at this time of day.
   W: That's a good idea.
2 B: Mom, I got only one question wrong on the Korean history exam!
W: Great! I was sure you would do well. Why don't

we go out to celebrate tonight?

B: Yes! Can we have pizza for dinner?

W: Of course, Joe. I'll call your dad.

Listen & Speak 1-B

A: What shall we do at the park?

B: Why don't we see a magic show?

A: That's a good idea.

Listen & Speak 2-A

1 B: Karen, let's practice our parts for the school play today.

G: O.K. What time shall we meet?

B: How about 4 o'clock, right after school?

G: Sounds good.

2 G: Do you want to play badminton together this afternoon, Mark?

B: Sure. Where shall we play?

G: How about at the park near your place?

B: O.K. See you there at 3 o'clock.

Listen & Speak 2-B

A: Let's go on a picnic this weekend.

B: Good idea. What time shall we meet?

A: How about 10 o'clock on Saturday?

B: O.K. Let's meet at the subway station. See you there.

Communicate A

Anna: Dad, guess what! I have no school next Wednesday.

Dad: Really? Why not?

Anna: It's our school's 75th anniversary.

Dad: Oh, I see.

Anna: Can we do something together that day?

Dad: I guess I can take the afternoon off. What do you want to do?

Anna: Why don't we go see a musical at Bravo Theater near your work? We can get a discount if we go on a Wednesday.

Dad: Good idea, Anna! Then, let's just meet at the theater.

Anna: O.K. What time shall we meet?

Dad: How about 12? Then, we can have lunch together, too.

Anna: You're the best, Dad!

Communicate B

A: What shall we do this afternoon?

B: Why don't we go see *Wonder Woman*?

A: Good idea! What time shall we meet?

B: How about 4 o'clock?

A: O.K. Let's meet at Moon Theater.

Progress Check

1 G: Jim, hurry up. It's already 10 o'clock.

B: Oh, we're going to be late for the movie.

G: Why don't we take the bus? The bus will be faster than the subway at this time of day.

B: That's a good idea.

2 B: It's very hot today. Let's go swimming, Julie.

G: Good idea! Where shall we meet?

B: How about at the subway station near my place?

G: O.K. See you there at 11 o'clock.

본문 TEST Step 1   p.09~10

01 Most Dangerous, World

02 Welcome, everyone

03 going, perform, opera

04 Like, other, Italian because

05 Before, like, storyline

06 appreciate, better if

07 of, beauty, cold as

08 who, marry, must

09 fails, die   10 has, been able

11 One, falls, at, sight

12 becomes, answer, riddles

13 However, marry, prince

14 nothing more than   15 then, of, own

16 asks, What

17 adds, correctly, die, incorrectly

18 before dawn, as, hers

19 to, until, finds out

20 most famous aria, whole   21 means, sleeps

22 No, sleeps   23 one, not even   24 secret, safe

25 No, will know 26 At dawn, will   27 prince's, is

28 learn, in time   29 watch, find out

본문 TEST Step 2   p.11~12

01 The Most Dangerous, World

02 Welcome, everyone

03 are going to, perform

04 Like, other famous operas, in Italian because, in Italy, 16th century

05 I'd like to tell, storyline of the opera

06 appreciate, better if

07 of great beauty, as cold as ice

08 who, marry her, three riddles

09 fails, must die 10 has ever been able to

11 falls in love with, at first sight

12 the first man to answer

13 However, to marry

14 nothing more than

15 her a riddle of his own

16 asks her, What

17 adds, correctly, agree to die, incorrectly, have to marry

18 before dawn, as difficult as hers

19 go to sleep until, finds out

20 the most famous aria, whole opera

21 means, sleeps

22 No, sleeps   23 not even you

24 My secret, safe

25 No one will know

26 At dawn, will win   27 prince's name

28 Will, learn, in time

29 Let's watch, find out

1 투란도트, 세상에서 가장 위험한 사랑

2 여러분, 환영합니다!

3 오늘 밤, 우리는 지아코모 푸치니의 오페라 《투란도트》를 공연할 것입니다.

4 다른 많은 유명한 오페라들처럼 《투란도트》는 이탈리아어로 되어 있는데, 오페라가 16세기 이탈리아에서 시작되었기 때문입니다.

5 시작하기 전에 오페라 《투란도트》의 줄거리를 알려 드리려고 합니다.

6 여러분이 즐거리를 알면 이 오페라를 더 잘 감상하게 될 것입니다.

7 중국의 공주 Turandot는 굉장히 아름다운 여인이지만, 그녀는 얼음처럼 차갑습니다.

8 그녀와 결혼하길 원하는 왕자는 누구든지 반드시 세 가지 수수께끼에 답해야 합니다.

9 만약 실패하면 그는 죽어야 합니다.

10 그 누구도 수수께끼에 답할 수 없었습니다.

11 어느 날, 어떤 용감한 왕자가 그녀에게 첫눈에 반합니다.

12 그는 세 수수께끼를 모두 맞힌 첫 번째 사람이 됩니다.

13 그러나 Turandot는 그 왕자와 결혼하길 원하지 않습니다.

14 그는 그녀에게 단지 낯선 사람일 뿐입니다.

15 그러자 그는 그녀에게 자신의 수수께끼를 냅니다.

16 그는 그녀에게 "제 이름이 무엇입니까?"라고 묻습니다.

17 그는 "당신이 맞게 대답한다면 나는 죽는 것에 동의하겠습니다. 만약 답이 틀리면 당신은 저와 결혼해야 할 것입니다."라고 덧붙입니다.

18 Turandot는 동이 트기 전에 답을 찾아야 하지만 그의 수수께끼는 그녀의 것만큼 어렵습니다.

19 그녀는 모두에게 "누군가 그의 이름을 알아낼 때까지 그 누구도 잠들 수 없다."라고 말합니다.

20 그리고 왕자는 이 오페라 전체에서 가장 유명한 아리아, Nessun Dorma를 부릅니다.

21 그것은 누구도 잠들지 못한다는 뜻입니다.

22 누구도 잠들지 못하네.

23 누구도 잠들지 못하네, 당신조차도, 공주여.

24 나의 비밀은 안전하다네.

25 누구도 나의 이름을 알지 못할 것이네.

26 동틀 녘에, 내가 이길 것이라네! 내가 승리할 것이라네!

27 왕자의 이름은 Calaf입니다.

28 공주는 그의 이름을 제때 알아낼 수 있을까요?

29 오페라를 보고 알아봅시다.

1 Turandot The Most Dangerous Love in the World

2 Welcome, everyone!

3 Tonight, we are going to perform Giacomo Puccini's opera Turandot.

4 Like many other famous operas, Turandot is in Italian because opera started in Italy in the 16th century.

5 Before we begin, I'd like to tell you the storyline of the opera Turandot.

6 You will appreciate it better if you know the story.

7 Turandot, a Chinese princess, is a woman of great beauty, but she is as cold as ice.

8 Any prince who wants to marry her must answer three riddles.

9 If he fails, he must die.

10 No one has ever been able to answer them.

11 One day, a brave prince falls in love with her at first sight.

12 He becomes the first man to answer all three riddles.

13 However, Turandot does not want to marry the prince.

14 He is nothing more than a stranger to her.

15 He then gives her a riddle of his own.

16 He asks her, "What is my name?"

17 He adds, "If you answer correctly, I will agree to die. If you answer incorrectly, you will have to marry me."

18 Turandot must find the answer before dawn, but his riddle is as difficult as hers.

19 She says to everyone, "No one will go to sleep until someone finds out his name."

20 The prince then sings the most famous aria of the whole opera, "Nessun Dorma."

21 It means no one sleeps.

22 No one sleeps.

23 No one sleeps, not even you, Princess.

24 My secret is safe.

25 No one will know my name.

26 At dawn, I will win! I will win!

27 The prince's name is Calaf.

28 Will the princess learn his name in time?

29 Let's watch the opera and find out.

4. I enjoyed its beautiful and moving songs.

5. The story was also as good as the songs.

6. If you are looking for a good musical movie, you should see this movie.

7. by Kim Jisu on Aug. 11

Write

1. Review of *Beauty and the Beast*

2. I saw *Beauty and the Beast* last Saturday.

3. It is about a beautiful girl and a beast.

4. I enjoyed it a lot.

5. The songs were great, and the love story was as beautiful as a gem.

6. If you like heart-warming stories about love, you will like it, too.

7. by Lee Minsu on Aug. 12

구석구석지문 TEST Step 1　　　　p.19

Link

1. How, our performance

2. amazing, seen, as great as, musical's

Write

1. Review of

2. saw, last Friday

3. is about, dreams, love

4. its beautiful, moving songs

5. was also as good as

6. are looking for, should see

7. by, on

Write

1. Review of

2. saw, last Saturday

3. beautiful girl, beast

4. it a lot

5. as beautiful as a gem

6. like heart-warming stories, will like, too

7. by, on Aug

구석구석지문 TEST Step 2　　　　p.20

Link

1. A: How was our performance?

2. B: It was amazing ! Actually, I've seen the musical *Cats* before, and your song was as great as the musical's.

Write

1. Review of *La La Land*

2. I saw *La La Land* last Friday.

3. It is about the dreams and love of Mia and Sebastian.

단어 TEST Step 1 p.21

01 초보자	02 해산물	03 실망한
04 점쟁이	05 혼자, 홀로	06 등
07 선호하다	08 반달	09 정책
10 문화	11 웃긴, 재미있는	12 육류, 고기
13 학자	14 정직함	15 전통의, 전통적인
16 상상의, 가상의	17 제안하다, 권하다	18 실내의
19 최근에	20 재료	21 추천하다
22 상징하다	23 신하, 하인	24 음식, 요리
25 화합, 조화	26 특별한	27 왕국
28 주문하다	29 모양	30 주로
31 신하, 관리, 공직자	32 다른	33 실외의
34 정치의, 정당의	35 세일 중	36 반면에
37 ~을 두려워하다	38 ~처럼 보이다	39 혼자서, 홀로
40 ~으로 뛰어들다	41 ~에 대해 걱정하다	
42 ~에 가 본 적이 있다		
43 ~의 이름을 따서 지어지다		

단어 TEST Step 2 p.22

01 traditional	02 culture	03 seafood
04 mainly	05 offer	06 official
07 different	08 servant	09 indoor
10 special	11 ingredient	12 alone
13 back	14 prefer	15 beginner
16 funny	17 political	18 fortune teller
19 half	20 disappointed	21 recommend
22 symbolize	23 harmony	24 policy
25 order	26 hit	27 honesty
28 half-moon	29 imaginary	30 scholar
31 kingdom	32 outdoor	33 party
34 recently	35 on sale	36 look like+명사
37 be afraid of	38 dive into	
39 on the other hand		40 by oneself
41 be named after		
42 be thinking of -ing		
43 become worried about		

단어 TEST Step 3 p.23

1 dessert, 후식   2 kingdom, 왕국
3 symbolize, 상징하다   4 imaginary, 상상의, 가상의
5 beginner, 초보자   6 prefer, 선호하다

7 ingredient, 재료   8 official, 관리, 신하
9 scholar, 학자   10 recommend, 추천하다
11 servant, 하인, 신하   12 culture, 문화
13 disappointed, 실망한   14 party, 정당
15 order, 주문하다   16 policy, 정책

대화문 TEST Step 1 p.24~25

Listen & Speak 1-A

1. anything, dessert / prefer, or / prefer / get, some
2. thinking of joining / prefer indoor or outdoor / prefer, last / Why don't you join / good idea

Listen & Speak 2-A

1. Excuse, looking for, recommend / have, cooked Italian / haven't, to try / how about, Italian, beginners, on sale / take
2. haven't seen, recently, recommend / Why don't you, big hit / action, recommend, comedies / how about / sounds

Listen & Speak B

recommend, for me / why don't you read

Communicate A

Have, been to / talking about / the one, about, ago, right / so, went, last / How was / ordered, different dishes, fried / recommend, for, tonight with / prefer, or / prefer seafood / should try, fried fish

Communicate B

Could you recommend, near / Do, prefer, or / prefer / try, at the end of

Progress Check

1. I'm thinking of getting / prefer, or / prefer, cute / give you one
2. looking for, recommend / What color, like / favorite colors / how about, on sale / take

대화문 TEST Step 2 p.26~27

Listen & Speak 1-A

1. B: Do you have anything for dessert, *Aunt May*?
   W: Yes, Johnny. Do you prefer pie or cake?
   B: I prefer cake.
   W: O.K. I have some chocolate cake. I'll get you some.
2. B: I'm thinking of joining a sports club.
   G: Do you prefer indoor or outdoor sports?
   B: I prefer indoor sports. I was in the badminton club last year.

G: Why don't you join the table tennis club, then?

B: That's a good idea. Thank you.

1. W: Excuse me. I'm looking for an Italian cookbook. Could you recommend one?

M: Well, have you ever cooked Italian food?

W: No, I haven't, but I want to try. I really like spaghetti.

M: Then, how about this Italian cookbook for beginners? It's on sale now.

W: Good! Thank you. I'll take it.

2. G: I haven't seen a movie recently. Could you recommend a good one?

B: Why don't you see *Iron Woman 2*? It's a big hit.

G: Well, I don't like action movies. Can you recommend any good comedies?

B: Then, how about *Funny Families*?

G: That sounds good.

A: Could you recommend a book for me?

B: Well, why don't you read *The Flying Pan*?

A: Great idea. Thanks.

Jaden: Have you been to the new Chinese restaurant, Ms. Park?

Ms. Park: Are you talking about the one on Main Street, Jaden?

Jaden: Yes, that's the one. They opened about two weeks ago, right?

Ms. Park: I think so. I went there last Friday with my friends.

Jaden: How was the food?

Ms. Park: It was great. We ordered many different dishes. I really liked the fried vegetables.

Jaden: Could you recommend a dish for me? I'm going there for dinner tonight with my family.

Ms. Park: Do you prefer seafood or meat?

Jaden: I prefer seafood.

Ms. Park: Then, you should try their fried fish. You'll love it!

M: Could you recommend a Korean restaurant near here?

W: Do you prefer hot or cold food?

M: I prefer cold food.

W: Then, you should try the naengmyeon place at the end of this block.

M: Thank you.

1. G: I'm thinking of getting a pet.

B: Do you prefer dogs or cats?

G: I prefer cats. They're so cute.

B: Great! I can give you one. I have seven cats at home.

G: Thank you.

2. W: Excuse me. I'm looking for a skirt. Could you recommend one?

M: What color do you like?

W: Blue and pink are my favorite colors.

M: Then, how about this blue one? It's on sale now.

W: Good! Thank you. I'll take it.

본문 TEST Step 1   p.28~29

01 Bite, Korean History   02 How, get, names

03 look like, half

04 There are, traditional food

05 Let's dive into

06 having, officials, something special

07 dish, colorful ingredients

08 Each, symbolized, political

09 that, in harmony like   10 was called

11 came from, policy

12 time, was, famous for

13 something wrong, afraid, telling

14 However, listened to   15 so, that, on

16 While, by himself, mainly   17 special pot, different

18 called, pot, in

19 because, like, imaginary, alone

20 time, last king

21 One, servants, strange

22 Something, written, back   23 like, full, half

24 fortune teller, What, mean

25 fortune, full, become smaller

26 On, other, grow bigger

27 became worried about

28 However, to, in, shape

29 Since then, have, shaped

본문 TEST Step 2   p.30~31

01 Bite, Korean History   02 How, get their names

03 Why, look like, half moon

04 There are, traditional food

05 dive into

06 was having dinner, officials, offered, something special

07 with four colorful ingredients

08 a different political party   09 in harmony like

10 was called   11 came from

12 was a scholar, was famous for

13 something wrong, was never afraid of telling

14 However, listened to   15 so, that

16 While, by himself   17 a special pot, together

18 called, the food in it

19 because, like, imaginary, lives alone

20 the last king

21 servants, a strange turtle

22 was written on its back

23 is like, full moon, is like, half moon

24 What, mean

25 fortune teller, become smaller

26 On the other hand, grow bigger, become, full moon

27 became worried about

28 However, in the shape of

29 Since then, have enjoyed, shaped rice cakes

---

20 백제의 마지막 왕 때였다.

21 어느 날, 왕과 신하들은 이상한 거북을 한 마리 발견했다.

22 그 거북의 등에 무언가가 쓰여 있었다.

23 그것은 "백제는 보름달과 같지만 신라는 반달과 같다."였다.

24 왕은 점술가에게 "이게 무슨 뜻인가?"라고 물었다.

25 점술가는 "보름달은 곧 작아질 것입니다.

26 반면에, 반달은 점점 커져서 보름달이 될 것입니다."라고 답했다.

27 왕은 자신의 왕국이 걱정되었다.

28 그러나 신라 사람들은 이것을 알고 매우 기뻐하며 반달 모양의 떡을 만들었다.

29 그 후로 사람들은 이 반달 모양의 떡인 송편을 즐겨 먹고 있다.

---

1 A Bite of Korean History

2 How did tangpyeongchae and sinseollo get their names?

3 Why does songpyeon look like a half moon?

4 There are many interesting stories about our traditional food.

5 Let's dive into the fun history of our food.

6 One day, King Yeongjo was having dinner with his officials and offered them something special.

7 It was a dish with four colorful ingredients.

8 Each ingredient symbolized a different political party.

9 Yeongjo wanted to say that the four parties should work in harmony like this dish.

10 This dish was called tangpyeongchae.

11 The name came from Yeongjo's policy tangpyeongchaek.

12 In the time of King Yeonsan, there was a scholar who was famous for his honesty.

13 When the king did something wrong, the scholar was never afraid of telling him so.

14 However, the king never listened to him.

15 The scholar was so disappointed that he went to live on a mountain.

16 While he lived there by himself, he mainly ate vegetables.

17 He made a special pot to cook many different vegetables together.

18 People called this pot and the food in it sinseollo.

19 That is because the scholar lived like a sinseon, an imaginary person who lives alone in nature.

20 It was the time of the last king of Baekje.

21 One day, the king and his servants found a strange turtle.

---

1 한국 역사 한 입

2 탕평채와 신선로는 어떻게 해서 그런 이름을 얻게 되었을까?

3 송편은 왜 반달 모양일까?

4 우리의 전통 음식에 대한 재미있는 이야기들이 많이 있다.

5 우리 음식의 재미있는 역사 속으로 들어가 보자.

6 어느 날, 영조가 그의 신하들과 저녁을 먹다가 그들에게 특별한 무언가를 권했다.

7 그것은 네 가지의 다채로운 재료로 만든 음식이었다.

8 각 재료는 서로 다른 당파를 상징했다.

9 영조는 이 음식처럼 네 당파가 화합을 이루어 일해야 한다는 것을 말하고 싶었다.

10 이 음식은 탕평채라고 불렸다.

11 그 이름은 영조의 정책인 탕평책에서 왔다.

12 연산군 시대에 정직하기로 유명한 한 학자가 있었다.

13 왕이 무언가를 잘못하면, 그 학자는 왕에게 그렇게 말하는 것을 절대 두려워하지 않았다.

14 그러나 왕은 그의 말에 전혀 귀 기울이지 않았다.

15 학자는 너무 실망하여 산속으로 살러 들어갔다.

16 그곳에서 혼자 사는 동안, 그는 주로 채소를 먹었다.

17 그는 여러 다양한 채소들을 함께 요리하기 위해 특별한 솥을 만들었다.

18 사람들은 이 솥과 그 안의 음식을 신선로라고 불렀다.

19 그것은 그 학자가 마치 자연 속에 홀로 사는 상상의 인물인 신선처럼 살았기 때문이다.

22 Something was written on its back.

23 It said, "Baekje is like a full moon, but Silla is like a half moon."

24 The king asked a fortune teller, "What does this mean?"

25 The fortune teller answered, "A full moon will soon become smaller.

26 On the other hand, a half moon will grow bigger and become a full moon."

27 The king became worried about his kingdom.

28 However, people of Silla were very happy to learn this and made rice cakes in the shape of a half moon.

29 Since then, people have enjoyed these half-moon shaped rice cakes, songpyeon.

구석구석지문 TEST Step 1 p.38

Work Together

1. Could you recommend
2. Do you prefer, or
3. prefer
4. Here you are
5. Thank

Write

1. Chocolate
2. something special
3. is made of, flour, nuts
4. a kind of
5. When, always think of
6. ago, fillings, decided to make
7. chance to remember

Culture Project

1. comes from, famous Chinese poet
2. During, to keep, for a long time
3. sweet and salty
4. Afterwards, or, became popular across

구석구석지문 TEST Step 2 p.39

Work Together

1. A: Could you recommend a salad for me?
2. B: We have two salads today. Do you prefer chicken salad or green salad?
3. A: I prefer green salad.
4. B: O.K. Here you are .
5. A: Thank you.

Write

1. Chocolate Songpyeon
2. My family eats something special on Chuseok.
3. It is made of rice flour, chocolate, and nuts.
4. It is a kind of tteok.
5. When I eat this food, I always think of my little brother.
6. Three years ago, he ate all the fillings for songpyeon, so we decided to make chocolate songpyeon.
7. This food gives us a chance to remember that funny day.

Culture Project

1. The word *dongporou* comes from the name of the famous Chinese poet Su Dongpo.
2. During his time in Hangzhou, he invented a way to keep pork fresh for a long time.
3. He made the pork sweet and salty.
4. Afterwards, dongporou or dongpo pork became popular across China.

14 daytime, 낮　15 electricity, 전기
16 charity, 자선, 자선단체

단어 TEST Step 1　　　　　　　　　　　p.40

01 단 하나의	02 주요한; 우두머리, 부장	
03 어둠, 암흑	04 퍼지다	05 전기
06 재단	07 놀이공원	08 대규모 정전 사태
09 주거지, 쉼터	10 불가능한	11 천장
12 널리, 폭넓게	13 구부리다, 휘다	14 자선단체
15 설치하다	16 외치다	17 발명하다
18 흔들다, 털다	19 마법의, 신기한	20 남은 음식
21 전체의	22 표백제	23 충분한
24 꽉 들어찬	25 인기 있는	26 놀랍게도
27 남아 있다	28 지붕	29 안전한
30 마을	31 작동하다	32 구하다
33 더 적은	34 놀라운	35 지불하다
36 최소한, 적어도	37 ~을 환하게 밝히다	
38 더 이상 ~ 않다	39 ~할 것을 잊다	40 (소리 등을) 높이다
41 ~ 덕분에	42 ~을 생각해 내다, ~을 만들어 내다	
43 ~와 꼭 마찬가지로		

단어 TEST Step 2　　　　　　　　　　　p.41

01 bend	02 ceiling	03 shake
04 charity	05 darkness	06 difficult
07 whole	08 blackout	09 widely
10 leftover	11 chief	12 less
13 impossible	14 shout	15 electricity
16 single	17 work	18 save
19 amusement park		20 foundation
21 roof	22 magic	23 shelter
24 village	25 popular	26 install
27 remain	28 safe	29 last
30 surprisingly	31 bleach	32 packed
33 enough	34 invent	35 light up
36 thanks to	37 not ~ anymore	
38 dry off	39 pay for	40 forget to부정사
41 come up with	42 turn up	43 fill A with B

단어 TEST Step 3　　　　　　　　　　　p.42

1 last, 지속되다　2 village, 마을　3 roof, 지붕
4 leftover, 남은 음식　5 blackout, 정전　6 save, 구하다
7 ceiling, 천장　8 popular, 인기 있는　9 lamp, 램프, 등
10 spread, 퍼지다　11 invent, 발명하다
12 bleach, 표백제　13 install, 설치하다

대화문 TEST Step 1　　　　　　　　　　　p.43~44

Listen & Speak 1-A

1. turn up / turn it up anymore, highest / Let, put, I've heard, works like / What an interesting idea, Let's
2. I've heard, is coming / right, favorite actress / played, chief scientist / can't wait to see

Listen & Speak 2-A

1. finished, meal / good / want to take, leftovers / please / Don't forget to eat
2. your plan for, winter break / I'm going to, with my parents / sounds exciting, going to do / going to go, amusement / to try all kinds / Don't forget to try

Communicate A

What's wrong / difficult / have to / a way to save / I've heard that, can save, by using less / I've heard that, too, stop using paper cups / can also use, to dry off / impossible, at least / shake, before, more than enough / try, next time / don't forget to shake, at least, times

Communicate B

I've heard, saving electricity, best way to save / heard that, too, save electricity / Why don't, turn off, when / Don't forget, turn off, when, leave

Progress Check

1. I've heard that, is coming / my favorite player / not going to, surprise
2. plan for, winter break / to visit, with / sounds exciting, going / spend, beach, seafood / Don't forget to try / won't forget

대화문 TEST Step 2　　　　　　　　　　　p.45~46

Listen & Speak 1-A

1. G: Can you turn up the volume on your phone? I like this song.
   B: I can't turn it up anymore. It's the highest volume.
   G: Let me just put your phone in a glass. I've heard a glass works like a speaker.
   B: What an interesting idea! Let's try it now.
2. B: I've heard that a movie star is coming to our school.

G: That's right. She's my favorite actress.

B: Oh, who is she?

G: Miranda Kim. She played the chief scientist in the movie *Jupiter*.

B: Wow, I can't wait to see her!

1. W: Excuse me, are you finished with your meal?

M: Yes, it was really good.

W: Do you want to take the leftovers home?

M: Yes, please.

W: Don't forget to eat the leftovers by tomorrow.

2. B: What's your plan for this winter break?

G: I'm going to visit Hong Kong with my parents.

B: That sounds exciting. What are you going to do there?

G: I'm going to go to an amusement park. I'm also going to try all kinds of food.

B: Good. Don't forget to try some dim sum.

Yuri: What's wrong, Jaden?

Jaden: My science homework is too difficult.

Yuri: What do you have to do?

Jaden: I need to find a way to save trees.

Yuri: That's easy. I've heard that we can save trees by using less paper.

Jaden: Oh, I think I've heard that, too. Then, I can just stop using paper cups.

Yuri: Yes! You can also use just one paper towel to dry off your hands.

Jaden: That's impossible. I need at least two or three paper towels.

Yuri: Just shake your hands before you use a paper towel. Then, one will be more than enough.

Jaden: Oh, that's a good idea, Yuri! I'll try that next time.

Yuri: Good! Just don't forget to shake your hands at least 10 times.

A: I've heard that saving electricity is the best way to save the Earth.

B: I've heard that, too. What can we do to save electricity?

A: Why don't we turn off the light when we're not using it?

B: That's a good idea. Don't forget to turn off the light when you leave your room.

1. B: I've heard that a famous baseball player is coming to our school.

G: That's right. He's my favorite player.

B: Oh, who is he?

G: I'm not going to tell you. It's a surprise!

2. B: What's your plan for this winter break?

G: I'm going to visit Vietnam with my parents.

B: That sounds exciting. What are you going to do there?

G: I'm going to spend some time on the beach and eat lots of seafood.

B: Good. Don't forget to try the fruit there, too.

G: O.K., I won't forget.

01 One-Dollar, Lamps   02 read, shouted, village

03 electricity, like, other, village

04 too, to pay

05 during, daytime, because, packed

06 things, because of, single

07 light up, without using

08 called, because, invented by

09 there were, blackouts

10 come, with, way, light

11 made for, lasts, about

12 also, safe   13 never start, fire

14 Surprisingly, easy, make

15 How, make, from   16 Fill, clear, with

17 Add, to keep, clear

18 roof, push, into, hole 19 Let, third, remain above

20 is bent, spreads around

21 in, widely used by   22 charity, local, how, install

23 Thanks to, thousands of

24 has, made, other, such

25 light up, for, years

01 One-Dollar Magic

02 shouted, in the Philippines

03 has no electricity, all the other houses

04 too, to pay for electricity

05 during, because, are packed close together

06 are changing because of

07 in the ceiling, light up, without using

08 is called, because, was invented by

09 were many blackouts

10 come up with, way to light

11 be made for, lasts for about

12 very safe   13 never start

14 to make   15 How to make

16 Fill, with

17 Add, bleach to keep, clear

18 push, into   19 a third, remain above

20 is bent by, spreads around

21 are widely used

22 The charity, how to make, install

23 Thanks to, thousands of

24 has, made, other countries, such as

25 light up, for many years to come

본문 TEST Step 3   p.51~52

1 1달러짜리 마법의 전구

2 "우와, 이젠 제 방에서 책을 읽을 수 있어요!" 필리핀의 한 마을에 사는 소년인 Marco가 외쳤다.

3 그의 집은 마을의 다른 모든 집들과 마찬가지로 전기가 없다.

4 마을 사람들은 너무나 가난해서 전기세를 낼 수가 없다.

5 심지어 낮 동안에도, 집들이 빽빽하게 들어차 있어서 그들은 어둠 속에 살아간다.

6 이제 플라스틱병 하나 때문에 상황이 바뀌고 있다.

7 천장에 있는 플라스틱병 하나는 전기를 쓰지 않고 방 전체를 밝힐 수 있다.

8 이 놀라운 플라스틱병은 Moser 램프라고 불리는데, 그것이 Alfredo Moser에 의해 발명되었기 때문이다.

9 2002년, 브라질에 있는 그의 마을에는 정전이 잦았다.

10 이 정전들은 그가 집을 밝히는 새로운 방법을 생각해 내도록 만들었다.

11 Moser 램프는 1달러 정도로 만들 수 있고 10년 정도 지속된다.

12 그것은 또한 매우 안전하다.

13 그것은 절대 집에 불을 낼 수 없다.

14 놀랍게도, 이 신기한 램프를 만드는 것은 매우 쉽다.

15 병으로 Moser 램프를 만드는 법

16 1. 투명한 플라스틱병에 물을 채운다.

17 2. 물을 깨끗이 유지하기 위해 표백제를 조금 넣는다.

18 3. 지붕에 구멍을 내고, 병을 구멍 안으로 넣는다.

19 4. 병의 3분의 1은 지붕 위에 남아 있도록 한다.

20 5. 햇빛이 병 속의 물에 의해 굴절되어 방에 퍼진다.

21 필리핀에서 Moser 램프는 My Shelter 재단에 의해 널리 사용된다.

22 또한 그 자선단체는 지역 사람들에게 램프를 만들고 설치하는 법을 가르친다.

23 이 자선단체 덕분에, 필리핀의 수천 가구가 이제 Moser 램프를 갖고 있다.

24 그 단체는 아르헨티나, 인도, 피지와 같은 다른 나라들에서도 Moser 램프가 유명해 지도록 만들었다.

25 Moser 램프는 앞으로 오랫동안 많은 사람들의 삶을 밝혀 줄 것이다.

본문 TEST Step 4~Step 5   p.53~56

1 One-Dollar Magic Lamps

2 "Wow, I can read a book in my room now!" shouted Marco, a boy in a village in the Philippines.

3 His house has no electricity just like all the other houses in the village.

4 People in the village are too poor to pay for electricity.

5 Even during the daytime, they live in darkness because the houses are packed close together.

6 Now things are changing because of a single plastic bottle.

7 One plastic bottle in the ceiling can light up a whole room without using any electricity.

8 This amazing plastic bottle is called a Moser lamp because it was invented by Alfredo Moser.

9 In 2002, there were many blackouts in his town in Brazil.

10 These blackouts made him come up with a new way to light his house.

11 A Moser lamp can be made for about one dollar and lasts for about 10 years.

12 It is also very safe.

13 It can never start a house fire.

14 Surprisingly, it is very easy to make this magic lamp.

15 How to make a Moser lamp from a bottle

16 1. Fill a clear plastic bottle with water.

17 2. Add some bleach to keep the water clear.

18 3. Make a hole in the roof, and push the bottle into the hole.

19 4. Let a third of the bottle remain above the roof.

20 5. Sunlight is bent by the water in the bottle and spreads around the room.

21 In the Philippines, Moser lamps are widely used by the My Shelter Foundation.

22 The charity also teaches local people how to make and install the lamps.

23 Thanks to the charity, thousands of homes in the Philippines now have Moser lamps.

24 It has also made Moser lamps popular in other countries, such as Argentina, India, and Fiji.

25 Moser lamps will light up the lives of many people for many years to come.

구석구석지문 TEST Step 1 p.57

Link-Share

1. make the lamp brighter
2. out of, another lamp
3. All the other steps
4. learned that, brighter than

Write

1. a lot of, with
2. can even make
3. fill half of, put, into
4. close, all of the sides
5. Finally, it, for about
6. is ready
7. make you happ

Culture Project-Share

1. like to talk
2. keeps food fresh
3. It, to make
4. put, inside
5. pour, between
6. let, dry off, cool

Culture Project-Share

1. We'd like to talk about a pot-in-pot cooler.
2. It keeps food fresh without electricity.
3. It 's very easy to make one.
4. First, put a pot inside a larger pot.
5. Then, pour sand and water between these pots.
6. Just let the water dry off, and it'll cool the food.

구석구석지문 TEST Step 2 p.58

Link-Share

1. We thought we could make the lamp brighter with a glass bottle.
2. We made one lamp out of a plastic bottle and another lamp out of a glass bottle.
3. All the other steps were the same.
4. We learned that the glass bottle lamp was brighter than the plastic bottle lamp.

Write

1. You can make a lot of things with a CD case.
2. You can even make a grass container.
3. First, fill half of the CD case with soil and water, and put grass seeds into the soil.
4. Second, close the case and tape all of the sides.
5. Finally, leave it in the sun for about ten days.
6. Now, your grass container is ready.
7. It will make you happy when the grass grows.

단어 TEST Step 1   p.59

01 (개가) 짖다	02 갈라지다, 금이 가다	
03 외치다	04 굉장한, 엄청난	05 도달하다, 닿다
06 썰매	07 릴레이 경주, 계주	08 특별한
09 기념하다, 축하하다		10 조부모님 댁
11 구하다	12 가슴 따뜻한	13 눈보라
14 실외의	15 구히다, 구조하다	
16 (사람들 사이로) 퍼지다		17 대략
18 얼어붙은	19 인기 있는	
20 경주하다, 달리다; 경주, 질주		
21 선두 개, 우두머리 개		22 가다, 이동하다
23 손녀, 외손녀	24 미끄러지다	25 코스, 흔적
26 방송	27 하이라이트, 가장 흥미로운 부분	
28 언어	29 우리	
30 발생하다, 일어나다		31 약
32 질병, 병, 질환	33 폭설	34 끔찍한
35 한 달에 한 번	36 개최되다, 일어나다	
37 곧바로, 즉시	38 계속하다	
39 ~에 참여[참가]하다		
40 ~을 기념[추모]하여		41 계속 ~하다
42 반드시 ~하다	43 ~가 되다	

단어 TEST Step 2   p.60

01 awesome	02 bark	03 heavy snow
04 crack	05 disease	06 language
07 slip	08 snowstorm	09 terrible
10 neck	11 frozen	12 happen
13 around	14 heart-warming	15 trail
16 race	17 celebrate	18 reach
19 spread	20 rescue	21 broadcast
22 cage	23 sled	24 medicine
25 outdoor	26 popular	27 save
28 shout	29 special	30 climb
31 live	32 go sledding	33 lead dog
34 granddaughter		35 take part in
36 in memory of	37 right away	38 keep -ing
39 take place	40 at least	
41 be interested in		42 once a month
43 go on a trip		

단어 TEST Step 3   p.61

1 snowstorm, 눈보라   2 terrible, 끔찍한

3 spread, 퍼지다   4 take place, 개최되다, 일어나다

5 race, 경주   6 trail, 흔적, 코스   7 continue, 계속하다

8 cage, 우리   9 rescue, 구하다   10 medicine, 약

11 slip, 미끄러지다   12 reach, 도달하다   13 sled, 썰매

14 disease, 질병   15 crack, 금이 가다, 갈라지다

16 relay, 릴레이 경주, 계주

대화문 TEST Step 1   p.62~63

Listen & Speak 1-A

1. What, doing / listening to / do you like / I'm not interested in, to sing, grandma's favorite songs / what a nice

2. Are you interested in watching, be sure to watch, live broadcasts, every night, enjoy, highlights, the most interesting

Listen & Speak 2-A

1. favorite / sometimes go swimming / How often, go swimming / Not very often, go swimming once a month

2. any special plans / going to play table tennis / How often, play / Every weekend, playing, How about / like playing, enjoy outdoor

Communicate A

special plans, winter break / to go, grandparents' place, go skating, sledding, winter sports / Good for, favorite / never played, I'm interested in learning, to play / how to play / awesome, the most popular / Everyone, loves, playing / How often, when / at least, three times / I'm sure, good at, can't wait to learn

Communicate B

What winter sport, interested in / interested in ice skating / How often do / once, twice a month

Progress Check

1. are, doing / practicing badminton / playing / not interested in, to pass, next week / Good luck

2. favorite / listen to / How often, listen to / Almost every day

3. It's, to show, How often, tell, that

대화문 TEST Step 2   p.64~65

Listen & Speak 1-A

1. B: What are you doing?

G: I'm listening to old pop songs.

B: Oh, do you like old pop songs?

G: No, I'm not interested in them. I just want to sing my grandma's favorite songs at her birthday party next week.

B: Wow, what a nice granddaughter!

2. M: Are you interested in watching the Winter Olympics? Then, be sure to watch MBS Sports to enjoy our live broadcasts from 6 p.m. to 11 p.m. At 11 p.m. every night , you can also enjoy our highlights of the most interesting games of the day.

Listen & Speak 2-A

1. G: What's your favorite sport, James?

B: I don't like sports much, but I sometimes go swimming.

G: How often do you go swimming?

B: Not very often. I only go swimming once a month.

2. B: Do you have any special plans for this weekend, Hana?

G: Well, I'm going to play table tennis with my dad and brother.

B: How often do you play?

G: Every weekend. I love playing table tennis. How about you?

B: I like playing soccer. I enjoy outdoor sports.

Communicate A

Anna: Do you have any special plans for the winter break?

Suho: I'm going to go to my grandparents' place in Pyeongchang. I'll go skating and sledding there. I love winter sports.

Anna: Good for you! I love winter sports, too. My favorite is ice hockey.

Suho: Oh, I've never played ice hockey, but I'm interested in learning how to play it.

Anna: Really? I can teach you how to play.

Suho: That's awesome. Is ice hockey the most popular sport in Canada?

Anna: Yes, it is. Everyone I know loves watching it and playing it.

Suho: How often did you play ice hockey when you were in Canada?

Anna: I played at least two or three times a week in the winter.

Suho: Wow, I'm sure you're really good at ice hockey. I can't wait to learn from you.

Communicate B

A: What winter sport are you interested in?

B: I'm interested in ice skating.

A: How often do you go ice skating?

B: I go once or twice a month.

Progress Check

1. B: What are you doing?

G: I'm practicing badminton.

B: Do you like playing badminton?

G: No, I'm not interested in it. I just want to pass the badminton test next week.

B: O.K. Good luck!

2. G: What's your favorite TV show, Jason?

B: I don't watch TV, but I listen to the radio.

G: How often do you listen to the radio?

B: Almost every day.

3. M: It's important to show your love for the people around you. How often do you tell everyone in your family that you love them?

본문 TEST Step 1   p.66~67

01 The Most Heart-Warming

02 early, biggest, takes place

03 It is called   04 Around, to, part

05 has, cover, from

06 take, than, through snowstorms

07 in memory, saved   08 cold, terrible, happened

09 got, kept spreading

10 needed, right away, any

11 had to, from

12 Because, heavy, way, medicine

13 race, began   14 Twenty-one, in, relay

15 On, others, at, points

16 of, 20th team   17 strongest, made, lead

18 finally, so, that, own   19 However, stay, trail

20 crossing, frozen, stopped

21 saw, cracking   22 whole, because, just

23 reached, final, sleeping

24 told, continue on

25 Here's, medicine, shouted

26 On, arrived in   27 was saved

28 is, celebrated, biggest sled

본문 TEST Step 2   p.68~69

01 Most Heart-Warming

02 every year, biggest sled dog, takes place

03 It is called　　　04 Around, take part in

05 has to cover, from, to

06 take more than, race through snowstorms

07 in memory of　　　08 a terrible thing happened

09 got, sick, kept spreading

10 right away, did not have any

11 had to get it

12 Because of, to get the medicine

13 the race to Nome　　14 in the relay

15 the others, at different points

16 of the 20th team

17 strongest dog, made, his lead dog

18 so, that, could not

19 However, able to stay on the trail

20 frozen, suddenly stopped

21 cracking　　　22 was saved, just in time

23 reached　　　24 to continue on

25 Here's, medicine, shouted

26 On, arrived in

27 was saved

28 is now celebrated, the biggest sled dog race

---

1 가장 가슴 따뜻한 겨울 스포츠

2 매년 3월 초에 알래스카(Alaska)에서는 세계 최대의 개썰매 경주가 열린다.

3 그것은 아이디타로드 개썰매 경주(Iditarod Trail Sled Dog Race)라고 불린다.

4 12~16마리 개로 구성된 80여 팀이 이 경주에 참여한다.

5 각 팀은 앵커리지(Anchorage)에서 놈(Nome)까지 약 1,800 km를 달려야 한다.

6 이 경주는 2주 이상 걸릴 수 있으며, 팀들은 종종 눈보라를 뚫고 경주한다.

7 아이디타로드 경주는 놈을 구한 개들을 기념하여 1973년에 시작되었다.

8 1925년의 어느 추운 겨울날, 놈 마을에서는 끔찍한 일이 일어났다.

9 몇몇 아이들이 매우 아팠고 병이 계속 퍼졌다.

10 놈의 사람들은 당장 약이 필요했지만 마을에는 약이 하나도 없었다.

11 누군가는 앵커리지에 있는 병원에서 약을 가져와야 했다.

12 폭설 때문에 개썰매 릴레이가 앵커리지에서 놈으로 약을 가져오는 유일한 방법이었다.

13 곧, 놈으로 향하는 질주가 시작되었다.

14 21개의 개 팀이 릴레이에 참여했다.

---

15 1월 27일에 첫 번째 팀이 출발했고, 나머지 팀들은 서로 다른 지점에서 기다렸다.

16 Gunnar는 20번째 팀의 몰이꾼이었다.

17 그의 팀에서 가장 강한 개는 Balto였기 때문에, 그는 Balto를 그의 선두 개로 삼았다.

18 Gunnar와 Balto가 마침내 약을 받았을 때, 눈발이 너무 거세서 Gunnar는 자신의 손조차도 볼 수 없었다.

19 그러나, Balto는 코스를 제대로 따라갈 수 있었다.

20 그들이 얼어붙은 강을 건너고 있을 때 Balto는 갑자기 멈췄다.

21 그때, Gunnar는 강의 얼음이 갈라지는 것을 보았다.

22 Balto가 바로 제때 멈췄기 때문에 팀 전체가 목숨을 구할 수 있었다.

23 Balto와 Gunnar가 마지막 팀에 다다랐을 때, 그들은 자고 있었다.

24 Gunnar는 Balto에게 계속 가라고 말했다.

25 "여기 약이 있습니다, 의사 선생님!"이라고 Gunnar가 소리쳤다.

26 2월 2일에 Gunnar와 그의 팀은 마침내 놈에 도착했다.

27 놈 마을 사람들은 목숨을 구할 수 있었다.

28 이 가슴 따뜻한 이야기는 세계에서 가장 큰 개썰매 경주인 아이디타로드 경주를 통해 오늘날 매년 기념되고 있다.

---

1 The Most Heart-Warming Winter Sport

2 In early March every year, the world's biggest sled dog race takes place in Alaska.

3 It is called the Iditarod Trail Sled Dog Race.

4 Around 80 teams of 12 to 16 dogs take part in this race.

5 Each team has to cover about 1,800 km from Anchorage to Nome.

6 The race can take more than two weeks, and the teams often race through snowstorms.

7 The Iditarod Race began in 1973 in memory of the dogs that saved Nome.

8 One cold winter day in 1925, a terrible thing happened in Nome.

9 Some children got very sick, and the disease kept spreading.

10 The people of Nome needed medicine right away, but the town did not have any.

11 Someone had to get it from a hospital in Anchorage.

12 Because of the heavy snow, a dog sled relay was the only way to get the medicine from Anchorage to Nome.

13 Soon, the race to Nome began.

14 Twenty-one dog teams were in the relay.

15 On January 27, the first team left, and the others waited at different points.

16 Gunnar was the driver of the 20th team.

17 The strongest dog on his team was Balto, so he made Balto his lead dog.

18 When Gunnar and Balto finally got the medicine, the snow was so heavy that Gunnar could not see his own hands.

19 However, Balto was able to stay on the trail.

20 When they were crossing a frozen river, Balto suddenly stopped.

21 Then, Gunnar saw the river ice cracking.

22 The whole team was saved because Balto stopped just in time.

23 When Balto and Gunnar reached the final team, they were sleeping.

24 Gunnar told Balto to continue on.

25 "Here's the medicine, Doctor!" shouted Gunnar.

26 On February 2, Gunnar and his team finally arrived in Nome.

27 The town was saved.

28 This heart-warming story is now celebrated every year by the Iditarod Race, the biggest sled dog race in the world.

Link-Share

1. Are you interested in learning the history of the marathon?

2. The first marathon was run by Pheidippides in 490 B.C.

3. The Greek army in Marathon ordered him to tell the people of Athens about their victory.

4. He ran 40 km from Marathon to Athens.

Write

1. One cold winter day, a man left home to get wood for a fire.

2. He slipped and broke his neck.

3. He could not move, but no one was near him.

4. His dog came to his rescue.

5. She barked and barked for 19 hours.

6. A neighbor finally heard the dog barking and called 911.

Culture Project-Share

1. Every winter, you can see many people jumping into the sea at Haeundae Beach.

2. It's a way of wishing for good health in the New Year.

Link-Share

1. Are, interested in learning

2. was run by, B.C

3. ordered him to tell

4. ran, from, to

Write

1. left, to get wood

2. slipped, broke his neck

3. not move, no one, near

4. came to his rescue

5. barked and barked for

6. heard the dog barking, called

Culture Project-Share

1. Every winter, see many people jumping

2. a way of wishing

MEMO

MEMO

MEMO

적중 **100** + 특별부록

Plan B

우리학교 최신기출

미래 · 최연희 교과서를 배우는

학교 시험문제 분석 · 모음 · 해설집

전국단위 학교 시험문제 수집 및 분석
출제 빈도가 높은 문제 위주로 선별
문제 풀이에 필요한 상세한 해설

중2-2
영어

미래 · 최연희

◎ 선택형 문항의 답안은 컴퓨터용 수정 싸인펜을 사용하여 OMR 답안지에 바르게 표기하시오.

◎ 서술형 문제는 답을 답안지에 반드시 검정 볼펜으로 쓰시오.

◎ 총 29문항 100점 만점입니다. 문항별 배점은 각 문항에 표시되어 있습니다.

[전북 ○○중]

01 다음 중 국가와 언어의 관계가 <u>어색한</u> 것은? (3점)

① German – Germany

② Vietnam – Vietnamese

③ Thailand – Thai

④ Spain – Spanish

⑤ France – French

[경북 ○○중]

02 다음 대화의 문맥상 자연스럽지 <u>않은</u> 것은? (4점)

Anna: Dad, guess what! I have no school next Monday.

Dad: Really? Why not?

Anna: ⓐIt's our school's 75th anniversary.

Dad: Oh, I see.

Anna: Can we do something together that day?

Dad: ⓑI guess I can take the afternoon off. What do you want to do?

Anna: ⓒWhy don't we go see a musical at Bravo Theater near your work? We can get a discount if we go on a Monday.

Dad: Good idea! Then, let's just meet at the theater.

Anna: O.K. What time shall we meet?

Dad: ⓓHow about 12? Then, we can have lunch together, too. The new Chinese restaurant opened about two weeks ago. Do you prefer seafood or meat?

Anna: ⓔI like meat more than seafood.

Dad: Then, we should try their fried fish.

Anna: You're the best, Dad!

① ⓐ ② ⓑ ③ ⓒ ④ ⓓ ⑤ ⓔ

[충북 ○○중]

03 다음 대화의 밑줄 친 (A)에 들어갈 영어 표현으로 알맞은 것은? (3점)

B: Mom, I (A)시험에서 한 문제만 틀렸어요!

W: Great! I was sure you would do well. Why don't we go out to celebrate tonight?

B: Yes! Can we have pizza for dinner?

W: Of course, Joe. I'll call your dad.

① only get one exam wrong on question

② only got one exam wrong on question

③ get only one question on the exam wrong

④ got only one question wrong on the exam

⑤ took only one question wrong on the exam

[서울 양천구 ○○중]

04 다음 대화의 흐름상 빈칸에 들어갈 가장 적절한 속담은? (4점)

Minsu: I'm so worried about my English project. I have to make a presentation file and memorize my script. I have a lot to do but I haven't started yet.

Junho: Why don't you think about the topic first? You know the *proverb, "_____ _____" I'm sure you can do it well if you start to do the first step.

*proverb: 속담

① What's learned in the cradle is carried to the grave.

② A man is known by the company he keeps.

③ A fool and his money are soon departed.

④ Children should be seen and not heard.

⑤ Well begun is half done.

[5~6] 다음 대화를 읽고 물음에 답하시오.

Anna: Dad, guess what! I have no school next Wednesday.

Dad: Really? Why not?

Anna: It's our school's 75th anniversary.

Dad: Oh, I see.

Anna: Can we do something together that day?

Dad: I guess I can take the afternoon off. What do you want to do?

Anna: Why don't we go see a musical at Bravo Theater near your work? We can get a discount if we go on a Wednesday.

Dad: Good idea, Anna! Then, let's just meet at the theater.

Anna: O.K. (A)_____

Dad: How about 12? Then, we can have lunch together, too.

Anna: You're the best, Dad!

05 위 대화의 내용과 일치하는 것은? (3점)

① Anna's Dad is 75 years old.

② There is a theater near Dad's work.

③ Anna can get a discount on tickets on weekend.

④ Anna has to go to school next Wednesday.

⑤ Anna's Dad will have lunch by himself next Wednesday.

06 위 대화의 빈칸 (A)에 들어갈 말로 가장 알맞은 것은? (4점)

① Where did we meet?

② What time did we meet?

③ What time shall we meet?

④ What are we going to do?

⑤ Where are we going to go?

07 다음 대화의 밑줄 친 부분과 바꿔 쓸 수 있는 것을 <u>모두</u> 고르시오. (4점)

A: What shall we do at the park?

B: <u>Let's see a magic show</u>.

A: That's a good idea.

① Shall we see a magic show?

② Are you going to see a magic show?

③ Why don't we see a magic show?

④ When does the magic show begin?

⑤ What about seeing a magic show?

08 What are the speakers going to take? (3점)

A: Liz, hurry up. It's already 6 o'clock.

B: Oh, we're going to be late for the concert.

A: Why don't we take the subway? The subway will be faster than the bus at this time of day.

B: That's a good idea.

① bus   ② taxi   ③ bike

④ subway   ⑤ airplane

09 다음 중 어법상 <u>어색한</u> 문장은? (4점)

① If you miss the bus, you'll be late for school.

② If you exercise every day, you will become healthy.

③ I can finish the work if you help me.

④ If it will rain tomorrow, I will stay at home.

⑤ If she does not hurry up, she will miss the train.

10 다음 ⓐ~ⓔ 중 어법상 옳은 것만을 있는 대로 고른 것은? (3점)

> ⓐ Tom is not so tall as his elder brother.
> ⓑ Unless you won't hurry up, you will be late.
> ⓒ You won't be on time if you will miss the bus.
> ⓓ If it will be fine tomorrow, I'll go on a picnic.
> ⓔ My grandmother is 90, but she's as fit as a fiddle.

① ⓐ, ⓑ   ② ⓐ, ⓔ

③ ⓑ, ⓒ   ④ ⓑ, ⓒ, ⓔ

⑤ ⓒ, ⓓ, ⓔ

11 다음 중 어법상 올바른 문장은? (3점)

① If it rains tomorrow, I will not play soccer.

② This winter is as colder as last winter.

③ The window broken by the storm.

④ Rome was not build in a day.

⑤ I couldn't find new anything in the room.

[12~13] 다음 글을 읽고 물음에 답하시오.

Turandot, a Chinese princess, is a woman of great beauty, but she is as cold as ice. (A) Any prince who wants to marry her must answer three riddles. If he fails, he must die. No one has ever been able to answer them. (B) One day, a brave prince falls in love with her at first sight. He becomes the first man to answer all three riddles.

However, Turandot does not want to marry the prince. (C) He then gives her a riddle of his own. He asks her, "What is my name?" He adds, "If you answer correctly, I will agree to die. If you answer incorrectly, you will have to marry me." (D)

Turandot must find the answer before dawn, but his riddle is as difficult as hers. She says to everyone, "No one will go to sleep until someone finds out his name." (E)

The prince then sings the most famous aria of the whole opera, "Nessun Dorma." It means no one sleeps.

12 위 글의 내용으로 보아 답할 수 <u>없는</u> 것은? (4점)

① What are the riddles of princess?

② Which country is Turandot from?

③ What does "Nessun Dorma" mean?

④ Who sings "Nessun Dorma" in the opera?

⑤ How many riddles does the prince answer?

13 위 글의 (A)~(E) 중 문맥상 주어진 문장이 들어가기에 가장 적절한 곳은? (3점)

> He is nothing more than a stranger to her.

① (A)   ② (B)   ③ (C)

④ (D)   ⑤ (E)

[14~17] 다음 글을 읽고 물음에 답하시오.

Turandot, a Chinese princess, is a woman of great beauty, but (가)그녀는 얼음처럼 차갑다. (A) If he fails, he must die. No one has ever been able to answer them. (B) One day, a brave prince falls in love with her at first sight. (C) He becomes the first man to answer all three riddles.
(나)_____, Turandot does not want to marry the prince. (D) He is nothing more than a stranger to her. (E) He then gives her a riddle of his own. He asks her, "What is my name?" He adds, "If you answer correctly, I will agree to die. If you answer incorrectly, you will have to marry me."

14 위 글의 (A)~(E) 중에 다음 문장이 들어가기에 가장 알맞은 곳은? (3점)

> Any prince who wants to marry her must answer three riddles.

① (A) ② (B) ③ (C) ④ (D) ⑤ (E)

15 위 글의 빈칸 (나)에 들어갈 말로 가장 알맞은 것은? (4점)

① So ② Therefore ③ Then
④ Since ⑤ However

16 위 글의 밑줄 친 (가)의 우리말과 같은 뜻이 되도록 다음 단어들을 배열할 때 다섯 번째 올 단어는? (3점)

> 보기
> as / cold / is / she / as / ice

① as ② is ③ ice
④ she ⑤ cold

17 위 글의 내용과 일치하지 <u>않는</u> 것은? (4점)

① Turandot는 굉장히 아름답다.
② 세 가지 수수께끼를 모두 답하지 못하면 죽게 된다.
③ Turandot는 어떤 용감한 왕자에게 반한다.
④ 수수께끼를 모두 맞힌 첫 번째 사람이 나온다.
⑤ 왕자는 자신이 수수께끼를 Turandot에게 낸다.

[18~19] 다음 글을 읽고 물음에 답하시오.

Welcome, everyone! Tonight, we are going to perform Giacomo Puccini's opera Turandot. Like many other famous operas, Turandot is in Italian (A)_____ opera started in Italy in the 16th century. Before we begin, I'd like to tell you the storyline of the opera Turandot. You will (B)_____ it better if you know the story.

18 위 글의 빈칸 (A)에 들어갈 말로 가장 적절한 것은? (3점)

① because ② before ③ but
④ so ⑤ or

19 위 글의 빈칸 (B)와 다음 두 예문의 빈칸 (C), (D)에 공통으로 적절한 한 단어를 쓰시오. (4점)

> • Background knowledge will help you to (C)_____ the musical.
> • Thanks for coming. I (D)_____ it.

→ _____

[20~22] 다음 글을 읽고 물음에 답하시오.

Welcome, everyone! Tonight, we are going to perform Giacomo Puccini's opera *Turandot*. Like many other famous operas, Turandot is in Italian because opera started in Italy in the 16th century. Before we begin, I'd like to tell you the storyline of the opera *Turandot*. You will appreciate it better (A)<u>if</u> you know the story.

20 위 글의 밑줄 친 (A)와 쓰임이 <u>다른</u> 것은? (3점)

① I don't know <u>if</u> she will come or not.

② I can finish the work <u>if</u> you help me.

③ <u>If</u> school finishes early, I will go see a movie.

④ <u>If</u> you exercise every day, you will stay healthy.

⑤ <u>If</u> it is sunny tomorrow, we can go on a picnic.

21 위 글을 읽고 대답할 수 있는 질문은? (4점)

① What is the lesson of the opera *Turandot*?

② What is the storyline of the opera *Turandot*?

③ Why are many famous operas in Italian?

④ When did the opera *Turandot* first begin?

⑤ Which country people usually sing the opera *Turandot*?

22 위 글에 이어질 내용으로 가장 적절한 것은? (3점)

① History of opera

② Performance etiquette

③ Introduction of singers

④ Life of Giacomo Puccini

⑤ Storyline of the opera *Turandot*

[23~24] 다음 글을 읽고 물음에 답하시오.

However, Turandot does not want to marry the prince. He is ⓐ<u>nothing</u> more than a stranger to her. He then gives her a riddle of his own. He asks her, "What is my name?" He ⓑ<u>adds</u>, "If you answer correctly, I will agree to die. If you answer ⓒ<u>incorrectly</u>, you will have to marry me."
Turandot must find the answer before dawn, but his riddle is as ⓓ<u>easy</u> as hers. She says to everyone, "No one will go to sleep ⓔ<u>until</u> someone finds out his name."
The prince then sings the most famous aria of the whole opera, "Nessun Dorma." It means no one sleeps.

No one sleeps.
No one sleeps, not even you, Princess.
…
My secret is safe.
No one will know my name.
…
At dawn, I will win! I will win!

23 위 글의 흐름상 ⓐ~ⓔ 중 낱말의 쓰임이 적절하지 <u>않은</u> 것은? (3점)

① ⓐ   ② ⓑ   ③ ⓒ   ④ ⓓ   ⑤ ⓔ

24 "Nessun Dorma"에서 나타난 the prince의 심경으로 가장 적절한 것은? (4점)

① angry   ② bored

③ hopeful   ④ scared

⑤ disappointed

[25~29] 다음 글을 읽고 물음에 답하시오.

Welcome, everyone! Tonight, we are going to perform Puccini's opera *Turandot*. Like many other famous operas, *Turandot* is in Italian because opera started in Italy in the 16th century. Before we begin, I'd like to tell you the storyline of the opera *Turandot*. You will appreciate it better if you know the story.

Turandot, a Chinese princess, is a woman of great beauty, but she is as cold as ice. Anyone who wants to marry her must answer three riddles. If he fails, he must die. No one has ever been able to answer them. One day, a brave prince falls in love with her at first sight. He becomes the first man to answer all the three riddles.

However, Turandot does not want to marry the prince. He is nothing more than a stranger to her. He then gives her his riddle. He asks her, "What is my name?" He adds, "If you answer correctly, I will agree to die. If you answer incorrectly, you will have to marry me."

Turandot must find the answer before dawn. She says to everyone. "No one will go to sleep until someone finds out his name."

(A)_____ Let's watch the opera and find out.

25 위 글의 제목으로 적절한 것은? (4점)

① The Most Dangerous Love in the World
② Cold as Ice
③ The History of Italian Operas
④ No More Love
⑤ Incorrect Answers

26 위 글의 첫 번째 문단의 내용과 일치하지 <u>않는</u> 것은? (3점)

① Turandot는 이탈리아어로 되어 있다.
② Puccini가 Turandot의 작곡자이다.
③ 오페라는 16세기에 처음 등장했다.
④ 이탈리아어로 된 오페라가 많다.
⑤ Turandot는 줄거리가 복잡하다.

27 위 글의 두 번째 문단의 내용과 일치하지 <u>않는</u> 것은? (4점)

① Turandot is a name of a princess.
② Turandot is a beautiful woman from China.
③ Anyone has to answer three riddles to marry Turandot.
④ No one could answer all the riddles before the prince.
⑤ Turandot has to solve the prince's riddle before the night comes.

28 위 글의 흐름상 (A)에 어울리지 <u>않는</u> 것은? (3점)

① Will the prince find her name on time?
② Will people be able to go to sleep?
③ Will the prince marry her or die?
④ Will the prince and the princess marry?
⑤ Will the princess find the correct answer?

29 위 글의 내용과 일치하는 문장을 아래와 같이 만들고자 한다. 빈칸에 들어갈 것은? (3점)

> The prince _____ the princess should marry him if she doesn't find out his name.

① wanted to learn that
② couldn't sleep because
③ had no idea that
④ gave no signal to the princess that
⑤ suggested that

◎ 선택형 문항의 답안은 컴퓨터용 수정 싸인펜을 사용하여 OMR 답안지에 바르게 표기하시오.
◎ 서술형 문제는 답을 답안지에 반드시 검정 볼펜으로 쓰시오.
◎ 총 26문항 100점 만점입니다. 문항별 배점은 각 문항에 표시되어 있습니다.

[충북 ○○중]

01 다음 글의 ⓐ~ⓔ를 우리말로 <u>어색하게</u> 해석한 것은? (3점)

Welcome, everyone! Tonight, we are going to ⓐperform Giacomo Puccini's opera *Turandot*. Like many other famous operas, *Turandot* is in ⓑItalian because opera started in Italy in the 16th ⓒcentury. Before we begin, I'd like to tell you the ⓓstoryline of the opera *Turandot*. You will ⓔappreciate it better if you know the story.

① ⓐ: 공연하다
② ⓑ: 이탈리아어
③ ⓒ: 세기
④ ⓓ: 주제
⑤ ⓔ: 감상하다

[경기 ○○중]

02 A 다음에 ⓐ~ⓔ를 배열하여 두 사람의 대화로 만들 때, 네 번째로 올 것은? (4점)

A: Dad, guess what! I have no school next Wednesday.

ⓐ Oh, I see.
ⓑ Really? Why not?
ⓒ I guess I can take the afternoon off. What do you want to do?
ⓓ Because it's our school's 75th anniversary.
ⓔ Can we do something together that day?

A: Shall we go see a musical at Bravo Theater? We can get a discount if we go on a Wednesday.

① ⓐ   ② ⓑ   ③ ⓒ   ④ ⓓ   ⑤ ⓔ

[경기 ○○중]

03 다음 대화의 빈칸에 들어갈 말로 가장 적절한 것은? (4점)

Kevin: Judy, let's practice our parts for the school play today.
Judy: O.K. _____
Kevin: How about 4 o'clock, right after school?
Judy: Sounds good.

① What time shall we meet?
② Where shall we play at 4 o'clock?
③ What will you do for the school play?
④ Where shall we meet right after school?
⑤ Why didn't you practice your part yesterday?

[전북 ○○중]

04 다음 대화 중 <u>어색한</u> 것은? (4점)

① A: Does Jenny prefer beef or pork?
   B: She prefers pork.
② A: Why don't we go out to celebrate tonight?
   B: I'll get you some tonight.
③ A: Where shall we play?
   B: How about at the park near your place?
④ A: Do you like soccer better than baseball?
   B: Yes, I like soccer more than baseball.
⑤ A: Could you recommend a movie for me?
   B: Well, why don't you watch *Harry Potter*?

05 다음 대화를 읽고 의미상 가장 <u>어색한</u> 표현을 쓰는 사람을 고르면? (4점)

Alex: The movie was very exciting. I like the main character. He was as strong as an ox on the screen.

Jenny: Yes, I think so. He was also as brave as coal.

Emma: How about the main actress? I think she was as cold as ice.

Jason: But she finally helped the main character. I think she was as wise as an owl.

Maria: Her action was very excellent, too. I think she looked cold, but she was as gentle as a lamb on the inside.

① Alex   ② Jenny   ③ Emma
④ Jason   ⑤ Maria

06 다음 대화의 내용과 <u>다른</u> 것은? (4점)

B: It's very hot today. Let's go swimming, Julie.

G: Good idea! Where shall we meet?

B: How about at the subway station near my place?

G: O.K. See you there at 11 o'clock.

① Today is very hot.
② The boy wants to go swimming with Julie.
③ The boy and Julie are going to meet at the subway station.
④ The boy's house is near the subway station.
⑤ The boy and Julie will meet at 12 o'clock.

[7~8] 다음 대화를 읽고 물음에 답하시오.

Anna: Dad, guess what! I have no school next Wednesday.

Dad: Really? Why not?

Anna: It's our school's 75th anniversary.

Dad: Oh, I see.

Anna: Can we do something together that day?

Dad: I guess I can take the afternoon off. What do you want to do? (A)

Anna: Let's go see a musical at Bravo Theater near your work. We can get a discount if we go on a Wednesday. (B)

Dad: Good idea, Anna! Then, let's just meet at the theater. (C)

Anna: O.K. (D)

Dad: How about 12? Then, we can have lunch together, too. (E)

Anna: You're the best, Dad!

07 위 대화의 (A)~(E) 중 다음 문장이 들어가기에 가장 알맞은 곳은? (4점)

What time shall we meet?

① (A)   ② (B)   ③ (C)   ④ (D)   ⑤ (E)

08 위 대화를 읽고, 답할 수 <u>없는</u> 질문은? (4점)

① Why does Anna have no school next Wednesday?
② Where is Bravo Theater?
③ What are Anna and her dad going to eat for lunch?
④ What are Anna and her dad going to do next Wednesday?
⑤ Where will Anna meet her dad next Wednesday?

[9~10] 다음 대화를 읽고 물음에 답하시오.

Anna: Dad, guess what! I have no school next Wednesday.
Dad: Really? Why not?
Anna: It's our school's 75th anniversary.
Dad: Oh, I see.
Anna: Can we do something together that day?
Dad: I guess I can take the afternoon (A)_____. What do you want to do?
Anna: Why don't we go see a musical (B)_____ Bravo Theater near your work? We can get a discount if we go (C)_____ a Wednesday.
Dad: Good idea. Anna! Then, let's just meet at the theater.
Anna: O.K. What time shall we meet?
Dad: How about 12? Then, we can have lunch together, too.
Anna: You're the best, Dad!

09 위 대화의 빈칸 (A), (B), (C)에 각각 들어갈 말로 적절한 것은?
(4점)

	(A)	(B)	(C)
①	off	for	on
②	off	at	in
③	off	at	on
④	on	at	in
⑤	on	for	on

10 위 대화의 내용과 일치하지 <u>않는</u> 것은? (4점)

① Next Wednesday is the 75th anniversary of Anna's school.
② Every Wednesday, the musical ticket is free.
③ Bravo Theater is not far from the father's office.
④ Anna and her dad are going to have lunch together.
⑤ Anna thought of going to a musical with her dad and he also liked it.

11 어법상 맞는 것을 <u>모두</u> 고른 것은? (4점)

Ⓐ They do not work as hard as we do.
Ⓑ If the weather is fine, I will go hiking.
Ⓒ I speak English as good as a native speaker.
Ⓓ If you don't get up early, you will see the sunrise.
Ⓔ If he exercises every day, you will become healthy.
Ⓕ Your trip to Rome will be more interesting if you know the history of Italy.

① Ⓐ, Ⓑ, Ⓕ
② Ⓐ, Ⓒ, Ⓔ
③ Ⓑ, Ⓔ, Ⓕ
④ Ⓐ, Ⓑ, Ⓔ, Ⓕ
⑤ Ⓐ, Ⓒ, Ⓔ, Ⓕ

12 다음 표의 내용과 일치하는 것은? (4점)

Name	Andy	Bobby	Clara
Age	15	15	13
English speaking score	90	100	100
100m speed	12 seconds	13 seconds	12 seconds

① Andy is as old as Clara.
② Bobby is as fast as Andy.
③ Clara can run as fast as Andy.
④ Andy can speak English as well as Clara.
⑤ Clara cannot speak English as well as Bobby.

13 다음 정보를 보고, 주어진 문장을 8 단어의 완전한 영어 문장으로 옮기시오. (4점)

the bus	the taxi
60km/h	60km/h

• 버스는 택시만큼 빠르다.

→ _____

[14~15] 다음 글을 읽고 물음에 답하시오.

Turandot, a Chinese princess, is a woman of great beauty, but she is as cold as ice. Any prince who wants to marry her must answer three riddles. If he fails, he must die. No one has ever been able to answer them. One day, a brave prince falls in love with her at first sight. He becomes the first man to answer all three riddles.
ⓐHowever, Turandot does not want to marry the prince. He is nothing more than a ⓑstranger to her. He then gives her a riddle of his ⓒown. He asks her, "What is my name?" He adds, "If you answer ⓓcorrectly, I will agree to die. If you answer incorrectly, you will have to marry me."
Turandot must find the answer before dawn, but his riddle is as ⓔeasy as hers. She says to everyone, "No one will go to s

14 위 글의 내용과 일치하는 것은? (4점)

① Turandot는 매우 부유한 중국의 공주다.
② Turandot는 용감한 왕자에게 첫눈에 반한다.
③ 왕자는 세 가지 중 첫 번째 수수께끼에만 답했다.
④ Turandot는 왕자의 수수께끼에 답하지 못하면 죽어야 한다.
⑤ Turandot는 동이 트기 전에 왕자의 수수께끼의 답을 찾아야 한다.

15 위 글의 ⓐ~ⓔ 중 글의 흐름상 낱말의 쓰임이 적절하지 않은 것은? (3점)

① ⓐ   ② ⓑ   ③ ⓒ   ④ ⓓ   ⑤ ⓔ

[16~17] 다음 글을 읽고 물음에 답하시오.

Welcome, everyone! Tonight, we are going to perform Giacomo Puccini's opera *Turandot*. Like many other famous operas, *Turandot* is in Italian (A)_____ opera started in Italy in the 16th century. (B)_____ we begin, I'd like to tell you the storyline of the opera *Turandot*. You will appreciate it better (C)_____ you know the story.

16 위 글의 빈칸 (A)~(C)에 들어갈 말을 바르게 짝지은 것은? (4점)

	(A)	(B)	(C)
①	if	When	while
②	when	After	if
③	because	Before	if
④	because	After	when
⑤	while	Before	when

17 위 글의 내용과 다음의 진술이 일치하면 T, 일치하지 않으면 F로 나타낼 때, 빈칸 (A)~(C)에 들어갈 말을 바르게 짝지은 것은? (4점)

• Many famous operas are in Italian. (A)____
• *Turandot* was composed by Giacomo Puccini. (B)____
• Giacomo Puccini will perform the opera *Turandot*. (C)____

	(A)	(B)	(C)
①	T	F	T
②	T	T	F
③	T	F	F
④	F	T	T
⑤	F	F	T

[18~19] 다음 글을 읽고 물음에 답하시오.

I'd like to tell you the storyline of the opera *Turandot*. You will ⓐunderline{appreciate} it better if you know the story.

Turandot is a beautiful Chinese princess, but she doesn't want to get married. Any prince who wants to marry her must answer three ⓑ<u>riddles</u>. If he fails, he must die. No one has ever been able to answer them. One day, a brave prince falls in love with her at first sight. He becomes the first man to answer all three riddles.

However, Turandot does not want to marry the prince. He is nothing more than a ⓒ<u>stranger</u> to her. He then gives her a riddle of his own. He asks her, "What is my name?" He adds, (A)"<u>If you answer correctly, I will agree to die. If you answer incorrectly, you will have to marry me.</u>"

Turandot must find the answer before ⓓ<u>dawn</u>, but his riddle is too difficult for her. She says to everyone, "No one will go to sleep until someone finds out his name." The prince then sings the most famous ⓔ<u>aria</u> of the whole opera, "Nessun Dorma." It means no one sleeps.

18 위 글의 문맥상 ⓐ~ⓔ의 영어 뜻풀이가 바른 것은? (4점)

① ⓐ appreciate: to thank for something that somebody has done

② ⓑ riddle: a question that is very confusing and has a humorous or clever answer

③ ⓒ stranger: someone who hates you and wants to harm you

④ ⓓ dawn: the early part of the night and the time to go to bed

⑤ ⓔ aria: a soft gentle song that is sung to make children go to sleep

19 위 글의 흐름상 (A)와 바꾸어 쓸 수 있는 것은? (4점)

① If you don't find out my name, you must die.

② If you find out my name, you must marry me.

③ If you don't find out my name, I'll agree to die.

④ If you find out my name, you don't have to marry me.

⑤ If you don't find out my name, you don't have to marry me.

[20~21] 다음 글을 읽고 물음에 답하시오.

Welcome. everyone! Tonight, we are going to ⓐ<u>perform</u> Giacomo Puccini's opera *Turandot*. ⓑ<u>Like</u> many other famous operas, Turandot is (A)_____ ⓒ<u>Italian</u> because opera started (A)_____ Italy in the 16th ⓓ<u>century</u>. Before we begin, I'd like to tell you the ⓔ<u>storyline</u> of the opera *Turandot*.

20 위 글의 흐름상 밑줄 친 단어의 우리말 뜻이 <u>어색한</u> 것은?(4점)

① ⓐ perform: 공연하다

② ⓑ like: ~처럼

③ ⓒ Italian: 이탈리아어

④ ⓓ century: 10년

⑤ ⓔ storyline: 줄거리

21 위 글의 흐름상 빈칸 (A)에 공통으로 들어갈 가장 알맞은 것은? (4점)

① for   ② on   ③ in

④ from   ⑤ by

[22~24] 다음 글을 읽고 물음에 답하시오.

Welcome, everyone! Tonight, we are going to ⓐ<u>performing</u> Giacomo Puccini's opera *Turandot*. Like many other famous operas, *Turandot* is in ㉮<u>Italian</u> because opera started in Italy in the 16th century. Before we begin, I'd like to tell you the storyline of the opera *Turandot*. You will appreciate it better if you ⓑ<u>will</u> know the story. Turandot, a Chinese princess, is a woman of great ⓒ<u>beautiful</u>, but she is as ⓓ<u>colder</u> as ice. Any prince who ⓔ<u>want</u> to marry her must ⓕ<u>answers</u> three riddles. If he ⓖ<u>fail</u>, he must die. No one ⓗ<u>has</u> ever been able to answer ⓘ<u>it</u>. One day, a brave prince ⓙ<u>falls</u> in love with her at first sight. He becomes the first man to answer all three riddles.

22 위 글의 내용과 일치하는 것은? (4점)

① Turandot likes to perform Giacomo Puccini's opera.
② The prince becomes the first man to fall in love with the princess.
③ Turandot is a Chinese princess who lived in Italy in the 16th century.
④ Knowing the storyline of the opera helps us to appreciate the opera a lot.
⑤ If a prince wants to marry Turandot, he has to solve three riddles that the king makes.

23 위 글의 ⓐ~ⓙ 중 어법상 어색한 것의 개수는? (4점)

① 4개   ② 5개   ③ 6개
④ 7개   ⑤ 8개

24 위 글의 ㉮Italian과 밑줄 친 부분의 의미가 같은 것은? (3점)

① David can count up to 10 in <u>Italian</u>.
② Ms. Lee loves <u>Italian</u> music and culture.
③ We can eat <u>Italian</u> food or Chinese food.
④ The star of the show was a young <u>Italian</u> singer.
⑤ I have been thinking of him as an <u>Italian</u> for years.

25 다음 글을 읽고 알 수 없는 것은? (4점)

Review of *La La Land*
I saw *La La Land* last Friday. It is about the dreams and love of Mia and Sebastian. I enjoyed its beautiful and moving songs. The story was also as good as the songs. If you are looking for a good musical movie, you should see this movie.
by Kim Jisu on Aug. 11

① 뮤지컬 영화를 보게 된 이유
② 라라랜드의 줄거리
③ 라라랜드를 본 요일
④ 라라랜드 주인공들의 이름
⑤ 뮤지컬 영화의 제목

26 다음 글의 내용과 가장 일치하는 것은? (3점)

However, Turandot does not want to marry the prince. He is nothing more than a stranger to her. He then gives her a riddle of his own. He asks her, "What is my name?"

① 투란도트는 왕자와 결혼하고 싶었다.
② 왕자와 공주는 그전부터 알던 사이였다.
③ 왕자는 투란도트에게 수수께끼를 내었다.
④ 투란도트는 왕자에게 수수께끼를 내었다.
⑤ 투란도트는 왕자의 이름을 알고 있다.

반 이름		점수

문항수 : 선택형(27문항) 서술형(2문항)

20 . . .

◎ 선택형 문항의 답안은 컴퓨터용 수정 싸인펜을 사용
하여 OMR 답안지에 바르게 표기하시오.
◎ 서술형 문제는 답을 답안지에 반드시 검정 볼펜으
로 쓰시오.
◎ 총 29문항 100점 만점입니다. 문항별 배점은 각
문항에 표시되어 있습니다.

[전북 ○○중]

01 다음 영영풀이에 해당하는 단어를 고르면?   (4점)

someone who is employed to work at
another person's home, for example as a
cleaner or a gardener

① servant   ② fortune teller
③ tutor   ④ scholar
⑤ official

[서울 동작구 ○○중]

02 다음 문장의 빈칸에 들어갈 알맞은 것을 고르면?   (3점)

I helped him many times, but now I don't
like him. Yesterday, I found his pencil but he
didn't _____ say 'Thank you' to me.

① less   ② have to
③ even   ④ suddenly
⑤ since

[대전 ○○중]

03 다음 대화의 빈칸에 들어갈 말로 알맞은 것은?   (3점)

J: Which animal do you prefer, cats or dogs?
L: _____

① I like cats better than dogs.
② You prefer cats to dogs, too!
③ My sister prefers dogs to cats.
④ This cat is as big as my hand.
⑤ What are these dogs eating right now?

[서울 송파구 ○○중]

04 다음 대화의 빈칸에 공통으로 들어갈 말로 알맞은 것은? (3점)

A: Do you have anything for dessert, Aunt
   May?
B: Yes, Johnny. Do you _____ pie or
   cake?
A: I _____ cake.
B: O.K. I have some chocolate cake. I'll get
   you some.

① prefer   ② get   ③ buy
④ think   ⑤ give

[충북 ○○중]

05 다음 대화의 흐름에 맞게 ⓐ~ⓓ를 바르게 배열한 것은? (4점)

B: I'm thinking of joining a sports club.
ⓐ: I prefer indoor sports. I was in the
    badminton club last year.
ⓑ: Do you prefer indoor or outdoor sports?
ⓒ: That's a good idea. Thank you.
ⓓ: Why don't you join the table tennis club,
    then?

① ⓐ-ⓑ-ⓒ-ⓓ   ② ⓐ-ⓓ-ⓑ-ⓒ
③ ⓑ-ⓐ-ⓓ-ⓒ   ④ ⓑ-ⓓ-ⓒ-ⓐ
⑤ ⓐ-ⓒ-ⓑ-ⓓ

[전북 ○○중]

06 다음 빈칸에 들어갈 알맞은 것은?   (3점)

• Sujin likes April better than _____.

① spring   ② Wednesday   ③ July
④ afternoon   ⑤ breakfast

07 다음 대화의 내용과 일치하지 <u>않는</u> 것은? (3점)

> A: Have you been to the new Chinese restaurant, Ms. Park?
> B: Are you talking about the one on Main Street, Jaden?
> A: Yes, that's the one. They opened about three weeks ago, right?
> B: I think so. I went there last Friday with my friends.
> A: How was the food?
> B: It was great. We ordered many different dishes, I really liked the fried vegetables.
> A: Could you recommend a dish for me? I'm going there for dinner tonight with my family.
> B: Do you prefer seafood or meat?
> A: I prefer meat.
> B: Then, you should try their fried meat. You'll love it!

① 약 3주 전에 신장개업한 중국 식당은 Main가에 있다.

② Ms. Park은 친척들과 중국 식당에 갔다.

③ Ms. Park은 Jaden에게 fried meat를 추천해준다.

④ Ms. Park은 fried vegetables를 맛있게 먹었다.

⑤ Jaden은 오늘밤 중국 식당에 갈 예정이다.

08 다음 대화에서 B가 가입할 동아리는? (3점)

> B: I'm thinking of joining a sports club.
> G: Do you prefer indoor or outdoor sports?
> B: I prefer indoor sports. I was in the badminton club last year.
> G: Why don't you join the table tennis club, then?
> B: That's a good idea. Thank you.

① 배드민턴   ② 탁구   ③ 배구

④ 테니스   ⑤ 농구

09 다음 대화를 아래와 같이 요약하고자 할 때, 빈칸 (A), (B)에 들어갈 말로 가장 적절한 것은? (4점)

> Girl: I haven't seen a movie recently. Could you recommend a good one?
> Boy: Why don't you see *Iron Woman 2*? It's a big hit.
> Girl: Well, I don't like action movies. Can you recommend any good comedies?
> Boy: Then, how about *Funny Families*?
> Girl: That sounds good.

> The girl has not (A)_____ any movies recently, and she asks the boy to recommend a good movie for her. She wants to see a good (B)_____ because she doesn't like action movies.

	(A)	(B)
①	gone to	horror
②	gone to	romance
③	seen	animation
④	seen	comedy
⑤	watched	animation

10 다음 대화가 끝난 후 일어날 일로 가장 적절한 것은? (4점)

> W: Excuse me. I'm looking for a skirt. Could you recommend one?
> M: What color do you like?
> W: Blue and pink are my favorite colors.
> M: Then, how about this blue one? It's on sale now.
> W: Good! Thank you! I will take it.

① The man will recommend a skirt.

② The woman will buy a new skirt.

③ The woman will try on a pink skirt.

④ The woman will go to another store.

⑤ The man will try to find a blue shirt.

[11~12] 다음 대화를 읽고 물음에 답하시오.

> Jaden: Have you been to the new Chinese restaurant, Ms. Park?
>
> Ms. Park: Are you talking about the one on Main Street, Jaden?
>
> Jaden: Yes, that's the one. They opened about two weeks ago, right?
>
> Ms. Park: I think so. I went there last Friday with my friends.
>
> Jaden: How was the food?
>
> Ms. Park: It was great. We ordered many different dishes. I really liked the fried vegetables.
>
> Jaden: Could you (A)추천하다 a dish for me? I'm going there for dinner tonight with my family.
>
> Ms. Park: Do you prefer seafood or meat?
>
> Jaden: I prefer seafood.
>
> Ms. Park: Then, you should try their fried fish. You'll love it!

11 위 대화를 읽고 박 선생님이 좋아한 음식과 Jaden에게 추천할 음식을 차례로 바르게 연결한 것은? (3점)

① 해산물 – 육류
② 야채튀김 – 생선튀김
③ 해산물 – 생선튀김
④ 야채튀김 – 육류
⑤ 해산물 – 육류

12 위 대화의 밑줄 친 (A)의 우리말과 같은 뜻으로 적절한 것은? (3점)

① cook
② symbolize
③ recommend
④ correct
⑤ perform

13 다음 중 문장 전환이 적절하게 된 것은? (4점)

① My dad is cooking dinner.
  = Dinner is being cooking by my dad.
② Many children read this book.
  = This book is read by many children.
③ My sister lookcd after my cats.
  = My cats were looked by my sister after.
④ Thomas Edison invented the light bulb.
  = The light bulb invented Thomas Edison.
⑤ Some children built sand castles on the beach.
  = Sand castles are built by some children on the beach.

14 다음 문장에서 'cold'가 들어갈 위치로 알맞은 것은? (3점)

> • Can (A) I (B) have (C) something (D) to (E) drink?

① (A)
② (B)
③ (C)
④ (D)
⑤ (E)

15 다음 중 어법상 바른 문장은? (4점)

① Was the room cleaned by her?
② Minsu didn't sent the letter last month.
③ The National Museum of Korea built in 1945.
④ My grandmother was planted these flowers.
⑤ The singer of the year was choosen by online voters.

[16~18] 다음 글을 읽고 물음에 답하시오.

How did tangpyeongchae and sinseollo get their names? Why does songpyeon ⓐlooked like a half moon? There are many interesting stories about our traditional food. Let's dive into the fun history of our food.

Tangpyeongchae

One day, King Yeongjo ⓑwas having dinner with his officials and offered them ⓒspecial something. It was a dish with four colorful ingredients. ⓓEach ingredients symbolized a different political party. Yeongjo wanted to say that the four parties should work in harmony like this dish. This dish ⓔwere called tangpyeongchae. The name came from Yeongjo's policy tangpyeongchaek.

16 위 글의 밑줄 친 ⓐ~ⓔ 중 어법상 적절한 것은? (4점)

① ⓐ　　② ⓑ　　③ ⓒ　　④ ⓓ　　⑤ ⓔ

17 위 글의 내용과 일치하지 <u>않는</u> 것은? (3점)

① 탕평채라는 이름은 영조의 정책인 탕평책에서 왔다.
② 영조의 한 신하가 영조에게 특별한 음식을 대접했다.
③ 탕평채는 네 가지의 다채로운 재료로 만든 음식이다.
④ 우리의 전통 음식에 대한 재미있는 이야기들이 많이 있다.
⑤ 탕평채는 네 당파가 화합을 이루어 일해야 한다는 것을 의미했다.

18 다음 중 제시된 단어와 설명이 알맞게 짝지어진 것은? (3점)

① official – a person specialized in a study
② mysterious – to represent with a symbol
③ symbolize – difficult to understand; unknown
④ imaginary – thinking something that is not real
⑤ scholar – someone who holds a position of authority

[19~20] 다음 글을 읽고 물음에 답하시오.

It was the time of the last king of Baekje. One day, the king and his servants found a strange turtle. Something was written on its back. It said, "Baekje is like a full moon, but Silla is like a half moon."
The king asked a fortune teller, "What does this mean?"
The fortune teller answered, "A full moon will soon become smaller. On the other hand, a half moon will grow bigger and become a full moon."
The king became worried about his kingdom. However, people of Silla were very happy to learn this and made rice cakes in the shape of a half moon. Since then, people have enjoyed these half-moon shaped rice cakes, songpyeon.

19 위 글의 제목으로 가장 알맞은 것은? (4점)

① What is Songpyeon?
② How to make traditional rice cakes
③ The scientific symbols of the moon
④ The history of traditional food: Songpyeon
⑤ The importance of knowing Korean history

20 위 글의 내용과 일치하는 것은? (3점)

① The last king of Baekje was a brave man.
② The king told people the future of Baekje.
③ The turtle wrote something on the ground.
④ Songpyeon is a full-moon shaped rice cake.
⑤ The turtle was found by the king and his servants.

[21~22] 다음 글을 읽고 물음에 답하시오.

It was the time of the last king of Baekje. (A)[One day / Some day], the king and his servants found a strange turtle. Something was written on its back. It said, "Baekje is like a full moon, but Silla is like a half moon."

The king asked a fortune teller, "What does this mean?"

The fortune teller answered, "A full moon will soon become smaller. (B)[At last / On the other hand], a half moon will grow bigger and become a full moon."

The king became worried about his kingdom. (C)[However / For example], people of Silla were very happy to learn this and made rice cakes in the shape of a half moon. Since then, people have enjoyed these half-moon shaped rice cakes, songpyeon.

21 위 글의 괄호 (A), (B), (C) 안에서 어법에 맞는 표현으로 가장 적절한 것은? (4점)

(A)　　　　　(B)　　　　　(C)

① Some day – On the other hand – However

② One day – At last – For example

③ Some day – On the other hand – For example

④ Some day – At last – However

⑤ One day – On the other hand – However

22 위 글을 읽고 답할 수 <u>없는</u> 질문은? (3점)

① What was written on the turtle's back?

② Who made Songpyeon?

③ Why were people of Silla very happy?

④ Who explained something written on a strange turtle?

⑤ Why did Silla look like a new moon?

[23~24] 다음 글을 읽고 물음에 답하시오.

Sinseollo

In the time of King Yeonsan, there was a scholar who was famous for his ⓐhonest. When the king did something wrong, the scholar was never afraid of ⓑtell him so. (A)_____, the king never listened to him. The scholar was so ⓒ disappointing that he went to live on a mountain. While he lived there by ⓓherself, he mainly ate vegetables. He made a special pot to cook many different vegetables together. People ⓔwas called this pot and the food in it sinseollo. That is because the scholar lived like a sinseon, an imaginary person who lives alone in nature.

23 위 글의 (A)에 들어갈 알맞은 말은? (4점)

① So　　　② However　　　③ But

④ And　　　⑤ Fortunately

24 위 글의 ⓐ~ⓔ 부분을 바르게 고친 것 중 <u>어색한</u> 것은? (3점)

① ⓐ honest → honesty

② ⓑ tell → telling

③ ⓒ disappointing → disappointed

④ ⓓ herself → himself

⑤ ⓔ was called → were called

25 다음 주어진 우리말과 일치하도록, 수동태 문장을 능동태로 바꿔 쓰시오. (4점)

・그 개는 그 고양이를 잡았다.
= The cat was caught by the dog.

→ _____

[26~27] 다음 글을 읽고 물음에 답하시오.

(A) One day, King Yeongjo was having dinner with his officials and gave something to ⓐthem. It was a dish with four colorful ingredients. Each ingredient symbolized a different political ⓑparty. Yeongjo wanted to say that the four parties should work in harmony like this dish. This dish was called tangpyeongchae. The name came from Yeongjo's policy tnagpyeongchaek.

(B) It was the time of the last king of Baekje. One day, the king and his servants found a turtle with ⓒ이상한 무언가 which was written on its back. It said, "Baekje is like a full moon, but Silla is like a half moon."

The king asked a fortune teller, "What does ⓓthis mean?"

The fortune teller answered, "A full moon will soon become smaller. On the other hand, a half moon will grow bigger and become a full moon."

The king became worried about his kingdom. ⓔ_____, people of Silla were very happy to learn this and made rice cakes in the shape of a half moon. Since then, people have enjoyed these half-moon shaped rice cakes, songpyeon.

27 위 글의 ⓐ~ⓔ에 대한 설명으로 옳은 것은? (3점)

① ⓐ 'them'은 'his officials'를 가리킨다.

② ⓑ 'party'의 뜻은 "Can you come to my birthday party?"에서의 뜻과 같다.

③ ⓒ '이상한 무언가'는 'strange something'으로 쓴다.

④ ⓓ 'this'는 '거북이 등에 쓰인 문구에 대한 점술가의 해석'을 의미한다.

⑤ ⓔ에는 글의 흐름상 'Suddenly'를 쓸 수 있다.

[28~29] 다음 글을 읽고 물음에 답하시오.

Sinseollo

In the time of King Yeonsan, there was a scholar who was famous for his honesty. When the king did something wrong, the scholar was never afraid of telling him so. (A)_____, the king never listened to him. (B)The scholar was disappointed enough to go to live on a mountain. While he lived there alone, he mainly ate vegetables. He made a special pot to cook many different vegetables together. People called this pot and the food in it the sinseollo. That is because the scholar lived like a sinseon, an imaginary person who lives alone in nature.

28 위 글의 빈칸 (A)에 들어갈 접속사로 알맞은 것은? (4점)

① Otherwise ② However ③ If

④ Though ⑤ Although

26 위 글의 (A), (B)의 공통된 제목으로 가장 알맞은 것은? (3점)

① Cooking Colorful Dishes

② Symbols of Korean Culture

③ A King Made a Special Food

④ Historical Stories of Some Dishes

⑤ Traditional Food with Different Ingredients

29 위 글의 밑줄 친 (B)와 같은 의미가 되도록 "so ~ that ..." 구문을 이용하여 주어와 동사를 갖춘 완전한 문장으로 어법에 맞게 영작하시오. (4점)

→ _____

◎ 선택형 문항의 답안은 컴퓨터용 수정 싸인펜을 사용하여 OMR 답안지에 바르게 표기하시오.
◎ 서술형 문제는 답을 답안지에 반드시 검정 볼펜으로 쓰시오.
◎ 총 31문항 100점 만점입니다. 문항별 배점은 각 문항에 표시되어 있습니다.

[전북 ○○중]

01 다음 빈칸에 들어가기에 <u>어색한</u> 것은? (3점)

• Do you prefer pizza or _____?

① lunch
② chicken
③ hamburgers
④ ramen
⑤ pasta

[충북 ○○중]

02 다음 중 반대말이 <u>어색하게</u> 연결된 것은? (2점)

① wrong   –   right
② ask   –   answer
③ dangerous   –   safe
④ difficult   –   easy
⑤ fortune   –   infortune

[경북 ○○중]

03 다음 (A)~(E)를 자연스러운 대화가 되도록 바르게 배열한 것은? (3점)

(A) That's a good idea. Thank you.
(B) I'm thinking of joining a sports club.
(C) Why don't you join the table tennis club, then?
(D) Which do you like more, indoor or outdoor sports?
(E) I prefer indoor sports. I was in the badminton club last year.

① (A)-(B)-(C)-(D)-(E)
② (B)-(C)-(D)-(E)-(A)
③ (B)-(D)-(E)-(C)-(A)
④ (D)-(B)-(C)-(E)-(A)
⑤ (D)-(E)-(C)-(A)-(B)

[경기 ○○중]

04 다음 대화의 내용과 일치하는 것은? (4점)

Jaden: Have you been to the new Chinese restaurant?
Amy: Are you talking about the one on Main Street?
Jaden: Yes, that's the one. They opened about two weeks ago, right?
Amy: I think so. I went there last Friday with my friends.
Jaden: How was the food?
Amy: It was great. We ordered many different dishes. I really liked the fried vegetables.
Jaden: Could you recommend a dish for me? I'm going there for dinner tonight with my family.
Amy: Do you prefer seafood or meat?
Jaden: I prefer seafood.
Amy: Then, you should try their fried fish. You'll love it!

① Amy prefers fried fish to fried vegetables.
② A new Chinese restaurant opened on Main Street last Friday.
③ Jaden wants to get Amy's recommendation about a dish.
④ Jaden enjoyed dinner with his family in a newly opened restaurant.
⑤ Jaden and Amy are mainly talking about each other's favorite food.

[전북 ○○중]

05 다음 대화의 빈칸에 들어갈 알맞은 것은? (2점)

A: Could you recommend a sport for me?
B: Well, why don't you _____ baseball?

① eat
② try
③ visit
④ study
⑤ experiment

[6~7] 다음 대화를 읽고 물음에 답하시오.

Jaden:	Have you been to the new Chinese restaurant, Ms. Park?
Ms. Park:	Are you talking about the one on Main Street, Jaden?
Jaden:	Yes, that's the one. They opened about two weeks ago, right?
Ms. Park:	I think so. I went there last Friday with my friends.
Jaden:	How was the food?
Ms. Park:	It was great. We ordered many different dishes. I really liked the fried vegetables.
Jaden:	(A) _____ I'm going there for dinner tonight with my family.
Ms. Park:	Do you prefer seafood or meat?
Jaden:	I prefer seafood.
Ms. Park:	Then, you should try their fried fish. You'll love it!

06 위 대화의 빈칸 (A)에 들어갈 말로 가장 알맞은 것은? (3점)

① Could you make a dish for me?

② Could you recommend a dish for me?

③ How can I get a discount on the dish?

④ How can I go to the Chinese restaurant?

⑤ Could you recommend a good restaurant for me?

07 위 대화에서 답을 찾을 수 없는 것은? (3점)

① Where is the new Chinese restaurant?

② Why does Jaden prefer seafood to meat?

③ When did the new Chinese restaurant open?

④ When did Ms. Park go to the new Chinese restaurant?

⑤ Which food did Ms. Park really like at the new Chinese restaurant?

08 What sports club will the boy join in the talk? (2점)

B: I'm thinking of joining a sports club.
G: Do you prefer indoor or outdoor sports?
B: I prefer indoor sports. I was in the badminton club last year.
G: Why don't you join the table tennis club, then?
B: That's a good idea. Thank you.

① table tennis ② baseball ③ soccer

④ badminton ⑤ basketball

[9~10] 다음 대화를 읽고 물음에 답하시오.

W: Excuse me. I'm looking for an Italian cookbook. ⓐ저를 위해 하나 추천해 주실 수 있나요?
M: Well, have you ever cooked Italian food?
W: No, I haven't, but I want to try. I really like spaghetti.
M: Then, how about this Italian cookbook for beginners?
W: Good! Thank you. I'll take it.

09 위 대화의 밑줄 친 우리말 문장 ⓐ를 영어로 가장 적절히 옮긴 것은? (3점)

① Can you recommend one for me?

② Can you recommend one of me?

③ Can you recommend me for one?

④ Do you recommend one of me?

⑤ Do you recommend me for one?

10 위 대화가 이루어지는 장소로 가장 알맞은 곳은? (3점)

① theater ② museum ③ bookstore

④ hospital ⑤ post office

11 다음 대화를 읽고 답할 수 <u>없는</u> 질문은? (4점)

Jaden: Have you been to the Chinese restaurant, Ms. Park?

Ms. Park: Are you talking about the one on Main Street, Jaden?

Jaden: Yes, that's the one. They opened about two weeks ago, right?

Ms. Park: I think so. I went there last Friday with my friends.

Jaden: How was the food?

Ms. Park: It was great. We ordered many different dishes. I really liked the fried vegetables.

Jaden: Could you recommend a dish for me? I'm going there for dinner tonight with my family.

Ms. Park: Do you prefer seafood or meat?

Jaden: I prefer seafood.

Ms. Park: Then, you should try their fried fish. You'll love it!

① When did the new Chinese restaurant open?

② What does Ms. Park recommend for Jaden?

③ When is Jaden going to the new Chinese restaurant with his family?

④ Which one does Ms. Park prefer, seafood or meat?

⑤ Who did Ms. Park visit the new Chinese restaurant on Main Street with?

12 다음 대화의 빈칸에 가장 알맞은 것은? (3점)

G: I haven't seen a movie recently. Could you recommend a good one?

B: Why don't you see *Iron Woman 2*? It's a big hit.

G: Well, I don't like action movies. _____
_____

B: Then, how about *Funny Families*?

G: That sounds good.

① Why do you like comedy movies?

② What is your favorite movie genre?

③ Do you want to be a movie director?

④ Can you recommend any good comedies?

⑤ When did you watch the movie 'Harry Potter'?

13 다음 중 어법상 <u>어색한</u> 것끼리 묶인 것은? (3점)

ⓐ Why does songpyeon look like a half moon?

ⓑ Let's dive into the fun history of our food.

ⓒ King Yeongjo offered special something to them.

ⓓ Each ingredient symbolized a different political party.

ⓔ Yeongjo wanted to say that the four parties should work in harmony like this dish.

ⓕ This dish was called tangpyeongchae.

ⓖ There is many interesting stories about our traditional food.

① ⓐ, ⓒ, ⓔ   ② ⓑ, ⓓ, ⓕ   ③ ⓐ, ⓒ
④ ⓓ, ⓔ   ⑤ ⓒ, ⓖ

14 수동태로 바꿔 쓸 수 <u>없는</u> 문장은? (3점)

① You look sad.

② I painted the picture.

③ She sent him a present.

④ Many people respect him.

⑤ The cat caught the mouse.

15 다음 (A)에 들어갈 가장 알맞은 것은? (3점)

go : gone = see : (A)_____

① saw   ② sees   ③ seed
④ seen   ⑤ seeing

[16~19] 다음 글을 읽고 물음에 답하시오.

It was the time of the last king of Baekje. One day, the king and his servants found a strange turtle. (its / back / written / on / was / something).

(가) The fortune teller answered, "A full moon will soon (A)[become / becomes] smaller. On the other hand, a half moon will grow bigger and become a full moon."
(나) The king became worried about his kingdom. However, people of Silla (B)[was / were] very happy to learn this and (C)[made / to make] rice cakes in the shape of a half moon.
(다) It said, "Baekje is like a full moon, but Silla is like a half moon." The king asked a fortune teller, "What does this mean?"

Since then, people have enjoyed these half-moon shaped rice cakes, songpyeon.

16 위 글의 괄호 (A), (B), (C) 안에서 어법에 맞는 표현으로 가장 적절한 것은? (4점)

	(A)	(B)	(C)
①	become	was	made
②	become	were	to make
③	becomes	were	to make
④	becomes	was	to make
⑤	become	were	made

17 위 글의 밑줄 친 괄호 안의 단어들을 바르게 배열하시오. (4점)

→ _____

18 위 글에서 문맥상 (가)~(다)의 순서를 적절하게 배열한 것은? (3점)

① (나)-(다)-(가)   ② (다)-(가)-(나)
③ (다)-(나)-(가)   ④ (가)-(다)-(나)
⑤ (가)-(나)-(다)

19 위 글의 내용과 일치하는 것은? (3점)

① 백제의 첫 번째 왕 때였다.
② 왕과 신하들은 이상한 기북의 등에 무언가를 썼다.
③ 신라는 보름달과 같지만 백제는 반달과 같다.
④ 점술가는 보름달은 곧 작아질 것이고 반달은 점점 커져서 보름달이 될 것이라고 답했다.
⑤ 백제 사람들은 이 반달 모양의 떡인 송편을 즐겨 먹고 있었다.

[20~21] 다음 글을 읽고 물음에 답하시오.

(A) In the time of King Yeonsan, there was a scholar who was famous for his honesty. (B) When the king did ⓐsomething wrong, the scholar was never afraid ⓑof telling him so. (C) However, the king never listened to him. (D) While he lived there by himself, he mainly ate vegetables. He made a special pot ⓒto cook many different vegetables together. (E) People called this pot and the food in it sinseollo. ⓓThat is why the scholar lived like a sinseon, an imaginary person ⓔwho lives alone in nature.

20 위 글의 (A)~(E) 중 다음 문장이 들어갈 곳으로 가장 적절한 것은? (3점)

The scholar was so disappointed that he went to live on a mountain.

① (A)   ② (B)   ③ (C)   ④ (D)   ⑤ (E)

21 위 글의 밑줄 친 ⓐ~ⓔ 중 그 쓰임이 <u>어색한</u> 것은?　(4점)

① ⓐ　② ⓑ　③ ⓒ　④ ⓓ　⑤ ⓔ

[충북 ○○중]

[22~23] 다음 글을 읽고 물음에 답하시오.

> Tangpyeongchae
> One day, King Yeongjo was having dinner with his officials and (A)_____ them something special. It was a dish with four colorful ingredients. Each ingredient symbolized a different political party. Yeongjo wanted to say that the four parties should work in harmony like this dish. This dish (B)_____ tangpyeongchae. The name came from Yeongjo's policy tangpyeongchaek.

22 위 글의 빈칸 (A), (B)에 들어갈 단어로 알맞은 것으로 짝지어진 것은?　(3점)

	(A)	(B)
①	offered	called
②	offered	has called
③	offered	was called
④	was offered	was called
⑤	was offered	has called

23 위 글을 읽고 답할 수 <u>없는</u> 질문은?　(3점)

① What was tangpyeongchae named after?
② How many colors are in tangpyeongchae?
③ What are the four ingredients for tangpyeongchae?
④ Why did the king give tangpyeongchae to his officials?
⑤ What did each ingredient in tangpyeongchase symbolize?

[전북 ○○중]

[24~26] 다음 글을 읽고 물음에 답하시오.

> In the time of King Yeonsan, there was a scholar who was famous for his honesty. (A) When the king did something wrong, the scholar was never afraid of telling ⓐhim so. (B) However, the king never listened to ⓑhim. (C) The scholar was so disappointed that ⓒhe went to live on a mountain. While ⓓhe lived there by himself, he mainly ate vegetables. ⓔHe made a special pot to cook many different vegetables together. (D) People called this pot and the food in it sinseollo. (E)

24 위 글의 밑줄 친 ⓐ~ⓔ 중에서 가리키는 대상이 <u>다른</u> 것은?　(3점)

① ⓐ　② ⓑ　③ ⓒ　④ ⓓ　⑤ ⓔ

25 위 글의 (A)~(E) 중, 주어진 문장의 위치로 가장 알맞은 것은?　(4점)

> This is because the scholar lived like a sinseon, an imaginary person who lives alone in nature.

① (A)　② (B)　③ (C)　④ (D)　⑤ (E)

[경기 ○○중]

26 위 글의 내용과 일치하지 <u>않는</u> 것은?　(3점)

① 연산군 때에 한 정직한 학자가 있었다.
② 학자는 왕의 잘못을 말하는 것을 두려워하지 않았다.
③ 연산군은 학자의 말에 귀 기울이지 않았다.
④ 산에서 사는 동안 학자는 주로 고기를 먹었다.
⑤ 신선로는 신선처럼 산 학자의 솥과 음식에서 유래했다.

[27~30] 다음 글을 읽고 물음에 답하시오.

Sinseollo

In the time of King Yeonsan, there was a scholar who ⓐwas famous for his honesty. When the king did something wrong, the scholar was never afraid ⓑof telling (가)him so. (A)[However / Therefore], the king never listened to him. The scholar was so (B)[disappointing / disappointed] ⓒthat he went to live on a mountain. While he lived there by (C)[him / himself], he mainly ate vegetables. (나)He made a special pot ⓓto cook many different vegetables together. People called this pot and the food in (다)it sinseollo. That is because the scholar lived like a sinseon, an imaginary person ⓔwho lives alone in nature.

27 위 글의 괄호 (A), (B), (C) 안에서 알맞은 말을 고르면? (3점)

	(A)	(B)	(C)
①	However	disappointed	himself
②	However	disappointing	himself
③	However	disappointing	him
④	Therefore	disappointed	him
⑤	Therefore	disappointing	himself

28 위 글의 내용과 일치하지 않는 것은? (3점)

① 연산군 시대에 정직하기로 유명한 한 학자가 있었다.

② 그 학자는 왕이 잘못된 것을 했을 때, 왕에게 그것을 말하는 것을 두려워하지 않았다.

③ 산속에서 혼자 사는 동안, 그 학자는 주로 채소를 먹었다.

④ 그 학자는 많은 다양한 채소들을 함께 요리하기 위해 특별한 솥을 만들었다.

⑤ 그 학자가 신선이 되었기 때문에 이 음식을 신선로라고 불렀다.

29 위 글의 밑줄 친 ⓐ~ⓔ에 대한 설명 중, 어색한 것은? (4점)

① ⓐ was famous for: '~로 유명했다'의 의미

② ⓑ of telling: 전치사 of 뒤에 동명사 telling이 옴

③ ⓒ that: 선행사 he를 수식하는 목적격 관계대명사

④ ⓓ to cook: to부정사의 부사적 용법으로 '~하기 위해'로 해석함

⑤ ⓔ who: 선행사 an imaginary person을 수식하는 주격 관계대명사

30 위 글의 밑줄 친 (가), (나), (다)가 지칭하는 것을 각각 본문에서 찾아 쓰시오. (6점)

조건

1. 본문에 있는 표현으로 쓸 것.
2. 영어로 쓸 것.
3. 단어 수 제한 없음.

(가) him → _____

(나) He → _____

(다) it → _____

31 다음 글에 이어서 나올 내용은? (3점)

How did tangpyeongchae and sinseollo get their names? Why does songpyeon look like a half moon? There are many interesting stories about our traditional food. Let's dive into the fun history of our food.

① 고려시대와 조선시대의 음식 비교

② 한국 전통 음식의 시대별 분류

③ 역사적으로 맛있는 전통 음식의 요리법

④ 역사적으로 대중들이 좋아했던 음식의 순위

⑤ 전통 음식에 관한 재미있는 역사적 이야기

◎ 선택형 문항의 답안은 컴퓨터용 수정 싸인펜을 사용하여 OMR 답안지에 바르게 표기하시오.

◎ 서술형 문제는 답을 답안지에 반드시 검정 볼펜으로 쓰시오.

◎ 총 30문항 100점 만점입니다. 문항별 배점은 각 문항에 표시되어 있습니다.

[경기 ○○중]

01 영영사전의 풀이가 올바른 것끼리 짝지어진 것은? (3점)

ⓐ blackout: a period when there is no light as a result of an electrical power failure

ⓑ bleach: a chemical that is used to make something black or dirty

ⓒ ceiling: the bottom surface of a room that you walk on

ⓓ leftover: food that has not been eaten at the end of a meal

ⓔ hanger: a curved piece of wood, plastic or wire with a hook at the top, to hang clothes

① ⓐ, ⓑ, ⓒ ② ⓐ, ⓑ, ⓓ ③ ⓐ, ⓓ, ⓔ

④ ⓑ, ⓒ, ⓓ ⑤ ⓒ, ⓓ, ⓔ

[경기 ○○중]

02 주어진 문장 다음에 이어질 대화의 순서로 가장 적절한 것은? (3점)

What's your plan for this winter break?

(A) That sounds exciting. What are you going to do there?

(B) Good. Don't forget to try some dim sum.

(C) I'm going to visit Hong Kong with my parents.

(D) I'm going to go to an amusement park. I'm also going to try all kinds of food.

① (A)-(B)-(D)-(C) ② (A)-(C)-(B)-(D)

③ (C)-(A)-(D)-(B) ④ (C)-(B)-(D)-(A)

⑤ (D)-(B)-(A)-(C)

[충북 ○○중]

[3~4] 다음 대화를 읽고 물음에 답하시오.

Yuri: What's wrong, Jaden?

Jaden: My science homework is too ⓐdifficult.

Yuri: What do you have to do?

Jaden: I need to find a way to save trees.

Yuri: That's ⓑeasy. I've heard that we can save trees by using ⓒless paper.

Jaden: Oh, I think I've heard that, too. Then, I can just stop using paper cups.

Yuri: Yes! You can also use just one paper towel to dry off your hands.

Jaden: That's ⓓpossible. I need at least two or three paper towels.

Yuri: Just shake your hands before you use a paper towel. Then, one will be more than ⓔenough.

Jaden: Oh, that's a good idea, Yuri! I'll try that next time.

Yuri: Good! Just don't forget to shake your hands at least 10 times.

03 위 대화의 주제로 가장 알맞은 것은? (3점)

① 에너지 절약 실천 방법

② 나무를 살리는 방법

③ 자연 보호의 필요성

④ 종이 수건 사용법

⑤ 손 씻기의 중요성

04 위 대화의 ⓐ~ⓔ 중 흐름상 낱말의 쓰임이 적절하지 않은 것은? (3점)

① ⓐ ② ⓑ ③ ⓒ ④ ⓓ ⑤ ⓔ

05 다음 개요를 대화문으로 표현하고자 한다. 개요와 대화문의 내용이 일치하지 <u>않는</u> 것은? (4점)

<개요>
• 과제: 나무 보호 방법 찾기
• 방법: 종이 사용량 줄이기
• 실천: 1) 종이컵 사용 중지
        2) 종이 타월 한 장만 쓰기
        3) 손을 씻은 후 10번 이상 손 털기

Yuri: What's wrong, Jaden?
Jaden: My science homework is too difficult.
Yuri: What do you have to do?
Jaden: ⓐI need to find a way to save trees.
Yuri: That's easy. ⓑI've heard that we can save trees by using less paper.
Jaden: Oh, I think I've heard that, too. ⓒ Then, I am going to try not to use paper cups.
Yuri: Yes! ⓓYou can also use just one paper towel to dry off your hands.
Jaden: That's impossible. I need at least two or three paper towels.
Yuri: Just shake your hands before you use a paper towel. Then, one will be more than enough.
Jaden: Oh, that's a good idea, Yuri! I'll try that next time.
Yuri: Good! ⓔJust don't forget to shake your hands within 10 times.

① ⓐ   ② ⓑ   ③ ⓒ   ④ ⓓ   ⑤ ⓔ

06 다음 중 가장 <u>어색한</u> 대화끼리 묶인 것은? (4점)

㉠ A: I'm going to go hiking tomorrow, but I'm worried about bad weather.
   B: Don't worry. It will be good.
   A: Thank you. I hope so.

㉡ A: Do you want to take the leftovers home?
   B: Yes, please.
   A: Don't forget not to eat too much.

㉢ A: What's your plan for this winter break?
   B: I'm going to visit Hong Kong with my parents.
   A: That sounds exciting.

㉣ A: Can you turn up the volume on your phone? I like this song.
   B: I can't turn it down anymore.
   A: Let me just put your phone in a glass.

㉤ A: Excuse me, are you finished with your meal?
   B: Yes, it was really good.
   A: Do you want to take the leftovers home?

① ㉠, ㉢   ② ㉡, ㉣   ③ ㉢, ㉣
④ ㉢, ㉤   ⑤ ㉣, ㉤

[7~8] 다음 대화를 읽고 물음에 답하시오.

B: What's your plan for this winter (A)break?
G: I'm going to ⓐvisit Vietnam with my parents.
B: That ⓑsounds exciting. What are you going to do there?
G: I'm going to ⓒspend some time on the beach and eat lots of seafood.
B: Good. Don't forget ⓓtrying the fruit there, too.
G: O.K. I ⓔwon't forget.

07 위 대화의 (A)break와 같은 의미의 단어는? (3점)

① vacation   ② clothes   ③ stone
④ food   ⑤ bread

08 위 대화의 밑줄 친 ⓐ~ⓔ 중 쓰임이 <u>어색한</u> 것은? (3점)

① ⓐ   ② ⓑ   ③ ⓒ   ④ ⓓ   ⑤ ⓔ

09 다음 대화의 내용과 일치하지 <u>않는</u> 것을 <u>모두</u> 고르시오. (4점)

Yuri: What's wrong, Jaden?

Jaden: My science homework is too difficult.

Yuri: What do you have to do?

Jaden: I need to find a way to save trees.

Yuri: That's easy. I've heard that we can save trees by using less paper.

Jaden: Oh, I think I've heard that, too. Then, I can just stop using paper cups.

Yuri: Yes! You can also use just one paper towel to dry off your hands.

Jaden: That's impossible. I need at least two or three paper towels.

Yuri: Just shake your hands before you use a paper towel. Then, one will be more than enough.

Jaden: Oh, that's a good idea, Yuri! I'll try that next time.

Yuri: Good!

① Jaden은 과학 숙제가 어렵다고 생각한다.

② Jaden은 나무를 심는 방법을 찾아야 한다.

③ Jaden은 종이컵 사용을 그만둘 수 있다고 말했다.

④ Yuri는 종이컵을 사용하기 전에 손을 털라고 말했다.

⑤ Yuri는 종이 수건 한 장으로 손을 닦는 것이 가능하다고 생각한다.

10 다음 문장 중 어법상 <u>어색한</u> 것은? (3점)

① You make me happily.

② Rainy days make me sad.

③ Being sick makes me upset.

④ Sunny days make me excited.

⑤ Music keeps me relaxed.

11 다음 빈칸에 공통으로 들어갈 말로 가장 알맞은 것은? (2점)

(1) I'll _____ my robot tell funny stories.

(2) Eating an apple a day can _____ us healthy.

① have　　② see　　③ ask

④ find　　⑤ make

12 다음 중 $\frac{3}{4}$ 을 영어로 바르게 옮긴 것은? (3점)

① three four　　② three fours

③ three fourth　　④ three fourths

⑤ third fourths

13 다음 중 어법상 <u>어색한</u> 문장은? (3점)

① Let it go.

② She made me smile.

③ Who let him go out?

④ Let me to play the guitar here.

⑤ I'll make my robot cook for me.

14 다음 중 어법상 올바른 문장을 <u>두 개</u> 고르면? (3점)

① I'll let you to go when it is finished.

② I had my robot clean my room.

③ I made my dad happily.

④ I helped him to move the desk.

⑤ She let the bird to fly.

[15~18] 다음 글을 읽고 물음에 답하시오.

"Wow, I can read a book in my room now!" shouted Marco, a boy in a village in the Philippines. His house has no electricity just like all the other houses in the village. (A)People in the village are too poor to pay for electricity. Even ⓐ_____ the daytime, they live in darkness ⓑ _____ the houses are packed close together. Now things are changing ⓒ_____ a single plastic bottle. One plastic bottle in the ceiling can light up a whole room without using any electricity.
This amazing plastic bottle is called a Moser lamp. (B)It was invented by Alfredo Moser. There were many blackouts in his town in Brazil. (C)(his / new / to / these / up / blackouts / him / come / a / way / light / house / made / with).
A Moser lamp can be made for about one dollar and lasts for about 10 years. It is also very safe. It can never start a house fire. Surprisingly, it is very easy to make this magic lamp.

15 Moser 램프에 관해 언급되지 <u>않은</u> 것을 <u>모두</u> 고르시오. (3점)

① 제작 비용　　　　② 사용 가능 기간
③ 환경에 미치는 영향　④ 처음 만든 사람
⑤ 램프 사용의 유의점

16 (A)와 (B) 문장을 같은 뜻이 되도록 바르게 바꾼 것끼리 짝지어진 것은? (3점)

① (A) People in the village are so poor that they can pay for electricity.
(B) Alfredo Moser invented it.

② (A) People in the village are so poor that they could pay for electricity.
(B) Alfredo Moser invented it.

③ (A) People in the village are so poor that they pay for electricity.
(B) Alfredo Moser invents it.

④ (A) People in the village are so poor that they couldn't pay for electricity.
(B) Alfredo Moser invents it.

⑤ (A) People in the village are so poor that they can't pay for electricity.
(B) Alfredo Moser invented it.

17 빈칸 ⓐ~ⓒ에 들어갈 말로 바르게 짝지어진 것은? (3점)

① for – because – because
② during – because – because of
③ during – because of – because of
④ during – because of – because
⑤ while – because – because of

18 (C) 문장이 '이 정전들은 그가 그의 집을 밝히는 하나의 새로운 방법을 생각해 내도록 만들었다'의 뜻이 되도록 주어진 단어를 재배열하여 쓰시오. (4점)

→ _____

19 다음 글의 밑줄 친 (1)~(5) 중 어법상 <u>틀린</u> 것 2개를 찾아 바르게 고치시오. (4점)

> **How to make a Moser lamp from a bottle**
> 1. (1)<u>Fill</u> a clear plastic bottle with water.
> 2. Add some bleach to keep the water (2)<u>clearly</u>.
> 3. Make a hole in the roof, and push the bottle into the hole.
> 4. Let a third of the bottle (3)<u>remain</u> above the roof.
> 5. Sunlight is (4)<u>bent</u> by the water in the bottle and (5)<u>spread</u> around the room.

( ) _____ → _____
( ) _____ → _____

20 다음 글을 읽고, 〈보기〉에 주어진 질문에 대해 주어와 동사를 갖춘 완전한 영어 문장으로 쓰시오. (4점)

"Wow, I can read a book in my room now!" shouted Marco, a boy in a village in the Philippines. His house has no electricity just like all the other houses in the village. People in the village are too poor to pay for electricity. Even during the daytime, they live in darkness because the houses are packed close together. Now things are changing because of a single plastic bottle. One plastic bottle in the ceiling can light up a whole room without using any electricity.

보기
Q. Why do people in Marco's village live without electricity?

→ _____

[21~23] 다음 글을 읽고 물음에 답하시오.

This amazing plastic bottle is called a Moser lamp because it was invented by Alfredo Moser. In 2002, there were many blackouts in his town in Brazil. These blackouts ⓐ그가 집을 밝히는 새로운 방법을 생각해 내도록 만들었다.
A Moser lamp can be made for about one dollar and lasts for about 10 years. It is also very safe. It can never start a house fire. Surprisingly, ⓑit is very easy to make this magic lamp.

21 위 글의 ⓐ문장을 주어진 단어를 재배열하여 바르게 완성하시오. (4점)

come up / him / made / his house / to light / a new way / with

→ _____

22 위 글의 ⓑit과 같은 용법으로 쓰인 것은? (3점)

① It is two kilometers from here to the office.
② Is it really spicy?
③ Was it difficult for you to find a job?
④ I found it hard.
⑤ It will be rainy and windy tomorrow.

23 다음 〈보기〉의 7개의 내용 중 위 글에서 언급되지 않은 것은 모두 몇 개인가? (4점)

보기
• Moser 램프의 발명가
• Moser 램프의 원리
• Moser 램프의 발명 계기
• Moser 램프의 전파
• Moser 램프의 생산 비용
• Moser 램프의 지속 시간(수명)
• Moser 램프의 안전성 여부

① 1개 ② 2개 ③ 3개 ④ 4개 ⑤ 5개

24 다음 글의 빈칸 (A)와 (B)에 들어갈 말로 적절한 것은? (4점)

In the Philippines, Moser lamps are widely used by the My Shelter Foundation. The charity also teaches local people the way to make and install the lamps. (A)_____ the charity, thousands of homes in the Philippines now have Moser lamps. It has also made Moser lamps popular in other countries, (B)_____ Argentina, India, and Fiji.

	(A)	(B)
①	Since	so
②	Next to	as
③	Thanks to	such as
④	In front of	for instance
⑤	According to	because

[25~27] 다음 글을 읽고 물음에 답하시오.

A Moser lamp was invented by Alfredo Moser. In 2002, there were many blackouts in his town in Brazil. ⓐBecause of these blackouts, he came up with a new way to light his house.
A Moser lamp can be made for about one dollar and lasts for about 10 years. It is also very (A)_____. It can never start a house fire. Surprisingly, it is very easy to make this magic lamp.

25 위 글을 읽고 알 수 없는 내용은?　　(3점)

① Moser lamp를 발명한 사람
② Moser lamp가 발명된 계기
③ Moser lamp의 제작 비용
④ Moser lamp의 지속 기간
⑤ Moser lamp의 제작 방법

26 위 글의 흐름상 빈칸 (A)에 들어가기에 적절한 단어는?　(3점)

① safe　　② cheap　　③ unique
④ expensive　　⑤ dangerous

27 위 글의 밑줄 친 문장 ⓐ를 아래와 같이 바꾸어 쓸 때, 빈칸에 들어갈 말을 쓰시오.　　(4점)

<주의 사항>
• 한 칸에 한 단어씩만 쓸 것.

→ These blackouts made _____ _____ _____ _____ a new way to light his house.

28 다음 글의 목적으로 가장 적절한 것은?　　(3점)

Hi, Mom! Hi, Dad! As you know, today is my 15th birthday. I haven't had a chance to deeply appreciate your supporting and trying

to understand me. You've truly been my friends and my teachers. I'm really proud to be your daughter.

① 감사　　② 충고　　③ 홍보
④ 통보　　⑤ 요청

[29~30] 다음 글을 읽고 물음에 답하시오.

"Wow, I can read a book in my room now!" shouted Marco, a boy in a village in the Philippines. (A) His house has no electricity just like all the other house in the village. (B) (가)People in the village are too poor to pay for electricity. (C) Even during the daytime, they live in darkness because the houses are packed close together. (D) One plastic bottle in the ceiling can light up a whole room without using any electricity (E)

29 위 글의 밑줄 친 (가)와 같은 의미인 것은?　　(3점)

① People in the village are so poor that they can't pay for electricity.
② People in the village save a lot of money to pay for electricity.
③ People in the village have enough money to pay for electricity.
④ People in the village are so poor but they always pay for electricity.
⑤ People in the village don't pay for electricity because they don't want to use it.

30 위 글의 (A)~(E) 중, 주어진 문장이 들어가기에 가장 알맞은 곳은?　　(4점)

Now things are changing because of a single plastic bottle.

① (A)　② (B)　③ (C)　④ (D)　⑤ (E)

◎ 선택형 문항의 답안은 컴퓨터용 수정 싸인펜을 사용하여 OMR 답안지에 바르게 표기하시오.
◎ 서술형 문제는 답을 답안지에 반드시 검정 볼펜으로 쓰시오.
◎ 총 29문항 100점 만점입니다. 문항별 배점은 각 문항에 표시되어 있습니다.

[제주 ○○중]

01 다음 밑줄 친 단어의 의미가 **잘못된** 것은?   (3점)

① The beach was packed with tourists. (~으로 꽉 들어찼다)

② There was a blackout, and I was in an elevator for an hour. (정전)

③ We'll try to come up with some ideas to solve the problem. (우연히 만나다)

④ Computers are widely used as communication tools. (널리 사용된다)

⑤ He decided to remain single. (계속 ~이다)

[대전 ○○중]

[2~3] 다음 대화를 읽고 물음에 답하시오.

Yuri: What's wrong, Jaden?
Jaden: My science homework is too difficult.
Yuri: What do you have to do?
Jaden: I need to find a way to save trees.
Yuri: That's easy. I've heard that we can save trees by using less paper.
Jaden: Oh, I think I've heard (A)that, too. Then, I can just stop using paper cups.
Yuri: Yes! You can also use just one paper towel to dry off your hands.
Jaden: That's impossible. I need at least two or three paper towels.
Yuri: Just shake your hands before you use a paper towel. Then, one will be more than enough.
Jaden: Oh, (B)that's a good idea, Yuri! I'll try that next time.
Yuri: Good! Just don't forget to shake your hands at least 10 times.

02 위 대화의 밑줄 친 (A), (B)가 가리키는 것으로 알맞게 연결된 것은?   (4점)

① (A): Science homework is too difficult.
   (B): We can save trees by using more paper.

② (A): Science homework is too difficult.
   (B): We can save trees by using less paper.

③ (A): We can save trees by using less paper.
   (B): Just shake your hands before you use a paper towel.

④ (A): We can save trees by using more paper.
   (B): You can use one paper to dry off hands.

⑤ (A): We can save trees by using less paper.
   (B): Science homework is too difficult.

03 위 대화의 제목으로 가장 알맞은 것은?   (3점)

① What Can We Do to Save Trees?
② How Are the Paper Cups Made?
③ What Is Yuri's Science Homework?
④ How Can You Dry off Your Hands Easily?
⑤ How Many Times Should We Shake Our Hands for Trees?

[전북 ○○중]

04 다음 밑줄 친 ⓐ~ⓔ 중 내용상 또는 어법상 바른 것은? (4점)

G: Can you turn up the volume on your phone? I like this song.
B: I can't ⓐturn up it anymore. It's ⓑthe higher volume.
G: Let me just put your phone in a glass. I ⓒhave heard a glass ⓓworks a speaker.
B: ⓔWhat a boring idea! Let's try it now.

① ⓐ   ② ⓑ   ③ ⓒ   ④ ⓓ   ⑤ ⓔ

[5~6] 다음 대화를 읽고 물음에 답하시오.

Yuri: What's wrong, Jaden?
Jaden: My science homework is too difficult.
Yuri: What do you have to do?
Jaden: I need to find a way to save trees.
Yuri: That's easy. (A)나는 우리가 종이를 덜 사용함으로써 나무들을 살릴 수 있다고 들었어.
Jaden: Oh, that's wonderful. Then, I can just stop using paper cups.
Yuri: Yes! You can also use just one paper towel to dry off your hands.
Jaden: That's impossible. I need at least two or three paper towels.
Yuri: Just shake your hands before you use a paper towel. Then, one will be more than enough.
Jaden: Oh, that's a good idea, Yuri! I'll try that next time.
Yuri: Good! Just don't forget to shake your hands at least 10 times.

05 According to the dialogue, which is NOT true? (3점)

① Jaden's homework is to find a way to save trees.

② Jaden thinks that he can save trees by using paper cups.

③ Yuri advises Jaden to use one paper towel to dry off his hands.

④ Yuri thinks one paper towel is enough to dry off hands.

⑤ Shaking hands at least 10 times can help us use fewer paper towels.

06 위 대화의 밑줄 친 (A)에 주어진 우리말과 의미가 일치하도록 다음 단어를 배열할 때, 9번째 들어갈 단어는? (4점)

(by, we, save, that, less, trees, I've, paper, using, heard, can)

→ _____

(주어진 단어를 모두 한 번씩 사용.)

① trees   ② heard   ③ using
④ save   ⑤ less

07 다음 대화가 자연스러운 대화가 되도록 주어진 문장의 순서를 바르게 배열한 것은? (3점)

W: Excuse me, are you finished with your meal?
a: Yes, please.
b: Don't forget to eat the leftovers by tomorrow.
c: Yes, it was really good.
d: Do you want to take the leftovers home?

① a - b - c - d   ② a - d - c - b
③ b - d - c - a   ④ c - b - a - d
⑤ c - d - a - b

08 다음 대화의 순서로 가장 적절한 것은? (4점)

(A) Oh, who is he?
(B) I've heard that a movie star is coming to our school.
(C) Robert Downey Jr. He played CEO of Stark Industries in the movie *Avengers: Endgame.*
(D) Wow, I'm really looking forward to seeing him.
(E) That's right. He's my favorite actor.

① (A)-(C)-(B)-(D)-(E)   ② (A)-(C)-(E)-(B)-(D)
③ (B)-(C)-(A)-(D)-(E)   ④ (B)-(A)-(E)-(D)-(C)
⑤ (B)-(E)-(A)-(C)-(D)

09 짝지어진 대화가 가장 <u>어색한</u> 것은? (4점)

① A: How often do you go swimming?

B: Not very often. I only go swimming once a month.

② A: I've heard that a famous singer is coming to our school.

B: That's right. I can't wait to see her!

③ A: Can you turn up the volume on your phone? I like this song.

B: It's the highest volume. Don't forget to turn it up right now.

④ A: What is your favorite sport, James?

B: I don't like sports much, but I am interested in basketball.

⑤ A: What's your plan for this winter break?

B: I'm going to visit Vietnam with my parents.

10 빈칸 ⓐ에 들어갈 표현으로 알맞은 것은? (3점)

Elsa: Excuse me, are you finished with your meal?
Anna: Yes, it was really good.
Elsa: Do you want to take the leftovers home?
Anna: Yes, please.
Elsa: ⓐ_____

① Be sure to bring the leftovers with you.

② I've heard that the leftovers taste good.

③ Don't forgot to eat the leftovers by tomorrow.

④ Keep in mind that you should take something to eat.

⑤ Remember to keep the leftovers in the fridge for a long time.

11 우리말과 같은 뜻이 되도록 다음 주어진 어구를 배열하시오. (4점)

• 엄마는 내가 친구들과 축구하는 것을 허락하였다.

let / my mom / friends / play /me / with / soccer

→ _____

12 다음 중 어법상 바른 문장은? (3점)

① He had his car wash yesterday.

② Mom will allow me go to the movies tonight.

③ She told the children to be quiet.

④ Your smile makes me happily.

⑤ I asked him to not close the door.

13 다음 중 어법상 <u>어색한</u> 문장을 <u>모두</u> 고른 것은? (3점)

ⓐ I need to have my ears check.

ⓑ My brother always makes me cleaned the room.

ⓒ He helped the old lady to carry the bag.

ⓓ She doesn't let her children play online games.

ⓔ She will have the wall painting this Sunday.

ⓕ Mom made I wash the dishes after dinner.

① ⓐ, ⓑ   ② ⓐ, ⓑ, ⓒ, ⓕ

③ ⓐ, ⓑ, ⓔ   ④ ⓑ, ⓔ, ⓕ

⑤ ⓐ, ⓑ, ⓔ, ⓕ

[14~15] 다음 글을 읽고 물음에 답하시오.

Marco couldn't read a book in his room because of no electricity in his house just like all the other houses. People in the village are too poor to pay for electricity. ⓐEven during the daytime, they live in darkness because the houses are packed close together. Now (A)things are changing because of a single plastic bottle. One plastic bottle in the ceiling can light up a whole room without using any electricity. ⓑThis amazing plastic bottle is called a Moser lamp because it was invented by Alfredo Moser. In 2002, there were many blackouts in his town in Brazil. ⓒIt is cheap to use this technology to produce electricity. These blackouts made him come up with a new way to light his house. ⓓA Moser lamp can be made for about one dollar and lasts for about 10 years. It is also very safe. ⓔIt can never start a house fire.

14 위 글의 밑줄 친 ⓐ~ⓔ 중, 전체 흐름과 관계 <u>없는</u> 것은? (3점)

① ⓐ   ② ⓑ   ③ ⓒ   ④ ⓓ   ⑤ ⓔ

15 위 글의 밑줄 친 (A)의 예로 추론할 수 있는 가장 적절한 것은? (4점)

① People can pay for electricity.
② Houses are packed close together.
③ Marco can read a book in his room.
④ Marco lights his house with electricity.
⑤ People live in darkness during the daytime.

16 다음 글의 제목으로 가장 적절한 것은?   (4점)

> 1. Fill a clear plastic bottle with water.
> 2. Add some bleach to keep the water clear.
> 3. Make a hole in the roof, and push the bottle into the hole.
> 4. Let a third of the bottle remain above the roof.
> 5. Sunlight is bent by the water in the bottle and spreads around the room.
> We can use the bottle as a lamp.

① The Importance of Bleach
② To Live without Sunlight
③ The Problems of Plastic Bottles
④ The Way to Make Water Clean
⑤ How to Make a Lamp from a Bottle

[17~18] 다음 글을 읽고 물음에 답하시오.

In the Philippines, Moser lamps are widely used by the My Shelter Foundation. ⓐThe charity also teaches local people how to make and install the lamps. ⓑThanks to the charity, thousands of homes in the Philippines now have Moser lamps. ⓒMany charities sent money to help people who are ill or very poor. ⓓIt has also made Moser lamps popular in other countries, ⓔsuch as Argentina, India, and Fiji. Moser lamps will light up the lives of many people for many years (A)_____.

17 위 글에서 밑줄 친 ⓐ~ⓔ 중, 글의 흐름상 <u>어색한</u> 것은? (3점)

① ⓐ   ② ⓑ   ③ ⓒ   ④ ⓓ   ⑤ ⓔ

18 위 글의 (A)에 들어갈 형태로 적절한 것은?   (3점)

① to come   ② came   ③ come
④ coming   ⑤ are coming

[19~25] 다음 글을 읽고 물음에 답하시오.

"I can read a book in my place now!" shouted Marco, a boy in a village in the Philippines. His house has no electricity just like all the other houses in the village. People in the village are too poor to pay for electricity. Even during the daytime, they live in darkness because the houses are packed close together. (A) Now things are changing because of a single plastic bottle. (B) One plastic bottle in the ceiling can light up a whole room without using any electricity. (C) This amazing plastic bottle is called a Moser lamp because it was invented by Alfredo Moser. (D) In 2002, there were many blackouts in his town in Brazil. (E)
A Moser lamp can be made for about one dollar and ⓐit lasts for about 10 years. ⓑIt is also very safe. ⓒIt can never start a house fire. You can't get an electric shock from ⓓit. Surprisingly, ⓔit is very easy to make this magic lamp.

19 위 글의 제목으로 가장 적절한 것은? (3점)

① Many Blackouts in Brazil
② The Importance of Saving Electricity
③ How to Make a Moser Lamp
④ A New Way to Light a House
⑤ The Inventor of a Plastic Bottle

20 위 글의 흐름으로 보아, (A)~(E) 중에서 주어진 문장이 들어가기에 가장 적절한 곳은? (4점)

These blackouts made him come up with a new way to light his house.

① (A)   ② (B)   ③ (C)   ④ (D)   ⑤ (E)

21 위 글에 드러난 Marco의 심정으로 가장 적절한 것은? (3점)

① bored   ② afraid   ③ pleased
④ worried   ⑤ disappointed

22 위 글의 밑줄 친 ⓐ~ⓔ 중 가리키는 대상이 나머지 넷과 <u>다른</u> 것은? (4점)

① ⓐ   ② ⓑ   ③ ⓒ   ④ ⓓ   ⑤ ⓔ

23 위 글에 언급된 단어가 <u>아닌</u> 것은? (4점)

① the inside surface at the top of a room
② the time of day when the sky is light
③ a period when lights are off because of an electrical power failure
④ an organization that gives money, goods, or help to people who are poor, sick, etc
⑤ a form of energy that provides power to motors and devices that create light or heat

24 위 글을 읽고 답할 수 <u>없는</u> 질문은? (3점)

① Why do people in Marco's village live in darkness even during the daytime?
② How long does a Moser lamp last?
③ Where does Alfredo Moser come from?
④ Who invented a Moser lamp?
⑤ Why were there many blackouts in Brazil in 2002?

25 위 글과 가장 관련이 깊은 속담은? (3점)

① Honesty is the best policy.
② Laughter is the best medicine.
③ Two heads are better than one.
④ Don't judge a book by its cover.
⑤ Necessity is the mother of invention.

[26~27] 다음 글을 읽고 물음에 답하시오.

"Wow, I can read a book in my room now!" shouted Marco, a boy in a village in the Philippines. His house has no electricity just like all the other houses in the village. People in the village are too poor to pay for electricity. Even (A)[during / while] the daytime, they live in darkness as the houses are packed close together. Now things are changing (B)[because / because of] a single plastic bottle. One plastic bottle in the ceiling can light up a whole room without using any electricity. This amazing plastic bottle is called a Moser lamp.

In the Philippines, Moser lamps are widely used by the My Shelter Foundation. The charity also teaches local people how to make and install the lamps. (C)[Thanks for / Thanks to] the charity, thousands of homes in the philippines now have Moser lamps. It has also made Moser lamps popular in other poor countries, such as Argentina, India, and Fiji. Moser lamps will light up the lives of many people for many years to come.

26 위 글의 괄호 (A), (B), (C) 안에 들어갈 말로 가장 적절한 것은? (4점)

	(A)	(B)	(C)
①	during	because of	Thanks for
②	during	because of	Thanks to
③	during	because	Thanks to
④	while	because of	Thanks for
⑤	while	because	Thanks to

27 위 글의 내용을 한 문장으로 요약하고자 한다. 빈칸 (A), (B)에 들어갈 말로 가장 적절한 것은? (3점)

- A Moser lamp can help poor people to make their houses (A)_____ with (B)_____.

	(A)	(B)
①	bright	electricity
②	safe	electricity
③	bright	a plastic bottle
④	safe	a plastic bottle
⑤	warm	power

28 Which is true about a pot-in-pot cooler? (3점)

We'd like to talk about a pot-in-pot cooler. It keeps food fresh without electricity. It's very easy to make one. First, put a pot inside a larger pot. Then, pour sand and water between these pots. Just let the water dry off, and it'll cool the food.

① 전기를 사용하는 제품이다.
② 음식을 신선하게 유지시켜 준다.
③ 항아리 한 개와 모래가 필요하다.
④ 만들기는 어렵지만 오래 사용할 수 있다.
⑤ 그릇에 모래를 넣기 전에 모래를 완전히 말린 후 넣어야 한다.

29 다음 ⓐ~ⓔ 중 글의 흐름상 가장 <u>어색한</u> 것은? (4점)

ⓐA Moser lamp can be made for about one dollar and lasts for about 10 years. ⓑMoser made a lamp out of a plastic bottle. ⓒIt is also very safe. ⓓIt can never start a house fire. ⓔSurprisingly, it is very easy to make this magic lamp.

① ⓐ ② ⓑ ③ ⓒ ④ ⓓ ⑤ ⓔ

◎ 선택형 문항의 답안은 컴퓨터용 수정 싸인펜을 사용하여 OMR 답안지에 바르게 표기하시오.
◎ 서술형 문제는 답을 답안지에 반드시 검정 볼펜으로 쓰시오.
◎ 총 29문항 100점 만점입니다. 문항별 배점은 각 문항에 표시되어 있습니다.

[서울 동작구 ○○중]

01 다음 중 의미상 나머지와 <u>다르게</u> 분류되는 단어는?   (3점)

① sled   ② boat   ③ car
④ travel   ⑤ plane

[대전 ○○중]

[2~3] 다음 대화를 읽고 물음에 답하시오.

Anna: Do you have any special plans for the winter break?
Suho: I'm going to go to my grandparents' place in Pyeongchang. I'll go skating and sledding there. I love winter sports.
Anna: Good for you! I love winter sports, too. My favorite is ice hockey.
Suho: Oh, I've never played ice hockey, but I'm interested in learning how to play it.
Anna: Really? I can teach you how to play.
Suho: That's awesome. Is ice hockey the most popular sport in Canada?
Anna: Yes, it is. Everyone I know loves watching it and playing it.
Suho: How often did you play ice hockey when you were in Canada?
Anna: (A)_____
Suho: Wow, I'm sure you're really good at ice hockey. I can't wait to learn from you.

02 위 대화의 내용과 일치하지 <u>않는</u> 것은?   (4점)

① Ice hockey is the most popular sport in Canada.
② Suho and Anna like winter sports.
③ Anna plays ice hockey better than Suho.
④ Suho will play ice hockey in Pyeongchang this winter.
⑤ There are many people who like ice hockey in Canada.

03 위 대화의 빈칸 (A)에 가장 알맞은 것은?   (3점)

① I played ice hockey with my friends.
② I have played ice hockey for 2 hours.
③ I lived in Canada when I was young.
④ I played it at least two or three times a week.
⑤ I liked to play ice hockey when I lived in Canada.

[서울 송파구 ○○중]

04 다음 대화의 순서로 가장 자연스러운 것은?   (4점)

ⓐ Well, I'm going to play table tennis with my dad and brother.
ⓑ Every weekend. I love playing table tennis. How about you?
ⓒ Do you have any special plans for this weekend, Hana?
ⓓ I like playing soccer. I enjoy outdoor sports.
ⓔ How often do you play?

① ⓒ - ⓐ - ⓔ - ⓑ - ⓓ
② ⓔ - ⓑ - ⓒ - ⓐ - ⓓ
③ ⓒ - ⓑ - ⓐ - ⓓ - ⓔ
④ ⓔ - ⓓ - ⓐ - ⓑ - ⓒ
⑤ ⓔ - ⓒ - ⓐ - ⓑ - ⓓ

[5~6] 다음 대화를 읽고 물음에 답하시오.

Anna: Do you have any special plans for the winter break?

Suho: I'm going to go to my grandparents' place in Pyeongchang. I'll go skating and sledding there. I love winter sports.

Anna: Good for you! I love winter sports, too. My favorite is ice hockey.

Suho: Oh, I've never played ice hockey, but I'm interested in learning how to play it.

Anna: Really? I can teach you how to play.

Suho: That's awesome. Is ice hockey the most popular sport in Canada?

Anna: Yes, it is. Everyone I know loves watching it and playing it.

Suho: (A)_____ when you were in Canada?

Anna: I played at least two or three times a week in the winter.

Suho: Wow, I'm sure you're really good at ice hockey. I can't wait to learn from you.

05 위 대화를 읽고 알 수 <u>없는</u> 것은? (4점)

① Anna and Suho love winter sports.

② Anna enjoyed the ice hockey when she was in Canada.

③ Suho wants to learn how to play ice hockey.

④ Suho will visit his grandparents' house with Anna.

⑤ People in Canada love ice hockey very much.

06 위 대화의 빈칸 (A)에 들어갈 말로 가장 알맞은 것은? (3점)

① Did you like to watch ice hockey games

② Were you interested in the ice hockey

③ What did you learn

④ Where did you play ice hockey

⑤ How often did you play ice hockey

07 빈칸 (A)에 들어갈 가장 알맞은 말은? (4점)

Gayeon: What are you doing?

Minjun: I'm listening to old pop songs.

Gayeon: Oh, do you like old pop songs?

Minjun: No, (A)_____. I just want to sing my grandma's favorite songs at her birthday party next week.

Gayeon: Wow, what a nice granddaughter!

① I like them a lot.

② I'm interested in listening to them.

③ I don't like singing K-pop songs.

④ I'm not interested in them.

⑤ I have loved them.

08 다음 중 짝지어진 대화가 가장 자연스러운 것은? (3점)

① A: What are you doing?
B: I'm not interested in music.

② A: What's your favorite sport, James?
B: I don't like sports much, but I sometimes go swimming.

③ A: How often do you go sledding?
B: I enjoy winter sports a lot.

④ A: Are you interested in watching the Winter Olympics?
B: No, the Winter Olympics interests me.

⑤ A: Do you often go to the movies?
B: I have an interest in comedy movies.

09 다음 대화문에서 주어진 문장이 들어갈 알맞은 곳은? (4점)

Anna: Do you have any special plans for the winter break? (A)

Suho: I'm going to go to my grandparents' place in Pyeongchang. I'll go skating and sledding there. I love winter sports. (B)

Anna: Good for you! I love winter sports, too. (C)

Suho: Oh, I've never played ice hockey, but I'm interested in learning how to play it. (D)

Anna: Really? I can teach you how to play. (E)

Suho: That's awesome. Is ice hockey the most popular sport in Canada?

My favorite is ice hockey.

① (A)   ② (B)   ③ (C)   ④ (D)   ⑤ (E)

10 다음 글의 목적으로 알맞은 것은? (3점)

Are you interested in watching the Winter Olympics? Then, be sure to watch YG Sports to enjoy our live broadcasts from 6 p.m. to 11 p.m. At 11 p.m. every night, you can also enjoy our highlights of the most interesting games of the day.

① to give advice

② to move people

③ to record memories

④ to entertain people

⑤ to advertise their broadcasts

11 다음 중 <u>어색한</u> 문장은? (3점)

① They will be here on Tuesday.

② After a short stop, he continued on the dog sled race.

③ Her parents always talk to him on Chinese.

④ The little girl was sitting on her father's shoulders.

⑤ It's freezing. Put your coat on.

12 다음 빈칸에 들어갈 수 <u>없는</u> 것은? (3점)

• Our teachers always _____ us to come to school on time.

① ask   ② get   ③ have
④ want   ⑤ advise

13 다음 문장을 4 단어로 알맞게 영작하시오. (4점)

• 나는 무언가 타고 있는 냄새를 맡았다.

→ _____

14 다음 중 어법상 올바른 것은? (3점)

① The strongest dog on his team were Balto, so he made Balto his lead dog.

② I heard my name called.

③ Be sure to watch MBS Sports to enjoying our live broadcasts.

④ This heart-warming story celebrated every year by the Iditarod Race.

⑤ Tim asked me helped him with his homework.

[15~17] 다음 글을 읽고 물음에 답하시오.

(A) When Gunnar and Balto finally got the medicine, the snow was so heavy that Gunnar could not see his own hands. (B) When they were crossing a frozen river, Balto suddenly stopped. (C) Then, Gunnar saw the river ice ⓐcracking. (D) The whole team ⓑwas saved because Balto stopped just in time. (E) (가)When Balto and Gunnar reached the final team, they were sleeping. Gunnar told Balto ⓒcontinuing on. "Here's the medicine, Doctor!" shouted Gunnar. On February 2, Gunnar and his team finally ⓓarrived in Nome. This heart-warming story ⓔcelebrated every year by the Iditarod Race, the biggest sled dog race in the world.

15 위 글의 (A)~(D) 중 다음 문장이 들어갈 곳은? (4점)

> However, Balto was able to stay on the trail.

① (A)   ② (B)   ③ (C)   ④ (D)   ⑤ (E)

16 위 글의 밑줄 친 ⓐ~ⓔ 중 동사의 형태가 <u>어색한</u> 것을 2개 고르면? (3점)

① ⓐ   ② ⓑ   ③ ⓒ   ④ ⓓ   ⑤ ⓔ

17 위 글의 (가)문장을 주어진 단어들을 이용하여 비슷한 의미의 5형식 문장으로 완성하시오. (4점)

→ When Balto and Gunnar reached the final team, Balto and Gunnar _____.
(see / the final team)

[18~20] 다음 글을 읽고 물음에 답하시오.

In early March every year, the world's biggest sled dog race takes place in Alaska. It is called ⓐthe Iditarod Trail Sled Dog Race. Around 80 teams of 12 to 16 dogs take part in this race. Each team has to ⓑcover about 1,800 km from Anchorage to Nome. The race can take more than two weeks, and the teams often race through snowstorms. The Iditarod Race began ⓒ_____ 1973 ⓒ_____ memory of the dogs that saved Nome.

18 위 글의 밑줄 친 ⓐ에 대한 설명 중 가장 올바른 것은? (3점)

① It can take more than 14 days.
② Around 30 dogs take part in it.
③ It is held in early March every two years.
④ It is the biggest sled dog race in Alaska.
⑤ Each team should race from Nome to Anchorage.

19 위 글의 밑줄 친 ⓑ와 의미가 같은 것은? (3점)

① Please put a <u>cover</u> over the food.
② She <u>covered</u> her face with her hands.
③ <u>Cover</u> this sleeping child with your coat.
④ They had to <u>cover</u> thirty miles by sunset.
⑤ You shouldn't judge a book by its <u>cover</u>.

20 위 글의 ⓒ에 들어갈 단어와 같은 말이 들어가는 것은? (3점)

① The daytime gets longer _____ the summer.
② Turn _____ the air conditioner when it is hot.
③ Our class won the relay race _____ the sports day.
④ This trail will lead us to the top _____ this mountain.
⑤ The car racer started to drive faster to catch up _____ the lead car.

[21~26] 다음 글을 읽고 물음에 답하시오.

In early March every year, the world's biggest sled dog race takes place in Alaska. ⓐIt called the Iditarod Trail Sled Dog Race. Around 80 teams of 12 to 16 dogs take part in this race. ⓑEach team have to cover about 1,800 km from Anchorage to Nome. The race can take more than two weeks, and the teams often race through snowstorms. ⓒ The Iditarod Race began in 1973 in memory of the dogs that saved Nome.

One cold winter day in 1925, a terrible thing happened in Nome. Some children got very sick, and the disease kept spreading. ⓓThe people of Nome needed medicine right away, but the town did not have any medicine. Someone had to get it from a hospital in Anchorage. ⓔBecause the heavy snow, a dog sled relay was the only way to get the medicine from Anchorage to Nome. Soon, the race to Nome began.

Twenty-one dog teams were in the relay. On January 27, the first team left, and the others waited at different points. Gunnar was the driver of the 20th team. ⓕStrongest dog on his team was Balto, so he made Balto his lead dog.

[A] ㉮ When Gunnar and Balto finally got the medicine, the snow was so heavy that Gunnar could not see his own hands. ㉯ When they were crossing a frozen river, Balto suddenly stopped. ㉰ Then, Gunnar saw the river ice crack. The whole team was saved because Balto stopped just in time. ㉱ When Balto and Gunnar reached the final team, they were sleeping. Gunnar told Balto to continue on. ㉲

"Here's the medicine, Doctor!" shouted Gunnar. On February 2, Gunnar and his team finally arrived in Nome. The town was saved.

[B] 이 가슴 따뜻한 이야기는 이제 세계에서 가장 큰 개썰매 경주인 Iditarod 경주를 통해 매년 기념되고 있다.

21 ⓐ~ⓕ 중 문맥 및 어법상 옳은 문장을 모두 고른 것은? (3점)

① ⓐ, ⓑ ② ⓑ, ⓔ ③ ⓒ, ⓓ
④ ⓒ, ⓕ ⑤ ⓔ, ⓕ

22 위 글의 내용과 일치하는 문장을 모두 고른 것은? (4점)

㉠ In 1926, a terrible disease kept spreading in Nome.
㉡ Gunnar and his dogs were the 21th team, and Balto was the lead dog.
㉢ Gunnar and Balto reached the final team, but they were sleeping.
㉣ A dog sled relay was the only way to get medicine.
㉤ Balto stopped after the river ice cracked and saved his team.
㉥ The biggest sled dog race takes place in Canada.
㉦ Gunnar's team finally arrived in Nome on February 27.

① ㉢, ㉣ ② ㉢, ㉦
③ ㉣, ㉤, ㉥ ④ ㉡, ㉣, ㉤, ㉥
⑤ ㉠, ㉡, ㉤, ㉦

23 ㉮~㉲ 중 다음 문장이 들어갈 위치로 가장 적절한 곳은? (3점)

However, Balto was able to stay on the trail.

① ㉮ ② ㉯ ③ ㉰ ④ ㉱ ⑤ ㉲

24 빈칸에 들어갈 단어가 위 글에 있는 것은? (3점)

① _____ the straw to use it easily.
(빨대를 쉽게 사용할 수 있게 구부리세요.)
② His father is the _____ of police.
(그의 아버지는 경찰서 최고직위이다.)
③ The old wall has started to _____.
(오래된 벽이 갈라지기 시작했다.)
④ The _____ is off because of the storm.
(폭풍 때문에 전기가 나갔다.)
⑤ The _____ helps poor children in our country. (그 자선단체는 우리나라의 가난한 아이들을 돕는다.)

25 [B]의 우리말을 영작할 때 다섯 번째 오는 조각은?　(4점)

heart-warming story	the biggest
in the world	sled dog race
by the Iditarod Race	every year
is now celebrated	this

① by the Iditarod Race

② in the world

③ the biggest

④ is now celebrated

⑤ every year

26 위 글의 내용을 기반으로 다음에 이어질 문장을 주어, 동사를 갖춘 완전한 문장으로 쓰시오.　(5점)

> • Balto is the greatest sled dog in the world because ＿＿＿＿＿＿＿＿＿＿＿＿＿＿＿.

[충북 ○○중]

[27~29] 다음 글을 읽고 물음에 답하시오.

(A)[When / Before] Gunnar and Balto finally got the medicine, the snow was so heavy that Gunnar could not see his own hands. However, Balto was able to stay on the trail. When they were crossing a frozen river, Balto (B)[sudden / suddenly] stopped. Then, (가)Gunnar는 강의 얼음이 갈라지는 것을 보았다. The whole team was saved because Balto stopped just in time. As Balto and Gunnar reached the final team, they were sleeping. Gunnar told Balto to continue on.
"Here's the medicine, Doctor!" shouted Gunnar. On February 2, Gunnar and his team finally arrived in Nome. The town (C)[saved / was saved]. This heart-warming story is now celebrated every year by the Iditarod Race, the biggest sled dog race in the world.

27 위 글의 밑줄 친 (가)에 들어갈 영어 표현으로 알맞은 것은?　(3점)

① Gunnar saw cracked the river ice.

② Gunnar saw the river ice cracking.

③ Gunnar saw ice cracking the river.

④ Gunnar cracked the river ice seeing.

⑤ Gunnar cracked the river and saw ice.

28 위 글의 (A)~(C)에 들어갈 단어로 알맞은 것은?　(4점)

	(A)	(B)	(C)
①	Before	sudden	was saved
②	Before	suddenly	saved
③	When	suddenly	saved
④	When	sudden	saved
⑤	When	suddenly	was saved

29 위 글의 내용으로 알맞지 않은 것은?　(3점)

① Balto는 얼음이 갈라지기 전에 멈췄다.

② 2월 2일에 Gunnar 팀이 Nome에 도착했다.

③ Balto 덕분에 전체 팀이 목숨을 구할 수 있었다.

④ Gunnar와 Balto는 마지막 팀에 이르러서 잠이 들었다.

⑤ 매년 위의 감동적인 이야기를 기념하기 위해 Iditarod Race가 열린다.

2학년 영어 2학기 기말고사(8과) 2회

반		점수	
이름			

문항수 : 선택형(25문항) 서술형(2문항)   20 . . .

◎ 선택형 문항의 답안은 컴퓨터용 수정 싸인펜을 사용하여 OMR 답안지에 바르게 표기하시오.
◎ 서술형 문제는 답을 답안지에 반드시 검정 볼펜으로 쓰시오.
◎ 총 27문항 100점 만점입니다. 문항별 배점은 각 문항에 표시되어 있습니다.

[경기 기출]

01 나머지 넷과 관련이 없는 하나는?   (3점)

① sled   ② doctor
③ disease   ④ medicine
⑤ hospital

[서울 강북구 ○○중]

[2~3] 다음 대화를 읽고 물음에 답하시오.

Anna: Do you have any special plans for the winter break?
Suho: I'm going to go to my grandparents' place in Pyeongchang. I'll go skating and sledding there. I love winter sports.
Anna: Good for you! I love winter sports, too. My favorite is ice hockey.
Suho: Oh, I've never played ice hockey, but I'm interested in learning how to play it.
Anna: Really? I can teach you how to play.
Suho: That's awesome. Is ice hockey the most popular sport in Canada?
Anna: Yes, it is. Everyone I know loves watching it and playing it.
Suho: _____ when you were in Canada?
Anna: I played at least two or three times a week in the winter.
Suho: Wow, I'm sure you're really good at ice hockey. I can't wait to learn from you.

02 위 대화를 읽고 대답할 수 없는 질문은?   (4점)

① What is Suho planning to do during the wintcr brcak?
② What kind of winter sport is Suho going to enjoy in Pyeongchang?
③ What is Suho interested in learning?
④ What is the most popular sport in Canada?
⑤ What is Anna's plan for the winter break?

03 위 대화의 빈칸에 들어갈 Suho의 말로 가장 알맞은 것은?   (4점)

① Where did you play ice hockey
② Did you want to play ice hockey
③ How often did you play ice hockey
④ How long were you playing ice hockey
⑤ Who taught you how to play ice hockey

[경기 ○○중]

04 다음 대화의 빈칸에 들어갈 말로 가장 적절한 것은?   (4점)

Brian: What are you doing?
Grace: I'm listening to old pop songs.
Brian: Oh, do you like old pop songs?
Grace: No, I don't. I just want to sing my grandma's favorite songs at her birthday party next week.
Brian: Wow, _____

① what a nice grandmother!
② you really enjoy listening to old pop songs.
③ I'm sure your grandmother will be proud of you.
④ there are so many wonderful pop songs these days.
⑤ I didn't know that you are good at listening to old pop songs.

[5~7] 다음 대화를 읽고 물음에 답하시오.

Anna: Do you have any special plans for the winter break?

Suho: I'm going to go to my grandparents' place in Pyeongchang. I'll go skating and sledding there. I love winter sports.

Anna: Good for you! I love winter sports, too. My favorite is ice hockey.

Suho: Oh, I've never played ice hockey, but I'm interested in learning how to play it.

Anna: Really? I can teach you how to play.

Suho: That's awesome. Is ice hockey the most popular sport in Canada?

Anna: Yes, it is. Everyone I know loves watching it and playing it.

Suho: ⓐ_____ ice hockey when you were in Canada?

Anna: I played at least two or three times a week in the winter.

Suho: Wow, I'm sure you're really good at ice hockey. ⓑ_____ from you.

05 위 대화를 읽고 문맥에 맞도록 빈칸 ⓐ에 들어갈 표현을 완성하시오. (4점)

→ _____

06 위 대화의 빈칸 ⓑ에 들어갈 표현으로 알맞은 것은? (3점)

① I can't wait to learn

② I can't want to learn

③ I can't stand learning

④ I'm looking for learning

⑤ I have no idea about learning

07 위 대화의 내용과 일치하지 <u>않는</u> 것은? (3점)

① Suho와 Anna는 겨울 스포츠를 좋아한다.

② Suho는 평창에서 스케이트와 썰매를 탈 예정이다.

③ Suho는 아이스하키를 배우는 것에 관심이 있다.

④ 캐나다에서 아이스하키는 가장 인기 있는 스포츠이다.

⑤ Anna는 겨울에 일주일에 적어도 두세 번은 아이스하키를 할 계획이다.

08 다음 대화의 흐름상 빈칸에 들어갈 말로 가장 자연스러운 것은? (4점)

B: What are you doing?

G: I'm listening to old pop songs.

B: Oh, do you like old pop songs?

G: _____ I just want to sing my grandma's favorite songs at her birthday party next week.

B: Wow, what a nice granddaughter!

① Yes, I want to be a singer.

② Yes, don't forget to listen to them.

③ No, I've never heard of them.

④ No, I'm not interested in them.

⑤ Yes, be sure to listen to them.

09 두 사람의 대화 순서가 바르게 연결된 것은? (4점)

(A) I'm practicing badminton.

(B) Do you like playing badminton?

(C) No, I'm not interested in it. I just want to pass the badminton test next week.

(D) What are you doing?

(E) O.K. Good luck!

① (B)-(A)-(E)-(C)-(D) ② (B)-(C)-(A)-(D)-(E)

③ (D)-(A)-(B)-(C)-(E) ④ (D)-(B)-(C)-(E)-(A)

⑤ (D)-(C)-(E)-(B)-(A)

[10~11] 다음 대화를 읽고 물음에 답하시오.

A: (A)_____

B: I'm going to go to my grandparents' place in Pyeongchang. I'll go skating and sledding there. I love winter sports.

A: Good for you! I love winter sports, too. ⓐMy favorite is ice hockey.

B: Oh, I've never played ice hockey, ⓑbut I'm interested in learning how to play it.

A: Really? ⓒIt's so difficult that you can't learn how to play it.

B: That's awesome. Is ice hockey the most popular sport in Canada?

A: Yes, it is. ⓓEveryone I know loves watching it and playing it.

B: How often did you play ice hockey when you were in Canada?

B: ⓔI played at least two or three times a week in the winter.

A: Wow, I'm sure you're really good at ice hockey. I can't wait to learn from you.

10 위 대화의 흐름상 빈칸 (A)에 들어갈 말로 가장 적절한 것은? (4점)

① Do you have any special plans for the winter break?

② Are you interested in winter sports such as skating and sledding?

③ Do you enjoy winter sports in Pyeonchang?

④ Do you know that Pyeongchang is famous for winter sports?

⑤ What kind of winter sports do you like best?

11 위 대화의 밑줄 친 ⓐ~ⓔ 중, 대화의 흐름상 어색한 것은? (3점)

① ⓐ ② ⓑ ③ ⓒ ④ ⓓ ⑤ ⓔ

12 다음 중 어법상 올바른 문장의 개수는? (4점)

ⓐ I heard someone called my name.

ⓑ His parents won't allow him staying out late.

ⓒ Do you want do it again?

ⓓ He told the children not to do it again.

ⓔ Kate smelled something to burn.

ⓕ He saw someone carry something heavy.

① 0개 ② 1개 ③ 2개 ④ 3개 ⑤ 4개

13 두 문장의 빈칸에 공통으로 들어갈 수 <u>없는</u> 것은? (3점)

• Tom _____ me to help him.

• Ms. Kim _____ the children to be quiet.

① wanted ② ordered ③ told

④ made ⑤ asked

14 다음 두 문장을 하나로 합치려고 한다. 같은 뜻이 되도록 빈칸을 채우시오. (4점)

• I saw Anna.

• She was crossing the street.

= I saw Anna _____.

15 다음 중 어법상 <u>잘못된</u> 것을 2개 고르면? (4점)

① I smell something burning.

② Jiwoo heard his name called.

③ Juhee saw somebody taken pictures of flowers.

④ We watched Jack get into his car.

⑤ Miso saw Suho to carry something heavy.

[16~17] 다음 글을 읽고 물음에 답하시오.

When Gunnar and Balto finally got the medicine, the snow was so heavy that Gunnar could not see his own hands.
(A) _____
"Here's the medicine, Doctor!" shouted Gunnar. On February 2, Gunnar and his team finally arrived in Nome. The town was saved. This heart-warming story (B)_____ every year by the Iditarod Race, the biggest sled dog race in the world.

16 위 글의 빈칸 (A)에 들어갈 내용의 순서로 가장 알맞은 것은? (4점)

(A) Then, Gunnar saw the river ice cracking. The whole team was saved because Balto stopped just in time.

(B) When Balto and Gunnar reached the final team, they were sleeping. Gunnar told Balto to continue on.

(C) However, Balto was able to stay on the trail. When they were crossing a frozen river, Balto suddenly stopped.

① (C)-(A)-(B) ② (A)-(B)-(C)
③ (A)-(C)-(B) ④ (B)-(A)-(C)
⑤ (C)-(B)-(A)

17 위 글의 빈칸 (B)에 들어갈 형태로 알맞은 것은? (3점)

① is now celebrating
② now celebrated
③ has now celebrated
④ is now celebrated
⑤ now celebrates

[18~19] 다음 글을 읽고 물음에 답하시오.

㉮ It was one cold winter day in 1925. ㉯ Some children got very sick in the town. ㉰ The disease kept spreading. ㉱ And situation was getting worse. ㉲ The people of Nome needed medicine right away. (A)_____ the town did not have any. Someone had to get it from a hospital in Anchorage. (B)_____ the heavy snow, a dog sled relay was the only way to get the medicine from Anchorage to Nome. Soon, the race to Nome began.
Twenty-one dog teams were in the relay. On January 27, the first team left, and the others waited at different points. Gunnar was the driver of the 20th team. The strongest dog on his team was Balto. (C)_____ he made Balto his lead dog.

18 (A)~(C)에 들어갈 말이 바르게 연결된 것은? (4점)

	(A)	(B)	(C)
①	Moreover	Because	So
②	In addition	Due to	Finally
③	However	Due to	So
④	However	Because of	Also
⑤	Therefore	Because of	Luckily

19 위 글의 ㉮~㉲ 중 보기의 문장이 들어갈 곳으로 가장 적절한 것은? (4점)

보기
A terrible thing happened in Nome.

① ㉮ ② ㉯ ③ ㉰ ④ ㉱ ⑤ ㉲

[20~22] 다음 글을 읽고 물음에 답하시오.

In early March every year, the world's biggest sled dog race takes place in Alaska. ⓐIt is called the Iditarod Trail Sled Dog Race. Around 80 teams of 12 to 16 dogs take part in this race. Each team has to cover about 1,800 km from Anchorage to Nome. The race can take more than two weeks, and the teams often race through snowstorms. The Iditarod Race began in 1973 in memory of the dogs that saved Nome.

One cold winter day in 1925, ⓑa terrible thing happened in Nome. Some children got very sick, and the disease kept spreading. The people of Nome needed medicine right away, but the town did not have ⓒany. Someone had to get ⓓit from a hospital in Anchorage. Because of the heavy snow, a dog sled relay was the only way to get ⓔit from Anchorage to Nome. Soon, the race to Nome began.

Twenty-one dog teams were in the relay. On January 27, the first team left, and the others waited at different points. Gunnar was the driver of the 20th team. The strongest dog on his team was Balto, so he made Balto his lead dog.

When Gunnar and Balto finally got the medicine, the snow was so heavy that Gunnar could not see his own hands. However, Balto was able to stay on the trail. When Balto and Gunnar reached the final team, they were sleeping. Gunnar and Balto continued on.

"Here's the medicine, Doctor!" shouted Gunnar. On February 2, Gunnar and his team finally arrived in Nome. The town was saved.

20 위 글에서 답을 찾을 수 <u>없는</u> 질문은? (4점)

① Why did Gunnar make Balto his lead dog?
② Where does the biggest sled dog race take place?
③ How was Balto able to find the trail in the snow?
④ How long does the Iditarod Trail Sled Dog Race take?
⑤ How many teams take part in the Iditrarod Sled Dog Race?

21 위 글의 문맥상 밑줄 친 ⓐ~ⓔ의 의미가 가장 적절한 것은? (4점)

① ⓐ: the world's biggest sled dog
② ⓑ: snowstorm
③ ⓒ: any sled
④ ⓓ: medicine
⑤ ⓔ: hospital

22 위 글을 다음과 같이 요약할 때 문장 (A)~(E)를 순서에 맞게 배열한 것은? (4점)

A disease spreaded in Nome.
(A) Gunnar and his dogs were the 20th team.
(B) The people of Nome needed medicine.
(C) Gunnar and Balto reached the final team, but they were sleeping.
(D) A dog sled relay through the heavy snow began.
(E) Gunnar and Balto continued on and arrived in Nome with the medicine.
Nome was saved.

① (A)-(B)-(D)-(E)-(C)
② (B)-(D)-(A)-(C)-(E)
③ (B)-(D)-(E)-(A)-(C)
④ (D)-(A)-(B)-(C)-(E)
⑤ (D)-(B)-(A)-(E)-(C)

[23~25] 다음 글을 읽고 물음에 답하시오.

One cold winter day in 1925, a terrible thing happened in Nome. Some children got very sick, and ⓐthe disease kept spreading. The people of Nome needed medicine right (A)_____, but ⓑ the town did not have any. Someone had to get it from a hospital in Anchorage. Because of the heavy snow, a dog sled relay was the only way to get the medicine from Anchorage to Nome. Soon, the race to Nome began.

Twenty-one dog teams were in the relay. On January 27, the first team left, and the others waited at different points. Gunnar was the driver of the 20th team. The strongest dog on his team was Balto, so he made Balto his lead dog.

When Gunnar and Balto finally got the medicine, ⓒthe snow was so heavily that Gunnar could not see his own hands. However, Balto was able to stay on the trail. When they were crossing a frozen river, Balto suddenly stopped. Then, ⓓGunnar saw the river ice cracks. ⓔThe whole team saved because Balto stopped just (B)_____ time. When Balto and Gunnar reached the final team, they were sleeping. Gunnar told Balto continue on.

23 위 글의 밑줄 친 ⓐ~ⓔ 중 어법상 올바른 것의 개수는? (4점)

① 1개　② 2개　③ 3개　④ 4개　⑤ 5개

24 위 글에서 답을 찾을 수 없는 것은? (3점)

① What was a terrible thing in Nome?
② When did a terrible thing happen in Nome?
③ Who is the driver of the first dog team?
④ How many dog teams were there in the relay?
⑤ Why did Gunnar make Balto the lead dog of his dog team?

25 위 글의 빈칸 (A), (B)에 들어갈 표현으로 알맞게 연결한 것은? (4점)

	(A)	(B)
①	on	in
②	on	for
③	away	in
④	away	for
⑤	away	of

[26~27] 다음 글을 읽고 물음에 답하시오.

In early March every year, the world's biggest sled dog race ⓐtakes place in Alaska. It ⓑis called the Iditarod Trail Sled Dog Race. Around 80 teams of 12 to 16 dogs ⓒtake part in this race. Each team ⓓhave to cover about 1,800 km from Anchorage to Nome. The race can take more than two weeks, and the teams often ⓔrace through snowstorms.

26 위 글을 읽고 답할 수 없는 질문은? (4점)

① Where is the race held?
② How long does the race take?
③ How many teams join the race?
④ How far does the team run on the race?
⑤ Where did the name of the race come from?

27 위 글의 밑줄 친 ⓐ~ⓔ 중 어법상 알맞지 않은 것은? (3점)

① ⓐ　② ⓑ　③ ⓒ　④ ⓓ　⑤ ⓔ

정답 및 해설

Lesson 5 (중간)

01 ①	02 ⑤	03 ④	04 ⑤	05 ②	06 ③	07 ①, ③, ⑤	
08 ④	09 ④	10 ②	11 ①	12 ①	13 ③	14 ①	15 ⑤
16 ①	17 ③	18 ①	19 appreciate	20 ①	21 ③	22 ⑤	
23 ④	24 ③	25 ①	26 ⑤	27 ⑤	28 ①	29 ⑤	

01 Germany - German: 독일 - 독일어

02 뒤에서 생선을 먹자고 하므로 ⓔ는 'I like seafood more than meat.'이 적절하다.

03 보통 부사는 수식하는 말 바로 앞에 쓰인다. 과거이므로 got을 쓰고 only가 one question을 수식하도록 한다.

04 아직 시작도 안 하고서 English project에 대해 걱정하고 있는 사람에게 해 줄 수 있는 속담으로 '시작이 반이다'가 적절하다.

05 'Why don't we go see a musical at Bravo Theater near your work?'라고 했다.

06 '12시가 어떠니?'라고 제안하고 있으므로 '몇 시에 만날지' 묻는 것이 적절하다.

07 '~하자, ~하는 게 어때?'라는 표현은 Let's+동사원형 ~., Shall we+동사원형 ~?, Why don't we+동사원형 ~?, What[How] about+동사원형+-ing ~? 등을 사용할 수 있다.

08 'Why don't we take the subway?'에 'That's a good idea.' 라고 했다.

09 조건을 나타내는 부사절에서는 미래시제 대신에 현재시제를 사용한다. will rain → rains

10 ⓑ won't → 삭제
ⓒ will miss → miss
ⓓ will be → is *as fit as a fiddle: 건강한(= very healthy)

11 ② colder → cold
③ broken → was broken
④ build → built
⑤ new anything → anything new

12 공주의 수수께끼가 무엇인지는 알 수 없다.

13 주어진 문장의 He가 가리키는 것이 (C) 앞 문장의 the prince이므로 (C)가 적절하다.

14 (A) 다음 문장의 he가 가리키는 것이 주어진 문장의 Any prince 이므로 (A)가 적절하다.

15 서로 상반되는 내용이 나오므로 However가 적절하다.

16 우리말과 같은 뜻이 되도록 단어들을 배열하면 'she is as cold as ice'이다.

17 어떤 용감한 왕자가 Turandot에게 반한다.

18 이유가 이어지고 있으므로 because가 적절하다.

19 appreciate는 '감상하다, 감사하다, 알아주다' 등의 뜻으로 쓰이며 (B)에서는 '감상하나', (C)에서는 '감상하다', (D)에서는 '감사하다'의 의미로 쓰였다.

20 ①은 명사절을 이끄는 접속사로 쓰였지만 밑줄 친 (A)와 나머지는 모두 조건절을 이끄는 접속사로 쓰였다.

21 'Like many other famous operas, *Turandot* is in Italian because opera started in Italy in the 16th century.'라고 했다.

22 'Before we begin, I'd like to tell you the storyline of the opera *Turandot*.'라고 했다.

23 그의 이름을 알아낼 때까지 그 누구도 잠들 수 없다는 것으로 보아 ⓓ의 easy를 difficult 정도로 고쳐야 한다.

24 'I will win!'이라고 하는 것으로 보아 ③번이 적절하다.

25 Turandot와 결혼하려면 수수께끼에 답해야 하고 답하지 못하면 죽어야 하므로 세상에서 가장 위험한 사랑이라고 하는 것이 적절하다.

26 Turandot의 줄거리가 복잡하다는 언급은 없다.

27 'Turandot must find the answer before dawn(새벽).'이라고 했다.

28 prince를 princess로, her name을 his name으로 바꿔야 한다.

29 'If you answer correctly, I will agree to die. If you answer incorrectly, you will have to marry me.'라고 제안했다.

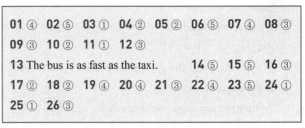

Lesson 5 (중간)

01 ④	02 ⑤	03 ①	04 ②	05 ②	06 ⑤	07 ④	08 ③
09 ③	10 ②	11 ①	12 ③				
13 The bus is as fast as the taxi.				14 ⑤	15 ⑤	16 ③	
17 ②	18 ②	19 ④	20 ④	21 ③	22 ④	23 ⑤	24 ①
25 ①	26 ③						

01 storyline: (소설·연극·영화 등의) 줄거리

02 다음 주 수요일에 수업이 없다는 말에 이어, 정말이냐며 왜 없는지 묻는 ⓑ가 이어지고, 이유를 설명하는 ⓓ가 나온 후, 알았다고 하는 ⓐ가 나오고, 같이 뭔가 할 수 있을지 묻는 ⓔ에 이어서, 오후 휴무를 할 수 있을 것 같다며 뭘 하고 싶은지 묻는 ⓒ가 이어지는 것이 자연스럽다.

03 '4시가 어떠니?'라고 제안하고 있으므로 '몇 시에 만날지' 묻는 것이 적절하다.

04 축하하러 외출하자는데 오늘밤에 조금 갖다 주겠다는 응답은 어색하다.

05 'as brave as coal'은 '석탄처럼 용감한'이라는 말이 되어 이상하다. 보통 'as black as coal(칠흑같은, 새까만)'로 쓰고 본문에서는 'as brave as a lion(매우 용감한, 사자처럼 용감한)'으로 쓴다.

06 G가 'O.K. See you there at 11 o'clock.'이라고 했다.

07 (D) 다음에 '12시가 어떤지' 제안하고 있으므로 (D)가 적절하다.

08 Anna와 아빠가 점심으로 무엇을 먹을지는 알 수 없다.

09 (A) off: (일·근무 등을) 쉬어, 휴가를 얻어, (B) 좁은 장소 앞에 at, (C) on+요일, 날짜: ~에

10 'We can get a discount if we go on a Wednesday.'라고 했다.

11 ⓒ as good as → as well as
ⓓ don't 삭제
ⓔ you → he

12 ① Clara → Bobby
② is as fast as → is not faster than
④ can → cannot
⑤ cannot → can

13 'as+원급+as'는 '…처럼 ~한'이라는 의미의 동등비교 표현이다.

14 'Turandot must find the answer before dawn'이라고 했다.

15 그의 이름을 알아낼 때까지 그 누구도 잠들 수 없다는 것으로 보아 ⓔ의 easy를 difficult 정도로 고쳐야 한다.

16 (A) 뒤에 이유가 나오므로 because, (B) 문맥상 '~하기 전에'를 뜻하는 Before, (C) 문맥상 '만약 ~한다면'을 뜻하는 if가 적절하다.

17 (A) 'Like many other famous operas, *Turandot* is in Italian'라고 했다.
(B) 'we are going to perform Giacomo Puccini's opera *Turandot*'라고 했다.
(C) Giacomo Puccini는 작곡자이고 글쓴이 일행이 공연할 것이다.

18 ⓐ appreciate: to like something because you recognize its good qualities
ⓒ stranger: someone you have never met before
ⓓ dawn: the time of day when light first appears in the sky
ⓔ aria: a song for one of the leading singers in an opera or choral work

19 이름을 맞게 대답한다면 나는 죽는 것에 동의하겠지만 답이 틀리면 당신은 저와 결혼해야 한다는 말은 이름을 알아내지 못하면 저와 결혼해야 하지만, 이름을 알아내면 저와 결혼할 필요가 없다는 말이다.

20 century: 100년, 1세기

21 in Italian: 이탈리아어로 in Italy: 이탈리아에서

22 'You will appreciate it better if you know the story.'라고 했다.

23 ⓐ performing → perform
ⓑ will 삭제
ⓒ beautiful → beauty
ⓓ colder → cold
ⓔ want → wants
ⓕ answers → answer
ⓖ fail → fails
ⓘ it → them

24 ㉮와 ①: 이탈리아어 ②, ③, ④: 이탈리아의 ⑤: 이탈리아인

25 영화를 보게 된 이유는 언급되지 않았다.

26 'He then gives her a riddle of his own.'이라고 했다.

Lesson 6 (중간) 1회

01 ①	02 ③	03 ①	04 ①	05 ③	06 ③	07 ②	08 ②
09 ④	10 ②	11 ②	12 ③	13 ②	14 ④	15 ①	16 ②
17 ②	18 ④	19 ④	20 ⑤	21 ⑤	22 ⑤	23 ②	24 ⑤

25 The dog caught the cat.   **26** ④   **27** ①   **28** ②
29 The scholar was so disappointed that he went to live on a mountain.

01 예를 들어 청소부나 정원사로서 다른 사람의 가정에서 일하도록 고용된 사람은 'servant(하인, 시종)'이다.

02 even: ~조차(도)

03 'Which do you prefer?'는 선호하는 것을 묻는 표현이며 ①번이 'I like A better than B.'로 알맞게 답하고 있다.

04 'Do you prefer A or B?'로 선호하는 것을 묻고 'I prefer ~'로 알맞게 답하고 있다.

05 ⓑ 선호하는 운동을 묻고 ⓐ 실내 운동을 선호한다고 답하고 ⓓ 탁구 동아리를 추천하자 ⓒ 좋은 생각이라며 감사하는 순서가 적절하다.

06 비교 대상은 어법상 대등한 것이어야 하므로 April과 비교할 수 있는 July가 적절하다.

07 'I went there last Friday with my friends.'라고 했다.

08 'Why don't you join the table tennis club, then?'이라는 추천에 'That's a good idea. Thank you.'라고 했으므로 '탁구' 동아리가 적절하다.

09 (A) 'I haven't seen a movie recently.'라고 했다.
(B) 'Can you recommend any good comedies?'라고 했다.

10 마지막에 'I will take it.'이라고 했으므로 ②번이 적절하다.

11 'I really liked the fried vegetables.'라고 했고, 'Then, you should try their fried fish. You'll love it!'이라고 했다.

12 recommend: 추천하다 symbolize: 상징하다 correct: 바로잡다, 정정하다 perform: 공연하다, 수행하다

13 ① cooking → cooked
③ looked by my sister after → looked after by my sister
④ invented → was invented by
⑤ are → were

14 -thing으로 끝나는 부정대명사는 형용사가 뒤에서 수식한다.

15 ② sent → send
③ built → was built
④ was planted → planted
⑤ choosen → chosen

16 ⓐ looked → look
ⓒ special something → something special
ⓓ ingredients → ingredient
ⓔ were → was

17 'King Yeongjo offered them something special'이라고 했다.

18 ① scholar   ② symbolize
③ mysterious   ⑤ official

19 전통 음식인 송편의 유래에 대한 글이다.

20 'the king and his servants found a strange turtle.'라고 했다.

21 (A) one day: 언젠가[어느 날](미래의 어느 시기나 과거의 특정한 날을 가리킴), some day: (미래의) 언젠가 (B) 상반되는 내용이 나오므로 On the other hand. At last: 마침내[드디어] (C) 상반되는 내용이 나오므로 However가 적절하다.

22 왜 신라가 새로운 달처럼 보였는지는 알 수 없다.

23 상반되는 내용이 나오므로 However가 적절하다. 뒤에 콤마(,)가 있으므로 But은 어색하다. But으로 시작하는 문장은 문맥상 'However,(콤마)'로 바꿀 수 있을 때 가능하다.

24 사람들이 이 솥과 그 안의 음식을 신선로라고 부른 것이므로 능동태로 써야 한다.

25 'by the dog'을 The dog으로 고쳐 주어로 쓰고 동사를 'be+p.p.'에서 caught로 고치고, 주어인 The cat을 목적어 the cat으로 쓴다.

26 (A) 탕평채와, (B) 송편의 유래에 대한 이야기이다.

27 ⓑ 'party'의 뜻은 '정당'이고 "Can you come to my birthday party?"에서의 뜻은 '파티'이다. ⓒ '이상한 무언가'는 'something strange'로 쓴다. ⓓ 'this'는 '거북이 등에 쓰인 문구'를 의미한다. ⓔ에는 글의 흐름상 'However'를 쓸 수 있다.

28 상반되는 내용이 나오므로 However가 적절하다.

29 'so ~ that ...'은 '너무 ~해서 …하다'라는 의미이다.

Lesson 6 (중간)

01 ①	**02** ⑤	**03** ③	**04** ③	**05** ②	**06** ②	**07** ②	**08** ①
09 ①	**10** ③	**11** ④	**12** ④	**13** ⑤	**14** ①	**15** ④	**16** ⑤

17 Something was written on its back. **18** ② **19** ④ **20** ④

21 ④ **22** ③ **23** ③ **24** ① **25** ⑤ **26** ④ **27** ① **28** ⑤

29 ③

30 (가) him = King Yeonsan (나) He = the scholar
(다) it = this pot

31 ⑤

01 비교 대상은 대등한 것이어야 하는데 lunch는 pizza와 비교하기가 어색하다.

02 fortune - misfortune

03 (B) 스포츠 동아리에 가입하려고 생각 중이라는 말에 이어 (D) 실내 스포츠와 야외 스포츠 중에 더 좋은 것을 묻고 (E) 실내 스포츠가 더 좋다고 하자 (C) 탁구 동아리를 추천하고 (A) 좋다고 하는 순서가 적절하다.

04 'Could you recommend a dish for me?'라고 했다.

05 try: (평가를 위해) 실제로 해보다, 도전해 보다

06 뒤에서 선호하는 것을 물은 후에 음식을 추천하고 있으므로 음식을 추천해 달라고 부탁하는 ②번이 적절하다.

07 Jaden이 왜 고기보다 해산물을 더 좋아하는지는 알 수 없다.

08 'Why don't you join the table tennis club, then?'이라는 추천에 'That's a good idea. Thank you.'라고 했으므로 'table tennis(탁구)' 동아리가 적절하다.

09 recommend A to[for] B: A를 B에게 추천하다

10 이탈리아 요리책을 사고 있으므로 '서점'이 적절하다.

11 박 선생님이 해산물과 육류 중에서 더 좋아하는 것이 무엇인지는 알 수 없다.

12 뒤에서 'how about *Funny Families*?'라고 추천했으므로 ④번이 적절하다.

13 ⓒ special something → something special
ⓖ is → are

14 look(~처럼 보이다)은 자동사이므로 수동태로 바꿔 쓸 수 없다.

15 'go : gone'은 '원형 : 과거분사'이므로 seen이 적절하다.

16 (A) will 다음에 나오는 동사이므로 become (B) people of Silla가 주어이므로 were (C) were와 병렬 관계로 made가 적절하다.

17 Something을 주어로 하여 수동태 'was written'으로 쓴다.

18 (다)의 It이 주어진 글에 나온 Something을 가리키므로 먼저 나오고, (가)의 The fortune teller가 (다)의 a fortune teller 다음에 나와야 하며 (나)에서 (가)의 결과에 대해 언급하므로 (가) 다음에 (나)가 나와야 한다.

19 '"A full moon will soon become smaller. On the other hand, a half moon will grow bigger and become a full moon."'이라고 했다.

20 (D) 앞에서 주어진 문장의 원인이 나오므로 (D)가 적절하다.

21 앞의 내용에 대한 원인이 나오므로 ⓓ는 That is because로 고쳐야 한다.

22 (A) 영조가 신하들에게 특별한 무언가를 권한 것으로 '능동'의 의미이므로 offered (B) 이 음식이 탕평채라고 '불린' 것이므로 '수동'의 의미로 was called가 적절하다.

23 탕평채의 4가지 재료가 무엇인지는 알 수 없다.

24 ⓐ의 him은 the king을 가리키지만 나머지는 모두 the scholar를 가리킨다.

25 주어진 문장의 This가 (E) 앞의 내용을 가리키므로 (E)가 적절하다.

26 'While he lived there by himself, he mainly ate vegetables.'라고 했다.

27 (A) 상반되는 내용이 나오므로 However, (B) 감정을 유발하는 경우 현재분사를 쓰고 감정을 느끼는 경우 과거분사로 쓰므로 disappointed, (C) by himself: 혼자서, 홀로

28 'That is because the scholar lived like a sinseon'이라고 했다.

29 ⓒ의 that은 'so ~ that ...' 구문에 쓰인 접속사 that이다.

30 각각 앞에 나온 (가) King Yeonsan, (나) the scholar (다) this pot을 가리킨다.

31 마지막에 'Let's dive into the fun history of our food.'라고 했으므로 '전통 음식에 관한 재미있는 역사적 이야기'가 이어질 것이다.

Lesson 7 (기말)

01 ③	**02** ③	**03** ②	**04** ④	**05** ⑤	**06** ②	**07** ①	**08** ④
09 ②, ④		**10** ①	**11** ⑤	**12** ④	**13** ④	**14** ②, ④	
15 ③, ⑤		**16** ⑤	**17** ②				

18 These blackouts made him come up with a new way to light his house.

19 (2) clearly → clear (5) spread → spreads

20 Because they are too poor to pay for electricity.

21 made him come up with a new way to light his house

22 ③ **23** ② **24** ③ **25** ⑤ **26** ①

27 him come up with **28** ① **29** ① **30** ④

01 ⓑ bleach: a chemical that is used to make something clean or white
ⓒ ceiling: the top part inside a room

02 겨울방학 계획을 묻는 주어진 글에 이어 (C) 계획을 말하고 (A) 무엇을 할지 묻자 (D) 하고자 하는 계획을 말하고 (B) 딤섬도 먹어 보라고 하는 순서가 적절하다.

03 'I need to find a way to save trees.'라고 하고 그에 대한 것을 이야기하고 있다.

04 이어지는 'I need at least two or three paper towels.'라는 언급으로 보아 ⓓ의 possible은 impossible로 고치는 것이 적절하다.

05 손을 말리는 데 종이 수건을 한 장만 쓰려고 손을 터는 데 열 번 이내로 턴다는 것은 어색하며 '적어도 열 번'이 자연스러우므로 'within'을 'at least'로 고치는 것이 적절하다.

06 남은 음식을 가져가겠다는 말에 '너무 많이 먹지 말 것을 잊지 말라'고 하는 것은 어색하며, 볼륨을 높여달라는 말에 '더 이상 줄일 수 없다'는 말도 어색하다.

07 (A)의 break는 '(짧은) 휴가'의 뜻이다.

08 'forget+~ing'는 '과거에 한 것을 잊다'라는 뜻이고, 'forget to 부정사'는 '앞으로 할 것을 잊다'라는 뜻이므로 'forget to try'로 고쳐야 한다.

09 'I need to find a way to save trees.', 'Just shake your hands before you use a paper towel.'이라고 했다.

10 목적격보어로 부사가 아닌 형용사를 써야 한다. happily가 아니라 happy가 적절하다.

11 목적격보어로 동사원형과 형용사를 받을 수 있으며 의미상 적절한 것은 make이다.

12 분수를 읽을 때 분자는 기수로, 분모는 서수로 읽는다. 분자가 복수일 경우 서수를 복수로 읽는다.

13 사역동사의 목적격보어로 동사원형이 나와야 한다.

14 ① to go → go ③ happily → happy ⑤ to fly → fly. 참고로 help는 목적격보어로 동사원형이나 to부정사를 쓴다.

15 '환경에 미치는 영향'과 '램프 사용의 유의점'에 대한 언급은 나와 있지 않다.

16 (A) too 형/부 to부정사 = so 형/부 that 주어 can't ~ (B) 수동태의 목적어를 주어로 하고 'be+pp'를 과거 동사로 바꾼 후 수동태의 주어를 목적어로 쓴다.

17 ⓐ '특정한 때'가 이어지므로 during ⓑ '절'이 이어지므로 because ⓒ '구'가 이어지므로 because of가 적절하다.

18 These blackouts를 주어로 하여 사역동사 made를 쓰고 목적격보어로 동사원형을 쓴다.

19 (2) 목적격보어로 형용사를 써야 한다.
(5) Sunlight가 주어이므로 spreads가 적절하다.

20 'People in the village are too poor to pay for electricity.'라고 했다.

21 사역동사 made의 목적격보어로 동사원형을 쓰는 것에 주의한다.

come up with: 생각해 내다, 만들어 내다

22 ⓑ와 ③: 가주어 ①, ⑤: 비인칭주어 ②, ④: 대명사

23 'Moser 램프의 원리'와 'Moser 램프의 전파'에 대한 언급은 나와 있지 않다.

24 (A) Thanks to: ~ 덕분에 (B) such as: ~와 같은

25 'Moser lamp의 제작 방법'에 대한 언급은 없다.

26 뒤에서 'It can never start a house fire.'라고 했으므로 safe가 적절하다.

27 이 정전들 때문에 그는 집을 밝히는 새로운 방법을 생각해 냈다. = 이 정전들은 그가 집을 밝히는 새로운 방법을 생각해 내도록 만들었다.

28 'I haven't had a chance to deeply appreciate your supporting and trying to understand me.'로 보아 '감사'하려고 쓴 글이다.

29 too 형/부 to부정사 = so 형/부 that 주어 can't ~

30 주어진 문장에서 '상황이 바뀌고 있다'고 한 후 그것을 (D) 다음 문장에서 설명하고 있으므로 (D)가 적절하다.

Lesson 7 (기말)

> **01** ③ **02** ③ **03** ① **04** ③ **05** ② **06** ③ **07** ⑤ **08** ⑤
> **09** ③ **10** ③ **11** My mom let me play soccer with friends.
> **12** ③ **13** ⑤ **14** ③ **15** ③ **16** ⑤ **17** ③ **18** ① **19** ④
> **20** ⑤ **21** ③ **22** ⑤ **23** ④ **24** ① **25** ⑤ **26** ② **27** ③
> **28** ② **29** ②

01 come up with: ~을 생각해 내다, ~을 만들어 내다

02 (A)는 앞에서 언급한 'we can save trees by using less paper'를 가리킨다. (B)는 앞에서 언급한 'Just shake your hands before you use a paper towel.'를 가리킨다.

03 '어떻게 하면 나무를 살릴 수 있을지'에 대한 대화이다.

04 ⓐ turn up it → turn it up
ⓑ higher → highest
ⓓ works → works like
ⓔ a boring → an interesting

05 'Then, I can just stop using paper cups.'라고 했다.

06 주어진 단어를 모두 한 번씩 사용하여 영작하면 'I've heard that we can save trees by using less paper.'이다.

07 식사를 끝냈는지 묻는 글에 이어, c에서 그랬다며 좋았다고 말하고, d에서 남은 음식을 가져갈 것인지 묻자, a에서 그렇다고 답하고, b에서 남은 음식을 내일까지는 먹어야 한다고 말하는 순서가 적절하다.

08 (B) 영화배우가 학교에 온다고 들었다고 하자 (E) 맞다며 가장 좋

아하는 배우라고 말한다. (A) 누구냐고 묻자 (C) 누군지 답하고 (D) 그를 만나고 싶다는 기대를 나타낸다.

09 '볼륨을 최대로 높인 것'이라고 언급한 후 '즉시 볼륨을 높이라'고 하는 것은 이색하다.

10 남은 음식을 집에 가져갈 것인지 묻는 말에 '그렇다'고 한 다음의 말이므로 '남은 음식을 내일까지는 먹으라'는 말이 적절하다. fridge: 냉장고

11 let은 동사원형을 목적보어로 취한다.

12 ① wash → washed ② go → to go
④ happily → happy ⑤ to not → not to

13 ⓐ check → checked ⓑ cleaned → clean
ⓔ painting → painted ⓕ I → me

14 전기 없이 방을 밝히는 Moser lamp에 관한 글에서 '전기를 생산하기 위해 이 기술을 사용하는 것은 싸다'라는 ⓒ의 글은 전체 흐름에 어긋난다.

15 'Marco couldn't read a book in his room'에서 '상황이 바뀌어' 'One plastic bottle in the ceiling can light up a whole room'이 되었다.

16 병으로 램프를 만드는 법을 설명하고 있는 글이므로 ⑤번이 적절하다.

17 필리핀에서 My Shelter Foundation에 의해 Moser lamp가 보급되고 있다는 글에서 '많은 자선단체가 아프거나 가난한 사람들을 돕기 위해 돈을 보냈다'라는 ⓒ의 글은 전체 흐름상 어색하다.

18 부정사인 'to come'의 형태로 'many years'를 수식하는 것이 적절하다.

19 플라스틱병 하나로 전기 없이 집을 밝힐 수 있다는 글이므로 ④번이 적절하다.

20 주어진 문장의 'These blackouts'가 (E) 앞의 'many blackouts'를 가리키므로 (E)가 적절하다.

21 '"I can read a book in my place now!" shouted Marco'에서 '기뻐하는' 것을 알 수 있다.

22 ⓔ는 가주어이지만 나머지는 모두 'Moser lamp'이다.

23 ① ceiling ② daytime ③ blackout ④ charity ⑤ electricity

24 왜 2002년에 브라질에서 정전이 잦았는지는 알 수 없다.

25 잦은 정전으로 인해 Moser lamp를 발명했다는 것이므로 '필요는 발명의 어머니'가 적절하다.

26 (A) 뒤에 'the daytime'이라는 '구'가 나오므로 during (B) 뒤에 'a single plastic bottle'이라는 '구'가 나오므로 because of가 적절하다. (C) Thanks to: ~ 덕분에

27 Moser lamp라는 플라스틱병 하나로 가난한 사람들도 전기 없이 집을 밝힐 수 있다는 글이다.

28 'It keeps food fresh without electricity.'라고 했다. ① 전기를 사용하지 않는다. ③ 항아리 두 개와 모래와 물이 필요하다. ④

만들기 쉽다. ⑤ 그릇에 모래를 넣은 후에 모래에 물을 부으면 된다.

29 Moser 램프의 장점을 설명하는 글에서 ⓑ의 Moser가 플라스틱 병으로 램프를 만들었다는 것은 흐름에서 벗어난다.

Lesson 8 (기말)

```
01 ④  02 ④  03 ④  04 ①  05 ④  06 ⑤  07 ④  08 ②
09 ③  10 ⑤  11 ③  12 ③
13 I smelled something burning.        14 ②  15 ②
16 ③, ⑤        17 saw the final team sleeping        18 ①
19 ④  20 ①  21 ③  22 ①  23 ②  24 ③  25 ①
26 he saved the people in Nome by carrying the medicine
   through a very difficult journey
27 ②  28 ⑤  29 ④
```

01 ① sled(썰매)와 ②, ③, ⑤는 의미상 사람들이 '타는 것'이지만 ④ travel은 '여행하다; (탈것으로) 다니다'라는 의미이다.

02 Suho가 이번 겨울 평창에서 아이스하키를 할 것이라는 말은 없고 'I'll go skating and sledding there.'라고 했다.

03 'How often did you play ice hockey when you were in Canada?'라고 물었으므로 횟수를 답하고 있는 ④번이 적절하다.

04 ⓒ 이번 주말 계획을 묻자 ⓐ 탁구를 칠 것이라고 답하고 ⓔ 얼마나 자주 치는지 묻자 ⓑ 주말마다 친다며 상대방에게 어떤지 묻자 ⓓ 축구를 좋아한다고 답하는 순서가 자연스럽다.

05 Suho가 Anna와 평창에 계신 조부모님 댁에 갈 거라는 말은 없다.

06 'I played at least two or three times a week in the winter.'라고 답하고 있으므로 '횟수'를 묻는 ⑤번이 적절하다.

07 'old pop songs를 좋아하느냐'라는 물음에 'No'라고 했으므로 ④번이 적절하다.

08 좋아하는 운동이 무엇인지 묻자 운동을 별로 안 좋아하지만 가끔 수영하러 간다는 의미로 자연스럽다.

09 'I love winter sports, too.'라고 하고 갑자기 'Oh, I've never played ice hockey'라고 하는 것은 어색하며 주어진 문장에서 'ice hockey'를 언급하고 나오는 것이 자연스러우므로 (C)가 적절하다.

10 'YG Sports'를 통해 겨울 올림픽 경기를 시청하라는 내용의 글이므로 '방송을 광고하기 위해'가 적절하다.

11 in Chinese: 중국어로

12 have는 사역동사로 동사원형을 목적격보어로 취한다.

13 smell의 목적격보어로 현재분사 burning을 쓴다.

14 ① were → was
③ enjoying → enjoy

④ celebrated → is celebrated
⑤ helped → to help

15 주어진 문장의 However로 (B)의 앞 문장과 상반되는 내용이 나오므로 (B)가 적절하다.

16 ⓒ told의 목적격보어로 to부정사를 쓴다.
ⓔ 수동태로 is celebrated가 되어야 한다.

17 saw의 목적격보어로 sleeping을 쓴다.

18 'The race can take more than two weeks'라고 했다.

19 ⓑ와 ④: (일정한 거리를) 가다[이동하다] ① 덮개 ③ 덮다 ② 가리다 ⑤ (책이나 잡지의) 표지

20 ⓒ와 ①: in ②, ③ on ④ of ⑤ with

21 ⓐ called → is called
ⓑ have → has
ⓔ Because → Because of
ⓕ Strongest → The strongest

22 ㉠ 1926 → 1925
㉡ 21th → 20th
㉢ after → before
㉥ Canada → Alaska
㉦ February 27 → February 2

23 주어진 문장의 However로 ④의 앞 문장과 상반되는 내용이 나오므로 ④가 적절하다.

24 ① Bend ② chief ③ crack ④ electricity ⑤ charity

25 영작하면 'This heart-warming story is now celebrated every year by the Iditarod Race, the biggest sled dog race in the world.'이다.

26 Balto는 어려운 여정을 뚫고 약품을 운반함으로서 놈에 있는 사람들을 구했다.

27 지각동사 saw의 목적격보어로 동사원형이나 현재분사를 쓴다.

28 (A) 의미상 '~할 때'의 When (B) stopped를 수식하는 부사 suddenly (C) 구해지는 것이므로 수동태가 적절하다.

29 'As Balto and Gunnar reached the final team, they were sleeping.'이라고 했다.

Lesson 8 (기말) 2회

```
01 ①  02 ⑤  03 ③  04 ③  05 How often did you play
06 ①  07 ⑤  08 ④  09 ③  10 ①  11 ③  12 ③  13 ④
14 crossing the street  15 ③, ⑤        16 ①  17 ④  18 ③
19 ②  20 ③  21 ④  22 ②  23 ②  24 ③  25 ③  26 ⑤
27 ④
```

01 sled는 '썰매'라는 뜻으로 '의사, 질병, 약, 병원'과는 관련이 없

다.

02 겨울 방학 동안의 Anna의 계획은 알 수 없다.

03 'I played at least two or three times a week in the winter.' 라고 답하고 있으므로 '횟수'를 묻는 ③번이 적절하다.

04 오래된 팝송을 좋아하지 않지만 할머니의 생일 파티에서 할머니가 좋아하시는 노래를 부르기 위해 오래된 팝송을 듣고 있는 Grace에게 해 줄 말로 적절한 것은 ③번 '할머니가 너를 자랑스러워하실 거야.'이다.

05 'I played at least two or three times a week in the winter.' 라고 답하고 있으므로 '횟수'를 묻는 'How often did you play'가 적절하다.

06 'I can't wait to learn(빨리 배우고 싶다)'이라는 말이 적절하다.

07 'I played at least two or three times a week in the winter.'라고 했다.

08 '그냥 할머니의 생일 파티에서 할머니가 좋아하시는 노래를 부르고 싶을 뿐'이라는 말이 뒤에 이어지므로 '오래된 팝송에 관심이 없다.'가 적절하다.

09 (D) 뭐하고 있는지 묻자
(A) 배드민턴 연습 중이라고 답하고
(B) 배드민턴을 좋아하는지 묻자
(C) 관심 없지만 다음 주 배드민턴 시험에 합격하고 싶을 뿐이라고 답하자
(E) 행운을 비는 순서가 자연스럽다.

10 뒤에서 자신의 계획을 답하고 있으므로 계획을 묻는 ①번이 적절하다.

11 뒤에서 'That's awesome.'이라고 했으므로 ⓒ는 'I can teach you how to play.' 정도가 되는 것이 자연스럽다.

12 ⓐ called → call[calling]
ⓑ staying → to stay
ⓒ do → to do
ⓔ to burn → burning

13 목적격보어로 to부정사가 있으므로 사역동사는 쓸 수 없다.

14 지각동사 saw의 목적격보어로 crossing을 쓴다.

15 ③ taken → take[taking]
⑤ to carry → carry[carrying]

16 (C)의 However로 앞의 내용과 상반되는 내용이 나오므로 제일 먼저 나오고 (A)의 Then이 (C)에서 Balto가 멈춘 때를 의미하므로 (A)가 이어지며 (B)에서 마지막 팀에 다다랐을 때, 그들은 자고 있어서 계속 달려 약을 전해주는 것으로 이어진다.

17 이야기가 기념되고 있는 '수동'의 의미가 되어야 하므로 is now celebrated가 적절하다.

18 (A) 약이 필요하지만 없었다는 상반된 내용이므로 However (B) '구'가 이어지므로 Due to나 Because of (C) 결과가 이어지므

로 So가 적절하다.

19 <보기> 문장의 A terrible thing이 ④ 다음에 'Some children got very sick in the town.'과 'The disease kept spreading.'으로 이어지고 있으므로 ④가 직질하다.

20 어떻게 Balto가 눈 속에서 코스를 제대로 따라갈 수 있었는지는 알 수 없다.

21 ⓐ the world's biggest sled dog race
ⓑ Some children got very sick, and the disease kept spreading.
ⓒ any medicine
ⓓ, ⓔ medicine

22 놈 마을에서 병이 퍼졌다.
(B) 놈의 사람들은 당장 약이 필요했다.
(D) 폭설을 뚫고 개썰매 릴레이가 시작됐다.
(A) Gunnar와 그의 개들은 20번째 팀이었다.
(C) Gunnar와 Balto가 마지막 팀에 다다랐을 때, 그들은 자고 있었다.
(E) Gunnar와 Balto는 계속 가서 약을 가지고 놈 마을에 도착했다.
놈 마을이 구해졌다.

23 ⓒ heavily → heavy
ⓓ cracks → cracking
ⓔ saved → was saved

24 누가 첫 번째 개 팀의 몰이꾼이었는지는 알 수 없다.

25 (A) right away: 즉시
(B) in time: 제시간에

26 경주의 이름이 어디에서 왔는지는 알 수 없다.

27 each는 단수로 받으므로 ⓓ의 have를 has로 고쳐야 한다.